# WORLD AFFAIRS
## National and International Viewpoints

# WORLD AFFAIRS

## National and International Viewpoints

The titles in this collection were selected
from the Council on Foreign Relations' publication:
*The Foreign Affairs 50-Year Bibliography*

Advisory Editor
RONALD STEEL

# POLITICS, ECONOMICS AND MEN OF MODERN SPAIN

1808-1946

by

## A. RAMOS OLIVEIRA

ARNO PRESS

A NEW YORK TIMES COMPANY

New York • 1972

Reprint Edition 1972 by Arno Press Inc.

Reprinted from a copy in The University of Illinois
Library

World Affairs: National and International Viewpoints
ISBN for complete set: 0-405-04560-3
See last pages of this volume for titles.

Manufactured in the United States of America

∽∾∼∽∾∼∽∾∼∽∾∼∽∾∼∽

**Library of Congress Cataloging in Publication Data**

Ramos Oliveira, Antonio, 1907-
    Politics, economics, and men of modern Spain,
1808-1946.

    (World affairs:  national and international view-
points)
    Reprint of the 1946 ed.
    1.  Spain--Politics and government--19th century.
2.  Spain-Politics and government--20th century.
3.  Spain--Economic conditions.  I.  Title.  II.  Series.
DP203.R3  1972      320.9'46'08      72-4285
ISBN 0-405-04578-6

POLITICS, ECONOMICS
AND MEN OF MODERN SPAIN
1808–1946

# POLITICS, ECONOMICS
# AND MEN OF MODERN SPAIN
## 1808–1946

by

## A. RAMOS OLIVEIRA

translated by

## TEENER HALL

LONDON
VICTOR GOLLANCZ LTD
1946

PRINTED IN GREAT BRITAIN BY PURNELL AND SONS, LTD. (T.U.)
PAULTON (SOMERSET) AND LONDON

# CONTENTS

# BOOK FOUR

## THE SECOND REPUBLIC

*Map at end*

# INTRODUCTION

THERE IS PERHAPS no nation in the world which has had less chance of deciding its own destiny than the Spanish nation. This is the first thing that needs to be taken into account by anyone trying to form a judgment on the political aptitudes of the Spanish race. For it is very frequently forgotten that, strictly speaking, Spaniards themselves have played but a small part in making the history of Spain, which has, more often than not, been made by events and accidents in which the Spaniard has had no hand and whose course he has not been able to govern.

Every nation owes its personality to diverse elements; physical, ethnical, historical, and so forth. But the proportion in which each of these elements shares in the formation of human societies varies in the highest degree. To some nations it has been given that their history should reflect their character with absolute fidelity, because no serious accident has occurred to disturb their spontaneous development. Other nations, on the contrary, are moulded to a great extent by history. Spain is one of these. Nations make their history; but history can also make, or mar, nations. In a word, there is no doubt that history—international relations, political institutions, forms of culture—can exercise on the destiny of a nation as great an influence as the *milieu* or the psychological factor.

The fate of the Iberian Peninsula seems to be to act as a battle-ground for any factions, nations and civilizations that have a quarrel to settle. In Spain, the destiny of Rome, the future of Christianity, the political structure of Europe, have been successively fought out—to a major extent, at least.

Carthaginians and Romans began the second Punic War in Spain, and afterwards, the factions of the Roman civil wars fought each other there. Islam discharged upon Spain all the energy of her expansion westwards. When the reconquest of the territory had been virtually concluded by the Christians in the thirteenth century, when Spain began to eliminate foreign bodies, France and England in the fourteenth century shifted

7

their secular struggle to the soil of the Peninsula. In the eighteenth century, during the War of the Spanish Succession, the European hegemony of the two great reigning continental Houses was decided on Spanish territory. At the beginning of the nineteenth century, with the blow dealt to Napoleon's power in the Peninsular War, the future of Europe was again decided in Spain. In 1823 the Holy Alliance, the outpost of absolutism, suffocated continental liberty in Spain by dispatching a French army of occupation. Finally, the memory is still green of how various Great Powers once more prevented the free play of Spanish political forces by imposing on the nation a predetermined form of government.

Less fortunate in politics than other nations, Spain, as we have seen, has rarely been free from the dislocating and disintegrating action of foreign agencies.

The truth is that it was only during the sixteenth and seventeenth centuries that Spain had a respite from foreign meddling. But though these centuries brought no historical disaster provoked by outside sources, the course of Spanish politics had already been determined, perhaps irrevocably, by a past in which Spaniards had had no choice.

The Saracen invasion in A.D. 711 (aptly called in the Middle Ages the destruction of Spain) was a political cataclysm much more disastrous in its consequences for the Peninsula than were the barbarian invasions for Europe 300 years before.

Under the Visigoth Monarchy (A.D. 476–711),[1] the political unity of Spain, propelled by innumerable factors and interests, had been accomplished within a single State embracing the whole Peninsula. Spain was already moving, with no cardinal difference, along the path of all the Western nations which had been civilized by the Roman soldier and the Roman lawgiver. There is no evidence that leads us to suppose that Spain, in the Middle Ages or in the Modern Age, would have differed fundamentally in her political and social institutions from other European nations, if the Visigoth drama had ended otherwise than it did.

But this process whereby Spain was being finally incorporated into the European current (just as the Peninsula had been incorporated into the Roman world, of which it became the most rapidly

---

[1] The founder of the Visigoth Monarchy in Spain was Eurico (467–83). The six Goth kings who preceded him ruled in Gaul. Eurico subdued the Suevi, consolidating the Goth power in the Iberian Peninsula, and in his days the Western Roman Empire disappeared (476). The constitution of the Visigoth State in Spain must, therefore, be fixed about this year.

latinized of all Rome's overseas provinces), this process, I repeat, was irreparably wiped out by the Arabs and Berbers in the eighth century. Spain, in reality, disappeared. Gone were unity of language and culture, religious unity, political unity: and the very existence of the race was seriously menaced.

Some authors are surprised that the Spaniards took eight centuries to expel the Saracens. But there is nothing surprising about it. The Arab army and culture were superior to the Christian. The domination of the Moors was intellectual rather than physical. They were better organized in everything; they had a cohesion and a vigour which were absolutely lacking in the European world. The Arabs brought with them a brilliant civilization, and instead of being conquered and absorbed by the vanquished, as happened to the German tribes, it was they who conquered and partly absorbed the peoples who fell under their sway.

For the rest, the enterprise of the Reconquista, which in another age would have fostered union among Spaniards (with more motive than the Napoleonic invasion, for example), worked, in the Middle Ages, in favour of the military and political disintegration characteristic of feudalism. Both circumstances— the Reconquista and feudal disintegration—which gave rise to the appearance of several states or kingdoms on the ruins of the single Visigoth State, conspired in the late Middle Ages to hamper every concerted and effective action of the Christians against the invader.

The Reconquista was a long military, religious and political process in the course of which Spain, as we know her at the end of the fifteenth century, modern Spain, came anarchically into being. And if there is reason to think of the Middle Ages as a Latin-Arab or Christian-Islamic epoch, Spain undoubtedly ought to be considered as the mediaeval country *par excellence* of the West. (Mediaeval and feudal are not necessarily synonymous.)

Spain's intimate connection with the Arab and the isolation which overtook her from the eighth century onwards, made the Middle Ages in Spain more genuine and intense in certain capital aspects than in other European countries. The incessant exercise of arms in an age when the military, the religious and the chivalrous came to be one and the same thing, made Spain the country of chivalry without rival. The secular struggle against Islam and the presence of countless Jews, more cultured, more numerous and richer than in any other part of the Western world, accentuated, beyond a doubt, the orthodox Catholicism of Spaniards. (In no other country did so many and so brilliant

A1

theological controversies take place as in Spain between the philosophers of the three religions; and the great influx of Jews in the Middle Ages was largely due to the attraction exercised over them by the enlightened tolerance of the Cordovan caliphs.)

The Reconquista, on the other hand, gave the Church in Spain an exceptional standing and engaged the Spanish clergy in military activities unknown to the clergy in the rest of Europe. If the warrior nobles of Spain were profoundly religious, the "religious" were also warriors. The military fortresses were monasteries: the monasteries were fortresses. The prelates led their troops in person. In such an atmosphere, the Spanish clergy were not only soldiers, they were also a political clergy.

Whatever the Spaniard did, or omitted to do, in the sixteenth and seventeenth centuries must, therefore, be analysed in the light of the exceptional features of the Middle Ages in Spain. With such antecedents, it is not difficult to understand the rôle which Spain was to play in the world of the Renaissance. The Spaniard countered the individualistic ideal of the Renaissance with mediaeval universalism. The values which Spain defended in the sixteenth century were typically mediaeval; in politics, the universal Catholic Monarchy; in philosophy, Aristotle and the Schoolmen; in ethics, chivalry; in economics, a pastoral economy.

The Spaniard was not interested in commerce or industry, which he held to be work for villeins. In conformity with the mediaeval ethic, his ideal was the nobleman. He sought the kind of wealth which was the obsession of the Middle Ages—gold, which Alfonso X tried to find with the philosopher's stone. The Spaniard, therefore, did not go to America in search of markets, but of gold nuggets: but he was also inspired by the ambition to convert millions of souls from the blood-stained religions of the heathen and to broaden the dominions of the Church. The excesses he committed in conquering and colonizing America were due to his primitive ideas and low degree of culture, which at that time was not much more advanced in the rest of Europe.[1]

[1] "In viewing the work of Spaniards in America, thought naturally turns to the later work of the English further north. Points of contrast at once occur. Since the first permanent Spanish settlement dates from 1493 and the first English settlement from 1607, both countries reproducing themselves in the New World, the England so reproduced was the England of the Stuarts and the Commonwealth, whereas the Spain so reproduced was that of the Catholic sovereigns and of Charles V. Spanish settlement coincided with the period of adventurous exploitation: English settlement followed the period of adventure. When the Spanish Conquistadores are accused of inhumanity and inefficiency, this difference of time must be remembered: all that has been

The power acquired by Spain in the sixteenth century did not spring from the fact that her political unity was accomplished before that of the other great nations (a very wide-spread error, for the England of Henry VII and the France of Louis XI had already succeeded in the previous century in achieving a political unity which was more real than the Spanish brand); it sprang from the passion for adventure of the Spanish people, who were, moreover, more accustomed than any other people to live dangerously and suffer hardships. The Spaniard had been trained in the hard school of eight centuries of war, eight centuries of ambushes and perils; and though the Renaissance stimulated all Europe to great adventures, the hazards of arms, conquests and discoveries called for executants which no other nation could then supply in the measure that Spain could.

The end of the war of Granada, the dynamic government of the Catholic sovereigns, the optimism of the epoch and various fortuitous circumstances, elated the soul of Spaniards at the close of the fifteenth century with unbounded enthusiasm and urged it towards great deeds. The Renaissance, therefore, did not entirely pass Spain by. She welcomed it in the fifteenth century with suitable honours, as we can see from the literature of the second half of that century and, above all, from the monarchy of Ferdinand the Catholic. But the intenseness of the Middle Ages in Spain had made her an infertile ground for the Renaissance revolution, whose object was the rediscovery of reason, the vision of man as the pivot of the universe, that is, humanism, doubt confronting dogmatic assertion. So that though Spain acquired a Renaissance monarchy, that monarchy was to serve the ideals of the Middle Ages and was soon to rest on such an essentially mediaeval institution as the Inquisition, which was revived in 1482.

Let us now see how the religious question presented itself in the sixteenth century.

The Spanish Inquisition in modern times came into being in order to supervise the religious behaviour of the converted Jews; only those Jews who, by force or of their own free will, had been converted to Catholicism. Spain was the country where the Jews had received the best treatment during the Middle Ages.

said—in the first instance by Spaniards—about that inhumanity and inefficiency is true, but not the whole truth. It may be noted that during the same period the English too were pursuing conquest and colonisation—in Ireland: and one would hesitate to claim that their work was more efficient or more humane" (F. A. Kirkpatrick, *The Spanish Conquistadores*, Chap. XVII, p. 345, London, 1934).

I shall return to this point later. But when in the fourteenth century the racial conflict became acute (it was more social than religious as far as the people were concerned: the product largely of the class struggle), the Church determined to solve the problem by means of conversion, mostly brought about by coercion. Conversion did not give the desired result, for the Spanish Jews, compatriots of the great Maimonides and well versed in their Books and ceremonies, mostly remained faithful in secret to the synagogue. The Church then decided to use the Inquisition to prevent the apostasy of converts, and the Crown supported the Church, thinking no doubt that the Inquisition would impose greater coherence on the State. But in spite of its harshness, the new Tribunal did not mitigate the racial struggle and, in any case, it lacked jurisdiction over the non-converted Jews, who were finally expelled in 1492.

For forty-three years, that is, until 1525, the Holy Office did not extend its jurisdiction to Christians. Moreover, the Inquisition not only allowed a certain freedom of conscience among Catholics, but it favoured the growing dissent in matters of dogma. Protestantism entered Spain with the books and letters of Erasmus "who had much in common with Luther and even went further than he did on occasions". It should be remarked that the first half of the sixteenth century was a period of theological confusion everywhere. In Spain, Fonseca, Archbishop of Toledo, and Manrique, Archbishop of Seville and Inquisitor General, were followers of Erasmus. So were also many of the Spanish *intelligentsia*. Erasmus, in fact, enjoyed the support of the Inquisition and of the Emperor Charles V. In Spain there were no Lutherans; there were Erasmians. That is to say, Spanish intellectuals were more impressed by the conciliatory doctrines of Erasmus than by the intransigence of Luther.

But all this was swept away by the hurricane blowing from Germany. The pace of the reformist movement ended by alarming the Church, and towards the middle of the sixteenth century the Catholic reaction began. Rome abandoned her confident attitude towards subtle innovators of the type of Erasmus and decreed the defence of the Catholic dogma, the whole dogma, as it had been handed down from the Middle Ages, without the subtraction of one jot or tittle. In Spain, on the death of the Inquisitor Manrique in 1538, reaction took the form of the implacable persecution of Erasmianism and was led by the religious orders. "It was then seen that Erasmianism was the work of a few 'intellectuals' without popular support. Rome encountered practically no obstacles in Spain, because the nuclei of anti-popular thought were scattered and weak."

Everywhere the Church was returning to pre-Renaissance times, and Spain was turning also to centre all her forces in that epoch. As we know, Spain became the champion and shield of Catholic dogma.

Given the militant spirit of the clergy since the Middle Ages and the extraordinary influence of the Church on Spanish society, it is not surprising that, when the Catholic world was split, Spain became one of the most stubborn centres of reaction against the Reformation.

From now on, Spain was going to be hermetically sealed against the current of the Renaissance (which no one personified better than Erasmus) and the persecution of Erasmianism was only one episode in the struggle against the new learning.

Intolerance, that religious frenzy, was then common to the whole of Europe, and in this respect Spain was not going to yield the palm to any nation. But not so long before, in other circumstances, Spain had given a very different example to the world.

As we know, the Cordova of the Caliphs had been the home of three religions—the Mohammedan, the Jewish and the Christian; and Mohammedans and Christians had even shared the same places of worship. Then in the twelfth century, the Spain which the Christians had won back was likewise the scene of the most complete tolerance. It was, in fact, a prince of the Church, Don Raimundo, Archbishop of Toledo and Grand Chancellor of Castile (1130–50), who encouraged the spread of Arab culture among the Christians in the reign of Alfonso VII. Alfonso the Wise (1252–84) demanded, and obtained, for his scientific works the collaboration of men of all three races; assigned to the Jews in Seville three mosques which they converted into synagogues; and founded in that city and in Toledo Chairs of Hebrew Language and Literature. And finally, the famous Colegio de Toledo, the laboratory where Jewish, Mohammedan and Christian scholars met, continued with magnificent lustre the admirable tradition of the Arab schools. What is more, during the eleventh, twelfth and thirteenth centuries, Moors and Jews lived perhaps more secure and respected in the dominions of the Spanish kings than the Christians had lived under the Arabs in the good days of the Caliphate.

This slice of Spanish history is a splendid canvas on which toleration stands out against a fearful background of religious hysteria, massacres of Jews, and the excesses of all kinds which can be laid to the charge of the Crusaders in the East, and even of those who paraded their arms through Spain. In Castile, the Jewish communities enjoyed the same laws and privileges as the rest of the community, and lived in harmony with Christians who were, like themselves, neither lords nor serfs, but units of an urban class, on a level with which the Israelitish world, with its enlightenment, its liberty and its wealth, functioned perfectly.

In Spain the Templars were not persecuted; nor did Spain share· the fury which was let loose in France against the Albigenses; on the contrary, a king of Aragon, the valorous Peter II, in whose dominions these heretics abounded, not only did not persecute them, but married one of his sisters to the Count of Toulouse, leader of the sect, and another to the son of the Count. He then marched at the head of his troops against the army of the Pope, commanded by the fanatical Simon de Montfort, and fell fighting at Muret in 1211.

To sum up, toleration and the spirit of religious compromise flourished in Spain in the Middle Ages at a time when the rest of Europe was led away by fanaticism and when even the Flemings (a people who were afterwards famous for their toleration of dissent) were burning synagogues in Constantinople.

We are bound to ask whether the spirit of toleration in mediaeval Spain would have been possible if Spain had been a nation of innate religious ferocity, as we are told she is. Would Spain have given such a lofty example of intellectual, spiritual and political moderation, for so long a time? The truth seems to be that Spanish tolerance, like Spanish intolerance, is determined by motives less bound up than is commonly supposed with the moral and ethnical constitution of the Spaniard; that, in some epochs, other nations have surpassed Spain in the persecuting and exclusivist religious impulse, while in others, Spain has been the most intransigent; and that if, in short, Spain confronts us with longer periods of persecution over the whole course of history up to the present day, this originality springs from historical facts which are also original and which cannot be analysed here.

But let us return to the sixteenth century. The Spaniard stuck to his mediaeval metaphysical attitude. He was the knight, the priest and the soldier, a profoundly anti-*bourgeois* character. Already at the end of the sixteenth century, the *hidalgo*, the cleric and the *miles gloriosus* were the plagues of Spanish society.

With these ideas, it was inevitable that Spain should fail as a nation, among nations where the Renaissance had introduced and imposed reason as the norm of thought, commerce and industry as the foundation of economic life, and work as the source of prosperity.

But the Spaniard was not now as isolated as he had been during the Middle Ages. However much the State willed it, it did not lie in its power to exclude entirely from Spain the stimulating and fresh breeze of the Renaissance. A great number of Spanish intellectuals had been to Italy, where the Renaissance had touched its greatest glory, and the revivifying breath of the epoch, which had already inspired the literature of the fifteenth century, but which had afterwards died down, now reappeared, though tardily, in the eminent literary production of the so-called *Siglo de Oro*. In *Don Quixote*, an essentially critical book, humanism triumphs, and with it the genuine emotion of the Renaissance. Cervantes saw Spaniards as they, absorbed in the cultivation of outworn values, could not see themselves. He laid bare a Spain enamoured of her anachronistic ideals and on the sure road to ruin herself in saving them. And with *Don Quixote*, Cervantes was obviously holding up the Middle Ages to public derision. Yet the author sympathizes with his hero (reason, a critical mind, humanism are not enough; hence the melancholy smile of Cervantes) and treats him with tenderness; for though the ideal is absurd, it is none the less noble.

The quixotic, mediaevalist, anti-individualistic and, consequently, anti-*bourgeois* chimera prevented any possibility in Spain of the rise of a social class with power rooted in commerce and industry. The revival of industry and commerce in Spain, which is apparent in the last years of the fifteenth century and the first half of the sixteenth, was stifled by the same anti-Renaissance reaction which suddenly cut short the revival of literature and religion. The expulsion of the Jews in 1492 had already dealt a tremendous blow to the Spanish middle class. The expulsion of the Moors in 1609 completed the liquidation of this commercial class. Strictly speaking, Spain only had two social classes—the aristocracy and the people. That is, Spanish society in the Modern Age was radically unbalanced.

The Spanish ruling class was recruited from the nobility. It could not be recruited from the middle class, for there was no middle class. And as was happening little by little everywhere, the nobility was losing its vigour also in Spain, more rapidly there than elsewhere, because the aristocracy did not intermarry with the lower classes. Into which class could it marry, if there were none on its level and equal to it in economic power? In the Middle Ages there had been frequent marriages between the ancient aristocracy and rich Jews. But already there were hardly any Jews left, and those who remained were not rich enough to tempt impoverished aristocrats.

The Spanish aristocracy was morally, intellectually and physically exhausted, and there was no class, I repeat, to to replace it in the leadership of society. In other countries when the nobility became decrepit, the middle class, the *bourgeoisie*, was on the spot to take over its place in politics and economics; or both combined—the aristocracy acquiring new blood and sharing, in a more or less subsidiary capacity, the responsibility of government with the *bourgeoisie*. If we seek in the seventeenth century in Spain (already in the seventeenth century!) a live and healthy social class, the depository of the virtues of the race, we shall find it in the people; but the people could not provide the ruling class that was needed.

Because the powers of leadership of the Spanish nobility were exhausted within a hundred years or so, Spain was practically without a State and without a Government. From then on, Spain was in a condition of anarchy, tempered by the fatalism of the race. This is the tragedy of Spanish decadence up to the present day—the lack of a middle class to take over the leadership of society from the degenerate and devitalized aristocracy.

When the absolute monarchy fell, at the beginning of the nineteenth century, when the sovereignty of the people was proclaimed, the tragedy of having no ruling class in Spain was revealed in all its crudity. That is the moment that I take to begin my study of an incomparable historical drama, which may have its counterpart perhaps in the ancient world, but not in the modern.

But I must make it plain that, contrary to what is generally supposed, there are no values or elements having a decisive function in this drama which are not of a strictly historical character. That is to say, whatever has happened in Spain from 1808 until today, can, in my view, be satisfactorily explained without the need to refer to any other science than History. Far from being faced with essentially original events, we find a theme which is profoundly classical in its broad outlines. Spain is not, in short, the first nation in history to stick in the morass of a secular civil war without being able to get out of it.

One of my main objects in writing this book has been, as the reader will see, to cut away from the history of Spain, and

16

especially from the history of modern Spain, those platitudes and prejudices with which a superficial and therefore, in this case, pessimistic literature has obscured it to the point of rendering it incomprehensible and absurd—a literature which is unfortunately abundant both inside and outside Spain. The idea that whatever, in politics or in the social order, happens in Spain lacks sense or originates in the unrestrainable inclination of the race to civil war is, therefore, false and unjust. Until the nineteenth century, England and France endured more years of civil war than Spain. (In the sixteenth, seventeenth and eighteenth centuries, France and England each suffered fifty years of fratricidal strife; Spain only twenty-three.)

To present the history of Spain during the last 130 years in strict accordance with the canons laid down for this kind of literature, that is, as a simple statement of events, would impose on the author an embarrassing silence regarding the ultimate origins of those events. To explain the facts without the necessary accompaniment of some reflections on their significance would be to abandon them to the usual vulgar interpretation, made in the confused light of the immense prejudices in vogue on Spain and Spaniards generally. I have tried to obviate this risk by writing history in the form of connected essays. This permits me to study at length, when their importance requires it, problems, events and personages. As far as possible, I have kept to chronological order; and reflections and narrative are linked by chronology and the whole bound together by the unity of the theme.

This book claims to be the history of an epoch in Spain; for historically the nineteenth century did not end in 1900; Spain is still painfully struggling out of it.

Such is the sequence of events and the indivisible historical unity of the epoch studied in this work that, if we disconnect or separate the different periods or phases of the Spanish drama that begins in 1808, we rob history of its principal virtue, its instructive purpose. And if we are to learn from history, it must be written impartially, without partisanship and, above all, without propagandist aims. In the case of Spain—where civil war has already deprived four generations of peace—the truth is something that needs saying. My motto, therefore, has been: *Amicus Plato, sed magis amica Natio.*

For the rest, the past is always being resuscitated in one form or another, and when we denounce a past evil or error, we are not condemning those who fell into it, because perchance they could not do otherwise, but drawing attention to what may perhaps be avoided if the opportunity occurs again.

I cannot conclude this Preface without expressing my gratitude to all who have helped me in one way or another with this work and especially to Miss Teener Hall, who has brought to the task of translation an energy and enthusiasm which have greatly facilitated the appearance of the book.

# BOOK ONE

# THE END OF THE ABSOLUTE
# MONARCHY

## CHAPTER I

## NAPOLEON IN THE PENINSULA

WHEN THE NINETEENTH century dawned, Spain was
not ripe to receive "French ideas", as the political philosophy
of the eighteenth century was aptly called in Madrid. The
Peninsula offered a violent contrast with France and the other
nations which were then carrying the torch of progress through
the world. France had 42,000 towns; instead, the curious traveller
would find 25,000 dispirited villages in Spain. There were not
forty Spanish cities with more than 10,000 souls. Madrid, with
fewer than 200,000 inhabitants, was a modest provincial capital,
the slack bond between *las Españas*, the home of the rural landed
nobility, the 'Change where tradesmen and shopkeepers with
a modest "turnover" met.[1] There was nothing in the capital
of the Spanish Monarchy to compare with the manufacturing
zone of the *faubourg* of St. Antoine in Paris. As regards the
general population, France had 27 million inhabitants, against
the 10½ revealed by the Spanish census.

No less sharp was the contrast between the two nations in the
vitally important question of an informed public opinion.
In the country of Montesquieu, there appeared during the
revolutionary period thirty-three newspapers, some of which
in the provinces, like *Le Courrier de Lyon*, ran into as many as
60,000 copies. But in Spain, where the huge majority of the
population was illiterate, the Press, which was almost always
parochial in character, fed the curiosity of the clubs but had
no influence over the people.

[1] Actually thirty years later, Larra could write: "If there is an industrial
and commercial middle class in Spain, it is not to be found in Madrid, but
in Barcelona, Cadiz, etc.; here there are now only the upper and the lower
classes." Article in the *Revista Española*, June 20th, 1834. According to the
same author, the Spanish middle class was composed of "decent office-workers
and artisans".

Moreover, books in Spain never achieved a wide circulation, owing to the extraordinary intellectual backwardness of the nation and the small number of inhabitants. A case like that of Necker's *Administration des Finances*, of which 80,000 copies were sold in France towards the end of the eighteenth century within a short space of time, would have been inconceivable in Spain at that epoch, and even today. The specialized theme of the treatise and its prodigious circulation indicate the enormous power which the French *bourgeoisie* already enjoyed on the eve of a change of régime. In the same way, the episode in which Mirabeau is shown at Marseilles opening a clothier's shop in order to curry favour with the Third Estate, throws an interesting side-light on the vigour of the French middle class. And such a significant event as that which occurred at the Beaucaire fair, when the merchants assembled there pronounced themselves in favour of Louis XVI's dethronement, would have been equally unimaginable in Spain.

In short, France had been converting herself into a *bourgeois* and enlightened nation ever since the reign of Henri IV, while Spain had gone in the opposite direction.

Spanish ignorance and the national decadence had followed a parallel course; and although in the eighteenth century, a philanthropic monarchy and its reformist Ministers had fostered enlightenment with all the means in their power, the practical results were not commensurate with the effort expended. Spanish society continued to be enveloped in thick darkness, impenetrable to the ray of light thrown on it by an enlightened minority which was exaggeratedly "frenchified" in its ideas, language and tastes. This minority was composed of a small group from each of the privileged classes—nobility, clergy and middle class. It was an intellectual stratum artificially superimposed on the general body of Spanish society, to which it never properly adhered. Between the *élite* and the people there was not, as in France, a middle class or *bourgeoisie*. Spanish intellectuals represented themselves, and no one but themselves.

It is not surprising that when a Chair of Economics was founded at Saragossa by the *Sociedad de Amigos del Pais*, a fierce controversy should have broken out about its functions, with the enlightened minority on one side and the nation on the other. The people saluted the event with ridicule and epigrams, and took sides for and against Economics. The affair was treated as a joke, at the time when, in France, financial treatises like the one already referred to were selling with astonishing rapidity.

What had happened was that profound ignorance had killed intellectual curiosity in the Spaniard. He neither knew, nor desired to know. He was a misoneist, opposed to anything new, to anything that tried to shake him out of his mental stagnation. Naturally, a man who displayed no interest in fiction or *belles lettres*, which are outside the range of an illiterate population, reacted suspiciously to more complicated processes of thought such as Economics, which were considered a dangerous innovation. War was waged on anything that called for mental effort. But this was not all. Like all other new ideas, political economy could only attract those who had need of such ideas in their struggle for a livelihood or for political power. In a nation of merchants and industrialists, economic questions arouse not merely curiosity, but a passionate interest. But in a nation like Spain, where as we shall see later, the last word on such subjects was spoken by the priest, the teaching of Economics provoked the frivolous hilarity of a society whose interests were adequately served by the Catechism of Christian Doctrine.

At the outset of the nineteenth century, stock-breeders, as a social force, took precedence over all other elements of the national wealth. That is, stock-breeding continued to be a factor of enormous weight in Spanish politics, and agriculture, industry and commerce had to give way to the interests of flocks and herds. Migratory herds were protected by the *Honrado Concejo de la Mesta*, the Honourable Guild of Sheep-Farmers, an institution of very ancient origin and curious lineage. The privileges of the sheep-farmers, which Campomanes had curtailed in the previous century and which were afterwards to be contested by the Cortes of Cadiz, were acutely prejudicial to agriculture, since the fields and crops were at the mercy of wandering herds, and the peasants, whose political power, as I have just said, was as yet inferior to that of the *Mesta*, complained in vain.

Agriculture was still but imperfectly developed. The deficit in the production of cereals was covered by the importation of grain—in the case of wheat, in considerable quantities. Land was for the most part held in the form of entailed estates by religious bodies, the nobility and the communes. There were 900,000 farmers, mostly tenants of these civil and ecclesiastical corporations, and a similar number of agricultural day-labourers. The peasants—day-labourers and tenants—lived a life of poverty, only palliated by what they could extract from the *bienes comunales*, that is, the lands owned communally by the local population. Lands belonging to the communes which were rented out to, and worked by, the peasants were known as *bienes de propios*. The communes were usually rich in both kinds of property. In the whole of Spain, there were hardly any small or medium proprietors, except in the Basque Provinces and in the Levante. Even in Catalonia, there was much waste land, and the lords of the cultivated land lived in the cities as absentees.

The number of the nobles and gentry (*hidalgos*) amounted to half a million, more than 400,000 of them in Old Castile. In regions where there was some industrial and mercantile activity, as in Catalonia and Valencia, the nobility was not much in evidence. But in the zones whose economy was based exclusively on the land, they formed an extraordinary army of parasites. There is no reason to see in this, as has been suggested, irrefutable proof of the charge of pride and contempt for work which has been laid at their door. The Spaniard bought his title to nobility, which was sold at a low price, as soon as he acquired any money, because the important Government posts were reserved for the nobles. The fact that a patent of nobility was necessary for entrance into the Civil Service or the military academies, constrained Spaniards, if it were economically possible for them, to enrol themselves in the *aristocratic* class, the monopolizer of the means of livelihood. (The same thing applied to the Church.) And the existence of an overwhelming number of patrician luminaries must be interpreted as the fruit of a social system whose roots go far deeper than the subsoil of individual psychology. It was not that the Spaniard was congenitally idle, but that that régime of privilege made him so. This was clearly seen when the régime changed and in thirty years Spain doubled her production of cereals—a magnificent advance for a country where the Roman plough was still in use, and one which moved Moreau de Jones to write that no other nation could have done as much.

Of the productive population, which represented about 50 per cent of the inhabitants, only a tenth part was engaged in industry. The Spanish *bourgeoisie*, properly so-called, was composed of half a million artisans and manufacturers and 25,000 merchants, most of them shopkeepers—less than the nobles and clergy combined. That is to say, the natural wealth of Spain was virtually neglected.

Commerce and industry were largely in the hands of foreigners, of whom there were 30,000 in Madrid and 8,000 in Cadiz. Commerce was hampered by innumerable stumbling-blocks in the way of tax regulations and by lack of communications. Roads were few, and those that existed were in a bad state of repair. Important coast towns like Vigo in the north-west had no trading relations with the centre. Transport was mainly carried on by pack-animals.

The coasting-trade was confined to French, British and Dutch ships. The whole merchant navy of Spain consisted of 900 ships of all kinds. Moreover, there were few ports worthy of the name.

Spain exported raw materials—iron, copper, lead, wool, silk—which the industrial nations converted into goods and sent back again. The textile industry, though modest, was the greatest focus of activity, especially the cotton mills of Catalonia and the silk looms of Valencia. In Castile, there were a few scattered cloth factories. In Andalusia, fifteen cities were engaged in the manufacture of textiles, especially silk. Metallurgy predominated in Vizcaya.

But the whole of Spanish industrial production remained far below the needs of the home market, though the people's standard of living could not have been more primitive.

The Spaniard had resigned himself to living without industry, without commerce and almost without agriculture; he had turned himself into a *hidalgo*, or a soldier, or a monk, and had left the care of his food and clothing to foreigners—for that was why they had been invited to come to Spain or had been sent the precious metals which arrived, ever less frequently and in less quantity, from the Spanish dominions in Central and South America. The traditional financial policy continued under Charles IV, who in 1807 raised a loan in Holland of 23 million florins in anticipation of the overseas remittances of gold and silver. For wheat alone, Spain expended 147 million pesetas, or three-quarters of the value of the bullion from America. The remainder of the income of all kinds from the New World was used to buy manufactured goods abroad, a portion of which passed through Spain to the Indies, on commission.

Spain was, in short, a country of shepherds. She not only lacked a middle class, but her economy was directed to the profit of the stock-farmer. And the shepherds of sheep ruled the nation in conjunction with the shepherds of souls. The number of clergy and monks in Spain was about 150,000.

The lack of a middle class and the all-pervading social influence of the Church were the principal causes why Napoleon failed in the Peninsula. In the rest of Europe, except in Russia, the people no longer blindly followed the nobility and the clergy,

23

who had, to all intents and purposes, been replaced in the moral leadership of society by an enlightened Third Estate. Hence, the people identified themselves spiritually with the middle classes and collaborated with them in the revolution or, at worst, did not resist the armies of Bonaparte.

The French Revolution, opening a path for itself in Europe by force of arms, only encountered a single obstacle—the mercenary armies under the sluggish leadership of the nobility in the dying feudal States. In every case, victory on the field of battle was enough for Napoleon to conquer the whole nation. Holland submitted without opposition to Dumouriez' troops, and when the English, at the instigation of Pitt, tried to attack France on Dutch soil, the Dutch resisted the English troops. Holland, which was a *bourgeois* nation, energetically frustrated British intervention and, by doing so, proclaimed that she wanted no Wellingtons.

General Custine occupied Metz, "where there were German democrats", without firing a single shot. Montesquiou took Savoy, in the same way, without opposition. Italy opened its arms to the hero of Toulon at Lodi. After Austerlitz, Austria fell. At Jena, Prussia surrendered. The fact is that all that separated the French Revolution socially from the European nations which were still living under the *ancien régime* was summed up in the ranks of the troops which fought, first, against the Convention and afterwards against the intrepid Corsican. Once the enemy armies had been defeated, opposition to France ceased. Even in Prussia, Napoleon was regarded favourably by the people, who did not consider themselves *a priori* wronged by the French and would never have risen (as is proved by the time that elapsed before they reacted) if Bonaparte's soldiers had behaved less licentiously.

But in the Peninsula a very different experience awaited Napoleon. Even the very cobblestones, so to speak, rose up against the "tyrant". The Spanish people only knew him in a second-hand version, as an enemy in every field—the patriotic, the religious, the political. The Spanish nation rose *en masse* against the invader.

Nevertheless, there is no doubt that Napoleon could have come to an agreement with what little middle class there was. And such was the intention of the *afrancesados* or francophiles, who placed themselves at the orders of the usurper king, Joseph, the brother of Napoleon.

The *afrancesados* who were bold enough to come out into the open were a minority within the enlightened minority, because

24

popular feeling against the French intimidated many. The people and the clergy were practically the whole nation, and to run counter to the nation obviously involved grave risks. For this and other reasons—among them the nervousness of the French, who, seeing themselves surrounded by enemies, ended by turning their arms against the civil population—the most clear-sighted among the Spanish progressives led the revolution against Joseph Bonaparte, whose policy coincided in general with that of the *intelligentsia*.

The anti-French cause found, then, determined and influential champions in men like Jovellanos, Quintana, Flórez Estrada, Martínez de la Rosa, the Conde de Toreno and—in a class apart—the immortal artist Goya.

The fury with which Spain rose and the vigour with which she attacked the French—even those who had resided for years in the Peninsula—can be explained by the single fact that the people drew their inspiration only from the old ruling classes, beginning with the clergy.

In conceiving his military campaign against the Spanish Monarchy, following, it seems, the treacherous counsel of Talleyrand, who, with Fouché, was simply laying an ambush for him, Napoleon fell into the unpardonable error of forgetting what he himself represented and committed the crime of betraying his own ideas. The man who realized that he had been born just at the right time and in the right country to fulfil his mission, should not for a moment have been unmindful of what he confessed later at Saint Helena—that his system was not applicable to Spain. In Spain, it was not enough to defeat the Army. When the Spanish troops were routed, the war continued, because the people took up the fight.

The story is well known and there is no need to repeat it here. The Spanish people shed its blood in torrents for King, religion and country. First, for the King, symbol of national sovereignty, as it was then understood. Then, for religion, against *l'Armée de Voltaire*, as commanded by the Church; and lastly, for the motherland.

When in the autumn of 1813, the French armies crossed the Bidasoa and were finally expelled from the Peninsula, "French ideas" had gained ground, but commerce, industry and agriculture were ruined. And the nation, though its "philosophers" had multiplied through contact with the invader, had lost what few merchants it possessed.

## CHAPTER II

# THE MEN OF CADIZ

Spain made her French Revolution, that is to say, her *bourgeois* revolution . . . without a *bourgeoisie*. The merchant aristocracy who gave France her watchword did not exist, as we have just seen, in the Peninsula when the Cadiz Cortes proclaimed the miraculous advent of the sovereignty of the people. Outside a few coastal cities, headed by Cadiz, Spain was entirely without a *bourgeoisie*. The Spanish revolution was, then, to be the Cadiz revolution—Cadiz, and part of the universal principles of the *Encyclopédie*, against the whole of Spain.

With the aid of geography, the Spanish revolution took refuge in that far southern corner, the only place besides Barcelona where the revolution could thrive and maintain itself in being, thanks to the mercantile character of the city. The Spanish revolution and Spanish philosophic patriotism remained locked in Cadiz, driven out of the rest of Spain by the French Revolution and French philosophic patriotism.

At that time, Cadiz outstripped even Barcelona in maritime traffic. In 1832, 721 ships entered her harbour, 167 more than in the Catalan port.

From the outset of the fight between Liberalism and the absolute monarchy, Cadiz was the bulwark of liberty. There the Constitution was conceived and came to birth. Cadiz organized Riego's rising and financed him with funds supplied by some of her merchants, among them, Don José Montero, an upright and energetic business man, and Don Juan Alvarez y Mendez, known to history as Mendizábal, manager of the firm of *Bertran de Lis*. In 1821, Cadiz refused to accept a Governor appointed arbitrarily by Ferdinand VII, and rebelled against the Crown. When, two years later, the whole of Spain bowed down, like a cornfield swept by the wind, before the passing of the insolent troops of Angoulême, Cadiz was the last bastion of Liberalism to submit, and then not without saving her honour. When absolutism was re-established, the Liberal heart of the city still beat, and Cadiz announced, through the mouth of a battalion of Marines, that there were still constitutionalists in Spain. Twenty years later Narváez rose against Espartero, and Espartero fell, but Cadiz sided *en bloc* with the defeated revolution. After another five years of anguish for the Liberals, the door of Parliament half-opened, and Cadiz was ready with her team of progressive deputies. Finally, Admiral Topete announced in 1868, in Cadiz, the overthrow of the monarchy of Isabel II. The Spanish revolution suffered its first serious setback when it abandoned its cradle. No sooner had the Cortes been installed in Madrid than it died a violent death *manu militari*, in 1814. Some ideas, like sickly individuals, find a change of atmosphere fatal.

The men of the Spanish revolution—names like Martínez de la Rosa, Alcalá Galiano, Toreno, Muñoz Torrero, Mendizábal, Istúriz, Argüelles, Quintana, Canga, Flórez Estrada, Lista— were the leaders of a group, not of a social class. Spanish Liberalism was not a movement, or even a party; it was a sect. Outside Cadiz, Barcelona, and other—very few—mercantile cities, it was lost. And as happens with a sect, no sooner was it born than it had to go underground. The history of Spanish Liberalism throughout its eventful life was, to an incalculable extent, the history of secret societies and, in particular, of Freemasonry.

Here was, without doubt, another tragedy. And this tragedy of Spanish Liberalism, which was to be that of contemporary Spain, originated in the fact that the Liberals were never a social class and had to grapple with the question of reform in Spain, without having enough strength behind them. But the first fact—the fact that they were not a social class—was not within the power of the Liberals to amend; and the second—the question of national reform—could not, in the urgent interest of Spain, be avoided. Hence the tragic background of the conflict which began in 1810.

Referring to the war against the Moors of Granada, Menéndez Pelayo asked himself whether the existence of the Mohammedan religion was possible in sixteenth-century Spain. And the answer was, rightly, "No". Neither, then, was an absolute monarchy in Spain possible in nineteenth-century Europe.

The ideal of the absolutists was to make of the nation an airtight chamber, shutting out every breath of wind from the outside world; a nation which would be uniform, not so much in its Catholic faith, which was never seriously menaced, but in its political creed. Needless to say, everything conspired against this absurd theory of life.

Tradition can only save itself through a compromise between

27

the old values and the new age. The claim to perpetuate the past literally, discredits it; because when its rules are applied to a society which has to take its place in its epoch, and when its standards are maintained as if they were a sacred duty, in a medium which can only be faithful to them by cutting its own throat, what is created is not a pious copy of the past which it is hoped to preserve, but a repulsive caricature. The monarchy of Ferdinand VII was, in effect, a hideous and mutilated mask of the Catholic Monarchy of the sixteenth century.

It is not surprising, therefore, that the traditionalist error of judging the actions of the nineteenth-century Liberals by sixteenth-century ideas—or, to put it better, by Recaredo's ideas—should be succeeded by Liberal intolerance in appraising the deeds of sixteenth-century kings by the standard of eighteenth-century philosophy. In the nineteenth century Philip II had been dead for a long time, and in the sixteenth century Voltaire would never have dared to have been born.

The enemies of "progress" in Spain—foremost among them, the Church—wanted the impossible; and they did not perceive that Spanish Liberalism posed a problem which was exclusively political in character—a fact that should have caused no surprise, since Spanish Liberalism, though it included half a dozen Voltairians in its fold, was Catholic by birth. It repudiated the Inquisition, as Ferdinand VII was soon to be forced to repudiate it, on the intelligent grounds that it had outlived its day and was a dangerous anachronism even for the Church. But the Liberals substituted for the Inquisition the *Tribunal de Defensores de la Fe* (Tribunal of the Defenders of the Faith).

The Spanish Liberals headed their first Constitution with a paragraph which might have come straight out of the liturgy: "In the name of Almighty God, Father, Son and Holy Ghost, Author and Supreme Lawgiver of Society . . ." and declared in Article 12 that "the Religion of the Spanish nation is, and always will be, the Roman Catholic and Apostolic Religion, the only true Faith. The nation shall protect it by wise and just laws and forbid the exercise of any other". Moreover, the Cortes decreed that the episcopal *imprimatur* should be compulsory for all publications of a religious nature. And, finally, the deputies heard Mass before beginning their sessions.

Neither the Cadiz Cortes nor the majority of the men who were representative of it, had ceased to be Catholic; and those who were not, were fully conscious that they were in a minority and would not have dared to challenge the Catholic Church on the subject of dogma. "One man", wrote Oliveira Martins, "declaims in the Cortes speeches learnt by heart from the French tribune and straight away goes home to repeat the Trisagion devoutly and is full of pious horror of Freemasonry. Another piles texts on texts, proofs on proofs, to show that in the eleventh or twelfth centuries Spaniards were already parliamentary Liberals and that the revolution consists in re-establishing the canons of the Councils of Toledo or the imaginary *Cortes de Lamego.* The confusion could not be greater; but it would be impossible to find greater candour or more sincere good faith."

Quintana, the author of the ode *Al Panteón de El Escorial,* a severe diatribe against fanaticism, included the compulsory teaching of religion in schools in his plan of Public Education. According to this document, the minds of schoolchildren were to be introduced to religious dogmas. And twenty years later, the Constitution of 1837, with Liberal consent, put the stamp on religious exclusiveness in favour of the Catholic Church.

But with the Church hostile, in spite of everything, to the political and economic revolution, and with its ranks closed to every gesture of reform, what was begun in the Cadiz Cortes with the greatest respect for religion was bound to become soon a painful struggle between clericals and anti-clericals. For the social power of the Church in Spain was greater than the social power of the Church in France. It was already obvious that anyone who wanted to destroy the Spanish political and economic *ancien régime* would have to deal first, not with *les aristocrats,* but with the clergy. And as there was no historic middle class in Spain, the group of reformers charged by the whims of history with bringing to a head the *bourgeois* revolution without a *bourgeoisie,* was fatally converted into a sect, and through a mischance of the revolution, into an anti-clerical sect. Their revolution was hardly more than a riot; and the revolutionaries were to end, not by hanging bakers and burning *châteaux,* as in France, but by killing monks and setting fire to convents.

CHAPTER III

THE CHURCH

THE STORMY EVENTS in Spain during the first twenty years of the past century altered, confused and complicated the national life to such an extent that the only thing which appears simple at first sight is a negative fact—the total ·destruction of the old State. As a result of the six years' war, a terrific upheaval took place, and everything that was inflammable caught fire and everything that was shaky crashed into ruins. But at the same time as the old institutions in Spain were levelled to the ground, the vital elements at opposite poles of Spanish society, warned by the phenomenon, were preparing to rebuild the edifice on a new plan.

The Liberals, in the name of a people who were hostile or indifferent to them, invoked a strong Spanish parliamentary tradition which only existed in so far as they distorted history to suit their own purpose; while the Church, as the spokesman of the party at the other end of the pole, also called tradition, which she purposely misunderstood, to her aid.

Yet the divorce between the past and the Church was not less flagrant at that moment than the lack of connection between the new and the old Cortes. Phrases which the nobles addressed to the kings, with a view to restricting the rights of royalty, were placed by the men of Cadiz in the mouths of the people of that time; presenting as a triumph what, when it actually happened, was a menace to the Third Estate, and forgetting in their present spite against the absolute monarchy of yesterday that, when the latter was born, it signified a notable political advance and enjoyed the support of the people. What is more, without the support of the people, it would never have been able to impose its will.

A similar stratagem was employed by the Church, which appealed to a past when she had served the grandiose political plans of the monarch (the universal Catholic Monarchy) in order to legitimize her old dream of supplanting the Crown and enthroning a theocracy on the ruins of the State. For it would be the grossest error to assume that the Church stood on the defensive during the crisis which Spanish society underwent with the Napoleonic invasion and that she would be satisfied with the humiliation of the Liberals. No; the Church had other ends in view. Spain was left without institutions, a fundamental consequence of the convulsion; the Government was prostrate, without a real master, and the Church, which had fought and lost great battles with the Crown during the eighteenth century, now set out to govern—no more and no less.

Already the first *Junta Central*, presided over by the Conde de Floridablanca, who had forgotten his *penchant* for reform, was recalling the Spanish Jesuits from their exile in Italy whither Charles III, who preferred his own despotism to theirs, had expelled them. The *Junta* appointed a new Inquisitor, suspended the sales of property belonging to the religious orders and prohibited the printing of all kinds of publications without previous licence. There were not lacking bishops who proclaimed themselves *de facto* king, like the Bishop of Santander, who placed himself at the head of the *Junta* of that province, called himself sovereign Regent of Cantabria, and insisted on being treated as a Highness. The clergy found themselves more than adequately represented in the other *juntas,* and in many cases they were the sovereign agent at the head of these particles of the secular power. No institution possessed more power at that time than the Church. She dictated decrees, led *guerillas,* inspired enthusiasm, and set the tone of the campaign against the French.

But the revolution which, when the hold of the monarchy was loosened and the contempt in which the hereditary nobility was held became evident, induced the Church to fight for theocracy, stimulated the enlightened minority to impose upon society the representative system. Liberals and ultramontanes were like two armies locked in a struggle for the government, both seeking to limit the sovereignty of the Crown; the former, in the name of the sovereignty of the people, the latter, tacitly founding their right to govern on their incomparable mastery over Spanish society. Hence, the immediate collision between the spiritual arm and the King and the simultaneous conflict between the constitutionalists and the Crown.

Ferdinand VII needed the Church in order to maintain his terrible and carefully-guarded absolutism; and the Crown found it was able to strike a bargain. There could be no other meaning in the appointment of his confessor, Father Victor Sáez, to be his Minister. Father Sáez was supported by the Jesuits, who hastened to install themselves as the decisive factor in the new situation. But it was subsequently discovered that the Church did not subscribe to this view. The monarchy was a hindrance to the Church's plans for a theocracy. In the first place, Ferdinand VII was a sovereign who believed in personal and autocratic rule. He was not a docile king like Philip III or a supine king like Charles II. More absolutist than the most absolutist of the Hapsburgs and more despotic than the most despotic of the Bourbons, Ferdinand would go as far in repressing the Liberals as the Church could desire. The terror which followed the restoration of absolutism in 1823 is well known. The sadistic persecution of the Liberals, of whom 120 were executed in eighteen days, forced the Diplomatic Corps accredited to Madrid to lodge a protest at Court. Even General Pozzi di Borgo, the Czar's confidential envoy at Madrid, intervened in order to curb the excesses of the police. Who could doubt that the most exigent among the clergy would be satisfied with the anti-Liberalism of such a king! Owing to the pressure put on him by foreign Governments, Ferdinand was not able to re-establish the Inquisition, as he would have liked to do. But the rôle of the Inquisition was efficiently taken over by new organisms, like the *Juntas de la Fe* and the *Junta Secreta de Estado*, presided over by the fanatical Bishop of Osma, leader of *El Ángel Exterminador*. These *juntas* were certainly no less zealous than the Holy Office in guarding the "purity of the faith". Nevertheless, nothing the King could do to please her would satisfy the Church, because the Church wanted to govern, and this could only come about if the power of the Crown was completely annulled, or if the throne was occupied by someone who would consent to be the submissive head of a theocracy. In short, the clergy wanted all the power for themselves, and as Ferdinand VII did not prove compliant, the Church invented Carlism, a movement which we shall study later with the attention it deserves.

Why did the Church aim at supplanting the monarchy in the first third of the nineteenth century? This anachronistic proposal originated, obviously, in the formidable social position enjoyed by the clergy in Spain at the precise moment when civil society was at its lowest ebb.

At the opening of the nineteenth century, Spain possessed 2,390 monasteries and convents. The monastic life had claimed 59,768 men and 33,398 women, and these, with the 50,000 secular clergy, raised the number of persons consecrated to religion to 143,398. The number of monks and nuns was on the increase, since in 1787 there had been 10,000 less. For every 91 inhabitants there was an ecclesiastic in Spain; while in Russia, there was one for every 153 inhabitants; in Italy, one for every 200; and in France, one for every 280. Spain, therefore, had twice the number of clergy as Italy and three times as many as France, in proportion to the census of inhabitants. In some Spanish cities the number of clergy was superlatively high, as in Valladolid which harboured at that time one servant of the Church to every sixteen laymen.

The economic power of the Church was twice that of the Crown; and her juridical strength was such that there was no court in the land which was not invaded by the clergy, nor was there any case in which the ecclesiastical tribunals did not have a hand, even though the business concerned was, by its nature, far removed from the province of the clergy.

The Church's landed property comprised 1,300,000 hectares.[1] Her annual income from land and urban rents amounted to 600 million *reales*; from tithes and first-fruits, 324 million; from casual fees and offerings, 118 million.

Nominally, the Church paid taxes, and it is possible that from 20 to 25 million *reales* from tithes went to the Crown, and that the tax on sales was effective in the majority of cases, as far as the religious orders which engaged in industry and commerce were concerned; but all this must be taken with a grain of salt.

Add to this economic power the political power which necessarily derived from it, plus that which flowed from the adhesion of the people to the clergy, and we shall have an exact idea of the impregnable social vigour of the Church at that time.

When the authority of the Crown was shaken in the upheaval of 1808–13, the Church, which had no rival in the economic field, which had assumed the leadership of the masses in the political sphere and which was able to scare off all competitors in the domain of jurisdiction, was only therefore claiming official confirmation of her effective omnipotence in the real life of the State. The Church was laying claim to the whole "imperium" for herself and giving the Crown notice to quit. In the name of a mendacious traditionalism, the prelates were claiming to rule the monarchy, to lay down the law to the King and the nation.

But this was not the Spanish tradition, unless we are going back to the times of the Visigoths. For under the Catholic Monarchy of the sixteenth century, there was "a government inspired by the interests of the Faith, but exercised through the civil powers". Moreover, the Church was associated with the State in one and the same supreme mission, when the best intellects in the land set the canons for the Catholic world.

But all this was impossible now, in the nineteenth century, since a Spanish Church-State could not declare itself an appanage of the other world without staging a ridiculous farce, nor was there still a Protestant Reform movement to be kept at bay, nor were the times the same. Nor, above all, did the Church astonish by the knowledge of her priests, but rather by her intellectual poverty.

[1] 1 hectare = 2½ acres.

Menéndez Pelayo proved· that during the whole of the first thirty years of the nineteenth century, not a single treatise on pure theology was published in Spain, a fact which is all the more eloquent as it leads one to ask what the 150,000 Spaniards who had consecrated their lives (or at least, their bodies) to religion were doing.

The best Catholic brains in Spain (except for a few rebels) were bent solely on preserving the material power of the Church. And if afterwards some doubtful luminary, like Balmes, appeared, his work, which stood out like a palm tree in the desert, was purely practical in its scope, an appendix to a social order which was based on an iniquitous distribution of wealth and charged with apprehension at dangers which were beginning to threaten private property in his time. Balmes' lucubrations could not be greater than the mentality of their author, and their author was a good Catalan *bourgeois*.

However, the Catholic genius of the nineteenth century in Spain was apparently not Balmes, but Donoso Cortés. The furore which the speeches and writings of the Marques de Valdegamas created in official Catholic circles in Spain was a measure of the barrenness of Catholic intellects. They courted this author for the socially reactionary character of his essays. This was what interested them. His most celebrated work, the *Ensayo sobre el catolicismo, el liberalismo y el socialismo, considerados en sus principios fundamentales* reflects the militant attitude of a social sector which was fearful of losing its privileges. Donoso Cortés was a convert from extreme Liberalism, who engaged in battle with the ardour inseparable from those who have been baptized in this Jordan. There is no possible comparison between this Catholic publicist and the best brains of Spanish Catholicism in its heyday. Neither his by no means impeccable style, nor his unoriginal ideas—as unoriginal as those of the Liberals—justified his instant success. When someone reproached him for his excessive use of Gallicisms, he replied "that no one can rise to the heights of metaphysics with a language which has never been tamed by a philosopher".

Donoso Cortés' admirers hailed him as the prophet of the new Catholicism, a Spanish genius, to whom the Liberals, those bad translators from the French, ought to take off their hats. But Donoso, whose merit consisted in having silently imported the ideas of Joseph de Maistre, was himself a translator.

The truth is that after the death of Sor Maria de Ágreda, the genuine Catholic tradition in Spain was bereft of intellectual vigour. Praise is due to the cultural work carried out by certain

Catholic writers and scholars, like Menéndez Pelayo, who commanded respect and admiration, but there was no official Catholic (Unamuno was not one) who could compete in freshness and originality of thought with the most modest of the Spanish theologians who took part in the Council of Trent. When the nineteenth century dawned, it was a long time since men like Vázquez Menchaca, Vozmediano, Cano, Suárez, Lainez, etc., had been seen.

It was obviously a disaster that in the supreme moment in the modern history of Spain, the Church should be so rich in worldly goods and so poor in intellectual values. When she was in her intellectual heyday, she was able to reform and to save herself, as witness the changes introduced into the ecclesiastical world by Cardinal Cisneros and Santa Teresa. It was in this way also that Spain avoided the impact of Protestant Reform.

On the threshold of the nineteenth century, the Church was the cornerstone of the social fabric in Spain; but she did not know how to confront a change from which Spain could not escape.

An enlightened Church would have initiated the most urgent political and economic reforms, as Cardinal Belluga desired to do in the eighteenth century, and this would have saved Spain and the Church. As this did not happen, both came to grief. If the reform of Spanish society was not brought about with the Church's consent, it would have to be done against her will; and the second alternative prevailed—this was the catastrophe. The ecclesiastical hierarchy completely ignored the rôle they ought to play. Like the Spanish-Roman clergy when Roman Spain disappeared, the Spanish clergy were politicians, probably because they could not cease being politicians; and, in justice, it was not this that they had to reproach themselves with, at the beginning of the nineteenth century. But they could have been better politicians than they were. Their ignorance and avarice made them the worst possible advisers, or incapable rulers, without any better title to rule the nation than their unmerited social pre-eminence. For Churchmen no longer monopolized knowledge as they did in the sixteenth century. And the inevitable conflict between the social power of the Church and her incapacity to administer it to the benefit of herself and of the nation, tended to translate itself into the rapid decline of the Church's popularity. The people lost all respect for an uncouth priest who preached political violence and executed it with his own hand. By leading police repression against a movement as inoffensive from the Catholic point of view as

Spanish Liberalism was at birth, the clergy seemed like the winds which heralded the tempests of tomorrow. The people began withdrawing their support from an institution which could reform nothing because it stood in need itself of a sweeping reform. And from attacking the Liberals, the people turned on the clergy. In 1834, there occurred the first murder of friars in Madrid, and the following year saw a repetition of the disorders. Already convents were burning in Barcelona, Saragossa, Reus and Murcia.

CHAPTER IV

# THE PRONUNCIAMIENTOS

SPAIN HAS ADDED the word *pronunciamiento* to the universal dictionary. And as words usually only become international when they have a typical, restricted and eloquent meaning which springs from the originality of the thing represented by them, it would seem as if Spain, with this word, had created a social phenomenon hitherto unknown to the world. We come back always to the same thing: the Spaniard is a singularly constituted being who loves civil war and, as soon as he dons a uniform, falls a victim to the morbid pleasure of rebelling against his civil institutions. Nothing could be farther from the truth. The presence of the Army in Spanish politics does not imply any psychological defect in the Spaniard, but the existence of the same tumour to which must be attributed all the fatal anomalies which may be observed in the functioning of Spanish society.

Two factors conspired to project the Army into Spanish politics. The revolutionary war of 1808–14 overthrew the fundamental institutions without new ones taking root. And this happened at a moment when the Army was at its apogee, at the hour when every Spaniard was donning a uniform, and when before the eyes of even the most modest there dangled the splendid prize of a general's rank. The coincidence of the decrepitude of the old State, defenceless and without moral authority, with the full-blooded ascendancy of the armed forces, converted both professional and amateur soldiers into arbiters of the destiny of Spain. Spain was in a state of anarchy.

When peace was restored, there remained at large a good number of generals and Army officers whose career had been brusquely cut short at the moment of their greatest glory. The

Liberals were reduced to seeking outside the law, in the cata-
combs of conspiracy, the force which public opinion had denied
them. The current feeling of the epoch, which was deeply
coloured by romanticism, favoured the proceeding, and the
amazing conduct of the Court seemed to authorize all the
excesses of its subjects. It was a providential occasion for dormant
ambition to unsheathe the sword once again in the pursuit of
fortune. Crown and subjects rivalled one another in flattering
the Army, the only decisive force left, once the civil and ecclesiastical institutions had been drained of their moral energy.

In the Spain of the last 130 years, revolutionaries and
reactionaries, Liberals and Conservatives, have confided to the
Army, the former, the revolution which the Liberal minority
were incapable of leading in a nation without a middle class,
the latter, the counter-revolution which the crumbling monarchy
could not carry out with its own feeble hands. In a healthy and
vital State, civil society watches over its prerogatives; in a
nation where these prerogatives pass to the armed forces, civil
society is corrupt. "The Army", declared Narváez, "is rotten
to the core." And it could not be otherwise. But at the same
time, the systematic incursion of the Army into public affairs
was a sure proof that not only the Army but the whole nation
was organically sick or corrupt, with a corruption or sickness
which went deep and which had nothing to do with administrative immorality or the decay of morals, but, as we shall see
later, was the fatal result of maintaining à outrance a system
of property which was harmful to the social order.

The constant intervention of the Spanish Army in public life
throughout the nineteenth century, coupled with present-day
events, has led many to think that Spain is a militaristic nation.
This is not so. The usurpation of the functions of government
by the military is a social phenomenon. In no country was the
Army more obedient to civil law than in Spain, so long as Spain
had a civil power which was morally unassailable. This is clearly
borne out by Spanish society in the sixteenth century, not only
in the Peninsula, but also in the remotest regions of the monarchy,
where the armed forces had the greatest inducements to go
astray. The conduct of Hernán Cortés in founding Vera Cruz
is an unsurpassable example of the humility of which Spanish
arms were capable in their dealings with civil society in the
Golden Age of both.

In ancient society, when the soldier was a citizen and the
citizen a soldier, and when the bearing of arms was a privilege

reserved to owners of property, the Army was very different from what it is today. But with all this, the Roman Senate took its precautions. When the legions camped on the Aventine, the Senate, seeing the spectre of anarchy and civil war (in which the patricians had everything to lose) loom before the city, yielded. But such prudence in a body which was traditionally jealous of the prerogatives of civil society may be excused by the peculiar constitution of the Army, which was not the military arm of the State, as it is today, but rather, the citizenry in arms.

The reaction which followed the assassination of the second of the Gracchi at a later date—the brutal reaction of an unjust Government, enemy of the invigorating reforms of the civil power—introduced armed force for the first time in Rome as a decisive element in the life of the State. Of the abjectness of this Government, Mommsen tells us that it was not possible to govern worse than did the Restoration in the years 117–109 B.C. Its baseness, he continues, was only exceeded by its incompetence. That was the epoch of the wars with the African petty king Jugurtha "who only told the truth, the pure and simple truth, when, on leaving Rome, he declared that if he had had enough gold, he could have bought the whole city".

The corruption of the Roman civil State invited the Army to enter the political lists. Marius set the legions to overthrow the aristocracy. Roman civil society was never to recover its ancient vigour in a sure and definitive manner. The civil power had degenerated, and Rome was to witness the disputes of the factious generals, fighting among themselves to establish their respective dictatorships (in the modern meaning of the word). Some, Marius and Caesar, were the generals of the democratic party; others, Sulla and Pompey, the champions of the aristocracy. In the analogous conflict of the nineteenth century, Spain was to have her Marius in Riego and her Sulla in Narváez. Avaricious Fortune, less generous to Spain than to Rome, denied the former the beneficent monarchy of Caesar and in its place substituted the complex and ephemeral regency of Espartero.

For a Spaniard, the political history of Rome, from the attempted reforms of Sempronius Gracchus to the triumph of Caesar, is very suggestive. In parts, this period of Roman history can be compared with Spanish history in the nineteenth century, which we have not yet outlived. That this was realized in Spain is proved by the fact that in 1854 Madrid was talking of the resurrection of the consulate, and Espartero and O'Donnell were referred to as "the Consuls".

The close parentage between events so distant in time as those which occurred in Rome's gravest crisis and those which have fallen upon the Spanish nation in our day, can be explained by the analogy between the social circumstances. And the parallelism is most marked in the character of the aggression of the armed forces against the civil government. The rivalry between Marius and Sulla was born on the battlefields of Africa, as the rivalry between Espartero and Narváez sprang from the first Carlist war. And in both cases, the political parties extolled the military glories of one general at the expense of the other. Political passion incited the parties to take their stand behind the generals, no doubt because they thought that the only force still unshaken was the military, or brute force.

By glorifying the respective generals in this way, the parties made them aspirants to the control of public affairs. And the mutual bitterness which was engendered in the struggle for the laurels of war was translated by the generals into the political arena, once they had been converted by the weakness of the Senate or the monarchy into arbiters of the political destinies of the nation.

The process of self-destruction of the civil State was the same in Rome as in Spain. The Roman Army, reorganized by Marius when he recruited the legions to fight in Africa, was no longer the republican militia of past days, but a body of armed retainers inspired by *esprit de corps*. When he incorporated into his columns the poorer citizens and made it possible for the most humble officer to become a general, Marius created a professional military force which opened the door, as volunteers, to innumerable individuals who had nothing to lose. This revolution in the life of the Roman Army had its points of contact with the revolution which occurred in Spain during the War of Independence, which threw up so many generals of the Marius type. In addition, coinciding, as I said before, with the relaxation of the civil power, Rome, like Spain, found herself entangled in wars abroad and at home, a circumstance which placed the nation in a state of permanent warfare, to the consequent advantage of the Army and the extension of its jurisdiction.

The first successful Liberal *pronunciamiento* in Spain took place in January 1820, under the leadership of Riego. Riego rose at Cabezas de San Juan at the head of 1,500 men who had been told (like the 22,000 men waiting to embark for America on the south coast) that if the revolution triumphed, they would be suitably rewarded. Here were, perhaps, new elements which completed the comparison between these forces and the troops of the conqueror of the Cimbri. Riego's army, like the armies of Espartero, Narváez and Prim later on, bore an unmistakable likeness to the Praetorian Guard. And in the subversive actions of Marius, the first general to raise a rebellion in Rome, factors were at play identical with those which influenced Riego. Mommsen's judgment on this point might apply *mutatis mutandis* to the Spain of 1820. "The Senate", he wrote, "was, or appeared, so powerless and discredited, so hated and despised, that Marius thought he would need no help in challenging it beyond his own immense popularity and hoped, if this assumption failed, to find support, in spite of the dissolution of the army, among the discharged soldiers, under promise of rewards."

The confidence of the conspirators of Cadiz and Seville was also founded, not so much on their military effectives, as on the disrepute into which the monarchy had fallen. And this faith gave them the victory. A major and half a company—at the end, Riego had only forty-five soldiers—were enough to overthrow that fiction of a civil State.

Spain suffered forty-three *pronunciamientos* between 1814 and 1923, thirty-two of which failed or were suppressed and eleven succeeded. And the number of these risings, which was only exceeded by the Roman Praetorian Guard, shows that in Spain there must be a social condition *sui generis* to account for the fact that the harmful phenomenon of the *pronunciamiento* is repeated there with much greater frequency than in other countries where the Army also intervenes in politics. The reason for Spain's lamentable supremacy in this field must be sought in the national characteristics of civil war, and one of the decisive factors was the theocratic nature of the Church. This itch to dominate civil society and keep it prisoner launched the clergy, armed, onto the battlefields and kept Spain in a state of permanent warfare throughout the nineteenth century. In no other nation among those which, in modern times, have endured the misrule of the Army, do we find this peculiar formation, which is the prototype of the Spanish conflict. This feature of the struggle will be drawn in clearer detail in the chapter dealing with Carlism.

## CHAPTER V

# THE ORGAN OF THE LIBERAL
# REVOLUTION

THE LACK OF a social *point d'appui* in constitutionalism made Spain a particularly fertile breeding-ground of secret societies. Moreover, with the ideas of the *Contrat Social*, there swept over Spain the wave of romanticism which Rousseau, as Belloc has observed, released, and everything combined to make the country a hotbed of declamatory sects and intrepid conspirators. The type of romantic conspirator is well known—one of those persons who lend most colour to an epoch. Romanticism saturates all the manifestations of life; in literature, it derides the old masters; in politics, it overrides conventionalism and scruples. A movement of rebellion and protest, it could not fail to shed its rays on Liberals and Carlists, at a time when Carlism was in a minority in the nation.

Secret societies and patriotic societies go hand in hand; and in Spain, when the century was already well advanced, the latter took the form of an imitation of the French Jacobins. But the imitation was to fail in the self-same way as all Spanish progressive movements failed. Jacobinism was a national movement, and the Spanish patriotic societies never achieved the status of more than a sub-sect. All the Jacobins of Madrid could have been contained in a single café. These rickety organs of the revolution, if we may call them so, however great their trouble-making capacity, lacked the support of the people, while the French Jacobins were basically a popular institution, with their 44,000 active and lively centres all over France. Strictly speaking, the Jacobins, as a popular force, took precedence, perhaps, of the Convention. Their proceedings, far from being merely the intrigues of a secret society, were published in the *Moniteur*.

In contrast, the Madrid patriotic societies shed no influence outside the capital, and even there, their activities appeared to be confined to provoking local disturbances.

In Spain, French Jacobinism, which was, as I have said, a mass movement, could not take root. But the Spanish Liberals wanted a revolution, and that revolution had to have an organ. The political parties of that modest middle class could not be such an organ because, however great an effort the enthusiasts made, they could never, to begin with, find elements among the nation to constitute anything on a national scale. And not only was Liberalism, through its divorce from the medium in which it worked, a sect and nothing but a sect; but it was conscious of the fact. This made it superlatively apt in sectarian practices, or, to put it in another way, in political occultism. On the other hand, the enormous social power of the clergy made it appear as if the Church were the principal, if not the only, obstacle which blocked the road to revolution. Reducing the problem to its simplest elements, the historic crisis came to be a conflict between the Liberal sect and the theocratic movement. The Liberals ended up as anti-clericals and the organ of the revolution became Freemasonry.

Some authorities assign the origins of Freemasonry in Spain to the eighteenth century. But this society, which blossomed out in the eighteenth century, was quite distinct from that which was later to head the Liberal revolution. There were freemasons in Spain before the arrival of the French with Joseph Bonaparte, but there was no masonic organization worthy of the name. The first lodges were formed by Joseph's Frenchmen and the *afrancesado* Spaniards under the authority and direction of the former. Towards the end of 1816, at the height of the terror unleashed by Ferdinand's *camarilla*, a new society, calling itself the reformed society, began to function at Granada. The French organization had suffered the amputations and additions which, in the judgment of the Spanish reformers, were rendered necessary by circumstances. The new society had no sharply-defined political character and was not founded in order to re-establish the Constitution of 1812. A lodge soon appeared in Madrid under the orders of the Granada lodge, and about the same time, another branch started its activities in Cadiz which, under the name of *Soberano Capítulo*, met at the residence of the Cadiz capitalist Don Francisco Javier de Istúriz. The success of the movement in this middle-class city led to the foundation of a central lodge under the high-sounding and ponderous title of *Taller Sublime* (Sublime Workshop).

During the three years which elapsed between the foundation of the reformed society at Granada and the *pronunciamiento* of Rafael del Riego, the secret assemblies did not cease to conspire. The Church launched a campaign against them and the Madrid and Granada lodges had to be dissolved, while in Valencia, General Elío suppressed a conspiracy of the same stamp with draconian severity.

It was in Cadiz that the sect found the atmosphere most propitious. There it had opened its doors to the Army, frankly assuming the guise of a political organization. Hardly had it established itself, than Freemasonry became the organ of the Liberal revolution. The Army officers of the Cadiz garrison (not the rank and file, because the society was not a democratic institution) joined the lodges, fully conscious of the fact that they had to do with a political entity. The arrival at Cadiz and the neighbouring ports of the expeditionary force which was to proceed overseas to suppress the secessionist movement in Spanish America, was an event from which Freemasonry swiftly reaped a rich harvest. The régiment which did not have its lodge was now an exception.

The introduction of the dogma of popular sovereignty in a nation which, on the dissolution of its institutions, spontaneously initiated the march towards theocracy because the clergy remained the sole repository of social power, was bound to make of the Spanish revolution an original drama. Fate had been steadily gathering together the diverse elements in this drama, and when Freemasonry became the leading organ of subversion, all the factors which go to make up the chaotic physiognomy of nineteenth-century Spain as we know it, were already present on the stage. Revolution was about to begin, by the hand of a sect which was incapable of carrying it through successfully.

The Cadiz lodges finally decided to re-establish the Constitution of 1812. This was a step of considerable political gravity; for if the revolutionary conspiracy triumphed, the Society was also going to triumph; and with victory, Freemasonry would become the *deus ex machina* of Spanish Liberal politics—a veritable catastrophe for Liberalism, as we shall see later.

With the plot going ahead, no one was allowed to participate in it who had not first become a freemason. In this way, the revolutionaries, unlike the Jacobins, kept out the popular elements and imprisoned themselves in a sectarianism which was later to ignore the interests of the people in essential economic reforms. The revolution against the Church was to be set on foot; but this did not necessarily imply that the people would gain thereby, as will be proved later.

From the first moment, then, the freemasons, by reason of their closed organization founded on the aristocratic principle, dispensed with the people; and the liberty they set out to conquer was to be imperilled as soon as won, because to gain it, they made use of a professional Army, very proud of its *esprit de corps*, very Praetorian, which envisaged revolution as a continuation of the adventure which had been interrupted by the departure of the French from Spain, and which enlisted in Freemasonry to evade a duty. This Army was as dangerous an enemy of civil society and liberty as the Church. Freemasonry mobilized the Army against the Church, but this type of Army could not be mobilized against the Church without being mobilized at the same time against the nation. The intervention of armed force in politics through the agency of the freemasons endangered any future simulacrum of a civil State which the Liberals may have proposed to set up.

An obscure personage—afterwards immortalized by martyr-dom—a major of the Asturian regiment of the garrison town of Cabezas de San Juan, rose with his troops at dawn on January 1st, 1820, and proclaimed the Constitution of 1812. This soldier, as I pointed out in the previous chapter, was Rafael del Riego, who had passed most of the War of Independence as a prisoner in France, after having given proofs of laudable fidelity to his leader. Riego was ordered to march silently on Arcos de la Frontera, but he preferred to operate on his own account and did not keep to the plan. On the following day, Colonel Quiroga rose at Alcalá de los Gazules. With Riego, there went over hill and plain the future financier of the revolution, Mendizábal.

The movement had triumphed and Freemasonry had struck a shrewd blow at absolutism.

Army chiefs and officers and the rank and file now hurriedly thronged to familiarize themselves with the sect. Spain once more had a Liberal Government. But another secret Government, formed by the representatives of the provincial lodges, was preparing to dictate policy to the Ministers, none of whom was as yet a mason. The sect had demolished absolutism and was jealously denying all non-sectarians the right to govern. The Government of the day was obstructing Freemasonry, and as it was also obstructing Ferdinand VII, absolutists and masons now agreed, at least up to a point. The masons were so impatient that they sent a special envoy—Alcalá Galiano—for an interview with Father Cirilo de la Alameda, General of the Franciscans and head of the absolutist Apostolic Party, an ecclesiastic who played a great part in the history of the nineteenth century. Father Cirilo proposed, on behalf of Ferdinand VII, to explore the possibilities of forming a homogeneous masonic Government. The negotiations did not bear fruit, for the moment; but the Government could not maintain itself without the acquiescence of Freemasonry—already the indisputable and powerful organ of the Liberal revolution—and several Ministers, among them Argüelles and Valdés, had to become members of the sect. The Ministers became masons, and Freemasonry began to split up. The Society's incapacity to direct Liberal policy made chaos of the revolution, since as a secret society it could not govern, but as the organ of the revolution, it arrogated to itself the function of electing the executive power.

The "Third Estate" of Freemasonry, the sector nearest the people, were not slow in deciding that the rite lacked a tradition in Spain and, romantically invoking the Liberal tradition, founded *Los Comuneros* or *Hijos de Padilla*. The *Comuneros* adopted a different liturgy; instead of the square and compass and other masonic symbols, they used other signs, with the castle as the centrepiece of the ceremony. The fact is that Spanish Liberalism could not disobey its sectarian conscience, in the purest meaning of the word. There is no doubt that, in parting company with Freemasonry, the men who founded the *Comuneros* aspired to set up a democratic organization. The mother sect, rigidly hierarchical, with its dogmatic scale of categories, the absolute-monarchist character of the leadership and the oath of blind obedience to the Grand Orient, was hardly compatible with the aspirations of the people. The new entity swept into its ranks all the non-commissioned officers. But the fact that the *Comuneros* persisted in using formulas of the masonic type and did not break away from Freemasonry and become a party proves, as I said before, how strong in Liberal circles was the sectarian sentiment.

Hereafter, Freemasonry and the *Comuneros* were to quarrel over their clientèle with the zeal of competitors in the same industry.

In 1822, Riego, now a general, became the leader of the freemasons, who set up a Government which was approved by Ferdinand VII, under violent protest from the sister sect, which could not reconcile itself to being deprived of ministerial representation.

Freemasonry must be reckoned an important factor in any impartial study of the Spanish pandemonium. The activities of this secret society would not have had any special significance in Spain, if fate had not decreed that the society should become the organ of the revolution. The Spanish revolution, difficult and chaotic enough in itself, became extraordinarily complicated through the part played by the lodges in the events of the day. The interests of Freemasonry were most certainly not those of the revolution; yet when the Liberals entrusted the transformation of the nation to this society, the whole work was bound to receive the imprint of masonic preoccupations and obsessions.

Freemasonry was spiritually prepared for a superficial type of politics, but neither its character as a secret society completely out of touch with the common people, nor its religious façade, rendered it capable of a more serious enterprise.

CHAPTER VI

# SYNOPSIS OF THE GENERAL CIVIL WAR (1812–1945)

ALTHOUGH WE ARE wont to speak of the Spanish civil wars, in reality there is only one civil war. What we understand by civil wars are merely military campaigns or exceptionally violent clashes in the great Spanish civil war whose point of departure is the Napoleonic invasion and whose end is not yet in sight. During the last 130 years, Spain has never known tranquillity. An unending tale of violence—*pronunciamientos* of every kind, terrorism, rebellion in the countryside, separatist movements—proclaimed on every occasion, even in the intervals when the military truce was in force, that the nation was living in a state of endemic civil war. We have, then, before us a single civil war, which appears sometimes in the guise of a localized conflict, sometimes of a nation-wide campaign; and more often than not, in the form of that secret collective rancour which is an unfailing premonitory symptom of social tempests.

Up to the present moment, this age-old struggle has fallen into thirteen periods, six reformist and seven anti-reformist, and is governed apparently by the swing of the pendulum between revolution and counter-revolution, which dislodge one another from power without either possessing sufficient strength to impose itself definitely on the community. The following table illustrates this point.

| Period | Years of Government | Character |
|---|---|---|
| Cortes of Cadiz | 1812–1814 | R[1] |
| Ferdinand VII | 1814–1820 | C |
| Restoration Const. 1812 | 1820–1823 | R |

[1] "R"=revolutionary or reformist; "C"=counter-revolutionary or conservative.

| Period | Years of Government | Character |
|---|---|---|
| Ferdinand VII | 1823–1833 | C |
| Marti. de la Rosa—-Toreno[1] | 1834–1835 | Transition |
| Mendizábal—Espartero | 1835–1843 | R |
| González Bravo—Narváez | 1843–1854 | C |
| Espartero—Madoz | 1854–1856 | R |
| O'Donnell—Narváez—G. Bravo | 1856–1868 | C |
| Serrano—Prim—-Republic | 1868–1874 | R |
| Restoration | 1874–1931 | C |
| Republic | 1931–1939 | R |
| Army—Falange | 1939–(?) | C |

We must now examine the core of each period and determine
the meaning of revolution and counter-revolution. In this way,
we shall see the civil war in its skeleton, stripped of its outward
and spectacular part.

REVOLUTIONARY PERIOD. 1812–14

(a) *Economic Aspect*. On general lines, the Cortes of Cadiz
proposed to abolish feudal and ecclesiastical privileges. The
spearhead of the revolution was to be the mobilization of entailed property among civil and ecclesiastical institutions. The
law of August 1811 decreed that jurisdictional seigniories should
be incorporated in the nation. A later decree suppressed the
*mayorazgos*, or entailed estates, worth less than 3,000 ducats,
but respected those of greater value, provided this did not exceed
80,000. In September 1813, it was decreed that the interest on
the National Debt should be covered, while the war lasted, by
the income from the Grand Masterships and the vacant *encomiendas*
or estates belonging to the military Orders, by the property of
the Inquisition, and by the surplus revenue of the monasteries
after meeting the expenses of worship and maintenance of the
monks. In January of the same year (I am following the thematic
and not the chronological order), the Cortes decreed the handing
over to private ownership of all the *bienes de propios* or lands
rented out by the communes, except the *ejidos*, or those within
a kilometre of the villages. In June, they proclaimed the freedom
of industry, and with it the death of the guilds. Finally, they
put up for sale the property of the monasteries. They took up,
at last, the cause of agriculture against the abusive privileges

[1] I give the most outstanding names for each period.

of the *Mesta*, ordering the enclosure of lands under private ownership and dictating other measures limiting the political power of the stock-breeders.

(b) *Political*. The Cortes introduced the Liberal Constitution of March 19th, 1812, the first that Spain had. This political Code was a copy of the French Constitution of 1791, save in its religious aspect, though in some ways it was more radical than the French model, as, for example, in the matter of the royal veto of the laws, which in France could extend up to five years and here was limited to two. The Cortes created the National Militia, also in imitation of the French National Guard. They established a Council of State with forty members. They decreed that the town councils should be elected by universal suffrage, and the single legislative Chamber by restricted suffrage, based on an income qualification. They founded the *Diputaciones provinciales*, or economic organisms for the provinces. They abolished the Inquisition. They ordered schools to be provided in all the villages of Spain and her colonies. They closed religious houses of less than twelve members and prohibited the existence of more than one convent of the same order in one place.

COUNTER-REVOLUTIONARY PERIOD. 1814–20

(a) *Economic*. Ferdinand VII repealed the law relating to juri dictional seigniories and restored the *mayorazgos*. He ordered the guilds to resume their functions. He restored to the clergy the property which had been sold, without compensating the buyers. He suspended all alienation of the *bienes de propios*, but the state of the Treasury compelled him to sell common lands and Crown property in order to meet the public debt.

(b) *Political*. He annulled the Constitution of 1812 and abolished the Council of State. He imposed on the municipalities the régime of 1808 and swept away the *Diputaciones provinciales*. The Inquisition was re-established. Finally, the Monarchy arrogated to itself all the prerogatives of absolutism, as understood by Ferdinand VII.

REVOLUTIONARY PERIOD. 1820–23

(a) *Economic*. The Cortes again put up for sale the estates belonging to the religious orders. By a decree dated October 1st, 1820, they abolished monasteries and monastic orders, monastic colleges, convents, military Orders (except the Knights Hospitallers) and applied to the redemption of the National Debt the surplus income of the existing religious houses and all the property of those which had been closed down. By a law of October 11th of the same year, ecclesiastical bodies were forbidden to acquire real estate, or to accept legacies and bequests. The Cortes again put into force the decree of 1813 which handed over the *bienes de propios* to private ownership. In 1822, these estates were ordered to be divided in such a way that each parcel could maintain five persons. Once more the Cortes proclaimed the freedom of industry. Where before certain *mayorazgos* had been abolished, now they were all abolished.

(b) *Political*. The Constitution of 1812 was re-established. The Council of State resumed its functions. Municipal liberties were restored, with full administrative autonomy. The *Diputaciones provinciales* were reinstated. The Cortes ordered the national territory to be divided into fifty-two provinces, on the French model. It was decided to expel the Jesuits and abolish the Inquisition. The Central University was founded.

COUNTER-REVOLUTIONARY PERIOD. 1823-33

(a) *Economic*. Ferdinand VII re-established the guilds. The religious orders regained their property in similar circumstances as obtained during the period 1814-20. The *mayorazgos*, the fount of the nobility's power, were restored. The reform of property was annulled in so far as was practicable. The law of 1831 deprived the villages of the right enjoyed by the local inhabitants of pasturing cattle on stubble and fallow.

(b) *Political*. The Constitution of 1812 was again abolished. The municipalities returned to the régime of 1808. The *Diputaciones provinciales* disappeared. The project to divide Spain into fifty-two provinces was set aside. The Council of State was declared extinct. The Jesuits returned to their monasteries, with the other Orders. The Universities were closed and teaching was declared to be the monopoly of the religious orders. Ferdinand VII took the *Juntas de la Fe*, the substitute for the Inquisition, under his protection.

INTERREGNUM OF 1833-5

(a) *Economic*. Status quo.
(b) *Political*. When Ferdinand VII died, there were 353 more religious houses than in 1808, but 38,000 fewer monks and nuns. Carlism rose in arms against the Queen. The municipal régime suffered modification. Those religious houses where a sixth

part of the community had joined the Carlist cause were closed. The National Militia was born again under the name of City Militia (*Milicia Urbana*). An amnesty was proclaimed. The Universities opened their doors again. Martínez de la Rosa promulgated the Royal Statute, with its Chambers of Grandees (*Próceres*) and *Procuradores*, in imitation of the French Charter of 1814. Toreno expelled the Jesuits and the State confiscated their property.

REVOLUTIONARY PERIOD. 1835–43

(a) *Economic*. The guilds were abolished once more. The law of October 11th, 1835, decreed the dissolution of the religious orders, except those engaged in teaching poor children, or in nursing the sick, or in training missionaries for the Philippines. In January 1836, the Government expelled the friars and took over their houses. The decrees of February 19th and of March 5th and 8th of the same year abolished all monasteries and such convents as housed less than twenty professed nuns, the monks and nuns who were expelled receiving pensions of three and five *reales*. These dispositions were upset by intervening political events; but the revolution returned to the charge and produced the law of September 2nd, 1841, which abolished all the monasteries, convents, colleges, brotherhoods and other religious houses for both sexes, and appropriated for the benefit of the nation all the property of the secular clergy, cathedral, collegiate and parish, except that of the prebends, chaplaincies, benefices and so forth under family patronage; brotherhoods and pious works proceeding from individual acquisitions; property dedicated to the use of hospitals, works of charity and education; churches and the adjacent dwellings of prelates and priests, with their grounds. The Constitution of 1837 provided for the total abolition of tithes and decreed in exchange that, as from the following year, the maintenance of the clergy and of public worship was to become a charge on the nation.

(b) *Political*. In August 1836, the Constitution of Cadiz was proclaimed. The nation adopted a new Constitution as the result of a compromise in June 1837. (It appears that the British Ambassador, Lord Clarendon, pointed out the English Reform Act of 1832 as a model for this Code of Laws.)

COUNTER-REVOLUTIONARY PERIOD. 1843–54

(a) *Economic*. By a decree of July 26th, 1844, the sale of property belonging to the secular clergy and to convents was annulled.

The law of April 9th, 1845, provided for the return to the secular clergy of any estates which had been alienated. Under the terms of the Concordat of May 13th, 1851, the sale of all Church property was suspended and the right of the Church to acquire other property was recognized. The estates due to be restored under the law of 1845 were returned to the Church. The prelates undertook to mortgage the property so restored and invest the proceeds in State bonds. (This part of the Concordat was never carried out; the Church did not dispose of the lands nor did the Treasury acquire any money.) A law was passed whereby 25 million pesetas were set aside annually for public worship and the clergy. Tithes were restored, half of which were to be paid over to the State.

(b) *Political.* A law was promulgated restricting municipal liberties (the same law which, when it was approved by the Cortes in 1840, was the immediate occasion of the Queen Regent leaving Spain). The National Militia was disbanded. The Government dissolved the Town Council of Madrid, the Congress of Deputies and the entire Senate. González Bravo founded the Civil Guard. The Charter of 1845, which revoked the principle of universal suffrage, was imposed on the nation. Narváez assumed dictatorial powers. In December 1851, Bravo Murillo brought in a Bill to reform the Charter of 1845, with a view to enabling the Crown to legislate in urgent cases. The Concordat of 1851 (already alluded to) was concluded with the Vatican. This Concordat affirmed that the Catholic religion should be the only one tolerated in Spain; and authorized the Orders of St. Philip Neri, St. Vincent de Paul and a third Order to be nominated from among those approved by the Pope, to reside in Spain—the famous clause which, by the expedient of leaving the third Order unnamed, served as a pretext for the Church to allow as many Orders as she wished to function in Spain.

REVOLUTIONARY PERIOD. 1854–6

(a) *Economic.* By a law of April 29th, 1855, the sale was decreed of all landed property belonging to the State, charitable establishments, schools and municipalities. The decrees of May 1st, 1855, and July 11th, 1856, authorizing the sale of all Church lands were promulgated. Under the afore-mentioned law of 1855, lands belonging to the communes, guilds and charitable institutions were included at this period along with Church property. By a special disposition, it was laid down that this enormous mass of property should be sold by auction and in small lots, so that the poorer classes would be able to acquire it. The latter were granted very easy terms of payment. They were required to pay only 10 per cent of the purchase price at the time of the sale; another 8 per cent in each of the two following years; another 7 per cent in the next two years; the remaining three-fifths of the price to be assured by mortgage at 6 per cent over a period of ten years. It was calculated that by paying these instalments, the peasant would become the owner of his land in fifteen years. The proceeds from the transfer of Church lands were to be converted into State bonds at 3 per cent in favour of the Church. The clergy were forbidden to possess real estate; but the Church was permitted to accept legacies and donations, provided always that State bonds were purchased with the proceeds.

(b) *Political.* The constituent Cortes then functioning drew up a draft Constitution which was never submitted to the Queen for approval or converted into law. The bishops announced their open opposition. The Holy See broke off relations with the Spanish Government on the grounds that the Concordat then in force had been violated.

COUNTER-REVOLUTIONARY PERIOD. 1856–68

(a) *Economic.* O'Donnell annulled Espartero's dispositions for selling Church property. An Order of October 14th, 1856, suspended the disentailing of ecclesiastical estates. On August 25th, 1859, a new Convention with the Holy See was signed, by which the right of the Church to acquire and retain all kinds of property and securities was recognized. Her title to the property restored by the Concordat of 1851 was confirmed, but on condition that she ceded it to the State in exchange for State bonds. (The first part of this agreement was carried out, but not the second.)

(b) *Political.* O'Donnell dissolved Parliament and the National Militia. He restored the reactionary Constitution of 1845, somewhat diminishing its anti-popular fury by an Act dated September 15th, 1856. He authorized the functioning of the Society of Jesus. Narváez proclaimed himself dictator and made the Carlist, Nocedal, Minister of the Interior. He annulled O'Donnell s reforming Act, and by another addition (July 1857) to the Constitution of 1845, accentuated the absolutist character of this political Code. Narváez' Act was revoked by the law of April 1864. A new conflict with Rome arose because the bishops

52

had circulated apostolic documents without the Government's knowledge, in violation of the Pragmatic Sanction of 1768 which was still in force. Gonzalez Bravo embarked upon his dictatorship in April 1868.

REVOLUTIONARY PERIOD. 1868–74

(a) *Economic.* All monasteries, convents and religious houses founded since the disentailing law of 1837 were ordered to be abolished and their property confiscated by the State.

(b) *Political.* General Serrano became Regent. The Society of Jesus was abolished by decree. Constituent Cortes. New Constitution in June 1869. Amadeo of Savoy occupied the throne of Isabel II. The Cortes and the Senate, sitting as one assembly, proclaimed the Republic.

COUNTER-REVOLUTIONARY PERIOD. 1874–1931

(a) *Economic.* Consolidation of property acquired by the break-up of the estates. Tariff protection. Definitive hegemony of agrarian interests over mercantile and industrial interests.

(b) *Political.* Foundation of the Constitutional Monarchy based on corruption of the suffrage. Caciquism. Growing centralization of the Government. Constitution of 1876. Promulgation of universal suffrage. Precarious supremacy of the civil power. Final defeat of Carlism on the field of battle and compact of the landed oligarchy with the Church. Return of the Jesuits and multiplication of the religious orders. Alfonso XII. Regency of María Cristina of Hapsburg. Alfonso XIII. Dictatorship of Primo de Rivera. Overthrow of the institutions of the Restoration.

REVOLUTIONARY PERIOD. 1931–9

(a) *Economic.* Agrarian reform and complementary laws. The State assumes the right to expropriate with or without compensation.

(b) *Political.* Proclamation of the Republic. Constitution of 1931. Tribunal of Constitutional Guarantees. Extension of suffrage to women. Reform of the Army. Dissolution of the Society of Jesus. Law prohibiting the religious orders to continue their educational practices or to engage in industry. Separation of Church and State. Abolition of the Budget for Public Worship and the Clergy. Concession of Statutes of Autonomy to Catalonia and the Basque Provinces.

(a) *Economic.* Suspension of agrarian reform and repeal of all laws contrary to the interests of landowners and capitalists. Law on trade unions decreeing the intervention of the Fascist State in the national economy.

(b) *Political.* Importation of the Italian Fascist system, with a *Caudillo* as head of the State and the Government, in imitation of the Nazi régime in Germany. Abolition of regional autonomy. Re-introduction of the Budget for Public Worship and the Clergy. Restoration of ecclesiastical privileges and legal recognition of the Society of Jesus. *Modus vivendi* with the Vatican.

This synoptic bird's-eye view—which does not claim to be a perfect summary—shows us, as I said at the beginning of the chapter, how revolution and counter-revolution obstinately and successively ousted one another from the Government, without either succeeding in strengthening its hold on the nation. But what was the final impression left on Spanish society by this weaving and unravelling? Up to what point did the Liberal revolution triumph or fail? This is what I shall try to explain in the pages that follow.

CHAPTER VII

# THE BREAK-UP OF THE ENTAILED ESTATES

The economic revolution initiated by the Spanish Liberals virtually ended in 1856. The first Republic did not bring any reform to a successful conclusion and the Restoration of 1874 established the counter-revolution firmly in power for an extensive period of about sixty years, interrupting the reform of property. But when in 1874 Spain set up new institutions, the Liberal revolution had already come to an end, since it had consisted in disentailing the entailed estates and there hardly remained an inch of land to disentail. It was precisely the disastrous end of the Liberal revolution which enabled Cánovas del Castillo to found the new régime which attempted to break with the tradition of the nineteenth century and ended in failure, as we shall see later, because it refused to persevere with a social transformation which had been a fiasco in the hands of the Liberals.

The work of freeing the entailed estates could not be the whole revolution, but only one of its sides or phases. But this unilateral reform was to create a new social class, whilst the landed nobility gained in strength; and these classes were to be a formidable obstacle, blocking the path of any subsequent attempt to continue the reform of the old régime of property which had, in fact, been bolstered up by the disentailing process. The Liberal revolution came to an end, but the civil war continued its course.

The Spanish revolutionary minority of the nineteenth century proposed to destroy the power of the nobility, curtail that of the monarchy, and lessen that of the Church. The resolutions passed by the Cortes and the Liberal Governments give us all the information we need about the design of the Liberals. But wishing was one thing, and doing another. We must not forget that this was a revolution which clashed with society. A considerable number of laws and decrees embodying reforms, which may have impressed the reader as wise and bold measures, remained a dead letter. In a word, society did not assimilate them. Laws dictated by a Government which lacks the power to enforce them, accomplish nothing. Spanish society of the nineteenth century—clerical, noble, and unlettered—was stronger than the Liberal State, and, as someone has pointed out, when the community clashes with the State, the community wins. The revolution was not to put through reforms. The structure of Spanish society was to remain the same in 1874 as it was in 1808, and the same in 1940 as it was in 1874.

The Spanish revolution had brains behind it in men like Flórez Estrada and Madoz and even perhaps Mendizábal, and it should have accomplished wonders . . . if it had not had enemies.

As was natural, those Liberal decrees which were able to take root and become a concrete reality were ones the community was prepared to accept more or less spontaneously. Every well-to-do Spaniard (and most men of means derived their wealth from landed property) sympathized with the disentailing policy. So did the proletariat, but for different reasons. Disentailing meant putting up for sale the property which was monopolized by ecclesiastical and civil corporations. The moneyed classes, who were able to acquire for an insignificant sum the lands of the clergy, the communes and the State, succeeded in combining in their conscience extreme piety with an eye for a good bargain; and among these men of means were the sceptical, blue-blooded aristocracy. The proletariat, for its part, though it was not going to benefit by the despoiling of the clergy,

55

applauded a measure which could not but be popular. And the anti-clericals, whether they benefited or not, saw in the break-up of the entailed estates a magic wand which was to rob the Church overnight of its social power. This was why the disentailing laws found ready acceptance in circles which were hostile to Liberalism. On this concrete issue, the Liberals and the community were at one, and the Church was relegated to the minority status of the Liberals. But so far, and no farther.

The economists of the hour toiled to throw all the entailed property into circulation. The principle would have been sound if the reformers' decrees had been carried out in their entirety. It was not enough to disentail. To destroy the landed power of the Church was not more important than to see that the expropriated estates were the foundation of a rural middle class. The Liberals, attentive to this necessity, regulated the distribution of the expropriated land by decrees like those proposed by Madoz. They erred, however, in not realizing that if it lay in their power to despoil the public corporations of their property, thus depriving the communes of considerable sources of income, it did not lie in their power, in practice, to compensate the local inhabitants for the spoliation involved in the disentailing process by the creation of a new popular economy. The first phase of the reform, the expropriation of the entailed estates, could be carried through with relative ease, because the municipalities and the proletariat offered no real resistance. The people—always supposing they could understand the chaotic state of affairs—hoped, no doubt, that the Government's promises to sell the lands in small lots on easy terms would compensate them for the economic shock they had suffered by the loss of the *bienes de propios* and the common lands. But if many were interested in the fulfilment of the first part of the Liberal Government's programme—the putting of wealth into circulation—few cared whether the people benefited by the change or not. The speculators and the wealthy classes flung themselves avidly on the disentailed property and the Liberal plan to parcel out the expropriated lands was swamped in the scramble which was only going to favour the strongest, that is, the richest.[1]

[1] In a pamphlet written in 1836, the poet Espronceda denounced the fatal results of the disentailing policy. "How did the Government dare", he wrote, "to dispose of the property of the State in favour of the creditors without thinking of alleviating the condition of the poor with it? And even these decrees have been carried out haphazard and with such lack of wisdom that they have not had the effect their author expected. We will not speak of the effect of the sale of national property, which deserved the criticism that our excellent economist Don Alvaro Flórez so rightly and wisely made of it,

The Liberals fell, therefore, into the error of destroying the popular economy which was linked to the old institutions, without being sure that they could revive it on new patterns. They were dogmatic on this point. They thought all the entailed property was harmful, without establishing the difference between the estates which by belonging to civil institutions were the indirect property of the people, and those other estates which, being the monopoly of private corporations, brought no profit to the proletariat. They exaggerated fanatically the necessity of breaking the entails.

There was probably no revolutionary purpose underlying the disentailing policy. The Liberal Ministers had to cope with the urgent problems of the day, and one of the gravest was the deficit which had reached astronomical proportions since the Peninsula War had cost Spain 12,000 million *reales*. To cover the deficit by issuing Government bonds was impossible, since the internal debt amounted to 18,000 million *reales* in 1833. This was one of the reasons why the lands were squandered. The State could not wait, and gave them away at bargain prices. On the other hand, the Carlists, as the party of the Church, announced that they would not recognize the sales. No one would want the estates, therefore, unless cheapness offset the risk.

Thus, all those Spaniards who already possessed wealth were able to become great landlords; and those who only possessed four rooms also became proprietors, though it was clear that they were only in a position to acquire a smallholding, a minute parcel, which would make them slaves for life.

With the disentailing policy, the Liberals were undoubtedly giving expression to an ancient national feeling and continuing the policy of the Governments of the eighteenth century. Shortly before, Charles III and Charles IV had applied the property of the Jesuits to the reduction of the National Debt and had expropriated charitable institutions, religious societies, pious foundations and benefices under lay patronage, in exchange for State bonds.

The pressing needs of the Ministry of Finance, on the one hand, and, on the other, the rigid Liberal criterion of the

and which, unless it is annulled by the Cortes, will increase both the fortune of the wealthy and the numbers and misfortunes of the poor. The Government, which ought to have aimed at the emancipation of this class—unfortunately so numerous in Spain—thought (if it ever thought in its life) that by dividing the property into small lots, it would avoid the monopoly of the rich and benefit the poor proportionately, without realizing that the rich would be able to buy up as many lots as together would form a considerable estate."

*Jovellanistas,* according to which the *bienes concejiles,* or common lands, and others of the same nature ought to disappear in favour of private property, made anarchy of the disentailing reform. The poor resigned themselves—for the moment—the rich heaped up wealth, and the Church defended its property with a tenacity surprising in those who professed other-worldly beliefs.

To judge by the commotion made by the clergy, and even by the Pope, who declared that those who were putting up Church lands to auction were guilty of sacrilege, the disentailing reform might have been exclusively a quarrel between the Liberal Government and the Church. A quarrel it certainly was, and an extremely bitter one, but the anti-clericals, in their struggle with clericalism, represented the expropriation of the clergy as a national emergency which, basically, it was not. That the Church was enormously wealthy, there was no doubt; the figures given in a previous chapter are eloquent of this. But the Church was not the territorial power the Liberals made it out to be. It was not the only power, or the greatest. When the revolution took on the character of a disentailing reform, the clash with the clergy was virulent and unavoidable, all the more so as the spiritual arm proposed to keep its property by hook or by crook. But the disentailing reform, locked in a vicious struggle with the Church, left the bulk of the national territory intact, divided into latifundia and minifundia, both equally pernicious. Ecclesiastical property amounted, as I said before, to 1,300,000 hectares; and something had to be done to reduce it. But the national territory amounted to 37 million hectares, in round numbers, and there were 27,100,000 hectares of lay property, most of which belonged to the nobles and the great civilian landowners;[1] and to this considerable amount of property there was due to be added, through the process of disentailing, the land remaining to the communes, the State, charitable institutions and religious communities. And the oligarchy, into whose power the estates mobilized by the reform were passing, knew no charity. It was an infamous class, which brought the nation to the pass it is in today.

In 1870, it was already possible to strike the balance of the economic revolution. Property to the value of some 3,000 million pesetas had been expropriated, of which Church property accounted for only 500 million, according to the register compiled

---

[1] The enormous extent of the landed property of the aristocracy was recognized by Wellington in 1813 when he referred to Spain as "a country in which almost all property consists in land, and there are the largest landed proprietors which exist in Europe" (*Dispatches,* VI, p. 261-4).

by the Ministry of Finance. The remaining capital represented the portion of the people's property, the property of the whole nation, which had been pocketed by a wealthy minority, "capitalists and shrewd, unscrupulous fellows" (Costa).

After the disentailing of the estates, the proletariat was more numerous and more poverty-stricken than before.

The Liberals had had the inspiration and strength to destroy part of an economic system, but they had lacked the power and dexterity to create another in its place.

As was natural, the revolution was to be more fortunate in abolishing formal privileges. Prerogatives dating from feudal times which were enjoyed by the clergy and nobles were abolished.

As a political class, the nobility hardly existed. But they enjoyed rights which were already inadmissible. In 1836, there were still 403,382 nobles, most of them impoverished *hidalgos*. In the census of the same year, they passed down to history as a social class with *fueros*, or privileges, and in 1857, and afterwards in the Constitution of 1876, it was laid down that nobles who aspired to a seat in the Senate must be men of considerable means.

With the suppression of the *mayorazgos* or entailed estates, the real aristocrats saw their privileges heavily curtailed. After much heartburning, this state of affairs came to be accepted. During the course of the century, the *señorios* were also abolished, though not entirely. There were in Spain 13,309 villages and places which were held in *señorio*, or with full manorial rights, with a rent-roll of 82½ million *reales*. Moreover, 50 per cent of the cultivated lands were under seigneurial jurisdiction.

But in its essentials, the reform was a failure. Spain ceased to be a feudal country *de jure*, but not *de facto*. In any case, if she ceased to be a feudal country, she did not thereby become a *bourgeois* nation. The revolutionaries did not desire, did not know how, or were not able to create a rural middle class, which was what history demanded of them. The structure of Spanish society underwent no basic change. In 1860, the number of landed proprietors just exceeded 2½ million—proprietors, mostly, of latifundia and smallholdings. In France, the Revolution had left behind it 4 million new landowners, mostly proprietors of medium-sized estates. The French *bourgeoisie*, which was already strong, had added to its numbers this respectable reinforcement of middle-class elements in the rural areas, which was so vital to its system of political liberty.

In Spain, where middle-class rural proprietors were more necessary than in France because of the lack of a powerful commercial and industrial class, the revolution accentuated the ancestral character of Spanish agrarian property.

The nobility and aristocracy, who lost their privileges in law, maintained them in practice, because not only did they preserve their lands, but in certain cases, as I have pointed out, they added to them those they had acquired by the break-up of the entailed estates.

Nevertheless, the change made a great difference. The people had been expropriated without compensation; and side by side with the old castes, there now appeared a new social class, the war profiteers who had enriched themselves in the tragic and disturbed years of the civil war, and not only thanks to the disentailing reform. With the blood of Spaniards, other Spaniards had made money. The new rich were rich at the expense of the Church, but also, in a great measure, thanks to the ruin of the lands belonging to the public corporations. As the century advanced, it could be seen that in spite of the din of battle and the transfer of properties, everything was still to do. The rural districts of Castile, Estremadura and Andalusia shook with approaching social earthquakes. In 1840, the first rural revolt for the division of the land occurred at Malaga. It might truly be said that the revolution had multiplied the number of the disinherited. And there was no doubt that the unfortunate landless peasant was not in the mood to accept the situation.

There was more hunger in the countryside than ever. The *braceros*, or landless labourers, became bandits, "generous bandits who robbed the rich to give to the poor", of the Robin Hood type. Groups of poverty-stricken peasants attacked persons and properties. Half-way through the century, 8,000 men without arms and without any bellicose incentive save their hunger, seized Loja, Narváez' birthplace, in the province of Granada. The peasants who seized Loja demanded the division of the land and the Government hanged six of them and sent 400 to the African *presidios*.

To remedy this state of affairs, the ruling social classes, each according to its nature, did what they could. The Liberals, as good philanthropists, founded the charitable society *Amigos de los Pobres* (Friends of the Poor), and the Conservatives, as has been said, founded the Civil Guard.

Without instruments of action, without organic support among the people, the revolution, which had begun by introducing the professional Army into politics, did not succeed in constituting even the shadow of a new civil authority. Nor did the civil power have any reality when the Government of the nation passed into the hands of the anti-reformers, because the civil State which the reactionaries endeavoured to embody had died at the beginning of the century. That simulacrum of power was, therefore, continually menaced by the monks or by the soldiers of one or the other faction, when it did not fall into their hands. The Praetorian generals were stronger than the revolution and the reaction. The Army, the only organized force, took turns in the Government under one or other political banner.

From the first moment, the Liberal revolution was lost in a *cul-de-sac* (from which it never succeeded in escaping in 130 years) and set up a tradition to which Spanish Liberals and Republicans have been faithful to the present day. The absence of a middle class in Spain was bound to sterilize any attempt at acclimatizing liberty. And in its turn, liberty would prevent a middle class from coming into being, for there are reforms which, by their profundity and amplitude, exceed the purely legislative capacity of Parliament.

When the first Liberals, who were also the most ingenuous, discovered that the people were making a chaotic use of liberty, they passed over to the reaction. Attacked on both flanks—by the ultramontanes who resisted the reforms, with perfect constitutional right; and by the impatient people, with equal constitutional right—the progressives gave way to panic.

Liberty, in short, is the privilege of people who have made their revolution.

The sincere masonic spirit of tolerance, brotherhood, and mutual aid which distinguished Spanish Liberalism from its first hour, placed liberty on the highest pinnacle. But liberty, in the conditions which were peculiar to Spain both then and now, led to anarchy.

Most of the men of Cadiz—Martínez de la Rosa, Conde de Toreno, Istúriz, Alcalá Galiano—abandoned the paths of reform. Even Mendizábal was a disillusioned man in 1847. His ideal already was for Narváez to allow the progressives to take turns in the Government. And with Mendizábal, Madoz, Cortina and many others ended by being overcome with the melancholy feeling which sooner or later creeps over all Spanish Liberals— the persuasion that revolution in Spain is sterile.

The only man of action among the civilian leaders of Liberalism was Juan Álvarez Mendizábal, a notable Jew. Mendizábal was born at Cadiz, and the Liberal revolution found in him its most influential champion. A revolutionary, but not *afrancesado,* since, on the contrary, he regarded the French with scant

61.

sympathy, he combined to perfection his rôle of business man with that of conspirator. Moreover, both characters showed him to be a genuine representative of the European middle class, among whom he would have played a political rôle with more success than in Spain where, as I have so often stated, the *bourgeois* revolution lacked a social class to give it impetus. An employee of the firm of *Bertrán de Lis*, Mendizábal, on the eve of the masonic conspiracy of 1819, was acknowledged as the heart and soul of the business, his influence being far greater than his position as manager would seem to warrant. He took part with Riego in the insurrection, as we have seen, and escaped to London when Ferdinand VII, thanks to the troops of Angoulême, recovered his decrepit throne in 1823. From London, he continued to conspire and to add to his personal fortune, amassing the sum, it is said, of £1,000,000 which he left in the care of someone who dissipated it in the absence of its owner.

When the King died, Mendizábal returned to Spain and impressed everyone with his knowledge of finance. At the moment when this remarkable financier took over the Government from the Conde de Toreno, the nation was once more seething with rebellious *juntas*; Mendizábal put out the conflagration. He then plunged deeply into the work of breaking up the entailed estates. "If ever in Spain", wrote a Spanish biographer, "a politician was able to found hopes of good results on the prestige and authority of his name, that politician was Mendizábal. His credit as a financier had been established in London, where his banking house achieved the greatest prosperity. The success of the Portuguese campaign had confirmed with extraordinary brilliance his reputation in the eyes of the world. Mendizábal, who had supplied the funds, was the real organizer of the expedition which seated the Queen Doña María de la Gloria de Braganza on the throne. The favour with which he was regarded by all the Cabinets of neighbouring countries which were interested in the throne of Doña Isabel—England, France and Portugal—added greatly to the prestige of the Prime Minister. The most powerful bankers of Europe were known to be favourably disposed towards him. This was one aspect; for the rest, his history as a progressive, which went back to Riego's rising in Andalusia and was linked with the first great shipwreck of the absolutist régime in Spain in 1820, was the reason why the rebel *juntas* in the provinces, the pillars of widespread anarchy throughout the nation, began little by little to abandon their insurgent activities. The moderates, who were in a majority in the Cortes, bowed down before the new star which was dawning with so much brilliance on the political horizon. The words of peace which Mendizábal was careful to address to them were as successful as might have been expected. For a moment, the Prime Minister succeeded in appearing before Liberals of all hues as the *deus ex machina*, the supreme arbiter of the will and destinies of Liberal Spain. To take one case, the never-to-be-repeated occasion of the *vote of confidence*—this was approved by the Cortes without real opposition, by an almost unanimous majority.

"But the hopes which the Prime Minister aroused in the Queen's partisans in the first moments of his administration were soon seen to be out of proportion to his actual gifts. No doubt, his skill in financial matters was real. No doubt, his knowledge of British constitutional practices was more direct than that of at least the majority of his friends. His ambition was great and was served by an unwearying activity and a boundless audacity. The Minister had a high opinion of himself, which made him view the future without apprehension. But, in spite of all this, he did not display the gifts of a statesman —not even of a ruler. Lacking a clear comprehension of the political issues pending, without aplomb and without fixity of purpose or a strong will, he also lacked, as a result, a sure orientation."[1]

In 1843, we find him leading the people of Madrid against Narváez, whose guns were thundering outside the city. All his inexhaustible energies were displayed in that lost battle.

The most important figure of the Spanish Liberal revolution was undoubtedly Don Baldomero Espartero, Dúque de la Victoria, Duque de Morella, Principe de Vergara, Conde de Luchana, Knight of the Golden Fleece, etc., who died in 1879 in retirement at Logroño, at the age of eighty-seven. He died loaded with titles and honours, this Spaniard who came the nearest to being the "hero" of the Liberal revolution, not by his own genius, but by the accident of history.

A native of La Mancha, Espartero was born among stubborn mules—his father was a carter with eight sons—in the heart of the genuine Castilian country of muleteers, Campo de Calatrava. At fifteen, he joined a battalion of students formed to fight against Bonaparte. Defying paternal authority, he refused to enter the Church and chose the alternative profession—the Army. The Peninsula War confirmed his career as a soldier.

[1] José R. Lomba y Pedraja, Prologue and Notes to the volume of Larra's *Articulos politicos y sociales*, Clásicos castellanos, p. xxix, xxx, xxxi.

On the death of Ferdinand VII, Espartero appeared on the political scene as one of the champions of the cause of Isabel II, and in the Carlist war he was a worthy adversary of the fanatical officers of the Pretender. He moved about the gorges of the North with the agility of a ·Zumalacárregui. In the military defeat of Carlism he played a decisive part; on the Queen's side, nobody understood the military tactics of the moment as he did. When the peace of Vergara was signed, he was hailed as the "peacemaker of Spain" and became the most popular man in the country.

In America and in Spain, he had had an excellent opportunity of making himself known. He was not an enigmatic man, with a complicated psychology. His two military virtues lay not so much in his gifts as a strategist, as in his unsurpassed personal courage and his affection for the common soldier, which no other Spanish officer equalled. In imitation of the Roman generals he distributed favours among his favourites, but as far as his personal integrity went, he had the reputation of being incorruptible. He had an overweening ambition, without which he would not have arrived where he did or scaled heights which must have seemed unscaleable to the son of a peasant. He was, in reality, King of Spain by virtue of his regency and could perhaps, if he had been so minded, been King in actual fact when Serrano, in 1869, offered him the highest office in a nation without a monarchy and without Republicans.

Espartero was a Castilian peasant, with the appearance, manners and stubbornness of a farmer from La Mancha. All his life he was the same. Neither his extraordinary career, nor his many honours, nor his entry to the *salons* and the Chambers, made the slightest impression on his rustic character. In drawing-rooms and in Parliament, he was ill at ease. Clad in resplendent uniforms, treading on thick-piled carpets, the *de facto* King of Spain, he was a peasant whom Fate had tricked into becoming a statesman. A man of the people, he loved the people above all else. He was swift, and at times inexorable, in his vengeance, and at such moments he would execute half a dozen men, bombard Barcelona or commit some other act of barbarism. But of all the generals of the time, the son of the carter was cast in the noblest mould. Narváez, an Andalusian with a heart of ice, never forgot a grudge. O'Donnell was disloyal. Serrano was an opportunist, a man without principles. Don Baldomero knew no rancour. Into the society which surrounded the Queen, among the elegant fops and the smooth, scheming generals, Espatero brought his slovenly dress, rough manners and the uprightness of his purpose. He made mistakes because he was bound to make them, because he was a stubborn peasant and a soldier of fortune, not a politician. What was said of Marius might well be said of him: "The first man of Spain and yet a novice in politics."

The conqueror of Zumalacárregui was conquered by his ex-protégé O'Donnell, a mediocre soldier, but an astute politician. And by Narváez, a lesser politician than O'Donnell but still superior to Espartero in social circles and in the councils of Ministers. Beside Don Baldomero, O'Donnell was a Ferdinand the Catholic in Machiavellism.

Espartero entered politics by chance, as it were, overborne by the pressure of circumstances; and when he came into power he showed himself irresolute and confused. For political reasons, no other Spanish general was ever more popular than he. The people, especially the people of Madrid, always supported him.

Don Baldomero did not succeed in canalizing the Liberal revolution, always supposing that such was his intent. His Government, which was in office from 1839–43, suffered from the lack of a fixed policy. It gave complete satisfaction to no one, and those who called themselves friends of the Regent, like his enemies, were able to manœuvre as they pleased in the barracks, in the chamber and in the haunts of the gossips. It was the attempt at government of a well-meaning man, who was yet incapable of preserving, still less of founding, a political movement. He did not know how to turn his unrivalled popularity into the executive instrument of a system which would establish him as the undisputed leader of the revolution and create the relative equilibrium without which Spanish society could not organize itself into a harmonious régime. No one, till then, had enjoyed, as Espartero did, the almost unlimited confidence of both people and Army. Yet the power slipped from his hands.

During the years 1854–6—the last great opportunity for reform—the Finance Minister, Don Pascual Madoz, a man of encyclopaedic knowledge, was preparing reforms, already alluded to in the preceding chapter, which were based on a more solid foundation than those of Mendizábal. But the forces of reaction, emboldened, were making use of the populace to agitate the nation or were intriguing in the Palace. Strife within the Government, rupture with the Vatican, the Praetorian Guards of the other generals impatient for a share in the booty— such was the situation. And at the head of the Government, for the last time, the liberator of Bilbao, dependent upon a Parliament of lawyers and intriguers.[1]

The inevitable end of civil wars won by democracy was repeating itself in the history of Spain. Espartero returned from the north with the halo of the popular hero, the hero whose destiny will not allow him to stop at military victory, but who is dragged into the political whirlpool to restore order and lead the nation. Thus, Caesar returned from Gaul, Cromwell from Naseby and Napoleon from Italy. But Espartero lacked the qualities to become the perfect hero—qualities which the others had in abundance; gifts of the statesman rather than the soldier.

When the "peacemaker of Spain" failed in politics, the Liberal revolution—the "paltry revolution", as Larra calls it—which, with him, had reached its highest peak, began to decline. It was defeated.

CHAPTER VIII

CARLISM

CARLISM HAS VERY little to do with the dynastic quarrel which arose on the death of Ferdinand VII. A social movement of much greater importance than if it had sprung from a mere vulgar dispute over the succession, its appearance goes back to the days which followed on the restoration of absolutism by the troops of Angoulême (April 1823). Six years before Ferdinand VII married María Cristina de Borbón, seven years before the birth of Isabel II, and ten years before the King passed to another world, Carlism was already in existence. It was created, I repeat, when the Church discovered that the monarchy of Ferdinand was opposed to Spain becoming that ideal theocracy of which the fanatics had been dreaming since the destruction of all the political institutions.[2]

In 1824 the clergy were already beginning their campaign against Ferdinand VII. They founded the *Partido Apostólico* (Apostolic Party) and *El Ángel Exterminador* (The Avenging Angel), its fighting organization. The *apostólicos* proposed a change of

[1] Richard Ford, the contemporary of Espartero, clearly saw the cause of his failure: "Personally brave and honest, his grand error was a wish to govern according to the Constitution in which even Hercules could not have succeeded" (*Handbook*, II, p. 860).

[2] "As for us, you do not annoy us, because we know you. Now you are going about in the mask of the pretender; but it is a lie; you existed before he did" (Larra, in the *Revista Española*, Feb. 18th, 1834).

monarch. In opposition to the monarchy, a *Junta Suprema del Principado* was formed in Catalonia, which began to launch the clergy on a rural crusade and made representations to the King, demanding imperatively the submission of the Crown to the Church. The *apostólicos* were seeking an obedient lord and they pinned their hopes to Ferdinand's brother, the Infante Don Carlos. Thus was born Carlism, in the lifetime of Ferdinand VII and in opposition to him.

Long before the death of Ferdinand VII, therefore, the Court of Don Carlos was set up in Madrid—an intimate, unofficial Court as opposed to the official and legitimate Court. The monarchy favoured by the Church found there its complete expression. Don Carlos was the supreme civil head of the Apostolic Party and The Avenging Angel.

Don Carlos was much superior to his brother in all the knightly virtues. There was no comparison between him and Ferdinand, beside whose frankly ruffianly personality he appeared unmistakably a gentleman. After the Carlists had taken to the mountains, more than once the Pretender stayed the fratricidal hand of his officers.

For the Church, he would have been the ideal king. He had not much will-power and unquestioning piety, which in him was not hypocrisy but a sincere feeling; and his feeble conception of leadership, combined with a passion to reign which was constantly fostered by his wife, made of him the docile instrument of the Church. A weak-willed prince, he needed the constant spur of a character stronger than his own, before he could be brought to act. Irresolute and fearful of responsibility—characteristics which were later to exasperate Zumalacárregui—it was certain that if he were to occupy the throne, he would end by being supplanted by a favourite—in all probability, a priest.

The *apostólicos* were swift to discover in Don Carlos the ideal king and adopted him as their candidate for the civil leadership of the theocracy they were planning.

But Carlism had another facet. It was not only an ecclesiastical movement; it was at the same time the reaction of the countryside against the city.

That the theocratic ideal was the sinews of Carlism, there is no doubt. All the evidence points that way; and if that were not enough, we have the participation of the clergy in the war, especially the monastic orders; while Cabrera himself, the indispensable leader of the cause, who ought to have known his own mind when he laid waste the Maestrazgo, corroborated the fact on his return from London in 1848 when, forswearing his old creed, he declared that the hour of the Inquisition and government by monks had passed.

But, as I have said, Carlism has another side, no less interesting. In his famous Memoirs, the British author C. F. Henningsen[1] emphasizes that Carlism was the rebellion of pious country folk against the corrupt inhabitants of cities. On its civil side, in effect, Carlism was a movement of peasants and shepherds against industry and commerce, with their sequel, Liberalism. Henningsen is repeating the sentiments of Zumalacárregui's headquarters when he tells us that Spain is divided into agricultural and industrial regions and that industrial Spain, like other industrial countries, produces nothing, lives on the sweat of the peasant and should be subordinated, by natural law, to rural society. All the more so, he adds, as industry forms only a tenth part of the Spanish population.

The reaction of the villages and towns to the call of the Pretender in 1833 confirms Henningsen's point of view as regards the political division of Spain. The insurrection of the Carlists of Bilbao, led by the friars of the monastery of San Francisco, did not succeed, because, as the Captain of Lancers observed, the population of Bilbao, like all mercantile populations, was two-thirds Liberal. San Sebastian, another capital, remained loyal to the Constitution. Vitoria, a rural and inland city, was divided in its attitude to Carlism. Pamplona remained in the power of the Queen's Party. All the great cities declared for the Queen, the British observer insists. The Queen's cause was espoused, he continues, by "the inhabitants of the coast of Andalusia and Catalonia, of the maritime towns and the larger cities which"—he consoles himself—"do not form a large part of the population." In Catalonia, the mountainous regions supported the Pretender; the Catalan coast and Barcelona were Liberal. The Carlist area extended from the Ebro to the Pyrenees, with a fraction of La Rioja inland and its foci of resistance in the heart of the mountain gorges.

There is another way of defining the Carlists, and that is by defining the men against whom they rose, the men who had become estranged from the peasant life of Europe by the nature of their education. It was against these men that La Vendée rose—that province which, politically and even geographically, is the French Navarre—and in Spain, the Carlists rose against their modest counterparts.

[1] *The Most Striking Events of a Twelvemonth's Campaign with Zumalacárregui in Navarre and the Basque Provinces*, by C. F. Henningsen, Captain of Lancers in the service of Don Carlos. London, 1836.

Modern European Liberalism, writes an English publicist, would not have been possible had not "the city, with its restless passion for change, replaced the countryside, with its hatred of innovation, as the primary source of legislation".

The cruelty of the Spanish civil war, which was not worse than the cruelty of the war between the Convention and La Vendée, can be explained by the fact that it was basically a war between peasants. The Spanish city, backward and not very populous, and the countryside were psychologically not very different. The Spanish middle class, the dwellers on the periphery and in the urban centres, had not had time to detach themselves from the land, from the peasant life; and the Liberal was a peasant with his rough edges smoothed over, his mind clouded by the exhalations with which Nature, especially in Spain, prodigal in rose-decked plains, granite peaks and torrential rivers, envelops man and makes him her own, like a spontaneous burgeoning of the earth, and rooted deep in the soil, like a tree or a flint monolith.

However, Don Carlos did not succeed in entering any large city. His officers did indeed cross the Peninsula in operations that were like hurried swoops, with the Liberals hot at their heels. But the town rejected Carlism.[1] On September 11th, 1837, Don Carlos, entering Arganda, approached the outskirts of Madrid, but the city militia and a platoon of soldiers, which were all the armed forces the capital could muster, sufficed to bar his way. The Carlist minority in Madrid made no move.

In the second Carlist war, thirty years later, the situation was repeated. The Pretender's Party continued to dominate the entire north. One by one, all the villages fell into his hands. After the fall of Estella, the capital of Carlism, the hamlets, villages and townships of Navarre, Guipuzcoa and Vizcaya surrendered. The great cities, on the other hand, remained faithful once again to the Liberals. Bilbao, San Sebastian, Vitoria, Tolosa, Irun, etc., heroic islands of constitutionalism in the midst of that aggressive Carlist ocean, encompassed, besieged, without communications with the centre, resisted stubbornly. And as often as the war was repeated, the same division occurred. The city, the great city, in Spain as in the rest of Europe, was Liberal.

Carlism, it must be remarked, was not an exclusively Spanish social phenomenon. Outside Spain, the political movement which

[1] "Carlism", said Larra, "is all the more robust and lusty, the farther away it is from centres of population" (Article in the *Revista Española*, Feb. 18th. 1834).

most closely resembled it was La Vendée. I have sometimes wondered, reading those ferocious campaigns of Turreau's "infernal columns", with the no less ferocious reply of the Vendean peasants, what France would have done if, instead of making the revolution with a powerful *bourgeoisie*, she had attempted to do it, like Spain, with a weak middle class. I think the answer would be that that indomitable focus of rebellion, La Vendée, a rebellion which was easily suppressed by the Convention though not without extreme severity, would have been in every detail the Navarre of France. What happened in France was that the crushing superiority of the "commercial *noblesse* with money in their pockets" had drawn the sting out of the Vendean movement, not with Turreau's or Rossignol's "raids", but long before, when the French *bourgeoisie* turned itself laboriously and silently into the nation. Thus, La Vendée, with its offshoots in lower Poitou and Brittany, met no response in the rest of the country, remaining as an excrescence on the body of France which was decidedly urban in its *Weltanschauung*.

The excrescence in Spain was urbanism. La Vendée was the geographical symbol of ignorance and clericalism among an enlightened people. The Spanish city was, on the contrary, the ostentatious gesture of enlightenment among an unlettered people.

Summing up what I have written, I think I have made clear the monastic-peasant character of the Carlist movement. Carlism had its roots in the monasteries and the villages. Its adherents were more numerous among the regular than among the secular clergy, among the monks than among the parish priests. The capitals, as we have seen, and even the big towns, were hostile to it.

The question arises—why did Carlism end by becoming a sort of regional ideology, and why was it confined to the north of Spain?

One of the conditions which determined this interesting fact was geography; the splendid nature of the terrain for guerrilla warfare and, above all, the proximity of the French frontier.

Potentially, the Spanish countryside was all Carlist when the Pretender struck in 1833; and while the north rebelled, part of Castile and Andalusia rose. In reality, the first revolt took place at Talavera, in the province of Toledo. But the power of the old aristocracy must be taken into consideration. A great part of this aristocracy, the part that may be called enlightened, though Catholic in many cases, was opposed to the extremism of

Carlism—as were also all those who, without being aristocrats, feared the promise made by the Carlists to restore to the Church her rural and urban property or to paralyse the disentailing reform which was the hope of innumerable persons who were about to pick up a good bargain for a song.

Spanish society was divided in its highest ranks, and the nobles, who usually lived in the cities, were not unanimous in their approval of the theocratic State. This had its repercussions in the villages where the landed power of the aristocracy had not lost its feudal character.

Was Carlist supremacy in the north due to a strategic and geographical reason?

History tells us that a small army could resist almost indefinitely in that epoch in the winding passages of the Borunda and the Amezcoas. Certainly, there were gorges, mountain ridges and craggy ground in many other regions of Spain. But no other Spanish zone enjoyed the proximity of the French frontier which was of inestimable value to the Carlists, who received from over the border an endless stream of arms, munitions and food, besides covering their retreat.

In contrast, war on the plains of Castile and wherever it could be waged in other mountainous regions, which were always easy to isolate, invariably turned out unfavourably for the Carlists. On the steppes, the war was bound to take on a mobile character, and the Carlists, inferior in numbers to the Liberals—partly due to the natural rivalry between soldiers and monks—could fight with the swift marches of Gómez or the devilry of the priest Merino, but they were always defeated. Zumalacárregui used to say that if the Carlists had all the men whom the famous priest had lost outside Navarre, Don Carlos would have entered Madrid.

The Carlists based their rebellion on the right of Don Carlos to the succession. Logically, his claim could not hold water. His supporters, who professed to be faithful followers of tradition, invoked the non-existent right of Ferdinand VII's brother to reign on the basis of the Salic law, which Philip V introduced into Spain, Charles IV repealed by the Pragmatic Sanction and Ferdinand VII acknowledged on his death-bed to establish his daughter Isabel as his successor. That the Carlists, known as traditionalists, should maintain that women could not reign in the country of Isabella the Catholic, was surprising, coming from that particular quarter. According to the Carlists, the duty of every traditionalist was to suppress French philosophy—

only to replace it by the Salic law which was also of French origin.

Let us now turn to history for the final, but no less necessary, touches in the description of this important movement.

No sooner had Ferdinand VII died than the first war began. The Carlist army was formed on the basis of the "Army of the Faith" (*Ejército de la Fe*), which, in its turn, arose out of another para-military organization, the Royalist Volunteers, counterpart of the National Militia. These Volunteers had been armed throughout Spain during the period of the French occupation which followed the restoration of absolutism in 1823. The Carlist army finally adopted the name of *Requeté* taken from the refrain of a marching-song of the 3rd Navarrese battalion, one of the battalions most esteemed by Zumalacárregui.

On its military and civil side, Carlism was an offshoot, therefore, of absolutism and was the new form adopted by the fanatical *Partido Apostólico*.

From October 1833 to August 1839, the battle raged boldly and fiercely in the bare hills of the Maestrazgo, in the mountain ridges of the Basque country, in the inaccessible places of Navarre, where often there were no signs of human habitation beyond a shepherd's cabin on the edge of a precipice—a shepherd who might, one day, become a priest.

The death of Zumalacárregui, who was wounded in the leg at the siege of Bilbao, when he was observing the enemy positions through his field-glasses from a balcony of the palace adjoining the Church of Our Lady of Begoña, was fatal to Don Carlos. From that moment, the Pretender, without the robust personality of his *caudillo* to hold his men together, proved incapable of leading his army.

At Vergara, the Carlist forces surrendered under conditions which did credit to Liberal clemency. Don Carlos abdicated in favour of his son, the Conde de Montemolín, who proclaimed himself Charles VI in 1845.

Until 1860, Carlism kept itself in being partly, like the embers of a still smouldering fire, by sporadic bursts of flame like that which occurred in Catalonia in 1847, and partly by insinuating itself tenaciously and by devious ways into the Court of Isabel II.

The policy of the reactionaries during the reign of Isabel II had as its *leit-motiv* the reconciliation of the monarchy with the Church, and ended inevitably in the subordination of the State to the spiritual power—which was what the Carlists wanted. Already the reconciliation of Vergara, colophon of the military

72

victory of the Liberals, represented, politically speaking, the triumph of Carlism. Bravo Murillo, Prime Minister at the time of the famous Concordat of 1851, attempted to win over the Carlists to the cause of Isabel II by his constitutional reforms. In 1856, we find Don Cándido Nocedal a Minister in Narváez' Government. Carlism had come into power.

Montemolín having left Spain, the leadership of his cause at Court was assumed by Don Francisco de Asís, the King-Consort, a puppet of the clericals and a man of such peculiar temperament that he was furious with Serrano for promoting the interests of the progressives at Court (when he was not supporting the reactionaries), but passed over the liaison of Serrano with his wife, the Queen, as an airy trifle. This Don Francisco de Asís now occupied the position which Don Carlos had held among the *apostólicos vis-à-vis* the Court of Ferdinand VII. He was the servile instrument of Carlism against his own wife, whose right to rule he placed in doubt.

Through the *Suprema Comisión Real*, with secret agents in all the vital centres of the State, innumerable positions of trust and authority were handed over to the Carlists. No one could govern then in Spain without submitting himself to the dictates of the Church. The true Government of Spain was composed of Sor María de los Dolores Patrocinio, Father Claret, the Queen's confessor, Father Fulgencio, the King-Consort's confessor and Fray Cirilo de la Alameda, leader of the *apostólicos* during Ferdinand VII's reign, he of the interview with Alcalá Galiano. Fray Cirilo was then Cardinal-Archbishop of Toledo; during the Carlist war he had been a Minister in the Pretender's Council.

Spain had then a theocratic Cabinet. Narváez, Bravo Murillo, O'Donnell, Sartorius, were all men of straw. The real Government of Spain consisted of the nun and the monks I have mentioned.

Isabel II was Queen only in name. The Crown was imprisoned in the meshes of Carlism which only respected the free choice of the scandalously self-indulgent Queen in one matter—her choice of lovers. The long-robed Carlists of the Court were behind the throne, holding the threads of political intrigue and making the Queen dance to the tune of the *Requeté*. It was they who advised her to sign the disentailing laws of Don Pascual Madoz in 1856 and then to throw out Espartero. The Queen, "whose ambition was limited to converting night into day, to embracing her lover of the moment and then receiving absolution from her favourite confessor", signed; and on the advice of the ecclesiastical sanhedrim, wrote to the Pope assuring him that the impious decision would soon be erased and the Church's property restored. The "Cabinet" of Fray Cirilo secretly persuaded the Holy See to break off relations with Spain, thereby aggravating the difficulties of the Espartero situation. To crown all, the statue of Christ in the Church of San Francisco began to sweat blood, an unmistakable protest from Heaven against the expulsion of Sor Patrocinio from the backstairs intrigues of the Court.

The Queen called on O'Donnell and the theocracy was formally constituted once more with all its tonsured Ministers as before. O'Donnell, once he had performed the service of restoring Sor Patrocinio to the Palace and saving the property of the Church, was replaced by Narváez, with the traditionalist Nocedal in the Ministry of the Interior. In due course, the Cabinet of clericals also expelled the proud ex-adjutant of Mina. Narváez got up in a towering rage, his eyes flashing, and declared that he was the bone and sinew of those gentry, ending his protest by saying in a voice of thunder: "Henceforth, I shall be more Liberal than Riego!"

However, not even by craft could a theocracy take root in Spain. Even disguised Carlism could not establish itself in power. The Queen was to pay with her throne for abandoning her prerogatives.

Meanwhile, Montemolín did not acquiesce in Fray Cirilo governing for him. Montemolín wanted to reign. In December 1860, General Ortega, Captain-General of the Balearic Islands, landed on the Catalan coast with 3,500 soldiers, the Pretender and his brother Ferdinand. The *coup* was a failure, but so many notable people were implicated in it that the Court had to hush up the affair and pardon everyone.

In order to gain his freedom, the Pretender had to renounce his so-called rights. He departed for Germany, and there published a recantation of his renouncement. But in the interval between his renouncement and the revocation of his renouncement, his younger brother Don Juan proclaimed himself Pretender. (This Don Juan showed alarming symptoms of Liberalism which scandalized the Carlist Party.) To all this, Montemolín replied by saying that Don Juan had not interpreted rightly his Catalonian pronouncement which was wrested from him under threat of imprisonment and therefore, according to him, not valid.

The quarrel was ended by the death of Montemolín, his wife and Don Fernando, all of them struck down within a fortnight by a malignant fever.

Having rejected Don Juan as a heretic, the Party cast about for a new leader. The mantle of Carlism fell on the son of Don Juan, Don Carlos María, who was made of more orthodox stuff and who, in 1868, when Carlist hopes were running high, took the title of Charles VII. Isabel II, who had already lost her throne, met Don Carlos in Paris and placed large funds at his disposal.

And here there enters again upon the stage Ramón Cabrera, "the tiger of the Maestrazgo", now transformed into the lapdog of Wentworth. Cabrera had married an Englishwoman during his exile in England. Charles V's fiery *guerrillero* had become a sober citizen, who spoke English, was possessed of no mean fortune, and recounted the exploits of his youth with the melancholy indulgence with which men are wont to excuse the follies of youth.

As I said before, Cabrera returned to Spain in 1848, and Catalonia trembled at the news that he had crossed the Pyrenees. But much to the astonishment of the Catalans, instead of issuing an aggressive Carlist proclamation, he announced that he had lost faith in the absolutist government of King and Church, that the age of depotism was past and that the Inquisition and government by monks were out of date. He preached a new sort of puritan Carlism, whose object was to purge the Court of dross. The civilized climate of England had changed this barbarian.

Cabrera continued to be a Carlist, no doubt because it was too much trouble to change his party. Charles VII was quick to secure his services; but the old *caudillo* made it a condition that it should be he who fixed the propitious moment for the attack— a moment which might never arise, to judge by the philosophy of the new Cabrera.

In spite of this agreement, Don Carlos entered Spain disguised, with the more impatient of his followers, in July 1869, and reached Figueras, where he realized his impotence and, disillusioned, retired to Paris. When he heard of the adventure, Cabrera broke into righteous indignation, resigned from the leadership of the Party and returned to London with his English wife.

Without a man of Cabrera's stature, the movement fell into a decline. Don Carlos hastened after him and once more enlisted his services. But Cabrera had become an honest constitutionalist who refused to collaborate unless Don Carlos first promised to govern with the Cortes and the Constitution. The Pretender yielded to the man of order and promised him, in effect, Constitution and Cortes. The Party then rose *en masse* against the advocate of constitutionalism, and Cabrera, when his right to select the King's advisers was disputed, shook the dust of Carlism off his feet for ever.

These incidents prove that Carlism knew that it was an anachronism. It had succeeded in Spain as far as it was ever likely to succeed. Nocedal himself advised Don Carlos in 1870 to enter into an alliance with the Republicans in order to overthrow Amadeo. Still, Carlism was bound to be a thorn in the flesh so long as the structure of Spanish society remained unchanged. But from 1860 onwards, it was no more than a disturbing element, unable to put its ideas into practice.

In May 1872, the Carlists returned to the fray with the cry of "Down with the foreign king!" Once more Don Carlos entered Spain. The displeasure with which the landed oligarchy regarded the Savoyard, the support given by the Republicans to the Carlists and the precarious state of the Government, helped Carlism in this its last bloody insurrection of the nineteenth century. In a few days the Pretender's army capitulated and signed the Convention of Amorebieta, an almost literal reproduction of the peace of Vergara. It was, however, no more than a truce and the war continued until February 28th, 1876, when Don Carlos recrossed the French frontier. Cabrera had already signified his allegiance to Alfonso XII, the new king, son of Isabel II.

Don Carlos María, fourth Carlist Pretender and grandson of the first, was succeeded on his death in 1909 by his son Don Jaime, who died in 1932 without issue. And the last king of the Carlists was Don Alfonso Carlos, brother of Don Carlos María and uncle of Don Jaime, who died in Vienna in a motor accident in 1936, at the age of eighty-seven. With him, the last male, the line became extinct.

Though the dynasty had died out, Carlism did not on that account interrupt its march. It was a movement which pre-dated the problem of the succession, and whether or no there was a Pretender—a minor factor—it would continue to live until Spain had created that mercantile and industrial environment which reconciled the rough soul of Ramón Cabrera to civilization.

Carlism, in brief, posed this question to Spanish society— was Spain to be a monarchy or a theocracy? I have already dwelt on some of the reasons which decided many Spaniards to fight the clergy and the shepherds and defend the throne of Isabel II. But this work would be incomplete if no mention was made of the terrific shake-up which the insurrection administered to the whole of Spanish society.

The absolutist aggression, under the banner of God, Country and King (with the King last and the Church first), ended by corrupting the meaning of the word Liberal. María Cristina de Borbón and some, if not all, of the generals and politicians who served her, found themselves compelled to assume the disguise of Liberals; for the conduct of the Church had cleft society into two halves—Liberals and Carlists. Most of the politicians and soldiers who belonged to the Queen's Party did not favour constitutional monarchy or the principle of the people's sovereignty. They were simply absolutists who repudiated theocracy, desiring a reactionary monarchy, but not one dominated and restricted by priests. The loyalty of Generals Llauder, Córdova and Quesada—the three with a command— to Isabel II at the time when the conflict broke out, has been attributed to base motives. It may be that personal ambition came into play; but this is not the whole explanation. These three absolutist generals enlisted against Carlism, as did so many other Spaniards, because they rejected the utopian and perturbing leadership of the Church. The consequence was that the Liberal or Queen's Party contained innumerable anti-Liberals, persons who would never have waged war on the clergy, if the clergy had not attacked them first.

In his *Discourse on the First Decade of Titus Livius* Machiavelli says: "When any difficulty becomes very great in a State or against a State, it is better policy to temporize with it than to combat it openly, since almost always what is done to extinguish it, increases and accelerates the evil which is feared." The difficulty which stood in the path of theocracy was obviously very great, and the endeavour to overcome it by a frontal attack, with the violent tactics of war, was bound to increase and precipitate the evil which the Church feared—the avalanche of liberty.

The insurrection of the monks placed the political power squarely in the hands of the people. The monarchy of Isabel II had to look to the people for support, and the people imposed the onerous condition of complete liberty. This the Crown had to concede—complete liberty to a people sunk in extreme poverty—and there soon remained not a single person in the Liberal camp, from the Queen downwards, who was not a demagogue. It was essential to make use of the people to fight Don Carlos, and so there was placed in their hands, not the vote, still less the land, but something infinitely greater in terms of sovereignty—a gun. The national militia, reorganized and significantly renamed the City Militia (*Milicia Urbana*), received the desperate sanction of the Crown. Anyone who

77

liked could enrol in it. Side by side with the regular Army, the other came into being with a membership of 200,000 men.

It was not a non-existent Liberal republicanism, or the people, who rose against the monarchy; it was the Church which supplied the spark which fired the train. This was the new situation. The Church, the only institution which had survived the general cataclysm at the beginning of the century, opened the flood-gates of chaos.

# BOOK TWO

# THE RESTORATION STATE
## (1874-1931)

### CHAPTER I

## THE NEW OLIGARCHY

We CAN FIX the birth of the new oligarchy in the neighbourhood of 1860. As the century passed its first half, the unhappy Spanish revolution, already in the last period of its ebb and flow, threw up upon the political strand a foreign body—the fantastic oligarchy which was to determine the fate of Spain for generations to come. This is a crucial hour in the history of Spain; for towards 1860 it became evident (we see it today with crystal clearness) what was to be the shape of contemporary Spain. The revolution was then in its decline; and its descent coincided logically with the rise of the new and the old rich who were getting ready to consolidate the property which the national upheaval had respected or created in its singular fluctuations.

The foundations of the political edifice of the Restoration were being laid. Fourteen years later, Spain already had new institutions—and what institutions!

The reign of the social class which, half-way through the century, was contending for the leadership of the nation, was ushered in by a soldier with a great deal of the politician in his make-up—Don Leopoldo O'Donnell. He was helped by, and obviously much under the influence of, a young lawyer from Malaga, a precocious individual, with a fluent pen and a fondness for history—Don Antonio Cánovas del Castillo.

Of all the generals who supplanted politicians in the reign of Isabel II, O'Donnell had the soundest instinct for politics.

And as the major part of O'Donnell's psychological traits are to be met with in his father, Don Enrique, we shall make rapid headway in our presentation of the former if we quickly sketch the political portrait of the latter.

Don Enrique O'Donnell, who was of direct Irish descent,[1] played an outstanding part in the Peninsular War. Of signal courage, like almost all his companions-in-arms in that extraordinary conflict, he distinguished himself in innumerable encounters. But his chief exploit—and the one which earned him his title—was when, with great daring, he brought food to besieged Gerona when the French under General Augereau were tightening the iron ring round the neck of Álvarez de Castro's immortal troops, with the threat of certain strangulation.

After that epic feat, O'Donnell followed Wellington in his invasion of France, with an army of his own choosing raised in Andalusia.

Years afterwards, on the eve of Riego's *pronunciamiento*, O'Donnell was going up and down the Andalusian coast, organizing the army which was to put down the rebels in Spanish America. He established intimate contact with the first conspirators and succeeded in gaining their confidence—so much so, that the latter regarded him as one conspirator more, and not the least illustrious. But when the time was ripe, he ordered the arrest of the conspirators and informed Ferdinand VII of the abortive plot. The King overwhelmed him with honours, granting him a pension from the Royal coffers and bestowing on him the Grand Collar of Charles III. In addition, he was made Captain-General of Madrid.

When Riego and Quiroga rose in Andalusia, the King, confident of O'Donnell's loyalty, ordered him to march to Cadiz at the head of the troops under his command and suppress the revolt. O'Donnell, convinced of the weakness of the absolutist cause, obediently set forth, but on arriving at Ocaña in the province of Toledo he joined the rebels and proclaimed the Constitution.

O'Donnell's brusque action opened the flood-gates, setting free the torrent which swept away absolutism in 1820.

The constitutionalists already knew Don Enrique; but Don Enrique, keeping a watchful eye on the game, made himself indispensable to both sides, since neither the Liberals nor the *serviles* (the name by which the absolutists were known) had so much advantage over their adversary that they could afford to

[1] The O'Donnells were descended from one of the Irish families who had taken refuge in Spain from the sixteenth century onwards.

despise the support which O'Donnell offered in the moment of an always vague and insecure victory. Thus it was that O'Donnell was once more entrusted with the defence of Madrid in 1823 when Angoulême's assault hovered over the capital. Don Enrique asked for and was given everything necessary to contain the French at the gates of Madrid. But the wind was now blowing against the Constitution; and the protean soldier, master, as we have seen, of this kind of tactics, passed over to Angoulême, abandoning the defence of the pass of Somosierra and discouraging the people with opportunely defeatist literature.

Retiring from the struggle for reasons of health, Don Enrique ended his days at Bayonne in 1834. The shooting of one of his sons, who was taken prisoner by Zumalacárregui at Alsasua, undoubtedly hastened his end.

Don Leopoldo O'Donnell, who was to influence Spanish politics, perhaps decisively, unquestionably inherited the moral lineaments of Don Enrique. Even in the timeliness of his retirement from public life and in his choice of a place to die he resembled his father.

As politicians, Espartero and Narváez (we will say nothing about Serrano) never reached the stature of O'Donnell—which does not mean that O'Donnell's politics were elevated. He owed much to the advice of Cánovas del Castillo, his inseparable lieutenant and co-founder of the Spanish State in the image and likeness of the new oligarchy. We shall see later what manner of man Cánovas was and in what his success consisted.

Undoubtedly this social class, of which O'Donnell and Estébanez Calderón's nephew were the spokesmen, perceived with sure instinct that it was a thing that was in process of being born. The name of Cánovas' newspaper *Las Novedades* was highly expressive. With that consciousness, sure of themselves and knowing what was at stake, O'Donnell and Cánovas entered the political lists. Their policy was iniquitous because it was to perpetuate civil war, putting the nation in deadly peril of death; but this oligarchy knew what it wanted—the indispensable key to success in life—while all the other parties were at the time in a state of crisis and bewilderment.

Cánovas del Castillo, the man of the future, was moving then in the shadow of the powerful figure of O'Donnell. That the soldier and the historian were at one in their ideas is notorious. One trait of O'Donnell's displeased Cánovas at times; his portentous capacity for intrigue. The General's exaggerated Machiavellism made Cánovas uneasy, for on occasions—as, for example, when O'Donnell surrendered to the Cabinet of monks, that is, to Carlism—he threw out of gear the whole policy of the oligarchy and might have ruined the work in which both were engaged.

The only inspiration which the new oligarchy brought to Spanish politics was a desire for repose. The old blue-blooded aristocracy—which had also reaped a rich harvest in the days of the fat kine when the estates were being disentailed—the families which had enriched themselves by fishing in the troubled waters of civil war, the old and the new monopolizers of the national soil, the merchants and high functionaries who had made their fortunes in Central and South America, from whence they were now returning, the "sensible" prelates, the higher ranks of the bureaucracy, the staff officers of that top-heavy army—all aspired to enjoy their possessions in peace in a pacified Spain. The oligarchy, therefore, as realists, shunned adventures in home policy. The dexterity of Cánovas, and what assured his personal triumph, lay in the fact that he could put out antennae, as it were, and sense, as no one else could, the desires and ambitions of the new social class. If a social class can on occasions be represented in all its virtues and moral defects, in its egoisms and in its insensate follies, by a single man, then Cánovas del Castillo was the miraculously exact personification of the new Spanish oligarchy. Above all, this young intellectual rightly interpreted—whether by reason or instinct, I do not know—that irresistible desire for peace which the Conservative classes were beginning to display just at the moment when he, hardly out of his teens, was crossing the threshold of public life. Cánovas was the living embodiment of the monstrous growth engendered by the revolution. It was only in intelligence and education, without which he could not have done what he did, that he had the advantage of that coarse and insensitive class.

But though Cánovas was in great measure the brains of O'Donnell, we must not lose sight of the General.

Like his father, Don Leopoldo O'Donnell was not a man to be tormented by the prickings of conscience. In that he also resembled Cánovas; for him, the end justified the means. These two persons had a policy (a thing no one had in Spain about 1860), and they were going to impose it on the nation. O'Donnell believed in nothing—unless, like Cánovas, he believed in himself. He entered politics on his own initiative, because of an irresistible vocation. In no wise did he resemble Espartero, who was forced into politics and took the popular cause seriously; or Narváez, who was profoundly convinced that his policy of severity was saving Spain from anarchy. If Narváez and Espartero give the impression that they were dragged into politics at the heels of destiny, O'Donnell's public acts were those of a man who needed a political career in order to use his exceptional talents as a courtier and his unusual gifts of command—the command of men, not of soldiers. O'Donnell, in short, was a politician even when he was directing the war; the others were soldiers even when they were directing the Government.

In 1854, O'Donnell revolted at Vicálcaro. The situation was ripe for the Radicals. But O'Donnell was an object of suspicion to the parties of the Left; he inspired no confidence in either reactionaries or progressives. What was his programme? What did he want, apart from power? The General found himself leading a revolt in the suburbs of Madrid. The capital, though nervous and confused, did not seem disposed to surrender. Then Cánovas del Castillo intervened (he was then twenty-six years old) and issued the famous Manifesto of Manzanares, with which he attached a Liberal label to the *pronunciamiento*. Madrid then opened her gates to O'Donnell, who was thus launched on the path of victory by his friend. But the victory belonged to the progressives, and the Espartero Government came into power, with O'Donnell as Minister of War.

O'Donnell had embraced Espartero in public; but no sooner had the Government been formed than he began to hatch with the Queen and the priestly *camarilla*, as we saw when we were discussing Carlism, the plot which was to overthrow him.

In 1856 O'Donnell rose with the Army, and the people came out in defence of Espartero. The National Militia was mobilized and barricaded itself into the Palaces of Vistahermosa and Medinaceli. The rebels were commanded by the illustrious Madoz and bombarded by Serrano.

In Barcelona, the battle lasted two days and cost 500 lives.

Such was the reaction of the oligarchy on perceiving that Espartero was exploiting—or might be trying to exploit—the Manifesto of Manzanares in favour of the revolution. But the Cabinet of monks, working behind the screen of the Crown, mellifluously dismissed O'Donnell, as we have seen, as soon as they saw that Church property was safe.

In spite of this, Cánovas' plan was making progress. Neither he nor O'Donnell were the men to admit defeat.

From '54 to '58, the new oligarchy, at war with the old policy —Carlism and *pronunciamientos*—was perfecting its technique, so that when in June 1858 the Queen once more charged O'Donnell to form a Government, the movement had reached surprising maturity. For the first time since the preceding century, Spain was going to have a stable Government, a Government which was to last five years!—a phenomenon so unusual and astonishing that the Cortes of the *Unión Liberal* was christened by everybody the "Long Parliament".

The political genius of Cánovas now had an opportunity of displaying all its arts, both good and bad, in what was evidently the political discovery of his day.

It should be repeated that the new oligarchy had one overwhelming desire—peace at home. Whatever militated against peace at home must be eliminated either by force or by compromise. The peasants might rise in Castile, Estremadura and Andalusia—the rebellion of Loja actually occurred when O'Donnell was in command—but this question did not cause him or his followers any concern; they considered it a private dispute between the *braceros*, the landless labourers and the Civil Guard. And the same thing was always to happen everywhere; because it was the firm intention of the new social class that the structure of Spanish society should remain unchanged "world without end. Amen".

Apart from this disturbing factor for the plans of the oligarchy, there remained three other principal agents of disorder with which it was necessary to come to terms: Carlism, or the Church's itch to govern; the *pronunciamientos*, or the Army's preoccupation with politics; and parliamentary opposition, or impertinent party criticism.

Cánovas did not conceal his admiration for the Carlists; but he was convinced that there would be no peace in Spain till the Church had renounced her claim to govern. His plan was to reach a compromise with the Church, on the basis of the submission of the spiritual arm to the civil power. For this purpose, he thought the Constitution of 1845 the most suitable, but with the addition of a Liberalizing element. Hence, the Act passed by O'Donnell in 1856, to which I have already alluded, whereby Narváez' Charter was lightened of its load of absolutism. Twenty years later, this formula reappeared in the Constitution of 1876. Cánovas held exactly the same views in 1897, when he was on the point of death, as he had held in 1860. He was a man impervious to the process of evolution, like some invertebrates, and in this also the editor of *Las Novedades* was the spirit of the social class which he represented in human shape.

Cánovas rejected Carlism because it was a notoriously utopian movement which, though it had no prospect of succeeding, yet threatened by its extremism the peaceful enjoyment of power by the oligarchy. As a realist, the Restoration statesman was prepared to go as far in his concessions to the Church as was compatible with the tranquillity of the nation, but no farther. Consequently, Cánovas, Ríos Rosas, Cortina, Alonso Martínez —the genuine civil representatives of the new oligarchy— withdrew their support from O'Donnell on a certain occasion, because the latter, like all persons of his idiosyncrasy, became entangled in the web of his own Machiavellism and once more cast in his lot with the absolutist *camarilla*. But their displeasure was, naturally, fugitive; for O'Donnell recovered quickly from his impolitic backsliding.

As regards the Army, Cánovas' aim was to expel it from political life, not only in deference to the sovereignty of the civil State, but also because military dictatorships brought in their train surprises and perils which, like those inherent in Carlism, disturbed the *dolce far niente* of the oligarchy. The result was that Cánovas, Ríos Rosas and the rest fought Narváez' dictatorship in 1864 and were banished.

The third element which contained the seeds of unrest was bound up with the parties opposing the policy of the oligarchy. These nuclei of rebellion must, therefore, be subdued—but how? By corrupting them. The famous Pact of El Pardo, which was not sealed in El Pardo, had its antecedents in the *Unión Liberal* of 1858.

The *Unión Liberal* already existed in the fancy of the new oligarchy on the eve of O'Donnell's *pronunciamiento* at Vicálcaro. The Manifesto of *Liberal regeneration*, which Cánovas drew up, was a call to agreement between the parties, with a programme designed to bring the march of progress to a standstill and leave Spain high and dry. That plan was frustrated by the intransigeance of the progressives, who wanted to go ahead with the disentailing of the estates. But in 1858 those inconvenient factors had already disappeared.

The *Unión Liberal* set out on the first stage of its government with a programme of unusual brevity—to wit, that no one should make a move in any direction. Its whole policy lay in ensuring that the country should be quiet. Concessions were made to the Church, the opposition was suborned, the Press was corrupted, the protests of the peasants were harshly repressed, and the Army was provided with a series of succulent adventures abroad.

The Government's physiognomy was that of the future Liberal-Conservative Party subsequently founded by Cánovas.

The whole policy of Restoration Spain was here roughly sketched out. This was its first dress-rehearsal.

The new oligarchy was born corrupt and born to corrupt; and it was to corrupt everything it touched.

O'Donnell formed his Government of all the notable cynics who revolved like dead suns round the man who brought to Spain, under a Liberal label, the policy of repose. From now on, anyone who had any initiative was looked upon as a disturber of the peace, and anyone who spoke of reforms as a common criminal. The *fin de siècle* scepticism, that apathy which quenched every vital spark of the national soul, was a specific malady of the new oligarchy, a disease which had already made its appearance in the period under review and which afterwards spread, by contagion, to the whole of Spanish society.

The miracle-Government of O'Donnell and Cánovas rested (the emphasis is on the word "rested") on corruption; not corruption in one particular direction, but the systematic corruption of all the organs of government. It was a Government without a policy properly so-called, without principles and without ideals. The oligarchy had no faith in Spain, nor did it believe in Spaniards.

The *Unión Liberal* was a nursery of disillusioned politicians, who were sick and tired of a struggle which appeared to lead nowhere; cynics, like O'Donnell and Cánovas, or schemers, like Posada Herrera. Beside these men, Narváez was a Quixote and the Carlists hopeless romantics. The new oligarchy, in fact, came to stifle everything that was vital in the Spanish character, the absurd as well as the discriminating, the good as well as the bad. O'Donnell offered a portfolio to everybody who counted; first, to his own entourage, in which disillusioned former progressives, called *resellados*, figured; then to the editors of opposition newspapers, to the most troublesome leaders of the opposition, to radicals who had the reputation of being incorruptible. Some accepted; others did not. But those who accepted were already corrupted.

Posada Herrera, who may be regarded as the founder of caciquism, the distinguished master of all the Romero Robledos of the future, undertook the corruption of the suffrage and the manipulation of the Parliaments.

To begin with, the "Great Elector", as he was called, took care that future Chambers should contain an opposition—not so numerous that it would endanger the Government, nor so weak that it would cause the Government majority to break up. Posada had a theory that a Chamber made up of the friends of the Government, that is to say, a unanimous Chamber, ends by becoming a house divided against itself. Moreover, the revolutionaries must have representation in Parliament; otherwise they would work against the Government from outside.

It was of prime importance that the friends of O'Donnell and Cánovas should be returned as deputies and senators. But it was no less important that the leaders of the Radicals and the ultramontanes should be elected. The absolutists, being nearest in sympathy to the Government, were assigned thirty seats in the Cortes; the Radicals, twenty.

Those lukewarm progressives who were the possessors of a biting tongue were given places in the Senate, or magnificent posts in the civil service, or sent on important missions to the colonies.

The Government did their best to satisfy everybody. No one could accuse them of lack of goodwill. All the same, they did not tolerate enemies, save those who were absolutely necessary to the functioning of the brand-new system. Every influential politician, journalist or soldier could thrive at his leisure. He could be a Minister, or a deputy, or a senator, or an editor, or a business manager, or a high official in Cuba. But woe to him who dared to obstruct the work of the Government! For those who bent the knee to the policy of O'Donnell and Cánovas —favours, pensions, rewards; for the incorruptibles—persecution and imprisonment.

Never did a Government and a Parliament last so long in Spain. The new oligarchy saw everything it had made, and behold, it was very good.

The new oligarchy did not propose to govern Spain; it proposed to enjoy power, which for it was an end in itself, and to dispatch, in passing, any business that might come its way. Its ideal was to compromise with the dissenting parties; but not the fruitful compromise of those who come to an agreement in order to get something done, but the demoralizing conspiracy of those who scheme to prevent anything being done.

The oligarchy's first transaction with the Church resulted in the Convention of August 25th, 1859, whereby the right of the clergy to acquire and retain all manner of property and securities was recognized. This was the most important point in the agreement, and one which the Church was most concerned to clear up.

By yielding the point, O'Donnell gained ground with the Carlists. He was to follow the same policy with the Army.

But the compromise with the Army was to be even more fatal. The oligarchy's solution of this other tremendous problem was implicit in its policy. Here again it followed a set course. Overwhelmed by the proximity of an unwieldy and politically-minded Army, the *Unión Liberal* decided to reopen the roads of Africa to Spanish arms.

The military intervention of Spain in Morocco was another item on the programme of the new oligarchy. Cánovas was the prime mover in this, too; for he had no need to interrogate the ruling classes in order to know their desires. In his *Historia de la Decadencia de España*, published in 1854, he had already discovered that "Spain may still be a great continental and maritime power" if certain events take place, and among these he includes expansion "through the neighbouring coast to Africa". It has been said that Cánovas was behind O'Donnell's policy in Africa, and this is undoubtedly true.

Nevertheless, the principal motive which inspired the oligarchy to pursue adventures abroad was not expansion, but, on the one hand, the necessity of employing a politically conscious Army which by its very size was in conflict with a policy of peace, and on the other, the need for distracting the people's attention with intoxicating visions of military glories to the benefit of tranquillity at home.

Spain could not afford such dangerous frauds. With a floating debt of 175 million pesetas, a budgetary deficit of 500 million, production ruined by taxes (which the oligarchy did not pay, as we shall have occasion to see), O'Donnell improvised as many military campaigns in Africa and Spanish America as could be carried out at the time. It was an unprincipled policy, a search for pretexts to inflame the country and distract attention from affairs at home.

As soon as the new oligarchy began to govern, it felt the need of a war. Its first idea was to send an army of 100,000 men to Italy to sustain the temporal power of the Pope and support the Prince of Parma whose throne was also menaced. But events in Italy moved too precipitously, and when O'Donnell wanted to intervene, the war was already drawing to a close and the Prince of Parma had lost his throne.

What was to be done, then, with an already mobilized army? The oligarchy agreed that the best thing to do was to teach the Moors a lesson, and in October 1859 O'Donnell declared war on the Sultan of Morocco—to avenge imaginary slurs on Spanish honour. In April of the following year, peace was signed, after Spain had lost 7,000 men. O'Donnell returned from Africa with a hero's halo, received the title of Duque de Tetuán, and was cheered in the streets of Madrid.

The African war would have been a venial sin, from which history would have absolved the oligarchy, had it not brought in its train other consequences. The worst was that Spain, disorganized and bleeding to death, fell into the African snare, to be weakened physically and morally for generations.

With his African laurels still green on his brow, O'Donnell launched out upon another adventure in support of the Republic of Santo Domingo against Haiti. For four years, Spain waged war in Santo Domingo and lost 10,000 men.

While the problem of Santo Domingo was still alive, O'Donnell and Cánovas resolved to seize another opportunity of keeping the people's attention fixed on events abroad and the soldiers occupied. Spain joined France and England in intervening against the Mexican Government of Benito Juárez. How events turned out is well known. In April 1862 the Spanish and British troops withdrew, leaving the French to their fate and their candidate to the throne of Mexico, Maximilian, to be captured and executed.

These vicissitudes abroad played no little part in maintaining the *Unión Liberal* in power. But that policy also had its dangerous side for the Government, which, in spite of all, was not yet omnipotent and irresponsible as it was to be under the Restoration.

In 1865, the *Unión Liberal* returned to power, and the Duque de Tetuán's Ministry again included Cánovas, Alonso Martínez, Posada Herrera, etc. This second innings only lasted a year, but the oligarchy already showed greater maturity. Sor Patrocinio was confined to her convent, Father Claret to his monastery. Posada Herrera brought to perfection his arts as an electoral magician. Important portfolios were offered to three editors of progressive newspapers, who refused them. Other progressives accepted posts in the Government and seats in the Chambers. The idea was, as it was ten years ago, to destroy the opposition, but not by carrying out its programme (always supposing that the opposition had one), not by winning over the nation by good works, but by corrupting it lock, stock and barrel, by associating every politically dangerous individual in the peaceful enjoyment of power, and persecuting those who refused to come into the fold.

We are already familiar with the foreign and home policy of the new oligarchy. (In 1865-6, O'Donnell and Cánovas repeated down to the last detail the experiment of 1858-63, this time getting involved abroad in a war with the republic of Chile). This is a rough outline of the kind of Government that Spain was to have from 1874 to 1923.

## CHAPTER II

# THE REIGN OF AMADEO OF SAVOY

CARLISM, WHICH WAS unable to dethrone Isabel II
by war, destroyed the Crown by other methods. By worming
its way into the Court and setting up an unofficial Cabinet,
presided over by the Cardinal-Archbishop of Toledo and Don
Carlos' ex-adviser, it no longer defied the "Liberals" on the
field of battle, but carried the fight onto a ground where, if the
monastic-peasant movement was to be conquered, the overthrow
of Isabel II's throne was an overriding necessity. The national
rebellion against the ultramontane absolutism which lurked in
the Palace was now, in the first instance, a general rising against
the person who before had symbolized the opposite movement.
Spain perceived one day with astonishment that she was being
ruled by a theocracy, and expelled the Queen who did not know
how, or was unable, to maintain the independence of the civil
institutions. What some Carlists had not achieved by force of
arms—"to raze monarchical institutions to the ground," as
Ferdinand VII said—others had succeeded in doing silently,
by the method of peaceful penetration. Nothing could be more
natural than that the forces which in 1834 had hastened to
succour the throne, should now declare their hostility to it.
The new oligarchy and those who had conquered Carlism in
1839 had not fought in order that Isabel II should pursue the
policy of Don Carlos. The situation was defined with eloquence
by the clergy themselves in that attempt to carry off the august
lady to the Basque Provinces, no doubt so that the most recalcitrant Carlists should see for themselves that she was one of
them. One by one, all the "Liberal" sectors abandoned the
Queen; and with the essentially Carlist dictatorship of González
Bravo the throne fell.

This is the real cause of the Revolution of September, 1868,
and not, as is commonly supposed, the love affairs of the Queen
which scandalized nobody, since, as far as such frailties were
concerned, everybody was engaged in doing likewise to the
best of his, or her, ability.

For the new oligarchy, the infiltration of Carlism into the
Government was a serious setback. O'Donnell retired to France,
to die shortly afterwards; but Cánovas and his friends did not
slacken their efforts till they had overthrown the monarchy

which was such a deadly obstacle to the policy of compromise and the tranquillity of the nation.

The conspiracy against the throne of Isabel II took on a national character; but the September revolt was led by the progressives, that is, by the middle class. The landed oligarchy had collaborated in the rebellion, isolating the Queen, leaving her alone with her Carlists, stimulating hostility to the throne by the pen, or through the mouth, of its spokesmen. But, I repeat, the new situation which was created when Admiral Topete's *pronunciamiento* succeeded at Cadiz with the assistance of Prim, Sagasta and Ruiz Zorrilla in person, and when some days afterwards Novaliches suffered the defeat of Puente de Alcolea—this situation was the work of the progressives or radicals and it was they who took the front of the stage during the regency of Serrano and the reign of Amadeo of Savoy.

Since Espartero retired from public life, the Progressive Party had been under the leadership of General Prim. Don Juan Prim was born at Reus in 1814. His father was a notary and a soldier. At the age of twenty, Juan enlisted in the voluntary militia against the Carlists and fought in the Carlist war, which gave him the opportunity to embark on a prodigious military career. When peace was signed, he was already a Lt.-Colonel. A man of action, bold, tenacious and grasping, Prim acknowledged no man his superior. He fought Espartero in 1839 and this resulted in his first banishment. He took part in the conspiracy of generals and progressives which overthrew Espartero in 1843. The Queen Regent rewarded his services to the dynasty with the title of Conde de Reus and the rank of General. Afterwards Prim opposed Narváez' régime and was out of Spain—in France and England—until 1847. When he returned, he was appointed Captain-General of Puerto Rico and afterwards military attaché in Turkey. He supported O'Donnell in the situation that arose following the *pronunciamiento* of Vicálvaro and the leader of the *Unión Liberal* promoted him Lt.-General. His achievements in command of the troops in the Moroccan war and the victory of Los Castillejos brought him a hero's renown and the title of Marqués of that name. From 1866 onwards Prim did not cease to conspire against Isabel II, his *coups* generally ending in fiasco, like those of Vilarejo de Salvanés and Valencia; but the luck which never abandons the persistent finally favoured him in the *pronunciamiento* of September 1868.

This soldier of fortune succeeded Espartero in the leadership of the Liberals. But he was not as popular as Espartero was.

In 1868 Prim must be regarded as the *caudillo* of the middle class. He had entered politics at a time when the Progressive Party had Espartero for its leader, and the voluntary retirement of the latter coincided with a bad period for the Radicals, who saw the doors of power closed to them. But Prim had sworn not to die until he had governed; and he was therefore a danger to any Government so long as, when every political faction already had its general, he was odd man out. This was why he must have appeared more disturbing and more ambitious than the other generals and was either given a post abroad or banished.

If O'Donnell's mentor and guide was Cánovas, Prim's advisers were Don Práxedes Mateo Sagasta and Don Manuel Ruiz Zorrilla, men of very different temperaments. Sagasta, who had better political gifts than Ruiz Zorrilla, now claims our attention, · because he is supremely representative of the most important Liberal nucleus at the end of the century.

He was born at Torrecilla de Cameros, in La Rioja, and came of a Liberal family. His father had suffered the rigours of persecution under the absolutists. Zurbano, the famous *guerrillero*, was an intimate friend of the family. Sagasta's father had a grocer's shop at Logroño, and this business enabled him to launch his son on a career as a civil engineer, in which he achieved marked success. When he was already a qualified engineer, the young Sagasta returned to the School of Engineering as a supplementary teacher, but he lost his post on refusing to sign a statement declaring his loyalty to the throne. However, he found employment with the Northern Railway Construction Company, of whose Board he became Chairman at the end of the century. In 1854, he was employed as Director of the Public Works of Zamora, in which post he took over the leadership of the Progressive Party. His political career began when he was elected deputy to the Cortes of 1854. Later, in Madrid, he became a contributor to *La Iberia*, and when Prim assumed the leadership of the Party, Sagasta became Secretary. On the death of Calvo Asensio, he took over the editorship of *La Iberia*, and as a result of his conspiratorial activities at the orders of the restless Prim, he was condemned to death in June 1866 for the incidents in the San Gil barracks. He managed, however, to trick his pursuers and escape over the French frontier. After a period of exile in Paris and London, he accompanied Prim in the ship which took them to Gibraltar, and obtained his first political post of responsibility when he was appointed Civil Governor of Cadiz in September 1868 after the triumph of the Navy's *pronunciamiento*.

By his home ties—the home of a modest shopkeeper—by his profession, by his ideas (he was a mason like most of the Liberal leaders), Sagasta was the perfect politician of the Spanish middle class in that late hour of the Liberal revolution, when the *social question* was transforming the relation of the political forces, and the thoroughly enfeebled middle class was about to surrender to the powerful landed oligarchy.

One of the sequels of the victorious *pronunciamiento* of September 1868 was the constitution in Madrid of a popular *Junta*, in which were included all the parties hostile to Isabel II, even those which had not participated directly in the revolution. No allusion to the form of government was made in the manifesto of this provisional organ of power. The programme of the *Junta*, in which Don Pascual Madoz made a final reappearance as President, embodied the aspirations of the middle class. It promised the nation universal suffrage, freedom of worship, teaching and the Press; the right of meeting and of association, decentralization, trial by jury, equality of all citizens before the law, inviolability of domicile and abolition of the death penalty.

As soon as Serrano and Prim arrived in Madrid, a Cabinet was formed with Serrano as Prime Minister, Prim as Minister of War, Topete at the Admiralty and Sagasta at the Ministry of the Interior. This was a middle class Government, a Government of progressives. As far as the Liberal claims as set forth by the *Junta* were concerned, the Government had hardly any objections. But they emphasized that the discredit surrounding the fallen dynasty must not be confused with the monarchical principle. Before the elections to the Constituent Cortes, the parties concerned issued in November a manifesto drawn up by Sagasta, in which he said: "The monarchical form of government is the form which most strongly and inevitably suggests itself if liberty and the needs of the Revolution are to be consolidated. The monarchy for which we are going to vote is a monarchy born of the people's rights expressed by universal suffrage—one which is the symbol of the people's sovereignty . . .; one which radically destroys the Divine Right of kings and the supremacy of one family over the people. Our monarchy is surrounded by democratic institutions and, for this reason, it is a popular monarchy."

This popular monarchy of which the Radicals dreamed was nothing less than the typical monarchy of the middle class, a monarchy in the Dutch style, a régime well suited to a nation with an all-powerful middle class, without a landed aristocracy or oligarchy. And this was what the monarchy of Amadeo of Savoy claimed to be.

In effect, if Isabel II ended by becoming the queen of the Carlists and Alfonso XII was later to be the king of the landed oligarchy and aristocracy, Amadeo was the king of the middle class. The Constitution of June 6th, 1869, with its postulates of parliamentary sovereignty, universal suffrage, freedom of worship and all the other freedoms, would have passed for an excellent instrument of government in any socially balanced country; but in Spain, where social inequality could not have been more strident, the Constitution of '69 and its centre-piece, limited monarchy, were demagogic gestures. These social institutions, like those of the Restoration, could have been sustained—though with greater effort—by fraud. But such was the weakness of the Spanish middle class, even this means was denied them.

It was not easy to find a king for Spain. Prim declared in the Cortes: ". . . In a country in this state of uncertainty; in a country which is in process of drawing up a Constitution, where things happen like the recent events we have witnessed— yesterday, a bloody revolt at Cadiz, then another at Malaga, then another veritable battle at Jerez; in one village, the Civil Governor murdered in church; in another, the municipal authorities lynched—in a country where these things happen which, though perhaps they may not mean much to us because we are used to them and worse, take on an extraordinary significance when they cross the frontier, is it strange that every prince who might be a candidate should say: 'Who is going to venture into such a country?'"

In fact, the violence and bloodshed to which Prim was referring augured ill for his experiment in constitutional monarchy, for they showed that the nation was not ripe to assimilate a system of institutions founded on liberty, as we shall see beyond a shadow of doubt when we study the Republican experiment.

Other candidates having been discarded, the choice fell— not without hazards and dangers for Spain—on Amadeo of Savoy, a prince of but twenty-six summers, but not lacking in character and skilled in all the duties of his office.

The new monarch's plan was to rule with his finger on the pulse of the nation. But he was not the king of the whole nation, or even the king of Spain's strongest class. The men of the moment, the Sagastas and the Ruiz Zorrillas (Prim had been assassinated the day Amadeo embarked at the port of Spezia for Spain) were bound to falsify the national will in order that the régime should not perish when it had hardly begun to live.

The first Parliament of the reign already contained an opposition which was formidable both in numbers and quality. Carlists, Republicans and *alfonsinos* were working in close alliance against the new monarchy. Sagasta provoked a national storm by placing 2 million *reales* from his Ministry's coffers at the disposal of progressive candidates. And in subsequent elections, when Ruiz Zorrilla was Prime Minister, progressivism achieved a miracle in that only seven opposition candidates made their appearance in the Cortes. Sagasta, Serrano, Ríos Rosas, Cánovas, Topete and Alonso Martinez lost their seats. Universal suffrage was, then, a fiction. Only a fraction of the electorate went to the polls. The withdrawal of the Conservative classes, who were thus also demonstrating their coldness to the régime, and the disdain of the proletariat for anything that was not revolutionary activity, together with the electoral machinations of the Government who were obliged, in order to secure a parliamentary majority, to make a reckless and unbridled use of power, showed up clearly the artificiality of the Constitution.

A monarchy of such a pronounced middle-of-the-road type could only appeal to the middle class. But the interests of the middle class, so eloquently defended in the Constitution, were not those of the Church, or those of the landed oligarchy, or those of the proletariat.

Cánovas had given a gala display of his exceptional political talents in the debates in the Constituent Cortes, but he was keeping the régime at arm's length. Inside and outside the Cortes, O'Donnell's ex-adviser was watching the swift disintegration of the system and was biding his time, sure of the future. Cánovas knew that this monarchy was in conflict with the nation and that its men, though so ingenious in cornering parliamentary majorities, were incapable of smoothing out this conflict. The social class which ruled in Spain was not the one in the Government, but the new oligarchy, master of the land; not the commercial and industrial middle class, but that other satiated, static class, which desired order and quietness and which he, Cánovas, knew so well.

The Italian King had been imposed on Spain by the middle class, in a moment of confusion, taking advantage of a crisis. What institutions—Cánovas must have thought—could be founded with a new dynasty, with no connections with the past, no appeal to tradition? Amadeo, faithful to his status as the monarch of liberty, comported himself with a modesty and behaved with a simplicity which shed lustre on the Crown. He was a white-collar King, a king who was also a functionary;

94

the ideal monarch, perhaps, whom Don Clemente, the father of Sagasta, might recommend to his friends in moments of leisure in his shop at Logroño.

Amadeo's Ministers were men of the middle class. It was they who had brought him to Spain; with them he reigned and only with them could he govern. What aristocrat who had any pride was going to put a foot in the Royal Palace? The nobility was pleased to look down on the Italian King and Queen, and with a foolish and intemperate *españolismo* did not let them forget that they were strangers. Carlism took up arms again; nor did the proletariat feel any attraction for an insipid régime which did not promise any sweeping reform. Amadeo lacked, therefore, any real forces on which to base his throne. And why should the Conservative classes embark upon the support of a monarch who appeared incorruptible and would not lend himself to countenance the oligarchic form of government? Amadeo was not a king given to compromise, one who could be suborned like those who came afterwards. For all this, the new oligarchy thought the less of him, and given these conditions, such a monarchy could not last. Its fate, from the beginning, was linked with that of the progressives. The régime of a party which was incontrovertibly in a minority was doomed to suffer the crises of progressivism. When the Radicals split into two groups—the moderate group under Sagasta and the advanced group under Ruiz Zorrilla—and hostilities broke out between them, Amadeo was left with no instrument of government. The monarchy was called a limited monarchy, and no one could doubt that it was indeed limited, when the possibilities of finding a person to undertake to form a Government under that unpretentious king were so swiftly exhausted.

When Ruiz Zorrilla dissolved the Corps of Artillery, Amadeo seized the occasion as a pretext to abdicate. Though opposed to the measure, he scrupulously observed the Constitution, signed the decree and departed for Italy. It was then February 11th, 1873.

On the same day, the Congress and the Senate met together—though this was contrary to the Constitution—assumed the character of a National Assembly and proclaimed the Republic by 258 votes to 32.

## CHAPTER III

# THE FIRST REPUBLIC

IT IS QUITE clear that the first Republic was an historic incident which merely delayed the process by which the social power of the new oligarchy was being crystallized into a new State.

The Republican régime was imposed on the nation by a Cortes bearing the monarchical stamp, elected as a monarchical assembly, and composed of an immense majority of Monarchists. This immense monarchical majority voted for the Republic, since the abdication of Amadeo had plunged the nation into the unexpected crisis of having quickly to provide a substitute for him, without the likelihood of finding anyone to fill the vacant throne. Where could another king be found for Spain, when, from September 1868 to November 1870, Prim's ill-starred diplomatic search through the Courts of Europe had proved the insuperable difficulties of the task? There were, therefore, incalculable drawbacks to renewing the search for a monarch who would be difficult to find; and even if one was found, the experiment of the young Italian King, whose reign had lasted little more than two years, did not augur well for the future of a new dynasty. The majority of the nation, whose resentment against the dethroned Isabel II was still hot, were determined that the Bourbons should continue to be excluded from the throne. And so the Republic was born, as the lesser evil, the last resort, after the possibilities of a monarchy had come to nothing. The Monarchists accepted it, in short, because it was the most conservative solution.

The middle class resigned itself to the experiment. Martos was unquestionably expressing the feeling of deputies and senators alike when he declared: "That without taking the initiative in proclaiming the Republic, the Radicals all accepted it and would vote for it with a good grace."

The Republic had summoned the inevitable Constituent Cortes by universal suffrage, but only a fraction of the electorate had gone to the polls. The Cortes decided without delay, by 210 votes to 2, that Spain should be a federal Republic. This aroused protests, because the deputies had not complied with the Rules of Procedure. Unitarian Republicans regarded their action as a *coup d'état*. The new Government's programme turned on the old postulates. The only thing was that the Republic—the highest expression of the people's sovereignty —could not agree to less than the complete freedom of the individual, a phalansterian or Fourierist liberty. While the Cortes was preparing to draw up a federal Constitution, Pi y Margall was expounding in the Chamber an initial scheme embracing the new liberties—the separation of Church and State, free compulsory education, reforms in Cuba, local autonomy. For the rest, it was understood that Spaniards should enjoy under this régime all the rights set forth in all previous Constitutions.

The draft Constitution which was submitted to Parliament in July 1873 took its inspiration from the desires of the federalists. Spain was to be divided into seventeen States; Upper Andalusia, Lower Andalusia, Aragon, Asturias, the Balearic Islands, the Canary Islands, New Castile, Old Castile, Catalonia, Cuba, Estremadura, Galicia, Murcia, Navarre, Puerto Rico, Valencia and the Basque Provinces. The Philippines, Fernando Po, Annabon and the African garrisons were to be called Territories.

The head of the federal State under the new Constitution was to be called the Co-ordinating or Harmonizing Power and he was to preside over a nation constituted in municipalities and regional States, with Church and State separated and complete freedom of worship.

However, the federal Constitution remained in draft; not so much as the first clause was ever discussed. The first Republic, therefore, fell back in the end on the monarchical Constitution of 1869. It was in reality a Republic without a President, headed by a chief of the Executive Power.

The new régime was symbolized by its leaders: four lawyers and professor-philosophers. It was a platonic Republic, conceived in utopian dreams by a band of philanthropists. The Government of Spain fell into the hands of a Cicero when Spain had most need of a Caesar.

The first Republican Prime Minister was Don Estanislas Figueras, a mild-mannered Catalan, an able lawyer, skilled in the cut and thrust of debate. Figueras owed his exalted state to the negative circumstance that he was the most colourless of the four persons who were disputing the post, and perhaps also to his position as leader of the *Unión Republicana*. A professional colleague of Pi y Margall, his experience as a lawyer availed him little in politics. The habit of command was not his; he was not made for action. In the end, responsibility overwhelmed him and he shook it off in the most original manner

**D s**

ever seen in the head of a State. He wrote out his resignation, sent it in a sealed envelope to the Deputy Speaker of the Cortes and took the train to France. And so the first Republican Prime Minister laid down his office. He had led the nation for four months. None of his successors lasted so long.

He was eagerly succeeded by Don Francisco Pi y Margall, one of his Ministers and one of the four leaders, the man with the strongest personality and the apostle of federalism—reasons why I shall leave it till later to sum up the man and his ideas. Pi y Margall only occupied his high post for a month and a half.

After this, Don Nicolás Salmerón took over the helm of that drifting ship. Under this Professor of Philosophy, the Republic dissolved, through his own demagogic action, into a police régime. The Government no longer paid heed to anything but public order, living from hand to mouth, only anxious that it should not be overtaken by general revolt. Salmerón entrusted the monarchical generals with the restoration of order throughout the country, called up 80,000 recruits (though the Republicans had promised to abolish compulsory military service) for the war against Carlism and the federalists, and reinforced the Civil Guard to an unaccustomed degree.

During his three months of office, Salmerón did to some extent put a curb on anarchy, but it was he—the enemy of capital punishment—who condemned the Revolution to death.

Next, Castelar immolated every principle on the altars of public order. Leaning on the forces which were hostile to the new régime, he exercised a veritable dictatorship from September to December '73. He continued the policy initiated by Salmerón with even greater energy and suppressed the insurrection of the Andalusian proletariat. This raised him above his predecessors in the Government in the estimate of the well-to-do classes. But was anything left of the Republic? The dictatorship of the Professor of History was the dictatorship of the oligarchs (whom he unconsciously served as an instrument), and not what it ought to have been—a sword against whoever, high or low, hindered reform. The transformation of the Republican régime, the régime of liberty and justice as understood by the philanthropists, into a system of tyranny induced the Republicans themselves to destroy it. On January 3rd, 1874, Castelar demanded a vote of confidence from the Cortes. Everyone knew that if he failed to get it, Pavía, the Captain-General of Madrid, would dissolve Parliament *manu militari* and set himself up as dictator. Yet the Republicans voted against Castelar. Deliberately, in cold blood, the Republicans were sentencing to death the

Republic which, twelve months before, had been proclaimed by the Monarchists. If the origin of the régime was paradoxical, its end was no less so.

The four men of note who had passed one by one through the highest office of the State while the Republic lasted, were probably second to none in personal integrity; but they were very far from possessing those statesmanlike qualities which might have saved the régime. They were the leading lights of the advanced middle class, men who lived in an ivory tower, learning everything they knew from books. They had seen the Republic triumphant in France and the Commune reigning in Paris and all this played no slight part in inciting them to follow the course mapped out by the neighbouring country. But the structure of Spanish society was not that of French society. The Paris Commune was an incident that was only made possible by the defeat at Sédan, and the French Republic came into being as the régime of what was perhaps the most robust middle class in Europe. In Spain, this class was but a sect, a class without political independence, a tributary, according to inclination, of the proletariat or of the landed oligarchy.

The first Spanish Republic, therefore, ended by being nobody's régime and so it died, painlessly and without glory. In the number and political quality of its sympathizers, it had even less luck than Amadeo's monarchy. The advanced middle class was only a fraction of the middle class as a whole, which, in its turn, was only a minority in Spanish society. The progressives would have nothing to do with the Republic, for the middle class saw in the social programme of the Republican régime a menace to property and, after all, they were a propertied class. The landed oligarchy was outraged and alarmed by the experiment. The Carlists took it for granted that the Republic's weakness guaranteed the success of a new bid for power. And the proletariat preferred not to wait for the legislative reform which had been promised in such profusion.

The Republicans represented no social class; they had all the classes against them. Their leaders were men of the University Chair and the lawyer's office, and it was not an accident that among them could be found no business man like Sagasta, no merchant like Mendizábal, no banker like Sevillano; it was not an accident, it was a symptom.

Because it was the régime of the advanced middle class, the Republic promised the proletariat fat concessions. Only the Republicans had a programme of social reforms. Their newspaper *La Igualdad* already expressed in its title a concept which was welcome to the multitude of the dispossessed. The federalism of Pi y Margall achieved popularity as a doctrine, thanks to its vein of anarchism. Pi y Margall is the father of Spanish anarchism; and the social interest of the first Republican experiment is bound up with his person and his ideas. The other leaders might be confused with the Liberals—not so the Catalan writer.

We shall now see what place Pi occupies in the Republican experiment, but in order to do this, we must first refer to the problem of property.

By observing the political forces of the end of the century, by weighing up the results of the Liberal revolution, and taking what we know of the national economy before and after that change, we can venture the hypothesis, in the absence of reliable statistics, that when the movement of landed property ceased, an exceptionally high percentage, for Europe, of the Spanish people possessed no property at all. That is to say, since the end of the nineteenth century the huge majority of Spaniards belonged to that class without property which was known in the Roman Republic by the generic name of proletariat (not the proletariat of Marxism); and in this must be included the smallholders, the poor proprietors (cruel paradox!) whose economic and civil state was, in general, as deplorable as that of the landless peasant, when it was not worse.

This huge and oppressed proletariat, nine-tenths of whom were peasants, had a standard of living equal to that of a Chinese coolie. Rome kept her proletariat at bay with distributions of grain; there was nothing of that sort in Spain. The landless population was left to the mercy of heaven; and the smallholders, who paid themselves a miserable wage for an endless day's work, could compare their daily lot with that of a beast of burden.

Had it always been so? These masses without property, the immense majority of the nation, did they exist in the sixteenth century when Spain dominated the world? The answer is, certainly, no. Three-quarters of this proletariat was new; it had already existed in the eighteenth century, but had multiplied in the nineteenth century. It was a proletariat born, in part, of the destruction of the popular economy, and, in part, of the concentration of landed property which had been encouraged by the disentailing of the estates.

Until the nineteenth century, Spain, as we have seen, did not develop her agriculture. The rural population was relatively sparse and managed to hold its own, though with difficulty, because the economic life of the municipalities was intense. The income of the farming population was supplemented by the common lands and the *bienes de propios*. "The system of the communal pasture-ground," says a Spanish historian, "on which the local inhabitants feed their livestock and where they all have at least a pig and a donkey, does not encourage wealth, but it regularizes its distribution and avoids the formation of a proletariat."

However, this system which kept away the proletariat, was shaken to its foundations as the century advanced. Moreover, the population of Spain considerably increased, and the nation, no longer able to count on the food and gold of America, set to and began to work. Uncultivated land was put under the plough.[1] A new class of expropriates was then created and, parallel to it, as I have previously pointed out, a new class of proprietors.

Some days before the Constituent Cortes of the first Republic met, the Republicans published the social programme of the new Government. The harm done to the poor by the spoliation of the disentailers was still so vivid in the popular mind that the revolutionaries of '73 construed the revolution as a reversion to the economic situation obtaining before the disentailing laws, and proclaimed as a result:

"The revision of the sale of common lands and *bienes de propios*; reversal of illegal sales and restoration to the villages of lands which have been illegally sold.

"Collective ownership of woodlands, grazing-lands and pastures under the inspection and guardianship of the municipality.

"Expropriation with compensation of owners of woodlands and pasture-lands which are to be put under collective ownership."

But the Liberal and Parliamentary Republic which began by proclaiming the sovereignty of the people in a country where there was only one really sovereign class, the landed oligarchy, fell into the old error of the middle class in heaping political rights on those who had no land. The Republican régime could not, therefore, carry out the revolution, nor had it the time to attempt to do so. It was, like the other Liberal systems in Spain, a demagogic régime. Liberty continued to devour the revolution; and this was not to be the last unhappy experiment.

We already have an idea of the structure of Spanish society when the first Republic came into being. Can we be surprised that that régime should perish, overcome by chaos? At the top of the scale, a minority, insignificant in numbers, but

[1] In 1803 there were 2,900,000 hectares under cultivation; in 1833, 5,137,000, and at the end of the century 6,937,675.

enormously wealthy; and between the minority and the great multitude of the expropriates, a feeble middle class, frightened, like the great estate-owners, by the social demands of the masses. There was no moral barrier between the wealthy proprietors and the dispossessed proletariat, unless it was the Civil Guard, armed to the teeth as if for international war.

The success of federalism in the countryside can be explained by the fact that it was more a social than a political doctrine, similar to that which had inspired the Paris communalists. But here we must turn to Pi y Margall and his ideas.

Don Francisco Pi y Margall was born at Barcelona while Spain was still occupied by Angoulême and his Frenchmen. Of very humble origin, he was, thanks to a will of iron, a self-made man. As a studious and hard-working young man, he had kept himself going on an exiguous income from private teaching, in the intervals of studying Law and voracious reading of such writers on social questions as Robert Owen, Saint Simon and Proudhon. He went to Madrid in 1847, one year before Figueras, to whom he was later attracted by strong ties of friendship and professional interests.

In person, he was diminutive, with small dark eyes hidden behind his glasses. Well-groomed, punctilious, very precise and orderly in his manner of living, always dressed in black, he was an enemy of violence, a pantheistic philosopher, an *amicus humani generis* who believed, like his idols Rousseau and Proudhon, in the innate goodness of man. Under his idealistic rule, Spain was convulsed with tumult from coast to coast.

Pi belonged to the period when his intellectual growth was fashioned, and that was the moment when the final rupture between the socialism of Marx and that of Bakunin had not yet occurred. It was a time of heart-searchings, of appraisals, the dawn of new ideas among mist and cloud. Pi called himself a Socialist, an "integral" Socialist; believed in the need for social revolution as the point of departure for organizing society on new patterns of justice; and accepted the State, which was to take over as many industries as were capable of nationalization. But Pi y Margall was a disciple of Proudhon and his federalism was libertarian, like that of the author of *La Philosophie de la Misère.*

Pi y Margall's stay in Paris as an émigré had no small influence on his spiritual development. He took up residence in the French capital shortly after Proudhon's death, when the theories of the anarchist philosopher were most in vogue. He translated into Spanish Proudhon's *Le Principe fédératif* and this set the final stamp on his ideas, though he never followed the master faithfully onto the social ground of pure anarchism. What attracted him chiefly in Proudhon was federalism, which was already an obsession with him.

Because of its disintegrating tendency, Pi's federalism had a marked social character. This explains its success among the proletariat. The people were groaning under an iron rule, and anything that would pulverize that rule, the rule of the State, was welcomed with open arms. A proletariat so numerous, and almost entirely illiterate, was excellent human material for Pi's Utopia which expressed, in political terms, the social faith of every primitive proletariat—a faith which fostered the belief that it was only necessary to strip off the husk in order to enjoy the fruit.

This anarchist federalism could count for support on the theories of the romantic writers who, avoiding a diagnosis, denounced Spanish national unity as artificial; on the no less favourable circumstance of the absence of stable institutions in Spain and, above all, on the desperate ignorance of the multitude. It was not the integrating federalism of Franklin and Jefferson, the creative philosophy of the great North American nation, but the disintegrating federalism of Proudhon. There was no question, in Spain, of the integration of a certain number of States in a superior framework, as in Switzerland and the United States, but of the partition of one State. The Spanish federalists were not proposing to constitute a nation, but to make of one nation in crisis, several. The word "federal" was improperly used, because it derives from the Latin *foedus*, that is, a covenant; whereas the federalism which Pi offered Spain was a breaking away; it disrupted, rather than bound together.

As might have been expected, such a doctrine dissolving the bonds of the State meant—though this was not Pi's intention—a revolt against the State. And the worst of it was, as Pi himself proved from his personal failure, that the Spanish federalist movement, once on the march, could not stop at regionalism, but, urged by its unconscious libertarian impulse, was to go on accentuating the division of territory, subdividing regions into cantons, cantons into villages, villages into tribes. Faithful to its Rousseauian origin, it was a return to nature, the total disappearance of the concept of the State, the realization of the anarchist's dream. It amounted, in short, to a reversal of history. For the law of civilization had imposed on Spain, as on the rest of the world, the contrary process.

Anarchist doctrines gained much ground in the second half of the nineteenth century, and the reason is not far to seek.

The spread of anarchism corresponded to the period in Europe of the greatest exploitation of the masses by all-embracing capitalism, a moment, be it noted, which pre-dated the advent of general education and social insurances. The lack of schools and the excess of injustices made anarchism the religion of the downtrodden. Natural man, the central concept of this philosophy, is man freed from the machine and the industrial State, man in a state of primitive liberty. Spain was a fertile ground for all kinds of Utopias, because poverty and ignorance could not be greater. The same thing happened in Russia— a fact which destroys the pretext that all the mystery of Spanish political individualism is concealed in the psychopathology of the Spaniard, rather than in the social conditions in which he lives.

With compulsory education and social reform, the hour of anarchism passed in Europe. But in Spain, time stood still. Exploitation did not cease, no social reforms were passed, nor was the door of knowledge opened.

The federalism of Pi y Margall spread like wild-fire. The Republic had the greatest difficulty in finally subduing rebellion in the rural areas. The proletariat of the townships proclaimed a primitive Communism, abolished private property and sallied forth to fight for the social Republic. Malaga, Seville, Granada, Cordova, Cartagena, fell into the people's hands. At Seville, the workers took possession of the arsenal, abolished private property and ruled over the city for several months. Salmerón sent General Pavía against the Andalusian, and Martínez Campos against the Cartagena cantonalists; it took Pavía a week to subdue the proletariat of Seville. He wanted to continue the expedition against Malaga, but Salmerón took fright and recalled him to Madrid. There had been too many casualties. Afterwards, Castelar decided to send Pavía to deal with Malaga, and the forces of the State finally prevailed.

The most troublesome focus of cantonalism was, as we know, at Cartagena, justly famous for the exploits of part of the Navy under Contreras, a general without naval experience, who went up and down the coast bombarding those cities which rejected federalism. The presiding genius of Cartagena was the philologist Roque Barcia, who had also learnt all he knew from books, and whose enthusiastic resolution, comparable to Contreras', was not belied even by his appeal to the United States for help for the cantonalists, impiously besieged by the federal Republic.

Coinciding with this saturnalia of liberty, which was fast engulfing the Republican leaders, the Carlist Catalans were advancing on Cuenca, Don Carlos was besieging Bilbao for the second time, and Barcelona was cut off from Madrid.

The first Republic succumbed, then, in the most unbridled disorder. The proletariat which, since the middle of the century, had been agitating against the new system of property, embraced, as we have seen, cantonalism and an obscure form of Communism, alarming by its attitude the propertied classes, both the landowners and the mercantile and industrial middle class. The hour of the Liberal revolution had passed; and not because it was no longer necessary (for it is still necessary today), but because the presence of the proletariat as an independent class, with aspirations apparently distinct from those of the middle class, put an end to the subversive activities of the latter. Sagasta was no longer going to risk his life at the barricades. The middle class was going to make a pact with the landed oligarchy. The *rapprochement* of both classes, a process which had begun in the days of Amadeo, if not sooner, now quickened, stimulated by the chaos in the Republic. In future, only the radical section of the middle class, represented by Ruiz Zorrilla and the Republicans, was to oppose the landed oligarchy in a systematic manner. It will be remembered that in the elections of September 1872, when Ruiz Zorrilla was Prime Minister, Sagasta, Ríos Rosas, Cánovas and Alonso Martínez had lost their seats. The fact is symbolic and throws considerable light on the transformation in the relation of the political forces then beginning to operate. Sagasta's moderates appear in conjunction with the political representatives of the new oligarchy in the repulse of the radical middle class. Already in the Constituent Cortes of 1869 it could be remarked how the moderate progressives were running in harness with the men of the *Unión Liberal* and with Cánovas. The most important of all the consequences that flowed from the Republican experiment was, therefore, that the middle class became conservative to a hitherto unimagined extent. Cantonalist Communism, permanent disorder, the disintegrating purpose of libertarian federalism, threw the historic middle class, the business men, into the arms of the landed oligarchy. The Restoration was to be a pact, tacit at first, afterwards openly acknowledged, between all men of property who were interested, before all else, in peace and order. What used to be the policy of Cánovas was now also to be the policy of Sagasta. This unnatural alliance between two classes with opposite interests to defend, was not to have the solidity of a contract between equals. But the Spanish *bourgeoisie*, constrained by the proletarian danger, could now do no more than utter a protest. Should the merchants and industrialists decide to fight the landed oligarchy's monopoly of power, their subversive impulse would be restrained by the fear that the proletariat would gather the fruit of revolution. The Republic, in short, accentuated the desire for tranquillity among all those sectors of Spanish society which had something to lose, closed the purely Liberal cycle of revolution, and awarded the victory to the policy of Cánovas. The balance-sheet, as we shall see, was tragic. Spain overthrew the absolute monarchy, only to fall under the domination of an absolute oligarchy.

## CHAPTER IV

## THE RESTORATION OF THE OLIGARCHY

THE PERIOD COMPRISED between the Sagunto *coup d'état* of December 29th, 1874, and the death of Alfonso XII on November 25th, 1885, is commonly known in the history of Spain as the Restoration. This is the name given, by antonomasia, to the restoration of the Bourbon monarchy. But what was then restored or re-established was not so much the monarchy of the Bourbons as the oligarchy of 1860, whose birth we have witnessed and whose form of government has been outlined. Although a son of Isabel II occupied the throne in 1875, this monarchy was the perfect mould of the oligarchic cohort, created by it and for it. "Property is the foundation of the system of institutions"; and the monarchy of Isabel II was born in the hurly-burly of the 'thirties, when there still was no civil State in Spain, precisely because there did not exist in that vortex where civil society was whirled to destruction, a homogeneous social class, or several classes, with common economic and religious interests. A monarchy built on chaos, without foundations, had, if it were to survive, to yield its prerogatives piecemeal—even its constitutional prerogatives— now to its own followers, now to the Army, and even on occasions, as finally turned out, to Carlism itself.

This Restoration monarchy must not be confused, therefore, with the monarchy of Isabel II. They err who discover a contradiction in the conduct of Cánovas, as when they write: "Perhaps Cánovas had forgotten the Manifesto of Manzanares and *El Murcielago*, his extremely effective contributions to the dethronement of the dynasty he was now about to restore." Cánovas had not proposed to overthrow the dynasty of the Bourbons, but the throne of Isabel II, which was what was hampering the plans of the class he represented. The Restoration monarchy claimed to be a new monarchy, and it was. Conscious of this, Cánovas, when he regained power, announced that he had come not to restore, but to conciliate.

In 1875, the authority of the new oligarchy had no rival. The social class which emerged from the revolution—that confused nucleus in which the decrepit old and the monstrous new met together—was already formed, as I have shown, in 1860; and fifteen years afterwards, those who had indignantly repudiated Isabel II now had sufficient substance to impose their will on the monarch, to reduce the proletariat by violence, to clip the claws of Carlism, and to persuade the Army that it was not the be-all and end-all of Spanish society. In the end, after long and violent disputes, the landed oligarchy was firmly in the saddle.

General Pavía's *coup d'état* smoothed the way for the restoration of the oligarchy's power. Cánovas was so sure of this that he refused to figure in Serrano's Government. He was content to bide his time. "So sure were the *alfonsinos* now of their strength", wrote an English historian, "that they were impatient with the exasperating slowness of their leaders. But Cánovas held them back. He wanted the comedy of the Republic to be played to a finish. By waiting a little longer, he thought, the experiment would end in such a way that it would serve as a warning to all ages."

As I have said, the political forces of the middle class took on a new orientation in the situation created by the shipwreck of the Republic. The mutual *rapprochement* of all the property-owning classes who desired tranquillity and feared the people took place overnight. Pavía had announced that the new Government would include representatives of all the parties, except— be it noted—the Carlists and the federalists, the two national sectors of expropriates, the two victims economically of the Liberal revolution—the Church and the proletariat.

What we are now witnessing is a final reconstruction of the fronts. The contours of the future are becoming plain. Sagasta's *fusionist* policy is taking shape—one step more towards the identification of progressivism, *en bloc*, with the *alfonsinos*. When the process of reorientation is complete, two political parties emerge; the Liberal-Conservative, with Don Antonio Cánovas del Castillo as its leader and presiding genius, and the Liberal, under the dexterous and suave hand of Don Práxedes Mateo

Sagasta. Cánovas aids the formation of the Liberal Party, while Sagasta co-operates in the concentration of the Conservative Party. What has happened is that the primitive *Unión Liberal*, now considerably reinforced by the admission of the *bourgeois* middle class, has blossomed out into two large groups.

Towards 1860, we saw O'Donnell grouping round himself men of various political hues, whose allegiance was prompted by two ruling passions—the first, to anaesthetize Spain at all costs, so that peace should not be disturbed; the second, to wax fat and prosper. The usufructuaries of power were absolutely agreed on these two points, though some placed the anaesthetizing of the nation before private gain. But in principle, one thing must be affirmed: the legislators of the new oligarchy were men of faith—they all believed in themselves. They came, not to govern, but to supervise an interment. Their attitude was one of weary distaste and melancholy scepticism. They thought Spain was defunct and they wanted to be the ones to organize the burial rites. In the meantime, while awaiting the exequies of the nation, they thought no harm in starting to dispose of the property of the deceased, before even the will had been read.

It did not square with the game of snatch-and-grab, nor yet with the policy of peace and quietness, that there should be only one party; and so there had to be two. The whole distance that separated the Liberals from the Conservatives could be contained, though only for a time, in the gap between the Constitution of 1869, Sagasta's ideal, and the Constitution of 1876, the long meditated dream of Cánovas. Such a slight difference was not going to be an obstacle to any Liberals who wanted to grow a Conservative shell, or *vice versa*. So we find Don Antonio drawing off the most important followers of Don Práxedes, and Don Práxedes seducing Don Antonio's best clientèle. There were free-trade Conservatives and protectionist Liberals; highly suspect generals in the Liberal camp, and zealous watchdogs of the civil power in the Conservative gallery. Historians might well ask themselves what hope there could be for Spain in a Liberal Party which contained generals like Weyler and landowners like the Duque de Veragua.

Cánovas rejected the idea of universal suffrage. Sagasta, more of the politician than his nominal adversary, approved of it and finally introduced it, thinking, no doubt, that it was a good thing to give the country the sensation, at times, that it was making great progress. The Liberal leader governed sometimes with a Conservative majority, and the Conservative Pharaoh relied occasionally on a Liberal majority. In 1891,

Cánovas declared that there was already no difference between the two parties. They were two groups, but a single political movement—an absolute oligarchy, facing both ways like Janus.

Before continuing, it would be as well to say a few words more about the two persons who ruled the destinies of Spain in the last twenty years, more or less, of the nineteenth century.

Don Antonio Cánovas del Castillo took his first steps in public life under the tutelage of his uncle, Don Serafín Estébanez Calderón, *El Solitario*. Don Serafín was a person of considerable influence in Madrid, a Councillor of State, a Judge of the *Tribunal Supremo de Guerra y Marina*, a Member of the Academy of History, a Senator, etc. He was a protégé of O'Donnell and spared no pains to place his nephew under his patron's protection, the sure path to the conquest of Spain. Cánovas was extraordinarily young and accomplished when he broke his first lance for power and fame. It was easy for Don Serafín Estébanez to put his nephew in the way of success, because Cánovas did not come to Court empty-handed; he came consciously prepared to triumph. A precocious genius, he had already at the age of twenty-five written inspired historical studies. He knew the history of Spain as few knew it and was a historian in the classical vein, mature in judgment and pithy in style. An excellent jurist, a notable speaker, a writer of much weight and an exemplary historian, Don Antonio Cánovas del Castillo might have served his country well, if his talents had not been offset by an unhappy defect of character. Cánovas was an incurable pessimist. He did not believe in Spain. "They are Spaniards", he once said, "who cannot be anything else." And when, in December 1895, there took place in Madrid that public manifestation against corruption and the sale of sinecures which both Conservative and Liberal ædiles practised in the municipality, and when Cánovas was informed that thousands of *madrileños* had lent their names to the protest which was known as the protest of "the honest men", he exclaimed: "But are there so many honest men in Madrid?" On occasions like this he displayed a scepticism which could easily be confused with the deepest contempt for his fellow-countrymen; and in truth, the particular nature of his character did not help to overcome this emotional deformity, for in Cánovas the head had developed at the expense of the heart.

In his inmost being, Cánovas was convinced that Spain was finished. He was not interested in the present, still less in the future, vague units of time which he suppressed *in mente*, either because they terrified him and that led to distress of mind, or because he thought that the past was the only thing left to Spain. Cánovas passed through the Government of Spain with the sole aim of shoring up the rotten fabric of Spanish society here and there, so that it should not fall on him unawares. All he did as a statesman was to botch things up. He knew nothing of what was happening in the metropolis or in the colonies, nor did he wish to know. He organized Spain on an iniquitous plan so that she could pull through for another forty or fifty years (this was certainly the most he would guarantee) and he fell into all the excesses he condemned in seventeenth-century politicians. He spread his ample cloak over all the greed and covetousness of his friends. He did not understand the gravity of the Cuban affair, not because he lacked intelligence, but because, in his secret heart, he had given up Cuba and Spain for lost, long before the *manigua* revolted. "It is folly to think", he wrote in 1854, "that nations, however noble, can rise to great purposes, make great sacrifices, be capable of supreme efforts, if they are oppressed and discouraged, without faith in the present or the future." Yet it was the author of that pronouncement who was guilty of folly. With his system of government, he wrought incalculable harm to the nation, emasculating it, oppressing it and making it lose what hope it still had in the present and the future.

There are few crimes less pardonable than that of the man who heads a Government or a system of government without faith in his country. No fraud can have worse consequences for a nation. Cánovas was that type of politician. And his style of ruler, obsessed by the idea of peace at any price at home, reluctant to act, and still more reluctant to think of the future, was bounded by, and pandered to, the sordid ambitions of the landed oligarchy, already eager, as I have said, to sit at the feast and enjoy the fat of the land in peace, without giving a thought to the reforms which would have been balm to the miseries of a ragged proletariat, or to the building of a State on firm pillars, or to the morrow which the Spanish people deserved.

A common pessimism bound Sagasta and Cánovas together; but while the pessimism of Cánovas was bitter, mordant and haughty, that of Sagasta was gentle, airy and hail-fellow-well-met. Don Práxedes had fought for liberty in the streets of Madrid and, as a progressive, he had then had contacts with the people which at least helped him to understand them. Cánovas was ignorant of the art of making friends and, except in the circle of his intimates, his frown was wont to be harsh. By contrast,

Sagasta had no intimates. He kept open house in the Plaza de Celenque to all his "colleagues"; and his colleagues were all those *madrileños* who liked to drop in at three o'clock in the afternoon for a word and a handshake. The secret of Sagasta's success lay not so much in his talents as in his manners; and manners are also a form of talent. Cánovas impressed by his creative genius, which, though it proved fatal in politics, could not be denied. His friends called him *El Monstruo*, an exaggerated tribute to his intellectual powers. Sagasta, on the other hand, had little book-lore, and the Conservative leader, who held Spaniards in such disdain, must have thought him lacking in culture. But an uncultured and lovable man wins esteem which does not fall to the lot of an intellectual and proud one. The great Liberal *cacique*, sleek in appearance and manner, won homage from the people which was denied to Cánovas. And not because the latter was a Conservative and the former a demagogue; for the cards were all on the table, and it was no secret that Sagasta, the left caryatid of the Restoration portal, was there to give symmetry to the oligarchic edifice. The rôles, in fact, were well distributed. Without the figure of Sagasta, that debonair cynic who also did not believe in Spain, but who never lost his cheerful smile even when the American Navy destroyed the Spanish Fleet while he was Prime Minister, the Restoration would have been more gloomy than it was. Don Práxedes was, in short, the cheerful pessimist, the man who reckons up his losses and finding the situation beyond repair, retires philosophically into his tub like Diogenes. Cánovas and Sagasta were both cynics; but the one inspired antipathy, the other, liking.

Now that the oligarchy knew itself to be supreme, it was going virtually to make an end of *pronunciamientos* and keep Carlism in bonds.

Carlism, which had been defeated in the last battle of the second war with the capture of Estella by Primo de Rivera in February 1876, lost the better part of its vigour when the Church finally realized that more could be gained by the compromise offered by Cánovas than by headstrong revolt. The Vatican hastened the disintegration of the theocratic movement by recognizing Alfonso XII, and during the Regency of Doña Maria Cristina or the minority of Alfonso XIII, the adhesion of the Spanish prelates to the Crown gave the *coup de grâce* to the crack-brained scheme of the monks to rule Spain in the twentieth century. The Carlist family went from one disaster to another; in 1888, Don Ramón Nocedal broke violently with the policy of Don Carlos, which he dubbed inadmissibly pragmatic. With Nocedal's defection, a good part of the clergy and twenty-four ultramontane newspapers, including *El Siglo Futuro*, deserted the Pretender. Nocedal's party henceforth called themselves *integristas*, acknowledging the Pope as their leader rather than Don Carlos.

Carlism, then, continued to exist, but in a state of open crisis, divided into several mutually hostile groups. "It was not only the higher ranks of the clergy", wrote Don Gabriel Maura, "who, as one man, accepted the established régime without mental reservations; this might have been attributed to a skilful handling of the weapon of the Concordat. But the parish priests, *especially the urban clergy*, and even the religious orders, which were then enjoying a respect practically never before accorded to them in that century, were also reconciled with the ruling authority. . . ."

The policy of Cánovas towards the Church, as towards the Army, was to make the greatest possible concessions, provided always that the favoured party admitted its subordination to the government of the oligarchy. This was in accordance with the Restoration policy, and its sole aim and object was to prevent the disturbance of internal peace. In exchange for the tolerance and favour with which the State paid homage to the spiritual institution, it insisted on the latter allowing it to govern.

The Church's bargain with the new State is of supreme importance, because her tacit agreement with the oligarchic form of government was to extend to present times. It should not be forgotten that the Constitution of 1876 and the government of the restored oligarchy were to last for forty-seven years.

During almost the whole of the nineteenth century, the Church had fought to govern the nation. For a given period of the reign of Isabel II, she had succeeded in that design, as we have had occasion to see. But under the Restoration, she changed her tactics almost abruptly. Her policy from 1808 onwards had been to impose a theocracy on the nation; but in 1876 she was already on the defensive. She had lost the stubborn, unending battle, *which was also a war against the new oligarchy*, and was now entering the path of compromise with the State, though not, it is clear, a compromise with such circles of dissent as existed in the nation.

The Church's aspirations towards the end of the century easily dovetailed with the political ideal of Cánovas and Sagasta and with the views of all sectors save the advanced middle class and the proletariat. The Church insisted, nevertheless, on reproducing in the Constitution of 1876 the formula of the Constitution of 1845, whereby the Roman Catholic and Apostolic Faith was declared to be the only religion of Spain. The clergy resigned themselves not to govern; but they were not disposed to admit toleration with a good grace, a concession which, from the Catholic point of view, implied an abandonment of theological principles. Compromise on this ground would have been too much to expect, had not Cánovas produced a similar solution for this problem as he had produced for the problem of universal suffrage and all the other problems.

The Church did not approve of toleration; but the Constitution of 1869 had proclaimed freedom of worship, thereby making it impossible to revert to the Constitution of 1845, especially after the final military defeat of Carlism. Under protest, therefore, from the prelates and the Pope, a clause was inserted in the Constitution of 1876 to the effect that "no one should be persecuted in Spanish territory for his religious opinions, or for the exercise of his religion, due regard being had to Christian morals" (Art. 11). The same Article laid down that the Roman Catholic and Apostolic religion was the religion of Spain, which was to be maintained out of the public funds.

We have already seen that the Church was not able to govern in the formal sense of the word. Now, the aim of the clergy was to prevent any Government from taking hostile measures against them. There was bound to be a fatal compromise on the law, though it may not have been acceptable to the clergy. But more important than the written law was its application, and here the Church had little to fear. For the State which Cánovas founded held the corruption of the law to be a normal thing whenever it hindered the peaceful course of the régime. The men of the new system were without principles, and the institutions they created were like them. They dictated laws with the avowed intention of not observing them when it was inconvenient to do so. The real compromise was made by the oligarchy with corporations and persons in defiance of their own laws, which were themselves in the nature of a compromise. So difficult was it to create a constitutional monarchy and a State founded on universal suffrage on the unjust and shaky structure of Spanish society, that the rulers could not stop for any kind of ethical consideration. Only by giving examples, like the one I have just quoted and others I shall give later, can the true nature of the régime be appreciated.

At the beginning of Alfonso XII's reign, the Cánovas Government passed a decree which infringed the liberties of the

Universities. Don Francisco Giner de los Ríos raised a public protest. Cánovas then privately requested Don Francisco to withdraw his protest, assuring him that the decree, though officially passed, would never be applied. But the famous professor refused to compromise and maintained his protest.

The incorruptible Don Francisco was not slow to feel the reaction of Cánovas. While he was ill in bed, police agents went to his residence, hustled him out into the street and carried him off to a fortress at Cadiz.

This kind of double compromise, which in the above-mentioned case did not succeed because one of the parties refused to play, was typical of the oligarchy's policy. The system was as follows: Cánovas agreed with the prelates to abolish freedom of teaching in the Universities, and dictated the decree. The ecclesiastics were satisfied. On the one hand, order was assured. But the measure naturally aroused the opposition of the professors. On the other hand, therefore, order was threatened. The Government tried to solve the difficulty in the way we have seen. In the case of Don Francisco Giner, the method failed; but men of his integrity are rare. Others—the majority—allowed themselves to be corrupted, for the alternative, as in the days of O'Donnell, was ruin.

The new régime's understanding with the Church was another double compromise. Cánovas met anti-clerical sentiment by decreeing that no one should be persecuted for his religious opinions or for practising a creed other than the established religion of the country. Order was thus preserved. But the Church rejected the precept—and so, order was endangered. The Government had given satisfaction to the Radicals; how was it now to appease the clergy? Cánovas pacified them by allowing the courts to ignore this part of the Constitution in their decisions.

Mustering all their powers of dissimulation, the Conservative hierarchy had fulfilled the promises they had made to the Pope and the Spanish prelates to placate them for Article 11 of the Constitution. Following his usual method, Cánovas had officially agreed to make a considerable increase in the Budget for Public Worship and the Clergy, to pay arrears due to the clergy, to suppress religious toleration and to restore the Concordat of 1851.

The compromise was not always favourable to the Church, as we have seen. If it had been, the civil power would have become a dependency of the spiritual institution and the disorders of the nineteenth century would have been repeated. The aim of the men of the Restoration was, on the contrary, to break with the nineteenth century. Did they succeed? This was the key to the success or failure of Cánovas' policy, and it is in studying the consequences of the system that we shall be able to pronounce judgment upon it.

Under the new State, the law was one more weapon of corruption in the hands of the oligarchic Government.

The Church saw immediately that the judiciary was not independent under the new régime and that political justice would annul in practice any legal precepts that might prejudice the social strength of the spiritual institution. The official religion of the country was the Catholic religion, and all others, which, strictly speaking, did not exist, could only be practised in private. What were the limits within which a religion could be privately practised fell to the courts to decide. But to mention, for example, in a newspaper or by way of a lampoon, the existence of a Protestant school was a criminal act, a public manifestation against the religion of the State.

From the ethical point of view, the alarming thing here was not the encouragement of intolerance, but the method by which Catholic exclusivism had its way, the demoralizing use of the law. The Inquisition was less of a corrupting influence.

The weakness of the new State was evident. The Restoration institutions, though stronger than those of the nineteenth century, were still not robust enough to make of civil society the undisputed ruling power. To be sure, when the new oligarchy installed its monarchy, the Carlist Church found herself face to face with something that had never existed before—a social class which, though vile, was powerful, compact, homogeneous. The same thing happened to the Army. But the strength of the new ruling class was purely physical and, therefore, unjust. Now, every unjust Government is bound to repose on brute force, thereby sacrificing its independence; neither can it, for political ends, ignore a conservative institution like the Church, which it relies on as an instrument of order. This forces the civil power into a compromise with its natural enemies, which will be all the more damaging, the less is its moral authority; for the principal fount of moral authority in the government of peoples is justice. The goal which Cánovas aimed at of dominating the Church and the Army was impossible in a régime which had to make a mock of its own laws in order to survive. The Church and the Army could only be expelled from politics by a strong civil power; but civil society lacks robustness when social inequality is marked in the highest degree. Only unjust Governments rely upon religion and the Army to sustain themselves in being. And what does this imply but to remove the Church and the Army from their private functions, throw them into the political scale, and remain ever afterwards at their mercy? This was Cánovas' great dilemma.

The leading topic in the first Cortes of the Restoration had been religious unity. But when the Church learnt with what manner of régime she had to deal, and had satisfied herself that the Constitution was not going to be put into effect, she calmed down and submitted to the new State. During the last years of Alfonso XII's reign, the oligarchy and the Church became reconciled. Both needed each other. The Church was to become one more cog in the oppressive machinery of the oligarchic system of government, and by so becoming, condemned herself politically.

The new official power of the Church culminated, as I said above, in the Regency. The clergy now supported the régime, not with resignation, but with real enthusiasm. New religious orders established themselves in Spain under the protection of that article of the Concordat which permitted three orders among those approved by the Holy See, while only mentioning two by name. Those orders already functioning multiplied their numbers. For the moment, this was perhaps to the advantage of the régime, which congratulated itself on winning the support of an institution which had been persistently hostile throughout the century. But were there not dangers for the new State in an attachment which, like that of the Army, was being bought at such a price? Might not the bishops and the generals be the ones to bring back the Republic again?

Let us now see what place the Army occupied under the Restoration. The Government followed the same policy with the military as with the Church.

The number of Army chiefs and officers was out of all proportion to the number of the rank and file. But nothing was done to create an efficient Army and much to flatter the generals, who, so long as they left the Government to govern, were allowed full scope for their freebooting instincts. In this, as in everything, the horror of reform passed belief. Spain had more than 90,000 men under arms, and this Army cost the nation as much as their respective armies of 500,000 men cost France and Italy.

Sagasta was afraid to appoint as Minister of War a well-known general on the active list, one who might conceive the idea of reforming the infinite ills which afflicted the military organization. So the Liberal leader, thinking he had found his man, appointed to this important post an obscure general with an excellent military record—Don Manuel Cassola. When the appointment was announced, everyone asked: "Who is Cassola?"—which was precisely why the Prime Minister had chosen him. But the new Minister lost no time in distinguishing himself by his talent (which had probably never been put to the test before), and in asserting himself as a precise speaker, an acute politician and a great patriot. Naturally enough, when he contemplated from his ministerial observation post the thing that was the Spanish Army, he conceived a series of bold reforms, among them compulsory military service for everyone, including even the clergy, the reform of the General Staff, the reduction of the thirteen Captaincies-General into which Spain was divided to eight—all of them reforms which could be readily carried out, but not without trespassing upon illegitimate interests then prevailing. Cassola took his plan to the Council of Ministers. Such audacity in that régime which only wanted peace and quietness was truly stupefying. On seeing the expression of surprise on the faces of his colleagues, this odd politician announced that if they did not accept his reforms, he would resign from the Government. He had supposed, in his ignorance, that those men were in the Government to govern. The case gave rise to much discussion at the time, and after a wordy warfare, Cassola resigned his office as Minister of War. Sagasta, that great cynic, added an amazing commentary to the affair: "Good God!" he exclaimed. "What a disappointment! There is danger in the most unlikely quarter. . . . The most scrupulous precautions are useless."

The danger was that anyone should dare to reform anything. That social class was obsessed, I repeat, with the idea of burying Spain, whom they thought was as good as dead; and any doctors who hastened to the sick-bed claiming to be able to reanimate or save the patient were angrily dismissed.

Since the oligarchy had set its face against any attempt at subsidiary reforms, how much more would it not harden its heart against any change connected with property! And there could be no salvation for Spain until the structure of agrarian property had been reformed. For if the Restoration did not touch on this problem, even in thought, it was clear that it was going to falsify the popular will. The régime of the absolute oligarchy was more disastrous to the nation than the absolute monarchy in this respect—that the former, because it could not avoid the representative system, founded all its institutions on the corrosive principle of the corruption of the suffrage and thereby corrupted the whole nation, at least politically; while the absolute monarchy, founded on the divine right of kings, or on force, which made it unnecessary to cloak its rule with any constitutional disguise, spared the nation the disaster of adulterated citizenship and was, therefore, a purer régime. This might appear to be a defence of absolute monarchy; it is, in reality, no more than a definition of the system of government implanted by the men of the Restoration, which was, when all is said and done, the worst régime any nation could have.

Caciquism was, therefore, a spontaneous offshoot of the imposture of granting political rights to a landless proletariat. There would have been less infamy in proclaiming the reign of despotism; but this was not possible.

The pattern of 1860 was now being followed; for the friends of the oligarchy, all kinds of gifts and rewards; for its incorruptible adversaries, savage persecution.

In each village, the local *cacique* was responsible to the Governor of his province for the submission of the people, with their civil rights, to the policy of government by rotation. The Governor, in his turn, answered to the Ministry of the Interior for the loyalty of the local *caciques* within the radius of his province. The authority of the local *cacique* derived from the support he received from the Government, either directly, or through the provincial satrap. And he proved his omnipotence by appointing himself or one of his henchmen mayor; he appointed the aldermen, elected the municipal justices and chose the employees of the municipal council. The provincial officers supported, riveted and welded the influence of the Governor, watching over, in tune with the delegate of the Government, the movements of the caciquist retinue in the zone. It was the business of the deputies to the Cortes to keep alive the connection between the rural *caciques* and the new Ministers. Every deputy to the Cortes operated as a Minister of a province in the indispensable function of distributing sinecures and pandering to local interests, some of them legitimate, others less so. The deputy appointed the high functionaries, among them the judges and magistrates, who it was important should be loyal, trustworthy and safe. For these judges and magistrates had to administer caciquist justice, making those who could not adapt themselves to the system feel the heavy hand of the law. Warrants for the arrest of defenceless Spaniards, caught by the steel tentacles of caciquism, from which few honest persons escaped, were issued in perfect order, with all the seals and signatures of a meticulous justice. Not infrequently, everything boiled over into stabbing affrays, shooting and formidable disturbances—the typical rustic drama attendant upon this kind of politics.

General elections were ordered, prepared and organized with amazing meticulousness by the Minister of the Interior. We have already seen how Posada Herrera managed them when the oligarchy was trying out its methods—an immense majority in the Cortes and the Senate for the Government, and a modest number of seats for the Opposition, to the end that the Government majority should not be demoralized or the occupants of the Opposition benches conspire outside Parliament. Cánovas' "Great Elector" was Romero Robledo, Minister of the Interior for almost the whole of the reign of Alfonso XII. On the Liberal side, the manipulator of the electoral levers was sometimes Don Venancio González, at other times Don Alberto Aguilera. Later it was to be Count Romanones, who married a daughter of Alonso Martínez, like Cánovas one of O'Donnell's old guard.

The reader will remember that Posada used to assign seventy seats to the Opposition. So faithful was the oligarchy to the policy of its youth that, surprisingly enough, the same seventy seats continued to be allotted to the Opposition in not a few of the Restoration and Regency Parliaments. In the elections of 1884, under the skilful management of Romero Robledo, 295 seats were won by the Conservative Government and 70 by the Liberal Opposition, neither Republicans nor Traditionalists having gone to the polls. In the 1886 elections, summoned by Don Venancio González, the inevitable seventy seats were assigned to the Conservatives. In this way, the national will, *freely expressed in the polling-booths*, endorsed the spirit of distributive justice in not giving Cánovas one deputy more or less than Sagasta.

The result of the elections was usually announced in the Government Press several weeks in advance.

Administrative corruption in the chief municipalities was on a par with this "Box-and-Cox" system of government. In the municipality of Madrid, scandals leaked out from time to time, whether the administration of the moment was Liberal or Conservative.

As supreme arbiter of power and of all the resources of the administration, the oligarchs treated the nation as if it were their private property and recreation-ground, created for their vicious pleasure. In this spirit, they paid nothing like the taxation they were liable for. The great landowners concealed their wealth from the revenue officials; and should any zealous servant of the State discover its exact amount, every effort was made to suborn him. But if he refused to be bribed, political influences were marshalled to ruin him. The avaricious oligarchs, therefore, exercised a veritable reign of terror against honest folk who refused to adapt themselves to official corruption. One owner of fields and hamlets entered 400 hectares of olive-groves as pasture, and 300 hectares of orange-groves as grass-land, on his tax returns.

In 1888, the taxable value of rural property, according to the owners' returns, amounted to 516,019,540 pesetas. But according to an investigation carried out by the Taxation Department, it amounted to 962,582,936 pesetas. The fraud involved, therefore, the concealment of 447 million pesetas; and in some places 78 per cent of the taxable property was not being entered on the tax returns.

Strictly speaking, the only persons who paid tax on their actual property were the humble labourers, and they, squeezed by the tax-collector, were paying for the great landowners. The peasant, with his modest and pitiful possessions, could not support such a burden; whereupon the cold machine of the oligarchy applied pressure with the threat of eviction. In April 1880, notice was given in the Cortes that 173,000 farms were about to be sequestrated for arrears of tax.

Another vicious aspect of the system was the creation of fictitious offices which only really existed in the budgets of the public corporations. In this way, countless persons, favoured by one or other group returning to power, were living at the nation's expense, in exchange for which they were expected to pronounce everything perfect and to cover up the disasters of the régime by verbal or written encomiums. Appointments and credentials were scattered broadcast among the corrupt crowd of lawyers, journalists, and a multitude of hangers-on, improvised functionaries of the State, the provincial government or the municipality. Enormous sums were spent on the services—and yet there were no services to speak of. In June 1876, the President of the Supreme Court informed the Senate that more than a third of the revenue from taxation was swallowed up in maintaining the apparatus of the tax-collecting bureaucracy.

The Andalusian countryside, as we have had more than one occasion to remark, had not ceased to warn the Government by its spasmodic outbursts of social violence that it was utterly impossible to produce any sort of harmony between the people and their masters, so long as the impious distribution of property persisted. Yet those legislators saw in the rural disturbances a symptom of the violent spirit of the race, for which the best remedy was the iron hand. Whenever the people rose, in the villages or cities, the rebellion was attributed to the ungovernable quality of the race—a slanderous and pessimistic view which at least served to justify the greatest excesses of the public authorities. The only way of dealing with the situation that occurred to the "Box-and-Cox" statesmen was to hang some of the peasants and imprison the others for life.

In 1883, the regions of the latifundia saw the flowering of a vast organization of the *Carbonari* type, called *La Mano Negra*, or "Black Hand", which sowed terror in the district. A virulent campaign of lightning aggression against the great landowners over a given period undermined their confidence in brute force. The wealthy classes hastened to save their skins, and left their *dehesas* and *cortijos* with fearful speed to take refuge in the great cities. The rumour spread through the fertile Andalusian plains that there were 50,000 armed *braceros* ready to rise in the most bloody insurrection that Spain had ever known. Such was the panic that hardly a rich man remained in the countryside; and if any stayed behind, they dared not move a step without a body-guard of police. This "Black Hand" was a Spanish *Carbonari* move-ment, a rural Ku-Klux-Klan, less terroristic than it was said to be, but sufficiently so to spread alarm and disturb that calm which was the whole aim of the Government of the landed oligarchy.

Penned in the midst of the fertile lands of Andalusia by the implacable violence of the State (a truly supernatural force), the miserable peasants, some of the most imaginative in the world, were ready to embrace any social Utopia as fast as their limited education allowed them to grasp its meaning.

In 1892, the Loja incident repeated itself; only this time, the city chosen by the peasants to try out their phalanstery was not Loja, nor did the *braceros* now march unarmed. In the outskirts of Jerez de la Frontera, some 400 peasants from the neighbouring townships of Arcos, Lebrija and Lajar met, each with whatever weapons he had been able to acquire—shot-guns, knives of all shapes and sizes, pitchforks, and other farm imple-ments. It was the classic peasant revolt. The *braceros*, thoroughly roused, were going to conquer Jerez and they had drawn up a military plan to this end. The attacking army divided into three groups. One was to attack the infantry barracks, the other the town hall, and the third was, with God's help, to set free the prisoners, this last a work of mercy which could not be shelved by those who, moved by the most primitive sense of justice, were going to storm the barracks with rakes and clasp-knives.

The crowd broke into the prosperous city of the vines with the cry of "Death to the *bourgeoisie*!", killing all those who they thought belonged to the heartless ruling class.

Nothing gives a better idea of the unsavoury character of

the Government than the fact that though they knew the conspiracy was on foot, they preferred, through pure sadism no
doubt, not to interrupt the preparations. Consequently, when the
misguided peasants penetrated into Jerez, they were met by
"conveniently posted" detachments of the Civil Guard and the
Army. After an hour's fighting, the peasants retreated with the inevitable casualties; but official precautions had not prevented the
rebels from wreaking vengeance on as many as crossed their path.

The military courts sentenced four of the ringleaders to death
and a great number to perpetual imprisonment.

When these melancholy events were discussed in the Senate,
the pious Bishop of Salamanca observed that revolts of this
character could only be avoided by reforming . . . the Penal
Code! . . . which in his opinion was entirely antiquated. The
devout cleric had the approval of Cánovas, who promised to
reform the Penal Code.

This epoch saw a renewed exodus of the peasant population to
other lands which appeared to the popular mind to be more
hospitable. The inhabitants of the southern plains, besieged
on all sides by hunger and caciquism, emigrated to French
Africa, preferably to Tunis and Algeria. The Andalusian
labourer had come to the conclusion that, in the conditions in
which he was forced to live, there was only one way of escape
from prison or the gallows, and that was to flee. With his
children on his shoulder, and leading his wife by the hand, he
turned his back on the virgin lands of the oligarchy. The proletariat of the north-east, a region suffocated by the bonds of
the minifundia, took the road to South and Central America.

Neither caciquism, nor the power of the State, nor that
valiant expedient of suspending the constitutional guarantees,
had sufficed to keep a nation in subjection. Cánovas and Sagasta
also needed adventures abroad, a current war at least, which
would absorb political commentary and concentrate the country's
attention far from the Augean stables of the oligarchy.

In 1893, a fresh incident with the Moors was on the point of
exploding into another sanguinary war. Spain only just saved
herself from such a disaster. It was only by the mercy of Providence that the 25,000 ill-armed and worse trained men whom
Sagasta's Government had sent to Morocco did not go into action.

The lynx-eye of Machiavelli had seen that conquests made
by badly organized Republics destroy rather than aggrandize
the conqueror. Spain lost the remnants of her Empire in America
and Oceania simply because if a disorganized Republic cannot

carry out conquests, neither can it preserve those which it achieved in times of good fortune.

With such a policy, Cuba, Puerto Rico and the Philippines were bound to be lost, and only by a miracle would other provinces closer to the heart of the monarchy not be lost too. A more absurd war, on Spain's part, than the Spanish-American war for Cuba in 1898 would be hard to find in all history, even bearing in mind that the United States were not then what they are today.

Clearly, the North American sugar companies were fighting for a foothold on the island; and it is also clear that the proximity of Spain in the Caribbean was not welcome to the United States. But, as is evident from the entire diplomatic proceedings, it was not the intention of the Government of the United States to end Spanish sovereignty in Cuba.

The worst was that the war with the United States not only threw the fate of Cuba into the melting-pot but also involved, by extension, Puerto Rico, where a rising of the natives against the Spanish authorities had been quickly subdued, and the Philippines in the Pacific, which had only recently been pacified.

It is a mistake to see in the loss of the Spanish West Indies and the Philippines the final episode in the fatal process of liquidation of the Spanish Empire. The truth is that half a century before, the Spanish-speaking countries of the American continent had broken away from Spain. But there were at least two reasons why this should have happened; first, that stronger Powers were interested in the secession; secondly, that when the metropolitan institutions were overthrown, when the State and the monarchy and the bureaucracy and the Army disappeared in the Peninsula, the symbols, the moral ties and the physical forces which maintained the bond with Spanish America dissolved into thin air. As soon as the first popular *juntas* in the most politically advanced colonies were set up, the separation began. In Spanish America, too, popular organs of power were germinating which, now that the Spanish State was destroyed, were going to replace a Peninsular power which had been extinguished in the chaos of the revolution. The dissolution of Spain implied the dissolution of the Empire, particularly since the Great Powers were not disposed to let slip so excellent an opportunity to indulge their expansionist desires. Now, Spanish America broke away from Spain because Spain remained without a régime and without a State. But Spain lost Cuba because she had a State and a régime which were intolerable. It was not the spectacle of a dying State in the Peninsula that incited the Cubans to rebel. Cuba, perhaps because she was an island and knew instinctively that because of her proximity to the United States she could never be independent, showed no desire for separation from Spain. On the contrary, it was only by an enormous effort that successive Spanish Governments succeeded in cutting her connection with Spain. The island was lost, therefore, not because Spain had no régime, but because the régime she had was disastrous.

If the evil had lain in the men and not in the régime, the catastrophe of '98 would not have had such importance. But the loss of Cuba, Puerto Rico and the Philippines was only an episode in the ruin of Spain under the misgovernment of the oligarchy. The gravest feature of the Spanish disaster was that it was the work, not of an erring Government, but of a corrupt system, and what was still worse, of a corrupt régime which it was difficult to replace. For among the evils of the system must be included the silencing of all the voices of vital and progressive opposition. There was no real opposition to the oligarchy.

"Except for a few irreconcilable Carlists and Republicans," writes an historian, "there was hardly anyone who did not recognize that Spain could not at present aspire to a better Government than that of the Restoration."

This, in other words, is what I have just said. But this singular situation had come to pass because the oligarchy had no scruples in resorting to the most reprehensible methods in order to rid itself of its political adversaries. The surrender of the *bourgeoisie* to the landowning Minotaur—a phenomenon which we shall finish analysing in the next chapter—was certainly a consequence of the revolt against property; but this, in turn, sprang from the faulty architecture of the social order which the new régime was engaged in buttressing. The Republicans failed through political inexperience; but also because they had to cope with a ruling class which was fomenting chaos with their perverse intractability, perhaps on the mischievous assumption that the experiment "would serve as a warning to all ages". It was not, therefore, that everyone recognized that there could not be a better Government, but simply that there could not be any other Government at all, for better or for worse, since for one reason or other any alternative to that régime had been virtually annihilated.

This was the only state of affairs which could make the government of the absolute oligarchy possible.

I said in the previous chapter that, from the time of the restoration of the oligarchy, the advanced middle class, which was represented in politics by philosophic republicanism, was the only one (leaving aside the proletariat for the moment) which opposed the régime in a systematic manner. This was a nucleus with a certain weight due to its intellectual and moral authority, but without followers, solitary and impotent. Liberalism, which had been bastardized by the *bourgeoisie* when they surrendered to the great landowners and the nobility—the Liberalism of the Liberal Party—had left vacant the seat which it had occupied on the Left, and it was this that the Republicans filled. The industrial and commercial middle classes were caught between a political Scylla and Charybdis, between the oligarchic peril and the proletariat; and they were to be known henceforth by the expressive name of the "neutral classes". After the completion of a century Republicanism, the depository of Liberal revolutionary principles, inherited the mission of the Cadiz reformers. The Liberal revolution had failed; it had not created a middle class and it had to start afresh. The *bourgeoisie* had finally renounced revolution—their revolution—which was still to make. And the fate of the reform of Spanish society fell into the hands of a divided philanthropic sect, as it had done at the beginning of the century.

There were four Republican groups under the leadership, respectively, of Castelar, Salmerón, Pi y Margall and Ruiz Zorrilla. Great differences separated them, for some devoted more attention than others to the social question. Leaders without followers, they still leaned on the proletariat which was soon giving them the cold shoulder, for workers and peasants had already begun to organize themselves into class parties.

At the close of the century, Castelar's group had become a Republican casualty. The possibilists, who defined themselves as "those who desired a Republic as a barrier against radicalism" ended by merging with Sagasta's party. Castelar thought that with the advent of universal suffrage, his life's ideal was realized. The famous orator left Sagasta no peace till he had extracted from him a promise of universal suffrage. He thought that in this way (*O sancta simplicitas!*) he was saving Spain.

For the most part, the intellectual flower of Republicanism formed a Puritan sect which trusted to education and civil progress to raise the nation. To this group, led by Don Nicolás Salmerón, belonged Don Gumersindo de Azcárate, Don Manuel Pedregal and Don Joaquín Costa.

Pi y Margall kept his federalist banner flying, now as faded as all the other Republican flags. The federalist, or anarchist, hosts of the first Republic were now enrolling as Socialists and revolutionary syndicalists. Marx and Sorel were replacing

Fourier and Proudhon. But the political power of the rampant proletariat was too feeble to offset the enormous havoc wrought by the alarm they aroused.

In conflict with all the Republicans, Ruiz Zorrilla, that anachronistic conspirator or belated romantic, strained every nerve from his exile in Paris to overthrow the monarchy by military *coups de main*. At the instigation of his *Asociación Republicana Militar*, there were military risings at Badajoz and Santo Domingo de la Calzada, while General Villacampa led a crazy revolt at Madrid, the Regency demonstrating the "benevolence" of the régime by granting him a free pardon.

Side by side with these Republican opposition groups, and sometimes in alliance with them, the diminished ranks of the Carlists were now peacefully pursuing their plans for a theocracy. The new Carlist policy, as proclaimed by Baron Sangarrén from his seat in Parliament was to keep within the bounds of the law.

On the fringe of the political ring, but touching it at a tangent, a noble, distinguished and select focus of opposition to the oligarchy had arisen—the *Institución Libre de Enseñanza*. Deprived of their University Chairs by the clerical reaction (though they were reinstated in 1881), Don Francisco Giner de los Ríos and other professors of the School of Philosophy of Sanz del Río, the sponsor of pantheistic Krausism in Spain, had founded a pedagogic sect, a private University in opposition to the official University, a haven for those stoics who wanted to avoid moral and intellectual shipwreck.

And facing this swarm of sects, without any organic national movement to menace its full control of power, the oligarchy ruled over the nation. At the end of the century, the strength of the oligarchic phalanx had no rival. The ruling class, master of the land and sovereign in the great enterprises subsidized by the State, advised and defended by men of undisputed political talent not impeded by any sort of scruples, was already enjoying its longed-for repose. The Church and the Army had been subdued, though at heavy cost. The weak-kneed *bourgeoisie* had surrendered. The proletariat was still protesting, but that was all. The calm was not absolute—far from it—and the oligarchy had to keep a watchful eye open. But the nineteenth century was a thing of the past, and those who remembered it found the new order Arcadian. Now one could live; or rather, that social class could live which since 1860 had alone had a dream and a programme—a dream which was now coming true; to sit and feast with their friends and enjoy, in the midst of the general poverty, the good things of the earth.

## CHAPTER V

# THE REBELLION OF THE MIDDLE CLASS

WE ARE NOW going to see how the new relations between the landed oligarchy and the *bourgeoisie* worked out in the economic field.

The form of production predominating in Spain is still wont to be called, with obvious inaccuracy, a pastoral economy. This is an anachronism. The Liberal revolution, though inadequate in other respects, was yet able to accomplish its design of eliminating stock-breeding as the leading element in the Spanish economy. The reign of the flocks and herds definitely terminated in Spain half-way through the nineteenth century. The political power of the cattle-breeders was superseded by that of the agriculturists. Agriculture stepped into the first rank of the national economy, and within the framework of agriculture, exercising a veritable tyranny over the rest of production, wheat- and olive-farming assumed, as it were, the command.

It must not be forgotten that, in the economic order, the Cortes of Cadiz and the Liberals of the beginning of the century, in general, pronounced in favour of agriculture as against stock-breeding; so much so that they were often more anxious to foster agrarian than industrial and mercantile interests. The reason no doubt was that the Liberals then understood progress as the predominance of agriculture over stock-breeding, thinking quite rightly that the excessive privileges of the stock-breeders constituted an archaic obstacle to the development of the nation.

When the revolution ended, therefore, stock-breeding had lost the eminent position it had enjoyed in the Spanish economy ever since the Emperor Charles V, yielding his better judgment to that of Spaniards, decreed in 1552 the subordination of the national economy to the supreme interests of the stock-breeders. As a result of the triumph of the landed oligarchy towards the end of the nineteenth century, the reverse situation arose; the agriculturists expelled the migratory flocks and herds from the lands where agriculture was most firmly in the saddle. And the reaction was so drastic that not only stock-breeding, but everything that conflicted with the cerealist economy was expelled; so that the economists hastened to deliver the warning that stock-breeding "was being driven off the land because of the ill-advised ploughing-up of unproductive areas, and that if the belief continued to be encouraged that Spain was a grain-growing country which might even in time export wheat, every head of cattle was doomed to disappear".

Those who called the Spanish economy pastoral fell, therefore, into grave confusion, since the opposite was certainly the case. Spain was suffering from a deficiency of live stock. She had passed from one extreme to the other. During the period 1922–31, the value of her imports of cattle products exceeded that of any other except cotton.

The Spanish landed oligarchy which assumed the leadership of the nation's destinies in 1874 was to demonstrate its unmistakable character by declaring war on anything that fell outside the framework of agriculture, and even in agriculture itself different classes existed. The oligarchs displayed a haughty indifference to those branches of production which did not enjoy the privilege of relationship with the influential family of cereals or the biblical olive. It was already clear that in the Spanish countryside there was to be no future save for those two aristocrats—the tall corn and the stocky olive-tree.

There is no need to say that the Restoration politicians were the mandataries of the grain and olive oligarchy. Professor Flores de Lemus, author of the sentence quoted above in defence of the stock-breeders, jeopardized his future as an economist by declaring himself an anti-cerealist. The "government-by-rotation" statesmen were long in forgiving him an indiscretion which was so damaging to official interests.

In 1891, there were 2,700,000 hectares sown with wheat and the crop amounted to 19,700,000 quintals. The following years saw a steady increase, until in 1933 we find 4,500,000 hectares under cultivation and a crop of 37,500,000 quintals.

Still more surprising was the increase in the cultivation of barley, which rose from 8,700,000 quintals in 1891 to 21,800,000 in 1933.

A similar rise took place in the olive industry, which in the last decade of the nineteenth century spread over 1,145,883 hectares and in 1933 had almost doubled its area.

It is curious to note that while the Spanish economy as a whole has been spontaneously prospering during the last fifty years, there are yet some branches of agriculture which are stationary and others that are deteriorating. The chapter we shall devote to the Spanish countryside will deal in detail with the victims of the grain and olive offensive.

In 1933, the wheat-growing area represented 26·6 per cent of the national territory. With the addition of the olive-groves, cereals already accounted for 29·37 per cent of the total area.

In this 29.37 per cent, the inexorable power of the Spanish ruling class had its roots. All interests outside cereals or olives were, in principle, at war with the oligarchy and the oligarchy was at war with them.

After the Restoration, the spheres of the Spanish economy were clearly demarcated. Politics were at sixes and sevens (though not so much as in the nineteenth century), because the middle class was hamstrung by a perpetual state of flux; but in the economic field, class warfare presented no obscurities for those who had eyes to see. The landowners were always at war with commerce and industry and with the proletariat. And not because the middle class continued to be a revolutionary class, but because the oligarchy subordinated the nation's economy to their grain and olive interests or arrived in most cases at a temporary compromise, without prejudice to their economic position, in order to maintain themselves in power. This was the reason why they compromised with industry.

In the first place, the oligarchy had not the slightest interest in the export trade. How could it be otherwise when they were a wheat-farming class and Spain did not produce cereals in sufficient abundance to supply the home market? Of the kinds of production in which the oligarchy had a direct and personal interest, only the olive industry allowed of a margin for exportation, and this was only 12·9 per cent of the national yield. Foreign markets, therefore, had no seduction for the ruling class. The importance of this fact cannot be exaggerated, since it was this that determined the policy of the "Box-and-Cox" Governments when the hour came to conclude or denounce commercial treaties.

Since the middle of the century, the free-trade controversy had aroused much feeling among all Spanish producers. The farmers were protectionists. So were the industrialists, or those who thought that Spain ought to devote more attention to industrial development than to mercantile prosperity. The commercial classes, on the other hand, were free-traders. The oligarchy's Press and the Press of the industrialists fought for protectionism, while the newspapers of the trading circles demanded moderate or no tariffs. The Madrid *El Defensor del Comercio* and the Cadiz *El Contribuyente* came out strongly in favour of free trade.

In the chapter on the reign of Amadeo of Savoy, I tried to show that that was the monarchy of the middle class, founded by the victorious middle class of the September revolution—

E s                                                                129 a monarchy of progressivism, led by Prim, the son of a notary, and Sagasta, the son of a grocer. Before Amadeo arrived in Spain, the progressive politicians had taken a hand in economics in the style that might have been expected of them. Desiring to foster the national wealth, they dictated a series of laws informed with the spirit of audacity, the "entrepreneur" spirit of their class. Among other measures, they decreed by a law of December 1868 that the first person to notify the existence of a mine could claim possession of it. But let us return to the struggle between the protectionists and the free-traders.

The men of the September revolution and of Amadeo's monarchy were, in general, free-traders by nature. In July 1869 they carried a very important tariff reform, introduced by Figuerola, which established a régime of moderate tariffs, highly beneficial to the commercial classes, but detrimental to the selfish interests of the farmers (that is, the oligarchy, which was then lying low) and the industrialists who, except in Catalonia and Vizcaya, counted for little.

The reply to the free-trade policy initiated after the revolution of 1868 by the Figuerola law, took the form of a series of rectifications introduced by the agrarians the moment they came into power with the Restoration. The war against commerce had begun.

In July 1877 the moderate tariff policy suffered its first modification. The régime had not yet been consolidated, and the agrarians feared a premature clash with the trading community. Sagasta himself had been given the mission of defending the middle class and he had not yet been completely won over by the landowners. In 1886 Moret, a Minister in the Sagasta Government, declared his intention of reforming tariff policy in a sense opposed to prohibitionism. But the Spanish middle class was a tributary of the landowners and could only govern as their sleeping partner by renouncing any independent policy, that is, by renouncing all idea of conducting themselves in power like a *bourgeoisie*. Only at this price could Sagasta, personally, continue his career; and so, for Moret, Montero Ríos, Martos, López Domínguez and the rest, he was soon to be the "renegade." Did Moret indeed propose to reduce tariffs? The real masters of the Government were there to prevent him. In the end, the Minister had to confine himself to renewing all the commercial treaties and the *modus vivendi* with England until January 1892, and to appointing a Parliamentary Commission to report on the gradual lowering of tariffs. In a word, the Liberals lacked the strength to oppose the policy of the landowners.

The Liberal Left, consisting of the men I have just mentioned, called Sagasta a renegade; but soon the critics themselves were to qualify for the epithet.

There can be no doubt that the politicians of the "dynastic Left", the discontented offshoot of Liberalism which had taken root, in opposition to Sagasta, in the principles of the Constitution of 1869, represented the last effort of the middle class in politics to escape from the onerous tutelage of the landed oligarchy. But all those who considered Sagasta a traitor passed themselves under the yoke of the oligarchy. This Liberal opposition, which was led by Serrano in the Senate and Moret in the other Chamber, flaunted a programme which included the reduction of taxes, the burden of the tradesman's song.

The *bourgeoisie*, I repeat, was in a blind alley; either it must bind itself to the chariot of the oligarchy, or it must enter the path of revolution with the proletariat. Should it choose the middle of the road and launch a protest on its own account, the protest of a class wounded in its interests, defeat lay in store for it, as we shall see later.

The Liberal Party contained an agrarian group, a kind of of rural middle class, led by Gamazo, and protectionist as a matter of course. This landowning nucleus found itself in a very singular position, for as it was composed of a poverty-stricken proletarian class of smallholders, which yet smacked of a proprietor class, it had interests in common with the progressives, but clashed with them over the aim of the *bourgeoisie* to foster the mercantile to the prejudice of the agrarian interest. For the rest, the modest landowners were an oppressed class, condemned, in economics as well as in politics, to be dragged in the wake of the great owners of the soil. Which was one more reason why Sagasta—every day more inclined to accept the programme of peace at any price—was to practise a policy opposed to his own class, in order not to exasperate the Gamazo party.

Fundamentally, the protectionist-free-trade struggle was a fight between the agrarians, allied for the occasion with the industrialists, and the trading community. For as a protectionist class, the Spanish industrial *bourgeoisie* was able to come to terms with the agrarians, towards whom they were impelled, in the same way, by another common factor—that of being an owner class menaced by the proletariat. Spanish commerce found itself in conflict with industry and agriculture over the question of tariffs, but at one with both in its quality as an owner class.

Now, industrialists and traders formed a dynamic, progressive class; they were the *bourgeoisie*. While the agrarians were a sedentary, static, reactionary class.

131

The grain and olive oligarchy brought into the Government a protectionist policy which bordered on prohibitionism. It was their reply to the régime which had attempted since the revolution of 1868 to establish itself with the Figuerola law. Nothing else could have been expected of a social class which, because the bulk of its production did not fall under the head of exportable commodities, had no direct interest in the interchange of merchandise with other nations—the exact opposite, for example, of England.

As exports of Spanish manufactures were also scanty, due to the fact that even the most highly developed industries did not cover the needs of the home market, Cánovas, the champion of protectionism, "the dogma of the Conservative Party", was a politician with a strong following in Catalonia. By contrast, he was hated by the trading community throughout Spain.

As the new règime of the Restoration found its feet, it began to unfold its anti-mercantile policy. We have already seen that in 1877 rectifications in the moderate tariff policy of 1869 had begun to be made.

In 1882 Sagasta decreed a rise in the taxes on commerce. The commercial classes raised a storm of protest and kept it up during the months of February, March and April. The traders of Madrid banded together in agitation, calling upon traders throughout Spain to resist; and all together succeeded in setting up a defensive organization whose function was suppressed with severity by the authorities. This crisis made it clear for the first time that Spanish commerce was as much an oppressed class as the proletariat, and like the proletariat, it was absolutely destitute of political power.

In 1889 the Conservative Minister, Fernández Villaverde, the typical financier of the wheat- and olive-farming school, requested Parliament to authorize an increase in the tariffs protecting grain and flour. The Conservatives were now planning their great offensive for tariff revision, a positive assault on the tumble-down mercantile blockhouse. The attack was not going to be only a mass assault on free trade, but also an offensive on shopkeepers' profits. Commerce was to receive its death-blow and no holds were barred. A powerful customs barrier was raised, therefore, to cut off its retreat, while a frontal attack was launched by the heavy artillery of taxation.

In 1890 the Conservatives once more came into power. We are now on the eve of an historic attack on Spanish commerce. The operation had been studied down to its last details. Cánovas was to break completely with the policy of moderate grain tariffs.

The Conservative Cabinet did not hesitate for an instant. Without more ado, it denounced the Commercial Treaty with France which was founded on the most-favoured-nation principle and was the linchpin of Spanish commerce abroad, being the model for all countries which signed commercial agreements with Spain. The final result was the severing of commercial relations with every nation and, in particular, with the neighbouring Republic. France was the largest market for Spanish wines, and the Spanish Government was not unaware that by taking this step they were bringing to the verge of ruin the viticultural industry, which of course did not fall within the radius of the immediate and most pressing interests of the oligarchy. In 1892 the new tariffs came into force, and the French market was lost.

Since the previous year, the trading community had seen disaster approaching and had once more raised the standard of revolt against the Government. The Chambers of Commerce from all over Spain met at Madrid. All kinds of protests were made, even an openly subversive street demonstration organized by the *Círculo de la Unión Mercantil* of Madrid to stir up the traders and public opinion against Cánovas.

The oligarchy suppressed the movement and the traders were officially declared to be hotheads, stirrers-up of strife and ungovernable. No doubt Cánovas was confirmed in his thesis that there were certain flaws in the race which made good government impossible.

The reform of 1892 "completely reversed the moderate free-trade policy which had been so beneficial to the foreign commerce of Spain from 1868 to 1892. The effects of this policy verging upon prohibition were soon sharply felt. Foreign exchanges rose, exports decreased, the railway traffic declined, and the commercial classes and consumers of foreign goods and products were loud in their protests. Industrial interests alone benefited, and imported more raw materials, chemicals and coal and coke, which naturally influenced the exchanges adversely."

The offensive against commerce did not end with the tariff reform of 1892, nor did the commercial classes who were without defenders in the Government cease to agitate.

After the radical tariff policy of Cánovas, it was now the turn of the "Liberals", and the same year Gamazo riveted new shackles on commerce with the creation of customs zones for foreign live stock, groceries (shades of Don Clemente Sagasta!), cotton, wool and silk textiles.

The afflicted traders redoubled their protests, and when they discovered, in addition, that the Government were putting a new tax on transfers of treasury bills and industrial and commercial securities in which commercial agents were concerned, the peaceable shopkeepers must have thought that the object was to rob them altogether of their livelihood. It was not surprising that the *Círculo de la Unión Mercantil* of Madrid, a respectable and patriotic *bourgeois* institution, should have organized revolts of the citizens.

From 1892 onwards, it was clear that the agrarians were determined on the annihilation of Spanish commerce. No less obvious was the tacit design to prevent a single industry springing up in addition to those already in existence. If commerce continued to survive and even to prosper, it was in spite of the policy of the two-headed grain and olive oligarchy and due to the irresistibly expansive nature of commercial and industrial activity or to the neutrality of Spain in the first world war.

In 1898 all the Chambers of Commerce throughout Spain met at Saragossa. The Spanish *bourgeoisie* was in the same straits as all the rest of the non-wheat-farming and non-olive-growing community (we have already seen to what a pass the viticulturists had come); and it was trying to regroup and discipline its forces for a defensive campaign.

The last show of revolutionary rebellion on the part of the Spanish *bourgeoisie*, trusting to its own resources as an independent class, took place in 1900. The traders had already exhausted all the peaceful means of combat. They had refused to employ a dangerous weapon—a strike of tax-payers—but now they were going to use it.

Cánovas was already dead, assassinated at Santa Águeda, where he was taking the waters, by an Italian anarchist. His mantle as leader of the Conservative Party had fallen on Don Francisco Silvela, another pessimist, but an honest one and superior to the oligarchy not only intellectually, as Cánovas was, but also morally. The Silvela Government could not fail to include the inevitable Villaverde. To a certain extent, Villaverde's tariff policy was as important as the protectionist measures of '92. It represented the continuation of the régime's economic policy which was founded in 1874. It was, in short, a merciless counter-revolution.

Villaverde announced that it was the Government's intention to balance the Budget and that all indirect taxation would be raised "with the sole exception of the taxes on agricultural and stock-breeding profits, which would be lowered in view of their already notoriously excessive nature".

The Government appealed to the nation's patriotism—an appeal which struck fear into the hearts of patriots, to say nothing of the traders, who no sooner heard the news of the balancing of the Budget than they returned to their barricades of public meetings.

Again the Chambers of Commerce met at Valladolid, founded the *Unión Nacional* party (the political organ they had lacked) and, in agreement with the Catalans, declared a strike of tax-payers.

If any doubt yet remained, this action of the commercial and industrial classes once more threw into relief the weakness of the Spanish *bourgeoisie*, which did not even succeed in begetting a party of its own. The Government broke the strike—and thus ended the last autonomous subversive action of the Spanish middle class.

The landed oligarchy had proved invincible.


CHAPTER VI

## THE MILITARY MONARCHY

THE SOCIAL INEQUALITY which had reigned in the rural areas of Spain since the middle of the nineteenth century was so insupportable that, since the necessary reforms were not forthcoming, a permanent army of occupation had to be kept in the countryside. This army of occupation could not be the regular Army; so the Civil Guard was created at an opportune moment, as we saw, two years after the first peasant revolt. There could be no more explicit recognition of the subversive character of rural property. Well might it occur to the oligarchy (which was monarchist at heart) that such outrageous social inequality could not find its political expression in a constitutional monarchy, however many resorts to dictatorship were permitted under the Constitution, any more than it found it in a parliamentary Republic. The progressive monarchy of Amadeo and the libertarian Republic of 1873 fell because they tried to found a free State on a slave society. The Restoration proposed to solve this contradiction by an iniquitous formula whereby the State and society were to be readjusted without touching property. Certain civil institutions were founded which had a longer life than previous ones because, though unjust, they represented a form of government—the oligarchic—which was more in harmony with the régime of property—also oligarchic.

But it was not government by consent, but government imposed from above; it had to rest on violence, since if liberty was effective, the institutions collapsed. The oligarchy's resistance to all reforms, the tyrannical exaltation of the interests of the great landowners over those of industry, commerce and the huge rural proletariat, irrevocably guaranteed the asphyxiation of the monarchical régime by stopping up those founts of civic energy which are the moral nourishment of the civil power. The social strength of the oligarchy was no doubt great; but not so great that a system of government, which by the enforced daily perpetration of injustices was alienating its authority, could take root. Much though it grieved the politicians of the Restoration, who boasted of having broken with the nineteenth century, they were obliged to use the Army in the delicate task of maintaining order at home. That fictitious civil State, which proposed to eject the generals from political life, found itself obliged to summon them to its aid with such assiduity that in time the Army became once more the arbiter of the nation's destinies. Cánovas, having satisfied himself that he had put an end to the *pronunciamientos*, refused to recognize that in the extraordinary and overwhelming number of Army officers and in the civil weakness of the State he had just founded, lay the seeds of that disequilibrium of forces which was to destroy the Restoration institutions. The soldiers were not in the Government, but their real power was none the less for that; and they used the liberty of movement they enjoyed outside the ministerial polygon at the close of the century to mould the mind of the boy king and to educate him and train him in the school of militarism. From the first hour, the Army besieged the Royal Chamber. Silently, in the tender person of Alfonso XIII, the military monarchy was taking shape in the Palace. The vigilance of Cánovas had protected Alfonso XII from the snares set for the sovereign by the natural enemies of civil society, and neither the Army nor the Church had had a definite hold on that, in other respects, discouraged and ephemeral monarch. During the Regency it was a woman who wore the Crown, and that favoured ecclesiastical influence at Court. But when Cánovas died, as if once more there were no ruling class, the Army seized its turn with the advent of the new king, and the Crown and the soldiers ended by ruling together.

During the nineteenth century, it was the theocratic *camarilla* which by taking prisoner the mind of the Queen, dragged down the monarchical institution into the abyss. Now the Church was only taking a secondary place (not the less lucrative for

136

that) in profiting by the weakness of the civil power—probably because the reigning monarch was a man, and therefore more susceptible to the clash of arms than to the murmur of prayers. But the process was the same. The Army wrecked the monarchy of Alfonso XIII for the same reasons as the Church brought disaster to the monarchy of Isabel II.

The monarchical institution was the cornerstone of the State which forced itself on Spain in 1874. This was, chiefly, because it was the régime of the landed nobility, an integral part of the oligarchy.

At no time was Alfonso XII, the first monarch of the Restoration, a really popular king, respected and loved by the people. He tried by every means he knew to counter the indifference of the middle class and the proletariat, because he was perfectly well aware that if the monarchy alienated the people's affection, it would lead a precarious life. But he did not succeed in winning the support of the masses. His goodwill, in the moments when he recovered his faith in his office (for he often believed in nothing, having been infected by the scepticism of the upper classes), was shattered against the obstinate reality of the system of government he was forced to preside over. More than once he risked his life in appealing to the sentiments of the people. On the occasion of the earthquake which wrought havoc in Andalusia in the winter of 1884, Alfonso, reduced to skin and bone by the malady which ravaged him, made a heroic physical effort and braved the inclemency of the weather to visit the devastated areas and succour the victims. In the following summer, the sinister appearance of cholera in New Castile and Andalusia provided him with another opportunity to display his affection for the poor. This was a truly catastrophic epidemic which cost the lives of some 100,000 persons. The King, who wanted to console and encourage the victims of the plague by a personal visit, was not to be dissuaded by the danger. He asked the Government's permission to visit the stricken regions and was forbidden to do so by Cánovas, who threatened to resign if he persisted in his rash plan. The King then proposed to replace Cánovas by Sagasta or Serrano, if either of them would allow him to visit the zones where the cholera was raging. But no politician would lend himself to the schemes of a king who was stubbornly bent on winning the people's affection for himself and the monarchy, with so little effect. In the end, State policy had to yield to the adventurous temperament of Alfonso, who very early on July 2nd wrote a letter of farewell to the Queen and set out for the station with one of his aides-de-camp. At Aranjuez he visited the hospitals and mingled with the threatened population in the streets. As was natural, the people responded with admiration and friendliness to the King's gesture. But the emotion of the crowds, which it had cost so much to arouse, melted away at the end of a few weeks.

It was useless for Cánovas and Sagasta to hymn the virtues of the King and to strain every nerve to make of the Spanish monarchy a respectable monarchy on the British model, established like a snowy mountain-peak in the upper regions of politics, where the air is clear and untroubled by the impurities of the struggle for power. The Spanish monarchy was paying for the windows which the knavish oligarchy had broken; and so no stratagem could make Alfonso XII an acceptable king to Spaniards.

The Restoration monarchy was plunged into a crisis almost the very moment it was born, and it was certainly only saved by the circumstance of the queen dowager being pregnant. Doña María Cristina was a woman of great moral character. Not very intelligent and completely dominated by the priests, she had nevertheless a good heart and common sense. She knew how to command respect; and the Spanish sense of chivalry —never so lively as among the common people—ordained that the Republican flag should be temporarily hauled down. As Castelar said, there were few who dared to fight an institution which was symbolized in a woman and a cradle. The oligarchy were quick to exploit the sentimentality of the people. For the time being, the sword was sheathed; but when Alfonso XIII ascended the throne, the controversy about the form of government broke out again.

Alfonso XIII had borrowed from the oligarchy their frivolity, their absence of faith in Spain, their avarice, their lack of interest in culture, and their liking for plebeian and colloquial expressions—the only thing the privileged classes had assimilated from the proletariat, as if in imitating popular speech they were seeking compensation for their lack of affection for the common people.

Alfonso XIII, I repeat, had all the defects of the ruling class, which in him were all the more conspicuous because of the lofty position he occupied. What was due to his education and what was congenital in someone whose personality, from a child, had been, as it were, a battleground for all those who were interested in using the monarchy for the furtherance of their personal or political dreams and ambitions, it is difficult to determine. But we can at least conjecture that if Alfonso had aimed at being the perfect king, he would not have kept his throne. The oligarchy needed a king who would turn a blind eye to their proceedings—a king in their own image and likeness. Morally, Alfonso XIII was the master the Spanish ruling class deserved. He was blamed because at times he threw the whole weight of his personal power into the balance. He was an active king, who had a finger in every political pie. If he had remained merely a spectator, as Unamuno once advised him to, he would have been held responsible all the same; his circumspection would have been called negligence and his prudence, cowardice. His office was condemned to failure in a nation shaken by the gusts of violence daily engendered by social inequality and the injustices of the oppressors. Everything conspired to make the kingly profession impossible in Spain.

The Army, being anxious to make the future monarch its own, made certain of the lion's share in the education of the prince. Swords and uniforms, parades and words of command—this was the atmosphere in which Alfonso XIII passed his youth.

By education or temperament, or both, the new monarch grew up a lover of everything military.

The policy of the oligarchy remained constant to its two ideals, as in the original days of *Las Novedades*. One part of the programme was that property should remain unalterable, and on this, agreement was general. But the other part—the enjoyment of power considered as an end in itself—gave rise to serious personal disagreements. Individual impatience sowed revolt in the two great parties. It was beyond measure astonishing to see the lack of shame with which the leaders and their henchmen sought power, putting forward no programme of government, but impudently basing their supposed right to take over the command on the expiration of the appointed term allotted to their adversary to sack the country. It could not but affect the nerves of believers in the system of government by rotation, which, in order to be effective and peaceable, demanded conformity in those who were temporarily dispossessed. In the end the sequence was broken, precisely because of this kind of greed.

The oligarchy of this period—worthy heirs of the followers of Cánovas and Sagasta—reduced their methods of corruption to a fine art. Where before they had been wont to look out for personal victims, they now applied their methods to whole classes. Few were surprised, for example, at a notice which appeared in *El Universo* of March 11th, 1911, saying that Canalejas and Count Romanones would have the greatest pleasure "in supporting the candidature of all journalists who presented themselves for election to the Cortes, because the priesthood of the Press stood for enlightenment and culture". The result was that some fifty journalists of varying political hues entered Parliament.

In both oligarchic parties, the quality of the leading personages was the same. The machine which Cánovas and Posada Herrera set in motion functioned prodigiously. We should not understand why certain men figured in the Liberal Party and not in the Conservative, and vice versa, if we failed to grasp the character of this political dualism. Don Segismundo Moret welcomed in his Government oligarchs like Rodríguez de la Borbolla, owner of great estates in the province of Seville; while another Liberal, Vega de Armijo, included among his Ministers grandees like the Marqués del Real Tesoro, a die-hard Conservative who would not have been out of place at the council-board of the Carlist Pretender. Now, as before, nothing divided the Liberals from the Conservatives. The clerical question? There was no more stubborn enemy of the *Ley de Asociaciones* than Don Niceto Alcalá Zamora, a supporter of Romanones and the owner of estates in the province of Jaen. The elections were manipulated with the dexterity of yore, if not with even greater skill, for practice had already raised the apprentices to the ranks of the master-craftsmen. So perfect was the organization for defrauding the public, that the inhibitions of the rulers did not detract from the perfection of the régime. "The workings of *servilismo*", writes an historian of the period, "and the mutual interest of the oligarchy facilitated to an extraordinary degree the choice of an Administration. This is proved by the fact that when municipal councillors and *Diputaciones* were elected during the Conservative term of office and municipal justices (whose influence on politics was vicious, but positive) were appointed under the same device, the Liberal Government had no need to modify these organizations and appointments. The fact was that the provincial *caciques* and their retinue preferred to support the system of victory by turns, which was more convenient for everybody than a fight."

Shortly after Alfonso XIII ascended the throne, Maura came into power with his theory of revolution from above and proposed to revolutionize the country "rapidly, radically, brutally". Don Antonio Maura could not be identified literally with the clownish oligarchy, and that, together with his arrogance and a misleading severity of manner, disqualified him for success in politics. But, as he himself said, he detested "sated stomachs" and had ideas—not so effective, however, as they appeared—

for ordering the nation. The first thing he did was to attempt to uproot corruption. He therefore relaxed official intervention in the elections of April 1903. The results were not slow in appearing. The Republicans triumphed in Madrid, Barcelona and Valencia. The King was annoyed with Maura and accused him of not protecting his interests. For the throne, like the rickety structure of the oligarchy, like the whole régime, could only maintain its tottering fabric by the adulteration of the suffrage. This was the point of departure for all the other corrupt practices. Caciquism could not disappear, nor could the monarchy be constitutional, so long as social inequality remained as it was. But no one was prepared to go to the root of the evil. The landless peasant continued his agitation in a series of melancholy incidents or, resigned to his fate, made known his miserable condition in other ways. Burning of ricks and farm-buildings and bloody encounters with the Civil Guard, today in this village, tomorrow in the other, perpetuated the signs of the rural anguish which made its appearance in the middle of the last century. One day the *braceros* of Cártama would be advancing on Malaga as if to begin a revolt, but "afterwards, their ranks scattered, they would be begging in the city". Another day, the people of Boada in the province of Salamanca would be humbly petitioning the Government for permission to emigrate *en masse*. And it showed a complete lack of understanding to claim that the evil was being remedied and that harmony could be introduced into Spanish society by means of laws like Maura's *Administracion Local*, which was described by its author as a "law to eradicate caciquism" and presented as the consecration of "the true and lively affinities of the *pueblos*, so that they can live their life and organize themselves in complete freedom". In the last analysis, Maura's conception of liberty would have meant increasing the political rights of the landless, and thus accelerating the rhythm of civil war. The fate of his political reform would have been that of all the Constitutions; if it had been genuinely carried out it would have let loose the revolution. But the law in question was stillborn. When it seemed to be already a reality, on the point of being approved by the Cortes, it was shelved.

The oligarchs did not govern nor did they allow anyone else to govern. Canalejas meditated reforming agrarian property, an aspiration less spectacular, but more intelligent, than the battle with the religious orders; but he soon had to bury the first in oblivion and draw in his horns over the second. Spain, in short, lacked an executive power. And there could be no salvation for the country while things continued as they were. For the absence of government is worse than erroneous government. What deals nations their death-blow is not a mistaken policy, but the lack of a positive policy. Error brings with it an implicit apology for past mistakes, and sooner or later things are put right. But when there is no attempt at anything, mistaken or otherwise, when all that is desired is to pull through somehow, to live a hand-to-mouth existence, to avoid difficulties without reforming anything, merely buying the silence of the critics with a seat in Parliament or with other degrading gifts, and applying force where blandishments fail—when this happens to a nation, that nation is without a Government.

During the period under review, Spain was *de jure* a constitutional monarchy, but she was also *de facto*, as Costa pointed out, a "parliamentary dictatorship". For whole years the nation lived under martial law, the various regions being delivered over to military jurisdiction, to the mercy of the Captains-General, viceroys in all but name. The people, excluded from the political game by the eliminating device of caciquism, and seeing the power taken over by the Army with a frequency which made it impossible to draw a dividing line between the normal and the abnormal, watched with more curiosity than anger the menace brooding over that derisory civil power. The military threat which had been averted during the first thirty years, more or less, of the Restoration, began to loom large with the advent of Alfonso XIII, as we have seen. The oligarchy was now mortally wounded in its privilege as ruler; for the Army had the Crown for an ally, and the militaristic leanings of the King were going to lead to the overthrow of the whole system. Such an important detail did not escape the oligarchs, and from the outset the Government Press took upon itself to admonish the throne. But the die was cast.

The encouragement which the generals received at the Palace, together with the actual power which the rulers conceded them in the course of the political struggle, puffed up the Army with pride, all the more so because, when they looked around, they were bound to discover that all authority paled beside their own.

On November 25th, 1906, some 200 Army officers at Barcelona attacked the offices of the weekly *Cutut* and the daily *La Veu de Catalunya*, which in their opinion were carrying on a persistent campaign against the Army and national unity. The Government had no means of punishing the outrage, in which other garrisons joined; and the immediate result of the incidents was the claim of the military to extend their jurisdiction to offences against the Army and the nation. The King refused to agree to measures which the Government of Montero Ríos had adopted against the violaters of the law, and the road was thrown open to brute force. The Chambers carried out the new measure under the constant vigilance of the officers' mess; and on March 20th, 1907, the *Ley de Jurisdicciones* was approved, Don Segismundo Moret being Prime Minister and Don Manuel García Prieto Minister of Justice. The Army was snatching from the civil power its essential prerogative of dispensing justice.

As the nation disintegrated, it was logical that the power of the military party should grow, through the decline of moral authority in the ruling class.

The events of July 1909, known as the disaster of the *Barranco del Lobo* and the *Semana Trágica*, or tragic week, in Barcelona, left the monarchy and the régime of the gormandizers in a very difficult situation. They suddenly cut short the public career of the most outstanding politician the system could count on, and stirred up opinion throughout Europe which had then no serious problems of its own to attend to.

What happened was briefly as follows. A Moor known as *El Rogui*, ruler of the tribes near Melilla, sold the iron-ore mines of Beni-bu-Ifrur to a Spanish syndicate founded for the purpose by Count Romanones and others. The *guelayas* or local Moors, considering themselves the legal owners of the mines, did not endorse the sale, broke with *El Rogui* and drove him out.

When the mining company began building a railway, the Riffs attacked the labourers, and this led to the intervention of the Spanish Army. The war in Africa therefore blazed up again. The Spanish Army at Melilla had to carry out a protective operation by establishing new positions beyond Monte Gurugú, which was occupied by the disaffected natives. The local garrison was wiped out in the early stages of the fighting. But the Gurugú had to be taken, and reinforcements were brought over from the Peninsula. Without stopping for food or rest, the troops disembarked at the port and were thrown at once into the battle. Technical deficiencies and the rash courage of the Spanish officers led to disaster on July 23rd. Then General Pintos, spurred on to a great pitch of enthusiasm by encouragement he had received at the Palace where he had promised to crown the precipitous promontory with the Spanish flag, went into battle with his men. He penetrated into enemy territory with such determination and lack of prudence that he perished in the rash enterprise. With him died many officers. The campaign was frankly disastrous—and the reason was the same as it had always been; the Spanish military machine did not function. The human material was excellent; officers and men displayed self-sacrifice and courage; but that was not enough. They lacked discipline, training and weapons. The Army was one more victim of the national confusion. Though it cost the nation vast sums, it was, nevertheless, ill paid; it was at once indulged and neglected.

Once more the Moroccan problem was on everyone's lips. The people saw in the enterprise the hand of the capitalists who were interested in the mines; so they opposed the war, demanding that Morocco should be abandoned. But what should have been abandoned was the iniquitous policy of the oligarchy. The truth was perhaps that Spain could not disinterest herself in Africa without loss of prestige and without compromising the defence of her *plazas* and consequently the defence of the Peninsula. Other reasons of a moral character counselled the presence of Spain in Morocco. But the oligarchy always considered that Spanish action should be first and foremost military, and tried, not to colonize, but to keep the Army occupied and to remain in Morocco because it seemed the right thing to do, or through vain pride.

But who could expect from the Spanish ruling class an African policy different from their policy at home? And in 1909 there arose this grotesque contradiction; a State carrying out a policy of economic imperialism (for what else was the Army's support of the exploitation of mines in the Riff?) with the ideas and technique of the Crusades. The Moor was viewed through the mediaeval prism, as befitted the angle of vision of a semi-feudal oligarchy, and the Moroccan war was presented, according to old and stale custom, as a war of religion. One of two things could be done: either abandon the mines or abandon the habiliments of Calatrava and Alcantara. For the fact was that the Knights of the old military Orders had once more taken out and dusted the last will and testament of Isabella the Catholic and risen against the infidel in Madrid, demanding to be mobilized against the enemies of Christendom and the Fatherland. No one hindered them, for the Government was not going to turn down volunteers. But how outmoded and ridiculous was the aspiration of these fossilized *señores* who, provided they were allowed to don the trappings of the Middle Ages (so well suited to their mentality), were prepared to repeat the exploits of Las Navas de Tolosa! We have perhaps given the incident too much importance; but it illustrates the mental decay of a dull-witted nobility, rising from the tomb of forget-fulness with a gesture that was meant to be virile and only succeeded in being ridiculous.

Because of the Moroccan incident, the nation was once more plunged into tragic turmoil. The people, with more sense than their rulers, grasped the fact that Spain was not prepared for war in Africa, and if their voice had been listened to, the Government would have thrown out feelers before mobilizing the soldiers of the active reserve, many of them fathers of families, who would have given everything for a less barren cause, but who felt no enthusiasm either for Morocco or for the Government. This was a blunder that was only surpassed by another—the drawing of troops from Catalonia, a region of endemic rebellion since the appearance of Catalan nationalism and given over to terroristic violence highly complex in origin, as we shall see later.

The protest against the war was led by the Socialist Party, a young organization which, through the mouth of its leader, Pablo Iglesias, pointed out that the enemy was not the Moors but the Government. Inflammable social material was there in abundance, and the fact that the proletariat—recently mobilized for political action—were spoiling for a fight, guaranteed that at the first spark the whole pile would burst into flames.

The discontent was most acute in Barcelona, the Mecca of Spanish demagogy. The departure of the troops for Africa provoked general unrest in the region, and on the 26th a unanimous strike of all the services began, leaving Barcelona without communications and without light. The movement had no visible leader, though it was the work of all the parties of the Left—Socialists, Anarchists, Syndicalists, Nationalists and Radical Republicans. It was, nevertheless, a negative rebellion, venting its rage on religious buildings. The wildest disorder lasted for a week, burning itself out more through lack of fuel to feed the flames than through any action on the Government's part.

The punishment of the revolutionaries was pursued with vigour, and the ringleader was declared to be Francisco Ferrer, a commercial clerk, a railway company employee at the time, and the founder and leader of the *Escuela Moderna*, an anarchist institution which scattered its explosive ideas among empty heads sustained by empty stomachs. Ferrer was a visionary, with the narrow mind of the sectarian, a nihilist, a fanatic and a freemason. He was the perfect example of the anarchist "intellectual", without the religious originality of the contemplative anarchist or the suicidal determination of the active anarchist. A strange person, therefore, apt in the arts of persuasion. He had an extraordinary influence over women. Married to the beautiful Teresa Sanmarti, he afterwards lived with Leopoldina Bonald, inherited from Ernestina Meunier the money with which he founded the *Escuela Moderna* and passed the last years of his life with Soledad Villafranca. I can find nothing noble in Ferrer. But the Government's treatment of him made him a martyr.

He was tried by court martial and condemned to death. It is said that the King advised clemency, but there is no evidence that he pressed his views and Maura approved of the verdict.

The proletariat of Europe and the philanthropic middle class made a terrific international scandal of the affair, which was fomented from inside Spain by the enemies of the oligarchy. But the person who paid at the time for the blunder of not pardoning Ferrer was the King. Maura had committed a gross mistake, and Spain—and the King—dealt justly with him, imposing on him a mild form of ostracism. A Minister who blunders so greatly puts himself out of the running for office. From that time on, Maura did not raise his head again in public life.

Maura, a man of dominating personality, kept the Crown in check for some time, reducing it to its strict rôle; which shows that Alfonso XIII might have been another sort of king if he had had another sort of ruling class. But history cannot judge Maura less harshly than his Ministers.

The events of July 1909 struck the oligarchic régime a blow to the heart and administered a severe shock to the monarchy.

CHAPTER VII

## THE PROLETARIAT

During the days of the first Republic, we find a proletarian agitation, at once amorphous and anarchical in character. It was not an organic movement, but the primitive protest of a class which was being mercilessly exploited. There were no large bodies of people united in the same intelligent purpose. Yet from the middle of the century, certain workers' societies, affiliated to the International Working Men's Association, functioned; and though it was too soon for it to have an appreciable effect on the events of 1873, there already existed in embryo the modern trade-union and political movement of the Spanish working class, whose different trends were even now beginning to take shape.

With the grant of freedom of meeting and association, the revolution of 1868 and the first Republic favoured the constitution of workers' societies. In November of that year, Fanelli, representing the "Alliance of Social Democracy" founded by Bakunin, came to Madrid. Fanelli's propaganda encouraged the formation of new groups of the International in various cities. In order to unite these in one national federation, a Congress met in June 1870 at Barcelona, which was attended by eighty-five delegates representing Sections of thirty-four localities. At this first Congress, anarchist ideology was the order of the day, and it was resolved that as "any participation of the working class in the ruling policy of the middle class could not produce results other than the consolidation of the existing order of things, which would necessarily stultify the Socialist revolutionary action of the proletariat, the Congress recommends all Sections of the International Working Men's Association to renounce all corporative action whose object is to effect social transformation by way of national political reforms, and invites them to employ all their activity in the federative constitution of the official bodies, the sole means of assuring the success of the social revolution. Such federation is Labour's true representation and must take place outside political governments".

The first Federal Council, elected by this same Congress, included the brothers Francisco and Angel Mora and Anselmo Lorenzo, the brain of Spanish militant Anarchism.

On September 9th, 1871, the Spanish Section of the International held a conference at Valencia, at which anarchist principles were reaffirmed: ". . . the true federal democratic Republic is collective ownership, that is, the free universal federation of free agricultural and industrial associations."

A new Federal Council was appointed, this time with José Mesa, Inocente Calleja and Pablo Iglesias.

The efforts of the emissaries of Bakunin to proselytize the Spanish working class were countered by Lafargue, the son-in-law of Karl Marx and the authorized interpreter of Socialist theories, who had temporarily taken up residence in Spain.

In January 1872 the Sagasta Government decreed the dissolution of the Spanish Section of the International, because they considered it to be the "philosopher's Utopia of crime". Nevertheless, the workers' movement continued to function.

In April of the same year there met at Saragossa the historic Congress at which occurred the rupture between Anarchists and Socialists, between the philosophy of Bakunin and the philosophy of Marx. The conflict which was afterwards to

147

assume international proportions and end with the expulsion of Bakunin at the Hague Congress, was solved by the Spanish proletariat when nine Socialist members, among them Pablo Iglesias, withdrew from the Alliance on May 2nd, 1872. It was significant that this group assumed the name of *Nueva Federación Madrileña*.

We shall go astray if we lose sight of the fact that these were the beginnings of the organized workers' movement. It had as yet no great following and existed in a nebulous state, though the seeds of rapid development were there. But it should be borne in mind that in Spain the International only grouped together 25,000 supporters.

The new régime of the Restoration was openly hostile to workers' associations, Socialism and Anarchism. The budding workers' movement passed, therefore, through a hard testing time and was forced, when on the point of annihilation, to go underground. Nevertheless, at the beginning of 1879, Pablo Iglesias' group, already more numerous, was on the march again and founded the *Partido Socialista Obrero Español*.

In 1886, the party weekly, *El Socialista*, first saw the light.

Two years later the first Socialist Congress met at Barcelona, and another Congress—also the first of its kind—the Congress of the General Union of Workers (*Unión General de Trabajadores*) took place about the same time. In 1889 this trade-union organization, with a Marxist bias, was composed of 73 sections and 15,000 members.

These events were paralleled by the rise of the anarcho-syndicalist workers' movement. The Federation of the Workers of the Spanish Region (*Federación de Trabajadores de la Región Española*) came into being at Barcelona, with its newspaper *Tierra y Libertad*.

At the opening of the present century both tendencies were already clearly defined in the social geography of the nation. One flourished in the soil of Madrid; the other was equally at home in Barcelona and Seville. It was already clear that the climate of Castile was not suited to Anarchism and that in industrial Barcelona and its hinterland and in the Andalusia of the latifundia, there was little place for Socialism. Or, to put it another way, let us say that, in the main, Catalonia and Andalusia plumped for Anarchism and Castile for Socialism.

The general line of Socialist aspirations, according to the programme approved by the founders in May 1879, may be summed up as the "possession of political power by the working class; the transformation of individual or corporative owner-

148

ship of the means of production into common ownership by the nation; and the constitution of society on the basis of economic federation, the scientific organization of labour and a comprehensive system of education for all individuals of either sex".

Revolutionary syndicalism, which ended by dominating not only Barcelona but, generally speaking, the industrial centres, was the offspring of Anarchism. Its doctrines must be looked for in the philosophy of Sorel and were born, therefore, outside Spain. Its tactics of direct action did not, as is commonly supposed, consist in the systematic use of violence, but in direct negotiation between employers and workers to the exclusion of third parties, whether political or not, having no stake in the specific interests of production in its two branches of capital and labour. That is, "that whenever workers have claims to put forward, or differences to solve, they should do it direct with the employers concerned and not accept the intervention of anyone not a party to the dispute, whether persons acting as friendly mediators, or official representatives, or State officials, or public authorities. If they arrive at an agreement—well and good; if not, then each party should make use of the means of pressure available in order to overcome the resistance of his adversary".

It is clear, however, that direct action, by eliminating arbitration by the public authorities, ends by establishing force as the solvent of social conflicts. Because of its anarchist, a-political, anti-State vein, Sorelian syndicalism is a social movement based on violence; while the Socialism which was soon to assume overwhelming predominance in the proletarian milieus of Castile was Marxist Socialism, fundamentally political, believing in the State, and pragmatic in its choice of methods of combat.

Why did the proletariat of Catalonia and Andalusia incline towards Anarcho-Syndicalism and the proletariat of Castile towards Socialism? Why was there Anarchism in Barcelona and Seville and none in Madrid? This is a problem of Spanish history which merits special attention.

The enigma is solved when we remember the economic structure of the nation. In Castile, the economic climate was temperate. Between the Duero and the Tagus, except for Salamanca, there were few great estates. The land was divided into smallholdings, with proprietors who earned little more than a *bracero*. The region was stabilized, as it were, at a level of general penury, equality of poverty being greater here than in the rest of Spain, without ever reaching the extremes of the property-owning system in Galicia. So much for the land.

In the cities, the advent of socialist ideas caught an archaic and patriarchal economic régime unawares. Castile had no industry and lacked a modern proletariat, the proletariat of Marxism. The workers did not work in factories but in workshops, and the employer knew them all by name. The workshop with a hundred operatives was a rarity. Castile was, then, without a *bourgeoisie*, and when the proletariat shouted "Down with the *bourgeoisie!*", because they had heard the phrase on the lips of their French, English, Belgian and German comrades, they meant something quite different. They meant "Down with the landowners!" For historically, this primitive proletariat of Castile was an ally (though they did not know it) of the *bourgeoisie*—also primitive, and like them, oppressed by the aristocracy and the great landowners.

The proletariat of Madrid was, obviously, still living in the age of the guilds. The employers maintained with their workers a kind of relationship which was already a thing of the past in the great industrial nations and in Barcelona itself. The building industry had not yet seen the day of the great enterprises. In short, the economy of Castile was based on handicraft. The workers were still artisans. And so the mediaeval terminology persisted. The employer was the *maestro* (master) and under him worked the *oficiales* (craftsmen) and the *aprendices* (apprentices). The employer himself was usually no more than the chief workman and at the end of the day, when the workers had left, this *capitalist* himself closed the door of the workshop, which was usually part of his own dwelling, and retired to spend the evening with his family or occasionally went on working.

The same sort of thing happened in commerce, which was still not organized on any definite scale.

Such was the social atmosphere of Castile at the beginning of the nineteenth century, and such it has been up to the present day. In these surroundings, there could be no place for the cold, mechanical and impersonal cruelty af capitalism. This was why Castile rejected Anarchism and why the anarchist philosophers who were born in these regions went to preach their phalansterian doctrines and their nihilist hatreds in the regions where social inequality was an eruptive force and where there existed a resentful industrial proletariat.

On the other hand, agrarian Andalusia and industrial Barcelona, though at opposite ends of the pole so far as their economic structure was concerned, had a fellow feeling in social matters, since in both districts the working class was the victim of a heartless exploitation and lacked the rudiments of education;

and neither the Andalusian peasant nor the Barcelona factory-hand knew the benefits of the social laws with which a powerful European capitalism, *master of political power* in the progressive nations, induced the labouring classes to embrace the moderate and evolutive doctrines of reformist Socialism. (Obviously, illiteracy and the absence of social insurances also obtained in Castile, but neither of these deficiencies produced as grave effects as in Andalusia and Catalonia, because the system of property was less harsh.)

With good reason did Anselmo Lorenzo in *El Proletariado Militante* attribute the failure of Anarchism in Madrid to the fact that there was no proletariat properly so-called in Castile. But if Anarchism was to make converts, it was not enough—as the general experience in Europe proved—that an industrial proletariat should exist. It was essential that this proletariat should serve an iron capitalism, socially primitive and protected by an unjust State or an unjust and corrupt régime like that of the Restoration.

Although Barcelona came to be the centre of Spanish Anarchism, none of the apostles of Spanish militant Anarchism was a Catalan. Anselmo Lorenzo was not, nor Ricardo Mella—nor was Angel Pestaña. But only in Catalonia and the industrial regions or in those other agrarian regions where tremendous inequality reigned, did their ideas succeed in taking root.

The position of the Andalusian peasant has already been sufficiently emphasized and the success of anarchist doctrines in a medium so propitious to their growth has been explained. Andalusian terrorism was related to the terrorism of Southern Italy, and the Andalusian bandits were a genuine product, like the Calabrian bandits, of a state of social disequilibrium in the land. (It might perhaps be useful to complete the social likeness between Italy and Spain, both in the rural south and in the industrial north, by pointing out in passing that Italy also had an industrial libertarian workers' movement and that the Italian Anarchists who were expelled or had fled from their country continued their terroristic activities in Barcelona.)

The social consequences of the existence of a huge, poverty-stricken agricultural proletariat were the same as those arising out of the existence of an exploited industrial proletariat, as was the European proletariat in the early stages of capitalism when the workers, blinded by despair, turned against the machine.

Catalan capitalism and, in general, the whole of Spanish capitalism, which lagged far behind the rest of Europe in making its appearance, never at any moment surmounted the bronze period of the Iron Age of exploitation. Even in our own times the pitiless exploitation of women and children went on in Spain, as it used to do in English and German factories towards the middle of the nineteenth century.

When the geographical distribution of the Spanish workers' movement could be confirmed with a certain degree of permanency, it was seen that Anarcho-Syndicalism dominated the whole of Catalonia, most of the industrial populations of the Levante, all the Andalusian plains, Gijon, La Felguera and other mining districts of the Asturias, Saragossa and its province, and Galicia—or, to put it in a nutshell, the majority of the industrial centres and the rural districts where poverty was greatest.

The Spanish working class brought to the fore in the twentieth century the social conflicts which Europe had known in the previous century. Spain wanted to have her political revolution without having preceded it by an industrial and commercial revolution; the consequence was she had neither. Hence the tragedy, which was due to the fact that the inevitable course of events forced Spanish society to run counter to the logic of history.

But let us resume the thread of our discourse. It should be repeated that the industries of Catalonia and the Basque Provinces were, as it were, excrescences on an essentially agrarian nation governed by a landed oligarchy. In such a state of things, it was inevitable that the countryside should gravitate socially towards the industrial zones, disgorging into them a poverty-stricken, unemployed mass, a cheap peonage, which knocked at the doors of the factories ready to work for any wages it could get. The landless labourer was attracted to the industrial cities as the moth is attracted to the candle; and his ignorance and need, coming into harsh contact with such an implacable force as nineteenth-century capitalism, made him an Anarchist. The economic livelihood of the industrial worker was constantly menaced by this multitude of potential blacklegs. The same thing happened in the building trade, in the ports and the mines. These illiterate, hungry labourers, migrating from the rural districts, were the leaven of Anarcho-Syndicalism. For their part, the employers adjusted their ideas on the value of labour to the known social reality; they could exploit the worker to their heart's content, since there was always a multitude of proletarians willing to work for less. This was precisely Karl Marx's industrial army of reserve, which in Europe had practically ceased to exist thanks to social insurance. But in Spain there is hardly need to point out that the industrial army of reserve, as in nineteenth century Europe, was permanently mobilized in the neighbourhood of the factories or begging in the streets.

For the tardy and timid Spanish social legislation could never be compared with the British, French or German social legislation. The *Instituto de Reformas Sociales* and the *Instituto Nacional de Previsión* owed their existence to an overriding need which the rulers—more intent upon preserving order than protecting the poor—could not ignore. But they never went so far as to create a system of unemployment insurance or decent old-age pensions for retired workers, or allowances for the orphaned children of the bread-winner, however many dependants he may have had.

The Government did nothing for the unemployed peasant, and when they were compelled to better the lot of the industrial workers, they took their time about it; for, as we know, the oligarchy had a horror of reforms.

There was obviously a superabundance of motives why the proletariat of Barcelona and its suburbs should be led astray into placing a crazy faith in violence. Political factors joined with social factors in converting the illustrious and splendid city into a playground for terrorists.

Terrorism in Barcelona had begun under the Regency, and its main cause undoubtedly was the Catalan question.

In 1892 the Catalan capitalists put the question of regional autonomy formally, for the first time, to the Spanish State. That same year, it will be remembered, the first bomb exploded in Barcelona. Thereafter, the dynamiters accelerated the rhythm of their activities in a horrifying crescendo until it reached white-heat.

On September 23rd, 1893, an Anarchist threw two bombs in the path of General Martínez Campos, while he was riding at the head of his troops on the occasion of a parade through the Gran Vía of Barcelona.

On November 7th of the same year another Anarchist was guilty of a really atrocious crime; he threw two bombs from the gallery of the Liceo theatre in Barcelona into the stalls while the performance was at its height. Fifteen of the audience were killed and many wounded.

At nightfall on Sunday, June 7th, 1896, another bomb exploded among the crowd forming part of the Corpus Christi procession, killing eleven persons and wounding many more, some of them children.

Without interruption, the series of political and social crimes went on in Barcelona, making the reign of Alfonso XIII a melancholy and turbulent period.

An anarcho-syndicalist workers' movement whose fighting weapon was a-political direct action carried the seeds of violence in its bosom. But the repulsive criminality of the terrorism in Barcelona exceeded the limits of class warfare, even in a stubborn industrial medium. The Andalusian peasant led a life of soul-destroying poverty. The workers in the mines and manufacturing centres all over Spain suffered cruel exploitation. That they and others should set their course by Anarchism was not surprising, nor need we seek an esoteric explanation for a perfectly rational phenomenon in the psychopathology of the race. But nowhere was there a social epidemic like the terrorism in Barcelona. It must be referred, therefore, to a specific cause; and that specific cause can only have its roots in separatism, under the leadership of the capitalists. This is borne out by the chronology of events; and it is one of the fundamental factors underlying the anarchist tendencies of Catalan society. However, we shall never be able to say with certainty whether the Catalan worker would have evolved towards a temperate class policy, if the *bourgeoisie* of Barcelona had not been at war with the State. The fact that Basque capitalism was not bound up with separatism no doubt freed that region from the horrors which rent Barcelona; and the same thing happened in the other industrial zones.

The specific terrorism of Barcelona was inherent in the Catalan problem, and it matters little who introduced it. When all is said and done, it was brought about by a complex historical crisis which was not Catalan, but Spanish and nation-wide, and which we shall study in due course.

In 1908 Anarcho-Syndicalism advanced one step farther in the development of its modern organization. The Anarchist Congress held at Amsterdam in the previous year led to the formation of *Solidaridad Obrera*, which celebrated its first regional assembly in Spain in September 1908, 122 associations being represented.

The year 1910 saw the birth of the *Confederación Nacional del Trabajo* and the *Confederación Regional de Cataluña*, entities which were to replace *Solidaridad Obrera*. Anarcho-Syndicalism prospered largely in that portentous shipwreck of justice, of ethics, of the very life of Spain. No proletarian organization dared dispute its control of the masses in Barcelona. It won over the obstinate by violence and killed in embryo with the fractricidal pistol any attempt at trade-union activities which threatened its totalitarian domination. Clearly, irresponsible separatism favoured its development and it seemed as if the capitalists took a delight in the perfidy of keeping the proletariat in a state of permanent exaltation. Thus was formed and grew to maturity a disquieting workers' movement—revolutionary in principles and reactionary in its consequences, martyr and hangman, idealistic and venal. Its violent character offered a vast field of experience to the desperate and the audacious. Its social utopianism seduced the mystics. And as no one was questioned about his antecedents before being enrolled, the *Confederación del Trabajo* was a mixture of the good, the bad, and the indifferent. It was the party of the open door. A proselytizing system which was so free of prejudice and caution was bound eventually to make Spain the only country in the world where the tribe of rogues and vagabonds could find sanctuary, in time of need, in a respectable working-class movement.

In the epileptic vicissitudes of Spanish politics, Anarcho-Syndicalism was always an unknown factor. Sometimes it hurried to the polling-booths; at other times it abstained from voting. Now it supported the autonomists of *Solidaridad Catalana* in Barcelona; now it supported Alejandro Lerroux, the official champion of national unity. It was an incalculable movement—drifting masses, without a real leader or a single intellectual value—it was all the same whether they served the revolution or the counter-revolution. And its character as an undependable social force, whose principles and ethical values were built on shifting sand, made the *Confederación* a rich reserve of popular energy to be wooed by the demagogues and the oligarchy.

The conduct of the ruling classes towards the Anarcho-Syndicalists was as unpredictable as that of the movement itself. It certainly did not escape the calculations of the privileged that it would be convenient to preserve this numerous a-political force, which was easy to move or to immobilize as circumstances required, thanks to a swarm of confidential agents and *agents provocateurs*. Accordingly the reactionaries were to practice a strange policy with that libertarian host, alternating flattery with the most savage repression. And it frequently happened that the oligarchy, in moments of peril, did not despair of using those bewildered multitudes to advantage, egging them on against the rest of the organized proletariat or inciting them to revolutionary action when disturbances least suited the interest of the workers.

Nor was it rare to see middle-class demagogues followed by an escort of Anarchists.

There in the public square was this negative, opaque force, called upon—sometimes with success, sometimes without— to decide the fate of democracy. The existence of a corrupt *plebs* fighting in the forefront of the political scene is inseparable from the régime of the degenerate oligarchy and aristocracy.

I will now conclude my description of the Socialist movement.

Socialism and those workers' organizations which owed their inspiration to Socialism had also advanced since the beginning of the century.

In the General Election of 1901 the Socialists polled 4,500 votes in Madrid. Seventy-three groups were represented at the Socialist Congress at Gijon in September of the following year. But certain workers' organizations still continued to be incorporated in Republicanism, since eighty-two delegates were present at the meeting of *Unión Republicana* in 1903. The Socialists celebrated their first electoral victory in November 1905 when the municipalities were reformed. Three Socialists, Pablo Iglesias, Ormaechea and Largo Caballero, were elected to the Madrid Town Council.

At the same time, the *Unión General de Trabajadores* was adding to its numbers. In 1890 it consisted of 7 sections and 2,000 members, and in 1908, 138 sections and 5,000 members. In 1912 the progress was still more marked, with 360 sections and 137,000 members.

The Socialist Party was developing more slowly, as befitted a political organization. But the half-dozen deputies, more or less, who represented it in Parliament when the reign of Alfonso XIII was already well advanced, were enough, if not to influence the voting, at least to cause a breeze in the oligarchic holy of holies with undoubted effect.

This party was born in the printing-offices, the workshop of the intellectual aristocracy of the proletariat. The staff-officers of Spanish Socialism, with certain exceptions, like that of the famous scientist Jaime Vera and the ex-plasterer Largo Caballero, were the typographers. The leader of the movement, Pablo Iglesias, was a typographer. This broad-browed, blue-eyed artisan, with his clear intelligence, incorruptible moral character and stubborn will, was the personification of the popular Spanish genius, of everything that was noble, vigorous and fairminded in the soul of the people. Iglesias was a man of action, a self-made man, who had imbibed a philosophy of history, set himself to observe four principles of social ethics, and launched a young political force, which was all the more necessary in Spain since the oligarchy was virtually without opposition.

Socialism encountered the same difficulties in Spain as Liberalism had done. Marxism came to a nation without a proletariat properly so-called, just as the principle of universal suffrage had been introduced a century before among a people without a middle class. Pablo Iglesias' mission lay exclusively in creating a regenerating and constructive movement; and this he fulfilled to perfection. He could not do more, and fate willed that he should not do less. The completion of the work, the wise use of that pent-up energy, fell to his successors. Iglesias' merit lay in having carried out the task with an illiterate, scattered and poverty-stricken proletariat. To put in motion a working-class political machine in France, England or Germany was an easy task, since the crowding of the proletariat into the great factories, the over-population of the cities and a better standard of education, meant that a practically ready-made movement was to hand. But Pablo Iglesias created a great party by writing in his own hand to every member by name. Thousands of letters came from his pen. Simple, paternal letters in which he exalted ethical values above everything. For the founder of Spanish Socialism had the temperament of a school-master, a teacher; and the people, conscious of this, called him not leader or *caudillo*, but *Maestro*.

The medium in which the first Spanish Socialists worked could not have been more hostile to political and social creation. On the one hand was the oligarchy: on the other, the anarchism which was latent in the living conditions of the Spanish proletariat—two negative and sterile forces, strongly resisting the advance of an organization with opposing aims.

Towards 1912 the Socialist Party and the *Unión General de Trabajadores* already had considerable weight in public life. Socialism had brought a new note into the tonelessness of the national policy. Spain was now shaking off the apathy into which the catastrophes of the end of the century had plunged her. There was entering upon the scene a disciplined proletariat which called itself, with childish pride, *consciente*. The Republicans received from this powerful solvent on the Left the stimulus they required. A gust of revivifying and refreshing wind cut across the gross pessimism of the oligarchy and the indolent scepticism of the middle class. The Socialists joined in the struggle against the oligarchy with a lively emotion which was lacking in the historic radical parties. There is no doubt that it was Pablo Iglesias, with his militant example and his inexhaustible activity, who shook up the dormant spirit of Republicanism. The dynamic nature of the proletarian force, its affirmative gesture, its implicit faith in the destinies of Spain, were reflected in a subdued middle class which had not only been infected by the grave-diggers of Spain with a disheartening pessimism, but, as we have had occasion to observe, were incapable of acting on their own initiative. Spain owes, therefore, to the Socialist Party the awakening of civic conscience in the proletariat and the re-emergence of the middle class in the ranks of the fighters. And this, in itself, was already a real revolution in a society which believed in nothing.

CHAPTER VIII

## JOAQUÍN COSTA

We have now arrived at the point in our history where our attention is claimed by the noble and extraordinary figure of Joaquín Costa, whose passage through Spanish politics and culture has left an imprint of originality worthy of the man who saw with most lucidity the problems of his country.

Don Francisco Giner de los Ríos, Pablo Iglesias and Joaquín Costa deserve to be called the founders of the new Spain. Each of them had his own personality. They could not be compared, because they were made up of heterogeneous values, though complementary one of the other. None was superior or inferior to the other two, and contemporary Spain owes the possibility of her salvation to the three of them.

But in this educational and revolutionary triad, the most universal and ambitious rôle fell to Costa.

Don Joaquín Costa Martínez (1846–1911) came from Monzón, a small village in Upper Aragon. The firstborn of a family of humble farmers, he was destined in the nature of things to follow in his father's footsteps in the battle of the land. His home was the typical home of the poor rural smallholders, that immense legion of the Spanish countryside which, as we shall see later, only earned a few hundred pesetas a year more than the landless labourer.

From his childhood Costa had a thirst for knowledge, and that spurred him on to seek new horizons. When still very young, he revealed himself as a man of action and of many studies. At the age of seventeen he entered the employ of Don Hilarión Rubio, an architect of Huesca, for whom he worked in exchange for board and lodging. By day Costa was a builder's

158

or a soapmaker's labourer; at night he studied for a degree, devoured whatever books came his way, and wrote. He had a passion for writing. He sent articles on agriculture to the local Press. He began to compose a treatise on this subject which was one of those dear to his heart. In 1867 he wrote a book on Christian Doctrine and one on Sacred History. He went to Paris as a workman employed on the Exhibition. He took his degree, and entered the ranks of the teaching profession as *maestro superior*—always without throwing off the poverty which was to dog his footsteps till quite late in life.

Costa, a prolific writer, lacked money to buy paper. He had no suitable clothes or shoes to go to Madrid where he could pursue the studies which he continued to extend by dint of perpetual demands on the purses of his long-suffering relations and friends. A man with a true love of learning, he was thorough in everything he took up—Law, History, Ethnology, Geography, Botany, Zoology, Mechanics, Mathematics, and so on. His talents soon attracted the attention of scientific and literary circles in Madrid.

But the prodigy from Aragon suffered from a congenital malady, a progressive primitive myopathy. He had a giant's frame with the hands and feet of a child—tiny, weak feet which could hardly support his body. He inherited the malady from his mother's side of the family, the Martínez. He had a noble and virile countenance, expressive of the prodigious intellect within. At the time when he began to conceive his projects for the regeneration of Spain, suffering had not yet begun to cloud his life—only his left arm had atrophied.

Costa was slow in invading the political scene as a combatant. His first vision of the Spanish problem was dominated, like that of almost all the reformers of that epoch, by an obsession with social education. The priest and the teacher—he thought in 1869—ought to unite in the same function of educating the people. His reaction to the Republic of '73 was unfavourable; he was one of those who said: "This is not what is wanted." The personal quarrels between Republicans made him angry. He condemned the hostility which Salmerón displayed towards Castelar and admired the latter as a politician (though he changed his mind later) because he ruled with the firmest hand. Already Costa was thinking as the leader of the "neutral classes", as he always called the middle class. The form of government did not worry him. His ideal was revolution brought about by the firm hand of the Government, without too much thinking about it. In March 1875 he called on Salmerón, whom he thought

"a politician who did not measure up to the needs of Spain"
He found the Republican leader "as pessimistic and sceptical
as Giner. He who feels he lacks the necessary strength", com-
ments Costa, "let him retire, like the great captains of Rome
in the war against Numantia; there would not be lacking a child,
a Scipio, to say: 'I dare'". Salmerón told Costa that the Aragonese had always distinguished themselves for their political talent.
Costa agreed; "and hoped to prove it", he said.

Costa already had his plans for reform ready. He thought
he could do what the Republicans had not been able, or had
not known how to do. A man intoxicated by patriotic ambition,
he was ready to dare.

His evolution from Catholicism to rationalism had been rapid.
He revered Giner and Salmerón as professors. He became a
Krausist and taught Political Law and Spanish History in the
*Institucion Libre de Enseñanza.*

In 1888 he became a notary, practising first at Jaen and
six years afterwards setting up an office in Madrid.

Up till 1890 he had studied and observed and ordered his
life with a fixed goal in view. Now he was going to throw himself
into the fight.

In 1896 he agreed to stand as parliamentary candidate for
Barbastro, as an agrarian. All the wrongs of that beggared
middle class, oppressed by the oligarchy, palpitated in Costa's
electoral programme and speeches. He aspired to be the representative of the commercial classes, and round them he hoped
to group all that was sanest in Spain, all good patriots, in order
to carry out the revolution. That moment saw the beginning
of the rebellion of the Spanish middle class, led by Costa,
which we reviewed in a previous chapter. In his electoral
campaign, Costa demanded that markets should be opened up
for agricultural produce, especially the French market for wines,
that agricultural credits should be made available, that the
sale of the village *bienes de propios* should be suspended, that social
security should be established, social insurances and pensions
for farmers and farm-labourers, and for artisans and traders
throughout the nation, and that the mercantile interests of
Spain should receive close and sustained attention. He wanted,
in short, to create that "merchant aristocracy" which accomplished the revolution in Europe, to remodel Spain on European
lines in the economic sphere.

All this was a challenge to the oligarchy and Costa did not
receive enough votes to be elected to Parliament. The local
*caciques,* once in the service of Cánovas, now in Sagasta's, saw

to it that the Government candidate, a fusionist, was returned.

The Aragonese statesman was not discouraged, but he was enraged with his countrymen who had voted for the fusionist candidate. He regretted not being able to enter Parliament where he might have helped to bring the Cuban war to a prompt and decorous close.

With Pi y Margall, Pablo Iglesias and the men of the *Institucion Libre de Enseñanza* he prophesied a colonial disaster, and when all was lost in the conflict with the United States, he coined his famous phrase: "The sepulchre of the Cid ought to be double-locked", that is to say, no more military adventures. It is an expression that will last, like his motto: "School and Larder."

Costa now aimed at creating a national party, to be the organ of the revolution, based on the neutral classes. He began by founding the *Cámara Agrícola del Alto Aragón* (Chamber of Agriculture of Upper Aragon) and the *Liga de Contribuyentes de Ribagorza* (League of Ribagorza Taxpayers). On November 13th, 1898, he issued a fiery manifesto to the "Chambers of Agriculture and Commerce, trade unions, guilds, centres and clubs of farmers, industrialists, traders, etc." demanding instant revolution from the seat of government in order to save Spain. In February of the following year his ideas bore fruit in the Assembly at Saragossa and the *Liga Nacional de Productores* was born. In January 1900 another assembly at Valladolid gave birth to the *Unión Nacional*. Costa had already dedicated himself to the service of the nation in a titanic struggle with difficulties of all kinds—not the least of which arose out of the weakness of the middle class.

He believed that the solution was to unite "the economic and intellectual classes" and to place them "on the path of frank and exclusive patriotism, without party labels, putting the country first and foremost". When the movement was a going concern, they would demand power from the Crown, form a government of the middle class and begin the national regeneration by "fostering production and education".

Costa found a sympathizer in Cardinal Cascajares, who wrote him a letter of encouragement. The famous cleric approached the Queen Regent on his behalf, who suggested that Costa should form a Government on condition that he shared the power with Gamazo, that is, with the oligarchy. This would have tied the hands of the reformer; and it is not beyond the bounds of possibility that it was done with a view to corrupting him. But Costa saw in Gamazo one of the authors of Spain's ruin and he rejected the offer with scorn.

Through the intervention of the Ateneo of Madrid, Costa began to collect materials for a report on "Oligarchy and Caciquism as the actual form of government in Spain, the necessity of changing it and the means whereby this may be done". There were few, however, who dared to collaborate, for the same reasons as the author did not succeed in imposing cohesion on the "neutral classes". Who would venture to defy the omnipotent oligarchy?

Costa's genius lay in his diagnosis of the national sufferings, in his historical identification of the reigning system of government in Spain (which no one had grasped before him) and in his crystal-clear perception of the fatal road along which Spain was being pushed under the oligarchic form of government. His vision was all the more acute since in that general state of stupefaction at the beginning of the century, everyone was inclined to think of Spain as a country with a Constitution. This danger did not escape Costa, and he called his countrymen's attention to the fact that the country was being attacked by a malady like the one he suffered from—progressive paralysis. He recommended "a surgical policy". The conduct of the Republicans exasperated him, because they were acting "as if Spain had a normal and regular government, like Belgium or England".

The Spanish parties, in fact, tended to align themselves on the European model and to work with programmes copied from their equivalents outside Spain. And the risk obviously was that they would forget that Spain was bleeding to death from a haemorrhage which had been going on for more than a century.

Costa failed in his design to found a great national movement with a limited and concrete programme of instant salvation. The "neutral classes" did not exist as independent social nuclei outside four great centres of population. The impotence of the mercantile classes was thrown into relief. Spain continued to be without a middle class. In 1914 the working population represented 39·1 per cent of the inhabitants, a lower figure than in the rest of Europe where the proportion of the working population in the *bourgeois* nations varied between 42·7 per cent and 51·5 per cent. Spaniards engaged in commerce and transport amounted to only 4·2 per cent of the working population, as against 7·4 per cent in Italy, 17·3 per cent in Holland and 23 per cent in England.

It should be remarked that the *bourgeoisie* was ruling in Europe, while in Spain it still had not a single representative in the Government and not even a political party, since the Republican philosophers, obsessed by anti-clericalism and other non-essentials, were very far from troubling their heads over commercial grievances.

The Catalan *bourgeoisie* was represented in politics, but though active and clamorous, its voice did not affect governmental decisions, apart from tariff reform.

Costa decided to go ahead with his plans, not only because he looked to the middle class for more efficiency than could be expected from the Republican parties, but also because he considered it to be a governing force. And he failed in everything; first, because he was an invalid, then because there was no vigorous *bourgeoisie* in Spain, and lastly, because there was a lack of trained men who could appreciate as he did the real historical situation of the nation. Costa saw the Spanish problem in its transcendental proportions; and as long as he could fight against his muscular atrophy, he did not despair of being the man to lead the national movement which was to bring down the oligarchy.

In the early days of the present century, Costa had still not abandoned the hope that the oligarchy itself would throw off its sloth and take a hand in the most pressing reforms.

In the end, the Aragonese reformer joined the Republicans and with him went his colleagues of the *Cámara del Alto Aragón*. Renouncing the formation of his ideal party, he brought his plan of government to the *Unión Republicana*. He knew quite well that Spain could not be a democracy founded on party politics. The first Republican experiment taught him that liberty stifled revolution. He had then begun to train himself for government, his plan being to "rule like a Cromwell, perhaps for ten years, until Spain was cured of her ills". He ended by hating Parliament, because under the oligarchy he thought it an infamous dictatorship which made a mock of the country, and under the revolution the greatest obstacle to reforms. After his electoral defeat in 1896, he swore never to sit in the Cortes. In 1903 he was elected deputy for Madrid, Saragossa and Gerona, but he did not take his seat in the Chamber. He had told Salmerón not to count on him for the Cortes. He was pleased by the attention, "but for me", he declared, "the elections and Parliament are two infamous jokes at the expense of the nation, in which I refuse to collaborate and which I much regret I cannot stop".

Costa had placed what little political faith remained to him in a rejuvenated Republicanism. But he had no illusions. He saw the poverty of the movement, and that, in his eyes, increased the importance of the leadership, which could only be filled by a really great man. He considered himself already incapable of this. Illness had crippled him. "My physiology—I say nothing of my psychology—is incompatible with these things", he murmured.

The clarity with which Costa discerned the causes of the nation's prostration made his illness more tragic. Chained to his armchair, he suffered, in a manner of speaking, the torments of Prometheus. A man of action immobilized by his disease, the Aragonese thinker was in despair. Spain could not defer her regeneration. Even if the revolution tarried only a little, thought Costa, it would arrive too late. Things were going in such a way that the Spanish Republicans would have no country in which to found a Republic, nor the Socialists a nation in which to make Socialism a reality. With the opposition parties disunited and separated by diverse ideals, who could guarantee that Spain would not disappear before his party was given the opportunity of governing with its own men and its own programme? Costa had this obsession—to unite and to act with all speed, as if he contemplated, with a vision which the others lacked, the complete process of the ruin of Spain in our time.

And in fact, the Spanish civil war of the nineteenth century had gained in profundity; now there was, over and above everything else, the struggle between the prosperous regions and Castile. The Basque Provinces and Catalonia, which had flown the Spanish flag in the Carlist wars, which had fought for a *Spanish* monarchy, despite its absolutist flavour, were falling rapidly into the hands of newly formed nationalist parties. Where a few years before the loudest hurrahs had been for Spain—that is, for the old Spain—now both the old and the new were execrated. The nation was falling apart, dying as a moral association because of the misgovernment of the oligarchy. This was the root of every problem. The restoration of the oligarchy had perpetuated the agrarian question, the agrarian question had led to caciquism and political corruption as the norm of power, and political corruption, together with the brutal affirmation of agrarian interests in the national economy, had exalted nationalism in the regions where capitalism and a wealthy middle class reigned.

It was a thousand pities that Costa did not enjoy perfect health; for no other Spaniard of his epoch was, like him, at once an intellectual, a man of action, a politician of genius and a fervent patriot.

In 1904, Costa was already persuaded that the Republican movement had no future, and, throwing over the Party, he retired to Graus. His malady grew worse, and he practically abandoned politics. He died in 1911. He left an enormous literary output, almost all of it on subjects hitherto little studied in Spain.[1]

CHAPTER IX

# FALL OF THE OLIGARCHY

WE HAVE SEEN the birth, development and system of government of the landed oligarchy, a conglomeration of men and social groups whose economic power since the middle of the nineteenth century was sufficient to impose a given political régime on the Spanish nation. The oligarchy built its police State on a system of outrageous inequality and, with an added touch of sarcasm, called it constitutional. Not only did it deny the people bread—it denied them also education. It corrupted everything—both persons and things—that could be corrupted. It waged war without quarter on commerce and industry. It lost the last jewels in the Spanish Empire's crown. It provoked

---

[1] The complete works of Joaquín Costa fill more than forty volumes. The English reader might like to know the titles of the more important works of this great Spaniard and so get some idea of his encyclopaedic knowledge of the questions which interested him and his extraordinary activity, little short of miraculous in a man affected by progressive paralysis. I hope that by enumerating here the works of Costa I shall add to what I have already written an important guide to the knowledge of his anxieties and preoccupations on Spanish affairs.

ON AGRICULTURE: *A Well-balanced Agriculture. Hydraulic Policy. Forestry and the Nation. The Land and the Social Question. Agrarian Collectivism in Spain.*

ON LAW: *The Life of the Law. Theory of Legal Action, Individual and Social. Legal and Political Studies. The Common Law and Popular Economy of Spain. The Problem of Ignorance of the Law. Outline of a History of Spanish Law in Antiquity. Problems of Aragonese Law.*

ON POLITICS: *Reconstitution and Europeization of Spain. Oligarchy and Caciquism as the Actual Form of Government in Spain. A Surgical Policy. Spain's Political Crisis (The Sepulchre of the Cid Double-locked). Spanish Commerce and the African Question. Nations under Tutelage in History. Regeneration and Social Tutelage. Geographical Policy. The Seven Standards of Government. Spanish-Moroccan Policy. The National Pessimism.*

ON EDUCATION: *Teacher, School and Country.*

ON HISTORY AND FOLKLORE: *Spanish Popular Poetry and Celtic-Spanish Mythology and Literature. Iberian Studies. The Religion of the Celtiberi. The Last Pagan God. "Islas libicas": Ciranis, Cerne, Hesperia. The Country of Viriato. Spanish Guinea.*

separatism in the regions which it could not dominate. It set out to conquer Morocco and only reaped failure and disaster, paving the desert with the bones of brave soldiers who deserved a better fate. Ignorant and sceptical itself, it served a frivolous and morally negligible monarchy. Avaricious and indifferent to the sufferings of the poor, it never felt any stirrings of charity. Its piety was hypocrisy; it believed in nothing. It did not know how to be sincere without cynicism. It came to put an end to the *pronunciamientos* and had to bow down in submission to the Army. It set out to defend the sovereignty of the Spanish State and ended up as a base satellite of the Vatican. It claimed to safeguard the civil power against the clerics and surrendered to a clergy without law. In short, it was the worst régime that any nation could endure, a system of national liquidation: the State supported on two infamous pillars—terrorism and corruption.

We are now about to witness the fall of the oligarchy. For it was written that this régime could not continue. Either the oligarchy fell, or Spain fell. The nation could not endure any longer. It was in the nature of things that the Restoration parties should disintegrate and die, destroyed by their own vices. And for the same reason, the victims of the system were mutually drawing together and forming a heterogeneous front of all colours—proletariat, Army, traders, industrialists, Republicans, Monarchists. The national movement against the absolute oligarchy was a historical necessity. It had been unconsciously forming ever since Cánovas and Sagasta declared war on all the sane and progressive forces of the nation. Costa's idea of a *Unión Nacional* had not perished, for it was more than an idea— it was a vital need. The union which had been taking shape since then was a spontaneous *rapprochement*, imposed by society's instinct for self-preservation. The Restoration institutions had to fall, as all worm-eaten things fall—crumbling away bit by bit.

In the process of the régime's decomposition, the wars acted as a powerful solvent. These hurricanes of death were what was needed to sweep away the rotten edifice. The colonial wars, the Moroccan war, the World War, shook the oligarchic sanctuary to its foundations.

The European war of 1914 did not make Spain a belligerent country, but two countries. The nation was split in half. The Right were germanophile, the Left francophile. Thanks to this equilibrium, Spain was spared the cataclysm. But no one could guarantee that the cataclysm would spare Spain. That world-wide violence had its repercussions in the Peninsula, creating

166

a multitude of new problems which the rulers obviously did not know how to solve. Bread and other essentials of life were scarce. The people rebelled. There were innumerable strikes and a recrudescence of terrorism, now made more complicated and obscure by espionage. The oligarchy could not cope with such an imbroglio. And these were the men who wanted a quiet life, to keep Spain standing still while they sat feasting at their groaning board, as Joshua commanded the sun to stand still until he had finished the battle with the Amorites! The revolution was marching on.

While the nations were fighting in Europe, the social classes were fighting in Spain. There were days when the casualties were higher in Spain than on the Western Front. In Spain, not a day passed without bringing something new. The proletariat, the commercial classes and the middle classes of Catalonia and the Basque Provinces were in a perpetual state of rebellion. The Spanish revolution, the national revolution against the landed oligarchy, was to come to a head in 1917, a year which was not only historic for Russia.

An unexpected event (unexpected in so far as anything could be unexpected in a nation where anything was now possible)— the rebellion, not of the Army, but of *the military middle class*, broke the sluices which were precariously holding back the revolutionary torrent.

It was not, I repeat, a *pronunciamiento*. The soldiers who organized themselves into the *Juntas de Defensa*, or kind of officers' trade unions, of 1917, did not aspire to govern, nor did they profit by the weakness of the civil power to take the lead in politics. They were the uniformed middle class, the infantry, the foot-soldiers, who also felt they could endure no more. Their protest was as legitimate as that of the capitalists, the traders, the employees and the proletariat. They were spurred on by their interests as an oppressed class. The Army was one more victim of the reigning system of government and took its place in the sum total of social classes and elements which longed for a radical change, a revolution. It was as simple as that.

The immediate origin of the military movement must be sought in the autonomy enjoyed by the Crown in its relations with the Army. The monarchy, whose military character grew more apparent every day, had escaped from the control of the oligarchy. Under Alfonso XIII the monarchy was to the end an independent power, offspring of the ruling class, yet divorced

167

from it. The King carried on a policy of his own, at his own risk and peril. This grave irregularity can only be understood if we do not forget that the ascendancy of the oligarchy over institutions and social classes was merely physical. Where force was ineffectual, deference disappeared; and those institutions which could only be subdued by moral suggestion were left to do more or less as they pleased.

The King's predilection for Army matters and his scheme to guard against perils which undoubtedly existed, since the oligarchy was incapable of defending anything but its own property, led him to persevere in wooing the Army. The Monarch was creating his own military force, his armed party, against the hour of crisis which he saw was coming.

Alfonso was not acting solely as nominal head of the armed forces, but as permanent Minister, in practice, of War and Marine. He therefore always insisted that the heads of these Departments should be persons who enjoyed his full confidence, figureheads resigned to a purely decorative rôle.

The Moroccan war was a splendid occasion for the King to make his personal power over the Army amply felt, often even in the direction of the military operations.

By a Royal Decree of January 15th, 1914, he authorized the generals, Army chiefs and officers to communicate directly with him, stressing the precept that "the King may intervene directly and constantly in anything concerned with his troops, as well as in appointments to commands and the promotion of officers".

In his hands, the prerogative to distribute honours and promotions became a fount of privileges for the Palace favourites, members of the military party. And where the injuriousness of the system was most clearly reflected was in the infantry. For the aristocratic branches of the Army, the artillery and the cavalry had had from of old their *Juntas de Defensa*, which watched over the interests of the Corps. Thanks to a rigid system of promotion, advancement was determined by years of service and there was less room for bastard glory.

The mere fact of being a soldier was sufficient to assure, in principle, the regard of the Crown. But the King's favourite was an artillery officer, the Marqués de Viana. The infantry officers, whose career was less costly and who were drawn rather from the ranks of the middle class than from the aristocrats and landed oligarchy, complained that they had to take a back seat. For a long time, they were refused permission to set up their *Juntas de Defensa*. The award of medals and promotions

168

for the Moroccan campaigns sowed unrest among the infantry, because it seemed that inefficiency and negligence were being openly rewarded.

The military leaders of the 1917 movement fixed the blame, not on the Crown (though they were really rising against the Palace military party), but on the oligarchy. And this would not have shown bad judgment on their part, had their passing over the person immediately responsible been due to high motives of policy and not adhesion to the monarchy.

The infantry's *Junta de Defensa* was set up in Barcelona, and on June 1st, 1917, the conspirators sent the Captain-General a document in which their wrongs and aspirations were set forth. Among other things they declared: "Not only the infantry, but the cavalry and the artillery are resolved that from henceforth only justice and equity shall prevail in the Army; they confirm their determination to assert their personality in order to defend and further their interests, renewing their most sacred oath on their banners and standards, that these interests are not egoistic and individual, but the sacred interests of the country for which they have been subjected and resigned for so many years to all kinds of sacrifices, even that of dignity since the disastrous end of the colonial campaigns. . . . Politicians who have wielded the supreme power have confessed on various occasions, some before the Cortes, some before the country, that our sacrifice has been useless, since those sources of wealth or of national life have not been regenerated. The administration has not improved and the Army is absolutely disorganized, despised and disregarded in its vital needs: (1) 'In its moral needs', which produces a lack of inner satisfaction and stifles enthusiasm; (2) 'In its professional or technical needs', through the absence of military knowledge, which there are no means of acquiring, through the lack of unity of doctrine to direct it, and the lack of material to carry out its ends; (3) 'In its economic needs', since officers and men are treated worse than in any other country and are even worse off than civilians in analogous circumstances in their own country."

The *Junta* was arrested and imprisoned in Montjuich.

But the oligarchy had no moral or material means of stifling this insurrection and had to set the prisoners free, recognizing the *Juntas* and approving their Regulations. It might have seemed that the Army was once more invading politics, in the old style, but anyone who studied the phenomenon with attention would perceive its special characteristics. For instance, one highly significant feature was that the rebellion was being led by a colonel—not a general—Don Benito Márquez, a Liberal who, months afterwards, when he felt the need to rehabilitate himself and when the *Juntas* were losing most of the democratic spirit which had at first animated them, appealed to "all those who in hours of affliction and of hope have dreamed of making a better Spain, to all those officers who, in order to remedy their helplessness, have constituted themselves into *Juntas de Defensa*, to all Spaniards, people and men in public life, to keep alive and vigilant their love of country and of liberty, which is one and the same love".

It is also interesting to note that the man who, six years later, was to lead the classic *pronunciamiento*—General Primo de Rivera—was hostile to the *Juntas de Defensa* set up by his own corps, the infantry.

The Catalan middle class, led by the capitalists of the *Lliga*, seconded the Army with a public act of rebellion. On June 15th they announced that they proposed to join in the general agitation, reserving, however, their liberty of action. They alleged that "the Cortes was the tool of the King. It was the preserve of the Court, functioning in the shadow of the Royal power. . . . The Spanish people hope to see another path opened, leading to great reforms". The capitalists were not thinking of setting up barricades, but of transforming society by means of a new Parliament. But they could not allow the opportunity of revolt to pass without affirming their revolutionary sentiment, although circumstances imposed on them the moderation inherent in a Conservative class. And once hostilities had broken out, it was to be Catalan capitalism which headed the revolutionary movement, of all the classes which were hostile to the landed oligarchy. Anything else would have violated historical reality.

The revolt began with a meeting of all the Catalan deputies and senators, who sent a note to the Government demanding a new organization of the State and warning them that if their demand was not acceded to they would summon all the senators and deputies of Spain to an Extraordinary Assembly at Barcelona. The Government rejected the demands of the Catalan parties (which, incidentally, had never been more Spanish than at that moment) and stigmatized their threat as seditious.

On July 19th there met at Barcelona sixty-eight deputies and senators of the opposition under the presidency of Don Raimundo de Abadal, one of the notabilities of the *Lliga*. The meeting insisted on the necessity of a Constituent Cortes convened by a government "which embodied the sovereign will of the country". The men who supported the motion were the living symbol of the *rapprochement* of all the oppressed social classes. It would not be untrue to say that Francisco Cambó was the mouthpiece of industrial capitalism; that Melquiades Álvarez, Giner de los Ríos (Don Hermenegildo), Lerroux, Rodés, Roig y Bergadá and Zulueta Gomis were the voice of the middle class, of all the business and professional men; while Pablo Iglesias spoke for the proletariat.

The historical value of the Parliamentary Assembly lay in the fact that it was a national front of classes with contrary and even widely separated economic interests, forced by historical circumstances to agree on the revolution against the State of the landed oligarchy.

The petty *bourgeoisie* wanted to go farther than the Parliamentary Assembly and committed itself more deeply to the revolution by joining with the proletariat in street demonstrations. The Reformist Party[1] had virtually replaced historic Republicanism and, with demagogic Lerrouxism[2] was the only

[1] Profiting by the mistrust of the "neutral classes"—the traders, the intellectuals and the functionaries—for the Republicans, Don Melquiades Álvarez, leader of the Asturian *bourgeoisie* and an orator of great eloquence, founded the Reformist Party. Strictly speaking, Reformism embodied the political doctrine of the men of the *Institución Libre de Enseñanza*, especially that of Don Gumersindo de Azcárate. Pragmatic as far as the form of government was concerned, Reformism aimed at attracting the middle class with an opportunist policy. As a party, it renounced revolution in favour of evolution. From the first moment, its ranks contained distinguished men: Azaña, the Azcárates, Pedregal, Zulueta; and it enjoyed the support of the commercial classes, which were represented at this period by Reformism more satisfactorily than by any other political organization.

[2] Alejandro Lerroux was the Spanish demagogue *par excellence*. An Andalusian from the province of Cordova, leader of the Radical Party, Lerroux came upon the political scene at the close of the nineteenth century, following in the footsteps of Ruiz Zorrilla, whose shoes he stepped into on the death of the latter, as if by transmitting the demagogic leadership from one to the other, the Spanish nineteenth century wanted to prolong itself, despite the Restoration, into the twentieth century. But the pupil outstripped the master in duplicity, in eloquence, and in the art of contracting debts and paying off his creditors by fresh borrowings. Lerroux might without imposture have called himself an Anarchist. But he preferred to remain a Republican, no doubt because he did not want to renounce the opportunities which were open to a turbulent Republican in Spain. To be a Republican was, in the last instance, to be nothing. It did not even necessarily imply hostility to the monarchy, or a desire to replace it by a Republic. This was why Spanish Republicanism housed all kinds of morally insolvent elements as well as revered apostles. Lerroux had grown up, so to speak, in the street, where he learnt everything he knew. It is open to doubt whether he ever read a book from beginning to end in his life, even when in his mature age he became a lawyer by sitting for a parody of an examination at the University of La

existing organization of the political movement of those neutral classes which did not belong to Big Business. The Socialist Party and the *Unión General de Trabajadores*, on the initiative of the Socialists, signed a revolutionary agreement with both groups.

The *Juntas de Defensa* and the Parliamentary Association were regarded by the public as related movements, and so they were in their ultimate motivation. The people looked with sympathy upon the military rebellion and not even the Socialist Party found cause to condemn it in the manifesto they issued over the crisis.

The Socialist Party and its offshoot, the trade-union organization, not only concocted a bilateral agreement with the Republicans, but concluded another one with the Anarcho-Syndicalists. In view of this double relationship of the Socialist Party, the rest of the opposition forces joined the plot.

The proletarian leaders overestimated the effectiveness of the general strike, which in a country like Spain—a nation without an industrial proletariat and with a workers' movement which was still too stunted to do what history required of it—could not be the infallible instrument of victory, as some thought.

The Government of the oligarchy had taken the measure of the workers' activities. They knew that there were bombs waiting to explode. They were not unaware that the revolution was following its course, and they did not, therefore, spare any pains to ensure that the general strike should break out before the preparations were complete.

The Anarcho-Syndicalist leaders having given notice that they could not hold back their followers any longer, the general strike broke out prematurely, on July 19th, at Valencia: whereupon Largo Caballero hastened to Barcelona to try to paralyse the precipitate action of the Anarcho-Syndicalists.

---

Laguna. His education, therefore, had been picked up from newspapers. But he had political intuition, a vivid imagination and knew how to make a glib use of the language of abstractions and generalizations which those who sway the passions of the mob employ. He understood the mind of the masses and played on their emotions with his warm theatrical tones. There was nothing like the Radical Party in Spain. It had no philosophy and no aims. It was strongest in Seville and Barcelona. In these two centres of national desperation, Lerroux attracted a following which consisted of the worst elements of the middle class and the proletariat. There was a certain body of opinion which would follow in the wake of the first great demagogue who presented himself and which fell in behind the Andalusian *meneur*. The Lerrouxist movement was in reality a vulgar imitation of the oligarchy, the moral and political corruption of the régime reflected in the gutter as in a mirror. For the rest, the party contained all kinds of persons, even some respectable ones.

Sporadic and anarchic strikes among the workers were grist to the Government's mill. This was what the oligarchy was looking for.

The insurrection of the proletariat lost its effectiveness through the impatience of the Sorelians. But it broke out in the end, in a general way, on August 13th. The strike was not unanimous, and the leaders had to reckon with important defections, notably that of the railway workers. Nevertheless, it would not be true to say that the revolutionary movement of the working class failed.

None of the acts which were levelled against the régime failed. But the revolution of 1917 could have taken on another aspect had the revolutionary parties had a clearer idea of the crisis, had there been greater courage among the middle class and the capitalists, and a national figure capable of canalizing that patriotic feeling, purging it of dross, and transforming it into a dynamic current. The task was prodigious; and only a really great man could have achieved it. The circumstances, though in all respects favourable, did not produce such a man. What would have happened if a Costa, physically master of himself, had been inside the uniform of Colonel Márquez? Once more a universal leader was lacking. There was no one to embody the collective spirit. Would a like opportunity occur again? The leaders of Big Business were now sitting cheek by jowl with the leaders of the proletariat and the middle class. Shortly afterwards the Catalan capitalists agreed to retire from the Cortes as a protest and entrusted the defence of their parliamentary interests to, among others, Julian Besteiro, the Socialist leader.

Spain went on trying to make her French Revolution. The *bourgeoisie*, hand in hand with the proletariat, was seeking a country which it did not possess, trying to be the nation, to give reality to that name, which every day lost some of its meaning in Spain.

All the manifestoes of the classes which the oligarchy had oppressed revealed in 1917 the same patriotic background. For the moment, all these classes, even the Catalans, abandoned their party programmes, their individual egoisms, merging them in the common aim of securing their own salvation by first saving Spain. The "internationalist" party made the voice of the collective spirit its own, and through the mouth of Pablo Iglesias expressed its desire to "remedy the misfortunes of our country" and to "raise the name of Spain". But that manifestation of the collective conscience was an exaltation and it did not last. A nation, like a human being, cannot stand on tiptoe too long. If there is no one to guide and inspire, to seize the historical "crescendo" in time to prevent regional, class or clan interests from raising their head, patriotic exaltation falls flat and turns to vulgarity, to pettiness, to the sordid egoisms which bring all great causes to defeat.

The uniformed middle class went farther than might have been suspected in demanding political reforms. *Esprit de corps* was at variance with the spirit of disinterestedness and patriotism and deprived the military movement of much of its greatness. The Army was monarchist and it was understandable that it should be so, not only through atavism or through affection for a spontaneously hierarchical form of government, but because of the special character of that monarchy, which gave the armed forces pride of place. But the infantry, which had risen in the first place against the oligarchy, did not forget the responsibility which attached to the Crown and the military party. The rebels were also challenging Alfonso's all-powerful faculties in military matters, and on July 2nd they forced the Government to pass a decree forbidding the Army chiefs and officers of the King's Military Household to hold their posts for more than four years. Even the inner life of the Palace felt the effects of the victory of the *Juntas de Defensa.*

The street revolution found itself up against the Army. The Government were able to employ the latter to quash the general strike without fear of the soldiers fraternizing with the populace. The military *Juntas* realized the inconsequence of their action— on the one hand, they were egging on the people against the oligarchy, while on the other, they were continuing to be the armed fist of the régime. There had been much bloodshed, more in isolated clashes with the armed forces than in pitched battles; and the soldiers' conscience was not clear. They tried to rehabilitate themselves in the eyes of the nation by blaming the Government once more, throwing on them the responsibility for the blood which had been spilt. The truth was that the Army wanted to overthrow the oligarchy, without harming the Crown. In contrast, most of the civilian rebels were acting directly against the throne. For them, the most important thing was to overthrow the King, after which the whole régime would come crashing to earth. If the opposite happened, and the oligarchy was eliminated, the consequences would be the same, for when all was said and done, the oligarchy was the linchpin of the Crown. As events proved, the reign of Alfonso XIII could not long survive the wreck of the political régime, government-by-rotation, faked elections, and so on.

It was, naturally, the successful military rebellion which laid the oligarchy low. The uniformed middle class was armed, and that lent force to its indictment—more so than in the case of the civilian middle classes. The revolt of the barracks could hardly be interpreted this time as a *pronunciamiento,* and the incidents which accompanied it sufficed to show that it was, in fact, something very different.

Melquiades Álvarez, on reading the comminatory protest of the *Juntas,* described it as "sedition triumphant, the natural fruit of an oligarchic policy which has corrupted everything". This was in the early days. Possibly, he did not immediately appreciate the fact that the revolution of the middle class which he was leading was gaining an ally who was going to decide the fall of the oligarchy. Months afterwards, this same Melquiades Álvarez maintained at the meeting of the parliamentary representatives in the Madrid Ateneo that the interests of the *Juntas* were likewise those of the Assembly. And he was right.

Having said all this on the negative factors which conspired against the success of the revolution, we must now turn to the really decisive act—the ultimatum of the military middle class to the oligarchy.

The real proof that the Army was not actuated, in essence, by its interests as a corps was shown by the nature of its political claims. The *Juntas* aspired to legal recognition, which they subsequently acquired. The Government of the oligarchy, under the leadership of Dato, approved their Regulations, giving them the force of law. Accordingly, with the recognition of the instrument which was to produce the improvements demanded by the Army, and with the obeisance of the Government to their sedition, the rebels had triumphed and the natural thing for them to do was to express their gratitude to the Government and retire, satisfied, to their barracks; not still holding aloof from public affairs, but interested, perhaps, in defending the amiable oligarchy against the continued aggressions of the middle class and the proletariat. But things did not work out like that. The *Juntas* were not content with the meagre caste rights they had just acquired. They insisted on putting the final touches to the revolution, which entailed no less than the overthrow of the oligarchic system. The patriotism and generosity of the military movement lay precisely in the obsession to regenerate political life without the direct intervention of the Army in the government of the country. This is what distinguished it fundamentally from the classic *pronunciamientos.* After the strike movement of August had been suppressed by the military, who were thus working against their own interests as an oppressed class, they considered it a point of honour not to leave the perverse régime of the absolute oligarchy standing.

On October 20th the *Juntas* addressed a message to the King, giving him seventy-two hours' grace "to entrust the Government to politicians capable of convening honest elections, and promising that the Army would once more dissolve the Cortes if the latter failed to observe their oath of loyalty to the Monarchy". This threat had no immediate effect. Accordingly, five days later an ultimatum was issued which the Crown could not continue to ignore.

The following day saw the fall of the Dato Government, the last Ministry in the "Box-and-Cox" system initiated forty years before.

The whole framework of the Restoration was crashing in ruins, for the peaceful rotation in the Government of the two great parties which had monopolized the nation, the lords of the great estates, was the cornerstone of the system founded by Cánovas and Sagasta. The monarchy's days were, therefore, numbered, though the soldiers may have thought that the civil death of the oligarchy meant liberation for the imprisoned Crown, and the Army in years to come spared no pains to save the throne.

The Army's zeal to divorce the Crown from the oligarchy was apparent in the approach made to Alfonso XIII in July by Colonel Márquez. "Hasten to carry out the revolution", he advised the King, "and you will have conquered the people, and the Army will applaud you. Do not forget, Sire, that if a king, with the support of his Army and his people, takes up arms against an oligarchy, that king strengthens his Crown; for the hour of monarchies has not yet passed."

Márquez proposed to the King a Government of the widest concentration which would convene the Constituent Cortes. This advice was rejected by the King.

It was about this time that the Catalan capitalists summoned to a meeting at Barcelona all the civilian opposition to the oligarchy. The agreement between the proposals put forward by the military *Juntas* and those drawn up by the delegates assembled at Barcelona was basically complete, and the Cabinet recommended to the King by the Army bore witness to the solidarity of the uniformed middle class with the civilian middle classes. Here are the names: Prime Minister, to be appointed by His Majesty; Interior, General Marvá; War, General Borbón;

Foreign Affairs, Santiago Alba y Bonifaz; Public Works, Agriculture and Commerce, Francisco Cambó; Finance, Urzáiz; Justice, Melquiades Álvarez; Education, Ramón y Cajal; Labour, Torres Quevedo.

That abortive government even contained a Republican name, though not a conspicuous one, and its anti-oligarchic character was not open to doubt. General Marvá had a weakness for social questions and his Liberalism was well known. General Borbón was to be the guarantee of the Cabinet's loyalty to Alfonso. Santiago Alba would be popular with the commercial classes. Cambó and Urzáiz would give satisfaction to the capitalists; Melquiades Álvarez, to the commercial and professional classes and to the intellectuals. The eminent histologist Ramón y Cajal and the famous engineer and mathematician Torres Quevedo set a stamp on the Ministry of intellectual superiority and respect.

As has been said, the King rejected Colonel Márquez' suggestions, refused even to receive his emissary, the chaplain Planas, and the crisis dragged on for some weeks more. Alfonso knew perfectly well that the fall of the oligarchy would leave him suspended, as it were, in a void, with no social force to support his throne. A Constituent Cortes which would have to decide the form of government, that is, which would bring the monarchical principle into question, alarmed him, and he would not even hear the subject mentioned. That would have been revolution, at least where the oligarchy was concerned; but the revolution could not dislodge the oligarchy from the Government without also dislodging the whole scaffolding of the State. Alfonso XIII did not like experiments—with reason; for whenever the Minister of the Interior weakened the device of caciquism, the Republicans triumphed in the great cities. The King perceived, therefore, that honest elections would bring about his certain overthrow. And the risk that free elections would lead to a Republic had already cemented the interests of the Crown and the oligarchy in the common goal of maintaining the traditional political régime. No doubt Alfonso thought that with the first breach in the fortress the garrison would be lost, and, after all, he was the most disputed figure among the defenders.

However, the *Juntas'* ultimatum of October 25th gave no scope for further hesitations or delays. The Army threatened to govern unless a regenerating Government was formed. And on this occasion the King fell back before the spectre of military dictatorship. The *Juntas* intimidated him. They were not the military party, but his antagonists.

On December 3rd, 1917, García Prieto formed the first Coalition Government. The Catalan *bourgeoisie* was represented in the Cabinet by Juan Ventosa, of the *Lliga*, and Felipe Rodés, of the Catalan Nationalist Party, a Republican organization.

Since the days of Amadeo and the Republic, the middle class had had no voice in the Cabinet councils; the *bourgeoisie* properly so-called had been excluded from the direction of the State. What could the new Catalan Ministers—Finance and Education, Costa's "larder and school"—have in common, historically and politically, with the rest of the Cabinet? The victory of the middle class was far from complete. The oligarchy was overwhelmingly predominant in the new Government. But the presence of Ventosa and Rodés was a guarantee that the oligarchy had been subdued, at least politically. The rot had set in and the fabric was crumbling away bit by bit. This Coalition Government was already not the traditional government of the landed oligarchy, uniform in its men and style. The Ministry of the Interior had been given to the Vizconde de Matamala, a judge of the Supreme Court, who until then had kept aloof from politics and now became a Minister for the first time.

But the oligarchy did not despair of being able to save its political skin, and mobilized all its economic power, spending 36 million pesetas on the new elections. Nevertheless, neither the Liberal Party nor the Conservative together obtained their classic parliamentary majority. The middle class, on the other hand, multiplied the number of its deputies. The *Lliga* now had twenty-three.

The García Prieto Government was shortlived. It called itself a regenerating government, and it was. The name was more than a label. With the interruption of the Liberal-Conservative sequence, the pulverization of the oligarchic parties, the regeneration was a fact.

The Coalition Ministry gave way to Maura's National Government of March 21st, 1918, after a dramatic moment of crisis. No one had been able to form a government to the satisfaction of the Army and of the nation, which continued to be in a state of rebellion, The political edifice of the Restoration was hourly disintegrating. Not so much the end of the "Box-and-Cox" system, already a thing of the past, but the end of the State and of the monarchy was foreshadowed in the comings and goings of the King and the politicians, in the agitation of the barracks and in the clamour of the streets. Finally, the National Government was formed. Before anyone could be found to lead it, and before the capitalists and the middle class could be induced to collaborate, the King had to threaten to leave Spain. During the whole of one interminable night, Alfonso concocted with his own hand the list of Ministers. When the new Ministry was formed, the King and the Infanta Isabel "embraced one another, with tears of joy".

Francisco Cambó was made Minister of Public Works, Agriculture and Commerce. Santiago Alba, "a politician of the extreme Left", according to Maura, became Minister of Education.

Alba had begun his political career in Costa's *Unión Nacional*, and had continued to be the more or less official paladin of the commercial classes, among whom his interests lay. He was not a likeable man and had the reputation of being a mischievous politician.

Shortly afterwards the capitalists acquired another Minister in the same Government—Ventosa, Cambó's lieutenant in business and in public life—through the elevation of the *Comisaría de Abastecimientos* (Commissariat of Supplies) to the rank of a Ministry.

As was to be expected, the new Ministers were filled with a burning desire to carry out reforms, and, on the part of the *Lliga* Ministers, not only for the benefit of Catalonia but for the whole of Spain. Cambó threw himself heart and soul into the study of great national economic problems in the search for a remedy. He drew up an ambitious plan of public works, visited the mining regions, proposed the nationalization of public services. Whether these projects hit the mark or not in every detail, it was evident that a new, progressive and alert force had entered the government of Spain.

In the year 1918 Catalonia seemed to have decided to pursue a national policy, to merge her destiny in that of the rest of Spain, as she did in the Peninsular War. It would appear that the expansive nature of capitalism was compelling the leaders of the *Lliga* to accept the historical law which was everywhere urging men of their class to destroy the vestiges of feudalism. In Spain this was for the Catalans a major need, for Catalonia could only be free when the rest of the nation, from whose fate she could not disinterest herself, was free. For the Catalans to turn their backs on the national revolution was equivalent to remaining at war to the end of the ages with the agrarian State. Were the Catalan capitalists choosing at last the path of success and of true independence? As if imbued with a new spirit, the staff officers of the *Lliga* visited other regions of Spain, aiming at creating a sister political movement. Cambó, Ventosa, Abadal, and other personalities of Catalanism, toured Andalusia,

Galicia, the Levante, speaking to the crowds. They wanted another Spain; and so did millions of other Spaniards.

But only the middle class (which did not really exist in the regions visited) could understand Cambó, and the *Lliga's* appeal woke no answering response. It was not speeches that were wanted but revolutionary reforms; and for these reforms to be effective, it was necessary for the anti-oligarchic elements to make themselves master of the Government and to govern dictatorially until a middle class had established its rule throughout the whole nation, as had happened in the rest of the world.

The national campaign of the *Lliga* failed, naturally enough, and the Catalan capitalists were bound to fail also in the Government. The economic power of the oligarchy remained unbroken and the revolution could not be accomplished in open forum.

The other new Minister, Santiago Alba, was not less diligent in suggesting educational reforms, *inter alia*, the grant of autonomy to the Universities, the reorganization of the secondary schools and the Technical Centres, the creation of 20,000 elementary schools, higher pay for teachers, and so on. This programme was also abortive, for the same reasons.

The National Government came to an end on November 6th, 1918, and the causes of its fall are worthy of note.

It was the personal and political incompatibility of the two Ministers who represented respectively industrial capitalism and the mercantile classes which first led to the splitting up of the Cabinet. The reason was that Alba, even discounting whatever personal animosity there may have been in his attitude, had undoubtedly raised the voice of the Spanish commercial classes against the *Lliga* when he tried, in competition with Lerroux, to man a front in Catalonia against separatism.

The conflict of interests between commerce and industry was repeatedly in evidence at the close of the century, because the high tariffs with which the oligarchy had endeavoured to tame the Catalan and Basque capitalists were prejudicial to trade. It was not that industry and commerce were, in principle, incompatible; but that the excessive protection enjoyed by the industries of the north harmed the mercantile economy by practically prohibiting the entry of foreign manufactures at prices which would have made them a commercial proposition in Spain. On top of this, the fact that an industry which enjoyed such protection at the expense of commerce and of the national economy should support an anti-Spanish movement irritated the non-Catalan commercial middle class and added insult to injury.

The resentment of the commercial classes was keen, though hidden, and like other resentments was bound to come to a head with the passing of the mood of collective emotion, which no one knew how to convert into the lever of the national revolution. The serious personal friction between Alba and Cambó, which ended with the former leaving the National Government, foreshadowed the end of the collaboration of the middle classes in the struggle against the oligarchy.

When the whole Ministry fell some days later, the Catalan capitalists returned to the Catalan fold. As was to be expected, Catalan nationalism received a new stimulus, for the moral dispersion of the nation in that crisis of government was being fatally hastened. Now the Catalans were insisting more imperiously than ever on autonomy. Apart from the reasons already mentioned, were there others?

Alba had entered the Government of the mortal remains of the oligarchy which had been formed after the fall of the National Government, and the *Lliga* saw in this a challenge—a threat as serious if not more so, than any homogeneously agrarian government could have been. For Alba was now Finance Minister and held the keys of tariff policy. With Alba in the Government was his friend Roig y Bergadá, a Catalan lawyer, an enemy of the *Lliga* and an exponent of the same policy. For the Catalan capitalists, this was a declaration of war by the traders who, *pari passu* with their official delegates in the Government (Alba was working on the reform of the taxation system) were noisily demonstrating their disapproval of Catalanist policy in the street.

And if the *Lliga* looked upon the commercial middle class as its chief enemy—a point of view which was to lead them into a fresh surrender to the landed oligarchy—the commercial classes, in their turn, now tended to regard the Catalan industrialists as more dangerous rivals to their class than the landowners. With the frustration of the national revolution, the inevitable had happened—Spain had fallen into the most stupid vulgarity.

The *Círculo de la Unión Mercantil* of Madrid announced the organization of a *Liga Nacional* which was to have as its motto: "With political liberty, tariff liberty and equality of taxation." The Madrid *Cámara Oficial de la Industria* followed suit with the demand that, if autonomy was granted to Catalonia, "a fiscal frontier" should be fixed "as compensation to the other provinces for the privileges extended to Catalonia in the last thirty years".

The National Government was a real revolution inasmuch as it shook the oligarchic system of government-by-rotation. But it could go no farther. It was too heterogeneous for it to be able to transform the nation, and without a reformist leader in supreme command the monstrous coalition of great landowners, industrialists, traders, autonomists, centralists, etc., was bound to dissolve in the first heat of discussion.

This conflict of interests which sometimes united the *Lliga* with the oligarchy against the commercial classes, and at other times united the commercial class with the oligarchy against the Catalan industrialists, now took on exceptional proportions, like all the other conflicts, because of the state of anarchy into which the country had fallen. With a disintegrating political régime and a State in ruins, the civil war developed into a free fight for all.

This was the state of affairs at the time of the fall of Maura's National Government. What came after was a social deluge.

The Cánovist and Sagastine fossils tried to govern, in a sterile longing to repair the device of the *turno*, or government-by-rotation. Legal equilibrium, either real or sham, existed no longer. The oligarchy continued to atomize itself politically. In order to keep itself in power, it had to employ more brute force every day. This is when chaos really began. The last glimmerings of law died out, and the State, in its impotence, delegated to the riff-raff, which it armed, the functions of judge and hangman. The oligarchy's death agony was an awesome spectacle. Under the terroristic command of General Martínez Anido in Barcelona, law suffered a total eclipse, delinquency was put down with delinquency, political crime with political crime. Darkness closed over Barcelona and blotted it out.

From 1918 to 1923, Spain lived in a frenzied state of social violence. Twelve Governments and three Parliaments came and went. It was anarchy which led nowhere, more terrible than the anarchy of revolutions, because the instinct for self-preservation which breeds revolutions seemed to have died in Spanish society.

The gun of the assassin ruled in the street, and Spain, as in the worst moments of her history, fully justified the line of the English poet:

> "A Land
> Where law secures not Life."

Those bankrupt Governments could not count on sufficient votes in Parliament to keep themselves in office. "We shall not last more than eight or ten days, because we can only count on forty votes", said Count Romanones when he formed one of such Cabinets.

He would be dull-witted who did not foresee that those institutions which had not yet fallen were doomed to complete destruction. Of all the political apparatus of the Restoration, only the monarchy remained standing. Its situation was desperate in the extreme, for it had no support to lean on. The King realized the danger the Crown was in, and cast about for a means to save it. He thought of a régime of organized force to act as a barricade against the oligarchy and the Republicans, both of whom he considered his enemies, the first because of their corruption and ineptitude, the second, on principle.

On May 23rd, 1921, the King made a speech at Cordova disparaging the parliamentary system. He implored the people to support "their King", so that the country might have a Government. The last hope of the throne was the Army; not the Army of the *Juntas de Defensa* now trivially engaged in the petty politics of the corps and on the point of dissolution, but the Conservative Army, the Army of the Palace military party, the Army of the generals who had ideas on how Spain ought to be governed and who hated the politicians.

A fresh military catastrophe in Morocco plunged the monarchy into a new crisis. General Fernández Silvestre's reckless action, encouraged by the negligence of the General Staff and the enthusiastic personal intervention of Alfonso, wiped out all the progress Spanish arms had made in the last twelve years, and the Moors were now at the gates of Melilla. The details of the disaster were horrifyingly macabre and a cry of grief and protest went up from the nation. And when the personal responsibility of the King became clear to the public mind, the precarious existence of the monarchy took on already the tints of sunset.

The defeat of the Spanish Army in Africa expedited an historical process which arose out of the nature of the national crisis. The chaos in Spain was more than enough to overthrow the monarchy, and the military dictatorship—now that the street revolution was in its death-throes—was the immediate solution imposed, on the one hand, by the power still enjoyed by the Crown and, on the other hand, but what still remained of the collective instinct of self-preservation, which was naturally strongest in the classes and bodies which had most to lose if, as seemed likely, the stage of social cannibalism was reached.

The Catalan capitalists, besieged in the streets of Barcelona by a demagogic revolution which, from being the political weapon of separatism, had now simply run amuck, were seeking shelter in the Army and the Crown; and Cambó was entering the Government which Maura formed immediately after the catastrophe of Annual. Weeks afterwards the *Lliga*, which had fought so hard for liberty and which had so often demanded the annulment of the *Ley de Jurisdicciones*, withdrew its representative, Bertrán y Musitu, from the Sánchez Guerra Government because it considered the re-establishment of the constitutional guarantees premature. From this epoch dates the change of front of the Catalan upper middle classes. From now on they were to be a reactionary force in Spanish politics. They were to implore the protection of the agrarians, to be their humble allies, to forget, in deference to their class interests, the liberties of Catalonia which they had been the first to exalt. The legend of Saturn was repeating itself: Catalanism, agent of anarchy, was devouring its own children. Forty years of struggle for the more or less radical independence of Catalonia were culminating in the submission of the *Lliga* to the historic enemy—the primitive agrarian State and its monarchy.

It was clear that the intensity of the movement's idealism had yielded to the greater weight of material interests, that if the *Lliga* defended itself against the landed oligarchy under the banner of autonomy, it hauled down that banner the moment the nearest peril proved to be not centralism, but the proletariat at war with property and persons.

Another interesting point to note is that the fluctuating middle classes had also long since taken their leave of the revolution. Unquestionably, those who most closely represented the commercial classes in politics were Santiago Alba and Melquiades Álvarez. Reformism had become monarchist, like the less transparent Leftist Liberalism of Alba; for the foundations of social life were in peril. In point of fact, Alba and Pedregal, the latter a notable figure of the Reformist Party, were included in the last Government of the régime. The "neutral classes" were classes of order, and, like the Catalan capitalists, were now tending to merge with the oligarchy in an endeavour to salvage the last vestiges of society. The monarchy, therefore, in that moment of pure crisis, was receiving unsuspected and valuable social reinforcements, which, together with the support of the Army, were to prolong its life artificially for a few more years.

The *Lliga*, at loggerheads with the non-Catalan, and even with the Catalan commercial classes, had no representation in any of these last Governments of the nation's liquidation whenever Alba or the Reformists figured in them. On the other hand, when men of the *Lliga* were included, the absence of the Reformists and of Alba was marked. This should be emphasized, because only thus can we understand subsequent events which, without this explanation, might appear strange.

The campaign of the Republicans and Socialists to fix the responsibility for the African disaster riveted the close bonds between the Crown and the Army. It was impossible to pass judgment on those immediately responsible for the catastrophe without at the same time condemning the King. And the Government which was formed on December 7th, 1922, the last of the Restoration régime, had promised the country to punish the guilty who were clearly indicted in the Report drawn up for the purpose by General Picasso. If the Crown and the Army wanted to stem a torrent of opinion which, unchecked by the impotent oligarchy, was going to sweep away the throne, there was no time to lose; all the more so because the Government of García Prieto, which not in vain included representatives of the middle classes, was not only announcing that it was going to expose the criminals, but also that it was producing its tardy plan of reforms; first and foremost, the reform of the Constitution. The hand of Alba could be seen in another promised reform—the reform of landed property, which was a persistent bugbear to the Catalan capitalists and would have predisposed them in favour of the military dictatorship, had they not already been so predisposed, body and soul, by the subversive action of the workers.

Alfonso considered leading the *pronunciamiento* in person, governing at the head of a team of generals. He was dissuaded by Maura, who perceived that this plan meant the final and rapid dissolution of the monarchy. But Maura had not the moral energy to divert the King's attention from the idea of the military dictatorship. In his heart of hearts, the old Conservative politician could find no other solution.

Don Miguel Primo de Rivera y Orbaneja, Captain-General of Catalonia, proclaimed himself Dictator on September 13th, 1923, with the consent of the Crown and the support of the Army and the Catalan capitalists, who had a considerable share in the plot and who promised Primo de Rivera (on whom the ruling classes looked with a benevolent eye) the most generous and determined aid. The spokesman of Catalanist apostasy was Puig y Cadafalch, President of the *Mancomunidad*.

The nascent dictatorship encountered no opposition in the country. Only the Socialist Party met the challenge with a manifesto, in which they declared: "What Spain rejects is what the seditious generals evidently want to impose. The people, therefore, ought not to support them."

The *bourgeoisie* bent the knee to the military régime, either with enthusiasm, complacency or resignation, as the case might be. The nation, torn by the struggle of all against all, was inclined to barter the presumed impunity of the guilty in the Moroccan affair for the sake of the peace which was being offered to Spain.

The military dictatorship counted, therefore, at its inception, on the formidable ally of the nation's weariness. It was not a counter-revolution, though it saved the monarchy for a certain time; for there was nothing positive about the agitation in the street, where the bloody grimace of a sporadic and aimless revolution filled the spectators with alarm. For all that, General Primo de Rivera did not have to unsheathe the sword of Sulla.

Lerroux, the demagogue, who approved of the King's speech at Cordova, greeted the military régime with benevolence and gratitude, like all those who longed for a respite. Other Republicans found occasion for relief in the *pronunciamiento* which saved the monarchy, because of their unconscious fear of the Republic returning to Spain during their lifetime.

In general, the country was not ill-advised in accepting the *coup d'état* with a good grace, for in the last resort it meant that the oligarchy was receiving notice to quit. Those who were learned in political and historical texts could always find matter for speculation in the question which would fall first—the throne or the oligarchy. The Crown had acquired new supporters and had survived on its pedestal by a change of posture. But the new platform was irreplaceable. If it split, Alfonso would remain without a people, without a ruling class, without an Army and without friends.

The decrepit oligarchy soon fell. It fell without glory, amid contempt rather, as might have been expected. Someone had to sweep it away. The revolution of 1909 unsettled it, finding out the chinks in its armour. The revolution of 1917, brought to a final conclusion by the uniformed middle class, struck it a shrewder blow, but was not able to dislodge it from the Government and condemn it to ostracism. The oligarchy continued, therefore, to be not only economically, but politically stronger than the middle class and the proletariat combined. Because the revolution could not directly eliminate it, that task had to be undertaken by either the Church, with a theocracy, or the Army, with a military dictatorship. The first was out of the question. The divorce of the Crown, an inconceivably autonomous power, from the oligarchy threw the King into the arms of the military, and both together annihilated the institutional

farce of the Restoration. From this point of view, the dictatorship of the King and the generals marked a necessary stage in
the Spanish revolution of our time. The dissolution of the
institutions founded by the landed oligarchy in 1874 was now
being consummated by the same people who proposed to defend
the monarchy. The régime was changed in order not to change
it. The oligarchy—the chief protagonist—was wiped out,
in order that the Crown—the lesser figure—should be saved.
Democracy might have willed otherwise, because the people's
hate and love are concentrated in symbols and for them, the
throne occupied the first place. But the order of events did not
have a decisive influence on the change. The oligarchy dug the
grave for the whole régime, and the King and the Army made it
certain that the régime would be interred in sections, leaving
the monarchy till the last.

If any doubt remained that it ought to be interred, the
oligarchy dispelled it by announcing, through the mouth of
García Prieto: "Now I have added a new patron saint to the
calendar—Saint Miguel Primo de Rivera, who has delivered
me from the nightmare of governing." That ruling class had a
final moment of lucidity before sinking contentedly into the tomb.

## CHAPTER X

# THE MILITARY DICTATORSHIP AND FALL OF THE MONARCHY

GENERAL PRIMO DE RIVERA had captured the feeling of
the nation in the manifesto which he addressed to the country,
the first official document of the rebellion and one which, if it
could not be considered the epitome of the future policy of the
military régime, at any rate testified to a complete knowledge
of what public opinion desired. The cardinal point of the new
policy was summarized in the motto of the Catalan *Somatén*,
which the Dictator made his own: "Peace, peace and again
peace." The walls of the disorderly Spanish Jericho collapsed
at the sound of this trumpet-call.

The proclamation pronounced sentence without appeal on the
oligarchs, a sentiment that was readily endorsed by the people:
"but in reality they accommodated themselves easily and
contentedly to the *turno* and their share of power, and settled the
succession between themselves."

The Crown was absolved from the notorious sins of corruption, the responsibility being thrown on the oligarchy; "The close-woven net of greed has enmeshed and held prisoner even the Royal will."

Though this was unusual in this kind of appeal, the manifesto contained prolix individual allusions which, by the unimportance of their nature, could only be explained as intended to satisfy a rancour which demanded urgent revenge. What availed it at such a solemn moment to speak of the "suspect tariff policy—all the more suspect because its manipulator flaunts his impudent immorality"? Its manipulator was Alba . . . "that depraved and cynical Minister". "The trial of Don Santiago Alba", the manifesto ran, "has now begun, in accordance with the unanimous voice of the country. . . ." Had the adhesion of the *Lliga* been partly bought with this bravado? In any case, the resentment against Alba which was thus being given outward form in the rebel General's proclamation, was not inspired by the barracks, but by certain administrative counsels.

In itself alone, this pronouncement on tariffs might foreshadow a policy, showing that the soldiers were not thinking of favouring the mercantile classes. And well might the Catalan capitalists consider they had triumphed when, on top of this, they could produce the counter of autonomy which—if Primo de Rivera's private assurances were to be believed—was to be one of the chief planks in his policy.

The General deceived the Catalan capitalists at many points; not because the politicians of the *Lliga* were excessively credulous, but because, as I have said, they also had opted for the peace of the *Somatén*. In this, as in everything else, the true nature of the régime was not slow in revealing itself.

The political system which was coming to an end had not been the product of improvisation. It had lived in the fancy of its inventors many years before it became a reality. To organize it, Cánovas had taken two years of plenary powers—a disguised dictatorship—and only when the work was on foot did he allow the country to be consulted by means of universal suffrage, the efficiency of the new institutions being seen in the overwhelming majority which the Government obtained for the Constituent Cortes. Universal suffrage disappeared from the Constitution of 1876, but Cánovas feared it because it complicated his methods not because it could not be made compatible with them. Thus he could boast, when years afterwards he was threatened with popular franchise, that there had never been a more docile

Parliament in Spain than the first Parliament of the Restoration. The dying régime was not, therefore, an empirical product, born of the national spontaneity, fruit of the Spanish psychology; but the conscientious work of a group of misguided or faint-hearted statesmen, without faith in the destinies of their country, detractors of the race, and therefore convinced that only in this way could age-old political chaos be remedied.

It took the new oligarchy ten or fifteen years to establish their dominance in politics. The refusal of the Church and the Army to admit the supremacy of a civil power retarded the triumph of Cánovas. But for those social classes, sovereign in the economic field, it was a matter of life or death to conquer the anti-State elements, to affirm their dominating position in politics, to restore order to the country and to create the stable institutions which would permit them to invest their money soundly and enjoy the proceeds. As Conservative classes, they feared that the Church or the Army would usurp the function of government; for both are, in power, a dissolving, and therefore revolutionary, force. And the military Directory was not going to belie this historical truism.

The politicians of the Restoration, mandatories of the great owners of the soil, when not the great landowners themselves, succeeded eventually in establishing a *modus vivendi* and in making it respected. The régime could not have been worse, but it was at all events a régime and to understand why it met with acceptance, we must not lose sight of the confusion that preceded it. We must not, therefore, judge it on its intrinsic merits if we want to fathom the mystery of the success of Cánovas, whose motto also was "Peace, peace and again peace." The men of the Restoration were obsessed by *legality* and they paid any price to acquire it. The reigning social inequality could not be the foundation of a robust state and the Government had to be unjust. But it was *legal*, and it succeeded in commanding obedience.

In his *Discourse on the First Decade of Titus Livius*, Machiavelli insists on "how useful and necessary to republics are the legal methods whereby the crowd can show its animosity to a ruler; for if no such legal methods exist, recourse will be had to extra-legal methods, which undoubtedly lead to worse results. And if a citizen is oppressed, even unjustly, within the bounds of legality, little or no disorder occurs; for the oppression is not the product of private violence or extraneous force, such as dispense with liberty, but of the fulfilment of the law, carried out by a legitimate authority which has its own limits and does not turn into something which might destroy the republic".

The Machiavellian legality of the Restoration rested on the scaffolding of caciquism, maker of Parliaments, and stay and support of the two great parties, which guaranteed the enjoyment of power by one social class and excluded the rest of the citizens from the government of the nation. For the ambidextrous oligarchy, it was essential not to let the political power slip from its hands. It could not authorize anyone else to govern for it, for it was itself the régime. Any other institutions which were not the caciquist apparatus, the manipulated Parliament, the Liberal-Conservative sequence in the Government unfolding with perfect precision, and the monarchy, reconciled to presiding over the farce, would put the oligarchs in an awkward situation. If the basic institutions of the Restoration were destroyed, the possibilities of *legal dictatorship* were exhausted. And this is why General Primo de Rivera's *coup d'état* was bound to have revolutionary consequences.

It was small comfort to the oligarchs to see the Government taken over by Conservative-minded men, when the latter were trying to install a system which dismantled their complicated and irreplaceable political machine. The generals were to fail in their attempt to create substitute institutions, that is, they were not to succeed in constructing a Conservative system.

The military dictatorship was not only born outside the law, but *ipso facto*, or by that very fact, placed the last oligarchic institution—the pseudo-constitutional monarchy—in that uncomfortable position too. Once more Spain was without institutions. In the political order, and perhaps in other orders, the nation was returning to the nineteenth century, a fact that was catastrophically reflected in the character of the opposition to the Dictator and in the second Republic.

As in the days of Isabel II, the oligarchy was going to have to renew the battle to recover its lost political power; except that history never exactly repeats itself, and a presentiment that they were never again going to govern with the absolute sovereignty they had enjoyed for fifty years, could not but assail the Conservatives (more dejected at their dismissal than the "Liberals"), who expressed their anxieties in the lines with which *La Época* greeted the military dictatorship: "We must all pray to God with all our strength that what has happened, though profoundly disquieting, will not unhappily prove overwhelmingly significant in the life of Spain." Thus spoke the newspaper of the aristocracy and the great landowners.

The Army took full possession of the State and invaded all the redoubts of the oligarchy. On September 30th they dissolved the municipal councils throughout Spain—"the seed and fruit of the two-party and caciquist policy"—and replaced them by *juntas* of associates and representatives of the military authority. They decreed that those who had been Ministers of the Crown, Presidents of the Chambers or Councillors of State were disqualified for public office. Parliament was closed, other bodies were dissolved, official representation in the great State-subsidized concerns was taken over by the military, and the hand of the Army eventually reached to the remote corners of public life through the Government delegates—captains, majors, lt.-colonels, etc.—who assumed the political command in provinces and townships as well as in the great cities, and carried out impertinent visits of inspection of *Diputaciones* and municipalities. The internal government of the latter was modified by provincial and municipal statutes. The Directory turned everything upside down, changed everything, overthrew everything—everything that could be overthrown, that is.

Neither in intelligence nor in virtue were the soldiers superior to the oligarchy, and they were entirely without experience in the art of government. Force, as always, was incapable of organizing anything. But this last deficiency had its positive side; there was no fear of a new system being invented as effective as the one that was dying.

For the rest, the Army's mission was not to govern the nation, but to complete the misgovernment of it. The more conspicuous was the absence of legality and the more the old skeleton was hammered, the less readily would the régime that had been overthrown be resurrected. The Army did not touch agrarian property and, consequently, did not completely eradicate caciquism; but the Minister-Generals, the Military Governors and the Government representatives upset the political machine so much that they put it out of action. They created new interests, giving preference to some *caciques* over others, or concentrating all influence in themselves. They took away and put back, changed, reformed, rewarded and persecuted. Sometimes out of stupidity, sometimes intentionally, they disorganized things that the oligarchy held in tender and sentimental esteem. Yesterday's high priests suffered terrible humiliations today. Spain was enduring an arbitrary régime, but it was no worse than the fallen régime either in arbitrariness or in any other kind of licence. On the contrary, the military dictatorship was making itself politically and historically responsible, even in the person of its leaders, for the crimes and excesses it was committing—something which never occurred under the system of the absolute oligarchy. Under the old system the people and the middle classes paid for the shamelessness of the oligarchs. Under the military dictatorship, there was a greater measure of democracy, because the rich and the grandees were also humiliated, persecuted and imprisoned. Only those suffering from amnesia could miss the liberty that had never existed. The country was under martial law. But the truth is that the oligarchy highly approved of such a state of affairs so long as it was the one to gather the fruits; and the manner in which it succumbed to the despotism of the sword could only be lamented, and only was lamented, by those who were free in the old régime, not by the people. Viewed in any light, the military dictatorship was a step forward compared with what had been abolished.

The Dictator himself was morally superior to the majority of the politicians he had supplanted. Primo de Rivera was a typical Andalusian; sensitive behind a gay and resolute mask, he was indiscreet, sensual, effusive and disinterested. Refusing to owe everything to his uncle, Don Fernando—Captain-General of Madrid and a party to the conspiracy when Martínez Campos led the revolt at Sagunto—he set out from his early youth to acquire his own personality and his own laurels. His education suffered from serious lacunae which were tacitly glossed over in view of the personal bravery which is traditionally, and perhaps rightly, considered to be the first attribute of a soldier. Primo de Rivera oftentimes put his courage to the test, winning his medals with his scars. His weakness for politics was as old as his weakness for good wine and women.

Under the military dictatorship the inevitable series of scandalous and corrupt practices continued without interruption. Administrative corruption at this stage was even more spectacular than under the oligarchy. Ethically there was really no great difference between one régime and the other. What varied was the style, which was more expeditious under the military dictatorship. With the latter system the attack on the public interests was fast and furious, without the check which the fear of scandal sometimes placed on the politicians of the "government-by-rotation" system and led them to practise suaver and more round-about methods.

Administrative policy did not improve with the formation in 1925 of the Government of civilians under Primo de Rivera, a team of volunteers who were anxious to make a career and to try out their hidden talents as statesmen in the shelter of a Cabinet Minister's office.

This Government of civilians was a change of front inspired by the desire to found institutions which would establish the dictatorship on a certain and permanent base. But the Dictator could not create a political party, though the *Unión Patriótica* was an attempt at it. He tried to found a representative organ with the *Asamblea Nacional*, but the country would have none of it. The truth was that the function of the dictatorship was purely one of liquidating a dead system. Primo de Rivera came, in the last instance, to dissolve the institutions of the Restoration, unconscious perhaps that that was his mission and that he was the sport of a mysterious force which occasionally directs the history of nations.

It must not, however, be understood by this that the military dictatorship was a régime with nothing but a negative interest. Its attitude in relation to the social classes merits special attention.

The soldiers who supplanted the oligarchs continued the class policy of the oligarchy. These generals and their civilian advisers were mostly great landowners. The Dictator, second Marqués de Estella, belonged to an ancient landowning family. There was not going to be, therefore, an agrarian revolution; more than that, the soldiers were not going to alleviate at any point the tragic lot of the peasant. For the Directory, as for the oligarchic Governments, the problem of the Spanish countryside did not exist. Except for an insignificant Royal Decree on the cultivation and tillage of the land, the dictatorship paid no attention at all to the agrarian question.

The economic and social policy of the dictatorship may be summarized as follows: continuation of the war of the agrarians against the commercial classes; a high degree of protection for cereals and olives and for industry; promotion of banking interests; complete abandonment of the landless peasant and protection of the industrial and mercantile worker at the obvious expense of commerce and industry.

As a régime, therefore, the dictatorship was as hostile to the middle class as the oligarchy. The structure of Spanish society continued to be the same. The oligarchy maintained its economic position, when it did not actually strengthen it, as in its financial branch. What changed was the form of government —a phenomenon which made of the oligarchic oppressors a politically oppressed class. This, as I said before, was of the utmost importance, for it imperilled the economic power of the landowners, which was only safe when it was supplemented in politics by undisputed mastery of the State. The policy of the dictatorship in this respect seemed to obey the motto of en-

G s

lightened despotism, as paraphrased in the sentence: "Everything for the oligarchy, nothing with the oligarchy." The military State was also the territorial State of the oligarchy. From this point of view, the counter-revolution begun by Cánovas was continuing under the Army.

The commercial classes were touched on the raw by the economic policy of the dictatorship, exactly as they were in the first years of the Restoration. It was the same offensive against the *bourgeoisie*, peculiar to the territorial State—an offensive which could only cease with the political triumph of the middle class.

The military dictatorship had no time to spend on governing, overburdened as it was with the pressing business of installing the régime; and until the Government of civilians was formed, with Calvo Sotelo as Minister of Finance, it did not throw its cards on the table. Its first measures restricting the mercantile economy appeared in January 1926. The Government proceeded with the taxation of shops and factories with a zeal far removed from that shown in taxing the landowners, now, as always, untouchable.

The State persisted in intervening in the mercantile and industrial economy, that is, cutting short, not losing sight of, preventing the unexpected development and appearance of a Liberal atmosphere in Spain. The rustic, bucolic and Carlist nation had to be preserved and watched over. All this meant, therefore, compelling merchants and industrialists to declare their securities, to submit to inspection, and, as a final touch, to keep a special new sales-book.

These decrees of January 1926 reduced the commercial classes to fury, but weak and oppressed as they were, they had no means of preventing them from coming into force. Nevertheless, when some months later Calvo Sotelo announced his new taxation proposals, they threw restraint to the winds and the *Círculo de la Unión Mercantil* came out in support of the interests of the traders with a mild protest: "The bad economic policy of pre-Directory times has been accentuated by this measure and by the present Government, causing an increase in the cost of living."

The reverse side of the Dictator's economic medal became clear in the summer of the same year. Protective tariffs on olive oil and grain were now raised to a point where they bordered on prohibitionism. In April imports of nuts and sesame-seed were limited to 40,000 tons. In May a tax of 10 pesetas per 100 kilos was levied on nut and sesame-seed oil. In December the importation of both products was totally prohibited.

As regards cereals, a fund of 25 million pesetas[1] was created in May to advance credits to wheat-growers. What amount of this fund reached the small farmers is difficult to say, since agricultural credits were always controlled by the great land-owners. In July the importation of wheat was entirely prohibited.

The social policy of the dictatorship was on a par with its economic policy. A Government of business men and lawyers of the *bourgeoisie* would have tended to protect the rural proletariat and would perhaps have been less generous to its own proletariat, the industrial and commercial proletariat. Consequently, the agrarian Government of Primo de Rivera adopted the opposite policy, the traditional policy of the oligarchy which it even improved upon. All its favours were reserved for the industrial and commercial proletariat and the peasants were abandoned, as before, to the mercy of the great landowners.

For the workers in the mines, factories, workshops, railways, and mercantile concerns, the dictatorship was a far more benevolent régime than that of the absolute oligarchy. It raised the standard of living for the working class in the cities and lent to the whole non-rural proletariat an attention which testified, first, to the interest of the Dictator in appeasing class warfare in the great centres of population, the theatre of continued strikes, and secondly, to his plan for imposing systematic order, as far as this was possible, in the world of labour and capital.

Conditions in Spain were not such as favoured Fascism, and Primo de Rivera could not have been a Mussolini; nor did he ever think of being one, though Alfonso XIII would have liked a more permanent sort of dictatorship than the military Directory, the last shot in the monarchy's locker. The Spanish workers movement was still in its infancy. There were only half a dozen Socialist deputies in Parliament; and though the elections were faked, this did not alter the fact that the Socialist *menace* was not a cause of alarm to the propertied classes as it had been in Italy where there were 156 Socialists in Parliament in 1920. Moreover there was nothing in Spain to compare with the occupation of the factories by the Italian workers in the same year. The social régime of property could not, by any stretch of the imagination, be deemed to be in peril; and the rich knew it.

Since 1909 revolutionary propaganda by all the opposition parties had been concentrated on the form of government. The immense majority of discontented Spaniards believed that, if

[1] 40 pesetas = £1; 1 peseta = 6d.

the Crown was overthrown, the revolution would be accomplished or would be so influenced by this event that everything would change automatically; there would be more social equality, Spaniards would learn to read and write and would, at last, be happy. Clearly, there would be much to do once the Crown was overthrown; the Constituent Cortes would have to be summoned, a progressive Constitution would have to be drawn up, a President of the Republic elected, the Jesuits expelled, and wise and just laws dictated. It was the demagogic vision of the revolution, born of the still reigning political philosophy of the nineteenth century. But this very fact lulled the fears of proprietors of all classes; and the conviction that the change would only affect the form of government not only prevented the military dictatorship from debouching into Fascism, but was also to be an important factor in the struggle of the wealthy classes against the military State.

Moreover the Restoration system had crystallized into the police State. Primo de Rivera took over a *strong* State, difficult to attack from the street. At no moment were the institutions in danger of falling through lack of public force, which was superabundant. Spain had police and guards and armed bodies of all descriptions, many of them unknown in the rest of the world—secret police, Civil Guards, Security Guards, *Carabineros*, municipal guards, rural guards and, moreover, *Mozos de escuadra* in Catalonia and the *Miqueletes* in the Basque Provinces. In addition, it was already customary for the Army also to watch over public order.

As in every corrupt State, the civil institutions, in spite of their weakness, were saved by an apparatus of violence unique in Europe. There would come a moment when physical force, however pompous and fantastic, would be incapable of prolonging that state of things, but until then, the police and armed bodies had saved the unjust State, and they were the only thing that had saved it. Because the police State still existed, the dictatorship did not, therefore, have to organize it or the propertied classes to clamour for it. All this enabled Primo de Rivera to be magnanimous up to a certain point and not to stain his name with cruel reprisals.

It was clear as time went on that the dictatorship was seeking peace with the urban proletariat. It could not declare war on everyone, all the more so as its mission was to persecute the political oligarchy, and it did not propose, because the historic interest of the territorial State was against it, to favour the middle class.

Primo de Rivera immediately got into touch with Manuel Llaneza, the Socialist leader of the coalminers, assuring him that the new régime would respect all the social gains of the workers. The trade unions would continue to function, the timid social laws passed by the oligarchy would remain in force, and the dictatorship would pass others even more favourable to the industrial proletariat. Llaneza came away from the interview satisfied. "There is nothing to fear," he said afterwards in public.

A difficult period, and one without precedent, was beginning for Spanish Socialism. But the Socialist leaders showed themselves worthy of the confidence reposed in them by the proletariat.

The Spanish Socialist Party had suffered the internal commotions which the repercussion of the Russian revolution had produced in international Socialism. The triumph of the Russian revolution was greeted with jubilation by the Spanish proletariat, perhaps with more enthusiasm than in other countries, because Spain was socially another nation of *moujiks* and, like Russia, without a middle class. The Socialist Party complacently accepted the fact that the new Russian régime was to be a dictatorship. The Spanish workers were in sympathy with the Russian revolution, without bothering their heads about "democratic government or the dictatorship of the working class". In June 1920 the Socialist Party summoned an Extraordinary Congress and by 8,269 votes to 5,016 and 1,615 abstentions agreed to join the Third International. But when the conditions laid down by Moscow for the incorporation of national sections in the new International came to be known, they changed their opinion. At the Extraordinary Congress of April 1921 the voting was very different. There were 8,808 votes against incorporation with the Communist International and in favour of the new Socialist International (the idea of founding another International was then being mooted), and 6,025 votes for the Communist International. This Assembly marked the beginning of the split.

The Spanish Socialist Party was pragmatical. It did not condemn the dictatorial nature of Bolshevism, but it rejected the instructions which were being launched from Russia to the rest of the world, without regard to the state of each country and the psychology of the various nations.

When the divorce was complete between those Socialists who approved Moscow's twenty-one conditions and the majority who rejected them, the Executive Committee of the Party issued a manifesto in the name of the latter, which was signed by Pablo Iglesias and which declared: "We are not in agreement with the conditions laid down by the Third International of Moscow, but we affirm today, as we did from the first day of the Russian revolution, that we identify ourselves whole-heartedly with that revolution."

Pablo Iglesias was not hostile to the seizure of power or to the so-called dictatorship of the proletariat. And in this Spanish Socialism differed at the time from the judgment of the leaders of the Second International, who condemned the methods of which Lenin availed himself in order to keep himself in power. That is, the Socialists of other countries invoked *external* democratic principles against the Russian revolution, while Spanish Socialism took its stand only against the twenty-one conditions, for *internal* democratic principles, for the autonomy of the Sections of the International, but not for a democracy that was more than dubious and in Spain simply suicidal, demagogic, an agent of civil war.

We already know, therefore, what was the spirit and doctrine of Spanish Socialism (the minority which left the Socialist Party and founded the Communist Party failed; so much so that up to 1930 there was no real Communist Party in Spain).

When the military *coup d'état* took place, the numerical strength of the Socialist Party was much less than its moral authority. The *Unión General de Trabajadores* had a membership of 200,000, many of them—the majority—peasants. The Socialist Party was infinitely less numerous, having only some 15,000 members.

As regards the Anarcho-Syndicalists, the dictatorship lost no time in imprisoning their principal leaders and declaring its hostility to the movement. This suited the Anarcho-Syndicalists better than the policy of the oligarchy which vilely assassinated them or used them through the agency of demagogues like Lerroux. In 1920, when Dato was Prime Minister, the corpses of twenty-one Anarcho-Syndicalists, dispatched to the other world by the mysterious hand of the Catalan capitalists and the Madrid oligarchs, were picked up within thirty-six hours in the streets of Barcelona.

From the outset, therefore, Anarcho-Syndicalism was in open conflict with the dictatorship or vice versa, and I repeat that this was preferable, for the honour of Spain and for the Anarcho-Syndicalists themselves, to the policy of the oligarchy, which had made of terrorism a political arm, using the Anarchists against other sections of the proletariat and buying the gunmen of the *Sindicato Único* who, incorporated with the *Sindicatos Libres* (blackleg organizations invented by the parties of reaction), placed their experience as terrorists, acquired in the *Único*, at the service of their paymasters. It was obvious that if things continued as they had been before the dictatorship, not a single Anarcho-Syndicalist leader would have remained alive in Barcelona. The most brilliant of them, Salvador Seguí, had been murdered by gunmen of his own organization who had been bribed to desert to the capitalist gang.

A past of such ignominy, a present teeming with dangers, and a future pregnant with promise for those who knew at what point in the history of Spain they were standing, counselled the Fabian tactics which Spanish Socialism adopted against the military Dictatorship. Like Quintus Fabius before the formidable host of Hannibal, the Socialists temporized. They fought without seeking a decisive battle, leaving time to wage a war of attrition on the powerful enemy.

Much was said then—and is still being said—about the collaboration of the Socialists with the dictatorship. But the terminology is inaccurate. To judge by the results of the prudent conduct of the Socialists, it would be more exact to speak of the collaboration of the dictatorship with the Socialists.

Primo de Rivera wanted to regulate the relations between labour and capital on an arbitral basis. He did not mind incurring the ill-will of the *bourgeoisie*, who thought any arbitral system onerous which placed the workers on a footing of legal equality with the employers. Certain capitalists wanted nothing less than the extermination of the workers' organizations, and the Catalan *Lliga*, as we have seen, had defended the terrorist policy of Martínez Anido. When there was talk of depriving the barbarous General of his command, Cambó protested, and even went so far as to say that that was the only possible policy which "met with the approval (according to him) of practically the whole of Barcelona". The military dictatorship was supported by the capitalists partly because it was supposed to be hostile to the workers' claims. In this, also, the Catalan *bourgeoisie* was deceived.

In this respect, Primo Rivera's most important initiative was the creation of the *Comités Paritarios* arbitral tribunals whose function was to intervene in conflicts between capital and labour. On November 26th, 1926, the law on the corporative organization of the nation was passed. The U.G.T., after exhaustive examination, agreed to issue a circular to all its

Sections advising them to accept this decree and to demand the setting up of *Comités Paritarios* in their respective trades. This measure of the dictatorship was the one which most favoured the workers' movement.

The capitalists never accepted Primo de Rivera's corporative organization with enthusiasm. They subsequently began a veiled Press campaign against the *Comités Paritarios*, which naturally confirmed the leaders of the U.G.T. in their opinion that the law favoured the workers.

When the monarchy fell, the wisdom of the Socialist Party's Fabian policy *vis-à-vis* the dictatorship became apparent. The trade-union organization of Socialism, which might have been destroyed by the military Government, increased its membership by 100,000. No better tribute could be paid to the tactics of the Socialists than the words which one of the intellectuals who had been persecuted by the dictatorship wrote a few years later: "Then came the dictatorship. The Restoration parties collapsed under the kicks of the jack-boot. Only the Socialist Party remained standing. And again there fell on it a torrent of taunts and maledictions. The Socialist Party obviously represented a class interest, as well as a political interest. To save the one, it could not sacrifice the other. Moreover, if it had succumbed under the dictatorship, the resurgence of Liberalism in Spain would have been delayed ten, even twenty years. The rapid mobilization of the progressive democratic forces, as soon as the squall of the dictatorship had passed, was carried out on the firm ground of Socialism."

If we consider the question carefully, we can say without reservations that the assets of Primo de Rivera's dictatorship exceeded the liabilities. Its chief merit lay in having destroyed the oligarchy politically, smashing the civil machine of the Restoration so thoroughly that the aristocracy and the great landowners were never to return to govern Spain by the systematic use of an instrument of power. The second important asset of the dictatorship was the conclusion of the Moroccan war.

Primo de Rivera always advocated abandoning Morocco. In this, as in so many other things, he reflected the opinion of the man-in-the-street, and to no one did he express it with greater frankness than to Webb Miller, the United Press Correspondent, who had a private interview with the General towards the end of 1924, during the bloody days of the retreat from Xauen. Miller quoted Primo de Rivera's opinion in his autobiography *I Found no Peace*.

"Abd el-Krim has defeated us," he said. "He has the immense advantages of the terrain and a fanatical following. Our troops are sick of the war and have been for years. They don't see why they should fight and die for this strip of worthless territory. I am withdrawing to this line (he drew a line on the map for me) and will hold only the tip of this territory. I, personally, am in favour of withdrawing entirely from Africa and letting Abd el-Krim have it. We have spent untold millions of pesetas in this enterprise and never made a céntimo from it. We have had tens of thousands of men killed for territory which is not worth having.

"But we cannot withdraw because England doesn't want us to. England has great influence over the King, and, as you know, the Queen was an English princess. England fears that, if we withdraw, the territory will be taken by France, which might nullify the command the British have of the Strait of Gibraltar with their great fortress on the Rock of Gibraltar. Command of the Strait is vital to England's imperial interests; it is the gateway to her Empire—India and Australia. England wants a weak power like Spain in possession of the territory opposite Gibraltar. They don't want a strong power like France there."

In November 1924 Primo de Rivera in fact ordered the retreat—which cost enormous casualties—to a more easily defendable line, letting the enemy overrun 180 positions. Abd-el-Krim's attack on the French positions eventually led to joint military action by Spain and France; and accordingly the naval, land and air forces of both countries routed the Riff chieftain in 1925. The Spanish army, with the support of its own navy and that of the French, was able to disembark in the bay of Alhucemas on September 8th, afterwards taking up a strong position on an extensive fortified line. The Moroccan war, that nightmare of the nation, had virtually come to an end. Primo de Rivera, who had been engaged heart and soul in the enterprise for months on end, officially ceased to command the African army on November 2nd. On May 27th, 1926, Abd el-Krim surrendered to the French authorities. On August 11th the Spanish troops recaptured Xauen. And in the spring of 1927 the work of extinguishing the last centres of resistance was put in hand.

The Dictator had promised to solve the Moroccan problem, and he had done so. The oligarchy would never have put an end to the African war—not because it suited it to prolong the adventure, but because it was irresolute and over-respectful to the interests involved, and because the Government, in its hands, never organized anything.

The pacification of Morocco was really the only constructive work of the dictatorship. In other directions the military State produced the evils inseparable from a dictatorial system without creative impulse and, needless to say, all those other evils inherent in the military State.

The dictatorship's heel of Achilles was its lack of a legal basis. Though it was basically no worse a régime than that of the Restoration, it appeared to be worse. The régime of the absolute oligarchy was an arbitrary system, but it was disguised by the trappings of legality. The dictatorship, while also being an arbitrary system, yet lacked formal legitimacy. Primo de Rivera found himself in the position which Cánovas had dreaded so much. His power derived from a successful military rebellion and every blunder he made reminded his ill-wishers of the irregular origin of his Government.

The Dictator, beset on all sides by enemies, came to realize at length the tragedy of not having succeeded in creating the weapon of *legality*. He could not use this weapon against the rebels and tried to justify himself by the applause he had been greeted with in those early days, at the same time throwing the responsibility on the Crown: "As the conspirators may possibly employ with the youth of the country, which is always vehemently or excessively credulous and ingenuous, the argument that this Government was a military rebellion, we can confirm this with pride as an historical reality; but our rebellion, which was the answer to the disintegration of the country and the disrepute into which it had fallen, was acclaimed by the people *and sanctioned by the King*, attentive to the dictates of patriotism and wisdom." A weak defence of a lost cause!

The oligarchy, though its material interests as a class had not been harmed, realized that a heavy blow had been struck at its political heritage and within a few weeks of the advent of the new régime, it was already raising its head and beginning the fight against the military State with the powerful means at its disposal.

The commercial and industrial middle class also was not slow in taking action, as soon as it perceived the contempt of the régime for mercantile and industrial interests.

The bureaucratic middle class was offended by the over-bearing ways of the military in the Ministries and other official Departments.

In the third year of the dictatorship, the "neutral" classes were already openly expressing their irritation with the régime. The importance of this could not escape Primo de Rivera, for it was essential for a Government like his to be able to count on the support of these non-party social classes. They had paved the way for the warm welcome the dictatorship had met with; now they were going to swell the opposition.

The intellectuals resented the lack of liberty, and the jokes of the Dictator. Primo de Rivera felt for the independent-minded intellectuals a special rancour—the rancour of the frustrated writer behind the make-up of the dictator, the rancour of the soldier invading a territory which was more the province of intelligence than of force.

The people in general were not yet at open war with the Government, but neither were they an active ally.

It was obvious that already in 1926 the dictatorship rested exclusively on the will of the King and of the barracks.

The first, treacherous and impulsive, began to fail Primo de Rivera a few months after the *coup d'état*. In the Palace, relief at the success of the *pronunciamiento* gave way to uneasiness at the legal abnormality of government by force. The King, as always, had no clear idea of the gravity of the step he had taken until after the historic event was a *fait accompli*. Then he wanted to repair the damage, if possible, by seeking the support of the monarchist Left and sometimes, also, of the people.

When the dictatorship had been in existence a year, General Cavalcanti, head of the King's Military Household, paid a series of significant visits to the fallen politicians. But Primo de Rivera cut short his perilous wanderings by sending him on an unimportant mission to Italy and Eastern Europe.

At no moment was the Dictator sure of the King. Alfonso may have been the chief author of the dictatorship; he was also the first to take fright at its consequences.

The oligarchy, as soon as it had recovered from the shock, began to conspire and attack, either with the King's help, or playing a lone hand. The Marqués de Cortina fired the first shot with an insidious article in *La Actualidad Financiera*, an error which he paid for with banishment to the island of Fuerteventura. The Duque de San Pedro de Galatino was the next to feel the heavy hand of the Government. And the first sanctions to be imposed on the Press fell, significantly, on *La Época*, the newspaper of the grandees, which was suspended indefinitely and fined 25,000 pesetas.

As I said before, the national front against the Dictator

was ready and in action by the end of 1926. All sectors of civilian opinion, some more aggressively than others, were working for a change of Government.

Alfonso XIII's game now was to prevent the fall of Primo de Rivera occasioning the end of the monarchy. The success of the manœuvre encountered insuperable obstacles, but the King plumed himself on being an expert at this kind of intrigue, which was a pastime to him, and there is no doubt that the comings and goings of the defeated politicians caused no surprise at the Palace.

Nevertheless, the Monarch was kept under observation ("Let him try no Bourbon tricks on me," Primo de Rivera is reported to have said), and his arts as a politician of the old régime relied upon a field of operations which was delimited by the Dictator.

Alfonso would have liked to return to legality before it was too late; to blot out the past and start afresh; to found a new constitutional era which would raise the monarchy from the slough into which it had fallen and set it again on the broad highway. Possibly, if he had been able to dismiss the Dictator in 1926, the Crown might have been saved, who knows for how long. For though the Conservative classes were anti-Dictator, they were not yet Republican. At the Republican banquet held on February 11th of the previous year at Madrid, no more than fifty persons were present. Republicanism was like —and, since the defeat of the middle class at the close of the century, had always been like—a ship waiting for a breeze to fill its sails. That breeze was to be the "neutral" classes; and not until the last days of 1926 did the sails of the anti-dynastic brig begin to belly in the wind.

No one, therefore, felt the pressing need of a *political* revolution so much as the oligarchy. Stripped of power, it was nevertheless not conquered. A multiplicity of motives spurred it on to fight; the need to defend itself, the itch to recover its political pre-eminence and the desire to save the King. The monarchical institution, if it survived the dictatorship, would serve to patch up the old régime. The oligarchic megatherium could be reconstructed from the bones of the monarchy. Time must be gained; and the oligarchy must stand in the vanguard of the revolution. Thus argued the most astute members of the olig-archy; and, reckoning on these lines, Count Romanones, the most representative politician of the fallen régime, appeared in 1926 at the head of the "Night of St. John" conspiracy, the most serious conspiracy to date.

The Count succeeded in uniting in a revolutionary *bloc* dismissed generals, out-of-work demagogues, offended intellectuals, ingenuous Republicans, incautious Anarchists, and other elements prepared to embark blindly on a conspiracy which, since it was under the leadership of the oligarchy, was, by its origin, a trap for democracy.

The Socialists, who had been asked to join both this and other conspiracies, refused to co-operate. They knew very well what the oligarchs were after.

The "Night of St. John" conspiracy was an abortive attempt at revolution conceived by the King and the oligarchs with the object of getting rid of the Dictator and saving the monarchy. The plot miscarried because the conspirators lacked courage. Moreover the Army was not yet prepared to withdraw its confidence from Primo de Rivera. The plotters, both civilian and military, made a great show of activity without actually doing much, and, as the Government held all the threads of the plot in their hands, they were able to break it up without bloodshed and with a certain arbitrary facetiousness. For the Dictator decreed that his rivals should be punished through their pockets and sentenced them to heavy fines. General Weyler was fined 100,000 pesetas; General Augilera 200,000; Count Romanones 500,000; Marcelino Domingo, a Republican, 5,000; Barriobero, lawyer of the Anarchists, 15,000; Benlliure y Tuero, journalist, 2,500; Lezama, journalist, 2,500; Dr. Marañón 100,000 and Amalio Quílez, Anarcho-Syndicalist, 1,000.

The plot bore the unmistakable monarchist stamp, and the plan of the conspirators was to *demand* that the King should hand over the government to General Aguilera, who was to re-establish constitutional legality. In company with Count Romanones, General Weyler, General Aguilera (who, if Alfonso had had his way, would have been dictator in 1923), there were lukewarm Monarchists like Melquiades Álvarez and Villanueva, demagogues like Lerroux (these last three took a back seat in the plot), wealthy intellectuals like Dr. Marañón, venal timeservers like Barriobero, and visionaries like Quílez. There was no lack of revolutionaries to work with the oligarchy to re-enthrone the system of the Restoration. And the worst was—so low had the political conscience of the nation sunk!—that few were surprised at such an astonishing alliance of plutocrats and Anarchists, fiery generals and fiercely anti-militaristic journalists, notorious demagogues and Palace envoys. Nor did the public wonder at the infinite love of liberty and democracy now expressed by the oligarchy.

Don José Sánchez Guerra, the leader of the Conservative Party, now set himself up as the Savonarola of political virtue. This proud man crossed the frontier in voluntary exile when the National Assembly was convened by the dictatorship, refusing to live any longer under a sky which remained impassive while a nation was being subjugated. But before he left, he issued a manifesto in which, making a copious use of phrases borrowed from Cánovas and Ríos Rosas, he recalled that the "Conservatives had always been in Spain the most convinced and most exalted defenders of the constitutional régime, of Parliament, and of the public liberties [sic]".

But whatever our judgment of the proceedings of the oligarchy, the fact remains that the military dictatorship was not an acceptable régime. Historically it had no reason to exist, once the Restoration State had crumbled away. Nor was Primo de Rivera able, nor did he know how, to create interests as vigorous as the resentments he aroused. He infuriated the aristocracy, persecuted the old politicians, displeased the middle class, and failed to win over the people. But he could not govern against the whole world, or without at least the support of a class which was either economically or socially powerful. The initial obedience of the Army was not enough, because the Army, which lived in contact with civil society and was influenced by it, ended by being divided in its counsels and making common cause with the opposition.

The dictatorship, therefore, had no effective force on which to rest, and once the period of longed-for national repose was over, the snowball of discontent began to roll, flattening out the military State and with it, inevitably, the monarchy.

A conspiracy of epigrams, sonnets, puns, anagrams, and jokes of all kinds had been undermining the régime from the beginning, and against this kind of offensive, cannon could do nothing. The military State was powerless before the irresistible aggression of the wit of a highly imaginative people.

It was also difficult to put down student revolts which, from 1927 onwards were a source of serious anxiety to the Government. The students had their own methods of striking a blow for liberty and were aided and abetted by the Republican professors. The police invaded the schools and universities or opened fire on them from the street in battles which boded no good for the dictatorship. For the political ebullience of the students was, in a way, the expression of the ruling sentiment of the wealthy classes, and a Conservative revolution is extremely difficult to subdue when the people cannot be relied on to help in suppressing it.

The clamour in the street found an echo in the barracks and military discipline received a rude shock.

By 1928 the possibility of saving the monarchy by dismissing the Dictator had faded, if indeed it had ever existed. Vast sectors of opinion, which until then had been only directed against the dictatorship, now decided to join the ranks of Republicanism. The "neutral" classes became Republican. And the Republicans, jolted into action by the influx of large middle-class reinforcements, regrouped their forces. Alejandro Lerroux was again in the limelight; and no doubt the rise in his private credit reflected the seriousness of the monarchy's position. Manuel Azaña, Civil Servant, distinguished man of letters and obscure ex-reformist politician, helped with his *Acción Republicana* to stiffen the growing anti-dynastic feeling. Republicans of varying hues united soon afterwards in the *Alianza Republicana* under the dubious leadership of Lerroux.

The oligarchs were not caught napping. They had seen which way the wind was blowing and were preparing to take the lead in opposing the Crown. The landed oligarchy was deserting the King.

We have seen that the dictatorship of Primo de Rivera was being strangled by the blockade of the interests it had harmed. Seeking air where he had drawn his first inspiration to begin his perilous march towards absolute power, the Dictator turned on January 26th, 1930, to the Captains-General and naval commanders: "The Army and the Navy first made me Dictator, either with their active support or by their tacit consent; the Army and the Navy should be the first to say whether I ought to continue or to resign my powers."

The armed forces did not renew their vote of confidence, and Primo de Rivera, openly humiliated, resigned on the following day, to the great satisfaction of the King, who was incapable of seeing that he had played his last card and had lost everything.

Then began the death-throes of the monarchical institution, the still visible mast of the submerged ship of the Restoration, most of whose crew were already making for the Republican shore in the lifeboats.

When the dictatorship fell, it left the monarchy isolated and unprotected, exposed to the fury of the revolutionary torrent. There followed a year of anxieties in the Palace, alarms and excursions, skirmishes, a political witches' Sabbath. No Government succeeded in pacifying the country, because the State had already arrived at that tragic cross-roads where liberty leads to anarchy and tyranny—to revolution.

Moreover, on the eve of victory, Spanish democracy was without a leader. It was a warren of parties, a nursery of small great men. Who could it find as a leader? Not Lerroux, because no one trusted him. Not a Socialist, because the property owners must not be alarmed. Tacitly, the people began to line up behind the deserters from the monarchy. The most conspicuous of these was Don Niceto Alcalá Zamora who, in April 1930, with genial opportunism, declared himself a Republican.

The oligarchy placed itself at the head of the revolution. It perceived that nothing could save the throne and prepared to assume command on the change of régime. At a time when the Catalan capitalists were supplying Cabinet Ministers to the dying monarchy, when they should, more than anyone, have been reconstructing the national front of 1917 and marching in the Republican vanguard, the old Restoration politicians, more astute and better informed, were boarding the Republican ship or beginning to signify to the Republican demagogues, with many nods and winks, that they wanted to entrust to them, at the appropriate moment, the defence of their interests.

Alcalá Zamora was now first in the field; the people were applauding him and the leaders of the middle class and the proletariat were hailing him as a heaven-sent leader. Yet the waves of the revolution could not have washed onto the Republican beach a castaway of the old régime with fewer qualifications to lead the new.

Still, he was accepted as the leader of democracy, firstly, because the Spanish people measured political talent by eloquence, and loved political rhetoric as a public show. Secondly, Alcalá Zamora was recommending a Conservative Republic, and it seemed to the majority that by supporting him, they were guaranteeing a rapid and peaceful change of régime by forestalling resistance among the wealthy classes. No one saw a danger, but rather an advantage, in incorporating in the Republican ranks individuals and social classes which, because of their past and the nature of their interests, were incompatible with the new régime.

Alcalá Zamora was fighting for a soulless Republic, as barren as Rachel—a Republic served, according to him, by "persons who have been, and are now, much more to my Right". "A viable, governable, Conservative Republic, which would attract the governing abilities of the Centre and of Spanish intellectuals —such a Republic I would serve, I would govern, I would propagate and defend", he said at Valencia on beginning his career under the new standard. He commended himself to San Vicente Ferrer and announced that he would gladly see the Cardinal of Toledo at the head of his Republic.

But the Republic, with or without the Cardinal of Toledo, could not be Conservative without committing suicide, as the monarchy had committed suicide through being Conservative.

It was patent that more than a century of civil war had taught nobody anything. There were just as many Republican and proletarian parties, if not more, than in the nations which were biologically mature. It was still assumed that Spain was another France or England. And the oligarchy was concerned that the Republic should be parliamentary and liberty general, because only thus could the real revolution—the revolution which was to write *finis* to the oligarchs—be avoided.

The dictatorship had thrust Spanish politics into a blind alley. It had directed them again into the channel of the pre-Restoration nineteenth century. And the opposition to the monarchy of Alfonso XIII was to be, till the end, an echo or almost literal transcript of the opposition to the monarchy of Isabel II. History was doing an about-turn, going back to its starting point of sixty years ago. By placing Spanish politics logically in the nineteenth century, Primo de Rivera was also annulling in this sense all the work of Cánovas and provoking among unwary democrats a reaction equivalent to that of the revolutionaries of 1868. The people and their tribunes were falling into a snare. The dictatorship had been overthrown in the name of liberty, and in the name of liberty the constitutional, parliamentary and anti-clerical Republic of 1873 was going to be reborn. Both times, the well-meaning had ignored the fact that a nation which throws out a dictator does not thereby acquire the right to set itself up as a Liberal régime; for liberty is not the recompense or moral reward of the enemies of tyranny, granted them because they hate tyranny, but a form of government which is denied, however ardently wooed, to nations where great social inequality reigns.

Spanish democracy had gone back with a rush to its position in the romantic epoch.

"We have come", ran the manifesto of the Provisional Government, "to overthrow the fortress in which personal power has immured itself, to relegate the monarchy to the archives of History and to establish the Republic on the basis of universal suffrage represented in a Constituent Assembly. From this Assembly, the Spain of the future will arise. . . ."

This archaic document ended with the words "Long live

Spain with honour!" which the poet López de Ayala had inserted in the manifesto of 1868.

The monarchy fell as the result of adverse municipal elections. "The voting in the Spanish capitals and chief urban centres has had the effect of a plebiscite against the monarchy and in favour of the Republic", declared the Republican coalition jubilantly.

The Republic issued, in fact, from the womb of the cities. The countryside had voted for the monarchy. And though this latter fact did not impair the legitimacy of the new régime—which was acknowledged by Greeks and Trojans alike—it was yet so serious an aspect of the realities of the Spanish situation that only politicians momentarily drunk with victory could belittle it.

At the residence of Dr. Marañón, Count Romanones, the last servant of the King, was relinquishing the reins of power, so to speak, to the *romanonista* Alcalá Zamora. The landed oligarchy was handing over the command to the landed oligarchy.

Alfonso XIII was already a fugitive. He had been abandoned. Every political régime has its support in social classes, and the social classes which had sustained the Restoration throne were seeking a last-minute salvation in dissimulation prompted by cowardice, or in the Republic whither their interests led.

For the sixth time in little more than a century, the gospel of popular sovereignty had been proclaimed. The civil war was continuing its course.

# BOOK THREE

# THE ECONOMIC GEOGRAPHY
# OF SPAIN

## CHAPTER I

## THE LAND

I AM INSERTING HERE the following two chapters on the
economic position of Spain for more than one reason; firstly,
because I cannot pass over such vital problems as the agrarian
and capitalist questions, and secondly, in order to present in
documentary form the social basis of the nation as it was in 1931,
at the moment when the political régime of the Restoration was
overthrown and the second Republic came into being. In this
way, we shall complete our understanding of the expiring system
and at the same time be able to sum up the Republic with more
exactitude, its *raison d'être*, its possibilities and its limitations.

### THE WEALTH OF SPAIN[1]

A few preliminaries about the wealth of Spain are unavoidable.
We must begin by inquiring whether the nature of the territory
is, or is not, to be considered a decisive factor in the fundamental
economic-political problem which so gravely compromises the
existence of the nation.

I think we shall find, if we have not already done so, that
Spain's unhappy plight cannot be attributed to an insufficiency
of natural resources. Gibbon called Roman Spain "the opulent
country"; and the first travellers and historiographers went even
further in their panegyrics on Spain. Strabo tells us that the
Ancients located the Elysian Fields in Andalusia "the habitation
of the Blessed". Alfonso the Wise begins his *Crónica General*
with an extravagant description of Spain, which he says is
"like the Paradise of God". Father Mariana, in his *Historia
General de España*, praises the soil and climate of his country
without moderation or discretion.

[1] Fairly exhaustive studies on this subject will be found in *El Potencial
Económico de España*, by Antonio de Miguel, Head of the Statistical Department of the Bank of Spain (Madrid, 1935), and in *España el País y sus Habitantes*,
by Leonardo Martín Echeverría. Mexico, 1940.

Naturally, Spain is not all this. But neither is she the opposite —neither a poor country nor a paradise; but simply a nation highly favoured by nature in some aspects and chastened in others. Spain, cleft by mighty rivers—the nine rivers of Eden —and crossed by majestic chains of mountains, enjoys more hours of sunshine than any country in Europe except Greece and Italy; she is the country beloved of Flora and Pomona, for in her various regions she has a climate and soil which favour the almost limitless cultivation of fruit; with physical features which raise her in beauty and enchantment far above other nations. She is also a country of bare rocks, steppes, pitiless deserts and desolation.

When we consider the enormous strides made by science, there is no doubt that Spain could succeed in becoming extraordinarily prosperous. Experts admit that her principal economic defects can be mitigated or remedied by the intelligent exploitation of her own resources. We must bear in mind that we are speaking of a nation where almost everything remains to be done.

The cardinal problem of the Spanish economy may be summed up in the fact that Spain has too much sunshine or too little rainfall. There is one area—the Cantabrian Mountains and Galicia—where the rainfall is heavy, but the temperature and the mountainous nature of the district militate against a flourishing agriculture; and another immense zone—two-thirds of the whole country—where the rainfall is insufficient to counteract the high degree of evaporation. In summer the soil of Andalusia, for example, exhales five times more humidity than it absorbs. To this phenomenon is due the prolonged drought from which the Spanish countryside suffers for most of the year.

From remote times, attempts have been made to solve the problem by making use of the rivers; and thanks to irrigation, the Levante zone has long been one of the most fertile in Europe. Throughout the dry regions of Spain irrigation works have been, or are being, carried out, or plans are being made to carry them out. There are at present 1,500,000 hectares under irrigation, 3 per cent of the national territory. In 1933 a plan was made to bring water to another 1,285,900 hectares. In all, probably 6,000,000 hectares could be brought under irrigation.

Spain is an agrarian country; and starting from this supposition (as if Spain could never be otherwise), the national economy has been judged solely from the viewpoint of the climate and the land. It is not surprising, therefore, to find in circulation innumerable technical and literary works giving a gloomy view of the picture; and an equally huge mass of publications countering this depressing effect with 'large doses of optimism. The controversy about the wealth of Spain—whether Spain is a poor country or a rich one—has always existed, with now the pessimistic and now the optimistic theory uppermost, generally according to the epoch. But because up till now Spain has lived almost exclusively by agriculture and has not known true prosperity, it must not be taken for granted that the possibilities latent in her subsoil, soil and climate have been exhausted.

Taken as a whole, the natural economy of Spain is very complete and well-balanced. But there can be no efficient agriculture without a certain development in industry and commerce—transport, tools and machinery, low rates of interest, credit—and in Spain no such development has taken place, even in the measure necessary to aid the countryside.

Nevertheless the basic Spanish economy as a whole does not justify the despair of our gloomy authors who have frequently blamed the geological formation of the country for the pessimism with which the political and social vicissitudes of Spain have inspired them. But these vicissitudes are another story. The convenient expedient of transferring the results of a fatal policy to Nature's broad shoulders might pass in a less scientific age; today it will not hold water.

The wealth that agriculture denies to Spaniards may come from industry. There is nothing to show that Spain ought to give up all idea of becoming an industrial country, as she has hitherto done. On the contrary, Nature suggests and urges such a course by endowing Spain with more abundant resources for industry than for agriculture. Though her agricultural products are not to be despised, Spain has been from primitive times more famous for her metals and raw materials than for the fruits of her soil. And the progress realized everywhere since the eighteenth century in the discovery and exploitation of all kinds of mines has not deposed Spain from the prominent place she has always occupied in the mining world.

Spain is still one of the nations which produce the most lead; in this respect, she takes first place in Europe. Spain is also, together with Germany, the greatest silver-producing country. Until recent years, no nation in the world produced as much copper, and today only certain countries of America and Asia surpass her in this field, and none in Europe. Enormous quantities of iron, of unsurpassable quality, lie in the Spanish subsoil. In Almadén, Spain has the richest deposits of mercury in the world, which have only recently begun to be rivalled by the Italian.

Spain has, therefore, great resources in the way of raw

materials. In fact, that chemical substance is rare which is not found to a greater or lesser extent in her territory. Stone in every form and shape, from granite to jasper, abounds in the Peninsula.

There is another element in which Spain is equally privileged —mineral salts. Common salt is present in dense and hard strata in many places. The immense new works at Suria, which cover an area of 350 square kilometres, are devoted to the production of potash, of which Spain is one of the greatest producers in the world. Spain is also very rich in sulphur, which she possesses in large quantities and which is perhaps the principal ingredient of the nation's young chemical industry.

From all this it can be seen that Spain is in a position, from the point of view of raw materials, to found important metallurgical and chemical industries. Applied chemistry, still in its infancy in the Iberian Peninsula, has offered a vast field of activity and wealth to countries which are poor in agricultural development. According to expert opinion, there is no reason why Spain should lag behind. Moreover Spain, so rich in metals and metalloids, possesses bituminous coal in fabulous quantities. The Spanish subsoil contains unlimited supplies of lignite, a more modern combustible than coal, and these supplies would make the large-scale development of the chemical industry in Spain a practical proposition. Spain—so the experts in these branches of engineering say—could obtain from this kind of coal respectable quantities of oil, since she possesses certain kinds of lignite which have been called solidified oil, exceeding 6,000 calories in some seams, while the German lignite, for example, which is much used in that nation's chemical industry, falls short of 5,000 calories. Nevertheless up till now, nothing has been done in Spain with regard to the distillation of inferior kinds of coal. The only step in this direction has been the utilization of 50,000 tons per annum of bituminous slate in Puertollano, producing a total of 750,000 litres of petrol, 2,300,000 litres of fuel-oil and 4,300,000 litres of creosote.

If we are to judge by drillings carried out up to the present, Spain has no oil wells. On the other hand, Spanish production of coal for industry does not meet the needs of the home market. Spanish coal suffers from excessive softness and breaks easily on being extracted. This is due to the peculiar formation of the strata. No less than 65 per cent of Asturian coal breaks into pieces. That means that, though Spain's position as regards solid fuel is not really desperate, like that of Italy, the lack of oil and the softness of her coal make her dependent on foreign imports in this aspect of her economy.

But the experts are unanimous in saying that this state of affairs can be remedied, and there is no reason why it should be an insuperable obstacle to the industrialization of the country, since Spain possesses enormous deposits of bituminous coal from which, as I have already pointed out, great quantities of petrol and heavy oils can be distilled. Moreover, the experts add, Spain has an incalculable potential wealth of hydro-electric energy. The Spanish rivers present serious obstacles to navigation, that is, they are not vehicles of commerce; the rapidity of their current prevents this. But it is precisely the great leaps of the rushing water through clefts and over precipices which make Spain a privileged country, if one day she decides to exploit her immense hydro-electric wealth. The hydro-dynamic value of the Spanish rivers is, in short, unparalleled; but up till now, this source of wealth has been practically neglected.

At the present time, some two million horse-power are generated, approximately a quarter by thermic and the rest by hydraulic power stations—much less than could be utilized, since an expert has asserted that Spain could make use of more than four million horse-power or probably, in the opinion of another expert, more than six million.

The importance of these figures is emphasized by the fact that Spain consumes only a third, perhaps, of her hydro-electric potential, even though almost the whole of the Catalan textile industry, that is, the whole of one region, has been electrified.

The electrification of Catalonia, begun in 1906 and virtually completed during the first World War, was carried out with Canadian capital. This kind of industrial installation obviously requires much capital. The same thing applies to the chemical industry; and the scarcity of capital is one of the causes of the scant development of both sources of wealth in Spain.

This does not influence the fact that Spain's future, if it is to be worth while, depends upon industrialization. And the industrialization of Spain is not practicable without the previous electrification of the country.

Here I will leave this summary presentation of the Spanish economy in general and turn to some fundamental aspects of the agrarian economy.

THE AGRONOMIC MAP

I have before me an agronomic map on which Spain is divided into six zones of cultivation: pasture-land, vineyards, cereals, orange-groves, olives and sugar-cane.

The zones of cultivation usually correspond to the regional divisions, a fact which cannot but have repercussions in the political sphere.

The pasture-lands embrace the whole of northern Spain, from fertile Galicia to the Cape of Higuer in Guipuzcoa.

The vine-growing region occupies all the north-east, with the eastern slopes of the Cantabrian Mountains, the Basque Mountains and the Pyrenees to the north, forming a triangle with its apices almost on the source of the Ebro in the west, Cape Creus in the east and the city of Teruel in the south. This zone is cut in two by the basin of the Ebro which flows, like almost all its tributaries, through vine-bearing lands. At Haro, with Alavese La Rioja on its left bank, it penetrates the wide valley of the vineyards; afterwards traversing the rich plantations of La Rioja itself, the adoptive country of Espartero and the birthplace of Sagasta, and, skirting the Navarrese vineyards at Tudela, flows on through the innumerable vineyards of Aragon at Borja and Tarazona, to the north of the plains of Plasencia. Farther on, the mighty river passes on its right bank the renowned vineyard of Cariñena, the most famous of Aragon. Only a part of the province of Teruel, where its frontier marches with New Castile, remains on the fringe of the vine-growing region which, for the rest, covers the whole of Aragon, except the desert of Los Monegros and El Somontano, a land scourged by the icy winds from the Iberian Mountains, principally from the Sierra del Moncayo.

The region of the vines ends near the coast of the Levante, just on the southern bank of the Ebro, and to the west, stops short of the border of the Maestrazgo. But from the mouth of the great river northwards, towards the Ampurdan (except for the fringe of coast from Tortosa to the Llobregat which is an orange-growing district), there extend the rich vineyards of the Tarragona countryside, el Panadés and el Maresme, pride of the *rabassaires*. Inside Catalonia the supremacy of the vine persists with the estimable wines of el Priorato and Vallés.

The region of the vineyards is formed, therefore, by Alava, Navarre, La Rioja, Aragon and Catalonia[1], in that order.

The orange-growing region begins at the Punta del Llobregat, south of Barcelona, and from Tarragona onwards, spreads triumphantly over the whole coast of the Levante as far as the Cordillera Penibética on the western approaches to Almería. Here, without entirely disappearing (the Andalusian orangeries

[1] Today the vineyards of La Mancha are more extensive than those of Catalonia, covering more than 350,000 hectares as against Catalonia's 250,000.

are among the most prosperous) the orange yields pride of place to the sugar-cane which occupies the whole Penibetic coast. But afterwards, it continues to monopolize the whole southern plain of the province of Cadiz where it stops short, perhaps out of respect for the inimitable and world-famous vines of Jerez.

The orange grows in compact masses and immense groves from the mouth of the Ebro to the valley of the Segura. In the Valencia *huerta* the orange-groves are especially dense and produce almost half of the total output of Spain. There are in the Levante belt about 27 million orange trees and 800,000 lemon trees.

A cursory glance at the map I have before me shows that the wheat- and olive-growing districts embrace little short of two-thirds of the territory. Hence the exorbitant power, as I have pointed out, of the Spanish ruling class.

The special political-economic protection extended by the monopolizers of power to the wheat and olive interests has stimulated the overriding and exclusive development of both products to the disadvantage of others, like the vine, which in Estremadura and La Mancha is beating a retreat before the encroachments of the olive tree, already wielding despotic power in Andalusia. For its part, wheat-farming is also tending to thrust beyond its present frontiers, penetrating into the Levante orchards, the fertile plain of Granada and the vineyards of Aragon.

The wheat-growing district comprises, roughly, all the Meseta, from the Cantabrian Mountains as far as the Sierra Morena and the border of Murcia, from north-west to south-east; and from the right bank of the Ebro near its confluence with the Segre, as far as the Guadiana, on the southern border of the province of Cáceres, looking at the region from north-east to south-west. Badajoz is already in the olive zone.

The wheat-growing district consists, therefore, of the whole of the central Meseta, the Maestrazgo and the rural areas of Cáceres and La Mancha in the province of Albacete.

The experts subdivide the grain-growing region into two zones, the northern and the southern, taking the central range of mountains as the line of demarcation. The northern zone is the grain-growing district *par excellence*, containing the most extensive and the best wheat-belts. The wheat of the Tierra de Campos is of excellent quality, only rivalled by its neighbours, the cornfields of the plain of León, of the Armuña in the province of Salamanca, of the Concha de Pineda in Burgos, and of the

Tierra del Pan in the middle valley of the Duero above Zamora. The steppes of Valladolid are an important wheat-growing centre. This northern zone—Old Castile, opulent granary of Spain—produces the proudest harvests and the most reactionary deputies.

Upper La Mancha and the Sagra of Toledo are also wheat-growing provinces.

The region of the olive tree covers the whole of Andalusia, except the slice occupied by the orange-groves of Almería, by the sugar-cane of the Cordillera Penibética and the orange, once again, of the province of Cadiz.

What the vine is to the Aragonese and Catalan landscapes, and the cornfields are to the scenery of the wide central Meseta, the olive is to the Andalusian countryside. If the Ebro is the river of the vines, and the Duero the river of the cornfields, the Guadalquivir is the river of the olive trees.

The Andalusian olive-groves take precedence over all others in Spain for richness and extent. They overwhelm the fertile countryside of Jaén with their enormous mass in the Sierra de Úbeda, the valleys of Baeza and Andújar and the plain of Martos; they extend, an immense vista, through the entire valley of the classic Betis, invading the mountains and dominating the flat arable land of Cordova, to penetrate into the district around Seville, where the most exquisite olives for the table are produced. In less profusion, the olive plantations spread far and wide over the whole region of Andalusia, over the fertile Tierra de Barros at Badajoz, the southern slope of the Sierra Morena at Huelva and the border of the Murcian *huerta* in the Levante, without forgetting the northern hills of Granada or the slopes of the Serrania de Ronda already in the province of Cadiz.

The olive-oil industry is the most important industry in Andalusia.

Such is the agronomic structure of Spain as a whole; it must not be interpreted in the sense that nothing else is cultivated in each region, but that the products I have mentioned are the dominating ones.

## LAND TENURE IN SPAIN—THE SATISFIED AND THE DISSATISFIED REGIONS

We must now consider the system of land tenure as it appeared at the fall of the Restoration State. I shall deal with the subject with reference to those regions where the distribution of landed property and the juridical form of land tenure are most sharply defined.

The structure of landed property in Spain is the same today as it was in the eighteenth century. The geometry of its distribution also appears identical. In both aspects, the progressivist revolution involuntarily confined itself to exaggerating the evils which Jovellanos was already denouncing. Qualitatively nothing has changed. As regards the distribution and ownership of the land, Galicia stands today where she stood then. The same can be said of Castile and of the Basque Provinces and of the Levante. Catalonia has suffered little change.

Taking the system of agrarian property as our subject—and here we are not concerned with anything else—we are bound to conclude that one part of Spain is organically healthy and another part, the greater part, organically diseased. Galicia, the two Castiles and Andalusia are diseased; the Levante, Catalonia and the Basque Provinces are sound.

For profound historical reasons, the Basques have enjoyed from of old a form of land tenure which may be classed as satisfactory; so much so, that it preserves a great likeness to the economic régime of Rome under the kings, and Basque democracy has been, strictly speaking, merely a reproduction of that system, without the aristocratic element which has never existed in the Basque Provinces for the exoteric reason that all Basques, even the most humble, always consider that the fact of being Basques confers on them a patent of nobility. Neither the passage of time nor history have fundamentally modified in recent centuries the rural economy of Vizcaya and Guipuzcoa, the nucleus of the region. The Basque peasant dwells in the *caserío* or isolated farmhouse, the cell of the community, to which is frequently attached a plot of ground large enough to support the family, which also benefits by the communal grazing lands and forests on the slope of some neighbouring hill.

The land is therefore reasonably parcelled out in the Basque country. There are fewer owners than landless peasants, but there is an enormous number of tenant farmers and the nucleus of agricultural day-labourers is proportionately small. The tenant and owner farmers are, therefore, in the majority. But the tenants are in practice the owners of their land because the long-term lease has been the rule in the Vizcayan and Guipuzcoan countryside and in part of Santander from time immemorial. The advantages of this form of land tenure for the labourer and for agrarian economy in general are obvious and only outweighed, where the farmer personally is concerned, by the advantages of outright ownership (where property is not abusive) or by communal farming. For the long-term lease means that the peasant becomes attached to his land and no longer has the threat of eviction hanging over his head like a sword of Damocles—all of which leads to the improvement of the land and to the peace of mind of the man who farms it. In spite of the freedom allowed by Spanish law to rural proprietors to dictate to the landless peasant any form of contract they please, the Basque landowners have never abused this inadmissible right—not because they are morally superior to landowners in other regions, but because any other sort of conduct could not be adjusted to the social framework of Basque rural life. As regards property, therefore, the Basque countryside shows a marked equilibrium. A kind of tribal society prevails there (the Basque is the most rural of the Spanish peoples), like that of the primitive Roman tribes; and this state of affairs is the foundation of the patriarchal Basque democracy which rests on the family system of land tenure.

We must exclude from this system a great part of the province of Alava, where the land is excessively parcelled out and there are fewer farmhouses. In Navarre there are two zones; the riparian, with a system like that of Aragon and La Rioja, and the mountainous, more akin to the agrarian economy of Guipuzcoa and Vizcaya.

In Catalonia the ownership of land is less evenly distributed than in the Basque Provinces; but nevertheless the region can be considered organically healthy in this respect.

The prevailing system in Aragon is similar, but the difference appears greater than it is, because the soil of Aragon is inferior to that of Catalonia, the region is a harsh one, with great expanses of steppes and an implacable climate which scourges the land and its inhabitants. All this helps to lend it an air of poverty and ruggedness.

The map of property has been regulated in these regions by the *fuero* of Monzón which goes back to the sixteenth century and serves as a buffer against excessive concentration and atomization of the land by limiting the right of inheritance. In addition, the Land Register (*Catastro*), dating from the beginning of the eighteenth century, has helped to regulate the agrarian economy.

Catalonia is a rich and productive region, thanks to the variety of the climate and soil. We have already seen that the chief interest of the Catalans is the cultivation of the vine. Consequently the Catalan agrarian problem is bound up with the vineyards. No doubt there are more great landowners than is desirable, and the distribution of the land is notoriously unjust. But it would not be beyond the powers of a stable Government to solve this question. On the whole, therefore, from the point of view of landed property, it cannot be said that Catalonia is a sick region. On the contrary, we might include it without hesitation among the sound.

The Castilian type of agricultural day-labourer is virtually non-existent in Catalonia. The only source of conflict, where agrarian property is concerned, is not, therefore, the landless labourer, but the leaseholders, the great army of the *rabassaires*.

The *rabassaire* is the landless peasant who obtains land from the owners on condition that he plants vines, the duration of the lease being determined by the life of the vine. The terms of the contract vary from province to province. Generally the labourer pays a sum agreed beforehand and afterwards hands over to the owner half, a third, or a quarter of the crop, according to the quality of the soil. There has always been discontent among the *rabassaires* whose legal situation as regards the enjoyment of the property has never been clear or stable. This has led to repeated disputes between owners and labourers, the most violent being at the end of the last century when the phylloxera plague killed an enormous number of vines. Countless land-owners tried to turn the disaster to their own advantage by cancelling the contracts, taking the view that legally the life of the vine was ended. The courts, after an obstinate and bitter controversy, decreed that, for the purposes of the leases, the life of the vine could not be taken as less than twenty-five years. The *rabassa morta*, in short, presses heavily on the shoulders of the direct cultivator whose logical ambition is to throw off the yoke and become one day the owner of the land.

Notwithstanding all this, I repeat that this problem, which has a great influence on Catalan politics, does not denote any incurable evil; still less can it be regarded as a symptom of an outrageous agrarian economy such as exists in other regions of Spain.

The last organically healthy region is the east; Castellón, Valencia, Alicante.

The Land Register, or system of classifying lands and their ownership, is fairly complete for this zone and gives us some very interesting information. The experts include the province of Murcia, together with Almería, in a separate region—the south-eastern. When I refer to the Levante, therefore, it must be understood that I am alluding to the provinces of Castellón,

Valencia and Alicante, although, as far as my arguments are concerned, there is no great difference between the Levante and the south-eastern region. The same line of reasoning would equally well apply to Murcia and Almería.

The Levante has the smallest number of large estates in all that part of Spain which has been surveyed and classified, among which is not included the classic region of the smallholdings, the crippled north-west. Estates of more than 500 hectares only occupy 6·6 per cent of the land in the Levante, while those of more than 250 hectares occupy no more than 14·56 per cent.

As we can see, land in the east is not concentrated in a few estates, but divided into innumerable farms. The type of estate prevailing is, as in the Basque country, the family farm, whose size and productivity is relatively satisfactory. It is a country, like the Basque Provinces, without either latifundia or excessive parcelling out.

We must now glance at the division of wealth in each region. Not all the Levante has been surveyed and classified and therefore the figures I give are incomplete; but they will serve as an illustration.

There are in the east 1,082 landowners with an income of over 5,000 pesetas a year, which represents 32 per cent of the total number of proprietors and only 15·78 per cent of the total wealth of the region.

If in the eastern provinces there are fewer large concentrations of territory than in the rest of Spain, except in the minifundist north-west, there are also fewer large accumulations of wealth. The 246 biggest proprietors of the province of Castellón only monopolize 8 per cent of the local income from land. In Valencia, without counting the coastal fringe (which if it were included would reduce the proportion), 17·40 per cent of the total wealth is in the hands of the privileged minority.

We now come to long-suffering Galicia, the smallholders' region *par excellence* and one of the most unhappy in Spain as regards the parcelling out of the land and the legal aspect of agrarian property. Galicia is a stricken region, mortally sick in this respect.

It is not entirely true to say that the whole of irrigated Spain is divided up into smallholdings, while the whole of unirrigated Spain is given over to the latifundia.

The chain of the smallholdings, consisting of thousands and thousands of small territorial links, stretches from the ancient

Asturias de Santillana, to the west of Santander and runs through the whole mountain range: Asturias, Galicia, Pais del Bierzo, north of León. But in Galicia, the chain is already a close-woven net of minute parcels, imprisoning the region like a coat of mail and holding it literally choked and submissive in poverty-stricken chaos. Here white bread is a delicacy and sugar and olive oil luxuries only enjoyed by the wealthy.

The medium proprietor possesses less than one hectare. A two-hectare plot counts as one of the largest estates; it is, for Galicia, a princely property. And the labourer who does not pay the *foro* is a privileged being.

Agrarian property in Galicia has been divided and subdivided from remote times. The *foro* or canon in kind, which the peasant pays the owner, is distinguished from the other *censos* prevailing in Spain in that it is hereditary and tied to the land, and is not affected by any legal relations that may be established between owner and tenant. The *foro* commonly remains in force for three generations, and though labourers and masters may die, the *censo* remains as part of the heritable estate. This particular form of *censo* generally consists of the payment to the owner of the farm of a fixed quantity of wine, rye, or other product of this lovely land. Once a year, as in the Middle Ages, the labourer goes to the village with his sack of rye, his wineskin, or other merchandise stowed away in the saddle-bags on his patient donkey, and pays his humble tribute, which for him is his own life-blood. Often his lord is a wealthy man, but sometimes he is a poor devil who has to share the tribute with another. There are rents of this kind which consist of the yearly payment of a hen. Whether in these cases subdivision is the rule and the hen has to be subdivided also, is a detail I have not been able to verify.

The *foro* and the *subforo* and the *subsubforo* have split the Galician countryside into atoms. There are plots measuring roughly 25 sq. yards in the irrigated parts and plots of a quarter of an acre are frequent in the dry parts—those between a quarter of an acre and 6¼ acres are innumerable.

Under the system of land tax in Spain, the lowest assessment is 6 pesetas. Taking Spain as a whole, these assessments of 6 pesetas represent 40 per cent of the receipts from land tax. Galicia, Asturias and León represent a fifth of that 40 per cent.

Each family usually works about 10 hectares which naturally rarely constitute a single estate; so that the peasants pass from one farm to the other, sometimes at great distances from each other, with a deplorable waste of energy and time, and consequent loss of wages. Not less serious is the economic waste involved in the erection of low mud walls to demarcate the inexorable boundaries of the property. A considerable area of land is lost for cultivation by this practice.

To sum up, Galicia is grievously afflicted by the atomization of the land and by the *foro*. She is saved from complete asphyxiation by the valiant sea washing her coasts, the prowess of her fishermen and the marvellous bays—the most beautiful in the world—whence her landless youth set out for America.

Cato demanded that slaves should work the clock round, with only an indispensable pause for sleep. The Galician peasant would have appealed to the exacting Roman as an ideal slave.

The other part of Spain which is organically diseased comprises two-thirds of the national territory: the two Castiles, La Mancha, Estremadura and Andalusia. Here 90 per cent of the oligarchs have their estates. The large proprietors of these regions are the richest landowners in the whole of Spain. The economic power of the old nobility is also concentrated in the central Meseta and Andalusia. The new rich of 1860, in their turn, founded their fortunes as landowners in these regions, the place where the monasteries and municipalities had the greatest number of estates.

THE LANDLESS PEASANT

Before examining the structure of property and the division of the soil in the territories of the ruling class, I must say a few words of a general character.

During the fifty-seven years between the restoration of the oligarchy and the advent of the second Republic, the only reforms carried out by the various Governments in the key problem of land ownership may be summed up as follows: On August 30th, 1907, there appeared a Government regulation which, under the ambitious title of *Ley de Colonización y Repoblación Interior* (Law for Internal Colonization and Repopulation) created 18 colonies in 29 years over an area of 14,470 hectares, and gave land to 1,679 colonists—a farce only surpassed by that of universal suffrage. On January 7th, 1827, the *Dirección Social Agraria* was empowered to buy land in private ownership, if any owner was willing to sell. In ten years, 37 estates covering 71,858 hectares were split up into 6,687 lots. But an inhuman Government insisted on the colonists paying 20 per cent of the value of the land in cash, and this was the reef, amounting to a veto for a peasant population which was among the poorest of the poor, on which the whole scheme was wrecked. Everything, therefore, remained a farce.

For the most part, the 2½ million landless peasants who go begging for work in Spain live in the *páramos* of central Spain and Estremadura and in the fruitful *vegas* and fields of Andalusia. These plains also house a numerous host of tenant farmers, while the small proprietors, almost all of them ruined by taxes, are legion. As we shall see later, the most pathetic aspect of the rural economy is that all the farmers are pitilessly reduced to the level of a proletariat. Day-labourers, tenant farmers and small proprietors are equally penalized by the harsh consequences of the property-owning system. Hence the considerable tragedy that not even in Spanish agriculture is there a middle class which is worthy of the name.

The principle that Might is Right, the law of the jungle, prevails in the Spanish countryside, and there, as in the ocean, the big fish devour the little fish. The reason for this is obvious. The ruling class in Spanish society did not want to put an end to this anarchy precisely because the strongest animal and the biggest fish were wearing the toga of the legislator. Every law has a restrictive sense; it is limitative. No law was ever passed to decree that everyone shall do as he pleases. So in the Spanish countryside every man was allowed to devour his neighbour, since there was no law to prevent him. But in the savage struggle the victory naturally goes to the strongest, and the strongest is the richest. This was why the landowning oligarchy, the monopolizers of political power, decided not to regulate the relations between the rural social classes in the legal sphere. Everything—persons and property—was hypocritically handed over to the power of the territorial dragon.

Incredible as it may appear, it is nevertheless a fact that, from the time when the oligarchy took over the helm of the Spanish ship until the overthrow of the institutions in 1931, not a single law was passed to check the power of the great landowners. No restraint was placed on the freedom of the arrogant throng to fix wages as they pleased, no measure taken to compel them to treat the *braceros* better than draught-animals, nor was a single word said on the subject of leases.

The only legislation for the protection of the worker in the period I refer to dealt with Spanish commerce and industry. Social insurance, wage rates, arbitral committees or organizations, were created or established for the benefit of the industrial and mercantile interests. The peasant was systematically ignored. As I said in a previous chapter, the dictatorship of Primo de

Rivera was prodigal of social laws, but all in favour of the great cities and their suburbs. *The Comités Paritarios*, the cornerstone of that social policy, passed agriculture by. The peasant continued to be utterly defenceless. No one could still doubt where the interests of the ruling class lay.

For the same reason the landowner can treat his property in Spain as he wills; no one can force him to cultivate it.

In the regions of the corn and olive, the land is cultivated on the large estates by labourers under the big landowner or a steward representing the absentee owner. In an infinite number of cases, it is the leaseholders who cultivate the land. In others, the small proprietors and their families supply all the labour. Frequently the labour is mixed; and there are even occasions when the same farmer is at once owner, leaseholder and day-labourer.

The day-labourer usually works a normal period of 160 days a year and 90 extra days at harvest time. A typical day's wages in 1930 was 3·25 pesetas and 5·50 pesetas at harvest time. If things went well, therefore, the average daily wage of the agricultural proletariat was 2·80 pesetas. On such an income, the peasant living on a fixed wage was practically reduced to starvation level.

The peasant worker has no defence against the landowner. If the local *bracero* refuses to work for the wage offered, the owner brings in labour from the neighbouring villages or, in the summer, gives preference to the Portuguese and Galician serfs who descend on the central plains, hungry for white bread.

The *braceros* are recruited in the villages in accordance with the needs of the countryside. The host of the landless assembles in the village square, where those required for the work on hand are chosen. Unemployment is rife in agriculture, so that the peasant ends by hiring out his labour for what it will fetch. It goes without saying that in choosing labour the political opinions of those seeking work are taken into account. The man who does not jump through the caciquist hoop is condemned to perpetual unemployment.

During the spring sowing and the summer harvest the countryside is animated, not only by the bright colours in which fecund Nature decks herself and by the song of the birds, but also by the presence of a rustic multitude, which bursts forth from the damp and tumble-down dwellings of Castile where it has sheltered from the frosts and snows, to earn its meagre bread for the whole year. An army of miserable workers, all clad alike in loose cotton jacket or black calico blouse, with sandals of hemp or esparto grass, awaits from the dawn the coveted offer of work—a veritable slave-market.

Another very numerous section of the agrarian population is that of the leaseholders. About half of all rural property is cultivated by tenant farmers, which shows the important place this system occupies in Spain. Nevertheless before the advent of the second Republic there was no law regulating leases. The fact that in an agrarian country where 50 per cent of the soil is cultivated by this method, nothing should have been done to protect the rights of the individual leaseholder, proves how strong is the hold of the big landowners. Unlike the conditions prevailing in the other regions of Spain already alluded to, in Castile, Andalusia, Estremadura and La Mancha the short-term lease is the rule, the most precarious form of ownership of the soil. Nothing restricts the freedom of the landowner to fix the terms of the lease as his caprice and egoism dictate except the general provisions of the Civil Code, and even these are a dead letter to anyone with political influence.

The economic position of the tenant farmer on a short-term lease is often no better than that of the casual labourer. The farmer obtains a plot of land for a limited period and pays the rent in money or in kind or agrees to some other kind of share-cropping contract with the owner. In practice, there is nothing to stop the proprietor from evicting him. Under the stress of poverty, the farmer presses his whole family into the task of extracting the greatest possible yield from the farm. The children cannot go to school (even if there is a school for them to go to) and the women grow old before their time. The system of property and its attendant poverty preys on them all. And it is dangerous to improve the farm, for the owner may then raise the rent or evict the hard-working farmer and lease his land to someone else at a better price.

The short-term lease which prevails in the territories of the oligarchy keeps the farmer in a state of desperate uncertainty and makes him the slave both of the irresponsible proprietor and of the harsh land.

But the misfortunes of the leaseholder do not end here, for the land tax grinds him down as rigorously as it does the small proprietor.

Spanish agriculture is subject to a single tax of 16·24 per cent of the net profits of agricultural property. This tax is exceptionally high, and we may well ask how it was possible for a ruling class, a landowning class, to have decreed such an abusive and unjust tax on land. On the face of it, it appears extraordinary. But if we look closer, we find that the oligarchy was not being guileless; on the contrary, the tax is one more proof of its devilish capacity to exploit the worker.

Because the tax is excessively high the big landowners, who are the only ones to evade it, keep the flock of leaseholders and small proprietors submissive by turning the financial screw. Whether the tax is high or low, matters nothing to the oligarchy. If anything, it prefers, as the ruling propertied class, that it should be high, since the big landowners can evade the tax-collector while the small proprietors have to pay up. So that the full rigour of the 16·24 per cent falls on the humble landowners and the tenant farmers. That is to say, the tax is one more weapon in the armoury of the oligarchs to ensure that the poor should not lift their heads but should bow them meekly to the rich.

## THE SMALL AND THE BIG LANDOWNERS

The small proprietors, who are very numerous in the two Castiles, fare no better than the tenant farmers. They are an indigent section of the community, on the level of a proletariat, always in the clutches of the moneylender or of the credit organizations controlled by the oligarchy.

In the wheat- and olive-growing districts, the system of the smallholdings is reproduced in a virulent form and the farms rarely cover the 15 or 20 hectares which are the minimum required to support a family in the unirrigated regions.

Of the 1,026,412 landowners in the regions included in the Land Register, 1,007,616 have an income of less than 8 pesetas a day, and 847,548 earn less than 1 peseta a day more than the *bracero*.

The total results by regions in the zones of Castile-León, the Central zone, Estremadura, La Mancha and Andalusia show the same appalling poverty as characterizes each province separately.

In the region of Castile-León, 260,423 proprietors make an average yearly profit of 151 pesetas, after deducting expenses and discounting what they would earn by working for others instead of for themselves.

Each of the 166,950 small proprietors in the Central zone earns 192 pesetas a year more than a day-labourer.

In La Mancha there are 264,673 small proprietors, each of whom is individually better off than the *bracero* to the extent of 120 pesetas yearly.

The average profits of the 171,486 modest proprietors in Estremadura amount to 255 pesetas.

In the Guadalquivir region the individual income of the 261,428 small and medium landowners does not exceed 161 pesetas.

The 155,908 small proprietors of the Penibetic region (Malaga and Granada) make an annual individual profit of 255 pesetas.

It can be readily seen that the difference between the income of the *bracero*, the tenant farmer and the small proprietor is not enough to make much difference in their standard of living. Apart from the big landowners, the Spanish farmers wring a heartbreaking existence from the soil; some beg for a day's work; others have to accept whatever terms the landlords impose, since land hunger gives rise to a tremendous struggle between those seeking work; and others live under the illusion that they possess something, though they are no less harassed than the others by sordid penury.

There are in the two Castiles, La Mancha, Estremadura and Andalusia, 1,325,446 medium and small proprietors, all earning less than 5,000 pesetas annually. On the other hand, there are 15,975 big landowners whose income exceeds this figure. Among these 16,000 big proprietors we find the old aristocracy whose fortune has its root in the land. Whether they are aristocrats or not, the big landowners are the heart of the oligarchy, which holds the multitude of day-labourers, small proprietors and leaseholders as in a vice. Let us see how these 16,000 potentates share the wealth of the regions they occupy, and how they partition the land.

In the region of Castile-León, 904 proprietors appropriate 31·26 per cent of the wealth of the district.

In the Central zone, 1,200 landowners take 32·96 per cent of the profits from agriculture.

In La Mancha, 2,132 *señores* pocket 35·46 per cent of the profits.

In Estremadura, 3,867 big landowners share out 57·71 per cent of the total wealth produced by the land.

In the Penibetic region, 1,857 proprietors take 41·81 per cent of the total wealth.

In the Guadalquivir region, 6,015 big landowners account for 56·20 per cent of all the income of the district.

The enormous inequality of income is progressive from north to south. Trifling in the wheat-growing districts of the north, it goes on becoming more marked, until in La Mancha it has assumed serious proportions. But from the middle valley of the Tagus to the mouth of the Guadalquivir, it reaches a stage which is disastrous to the nation.

In Castile the number of big landowners is not large, except in Salamanca, which the experts liken in this respect to Estremadura. But the poverty of the rural population is very marked (these are the regions where the modest landowners have the lowest incomes) and the subjection of the ruined farmer to the great landlords is actually not less effective and complete than in the south. The average for the region—31·26 per cent of the total wealth is in the hands of the big landowners in Old Castile —is not low. Valladolid has not many big landowners. Soria, Guadalajara, Avila have wretchedly poor agricultural populations. But in Segovia, the big proprietors take 42 per cent of the income of the province. The tragic feature of these zones, as of the others, is the beggar proprietor; but the contrast between big and small property is less violent. We find suffering which is different from that which holds the south in its grip, but which is no less fatal in its consequences.

In Albacete and Toledo, the big landowners appropriate 38 per cent of the total income.

In the whole of La Mancha, 2,132 powerful landlords divide about 30 million pesetas a year among themselves, while 264,673 small proprietors have an individual income of less than 100 pesetas over and above what a *bracero* earns.

The inequality is more serious in Estremadura, as I have pointed out. The great landowners of Badajoz take 60 per cent of the agricultural income of the province; those of Cáceres 57 per cent. The income of the great landowners in Estremadura amounts to some 18,000 pesetas a year; that of the small proprietors to 150 pesetas (here there are in reality no medium proprietors).

Lower Andalusia is already, in this respect, a volcanic zone, the region of bloody peasant revolts. Five per cent of the landowners in Seville share 72 per cent of the total income of the province! In Cadiz, 3 per cent of the landed potentates share 67 per cent of the total wealth! In Cordova, the large proprietors account for 52 per cent. This is the Betica region where 6,015 landowners appropriate between them over 100 million pesetas a year, and 261,428 modest proprietors share 42 million.

THE LANDOWNING ARISTOCRACY

I have already pointed out that almost all the estates belonging to the ancient nobility are concentrated in these regions of the governing oligarchy. Eight dukes, three marquises and three counts own 383,062 hectares of cultivable land, which is only one part of their territorial domains. Some are lords of 80,000, 50,000, 40,000 and 30,000 hectares.

In voluntary flight from civil society, they have kept at a distance from everything that is vital in Spanish life, refusing to admit regenerating elements which they have always regarded with unyielding hostility. In England, merchants and financiers can, and frequently do, enter the ranks of the aristocracy; and in this way the ancient nobility is renewed by inter-marriage with the new aristocracy or by frequent social contacts. But neither in Castile nor in Andalusia does there exist a middle class which could aspire, on account of its extraordinary wealth, to rub shoulders with the aristocrats of the blood. The power of the purse, which storms so many fortresses, is in the hands of the great landowners, among whom the aristocrats occupy the front rank. And the economic superiority of the nobility, who own the largest estates and the pick of the land, confirms them in their pride and social aloofness.

Should any grandee, remaining by a rare chance uncorrupted, remember his country on his death-bed and bequeath to the nation some money for education, like the Marqués de Cartagena, his deed is recorded in the annals of Spain as the Ancients recorded portents.

The Spanish aristocracy occupies itself, not without avarice, in collecting large rents from its extensive domains and practises absenteeism on a grand scale. A steward deals with the tenants or day-labourers. Some landowners vegetate in Madrid for some months of the year; others pass their time at fashionable European resorts or trail round Europe with the aimlessness of the man who has nothing to do. For the Spanish aristocrats think there is nothing to do.

I have already pointed out that the hereditary nobility have no moral or intellectual influence on Spanish society. They are an exhausted and sedentary class, with commonplace minds —not the kind of class which produces, as in other times, a Maecenas or an Archelaus. They engage in no activities, not even, for the most part, in sport. Physical and mental sloth has brought them to such a pitch of irresponsibility that they foolishly imagine that whatever benefits their outrageous egoism must be for the good of Spain. *They* are the nation; and the hard-working hungry people are *la chusma encanallada*, the rabble. Because of all this, because they are degenerate, because they have not laid aside their arrogance, because they have made money hand over fist, the old nobility is the class which is playing the foremost part in ruining Spain.

The Spanish aristocrat has seen that the English nobles own huge estates, and he does not want to lag behind his English counterpart. But he forgets that in England the land is not the basis of the national economy. And here we may digress a moment, for it is well known that the Spanish aristocracy admires English traditions and extols aspects of English life which, when reproduced in Spain, have quite another significance and produce very different results. An English ducal landowner with estates covering thousands of acres is socially inoffensive compared with a Spanish duke owning 80,000 or 40,000 hectares of fertile land. Large accumulations of landed property do not create poverty in England, for the nation lives—and has lived up till now—on industry, commerce and foreign investments. Agriculture is neglected—or has been neglected until now—in England. The English have been able to do without cultivating the land; and there can be no agrarian question in a nation where only a negligible proportion of its inhabitants depends on home-produced agricultural products. The British citizen, therefore, regards the distribution of the land as a problem which does not affect him personally. An industrial or commercial crisis hits the British workman hard, and he is loud in his complaints; but if he reads in his newspaper *à propos* of something that has nothing to do with agriculture, that the Duke of Blankshire's estates are enormous, he receives the information with indifference, or at most, curiosity. The Englishman does not feel that he has to go without land because the nobility have too much of it. Apart from which, he knows that large incomes are heavily taxed (a subject we shall return to later), and the certainty that in the course of two or three generations the State will have claimed most of the duke's fortune, has finally convinced him that the aristocracy are doing no one any harm.

But in Spain, commerce and industry provide a livelihood for only a minority. Agriculture is practically the pivot of the whole Spanish economy; and the Spanish duke, who excuses his action in accumulating vast estates by pointing to the example of the English dukes who own as much or more than he, ignores the fact that the English duke is a man who possesses a gold watch in a country where everybody has one of more or less precious metal, while he, the Spanish duke, flourishes his eighteen-carat timepiece in a nation where the immense majority have no watch at all.

The social consequences of monopolizing arable land are one thing in England and another in Spain. In England, they do not condemn anyone to semi-starvation; in Spain, they do. In England, large landed estates are a luxury which can be permitted by a nation which is accustomed to live on commerce, industry and banking, and which imports most of the food it needs. In Spain, large estates are a crime, because they can only exist by taking the bread out of the mouths of countless peasants, whose only medium of subsistence is agriculture.

The profits from Spanish agriculture are such that only those who cultivate the land can get a livelihood from it. And as many as live off the land without cultivating it are progenitors of poverty. For the annual value of agricultural products in Spain is little more than 10,000 million pesetas, which, if divided equally among the 5 million farmers and *braceros* would give each one 2,000 pesetas a year. Subtracting 20 per cent for taxes and expenses, there remain 1,600 pesetas. And dividing 1,600 pesetas by the 365 days of the year, every farmer is left with a daily income of about 5 pesetas.

However, as the land only produces enough to feed those who cultivate it and as there is an oligarchy which insists on living off it without cultivating it, in the style of an Eastern potentate, the average daily wage of the *bracero* is 2·80 pesetas, if things go well all the year round. The small proprietors of the minifundia and the tenant farmers earn little more. All are poor; and there are few indeed who earn the 5 pesetas to which they would be entitled if agricultural products were sold on the open market, and the proceeds distributed among those who farm the land.

It is clear, therefore, that land rents in Spain are a social enormity.

I am not concerned here with denouncing the well-established fact of the exploitation of man by man. The point is not only that a parasitic minority should reap the fruits of the labour of the majority. No; the point is that in Spain the land does not allow sufficient margin for the payment of rent, so long at least as the social and technical revolution hangs fire; it does not produce enough to provide a livelihood for those who cultivate it and those who do not. If those who do not cultivate the land gather some of its fruits, the labourers who till the soil have to beg their bread. This is the situation.

Irresponsible absenteeism gives the keynote to the whole oligarchic system. This state of affairs has created *señoritismo*, an eruptive social affection which is characteristic of the kind of economy I have alluded to. *Señoritismo* has spread by contagion to all the social classes, since every nation is imitative in the sense that it takes its tone from its ruling class. *Señoritismo*, therefore, is a pathological excrescence of absentee landlordism; the projection onto the city of a barbarous rural economy. It is present in Poland, in Hungary, in Rumania and the Latin-American countries. Spain has a brand that is frankly degenerate.

But *señoritismo* is not the only rotten fruit of a property system in which wealth is sedentary by nature, runs no risks, and is concentrated in the hands of an oligarchy.

The division of society into two groups, the privileged minority and the landless majority, inevitably brings in its train ostentatious luxury in the strongholds of absenteeism—Seville and Madrid—and extreme poverty in the other cities.

But let us return to the main theme—agrarian property in Spain.

## THE LATIFUNDIA

We have seen the impious distribution of rural wealth. We must now consider another important aspect of the rural economy, another internal lesion which is gnawing at the entrails of Spanish society; the unbelievable parcelling out of the land in the regions where the oligarchy has its seat.

Leaving aside that part of the Levante and south-eastern zone which is entered in the Land Register, and where property is better distributed and the land more evenly divided, we find in Castile, Andalusia, Estremadura and La Mancha that estates of more than 250 hectares cover an area of 6,608,759 hectares; that is, about 7 million hectares are absorbed by the latifundia, the huge estates.[1]

Small and medium proprietors (again exclusive of the Levante and south-east) own 12,521,921 hectares in farms of 250 hectares and less.

Including the Levante and the south-east, the Land Register shows that farms of less than 10 hectares cover an area of 8,014,715 hectares. Even discounting the smallholdings of the Levante, which cannot amount to much more than half a million hectares, the volume of the smallholdings in the two Castiles and Andalusia, especially the Castiles, would suffice to strike despair into the heart of the most courageous statesman. For there are more than 8 million hectares divided up into farms of less than 10 hectares. This is a problem of greater seriousness than the problem of the latifundia. Far from the classic region of the north-western smallholdings, the same plague which

[1] We must remember that 1 hectare=2½ acres.

paralyses Galicia spreads through the heart of Spain, throttling the rural economy and plunging into poverty the inhabitants of the dry land.

The typical regions of the latifundia, on the other hand, are La Mancha, Estremadura and Andalusia.

In La Mancha (Toledo, Ciudad Real and Albacete), 28·81 per cent of the land is covered by large estates of over 500 hectares. Those of over 250 hectares cover over 38·8 per cent of the land. The 1,848 big landowners of this region own 1,870,213 hectares in farms of over 250 hectares.

In Estremadura, farms of over 500 hectares account for 19·31 per cent of the land, and those of over 250 for 35·84 per cent. Therefore, 1,775 landowners are lords of 1,238,852 hectares in farms of over 250 hectares.

The question of the latifundia becomes more acute in the Guadalquivir region. Here 31·48 per cent of the land is divided into immense lots of over 500 hectares and estates of over 250 hectares account for 46 per cent of it.

In the Penibetic region (Malaga and Granada) 30·42 per cent of the land is covered by estates of more than 500 hectares and 43·34 per cent is parcelled out into properties of over 250.

In the two Andalusias, 3,343 proprietors own 3,279,376 hectares in farms of over 250 hectares—a state of things which is simply fantastic.

If we study the problem by provinces, we find that Granada has 33 estates of more than 500 hectares, of which 10 are over 5,000 hectares. Forty-six per cent of the area of the province consists of large estates. Jaén has 10 estates of 1,000 hectares and 355 of more than 500 hectares. In Seville, 50 per cent of the land is divided into enormous estates; there are 426 estates of more than 500 hectares, occupying 33 per cent of the area of the province; 104 of more than 1,000 hectares and 13 of more than 2,500.

In Cadiz, 624 landowners monopolize 58 per cent of the province, with 271 estates of more than 500 hectares, 32 of more than 1,000 and 3 of more than 5,000.

CONCLUSIONS

Thanks to the fantastic system of property prevailing there, Galicia and the central and southern regions are diseased parts of the national body. Outside the Basque Provinces, Catalonia and the Levante belt, that is, in the remaining three-quarters of Spanish territory, there is no rural middle class. Nor do the regions without a rural middle class enjoy a flourishing industry and commerce. How can a nation, where 1 per cent of the landowners possess 50 per cent of the land, and where more than 50 per cent of the peasant population have no land at all, hope to escape great social convulsions?

## INDUSTRY AND BANKING

THE GROWTH OF Spanish industry continued painfully throughout the nineteenth century, among the alarms and excursions of civil war. After the peace of Vergara in 1839, the first railways began to be built. And in the period between the end of the first Carlist war and the revolution of 1868, the whole of the economic life of the nation experienced the stimulating effect of peace at home and the great expansion of international capitalism. The loss of the colonies also played its part in leading to the repatriation of capital. At the close of the century the country, as compared with what it was in 1814, had progressed so far as to give rise to the illusion that Spain was on the road to industrialization, an effect that was singularly heightened by the success of the International Exhibition at Barcelona in 1888.

But if we bear in mind the swift and complete industrialization of other countries in the same period, it is obvious that what had happened in Spain was not an industrial revolution but a modest and distinctly slow advance. Only in Catalonia and Vizcaya was the improvement tangible and authentic.

The civil wars and the increase of industrial activity brought into being a new plutocracy. Great fortunes, like that of the Urquijos, were made in those days out of Army contracts, by gambling on the Stock Exchange and the instability of the markets. Bilbao banking increased its assets enormously with the money flowing in from exports of iron ore and the startling development of the local iron and steel industry.

But this plutocracy came on the scene at the moment when the romantic Liberal capitalists of the type of Mendizábal and the banker Sevillano had been decisively defeated by the agrarian oligarchy of the Restoration. And the Liberal capitalists of Bilbao were displaced by an aggressive generation of business men who were exclusively interested in banking, with no idea in their heads save to make money. In some cases, family tradition meant that the political ideals of the father were carried on by the son, as in the case of the millionaire Don Horacio Echevarrieta. But the budding financiers of Asturias and Bilbao hastened to join hands with the landed oligarchy and to sit with the aristocracy on the Board of the Bank of Spain. Thus was formed a brand-new financial oligarchy of men from Bilbao and Asturias, the aftermath, in some cases, of the old industrial dynasties. The new generation was, in general, less enterprising and less idealistic.

The Catalan capitalists did not possess their own banking system and were at war with the oligarchs and their monarchy.

The aristocracy and the great new financial *bourgeoisie* now combined, at the beginning of the twentieth century, to make life unbearable in Spain for everybody but themselves—and they succeeded. The banking oligarchy of Asturias and Bilbao, taking their inspiration from the counter-revolutionary, or anti-commercial and anti-industrial, policy of the agrarian oligarchy, turned credit into a monopoly. Division of labour was tacitly agreed upon in the Spanish economy; the landed oligarchy was to exploit the farmers and the financial oligarchy was to exploit the artisans and traders. We find, therefore, the financial oligarchy of the Spanish "capitalists standing alongside of, and on a par with, the political oligarchy".

Spanish financial capitalism was to be a sedentary capitalism, a pseudo-capitalism, with all the defects and none of the virtues of English, French, German or American capitalism.

Like everything else in Spain, the economic life of the nation suffers from lack of leadership. It lacks continuity, method and meaning. In order to pacify the capitalists, the landed oligarchy surpassed itself in granting concessions, which cost it nothing personally, but which made anarchy of the national economy and turned capitalism into a huge parasite of the State. To penetrate into the world of Spanish capitalism, therefore, is to enter a virgin forest, where the vegetation runs riot and where not only is it hard to force a way, but it is necessary to keep a cool head and not lose one's composure at the sudden appearance of gorgons and monsters much more horrifying than those in the Greek legends. It is a logical state of affairs in a nation which has had more than a hundred years of civil war and in which a corrupt agrarian State gave the capitalists a free hand to hold the community up to ranson in exchange for leaving the Government in peace and allowing it to subject all the social classes politically.

The result of this economic anarchy is that though Spain lacks industry and commerce in proportion to her wealth of raw materials, the industry she has is excessive. In other words, Spain has little industry, but what she has is too much. In 1932, the output of the steel industry was sufficient to supply six, seven or eight Spains; and the Catalan textile industry could have supplied the annual needs of the home market—95 per cent of its manufactures—with four months' work.

Not that, of course, Spanish industry is excessive in absolute terms, or that the Spaniard is content with a single steel ingot or a single pair of socks. The cause of such a pathetic anomaly is to be found, not so much in the disproportionate growth of the steel or cotton industries, a relative phenomenon, as in the staggering circumstance that a nation of 25 million souls does not form a market capable of absorbing a production which is manifestly inferior to the national needs. When we have said this, we have said all that remains to be said on the subject of Spanish penury. Spain does not consume goods; she does not go shod, she does not clothe herself, she does not build, she does not make machinery.

And there is no market, because wages, both in the rural areas and in the cities, do not rise for the most part above the poverty-line.

I have already pointed out that the average daily wage of the agricultural worker is 2·80 pesetas. At the same time, wages in commerce and industry are among the lowest in the world. Taking real wages in England as an index and giving them a value of 100, we find in 1930, according to the *International Labour Review*, that the American worker earned 191; the Australian 145; the Danish 104; the Swedish 101; the Irish 85; the *Spanish* 45; the Esthonian 41; and the Portuguese 32.

But the fate of Spanish industry is bound up, first and foremost, with the fate of the peasant. And since, in addition to the fact that there is practically no market outside the great cities, the urban worker's daily wage is among the lowest in Europe, it is obvious that the cities cannot offer any considerable market either.

The repercussion of wages policies on the rhythm of textile production has always been very swift in Spain. "A good crop of olives in Andalusia coinciding with high wages means a marked increase in the demand for textile goods." In the two first years of the Second Republic, increased wages meant that large factories in Barcelona had to work more shifts, even night shifts. Even timber merchants felt the benefits of a policy of higher agricultural wages.

This was in exceptional times. Normally—that is to say, under the absolute command of the oligarchies—the mass of the Spanish workers hardly consumed anything; they had no money to make the wheels of industry turn.

A buoyant home market was unquestionably in the interest of native capitalism. But not being able to introduce a policy of decent wages in agriculture, which was the preserve of the landed oligarchy, and being naturally not disposed to open their own purse wider, the industrialists fell back on the alternative policy of owing a false prosperity to the State. This solution pleased the oligarchs; they preferred it to increasing the wages of the *braceros* so that the nation's industry might live. Agrarians and industrialists, the former stretching the bow of protection to its farthest limit, the latter demanding new concessions every day, were able to agree, though their accord might be less firm than that between the landed oligarchy and the financial oligarchy. The aristocratic-oligarchic State said in effect to the industrialists: "It does not matter that the Spanish people have no money to buy your goods; we will do our best to prevent your going bankrupt."

The result was the raising of a tariff wall high enough to keep out of Spain all foreign goods. This prohibitionism, rather than protectionism, was called "protecting the home industry". In principle, protection is justifiable and necessary. But when it is so stringent that it resolves itself into a situation where a nation which is exceedingly rich in iron ore cannot make machinery because the price of steel is exceptionally high, capitalism is working against itself and industry, artificially fed, is being stifled for lack of markets. And when, for identical reasons, Spain, with all her wealth of lead, offers it at the highest prices in the world; and the sugar industry, with a frequent margin of overproduction, sells sugar to a nation of paupers at prices higher than any others in Europe, it may well be thought that, though the existing industry is meagre enough, it is preferable to have no industry at all.

In its organization at the top, Spanish capitalism has all the features of great monopolistic capitalism in Europe and the United States. The chief Spanish industries and banking move in a world of cartels and combines. As if high tariffs are not enough, the capitalists have united in cartels and combines, so that neither from outside nor in the internal development of industry and finance can the breath of competition enter. Private banking lives by a system of combines, which has a tremendous effect on the world of commerce and industry. For their part, the steel, lead, paper and sugar monopolies have also formed their cartels and agreed to share out the national market. We find, therefore, a capitalist economic dictatorship whose effect on the material progress of the nation is as overwhelming as is the influence of the landed oligarchy's dictatorship in agriculture and politics.

Landowners and plutocrats alike have conspired to throw the nation's burdens onto the shoulders of the poor and the lower middle classes. The rich—agrarians and capitalists—do not pay anything like the taxes they should in equity pay. Spain is, in fact, a fiscal paradise for the plutocracy. According to *La situation économique mondiale* (League of Nations, 1931–2) the percentage of State revenue represented by receipts from property and income tax in the following countries was: United States of America 67·7; England 55; Holland 43·8; Denmark 35·1; Italy 36·2; *Spain* 30.

As can be seen, the proportion in which the citizen contributes to the expenses of the State by payment of income tax is lowest in Spain and altogether ludicrous in comparison with the United States, England or Holland.

I shall refer later on to the fact that the Second Republic imposed a tax on unearned income and the *rentistas*, without stopping to give the matter much thought, decided that it was preferable to risk their necks in another civil war rather than pay a modest tax, even though the tax meant that a man with a million pesetas would have paid less than 70,000, while the same individual in Great Britain would have had to part with 241,000.


HEAVY INDUSTRY

As I have already pointed out, Spain is exceedingly rich in iron ore. The most famous deposits and those which have been worked with the greatest regularity from remote times are to be found in Vizcaya. The Vizcayan mining zone produces excellent rubies, a mineral of a superior order which has always found a ready market in Great Britain. Moreover explorations carried out in territory near the present mines attest the existence of new deposits, so that the exhaustion, as yet distant, of the old workings can be viewed without alarm.

Next in importance to the iron mines of Vizcaya are those in the province of Teruel. There are two zones in this region, both practically virgin, and of immense importance to the

Spanish iron industry. One is that of Ojos Negros-Almoja, the other that of the Sierra de Albarracín. The Ojos Negros mine, which today is practically at a standstill, produced a million tons of iron ore in 1913. But the most productive mines in this region are those of the Sierra de Albarracín, which with their *hematites*, more than 70 per cent pure ore, are a veritable gold mine to Spanish industry. Nevertheless the Sierra de Albarracín mines are closed down owing to lack of communications.

Of inferior quality, though abundant, are the ferriferous minerals of the Cartagena region.

In Andalusia there are two important ferriferous zones, extraordinarily prolific in ochres and oxides for painting. These also are virtually abandoned.

At the beginning of the century, Spanish iron-ore production was reinforced by the Riff mines, which surprised the experts by their splendid possibilities and the high quality of their ores.

Spain, therefore, as we have seen, takes a high place among better endowed nations in this branch of natural resources. The Spanish subsoil contains in abundance material of the highest quality. But this kind of wealth, if it is to be turned to advantage, calls for a good transport system and an industry to convert the raw materials into goods, based economically on an extensive market.

The great towns of the province of Bilbao grew up in the last decades of the past century round the mining districts of Somorrostro, Ortuella and Gallarta, in the vicinity of the river Nervión. Bilbao owes its present wealth to these mines, which reached their greatest activity about 1880 when about 5 million tons of iron ore were being exported annually.

The same mines have also been the foundation of Vizcayan industry, which represents about 85 per cent of the Spanish steel industry.

The providential circumstance that Great Britain was a coal-exporting nation and Vizcaya an exporter of iron ore was of inestimable benefit to the merchant fleet, the mines and industry of Bilbao. The ships discharged iron ore at the British ports and returned with coke. Later, coke began to be manufactured in Vizcaya, but some coal continued to be imported from Great Britain.

The advantageous conditions I have mentioned, on the one hand, and, on the other, the protection granted by the Spanish State to industry from 1892 onwards (mentioned in another section of this work) gave a powerful impetus to iron and steel production in Vizcaya.

241

The expansive rhythm of the Spanish iron and steel industry, which was regular and constant from 1876 till 1913, stimulated by national and international factors quickened its pace until it became almost an industrial revolution on the outbreak of the first World War. Spain's neutrality attracted to Bilbao and the Asturian manufacturing centres a veritable river of gold. The production of iron and steel ingots which had amounted to little more than 600,000 tons in 1813 exceeded 800,000 tons in 1917.

In short, as a result of the first World War, the Spanish steel industry took its place among the great modern industries.

The Spanish capitalists, blinded by the present opportunities for money-making, and intent upon their dividends, paid no heed to the future of industry. No doubt they thought the war would never come to an end and built up a considerable industry on the shifting sands of a demand which would cease abruptly when peace was declared. The expansion of the Spanish iron and steel industry which had come about in response to an exceptional state of affairs, without plan or intelligent agreement from the point of view of the nation's needs, ended by ruining both industrialists and the nation.

The basis of the capitalist system is the market—a market to absorb production. In the nations where industry developed by its own means and succeeded in constituting a respectable force in the capitalist form of production, the *bourgeoisie* created, to begin with, a national market and consolidated it with revolutionary reforms, destroying from the seat of government the obstacles and impediments which the old classes put in the way of the nation's economic progress. And just as the *bourgeoisie* assured the home market, so they sought in countries with a primitive economy the markets that were needed to heap up profits and affirm the domination of the middle class over the aristocracy and other landed proprietors.

We must remember that in Spain the contrary process took place. The industry of the nation rested, during the first World War, on the fortuitous basis of the international market. And there arose the paradox of a nation with a primitive economy, a mediaeval, agrarian nation, possessing a heavy manufacturing industry living largely on the European market. No more delicate situation could be imagined.

The exportation of iron ore—an item of prime importance in the Spanish economy and especially in that of Vizcaya—was reduced in 1933 to 15 per cent of what it had been in 1913! In 1933 exports only amounted to 1,400,000 tons. In the history of the Spanish iron-ore mining industry, there was no more tragic situation than that of the first three years of the Second Republic; in none of these years did exports touch the 2 million-ton mark.

As regards iron and steel production, the index number fell to what it had been during the war years, a no less disastrous fall when we remember that the industry's productive capacity had doubled itself since then. Altos Hornos in Bilbao, whose output fluctuated in 1917 between 200,000 and 300,000 tons, was able to manufacture 400,000 tons in 1935. And the yield from the ore, which in 1919 had been 47 tons of pig iron for every 100 tons of ore, had already increased to more than 50.

Altos Hornos, which still employed 8,300 workers in 1930, only employed about 5,000 in 1934. The firm's profits, which in 1917 and 1918 had amounted to 100 or 150 million pesetas, had been reduced to 5 million pesetas, a miserably inadequate profit in view of the company's financial commitments.

Spain's heavy industry was bankrupt.

For reasons which had their root in the international situation and had no connection with the new régime, the Second Republic coincided with the gravest crisis which had ever afflicted Spanish industry.

The iron-ore mines and heavy industry of Vizcaya, the life-blood of her economic life, contracted to an extent that was frankly catastrophic.

### THE TEXTILE INDUSTRY

I have just described the extent of the Spanish iron and steel industry, which is enormous and even apparently excessive for Spain, but small in absolute terms when we consider that Spanish iron industry normally produces half a million tons of pig iron a year compared with the 10 million produced by Great Britain or France. The same observation applies to the textile industry.

From the middle of the nineteenth century, about 90 per cent of the manufacture of textiles has been concentrated in Catalonia, and within that region, in Barcelona and the surrounding province.

In 1850 the entire textile industry of Spain employed 37,301 looms and 900,099 spindles. 73,208 workers were engaged in the industry.

Ten years later, according to Orellana's survey, Catalonia possessed 37,000 looms of all kinds and 1,075,414 spindles. The number of workers employed had risen to 125,000.

Another investigation carried out in 1867 by Alonso Martínez showed that there were 1,050,000 spindles, 44,402 looms and 99,745 workers.

The data submitted in 1918 by Government inspectors throw considerable light on the situation of the textile industry in general, for they show that there were then in Catalonia 45,000 cotton looms, and 5,000 in the rest of Spain. The number of spindles was 2 million.

Years afterwards, Aguilera's inquiry showed, with reference to the Catalan industry, that there were about 2 million spindles and 56,000 looms, giving employment to 110,000 workers. As regards the silk, woollen, hemp and jute industries—also in Catalonia—there were 10,110 looms and 308,920 spindles, employing 37,350 workers.

Hence, there were in all 66,110 looms, approximately 2,300,000 spindles and 147,350 textile workers in Catalonia.

The war of 1914–18 gave the Spanish textile industry its chance, though the demands of the foreign market did not exert such heavy pressure on textile production as they did on iron and steel. Catalan goods found a temporary market abroad which helped to stimulate the expansion of the industry.

The conditions in which Catalan industry had to work could not have been more favourable to its development, since in the first twenty years of the present century, the electrification of Catalonia was carried out with extraordinary rapidity.

Let us now glance at the volume and distribution of the Catalan textile industry during recent years.

The province of Tarragona has little manufacturing industry. The most important city from this point of view is Reus, which in 1930 possessed five silk textile factories.

In the province of Gerona there were thirty-five factories employing 2,300 workers.

Lerida hardly ever had any textile industry.

The main industrial zone is Barcelona and its suburbs where almost the whole of the cotton, woollen and silk industry of Spain is concentrated.

In 1930 the most important industry was still the cotton textile industry which then disposed of 2,100,000 spindles and 99,500 looms, 5,800 of which were automatic. 125,000 workers were employed. (In 1918, as we saw, there were in the rest of Spain 5,000 looms manufacturing cotton goods. There is no reason to think that the number had risen to any great extent by 1930. The marked disparity between this number and the 99,500 Barcelona looms engaged in the cotton industry should be noted.)

The woollen industry was situated almost entirely in Sabadell and Tarrasa. The yarn was spun on 275,000 spindles and the cloth woven on 6,900 looms distributed between Sabadell (3,400), Tarrasa (2,500) and Barcelona (1,000). The number of workers employed in the Catalan woollen industry was, in round figures, 50,000. (In the rest of Spain, there were in 1930, 4,000 looms for the manufacture of woollens, the industry being the least concentrated in the principality.)

The Barcelona silk industry was spread over thirty-five factories with two or three thousand looms and rather more than 6,000 operatives.

The number of spindles in use in the hemp, flax and jute industries amounted to 34,000; and there were 2,186 looms, all installed in factories in the plain of Barcelona. 5,000 workers were employed in these industries.

To sum up, the textile industry was concentrated, and still is concentrated, in Barcelona.

Having emphasized this, we must sum up what has gone before, the better to appreciate the dimensions of this Barcelona industry (a more exact term than Catalan industry). We shall find that the aforesaid production in its entirety comprised, at the advent of the Second Republic, 2,409,000 spindles, 110,580 looms and 186,000 operatives—figures which are satisfactory from any standpoint, especially if we remember that all this manufacturing activity was confined to a single city and its environs.

The capital faults of the textile industry are, in substance, the same as those of all large-scale industry in Spain—the weakness of the home market and high prices by comparison with those in other countries. If Spanish textiles are to compete in price in the international market, there will have to be a new revolution in industry and another revolution in the property system, especially agrarian property—two revolutions which the capitalists have not known how, or have not wanted, to bring about.

In quality Catalan textiles are excellent, despite the fact that the industry as a whole has not been completely modernized. The woollen industry of Sabadell, which is devoted to the production of fine woollen goods, manufactures magnificent cloth which can stand comparison with any in the world.

Before leaving this subject, I must say a few words about the basic factor of the cotton textile industry—raw materials.

A cotton manufacturing industry employing more than 2 million spindles and more than 100,000 looms runs grave and obvious risks in depending entirely on foreign imports in such a fundamental matter as raw materials. This is another vulnerable flank of the Spanish textile industry. Spain imports annually about 100,000 tons of raw cotton, the cost of which—exceeding 200 million pesetas—affects her balance of trade adversely. The question has been a source of anxiety to industrialists and also, according to their own account, to the country's rulers; but little has been done to encourage the cultivation of cotton in Spain.

There is abundant evidence, however, that Spain could produce, if not all, at least the major part of the cotton used by her industry. Undoubtedly the variety of the Spanish climate and soil is such that there are many places suitable for growing cotton. But it is also a fact that the cultivation of cotton will not prosper, in common with so many other things in Spain, so long as the national chaos, and the State which is the embodiment of that chaos, continue in being.

## THE PAPER INDUSTRY

The bulk of the Spanish paper industry is situated in the Basque province of Guipuzcoa, at Hernani, Tolosa and Villabona. There are six factories at Tolosa alone. The proximity of the port of Pasajes and an abundant supply of water power, the mainstay of this famous industry, make the province of Guipuzcoa the ideal region for the production of paper. And the leaders of the industry have not been idle in exploiting such favourable circumstances or in using them as the basis of an excellent distributive machinery.

The modern features of this industry, the best organized in Spain, are due to *La Papelera Española*, a society founded in 1901.

The first World War opened up to the Spanish paper-makers a new and ample market, which had a decisive influence on the development of the paper industry. Fortunately for the Spanish paper-makers, Sweden and Norway, pulp-producing countries, were not drawn into the conflagration. Like the other Spanish manufacturing industries, the paper industry was working at full pressure.

When the war ended, the industry had suffered considerable changes, at least in its financial structure. Thanks to the influence of *La Papelera*, the whole industry had formed itself into a cartel. In 1919 the cartel was officially set up under the title of *Sociedad Cooperativa de Fabricantes de Papel de España*, but in practice it had already existed from the beginning of the war. The strongest factories had established price uniformity and the division of labour, and had divided up the national market among themselves.

When the European war came to an end in 1918, the first problem the cartel had to meet was that of overproduction. The disproportion between the needs of the home market and the productive capacity of the factories reappeared now in an aggravated form. But the paper industry had defences which were denied, for example, to the iron and steel and the textile industries: and besides, the paper cartel, which enabled the industry to manœuvre as best suited its interests, helped to combat the crisis.

To begin with, three or four important factories, like that of Ruiz de Arcaute at Alegría, closed down, and the *Cooperativa de Fabricantes* indemnified them to the tune of 50,000 pesetas a year, a premium on enforced idleness, on the "standstill", a Big Business expedient which the Spanish paper-makers borrowed, thus proving that the refinements of the higher ranks of capitalism existed in Spain side by side with the Roman plough in Castile and the domestic oven of the days of Agamemnon and the Trojan War, in Galicia.

Obviously the cartel did not altogether solve the problem of the contraction of the home market. But since the paper industry was in the hands of enterprising men—and *La Papelera Española* did not lack shrewd captains of industry—there was always the possibility that it might convert itself (as indeed it did) into its own customer and use excess production to set up establishments which would consume its own products. For if there was not a big enough market for virgin paper, there was one, so the argument ran, for books and newspapers. Don Nicolas M. Urgoiti, a wizard of the business world, author of the cartel and moving spirit of the great Bilbao undertaking, perceived, with the perspicacity of the man of enterprise who is not a stranger to the things of the spirit, that *La Papelera* could only correct the slackness of the market by diverting its formidable productive capacities, or part of them, to undertakings of its own making. This sane and, in a way, desperate resolve led to the foundation of a great morning daily newspaper *El Sol*; another evening paper *La Voz*, and two publishing houses *Espasa-Calpe* and *Gráficas Reunidas*.

What *El Sol* came to be to the newspaper world, *Espasa-Calpe* was to the world of books. Installed in splendour, with its huge and magnificent offices in the Gran Vía of Madrid, *Espasa-Calpe* brought a new tone into the Spanish book trade. Its popular editions of the classics, its collection of Spanish and Spanish-American biographies and, above all, its great Encyclopaedia (which was not, however, free from reactionary tendencies in history and politics) have enriched the libraries and culture of the Spanish-speaking world.

This monumental Encyclopaedia is, if we consider the matter closely, another disturbing aspect or trustworthy proof of the paradoxical disequilibrium of Spanish society. For is it not astonishing that Spain, the nation with the greatest percentage of illiteracy in Europe, should have produced a work of the range of the *Enciclopedia Espasa*, which for size and sumptuousness has not its equal in the world? Such were the prodigies performed by *La Papelera España*, an enterprise of unusual vigour, which, for lack of a market, became its own customer and wrought in the newspaper and book trades as great a revolution as it had already accomplished in the paper-manufacturing industry.

COAL-MINING

Much has been written about the quality of Spanish coal. But from analyses and comparisons recently made, it is clear that the inferiority of Spanish coal does not lie in its chemical composition which, as far as certain classes are concerned, admits comparison with, and is even superior, in fixed carbon and calories to the English "Welsh Steam".

Anthracites are excellent, exceeding 8,000 calories.

Spanish lignite, as I have already pointed out, is superior in calorific value to most foreign lignite.

From this aspect, Spanish coal mines in general are not far behind the best foreign mines. And as far as quantity is concerned, the Spanish seams are practically inexhaustible. In fact, the Canadian Geological Congress in 1913 designated Spain as a coal-producing country, putting her reserves at 5,500 million tons, an estimate which recent research has raised to 9,000 million.

As far as natural resources go, Spain, I repeat, is extraordinarily rich. But the conformation of the seams and the softness of Spanish coal are, as I have already pointed out, radical defects which make Spanish solid combustibles inferior to the English, French, German or American.

Coal-mining in Spain employed about 50,000 men in 1933. Production amounted to about 7 million tons which were consumed by the home industry. About 900,000 tons of coal were imported in that year, 75,000 of them from England. Strictly speaking, Spain was self-supporting in coal, but deficient in coal products, like coke, which until a short while ago was obtained entirely abroad. The importation of English coal at a reduced tariff can be explained more for reasons of commercial interchange—in the interests of the fruit exporters of the Levante—than for the sake of the Spanish market.

248

The changes imposed on coal-mining by the first World War were as radical as in the other branches of Spanish industry. In 1913, when Spanish industry was beginning to develop, Spain imported about 3 million tons of coal, without counting coke and briquettes. It is interesting to note how imports have continued to fall, in spite of the growth of industry, until in 1933 they amounted to less than 900,000 tons, including coke and briquettes.

Coal output has continued to rise steadily during the last thirty years. In 1914, 4½ million tons of coal were mined: in 1933, 6½ million.

The war of 1914–18 hastened the rhythm of production. No coal could be obtained abroad where, on the contrary, Spanish coal was worth its weight in gold. At the same time, Spanish industry was consuming much more, for the foundries were working three shifts. The Spanish coalowners were the absolute monarchs of the home market. Between 1914 and 1918, prices were quadrupled. We find also a corresponding rise in wages, fruit of the public and tangible prosperity of the industry which made the Asturian region and its workers, like the Vizcayan, a privileged community.

When the war ended, coal-mining inevitably suffered the effects of the general crisis.

The slump of 1929 hit the mines as hard as it hit the blast-furnaces. After this fatal year for production, demoralization set in in the coal industry. Consumption declined, as could be foreseen, and prices fell disastrously. Spanish coal, which in 1929 had been 19 per cent dearer than English, was in 1932 45 per cent cheaper than German, hitherto the cheapest in Europe.

Due in part to the natural characteristics of the industry, and in part to the bad management of the capitalists, the Spanish coal-mining industry is a synonym for disturbances.

The struggle between capital and labour is here more bitter than in any other industry. It is certainly not helped by the instability of the Governments and the perennial political crisis of the nation—factors which operate continuously on the excitability of those engaged in an insecure industry which is extremely sensitive to outside disturbances.

In every nation where coal-mining reaches a certain pitch of development, this is the most complex branch of production and one that requires the greatest vigilance—particularly so in Spain, owing to the peculiar natural structure of the industry. Since it is an instrument which is extremely susceptible to outside interference, and since the state of the nation's trade is automatically reflected in it, the coal-mining industry must be scrupulously administered and its technical and commercial side conscientiously managed—two virtues which have been lamentably absent from coal undertakings in Spain.

The Spanish railways had to contend from the beginning with three formidable enemies; the general slackness of Spanish economic life or lack of capital; natural obstacles due to the irregularity of the country's physical features; and the absence of plan or political-administrative chaos.

If railways are to prosper, there must be a numerous population, evenly spread over the country, and a flourishing commerce and industry. The transport of large masses of people and great quantities of merchandise has everywhere been the foundation of a prosperous railway system. But we have already seen that Spain is not a nation with large urban agglomerations or any unusual industrial and mercantile activity. The need creates the instrument; and the depopulation of Spain, most of whose inhabitants are dispersed in tiny, widely scattered hamlets, is not an incentive to the construction of railways.

The total area of Spain is 505,550 sq. kilometres and there are 16,861 kilometres of railway open to traffic. Italy, with an area of 200,000 sq. kilometres, has 5,000 more kilometres of railway than Spain. And Switzerland, in spite of the mountainous nature of the country, has about half the length of the Spanish railroads in an area of 41,000 sq. kilometres. Spain is the third largest nation in Europe, but in railway development she takes sixth place.

Until a short time ago, that is, until the war of 1914–18, the Spanish railways were run by foreign capital. This had been the case since the founding of the first companies in the middle of the nineteenth century, a period of resounding scandals everywhere, due to financial speculation following on the subversive presence of the steam locomotive which, like all innovations in transport, changed the face of the planet. Spain's neutrality in the first World War enabled Spanish capital to supplant foreign capital in the possession of the nation's railways. Today the railways are almost all owned by Spaniards. Of all the infinite opportunities which that war, or rather, that neutrality, offered Spain to put her economic house in order, this was perhaps the only one she really benefited by. With the exception of a few small companies, like that of the Lorca-Baza–Aguilas line which is financed by English capital, and others connected with the mining industry, also financed by English or French capital, the financial control of the great undertakings—though there is still some French and Belgian capital, especially in the form of debentures—belongs conclusively to Spaniards and largely to the State.

The major defect in the management of the Spanish railways is the complete absence of cohesion in the general lay-out. As a result of this anarchical development, there are a great number of lines with no inter-connection and consequently an extraordinary number of separate enterprises. Barely 17,000 kilometres of railway in Spain are operated by about eighty companies—eighty companies with their corresponding boards of directors.

The eight largest companies operate 11,831 kilometres. That leaves seventy-two companies to 5,020 kilometres of track. Of these 5,020 kilometres, fourteen companies operate 2,394; the largest, controlling 312 kilometres, is *Ferrocarriles de la Robla* and the smallest, with 103 kilometres, is the *Villena a Alcoy y Yecla*.

The State has the direct control of 402 kilometres. The remaining 2,224 kilometres are run by *fifty-seven* companies all of which control less than 100 kilometres and some less than 20.

Obviously the distribution of the nation's railways between eighty companies is a formidable obstacle to progress and the prosperity of the industry. Even if the profits from the railways were greater than they are, they would not be enough to satisfy such an enormous and greedy horde of directors, legal advisers, technicians and bureaucrats of all sorts and descriptions.

All the companies, small as well as large, keep up a bureaucratic apparatus regardless of cost. The managing director of the Lorca-Baza and Aguilas Company, which operates 168 kilometres of broad-gauge track, receives approximately the same salary as the director of the great Northern Company.

Recently the Falangist State has nationalized the railways, but there are no means of telling what changes it has wrought in the organization of this service, whose fundamental defects are not likely to have been remedied by a corrupt régime like that of General Franco.

I have now dealt with five important industries in Spain; by them, the rest can be judged. We must now turn to an aspect of Spanish capitalism—the financial aspect—which is of superlative interest to the study of modern Spain.

The organization of credit is so important to the development of a modern nation that even a lyrical poet like Coleridge attributed the social health of the English nation, that is, its equilibrium, to the loyalty of the people to their institutions, a "loyalty which is linked to the very heart of the nation by the system of credit and the interdependence of property".[1]

The problem of credit in Spain has as far-reaching effects as the agrarian problem.

Although Spain is a predominantly agrarian country, agricultural credit is as primitive, paltry and unjust as the system of land tenure and cultivation of the soil. There are no *Cajas de Crédito* in Spain, like the German *Reiffeisen* or the French *Durand*, genuine people's agrarian banks, which advance loans at moderate rates of interest to small and medium proprietors and long-term leaseholders out of their deposits, which are often the property of the great landowners who thus come to the aid of the small farmer.

The absence of specifically agrarian credit in Spain is one of the most typical features of rural penury and of the heartless system of land tenure.

The system of agrarian credit prevailing in Spanish agriculture is that of the *Pósitos*, languidly functioning organizations, the most rudimentary manifestation of this kind of credit. The *Pósitos* are run by the municipalities with the half-hearted support of the State.

The official credit organization has a competitor in the *Confederación Nacional Católico-agraria*, an institution which is under Church patronage, of marked clerical stamp as its name indicates, and whose activities are not confined to loans in cash and kind, but extend to everything connected with agriculture and stock-breeding. In 1926 (I do not know the figures for later years), the deposits and loans of the *Confederación* amounted to 250 and 200 million pesetas respectively.

But this entity's financial radius of action is limited by the system of land tenure. Its field of activity covers especially Old Castile and León—wheat-farming zones, the granary of Spain. In these regions, large estates, let us remember, are few and far between. Except for the province of Salamanca, the rest of the region is populated by some thousands of medium proprietors and an infinite number of smallholders. Here the *Confederación Católico-agraria* has a large and submissive *clientèle* and the Church

[1] Coleridge, *Biographia Literaria*, pp. 111 and 112.

naturally has considerable political authority, partly due to the situation of the peasant, who is in need of help of all kinds which is obviously only forthcoming if he accepts spiritual help as well.

The work carried out in the economic sphere by the Catholics deserves more attention than I can give it here. But however remarkable it is from the point of view of credit, it does not extend to all the rural areas of Spain, like the ramifications of agricultural credit in other countries, and, in essence, it has a particular character which makes the banks of the *Confederación* very different organisms from the agrarian banks already referred to.

There are no other agricultural credit institutions in Spain worthy of mention.

As regards credit in general, on which depend the mercantile and industrial life of the country, the exploitation of virgin wealth —in a word, the prosperity and size of the middle class (all this intimately linked with the form of government)—the situation is even more discouraging in Spain.

Spanish banking, like Spanish industry, has come into being and developed during the course of the last two generations. The great private banks of today were founded at the end of the nineteenth century or in the first decades of the present century and consolidated their position, alongside great industry, during the first World War.

The new solidarity which has succeeded in merging in one supreme reactionary nucleus the great landowners and the bankers—both classes being to a certain extent historically incompatible—is expressed provocatively in the privileged economic situation of the absentee landlords and the usurers of the banking world. Really great wealth is not to be looked for in Spain outside banking and landowning circles, because it does not exist. A Juan March or a Cambó are exceptions, and even the former is also a banker.

The whole nation works for the bankers and the great landowners, who may rightly be called the parasites of the national economy.

The Spanish banking oligarchy has its origin chiefly in Asturias and the Basque Provinces, as I have already pointed out. Neither in Galicia, nor in Catalonia, nor in Castile, nor in the Levante, nor in Andalusia, is there a financial *bourgeoisie*. In these regions there are, no doubt, bankers, not more enlightened —on the contrary, even more avaricious—than the Basque or Asturian bankers; but the main pillar of the financial oligarchy rests on the four northern Banks.

The four banks which, in a fraudulent conspiracy with the Board of the Bank of Spain, practically control the industry and commerce of the nation, are the Banco Urquijo, Banco de Bilbao, Banco de Vizcaya and Banco Herrero. Sixteen directors of these banks are also directors of about 400 companies of all kinds: railway, electrical, banking, chemical, mining, oil, etc. Some of them, miraculously defying the dimensions of time and space, sit on the Boards of about fifty companies—a feat which is certainly without parallel elsewhere.

Such an accumulation of directorships bears witness to the fact that these sixteen citizens, with about half a dozen other bankers, are the dictators of credit; that without their benevolent ruling, no industry can borrow a *céntimo* from the private banks nor can the other banks count on the indispensable collaboration of the Bank of Spain.

The event proves, moreover, how acute is the dearth of capital in the Spanish mercantile and industrial world—not because cash is short, for the banks do not know what to do with the money, but because, save in special circumstances, it is withheld from industry and commerce by an arbitrary and deplorable dereliction of duty on the part of the bankers.

Given the mentality of the Spanish bankers, which is, after all, that of the agrarians, it is not surprising that they prefer to keep capital unproductive rather than employ it in the liberal function of revitalizing the national wealth, which it has in nations where banking is civilized. Spain is the country of dear land and dear money; of waste land in the midst of necessitous populations, and of hoarded money in the midst of an economy hopelessly handicapped by lack of capital. What has happened, in effect, is that the absentee spirit has spread to the banks—a not altogether surprising occurrence in view of the close association between the landed oligarchy and the financial oligarchy. The Spanish banker is also, in his medium, an absentee.

To take a concrete example, the first thing that depresses the observer in Spain is the price of money—the highest in Europe. The official rate of discount in Spanish banking in 1935 (it would be useless to base any study of the Spanish economy on the abnormal conditions of later years) was 6 per cent. But taking into account stamp duties, taxes, etc., the real rate of discount was not less than 8 per cent. This is a really prohibitive figure; and there is no doubt that to lend money to commerce and industry at a rate that practically amounts to 8 per cent verges on usury, a practice which was severely condemned by the

254

Fathers of the Catholic Church in the dawn of capitalism, an epoch in which, to all appearances, Spanish banking is still living, even if the Catholic Church is not.

In the year referred to, the bank rate in England and Switzerland was 2 per cent; in France, Denmark, Holland and Sweden 2½ per cent; in Italy 3 per cent; in Belgium 3½ per cent; in Germany 4 per cent; in Portugal 5½ per cent and in Rumania 6 per cent.

As we can see, except in Rumania (not very inspiring company, to be frank), money was cheaper in all the countries mentioned than in Spain.

This fact is enough to explain the poverty of Spanish commerce, for in principle, wherever money earns a high rate of interest, commerce is not developed—it is in its infancy.

## FOREIGN CAPITAL

Though there is no question but that multiple factors abroad conspired against the second Spanish Republic, it is equally certain that the complaints and exhortations of foreign companies domiciled in Spain found a swift and sinister echo in the chancelleries. The asphyxiation of the Second Republic was the work also of the international trusts with ramifications in the Peninsula; not only in 1939, when the more cautious Powers who had not yet recognized the Falangist régime proceeded to take this step, but from the first days of the Republic, as soon as it became clear what disastrous concessions the dictatorship of Primo de Rivera had made in order to attract foreign capital to Spain. This dictatorship aggravated the dependence of Spain upon more powerful nations, not so much because it smoothed the way for foreign capital eager to take advantage of nations whose economic life was little developed, but because of the form in which this capital was admitted. Spain shed a little more of her national sovereignty and Spanish politics were complicated to an extraordinary degree by the presence of new foreign and obscure forces.

Spanish capital has always been scarce; nor has foreign capital been particularly attracted to Spain on account, no doubt, of the political disturbances. It was not until the middle of the nineteenth century that foreign capital began to take a timid interest in the possibilities of profit in Spain. The first immigration of capital worthy of note was in connection with the construction and running of the railways, which attracted mainly French capital.

On the eve of the war of 1914–18, the tendency of international capital to turn its attention to Spain became more marked. This was only to be expected at the moment of international capital's greatest expansion, the pinnacle of imperialism, when the world had already been divided up. The number of foreign companies in Spain increased, the year 1913 being especially significant in this respect. New companies domiciled in France, Belgium or England were founded in Spain, with a total capital of 68,754,400 gold francs. Foreign capital covering new issues in Spain during the same year amounted to 149,327,000 gold francs—in all, 218,981,400 gold francs.

The war rapidly diminished the influx of foreign capital and brought Spain abundant money, as we have seen, with the rise in her exports. The foreign debt was repatriated. Railway shares, as I have already pointed out, became Spanish property. Most of the shares of the great railway companies were taken over by the banks of Vizcaya and Catalonia. The ownership of the railway debentures is, however, problematical at this date, but they probably remain in foreign hands. It is difficult to get an exact idea on this point, for the Spanish banks confine themselves to printing briefly *Valores en cartera* on their balance-sheets, without naming these securities, still less giving their current price.

Thanks, therefore, to her neutrality in the first World War, Spain recovered precious slices of her independence in the financial sphere. But shortly afterwards came the relapse, with the mischievous policy of Primo de Rivera's dictatorship. The dynamic and adventurous character of the Dictator's administration, inordinately enamoured of monopolies and eager to capture stray foreign capital (ás if that was equivalent to a positive political triumph for the régime), brought a shower of foreign capital amounting to 800 million pesetas on Spain, speculative capital which was as ready to take flight as it had been to come, and which helped to bring the dictatorship and Spain into that impasse which ended in the disastrous fall of the peseta.

But this was not the most serious incident in connection with foreign capital that occurred during the military Government. The action most fraught with political consequences was the installation of the automatic telephone, which first introduced American capital into Spain on a large scale and so directed the attention of the Government of the United States to Spanish domestic policy for the first time since the war of 1898. It is with this theme that I propose to end the present chapter.

When the Second Republic was born, German capital in Spain was insignificant. Most of it was invested in the *Compañía Sevillana de Electricidad*; the rest, on a small scale, in the motor industry and in electrical undertakings.

Italian capital was also strictly limited. The companies under Italian control were the *Sociedad Española Puricelli* (with a capital of 3 million pesetas) and *Comercial Pirelli* (with a capital of 7,500,000 pesetas).

As was to be expected, innumerable businesses and services fell into German and Italian hands when General Franco's rebellion momentarily triumphed and the Falangist State was set up. But like the majority of the changes introduced into Spanish life by the Fascist régime, the economic penetration of the Italians and Germans will be the flower of a day. When Fascism is ousted, the concessions and favours granted to the foreign ally will also come to an end. Let us, therefore, disregard the episodic and the subsidiary and concentrate on the permanent.

There is undoubtedly a great deal of foreign capital invested in Insurance Companies in Spain, mostly of English and French origin. If we were to try to ascertain how much foreign capital and how much Spanish capital are invested in the same company, whether of Spanish or foreign nationality, we should lose ourselves in another labyrinth of Minos and come out as confused as we went in. In the last analysis, it is enough for us to know approximately the amount that leaves Spain every year under the head of insurance to realize how serious for the economy of Spain is the activity of non-Spanish capital in this branch of industry. The Insurance Companies, in effect, take out of Spain 250 to 300 million gold pesetas annually.

Belgian capital invested in Spain or created partly in Spain, though ultimately of Belgian origin, amounts to about 500 million francs. There are Belgian technicians and Belgian shareholders in the timber industry, in the tramways, in the railways. The *Sociedad Madrileña de Tranvías* (capital 75 million pesetas) is partly controlled by Belgians. The *Compañía de Tranvías y Electricidad de Bilbao* (10 million francs); the *Consorcio de Almagrera* (20 million francs); the *Compañía Asturiana de Minas* (279 million francs); the *Minas de Volframio de Balborraz* (1,750,000 francs); the *Sociedad Anónima "Verreries Espagnoles"* (4 million francs) are financed entirely by Belgian capital. The Belgians (the international trust) also have a large share in the potash mines of Suria (30 million pesetas).

I s                                                                257

French capital controls, chiefly, various important mines; it is also invested in the textile industry, in fertilizers, explosives, etc.

Part of the capital of *La Seda de Barcelona* (16 million pesetas) is French, and the French also have an important financial interest in the *Unión Española de Fábricas de Abonos de Productos Químicos y de Superfosfatos* (20 million francs) in the profitable company *Unión Española de Explosivos* (60 million pesetas); and in the Spanish company *Minas del Castillo de las Guardas* (12 million pesetas).

The ownership of *Minero y Metalúrgica de Peñarroya* (309 million francs) and of the *Compagnie des Mines de Cuivre de San Plato* (7 million francs) is also French.

Canadian capital is invested in Spain on such a large scale that it deserves special mention.

The powerful company known as *La Canadiense* controls 80 per cent of the hydro-electric industry of Catalonia. The capital of the Barcelona Traction, Light and Power Co. amounts to about 200 million pesetas. In 1914 this company's output was 145 million kilowatt-hours, taking thermic and hydraulic production together. In 1931 the output had risen to 611 million kilowatt-hours.

Through *Riegos y Fuerzas del Ebro* S.A., with a branch also at Toronto, *La Canadiense* participates in thirteen hydro-electric undertakings in Catalonia, with a paid-up capital of 114 million pesetas. This all-embracing company, with a capital bordering on 600 million pesetas, to take the lowest estimate, supplies electrical energy to practically the whole of the Catalan textile industry. It is also interested in *Luz y Fuerza de Levante* with a capital of 70 million pesetas.

British capital which, before the establishment of the American Telephone Company, had the most influence on the Spanish economy and therefore on Spanish politics, is invested in *Ferrocarriles de la Carolina y Prolongaciones* (3 million pesetas); in *Insular Colonial de Electricidad y Riegos* (12½ million pesetas); in *Minas del Centenillo* (12½ million pesetas); in *Minas de Rodalquilar* (auriferous quartz) (5½ million pesetas); in *Sulfatos de Logrosán* 4½ million pesetas), where English interests are represented by the firm of Vickers, which also participates in the *Sociedad Española de Construcción Naval*.

British capital entirely controls The Seville Waterworks Co., Ltd. (12 million pesetas); *Compañía General Canaria de Combustibles*

($1\frac{1}{2}$ million pesetas); The Tharsis Sulphur Copper Mines Ltd. (60 million pesetas); *Compañía de Río Tinto* (150 million pesetas); *Manufactura de Corcho Armstrong*, S.A. (35 million pesetas).

To sum up, British capital controls the water supply of Seville, almost all the copper output of Spain, which means a large part of the world output of copper, and a considerable portion of the manufactures of Spanish cork.

British capital has also gained a hold in the iron-ore mines of Vizcaya, where it controls the Iron Ore Co. and Luchana Mining.

In this branch of industry, the mining industry, the Spanish State has shown itself lamentably inept and negligent in opening the way to foreign capital, granting valuable concessions or selling the mines outright for derisory sums. Río Tinto is a case in point.

On March 29th, 1873, the Spanish State sold the copper mines of Rio Tinto to an English company for the modest sum of 92,800,000 pesetas.

The Río Tinto Company has issued and redeemed with the greatest facility in Spain debentures to the value of 100 million pesetas. In 1931 the company issued new debentures in London for £2,000,000, and the following year it had already redeemed £62,516. In spite of the fall in the price of copper, which was quoted in London at £32 per ton (as against £82 and £89 in 1928 and the following years), Río Tinto was able in 1932 to allocate 24 million pesetas to the Reserve Fund and 40 million more to the general Investment and Development Fund.

According to the company's public balance-sheet, the profits of the Río Tinto Company during the second decade of the present century amounted to a yearly average of £1,500,000. These figures show, therefore, that in little more than any two years during the period mentioned, the company's profits enabled the British capitalists to recoup the 93 million pesetas they had expended in acquiring the mines.

This company has distributed to its shareholders between 90 and 100 million pesetas annually.

From 1910 to 1932 the net profits of Río Tinto amounted to the enormous sum of £21,912,672. Ignoring the fluctuations of the peseta and assuming the rate of exchange to be 25 pesetas to the £, the profits of the company in the aforementioned period amounted to about 600 million pesetas.

The profits of the mines administered by The Tharsis Sulphur Copper Mines Ltd., though less startling than those of Río Tinto, have also followed an upward curve.

Around the copper mines the British have accumulated a wealth of property that cannot be estimated,—railways, buildings of all kinds, residences for the British personnel, and acres and acres of forest land, which virtually make these alert colonizers an economic power on Spanish soil and turn the province of Huelva into an English province in the Roman style, a sovereign enclave.

I have already said that American capital in Spain was negligible before the installation of the automatic telephone by The International Telephone and Telegraph Corporation. The Americans controlled, as they do today, the Standard Electric (30 million pesetas) and participated in the *Sociedad Ibérica de Construcciones Eléctricas* (20 million pesetas) and in *Firestone Hispania*, S.A. (10 million pesetas). But the foundation of the *Compañía Telefónica Nacional de España* has made American capital such a potent financial and moral factor in Spain that it must be admitted that not only has the ground gained by the transference of capital and industry to Spanish ownership through Spain's neutrality in the first World War been lost, but more ground has been yielded. In a word, Spain's situation had deteriorated in this respect, even without the disaster of the civil war.

Under a contract signed in 1924 between the Spanish Government and the I.T.T.C., this company was given the monopoly of telephonic communications in Spain for twenty years. At the end of this period, the Spanish Government could take over all the installations of the *Compañía Telefónica Nacional de España*— in theory; but in practice, Spain would have had to refund to the I.T.T.C. all the capital expended, plus 15 per cent interest, and would have had to pay the whole in gold! In 1944, the year when the contract expired, the capital of the American telephone syndicate in Spain probably exceeded 1,000 million pesetas. But Spain had no gold. How could she then take over the telephone service on the expiry of the concession?

Nevertheless, at the beginning of April 1945, General Franco's Government announced that a satisfactory agreement had been reached with the I.T.T.C. which would enable the State to take over the telephone system. The Spanish Government, according to the British Press, was to acquire 80 per cent of the shares of the *Compañía Telefónica Nacional de España* at a cost of £14,250,000; £12,500,000 in State bonds and the rest in cash.

From the foregoing we cannot deduce with any certainty the exact significance of the agreement arrived at, without publicity, in secret, between a weak Government and the powerful I.T.T.C. Knowing the terms of the 1924 contract, which were very unfavourable to the Spanish Government, we are bound to suspect that the *de facto* control of the Spanish telephone service will remain in the hands of the Americans and that Spain will have what she has hitherto never had; a foreign debt with the United States, a power which seems to have recently chosen Spain as a zone of expansion for her economic imperialism.

The flow of American capital to Spain would not be a cause for dismay if it came with more liberal pretensions than those embodied in the concession for the telephone monopoly.

BOOK FOUR

# THE SECOND REPUBLIC

CHAPTER I

## THE NEW SITUATION

A<small>PRIL</small> 14<small>TH</small>, 1931, saw the beginning of a new national drama, or rather, a new act in the old drama which began with the Cortes of Cadiz in 1810.

The Republic was born without paying the heavy tribute of bloodshed which history usually exacts from nations which change their form of government. The Spanish people greeted the end of the monarchy with an outburst of joy. In the crisis of authority the defence of life and property was undertaken by the people themselves, as in 1868 when Madrid offered a similar spectacle with an improvised popular police force guarding the doors of the banks. On this memorable April 14th the Royal Family was given a bodyguard of young Socialists. For the reigning obsession was to avoid dishonouring the nascent Republic with disturbances and acts of vandalism. Both Spaniards and foreigners commented on the magnanimity and discipline of the people who, on reconquering liberty and power, made no use of their conquest to destroy or humiliate their erstwhile oppressors. And although magnanimity is not always a virtue in politics, it is still true that cruelty, as Talleyrand observed, may be not so much a crime as something far worse—a mistake. If the people were now irreproachable in their conduct, they had on occasions been less master of their impulses during the tumults of the past century—and nevertheless the revolution made no progress. This proves, perhaps, that the victory of democracy depends not so much on the temper of those below as on the use which those at the top make of their possession of power. All that can be said is that the behaviour of the Spanish people in April 1931 was beyond reproach. In the crisis, they acted as they should have done.

As in life and art, so in history, tragedy ripens in the womb of the irrevocable destiny of individuals. Since Spanish democracy is always the unfailing reply to tyranny, from the very moment of its rebirth the advent of the reign of complete liberty is taken for granted. The dark night of absolutist dictatorship is followed by the bright day of the people's *saturnalia*, or the carnival of the Rights of Man. The struggle against despotism in Spain is a fight for liberty in the abstract, liberty as an end in itself. Consequently, as soon as liberty has been achieved, the democratic movement comes to nothing. The revolution has been made; liberty has been attained; the urge for action has already passed. Everything that could not be said during the last ten years has been said in the last ten days, and continues to be said. With the haste of men who think that nothing remains to be done, the leaders of liberty consume their energy in speech-making.

It is natural that an oppressed people should aspire to be free and should take steps to achieve its freedom the moment tyranny ceases. But this attitude impedes the necessary concentration of authority without which the reform of property comes to naught. Thus, reaction and revolution in Spain follow one another like the links of a chain, without either achieving its objective. It is a problem without a solution, unless democracy can succeed, by extraordinary and not easily discoverable methods, in breaking the logical process which, if prolonged as it is in Spain, can exhaust a nation. However, the miracle was not going to be achieved under the Second Republic. Liberty had triumphed; and all the rest, beginning (as had so often happened before) with the revolution, was going to be subordinated to the principle of the sovereignty of the people.

The conclusion of the Pact of San Sebastian in August 1930 marked the taking of a step which was of the gravest import. The leaders of Spanish democracy (both historic leaders and recent converts) had agreed on the basis of an alliance whose aim was the proclamation of the Republic, the organization of which, once the monarchy was overthrown, was to be entrusted to a Constituent Assembly elected by universal suffrage.

Four months later, the Revolutionary Committee, functioning as a provisional Government, issued a manifesto on the lines of the proclamation of the revolution of September 1868, and announced that the object of the revolution was to establish the Republic on the basis of the people's sovereignty represented in a Constituent Assembly.'' They might as well have announced that they were going to preside over another civil war.

Spanish democracy had returned to power, but it did not return more intelligent or better led.

It would not be superfluous to recall that the Republic was being hatched in the cities during the military dictatorship and was brought to birth by the cities. It was the creature of the middle class or *petite bourgeoisie* and the urban proletariat. In the change of régime, it was the small business man who played what was probably the decisive part.

Towards the end of the dictatorship, the mercantile classes, defrauded, or to put it better, antagonized, as we have seen, by Calvo Sotelo's administration, lost confidence in the régime. And while the blunders of the dictatorship in the economic and financial sphere aroused the hostility of the trading community, the series of spasmodic crises which attended the monarchy after the fall of the dictatorship, with the inevitable threat to public order, led this section of the middle class to throw in their lot with the Republicans. The Republic came to be the most conservative solution at that moment for the commercial classes; as it was for part of the oligarchy, for General Sanjurjo, who placed the Civil Guard at the service of the new régime, and for the Church which, in the words of *El Debate*, proclaimed the nation to be above forms of government.

In 1923 the industrialists had greeted the military *coup d'état* with frank enthusiasm, primarily because it promised law and order, so necessary to trading activities. In 1930 the budding Republic was a better guarantee of peace than the unpopular monarchy, and the *petite bourgeoisie*, without clearly defined political, ideals adopted Republicanism.

This social class, with no direct representation in politics, oppressed by the landed oligarchy under the Restoration régime, was, I repeat, a factor of supreme importance in the new situation created by the overthrow of the institutions of 1874. Precisely because it lacked a party, it was to exert an extraordinary influence in the *dénouement* of the national crises, because it shook the system of the two-headed oligarchy. In a Spain without political institutions, the mercantile classes, though much less powerful in the economic field than the oligarchy and less numerous than the proletariat, influenced the moral atmosphere of every régime by favouring now democracy and now reaction. These neutral classes, as they were properly called since the beginning of the century, had no fear of revolution as such. The merchants and industrialists had nothing to lose by a reasonable distribution of agrarian property, or by the reform of the banking system; on the contrary, all this would be in their interests. But these classes are proverbially sensitive to demagogy. The Republic, therefore, had to endeavour not to alienate the sympathy of this social class, whose principal enemies were the landed oligarchy and chaos.

Commerce is by nature Liberal in its sympathies; and Spanish Republicanism, in spite of the demagogic vein which runs through it, was often by force of circumstances the refuge of the mercantile classes. In their struggle with the landed oligarchy, the merchants sometimes retaliated by voting for Republican candidates and seeing them triumph in the most important capitals, where the electoral farce was less violent. But the anti-dynastic movement did not systematically include the trading community. They might vote Republican in a moment of desperation, but they did not serve in the ranks of Republicanism. For which class, then, did the Republican politicians speak? As a hard and fast rule, for none. They did not represent interests, but ideas. But this will be discussed in the following chapter.

In 1931 the Spanish people reaped the harvest of the 1917 revolution. What were to be the fruits of the revolution of 1931? Let us review the situation.

The landed oligarchy had lost its political power, but it was still very strong—by far the strongest class in the nation. The countryside had voted for the monarchy, that is, for the oligarchy which dominated it. The provinces and not a few of the cities of Castile and Andalusia—the political hunting-ground *par excellence* of the oligarchy—had given their verdict against democracy. The perils which beset the Republican régime from the moment of its birth were obvious. If the Republic did not destroy the oligarchy before it recovered from its discomfiture, the oligarchy would destroy the Republic once and for all.

The classes which were politically and economically oppressed could not afford to lose an hour. The Republic had to subordinate everything to the revolution against the oligarchy. And for that, the ideal would have been to revive the national union of 1917, a front which would include all the democratic parties from the rural proletariat to the industrial middle classes, and which would embody the common aspirations of all without unduly stressing those of any particular party. As we have seen in the preceding chapters, all the problems of Spain could be resolved—and can still be resolved—into one: the agrarian problem. For as long as the land belongs, on the one hand, to the old nobility and other great landowners, and, on the other, is divided and sub-divided among myriads of beggar-proprietors, there can be no citizens in Spain, nor can the nation be organized within a system of liberty, nor is it possible to build a State of any shape or form, still less to found a democracy.

This was the only problem—the fountain-head of all the others. The problem of the Army and the clerical problem originated in the weakness of civil society, and this, in turn, sprang from abysmal social inequality. Separatism, on the other hand, was the natural enough desire of certain parties in the socially healthy, balanced and industrial regions, to break with a nation which was socially unsound, unbalanced, and oppressed by an agrarian oligarchy.

Yet there did not exist in 1931 a national movement similar to that which existed in 1917; and this was, no doubt, in the natural order of things. What is necessary is not always easy, even when the life of a nation is at stake. The great Catalan *bourgeoisie* had fallen back before the Castilian-Andalusian oligarchy, after having accused it for forty years of causing the ruin of Spain; and the oligarchy had succeeded in gaining admission to the Republic. Those who ought to have been in the Republic were not there; and not all those who were there ought to have been.

The capitalists of the Catalan *Lliga* had definitely abandoned their allies of 1917. They were now more afraid of the hypothetical menace of the workers' revolution than the real and degrading yoke of the oligarchy. Thus we have the paradoxical situation that at the moment when at least part of the oligarchy had abandoned the King in order to survive, the great Catalan *bourgeoisie* which, if it were true to its historical past, should have led the national revolution against reactionary power in landed property and banking, gave Ministers to the Crown and exerted itself to save what was not worthy of salvation. When the monarchy expired, Cambó and Ventosa appeared as the co-founders of a monarchical party whose aim was to "renew the institutions". They wanted to shore up an institution which they ought to have helped to overthrow. The National Committee of this untimely and misbegotten party consisted of Ventosa, the Marqués de Figueroa, Silió, Goicoechea and Montes Jovellar, all, except the Catalan, representatives of the Restoration régime of greed and landed interests.

The national front had lost the Catalan capitalists, but, as I have said, it had gained the collaboration of those oligarchs who were beginning to be uneasy.

It must be remembered that the Republic rose on the ruins of the oligarchy, which had been politically pulverized by the military dictatorship. In the Restoration State, the ruling class had been represented politically by two groups which, acting in concert, had taken turns at government, by means of the famous "Box and Cox" arrangement. Those two mutually dependent parties had now been converted, as will soon be seen, into two different nuclei, with divergent methods of appraising the struggle against the revolution. But the oligarchic constellation had thrown off a meteorite or asteroid—the group which was led by Don Niceto Alcalá Zamora.

Alcalá Zamora was the leader of an insignificant oligarchic group, the head of the small party which passed over to the Republic with the aim of governing it, of making it an old-fashioned Conservative régime. Romanones' ex-Minister had founded a party, the Republican Liberal Right, to accommodate the "historic Liberals". As Alcalá Zamora himself declared on March 20th, 1931, "he had procured the incorporation into the movement of the historic Liberal elements in order to guarantee the existence of a Conservative Republic".

Alcalá Zamora was one of the most muddle-headed and obstinate leaders of the old régime. A lawyer and a landowner, the *cacique* of the province of Jaén and an impenitent oligarch, he was to be a perpetual menace to the Republican régime and the despair of Republicans who aspired to new political methods. Thrown into the arms of the revolutionaries, like so many others, by an impotent feeling of resentment against Alfonso XIII, the President of the first Republican Government brought only negative talents to the Republic. His aim was to continue the policy which the dictatorship had prevented him from following —to recover for the oligarchy the political power it had lost. An excellent family man (a fact which may be of no interest to historians), he was not lacking in good feeling, but as a politician, he was incorrigible. Even under the old régime, which he undermined with his factious manipulations, he had been incorrigible, and he would have been the same under any régime. His ambition was vanity; his eloquence, artifice; his talent, dexterity; his Catholicism, superstition. In a Republic which was born with the stern mission of regenerating Spain, Alcalá Zamora was a crowning blunder. With such a hero, the revolution was already on the way to becoming an imposture.

# THE PARTIES OF THE RÉGIME

Alcalá zamora presided over a coalition of parties of the Liberal middle class in which the Socialists, with three Ministers, were represented.[1] Undoubtedly the first Republican Government contained men who would have played a worthy part in a nation which was organically healthy; but in Spain these politicians were to wear themselves out battering against the wall of historic problems which a parliamentary régime is incapable of solving. It was not the men who were at fault, but the system. No politician on earth could have succeeded in such circumstances. The statesman who, in a revolutionary situation, attempts to govern like a statesman in countries which have succeeded by exceptional methods, at a certain moment of their history, in mastering the forces of revolution, is showing an obstinate propensity to suicide.

Moreover the first Republican Cabinet included men who were bound to trouble the democratic waters. Besides Alcalá Zamora, there was Lerroux with his party, a sure pledge of the impotence of the regenerating movement.

Lerroux was at that time a tired agitator. The hazardous existence of the political adventurer, without principles, faithless, pursued more often by creditors than by the police of the monarchy, had consumed, with the years, his passion for the fight. The Republican lion turned lamb had only one ambition: to lie down and rest. His programme of government was reduced to being head, if possible, of a Government, paying his debts and, once he could obtain credit again, looking forward to a settled future. Lerroux believed in nothing. He now lacked even the only faith he had ever had in his life—the cynic's creed, faith in himself.

In the recent conspiracies, in the counsels of the Revolutionary Committee, Lerroux agreed to whatever the others proposed.

[1] The first Republican Government consisted of: Niceto Alcalá Zamora (Conservative), President; Alejandro Lerroux (Radical), Foreign Affairs; Fernando de los Ríos (Socialist), Justice; Manuel Azaña (Left Republican), War; Santiago Casares Quiroga (Galician Autonomist), Marine; Indalecio Prieto (Socialist), Finance; Miguel Maura (Conservative), Interior; Marcelino Domingo (Radical Socialist), Education; Alvaro de Albornoz (Radical Socialist), Public Works; Francisco Largo Caballero (Socialist), Labour; Luis Nicolau d'Olwer (Catalan Autonomist), Trade; and Diego Martínez Barrio (Radical), Communications.

He questioned nothing. He had no doubts, because he had no faith. He said yes to everything because he was the first to doubt whether the Republic really was on the way. It goes without saying that Lerroux's mission was to lead, not the revolution, but the counter-revolution. The revolution would be led by the Incorruptibles—a word that evokes the sharp profile of Robespierre. And who can name Robespierre without recalling the Jacobins who were to set the standards, tone, and course of the Revolution and give it its soul?

"History teaches us", wrote Hegel, "that man learns nothing from history."[1] Applied to the Spanish radical middle class, this phrase has all the force of an axiom. Philosophic Republicanism under the second Republic showed no trace of having suffered the slightest change during the past 130 years. The Liberal middle class in Spain wrote and spoke as the Spanish Liberals used to write and speak in 1810. It was a case of mental stagnation at its worst. They thought in all good faith that men could only begin to live in Spain on the day when the Church was separated from the State. Whatever fell outside the ecclesiastical question was, for them, a subsidiary matter.

Azaña—to whom I shall devote a separate chapter—was to a certain extent an exception. In him, Spanish Liberal demagogy was refined in the fiery crucible of the artist's personality, full of intellectual dignity and tempered by the sober Castilian strain.

The Socialist Party was the most outstanding political force on which not only the democratic movement, but the nation as a whole could count. It reckoned among its ranks a disciplined and relatively enlightened proletariat; and in addition to this politically-minded proletariat, a brilliant group of men from the middle class, some of them famous intellectuals, who lent authority and solvency to the movement. As a party, it excelled both in the quality of its leaders and the number of its adherents, in contrast to the purely Republican parties which were always poor in numbers. Everything seemed to indicate that if in future a man should arise in Spain who could bring order to the country, he would come from the ranks of the Socialist Party.

But this party, which was represented unofficially in the Pact of San Sebastian by Indalecio Prieto, tended to avoid responsibility. This reluctance to participate in the Government and

[1] Gibbon said the same thing: "The experience of past faults, which may sometimes correct the mature age of an individual, is seldom profitable to the successive generations of mankind" (Bk. IV, chap. xli).

assume the leadership of the régime, which was insurmountable in some of the Socialist leaders and manifest in them all, was only overcome by force of circumstances. In the first place, the soldiers who took part in the revolutionary conspiracy of 1930 demanded the participation of the Socialists in the Government as an earnest of good faith.[1] The truth was that, as Spain was weak in middle-class elements, the Republic could not make headway without the services of such a numerous and disciplined party or do without many of its leaders. Fate decreed, therefore, that Socialism should be the axis of the new régime, and the efforts of the Socialists to disinterest themselves in a historic situation which affected them so profoundly were bound to be in vain.[2]

Nevertheless the leading rôle of Socialism in the Republic was limited, on the one hand, by its own quality of a party based on class (though it did not intend to follow a class policy) and, on the other, by the conception that not a few Republicans had formed of the Republic. The Socialists were debarred from governing the Republic, however much they conducted themselves as Liberals. A Socialist Government, even if it did no more than was acceptable to the Republicans, would alarm the Conservative classes, a disaster the Republican politicians wanted to avoid at all costs. Consequently the future mission of the Socialist Party appeared to lie, by tacit and universally accepted agreement, in supporting the Republicans and acquiescing in their policy—in a word, in being one more Republican party, though, in practice, with fewer rights.[3]

This solution was assured in advance of the goodwill of the Socialists, who were conscious of how much conspired against Socialist policy and who were, as we have seen, in no wise interested in overburdening themselves with responsibilities, still less in embarrassing the Republic. But what chiefly facilitated the collaboration of the Socialist Party with the Republicans was the relative coincidence of their points of view as regards fundamental questions of policy. Part of the Socialist Party's programme, as well as the political vision of its leaders

[1] Indalecio Prieto, speech in the Cortes, June 20th, 1934.
[2] As it happened, the man who carried resistance to collaboration in the Government to its furthest lengths, Don Julian Besteiro, was precisely the one who had to accept a post entailing the most delicate responsibilities, such as leading the Cortes and deputizing on occasions for the President of the Republic.
[3] For example, the Socialist Party was to have Ministers, but not Civil Governors, the idea behind this restriction being the same desire not to make the presence of Socialists in the Government too much felt.

in general, paid tribute to the Liberal tradition. It was at that time of little import that Republicans and Socialists should have different and even opposite ideas on the subject of property, since no one proposed to carry out a real revolution in that field. For the rest, the Socialist attitude towards the Church, national unity, Parliament, the form of government, approximated to the attitude of the Republicans, where it was not exactly the same. The fact was that the radical middle class had great influence on the direction of the Socialist Party, whose unmistakable personality derived partly from the fact that the bulk of its adherents were proletarian and partly from having maintained its opposition to the monarchy in a purer and more compact form than the Republican. Moreover there ran through the Socialist Party, as a legacy from its first founders, a vein of morality and seriousness, which was very Spanish, and which gave the finishing touches to its personality.

For the rest, Spanish Socialism was associated in the international sphere with the Second International, thus recognizing its relationship with parliamentary, Liberal and progressive Socialist parties in other countries.

In reality, therefore, the Spanish Socialists undertook to support the Republic and provide Socialist Ministers and deputies, because their programme and tradition tended this way and because Socialists in other countries had done likewise.

So long as the Socialist Party was free of governmental responsibilities or had only to give its opinion on the outstandingly important problem of the national Constitution, it could, without consequences to itself or the nation, do what the Socialist parties of the industrial countries were doing. But when the oligarchy fell and Spanish democracy came into power, there arose formidable questions which did not exist for Socialist parties in nations whose social order was relatively stable, like England, France and Belgium. In none of these countries did the fall of a Conservative or Liberal Government and the return of a Socialist Government or the admission of Socialist Ministers to the Government, have such grave significance as in Spain. English, French or Belgian Socialists could *govern* without changing the real and basic constitution of society —the Spanish Socialist (and, for that matter, the Spanish Republican) could not. The first question which confronted Spanish Socialism on assuming directly or indirectly the responsibilities of government concerned nothing less than the form of government. Up to that point, the example of Socialists abroad was useful and could be followed without untoward

271

results; but beyond that, Spanish Socialism, the pivot of Spanish democracy, had to be guided by its own light, in harmony with national problems which had no equivalent outside Spain. The undertaking was hard in the extreme. It matters little that a party should know how to order world affairs, if it lacks practical solutions for the grave and immediate political problems of its own nation. By its gravity and urgency, the Spanish national problem was, as events were to prove, *sui generis*. During the lapse of the last 120 years, fundamental laws of political biology had been violated in Spain, and they could not continue to be violated without Spaniards bringing the world crashing about their ears, as happened in 1936. Let us see what the situation was in so far as it directly affected the Socialist party; let us go to the heart of the matter.

The tragedy of modern Spain (*nunquam nimis dicitur, quod nunquam satis dicitur*, as Seneca says) originated in the plan to found a Liberal State while the nation lacked a sufficiently strong *bourgeoisie* or middle class; and as Spain continued to be without a middle class and as the Middle Ages began at the outskirts of Madrid, the insistence of the democratic parties upon governing the country on the basis of universal suffrage perpetuated the catastrophe. Moreover, while this organic and insuperable conflict was still unresolved, a further complication arose in the presence of Marxist ideas in a pre-capitalist medium. As political liberty in modern constitutional practice pre-supposes the existence of a middle class capable of translating it into reality[1], so Marxist philosophy, in its turn, assumes the pre-existence of a *bourgeoisie* or capitalism and the corresponding proletariat. Now it is evident that Liberalism came to a Spain which was without a *bourgeoisie* or even a rural middle class— except in certain regions—and that Marxism came to a Spain without a modern proletariat, except in certain zones. The consequence was that the proletariat in Spain began an organized fight against private property in general, when the weak Spanish *bourgeoisie* had not yet succeeded in overcoming the aristocracy economically or in founding the *bourgeois* or capitalist State. In 1931 more than 72 per cent of the working population in Spain were agricultural, or, which is the same thing, less than 28 per cent were industrial and mercantile. As can be seen, the urban proletariat were insignificant compared with the huge mass of the rural proletariat. In addition, as I said before, there were more than 2 million landless peasants, a phenomenon without equal in the West, at least as regards numbers.

[1] See Rousseau, *Contrat Social*, Bk. II, chap. xi.

Spanish society, therefore, was still predominantly rural and full of inequalities; and it goes without saying that in this type of society, the mercantile and industrial *bourgeoisie* exercises, by the mere fact of its existence, a revolutionary function. For it modifies its surroundings by liberalizing them, in the same way as the tree influences the humidity of the atmosphere. Spain was still at that stage of social evolution when anyone who opened a shop, founded an industry or built a factory, was performing a progressive action. Moreover, without industry or commerce Socialism could hardly exist, or it would be a primitive Socialism to which the development of an industrial and commercial middle class would always be advantageous. Lastly, the need for destroying the agrarian-aristocratic oligarchy was, too, in Spain common to both workers and industrial capitalists. Such solidarity of moral and political interests between the historic middle class and the proletariat in the period of bourgeois ascendancy was clearly manifest in the French Revolution; both social strata fought together against the medieval world of *les aristocrats*. Spain is still in eighteenth-century France, so to speak, though her middle class is weaker than the French *bourgeoisie* at that time. The irruption of Socialist theories of all kinds intensified in Spain (prematurely, from the point of view of the normal play of politics) the collision between the proletariat and the *bourgeoisie* properly so-called, the latter finding itself forced, the more so as it lacked political genius, to seal a bargain with the aristocracy in order to defend itself against the class revolution of the proletariat, the revolution of organized Socialism and Anarchism.

Pursuing this analysis to its logical conclusion, it is un-questionable that, given the special conditions of the development of Spanish society, the industrial proletariat, by introducing class warfare in the terrain in which it had been introduced by the working classes of the capitalist nations—a thing Spain never was—sacrificed to a certain extent the interests of a vast rural proletariat to the political ideals of a small industrial proletariat. The interests of the Spanish peasant—in an exalted historical sense—were merged with the national interests, inasmuch as they consisted in throwing off the yoke of the landed oligarchy—a need which was common to the whole of non-oligarchic Spanish society and, therefore, to the industrial and mercantile *bourgeoisie* itself. The interests of the industrial worker were less universal and even conflicted with the general political interest, since this proletariat was urging an anti-capitalist revolution which would consolidate the landed oligarchy because it would then have the support of the bourgeois middle class. This particular inter-influence of the social classes only exists now in countries whose development in the social order is abnormal. And there can be no doubt that the anarchist terrorism in Barcelona, the violent strikes and what amounted to the aggression of the industrial proletariat against the capitalists, retarded the emancipation of the rural proletariat in Spain. Up to a certain point, this was, for the most part, inevitable. Historically it was as if, during the French Revolution, Babeuf's Communists had supplanted the middle class in the leadership of the revolution, or as if the English Levellers had been sufficiently strong to frighten the Puritans into uniting with the aristocracy and the Presbyterians for the defence of private property. In all probability, the middle-class revolution, both in England and France, would have failed; or would not have been so complete, to the ultimate advantage of feudalism. That is, more or less, what happened in Spain.

Hence the disagreement between Joaquín Costa and Pablo Iglesias at the beginning of the century. Costa foresaw or had a presentiment that the class organization of the proletariat would frighten the middle class and convert it from a potentially revolutionary and anti-oligarchic social sector into a reactionary class—as indeed happened. But Pablo Iglesias was a man of his time; and at that moment, only a popular political movement with Socialist ideas could hope to make headway. Costa failed; Iglesias did not. The tragedy was that, with Costa's *national* ideas, aimed at destroying the powerful landed oligarchy by means of a general movement of all the progressive classes, the historic Spanish problem, as it appeared at the end of the nineteenth century and continues to appear, would have found a solution; but these ideas were not fitted to mobilize the masses politically—a no less urgent and laborious task, since at that time all Spaniards were paralysed by an apathy or moral weakness which caused them to stand aloof from public strife.

I repeat that all this—Costa's failure, class warfare in imitation of the advanced nations, and so on—was in the highest degree fatal. And it was likewise fatal that Spanish Socialism should conduct itself like the British and Belgian Labour Parties. But with all this, the fact cannot be refuted that the masses which in Spain were attracted by Socialism—the party of countless multitudes without land—were not the industrial workers of British or Belgian Labour; that what Spanish Social-ism had to confront was not a sovereign and wealthy *bourgeoisie*

274

like the English, but a much less prosperous *bourgeoisie*, frequently menaced by bankruptcy, and *politically* oppressed by the landed and financial aristocracy.

Only in the Russia of pre-revolution days was Socialism confronted by a similar national situation, and on this I shall say a few words later. But even if the circumstances were the same in all the countries where Socialist philosophy had made progress before the existence of a triumphant *bourgeoisie* had provoked it, the consequences of violating the given stages of political and economic evolution may vary considerably. For Spain, ruled for nearly sixty years by an absolute oligarchy, it was, and still is, vital to reduce the landed and financial aristocracy to economic impotence. Everything hinges on this, beginning with national unity and ending with the very fate of the race. For if an end is not put to the age-old civil war, who knows whether Spain will not soon cease to exist as a nation? Never has the life of a great people depended on a revolution so much as today the life of Spain hangs on the elimination of the oligarchy which oppresses her. These pages will, I hope, show the truth of this. Now let us glance at the case of Russia.

Before the memorable events of October 1917, Russian Socialism in general encountered a similar situation to that of the Spanish Socialists in 1931. The Bolshevists were working, in a nation of *moujiks*, with ideas derived from the epoch of Big Business. Lenin understood the anomaly; and his view was in substance that, for the benefit of the proletariat itself, capitalism should be built up in Russia.[1] Undoubtedly, Lenin did not foresee the course the revolution would take. But the Russian middle class subsequently proved inept or impotent in delivering the nation from the impasse and the course of events gave the Bolshevists the opportunity of carrying out a sweeping revolution with Socialism as its goal.

In 1931 the Russian method was not applicable to Spain, even if the Spanish Socialists had thought of trying it—and the same holds good today. For an incalculable part of a nation's problems impinge on the international sphere. The Communist Revolution triumphed and was able to consolidate its position in Russia owing to a concatenation of exceptional circumstances —primarily, the immensity of Russia itself and the war-weariness and exhaustion of the intervening Powers. Wherever else in Europe Bolshevism attempted to get a grip, it could

---

[1] Lenin, *Carta de despedia a los obreros suizos.* Henri Rollin, *La Revolución rusa. Su génesis histórica.* Editorial España, Madrid.

not survive, principally because of hostility from without. In addition, the Russian Communist movement was particularly rich in men of action.

Basically the Socialist position in Spain in 1931 *vis-à-vis* the Republic was that recommended by Lenin before the Russian revolution of February—support for the middle class with the aim of carrying out the democratic revolution. It would, in fact, have been no small gain for the Spanish Socialists if the Republic had been able to accomplish, for example, the electrification and industrialization of the country, even though on a capitalist basis. The difficulty was that the courageous enterprise was not capable of realization until the oligarchy had been stripped of all power, and this, in its turn, exceeded the capacities of the parliamentary system.

Apart from the fact that the international situation was favourable to them or not irremediably hostile, what saved the Russian revolutionaries was the form of government they adopted. Kerensky's political solution was utopian and not a solution at all. If neither in England nor in France—nations with a powerful middle class—it had been found possible to carry out a revolution in a system of political liberty, how could it be possible in Russia where the abyss separating the social classes was so wide and deep? By concentrating power in one hand—an expedient which is always necessary if a nation is to make radical change in the structure of property[1]—the Bolshevists solved the most pressing problem of the revolution. Kerensky and the middle class had no eyes for this, nor had they men of action; and sooner or later the middle class would have been overthrown, as it was to be in Spain in the manner which will be revealed.

In Spain, as we have seen, a Government with plenary powers could not have relied on the Socialist Party to play the principal part, even if the Socialists had advised this solution. But for a Socialist, more perhaps than for a Republican, it seemed to be axiomatic that the second Republic, pledged to universal suffrage, should have a short life and perish as the first Republic perished. There were not lacking those who saw this happening and said so; but with some of the Socialists paralysed by fatalism and others seduced by the same illusions as inspired the Republicans, they were all heading for the rocks.

For the moment the Spanish Socialists had renounced the design to introduce Socialism, as they were bound to do. The history of Socialism under the Republic was a long string of

[1] See Machiavelli, *Discourses on the First Decade of Titus Livius*, Bk. I, chap. ix.

renunciations, as we shall have occasion to show. The error lay in discarding Marxist principles in favour of others no less inapplicable to Spain.

More than any other party of the régime, the Socialist Party, because it was an anti-bourgeois organization and at the same time the corner-stone of Spanish democracy, was to find itself often under the Republic in a state of extreme perplexity. This lack of sureness in the policy of the Socialist Party inevitably weakened the pulse of a movement which was charged by history with responsibilities of unaccustomed magnitude; largely, perhaps, because since the death of Pablo Iglesias, Spanish Socialism lacked that supreme leader, respected by all, who is so necessary to a political organization in a historic crisis.

Here we should say a few words about the other parties of the Republic.

If the great Catalan *bourgeoisie* was far from rising to the occasion, so was the *petite bourgeoisie*. This social class was impatient to secure regional autonomy. Autonomy, or independence, was the only interest which bound the Catalan middle class to the Republic. For these Catalans, who had learnt nothing from history, the national revolution meant a superficial and purely political change of form. There appeared to be certain difficulties in the way of understanding that the conquest of Catalan liberty was a more arduous and serious enterprise than the extraction of a document or statute solemnly approved by the Cortes from the Madrid politicians. When Maciá told the Catalans: "*Soms lliures*" (We are free), he uttered an empty phrase. The Catalan Nationalists did not stop to consider that so long as the anatomy of property south of the Ebro remained the same as it was in the nineteenth century, there could be no Liberal Constitution in Spain or Statute of Autonomy in the more prosperous regions. Catalans could not be free while the Andalusian *bracero* was a slave. And the more the discontented regions disinterested themselves in the rest of Spain, the more links they forged in their own chains and those of other Spaniards.

However, the fact is that the defection of the great Catalan *bourgeoisie*, which, as we have seen, enslaved itself to the Castilian-Andalusian oligarchy, left the *petite bourgeoisie* to hoist the standard of autonomy, separatism, or whatever else it was called. And so we have the situation of sixty years ago. In 1873 the Republican leader, Figueras, who was living in Madrid, had to depart hurriedly for Barcelona to request the hotheads to take down the federalist banner and renounce the Catalan State they had cheerfully proclaimed. The same thing happened in 1931. Maciá and Companys announced the miraculous birth of the Catalan Republic and Alcalá Zamora, following in Figueras' footsteps, went with another message of concord to restrain the secessionist movement, the avalanche which always threatens to engulf Spanish democracy every time it is reborn.

In the Pact of San Sebastian the Catalan middle class exacted a pledge from those party to the agreement, that the Catalan question should be solved "on the basis of the principle of self-determination", and for greater security they insisted that it should be put in writing. For these Catalan parties, as for those who granted them liberty before being free themselves—a situation which was not modified by the fact that they were about to become the Government—the Spanish revolution was reduced to a mere business of stipulations and signatures.

The inflamed nationalism of the Basques had no part in the ministerial coalition which was to regenerate Spain. This separatist movement was neither monarchical nor republican. The Basque Nationalist Party wanted to have nothing to do with Spain, as they called the territory inhabited by Spaniards of less vigorous *españolidad*, perhaps, than themselves, making no distinction between the oligarchy and the rest of the nation. The error of separatism is here clearly manifest. The Republic needed the combative ardour of this Basque middle class for the common and saving task of destroying the power of the oligarchy. But the Basque Nationalists would only support a Government which would undertake in writing to open up for them the path of secession. In the discussions at San Sebastian, from which the followers of Sabino Arana were absent, objections were raised to this brand of separatism; for it was not a separatism of the Left like the Catalan, but of the Right, and the Basque Nationalists were at that time entrusting their future to certain negotiations with the Carlists, their brothers of yesterday and their ferocious adversaries of tomorrow. These two sister movements could not agree, for though they were in essence the same thing, Basque nationalism represented centrifugal traditionalism and the Navarrese centripetal traditionalism. The former wanted not to depend on Spain for anything; the latter wanted the whole of Spain to depend on them.

Ignoring historical realities, the Catalan middle class and an important sector of the Basque middle class fought and bargained for *their* liberty; but in Spain, liberty is indivisible.

The Republican autonomists of Galicia, like the Catalans, were represented in the first Government of the Republic. But there is no doubt that the Home Rule question was not a pressing one in Galicia. Till then, the radical middle class in that region had not succeeded in creating or inventing a grievance which had any backing among any of the more important social classes in the north-west. Galician nationalism was purely intellectual and imitative, outside the structure of Galician society—a society which in no way, like the Basque and the Catalan, clashed with the oligarchic character of Castilian-Andalusian property.

I shall deal with the regionalist and separatist movements at length later on.

I think I have said enough to indicate the conditions in which Spanish democracy had to found a State and how it began to govern. It only remains for me to say a few words about the political stature of the men who embodied the régime.

I have already pointed out that the Republic, from its inception, had at its service men who would have passed for acceptable, and even illustrious rulers in a Europe dominated by the Third Estate. But the gravity of the historic crisis in which Spain was floundering called for exceptional qualities in the Spanish politician. And if, in absolute terms, the statesmen of the new régime deserved the confidence the people placed in them, on a relative plane, measured by circumstances of which the people, and even many of their leaders, did not perceive the full dramatic significance, these rulers were like Gulliver in Brobdingnag. In the light of the immediate past, the commanding cadres, not only of democracy but of Spanish policy as a whole, appear frankly impotent. The oligarchy had no Cánovas; not even a Silvela. The middle class could produce no thinker and man of action to approach the gigantic personality of Joaquín Costa. The proletariat had lost Pablo Iglesias and there was no one to fill the gap. Nor could there be found among the more or less libertarian Anarchists anyone of the stature of Pi, no one who could even reach to the knees of that diminutive great man, of whom it was said that he was as short as his name. And if the men were smaller, the problems had grown bigger and more complicated.

To my way of thinking, this was to be one of the most serious aspects of the Spanish situation in the period we are about to study. There can be no doubt—and I believe that events will confirm this impression—that the relative and rapid impoverishment of Spain in political personalities or leaders was to be a factor of enormous weight in the ripening of the catastrophe which overwhelmed the nation in 1936. The decline of the conservative parties in this respect was to be, perhaps, decisive. Never was the oligarchy more vulnerable to attack than it was now; never were its leaders more incapable or the class, in the aggregate, more despicable.

## THE ·CONSTITUTION

I T M U S T B E admitted that a nation's gravest and most solemn hour is that in which it establishes itself as a régime of liberty and justice. In Spain this rite has been repeated so often that it is rapidly becoming a farce. And it is repeated so often because, for Spanish democrats, a nation becomes a régime of liberty and justice through the approbation, in an extraordinary session of the Cortes, of a hundred or so Articles containing a definition of Spain which is totally at variance with what Spain really is and can be. In the Constitution of 1931 we find this: "Spain is a Republic of workers . . .", when it should read: "Spain is a Republic of fellaheen, tyrannized over by the landed oligarchy."

The Constitution which does not sanction a real state of affairs is a mere lawyers' pastime, and a fatal pastime at that, since it spreads the illusion, among others, that the rights which are registered in the constitutional code of laws have been achieved. "A Constitution is born, not made," wrote Savigny.

The Spanish democrats would have died for the Constitution, under the impression that they were dying for the revolution. Never was such importance attached to a document. The Constitution in Spain wore a halo, it was an icon, a Liberal Huizilopochtli. Heterodox Spaniards ended by idolizing this Bible of the Rights of Man, this kind of Vulgate for those who, having ceased to be Catholics, had yet not become Protestants. Having lost their religious faith, the Spanish intellectual and bureaucratic minority made a fetish of the Constitution. And to this fetish there were sacrificed periodically in Spain fantastic hecatombs of men, women and children, as in Carthage sacrifices were made to the glory of Baal.

Foremost among the factors which prevent Spain from organizing herself politically are Constitutions and Constituent Assemblies; in part, because the time necessitated by the conception, drawing up and parliamentary approval of the constitutional code of laws is approximately that required by the oligarchy to come out of its stupor and give battle to the revolution on sure ground. When the happy birth of a new Constitution is announced to the people with the customary ingenuousness, the revolution is already beating a retreat. In the struggle between the *rights* of the people which only exist on paper, and the *power* of the oligarchy which has its roots deep in society, the people naturally are bound to lose, and they do lose. In the second place, the obsession for constitutionalism forces the reformers to define their attitude on all the problems, some of which are not pressing, and on all the social classes, some of which could be allies of democracy in the revolution against the sector which enjoys most power and which it is of paramount importance to bring into subjection.

To put the Constitution first is to put the cart before the horse, besides irritating formidable social forces without being able to destroy anything or anybody.

In 1931 the Spanish people handed over the revolution to the revolutionary Government, and the revolutionary Government handed it over to the lawyers. The men of law were called in "when it was not a question of law or no law, but of life or no life".

The lawyers took over the already inanimate revolution and busied themselves for several months in carrying out a meticulous post-mortem. After infinite labour necessitated by the difficulties of finding the correct formulas, the legal sanhedrin submitted to Parliament a document which, under the title of a draft Constitution, was the death certificate of reform in Spain.

Like all unhappy nations where justice is unknown, Spain is superlatively rich in lawyers. Plato thought this was the unmistakable sign of a corrupt republic. It is not that the ancient profession of the law is useless or harmful in a well-ordered republic; men as famous and respected as Abraham Lincoln have belonged to it. But it is obvious than an excess of lawyers is as much a herald of disease in a nation as a superfluity of priests and monks, if not more so. A republic which has regard for its interests ought not to aim solely at diminishing religious communities, but also at placing a limit on those congregations of bishops, canons and sacristans of the law. In the second Republic the lawyers were to succeed in cornering the whole Government, under the ineffable leadership of Señor Samper.

One of the first decisions of the revolutionary Government was to appoint an advisory Juridical Commission, an idea which was certainly hatched in the fancy of the lawyer-Ministers. It was clear that the revolution was going to be flattened out under a pile of documents, as a man crushes a buzzing and irritating insect.

The Juridical Commission drew up a draft Constitution which did not satisfy the most advanced of the Ministers. It was the work of a typical lawyer, the patriarchal Don Angel Ossorio y Gallardo. Ossorio and his assistants had found an almost perfect formula—that the State "should base its laws and acts on the principles of Christianity". The resurrection of the Senate and other bold measures proposed by the legal advisers revealed the skeleton of the Constitution of 1876. Was it for this that a revolution had taken place?—for it was believed that there really had been a revolution. Ossorio's plan was a dismal failure.

The drawing up of a new draft Constitution was then entrusted to the Socialist lawyer Jiménez de Asúa, who was assisted by other lawyers, some professional and not a few honorary. This new team, a mixture of legal and lay authorities, passed in rapid review all the Constitutions of the world. The result was a digest of political codes which would have astonished Rousseau. Without greater effort than the enthusiasm of the lawyers, Spain was achieving the perfect democracy.

When Sieyès presented Napoleon with the draft Constitution of 1799, the First Consul remarked: "You, my dear friend, have created a world of visions." And if that was a world of visions, what can be said of the political Code of the Spanish Sieyès?

In that Constituent Assembly, which was going to constitute nothing, there was no one to say: "It is now a time to speak, or forever hold the tongue. The important occasion now, is no less than to save a Nation, out of a bleeding, nay almost dying condition."[1]

Since 1810 Spain had also been a nation "in a bleeding condition". But the Constituent Parliament elected in June remained inactive at least until September. They discussed what kind of things they ought to discuss. They passed judgment on Alfonso XIII, as if he had not already been tried and sentenced, and the sentence carried out. Men turned eagerly to the past, because none dared look the future in the face. The Chamber delayed, waiting for the lawyers to produce the draft Constitution.

From September to December the Cortes and the Government were plunged in the sterile task of scrutinizing, amending

[1] Cromwell, speech in the House of Commons, 1644 (Carlyle, p. 160).

and polishing the draft Constitution. They made eloquent speeches. Feeling ran high. The Government majority attacked what it ought not to have attacked, at least for practical reasons. The Opposition defended what it ought to have been a crime to defend.

In the end, on December 9th, the Constitution was promulgated.

The Republic had lost precious and irrecoverable time. For nine months it had been asking the oligarchic goose what sauce it would like to be cooked in. Naturally the oligarchic goose decided not to be cooked in any sauce at all.

But let us be reasonable. Nothing could be done before the constitutional entity had been established. For who begins a revolution without knowing if Parliament will ratify his action, without keeping the Constitution in view, and without having a President of the Republic?

These men, as was said of others, would have gone beyond the bounds of legality, if that had not been illegal.

In the meanwhile civil war was already on the march.

CHAPTER IV

# THE OLIGARCHY UNDER THE REPUBLIC

WITH THE CONSTITUTION, the democratic parties gave definite expression to the temerity with which they had ignored the characteristics of Spanish society in the manifesto of 1930. There was now no escape. Like Actaeon, torn in pieces by his own hounds, the Republic, like that of 1873, was to be devoured by the principle of the sovereignty of the people.

In an extraordinarily dynamic and revolutionary medium, the Republic was the very image of slowness. After the passage of seventeen months, reckoning from the fall of the monarchy, there was still no agrarian reform, even on paper. On December 31st, 1934, after two and a half years of the Republic, the revolution had only given land to 12,260 peasants.[1] Yet $2\frac{1}{2}$ million *braceros* were awaiting their turn. I shall come back to this when I deal with the agrarian laws. For the moment, let us uncover the general causes of such a glaring failure.

First we must see how, in practice, the forces of counter-revolution, both conscious and unconscious, come into play

[1] Instituto de Reforma Agraria, *La Reforma Agraria en España*, p. 35.

when a Liberal State takes up the challenge of a semi-feudal society. The Republic was between two fires. The fate of a Liberal Republic in a nation without a middle class is to be assailed by millionaires and beggars alike, or, which is the same thing, by almost the whole of the community. The events that are about to be related will confirm this social law. Even the industrial and commercial capitalists, compelled by the violence of class warfare, were to end by making common cause with the landed aristocracy against the Republic. When the revolution of the middle class is impotent, it is inevitable that the nation should divide, outside the Republican ambit, into two warring factions —those who have something to lose and those who have nothing to lose. The constitutional and parliamentary Republic was finally estranged from the economic middle class and remained a political skeleton of doctrinaires, men standing on the verge of an abyss.

The second Spanish Republic, like the first, was to be continuously attacked by the landed oligarchy and the anarchists. We shall deal with anarchism in the following chapter. Here we have to discover how the oligarchy behaved under the new régime.

It is superfluous to repeat that, under the Republic, the Castilian-Andalusian landed oligarchy continued to be the most powerful class in the nation. As I said before, the oligarchy had thrown off a group, led by Alcalá Zamora, which, though insignificant in numbers, was to have great weight in the new régime by reason of the high place it occupied with the consent of the Republicans. Socially Alcalá Zamora hardly attracted attention, and his party never at any time reached ample proportions. But the personal power wielded by Romanones' ex-Minister and his unquestionable influence on the course of the revolution, made this chip of the oligarchy a supremely disturbing element in the functioning of democracy. The design of the landed oligarchy was obviously to prevent the revolution, since it was itself the sole target at which the revolution should have aimed. However, the mode of appraising the struggle against reform divided the reactionaries into three principal sections. Under the Republic, the oligarchy acted with all the spontaneity which danger calls forth in political movements; it had its left wing, its centre, and its right wing. Alcalà Zamora was the left wing of the oligarchy. His policy was to fight the revolution by leading it. This policy had its risks, like everything which is at once frank and crafty, and Alcalá Zamora did not succeed in commending himself to the historic

Liberals who saw in him an apostate or a self-deluded man. The bulk of the oligarchy preferred to fight the revolution by other methods.

In order to make a sharper distinction between the oligarchic forces and interpret future events more clearly, it must be pointed out that the forces of opposition to the Republic represented by the reactionary faction were grouped round the great daily papers *El Debate* and *ABC*. Both newspapers spoke for the same social class, the landed oligarchy, but each represented, inside this social class, a specific economic interest and a different political tendency.

*El Debate* was not only the recognized organ of official Catholicism; it was, in addition, the mouthpiece of the Castilian grain-producing oligarchy, united to the Church in the *Confederación Nacional Católico-Agraria* by moral and political bonds. The Church, by intervening in the economic life of the countryside, organizing the agricultural labourers, interesting herself in their problems and helping to solve them, was inextricably involved in the agricultural movement in Castile, without actually being a landed proprietor. No newspaper in Spain, not specializing in the subject, dedicated so much space to agrarian questions or gave such a wealth of information on them as did *El Debate*. Its two great themes were religion and the countryside, agriculture and the Church. In Castile the bishop was as much master of the spiritual life of the peasant as the landowner was of his social life. In these wheat-growing regions, the Church was the pivot of the political world, as she was in the Middle Ages. Castile, strangled by the poverty engendered by the dry-land smallholdings and partly also by the large estates, was kept in submission, like a dumb flock, by the great landowners and the clergy. And the province of Salamanca, the principal seat, together with the region of La Mancha, of the great Castilian landowners, was the magnetic centre of the agrarian and Catholic movement in these regions.

The Castilian wheat-growing oligarchy, inspired by *El Debate*, joint creator with the Church of the *Confederación Nacional Católico-Agraria*, and led by José Maria Gil Robles, Professor in the University of Salamanca and contributor to the great Catholic daily, had as its political Egeria the Vatican. It professed to be neither Monarchist nor Republican; as regards the form of government, it was pragmatic and opportunist. The Holy See glimpsed incalculable dangers in an open and violent challenge to the revolution. The tactics of the Catholic wheat-farmers, therefore, were to endeavour to open a breach in the Republic through which to invade the régime cautiously, purging it of its revolutionary elements and installing the dictatorship of the clergy and the landowners.

The other oligarchic nucleus, that represented by *ABC*, was the party of assault. It was the faction of the old aristocracy and the plutocracy who met on the Board of the Bank of Spain. For *El Debate*, the form of government did not constitute a real problem. The contained, not the container, was what mattered. There is only one King, says the Church, who cannot abdicate or be dethroned, because He is not crowned by men; only the reign of Christ is eternal. But for *ABC*, the form of government was essential; and that form was the monarchy, "consubstantial with Spain".

*ABC*, founded by Don Torcuato Luca de Tena, Marqués de Luca de Tena, with a fortune that originated in the olive-groves of his Andalusian properties, was the true voice of the aristocracy of the olive-groves and the great landowners of southern Spain. The nobility of the Spanish latifundia could not do without the monarchy. *Pas de roi, pas d'aristocrats*. And they defended the continuity of the institution, because without the apex of the monarchy the Pharaoh's pyramid of Spanish property was truncated and incomplete.

The oligarchic movement represented by *ABC*—of which an edition appears in Seville, and nowhere else—had as its basis as I have just indicated, the great landowners of southern Spain, among whom the aristocracy was conspicuous. But it also included the most influential and powerful bankers who had been propitiated by the monarchy with titles of nobility.

Thus we have the picture of the oligarchy under the Republic. It was not now double-faced as it had been under the Restoration régime, but double-headed—a two-headed hydra. And it appeared without a pseudo-constitutional disguise, without a Cánovas, and without a place in the Government. But the oligarchy was not defeated; it was meditating revenge and preparing to defend itself.

From the first moment, the oligarchy held the Republic up to ransom with its economic power; but the Republic, in its turn, kept the oligarchy a political prisoner.

For the aristocracy most particularly, being monarchist by nature, the Republic was a declaration of war. Moreover the Republican Government, without being sufficiently strong to destroy this class, was foolish enough to set out to humiliate it. Titles of nobility were abolished as in 1873 (everything was done on the 1873 model), and dukes, in law at least, became simple citizens—simple citizens possessing immense tracts of national territory. Not so simple, in fact.

What can be said of this oligarchy which has dominated Spain since the middle of the nineteenth century? Cruel, avaricious, vengeful, ignorant—no country in our time has endured, perhaps, a more dangerous ruling class. These social classes would have stopped at no crime, however unpatriotic in order to get back their power.

Certainly the Spanish aristocracy stood for nothing constructive. Sluggish and undistinguished, no one would have said that Spain still had a nobility. Its moral influence was nil; and it appeared inoffensive because it had disappeared as a political entity. But it still had vast possessions and was too proud for the Republic to affront it with impunity. All this we have said before. The aristocracy placed itself at the head of the counter-revolution; and from April 15th, 1931, it began to organize civil war and prepare to give battle. The nobility, psychologically, morally and intellectually worthless, was not going to give up its economic privileges without a struggle.

Yet the revolution could not have been more urbane; or, to put it better, there was not going to be, and no one wanted there to be, a *revolution*. But Spain did have a Government which proposed to govern. Any Government worthy of the name, however conservative it was, would have had to do more or less what the Republican-Socialist coalition started to do. No doubt the Constitution injured interests and wounded feelings, but it also fixed the procedure for its revision. That is to say, the legal path had been cleared of obstructions. Everything was revisable in this régime. But certain measures of the Republic, though revisable, should not have been rectified if there was going to be peace in Spain. The fate of Spain, her well-being or her ruin, lay in the hands of the Conservatives.

The Government had not remained inactive since April. The revolution had dissolved into thin air, but the Government had been governing since it came into power. The mistake it made was in ruling Spain, not as a revolutionary Government, but as the normal and regular Executive of a country run on constitutional lines, which Spain was not, even after the promulgation of the Constitution.

To govern is to reform. But reform is one thing and revolution another. Revolution means a new structure of society. In France at the end of the eighteenth century, it meant the creation of 4 million new rural proprietors, an Army, an Estate. In Spain the reformers were busy; but they neither founded nor created. For example, they did not create an Army; they reformed the Army of the monarchy, as we shall see. A grave mistake, like those implicit in other reforms; for the revolution needed its Army, its own militia. But we have already said that the pretence of making a revolution had been abandoned.

The whole menace which brooded over the agrarian-plutocratic oligarchy consisted in the fact that Spain had a Government, for better or for worse, but at least a Government, such as had not been seen in the Iberian Peninsula since the eighteenth century. Hitherto there could be no Government, because the *señores* abominated reform. They preferred anarchy. Spain was an anarchy, buttressed by caciquism. The horror of order felt by the supporters of law and order in Spain led them to oppose any real Government which, by governing as it ought, would deprive them of privileges which were harmful to the nation.

In their inmost being, these great Spanish landowners were still inspired by the ruling classes of another epoch—turbulent, anarchist men of prey—the nobles or *caballeros*. "And in this case, I call nobles or knights", said Machiavelli, "those who live idly on the rents of their numerous possessions, without troubling at all to cultivate them, without having any other occupation or profession among those necessary to life. The Kingdom of Naples, the province of Romagna and Lombardy", he added, "are full of these two classes of men, which is why there are no republics in these districts or any stable government, since such men are complete enemies of any ordered régime."

Machiavelli goes on to quote the example of Tuscany, where there were three republics—Florence, Siena and Lucca. "The peace of these republics springs from the fact that in this province there are no, or few, nobles, but such equality that it would be easy for a wise man familiar with ancient political institutions to establish a liberal régime."[1]

It should be noted in passing that Machiavelli mentions equality as a necessary condition for a liberal régime. But here I am not so much concerned with returning to this theme as in completing the portrait of the oligarchy, by recording that "such men are enemies of any ordered régime" and of all "stable government".

The Spanish *caballeros* were dismayed at the prospect that there was at last going to be a Government in Spain, that is, that there were going to be reforms; because no one can govern,

[1] Machiavelli. *Discourses on the First Decade of Titus Livius*, Book I, chap. LV.

I repeat, without reforming what demands immediate reform. They did not fear the revolution, in which they themselves did not believe; and the prospect of civil war pleased them. The aristocratic section of the oligarchy, the *caballeros par excellence*, thought the shortest way to deal with democracy was by civil war. This will become plain, if the reader has patience.

The first decrees of the first Republican Government had not yet appeared before the great landowners were already abandoning their country seats, partly out of fear of the rural proletariat (and they may have had cause for fear), and partly as a declaration of war on the régime. In many places these great landowners ordered the suspension of agricultural work and left their lands without labour.

On the other hand, many of the aristocracy went abroad. The flight of capital began. *El Debate*, which recommended the Fabian tactics of destroying the Republic without violence, deplored the insensate spectacle of those who fled from Spain and took their capital with them.

The grandees who had not fled, and even those who had crossed the frontier, had broken with their habit of ease; now they were unwearying. For even in Spain, in spite of the reputation Spaniards have, to organize and unleash civil war requires great effort and considerable patience. But what cannot be achieved by persistence?

The Republic had hardly come into being before Monarchist emblems were being displayed in the streets and the *Marcha Real* played on open balconies, no doubt so that the people who had behaved so admirably to their oppressors should realize that what they had thought dead was still alive and breathing defiance. The expatriated King was acclaimed. In short, street incidents were fomented by every means and disorder propagated. Everything was done to prevent the Republic, which had challenged no one, from living at peace.

The insolence of the Monarchists provoked the events of May 10th in Madrid. From the offices of *ABC*, fire was opened on the crowd and two people were killed. And on the following day the people rose over practically all the country. Churches and convents were burnt to the ground.

But isolated incidents were not enough to bring civil war to a head, which was what the *caballeros* urgently needed. Without further delay, they began to organize it conscientiously with generals and Army officers.

In 1932 the absentee aristocracy was desperately anxious to destroy the Republic, because the Government were persevering in dictating decrees to regulate rural leases, raise the wages of the landless peasants and order the compulsory cultivation of estates; and what was worse for the landowners, the Cortes was discussing agrarian reform.

The drawing-rooms were enlivened these days by the presence of a crowd of Army officers, retired Monarchists, who received every month the same pay as if they were still on the active list —a liberal gesture on the part of the Republic, which asked nothing in exchange, not even that these soldiers should refrain from trying to overthrow the Government.

Hints had been dropped in Parliament that agrarian reform would become law, at the latest, in September. The great landowners were due to lose some thousands of hectares and would receive the full value as compensation in State bonds at a high rate of interest.

In August the *caballeros* could wait no longer. General Sanjurjo unsheathed the sword in Seville—the obvious choice of locality!—appointed himself Captain-General, declared martial law and seized the capital without meeting any resistance. But in the rest of Spain the rebellion was a fiasco.

The Monarchist faction saw that it had acted precipitately and lamented that Spain was not yet ripe for civil war. I shall return to this when the moment comes to describe the conspiracy of the aristocrats which ended by setting in motion the most terrible disaster which Spain has known in all her civil wars.

In view of the situation which was created in Spain when— the revolution having been rejected—the enactment of reforms was entrusted to Parliament as the organ of the people's sovereignty, civil war was inevitable from an objective standpoint. Only revolution, by overcoming and disarming the oligarchy in the instant most favourable to the democratic parties, could have rescued Spain from such a tremendous danger. The most elementary prudence should have counselled the Republic not to shrink from any audacity.

Once the revolution proved abortive, the fate of the régime was, as we have seen, to be assailed ceaselessly from above and below. When the oligarchy gave ground, anarchism took up the attack. But this belongs to the next chapter.

## CHAPTER V

# THE "CLIENTS" OF THE ARISTOCRACY

IT IS NOT recorded in the annals of the dying monarchy whether any democrats asked themselves what was going to happen to the Republic when the advent of the reign of popular sovereignty was announced to the countless numbers of the landless peasants. For the huge mass of the people without property, for the world of beggars, political liberty could have no other meaning than the immediate amelioration of their situation *vis-à-vis* the exiguous minority of great landowners, the world of millionaires. It was for this profoundest of motives that social tension in the countryside was hardly distinguishable from civil war in the first months of the Republic. Given the structure of property and the liberal character of the Republican State, the peasant could not wait indefinitely for legal reforms which seemed to him to proceed with excessive slowness, nor did the Government possess the means to coerce the great landowners, for whom the reforms came only too fast.

In all its fundamentals, the old régime had remained as it was. And the functioning of the new order, as could have been foreseen, encountered the obstinate resistance of the proprietors and the excusable impatience of the needy. The executive power of the Government did not extend beyond the thresholds of the Ministries. In practice, it was practically impossible to force the landowners to cultivate their lands or to oblige them to treat leaseholders liberally, or not to import labour from other regions in order to bring recalcitrant peasants to heel, through hunger. It was not surprising, therefore, that the farmer should refuse to pay his rent or that the landless peasant should invade the abandoned estates in order to plough them up. Even if the rural proletariat exceeded official instructions and occupied lands, anticipating agrarian reform, did it not show the Government their mistake in installing a popular Republic when the people possessed no property? Or a political democracy, when economic democracy did not exist? At bottom, the peasant had a better notion than the legislator of what constituted a lawful State, and tried instinctively to create the basis that was lacking in the constitutional Republic, by the act of entering into possession of the land.

With those relationships between the classes, a harmonious existence in a free society became a philanthropic dream. Legal equilibrium was undermined by social disequilbrium. The land-owner made a mock of the law, resisting it with his immense local power; the proletariat interpreted the law in the light of their own needs.

In the civil order the peasant found that, when he wanted to make use of his liberty, he was as much a prisoner as before. The Republic granted him *rights* on paper which could only be enforced against the *power* of the landowners. The rural areas continued to be occupied by a police force which carried out the orders of the property owners. In such circumstances, the peasant could not exercise his political liberty, without exposing himself to serious reprisals.

The complete political liberty which had just been introduced was irreconcilable with the existing economic vassalage and the dissociation between the State and society was to be fatal to the Republican régime.

Civil war in the rural areas took on its own aspect—the aspect of a cruel and primitive struggle. Clashes, skirmishes and affrays with the police were the order of the day.

Among a succession of events which infuriated the people, one which stood out from the rest was the tragedy of Castil-blanco, a typical and eloquent symptom of a frightful state of affairs. Castilblanco is a poverty-stricken village on the fringe of the Sierra de Guadalupe in Estremadura, in the region of the large estates. In January 1932 the peasants of this place decided to go on strike, as the *braceros* of Badajoz had already done, and called a meeting in the village square. The police force of Castilblanco—four Civil Guards—tried to prevent the meeting taking place. The villagers insisted on holding their demonstra-tion; the Guards blocked their way; and the population ran riot, attacking the Civil Guards and killing them, and profaning the corpses with the peculiar fury of the primitive man who is at the same time oppressed.

A year later there occurred the horrifying tragedy of Casas Viejas, a wretched hamlet, forgotten by the authorities, situated in the province of Cadiz in the middle of the feudal latifundia.

In Casas Viejas the peasants rose and besieged the barracks of the Civil Guards. In the ensuing battle, one of the Guards was killed and several of the rebels. Assault and Civil Guards were brought in from Cadiz and the neighbouring villages, and the siege was raised without any difficulty. But some of the rebels, barricaded in one of the hovels, continued to resist and the police reduced them to submission by setting fire to the place.

Having stamped out the rebellion, the Guards went from

house to house, seized the men and boys they thought were implicated in the revolt, handcuffed them, took them to the smoking hut and shot them out of hand.

Events like this created very awkward problems, which ended by proving fatal to the régime.

Civil war which, as we have just seen, took on such a deplorable aspect in the countryside, had a different but no less stubborn character in the cities. The bulk of the working population of the cities consisted of that varied and complex multitude, the unskilled workers, whose standard of living was not much higher than the abject poverty of the peasant. The wages of the Spanish worker were among the lowest in the world, as we have seen, though in some industries they were relatively high. And it should not be forgotten that the Republic was proclaimed at a moment which was exceptionally unfavourable, from the economic standpoint, for those undertakings which paid better wages. The principal mining and metallurgic industries were feeling the effects of the world crisis and some were frankly on the verge of bankruptcy. That is, the industrial and mercantile economy of Spain, like that of other nations, was going through a very difficult period—a circumstance which helped to intensify the conflict between labour and capital in the regions where skilled labour was to be found and the people's standard of living was more satisfactory.

It is also important to recall that in Spain neither peasant nor worker enjoyed the mitigating effects of social insurance. In practice, the only patrimony of the worker was his bare wages . . . when he could find work. I leave the reader to imagine how an unemployed worker lived, or a widow with three, four, or five children—as is often the case in Spain—without social insurance. Their only recourse was to beg, more or less openly.

The poorer classes only knew society and the State in their coercive aspect; to the downtrodden, they never presented an amiable facet, but only violence in its most hateful form. Hence, anarchism in Spain was not confined to the anarchists, but claimed many more than those who actually called themselves anarchists. On the other hand, the ranks of organized anarchism or the mass of those who thought to discover in negative violence the only path of salvation, were less numerous than might have been objectively expected in a country where the ignorance and poverty of the people competed, over the yawning gulf that separated them, with the impassive cruelty of the ruling classes. From one of Azaña's speeches in the Cortes, we learn that there were Socialists in Casas Viejas who fled from the village when the anarchists rose. That is to say, in those hovels, in that poverty, in that ignorance, there were men with moderate political opinions. Should they not all have been anarchists? That they were not, proves how tenacious are the conservative temperament and moral resistance to desperation among the Spanish people. We must wonder, then, not that there were so many anarchists in Spain, but that there were not more. It must be recognized that, given the conditions under which the proletariat lived, the weapon of terrorism could not have been more tempting. That a considerable section of the working-class was not seduced, that it accepted instead the temperate message of opportunist Socialism, was without doubt a more significant fact than the facility with which other sections were captivated by the utopian idea of a perfect society, without a State, without authority or criminals, achieved by a-political violence.

Anarchist policy was not really a policy, but a state of systematic rebellion against society, a revolt against an intolerable life. It was a social phenomenon which pre-dated the philosophy of anarchism. Anarchists existed among the proletariat, in Spain and in other countries, in modern times and in antiquity, before the existence of a theory specially formulated for them. Anarchism was the primordial and elementary manifestation of the discontent of the exploited. A proletariat which is primitive in all its aspects reacts, in general, against society as a whole.[1] One of the greatest merits of Marxism is that it has delivered the working classes, even those most oppressed by the social organization, from the disorientation and perplexity from which they suffered before the appearance of the Communist Manifesto. With the advent of Marxist philosophy, the modern proletariat ceased to be an amorphous and generic mass, as it had been up till then. Socialism reconciled the working class—and what was still more important, the rural proletariat—to civilization, because it kindled in it a serene and confident hope in the future, a positive hope, founded on a critical analysis of society. The anarchist current (and up till then everything had been anarchism more or less violently expressed) was immediately absorbed by

[1] In my view, anarchism eloquently and conspicuously confirms the social contract theory. "The social state is only advantageous to man if all possess something and no one has too much" (Rousseau, *Contrat Social*, Bk. I, chap. ix). The anarchist reaction against society as a whole must, therefore, be interpreted as the impulse to dissolve the contract and return to the primitive state, the natural society—an aspiration, for the rest, which is manifest in modern anarchist theories; and this because, as Rousseau pointed out, civil society has nothing to offer the miserable and exploited masses.

the new ideological mainstream. Idealist subjectivism gave way to a cheerful rationalism in the interpretation of class warfare. In his belief that he glimpsed the light of a future world, Marx mocked the gloomy frown of Proudhon. The philosophy of poverty denounced the poverty of a philosophy which set out to confuse the proletariat, overwhelming it with an explosive pessimism.

Nothing was more logical, then, than the anarchist character of the First International. In Spain also, as we already know, the first workers' organizations, sections of the International, were in communion with anarchism; and in the case of Spain, we can appreciate the immediate and salutary consequences of the appearance of Marxist theories.

In a word, anarchism was the moral and political reaction typical of a primitive proletariat, whether rural or urban. The slaves of antiquity were anarchists. The *plebs* who followed Catiline and tried several times to set fire to Rome from the four points of the compass were anarchists. The youth of Carthage who made their little revolutions every day were anarchists. The legions of extremists in the religious wars of the sixteenth and seventeenth centuries were anarchists. And in the England of the Stuarts, which has so many points of contact with nineteenth-century Spain, anarchism became so much the national habit that, perhaps on that account, Cromwell was led to pronounce England an ungovernable nation.[1] Finally, during the French Revolution, anarchism swept the country with its frenzy of burning and its "infernal columns". Shortly after, as we have seen, the European proletariat, oppressed by a semi-feudal and semi-capitalist society, in a crisis of transition, also displayed a tendency to anarchism which was checked by a combination of Marx, Engels and social insurance.

At the beginning of the nineteenth century, before there existed in Spain any anarchist organization, the most wretched among the Spanish proletariat behaved like anarchists and did what the present-day body of anarchists do within or on the fringe of the *F.A.I.* and the *C.N.T.* The *Federación Anarquista Ibérica* and the *Confederación Nacional del Trabajo* are merely the names of a social phenomenon which was inevitable in the economic and moral conditions of Spain. And this proletariat which, described as federal, made the functioning of the first Republic impossible, was going to impede the course of the second. The disquieting reality of an anarchist body, whether organized or no, the enemy of every known and still to be known régime, enamoured of violence, the inflammable material of demagogy,

[1] Cromwell, speech, Jan. 25th, 1657-8 (Carlyle, III, p. 316).

was as inherent in contemporary Spain—the Spain of the oligarchy—as it was in other nations attacked by the same functional vices and organic defects as Spain. The modern organization of this part of the proletariat, as well as the dialectic methods employed in its making by the thinkers, writers and orators who have worked for it and set its bounds beyond the stars, have not changed the chaotic nature of the phenomenon, its character as a pathological social product, born of a diseased society.

In such conditions it was obvious that to try to carry out the revolution in Spain through a system based on the principle of popular sovereignty implied the renunciation of all fruitful reforms. To be precise, the revolution was handed over to the demagogues.

Under the Restoration régime (1874–1923), the Government had taken demagogy into its service. The demagogues aided the authorities chiefly in counteracting the obscure separatist agitation in Catalonia. When the monarchy fell, they continued to favour the oligarchy, and, whether or not they were paid by the rich, they were a menace and an insult to the Republic.

No sooner had the Republic come into being than, as if by magic, a crowd of demagogues set up camp in the public square, most of them novices in politics, some of them party-men, others not. The fact that these agitators had little in the way of ideas to offer was not an obstacle to their success, which was assured beforehand in the regions of the latifundia and among the inhabitants of cities like Barcelona who had been demoralized by political corruption. It was considered natural, if novel, that the most varied assortment of persons should mount the revolutionary tribune, from the street-corner hero proclaiming the social millennium, to the marqués pronouncing himself to be an anarchist. Less notorious, though not less deadly, was private demagogy. The Conservatives or their agents were proselytizing among the people in favour of anarchism.[1] They were preaching *sotto voce* what Lerroux had preached, without unduly alarming the oligarchy, in his youthful days. For that unscrupulous class always made use of anti-clericalism in order to turn away the people's wrath from the palaces and the banks. Since the nineteenth century the Church had been the providential lightning-conductor which saved the oligarchy from the fearful consequences of social misery.

Official and unofficial anarchism was an incalculable factor in Spanish politics. When the Republic first came into being,

[1] Henry Buckley, *Life and Death of the Spanish Republic*, p. 78.

Anarchists and Anarcho-Syndicalists greeted it with hostile salvoes. They were fighting, they said, for the social revolution; Republican and Socialist politicians were no more worthy of confidence than the politicians of the monarchy. So the *F.A.I.* and the *C.N.T.* threw themselves fiercely into the task of fomenting and preparing the ground for social revolution. But for the Anarchists, permanent agitation, disturbances, terrorism, public alarm, were an end in themselves. Political power did not interest them. The goal of libertarian Communism was Utopia, and the revolution of the *F.A.I.* and the *C.N.T.*, whose ideal was indiscipline, could not but be accompanied by public unrest and social chaos. And in this, as I have pointed out, the views of the aristocracy coincided, for the time being, with those of the Anarchists. The programme of action of the Spanish *optimates* was similar to that of the Anarchists in that it aimed at making the life of the Republican Government impossible and preventing the consolidation of the Republic. As the Anarchists, launched upon revolution, set sail for unknown seas, so the Monarchists for their part, were not certain what was to be their destination. They were the first to be convinced that circumstances, then and for some time to come, would not favour the return of the monarchy.

The fatal coincidence in policy of the Anarchists and the Right-wing extremists of the oligarchy was due to the fact that these social classes, though poles apart, focused their criticism on the same spot. As one man, anarchists and aristocrats stigmatized the Republican Government as a Socialist dictatorship. If General Sanjurjo's manifesto and the anarcho-syndicalist Press were to be believed, neither party rose against the Republic, but against the Government.

Consequently, during the constitutive period of the Republic, the oligarchy and this section of the proletariat arranged their insurrections against the Government in echelon. When the Monarchists or the generals were not attacking, the Anarchists attacked; and sometimes they all attacked together. The Government spent their time in repressing anti-Republican plots. The stratagems and violence of the aristocrats will be dealt with at length in a separate chapter. Here we have to do with the subversive action of the Anarchists.

The first act of aggression executed by the *C.N.T.* and the *F.A.I.* against the Republic—an indirect aggression—was the telephone strike, a revolutionary conflict in view of the service involved, and one that had extraordinarily disturbing effects on the régime.

The telephone strike of June 1931 merged into the general anarchist rising of September, after a protracted struggle in which the strikers were actively engaged in the background in sabotage, blowing up telegraph poles, destroying apparatus, cutting wires, etc. In July the strike gave rise to bloody encounters in Seville. The Army attacked with artillery the offices of the *C.N.T.*, and the police, as usual, committed deplorable excesses. Thirty people were killed and 300 wounded. In Barcelona the events of September caused sixteen deaths.

The strike agitation in all the zones and factories where anarchist influence was predominant continued at fever-heat until the beginning of the civil war. In 1935 the Government gained time by pointing out what industries or factories were working, instead of mentioning those which were paralysed by strikes.

At the beginning of 1932 there occurred the insurrection of the *F.A.I.* in Catalonia. Libertarian Communism was proclaimed in the valley of the upper Llobregat; the revolutionaries seized the official centres in Berga and the Army had some difficulty in suppressing the rising.

But the anarchist rebellion which most disturbed and shook the Republican Government was that of January 1933. This time, apparently, a really serious effort was made to install libertarian Communism in Spain, and to this end the promoters of the project organized a kind of "Voyage to Icaria" with an obbligato of assorted explosives. The whole of Catalonia was paralysed by the general strike and there was street-fighting in Barcelona with ten dead and seventeen wounded.

In Andalusia also the public peace was disturbed, though the consequences were not so serious, except for the fatal episode of Casas Viejas, a tardy spark from an already spent conflagration; but a spark which, tardy or not, almost destroyed the Republic.

No one could have any doubts that the constitutional and parliamentary Republic was not in a position to contend with the two-fold and persistent rebellion of the rich and a great section of the people.

At various times the Government defended itself against the oligarchy by suspending its publications and shutting its political centres, and even by dissolving the Monarchist parties. It did the same, in substance, with the Anarchists. Equally, on several occasions, it banished hundreds of persons to the Spanish possessions in West Africa, some of whom had been concerned in the rebellion of August 1932, others in the libertarian attempt of the following year.

But these severe measures did not touch the root of the problem. The structure of society remained unaltered; the great land-owners were more to be feared in prison than out of it, while the Law on Vagrants and Malefactors, directed against the fringes of anarchism, infuriated the rogues and vagabonds without diminishing their numbers.

When, as inevitably happened, the counter-revolution triumphed in 1933—a fact which will be examined later—the moral and political debt which the oligarchy had contracted with anarchism was not easily liquidated. They owed half their victory, perhaps, to the Anarchists. But the Anarchists were then preparing to be the heroes of the Republic (and some of them genuine heroes) in the fight against Fascism.

Nevertheless, the damage was already irreparable. In reality, the chief fault lay not with the Anarchists (and I use that name to designate the whole mass of the people to whom it might apply, whether organized or not in the *F.A.I.* and the *C.N.T.*), but with the Government. What happened was bound to happen. The peasants of Casas Viejas were bound to be Anarchists and were bound to rebel. The strange thing is that there were not more Casas Viejas.

A proletariat like the one I have described cannot be or act otherwise, unless Spanish society suffers a profound change. Moreover Anarchism appeals in all countries and in all ages to a rabble without honour which thrives at large in a violent and irresponsible social movement without guiding principles. This corrupt rabble is, above all, a pathological social feature inseparable from the régime of a degenerate oligarchy and aristoc-racy. We have already seen that in Spain the oligarchy did not fight democracy exclusively with its own weapons. It counted in the political field on a compliant *plebs* as its ally, the "clients", as it were, of the aristocracy.

In the worst epoch of the Roman Republic there was a plebeian class, the class of the "clients", who were active in politics on the orders of the aristocracy. These clients of the patricians were then a dubious mob of parasites, footpads and beggars, whose mission was to corrupt and undermine democracy. The oligarchy supplied them with funds and, in its turn, followed up their political moves (Mommsen, Bk. III, ch. xi).

The group of Spanish "clients", flattered by the oligarchy, protected politically by this class and paid by them—more often than not with State funds[1]—succeeded under the cloak of the

[1] On November 30th, 1932, Indalecio Prieto, Minister of Public Works, revealed in the Cortes that in the port of Huelva there was an annual deficit

spontaneous and legitimate radicalism of a section of the people in provoking, without arousing too many suspicions, the disturbances, riots and bloody affrays which the plutocracy could not directly provoke. By making use of the Anarchists, the aristocracy held in their hands the threads of counter-revolution in the streets. In reality the oligarchy controlled almost the whole of the anti-Republican movement; what it could not do itself against the Republic, its "clients" did for it.

CHAPTER VI

## AZAÑA

SOONER OR LATER there was bound to be at least a partial rupture between Alcalá Zamora and the democratic parties. This politician, already a sexagenarian, a man of another epoch and another style, could not change even if he had wanted to. Triumphing personally in the revolution, he may have thought that anyone who had not known the *ancien régime* had not savoured the sweets of living, as Talleyrand said, himself also triumphant in similar circumstances. Thus, after the preliminary period of generalities and effervescent rhetoric, when the moment arrived for concrete and definite solutions of burning and real problems, Alcalá Zamora revealed his inadaptability. His invariable method of confronting questions was to seek inspiration in the past. Each one of his speeches was a flight to the dawn of the century. He wanted to resuscitate the Restoration system. He could not conceive a Republic

---

of a million pesetas that the *Junta de Obras* of the port, which until three or four years ago had a credit balance of 8 millions, now showed this alarming deficit; that in the port of Huelva "sometimes through complacency, sometimes through fear and at other times through profoundly suspicious combinations", the civil list of anarchism had been included in the budget of the port *Junta de Obras*; that any anarchist of any importance was receiving remuneration from the *Junta de Obras*; that there a contract had been made with anarchism, promoter of all kinds of disorder, paid by State funds, though no work of any description had been performed by the Anarchists; that he, Prieto, had never credited the supposed alliance against the Republic of unruly Right-wing extremists and Leftist elements who respected no political or social principles, but that he had just seen that all the anarchist leaders of Huelva "were receiving State funds from the hands of representatives of the *Junta de Obras*, men who patronized religious organizations and directed institutions belonging to the extreme Right, with the object of forming a focus of disorder throughout the city".

without a Senate. A political régime without *compadres* was bound to strike him as an unsanctified thing.

Even before the Constituent Cortes opened, Alcalá Zamora was in conflict with those parties which most particularly personified the spirit of the new situation. And when Parliament was sitting, friction was a daily occurrence. He had to accept, much against the grain, the one-Chamber system; but he voted against other innovations which were unacceptable to a "historic Liberal". Until one day, having been worsted in the debate on Article 26 of the Constitution referring to the Church, he leapt from the ministerial bench and left the Republic for some hours without a Government

Amid the surprise of many, the displeasure of a few, and the expectant curiosity of almost all Spaniards, Don Manuel Azaña became Prime Minister. The conqueror displaced the conquered, as in a game of skill. The combat between the old and the new politics, between a Republic vicious with restorationism and a Republic determined not to yield to an outworn and crumbling system narrowed down to an oral duel between Alcalá Zamora and Azaña. Azaña found a formula which the others had sought in vain. The Cortes surrendered to him, and with it, the fate of the Republic. From that moment in October 1931, Azaña was the Republic and the Republic was Azaña.

A political creation is rarely without the marks of a personal stamp. Politics are like a plastic art; they have, in fact, a touch of all the arts, and the creator of a régime or the moulder of a people tends to put himself into his work as all artists do. The political artist leaves the print of his personality on the régime he has created himself or at whose birth he has assisted. And the moral lineaments of the most detached politician will always serve as a guide to a régime or a people at any given moment of its history.

Consequently, whoever wants to know what the second Spanish Republic was like in its most characteristic instant, in the moment in which it acted with greatest spontaneity, what its morale was, what its tastes, its passions, its mode of administration, what, in short, its virtues and defects, must familiarize himself with the figure of Azaña. Azaña's faults were the faults of the Republic; the merits of the Republic were also Azaña's personal merits.

The Republic found Azaña in the prime of life, in "the fruitful maturity of autumn", at the age of fifty; a time of seasonal ripeness, the hour when men are most apt for great

301

creations. Yet Azaña was not to bequeath to posterity a great book, though some of his writings are notable for their style; nor was he to leave behind him a nation which had been redeemed. Nothing of that. Azaña was to be a failure. An undoubted failure in politics; a failure, perhaps, in literature, since he could doubtless, with his talents, have produced a great work. I mean that when the monarchy fell, Azaña was at the height of his mental powers, at that critical and unique moment in the life of the complete and mature man when he can achieve his ambitions to the full measure of his capacity.

Azaña was born, as is well known, at Alcalá de Henares. He came from a middle-class and well-to-do family, half artisan half landowner—a traditional home of Liberalism. "I remember", he said once, "that I used to amuse myself as a boy by irreverently playing with a soldier's helmet with a majestic plume, and a silver buckle which was part of the panoply. . . . The wearer and owner of these military trophies was my grandfather; and with them I received, across the dark gulf of the past century when all Spain was ablaze with the fight for liberty, the impression of something epic, indescribable and, to a child's mind, ineffaceable which for me, ever since my childhood, has been inherent in the annals of Spanish Liberalism."[1]

From his student-days among the Augustinians of El Escorial dated those first searchings of conscience and spiritual doubts which Azaña has described, in prose as yet a trifle unpolished, in *El Jardín de los Frailes*. The Church could not capture his soul, nor did it seem to inspire him with any affection. El Escorial purified and refined the artistic sensibilities of the writer, while, at the same time, it planted in his soul the desire for a faith sustained by reason.

The smallness of the family fortune, which had become more slender with the lapse of time, imposed on Azaña the usual career of Spaniards of his class. What a remedy! He knocked at the doors of the State, seeking a place in the bureaucracy. Examinations passed with brilliance, a safe job; and on this economic basis, a life of literature and politics. As a high State official, Azaña had half the day and half the night free and employed them in study and polemics. He wrote books which never reached the great public, gave lectures, took a secondary place in the Reformist Party.

Lastly, we must mention his literary dignity as an assiduous and excellent member of the Ateneo and, later, his impregnable position as secretary of that restless institution.

[1] Speech in *El Sitio*, Bilbao, April 9th, 1933.

Although, it seems, Azaña would not admit it, his irruption into politics under the Republic, being as he was then unknown to the people, had the character of a revelation. "I did not need to reveal myself to anybody," he pointed out, "and no one reveals himself except as a worker." In effect, what brought him to the highest office in the Republic, this man who was to lead the régime, was the result of a great effort carried out in silence. Azaña reached his full intellectual stature in the Ateneo of Madrid, which he first started to frequent at the opening of the century with all the intellectual curiosity of his twenty years. "The Ateneo", he tells us, "stimulates and sets free the enquiring and sensitive mind, creative fancy and critical spirit." There he exercised and kept in trim his weapons as an orator and politician; and during the truce to civil war which the military dictatorship bestowed on the nation for nearly a decade, Azaña followed his own star with a clear end in view. He knew what he wanted and where he was going; and he lacked neither the ambition nor the will nor the character to succeed. Azaña left nothing to chance; he did not work by the kind of inspiration which responds to the changes of the seasons, as a flower opens to the sun. His triumph in politics was due to a variety of circumstances, like all others of the same kind; but the chief cause was the methodical and silent labour of many years. "In the last analysis", wrote Balzac, "genius is no more than an infinite patience." Whatever scale is adopted, this is true of Azaña.

For the rest, we must ask ourselves whence Azaña drew the strength to persevere in politics. His past as a *reformista* had not exactly earned for him great personal successes. The vicissitudes of Spanish politics had doomed him to be a mediocre figure in the movement. The leader of the Party held him in scant esteem, less, no doubt, than he merited and less than he thought he merited—a fact of some importance. It came to his ears that he was not considered to be of the stuff that deputies to the Cortes are made of. And may there not have been behind the eagerness with which Azaña prepared himself to govern, a burning desire, perhaps unconfessed, to get even with his detractors? There are some affronts which so sting a man to the quick that he can move mountains.

But what kept Azaña in public life was not a feeling of inferiority, though perhaps his past experience lent at times a controversial and acid tone to his speeches under the Republic. In any case, there could be discerned among Azaña's personal traits as a figure in the Republic, a certain intellectual arrogance, an aggressiveness of speech and mien which made him seem more dangerous to his enemies than he really was—an attitude which bore bitter fruits where the success of his policy was concerned.

In truth, Azaña was a militant politician through the tyranny of circumstances. His real vocation was literature. It was that public virtue which is so entirely alien to the Spanish oligarchy—I mean patriotism—which launched him, like so many other Spaniards, into politics. For a sense of patriotism, exacerbated by the country's tragic plight, brought into Spanish politics many citizens who, in another country or in another epoch of Spain's history, would have lived secluded from public life. Either because patriotism kindled a vocation and it seemed a moral obligation, in view of the notorious lack of men, not to stand aloof from the affairs of the State; or because he was inextricably caught in the tangle of social relations, it was rare that a Spaniard of any authority turned his back on militant politics. No citizen of sensitiveness and discernment could look unmoved upon the crisis of a nation which staggered from disaster to disaster. Art, science, and all the rest, were abandoned, therefore, for the political struggle; and whoever persisted in not leaving his ivory tower was, after all, no better than Archimedes, who was so wrapped in his studies that he did not notice his house was being set on fire.

In my view, Azaña was the type of citizen who, in a Spain that was normal, properly constituted and prosperous, would not have engaged in politics, much less taken a leading part in them. He might, perhaps, have written a masterpiece. As we shall see, he was not a man of action, though he may sometimes have given the impression that he was. The real Azaña was conscious of his timidity—for he was not entirely without knowledge of himself—and more than once confessed as much in public. He, too, was aware that he was not a man of action. "If I were a man of action . . ."[1]

In his inmost heart, Azaña was an artist, that is, a man of aesthetic sensibilities—no more and no less. His "politician's soul kindles like the soul of an artist in contemplating a beautiful conception."[2] The people were, for Azaña, "the raw material in which the artist works".[3]

But where Azaña reveals most openly his secret is, perhaps, in his pleasing essays on Don Juan Valera. The personality of

[1] Speech in the *Frontón Central* of Madrid, Feb. 14th, 1933, and Speech in the Cortes, Oct. 2nd, 1933.
[2] *La Velada en Benicarló*, p. 82.
[3] Lecture in *El Sitio*, Bilbao, April 21st, 1934.

the writer from Cordova filled his mind and impressed him as did no other Spaniard, the reason being that both looked at Spain from the same angle. In essentials, their characters were the same. If they had lived together, it would have been apparent in their intimate and personal reactions to Spanish society and the Spanish landscape that they had identical tastes and opinions. Azaña discovered in Valera virtues which were also his in his mature age. "Modesty, moderation, the careful preservation of personal intimacy; purity of line, clarity, order, the perpetual appeal to good sense, simplicity, grace; with a corresponding aversion from all that is noisy and disorderly."[1]

As with Valera, so with Azaña, the conflict between the man and his surroundings had an aesthetic origin. Valera felt a proud aversion from Spanish society which seemed to him primitive, coarse, presumptuous and ignorant. He perceived, above all, the aesthetic, or anti-aesthetic, aspect of Spanish things—a quality which was also prominent in Azaña. Over a long period, much the same thing happened to Azaña in politics as happened to Valera. There is no doubt at all that "his mental fineness", as Azaña wrote of the Cordovan writer, "prevented him from being fanatical; his personal dignity did not permit him to elbow his way among the throng." And did not Azaña perhaps describe his own position in the Reformist Party with these lines on Valera: "Among the parties, he could not step beyond the secondary rank allotted to those who shine outside politics, feared and at heart disliked for their intelligence, objects of suspicion to their colleagues."

In the same way Azaña the adherent of a Reformist Party which aimed at liberalizing the monarchy, reminds us of Valera attaching himself to the moderates with the object of introducing a liberal spirit among them.

In both men we find the same tendency "to show off their intellectual brilliance, a certain indulgence of the man for whom nothing any longer holds any terrors." Valera confronted the Cortes with the remark: "I belong to the doctrinaire Liberal school!", just as Azaña took pleasure in prodding his parliamentary audience by announcing: "I am not a Liberal", or on another occasion: "If they conjure up the bogy of social chaos, I just laugh." Both men delighted in this sort of *boutade* or sally; but for Valera, the *franc-tireur*, the mere deputy to the Cortes, there were no untoward consequences.

[1] See Valera, in the volume *La Invención del Quijote y otros ensayos*, Madrid, 1924. The English reader will find an interesting study of the person and work of Don Juan Valera in *The Soul of Spain* by Havelock Ellis. Constable, 1908.

Nor did the concept of revolution visibly separate them, taking into account the respective times in which they lived. Azaña said of Valera that "of the revolution, he accepted the critical principle of discursive reason, the destructive and at the same time reconstructive principle, directed against traditional forms. The advent of the *bourgeoisie* to power was, for Valera, the final, if not the perfect, form of society." Azaña, man of a more advanced hour, probably beyond the conception of the Andalusian writer, did not think on exactly the same lines, but the basic concurrence was absolute in both.

Where their ways radically diverged was in their personal destiny. Valera went into politics with an aristocratic liberalism and a confused notion of the rôle he was to play, but certain that he was going to rule the nation from his deputy's bench. Yet he accomplished nothing; he belonged to another epoch and the impulse was lacking. Here the destiny of these two personalities branched off and Azaña forged far ahead of the man from Cordova, who ended by burying himself entirely in literature and diplomacy.

Like Valera, Azaña was a classical spirit confronted by the aesthetic disorder of Spanish society. The nation which to others appeared an abortion, misshapen and monstrous, he wanted to remodel with greater purity of line. Personal ambition, love of power, the desire for justice—incentives which spur on most politicians—had a subsidiary place in Azaña's protestation of faith; instead, while he was preparing himself for the work of government, he was lost in a dream, like a man who conceives a work of art. Like Valera, Azaña was more irritated by ordinariness and vulgarity than by the other defects of Spanish society. And even if he abandoned books (not that he did abandon them, for he wrote always, with ever greater emphasis on style), he did not break with art. For him, politics came to be, in an exalted sense, a prolongation of literature. The same obsession led him to saturate his literary works with politics.

The almost poetical ideal which Azaña sought to realize in politics crops up over and over again in his speeches:

"If you take a Spanish heart in your hand, it will tell you that it is poor, that it is hungry, that it has no work; but it will also tell you things of which it is not perhaps aware itself— a sort of racial lament, handed down from century to century; for the ancient Spanish spirit is bowed beneath twenty-five centuries of civilization, and while half Europe lay in savagery and barbarism, in this land Latin civilization had already lit those stupendous lamps which still illuminate our way. I tell you, gentlemen, the Republic, in its highest values, in its national potential, is the resurrection of Spanish civilization, the breath of the Spanish race, the opening of an immense and wide highway for the creative genius of the Spanish people. Yes, I am persuaded of this; I am persuaded, because I go, not by hearsay, but by what I have observed for myself in the panorama of the Spanish landscape. This evening a friend reminded me of an ancient poet, a fellow-countryman of mine, who said, singing God knows what follies of his youth:

"'By the banks of the Henares, I sowed my wild oats. . . .' How sad that is! The old poet, remembering his youth, between the flax-field and the grove! . . . But this same poet, wild, untamed, a great lover, climbed the *sierra;* and there on the mountain heights, battered by the winds, scorched by the suns of Madrid, he howled defiance to life; and between the river and the mountain, there remained an immense space, covered by a blossoming and smiling civilization, not sung by the history of great empires, but felt by Spaniards who know the history of their country and hail in it the best fruits of civilization and of the life of their time.

"The years passed, my friends, and I also went, as the poem says, 'to sow wild oats by the banks of the Henares'; and I sowed them. I sowed those wild oats at the beginning of the century, when all was scepticism, pessimism and negation, when it was elegant to deny the name of Spaniard, when it was distinguished to say the history of our country was finished, when it was brilliant to wash one's hands of all social responsibilities. This was the food on which the youth of my time was nurtured; and I also, at that time, followed the old road of the *arcipreste* and saw the sadness of the destruction which the negligence of centuries had wrought in my country. But from the Toledan sadness, we climbed the *sierra* with the masters who taught us to love the face of Spain, and in that immense solitude, battered, like the old *arcipreste*, by mountain gales, we felt ourselves at one with him and all his story, only because, with the same landscape under our eyes, we were filled with the same lacerating emotion."[1]

The crumbling bricks and mortar, the unutterable sadness of the countryside, the melancholy of the waste lands, the desolation of the landscape, whatever gives Spain a look of disorder, of abandonment, of disequilibrium, was what Valera would have tried to remedy and is chiefly what fired the patriotism of Azaña.

[1] Speech in the *Frontón Central* of Madrid, Feb. 14th, 1933.

Azaña's rôle in politics was assured by his command of language. He had already impressed his personality on the Ateneo by his originality of speech, his astonishing logic and his elegant sophisms. And there is no doubt that his successes among the unruly literary crowd in the Byzantium of the Muses strengthened his faith in himself, his confidence in his polemical powers.

We find a writer who can draw from the instrument of language notes of a rare and delicate lyricism, as his essays show. In his polemical speeches, too, he succeeded, whether in attack or defence, in putting his arguments with such force and with such dazzling lucidity, that his adversaries were completely routed. Azaña himself held that speech, "the great instrument of political creation", was action. "I do not know which comes first, speech or action; but happily, in politics, words and deeds are the same thing."[1] This is only true in part, and at times, not even in part, as Azaña was to recognize in another place when he said "that there have been eminent politicians in history who have always maintained a profound silence".[2]

In politics, speech is not enough, and often too much. The worst that can befall a politician is to think himself a man of action because he can pacify or rouse the mob, draw crowds or carry his audience with him. Speech is not a guarantee of action but of thought, which are different and frequently conflicting things; and success in criticism or analysis does not ensure success in execution.

Reference has been made to the passion which impelled Azaña to take an active part in Spanish politics. It was patriotism; the desire to regenerate Spain, a passion and a purpose common to all Spaniards of feeling and often present in those worst armed for this kind of task. But when a fire breaks out, no one asks if he is qualified as a fireman. We saw also that what spurred Azaña to seek to change the face of his country was chiefly the longing for harmony and beauty, the preoccupation of the artist rather than the politician, the ambition of a man with the soul of a poet rather than the urgent need of the man of action. This second point needs stressing.

In 1918 we find Azaña plunged in the study of military questions. At that date, he was charged with drawing up a report for the Reformist Party on Spanish military affairs. He gave several lectures in the Ateneo on French military politics which he had recently studied in France.

[1] Speech at Valladolid, Nov. 14th, 1932.
[2] Lecture at *El Sitio*, Bilbao, April 21st, 1934.

Azaña tells us himself that he took up the study of military problems "for two reasons; firstly, for internal reasons of policy; secondly, because of the world importance which these military questions assumed at the outbreak of the European war. And I must confess that my chief anxiety was connected with home affairs."[1]

Hence, at the outset of his political career, Azaña began by singling out from all the other Spanish problems the military problem. The reformist politician devoted himself not to the agrarian question though he had been interested in farming in the unregenerate days of his youth; nor to the financial question, nor to teaching. Why did Azaña specialize in military problems which, at first sight, must have been the least attractive to an artist, to a writer who, in politics, pursued an aesthetic ideal? Precisely for that very reason.

It was natural that Azaña should choose the military question, since for a temperament like his, nothing could have been more "noisy and disorderly" in Spain than the invasion of public life by the Army. There could not have been a more genuine manifestation of disorder or cacophony for a spirit on which the morphological disequilibrium of the component elements of a work (in this case, society) exercised exceptional violence. This was what most affected Azaña. The Army outside its orbit, transgressing its lawful bounds, disturbing and altering the national life, outraged his feelings as an artist. To put it simply, the Army did not allow him to write, to fulfil himself, in a grave and noble sense; the Army was the major obstacle which prevented Spain from realizing her destiny. Could there be anything more opposed to order, to thought, to dreams, than the military rabble turning the nation into a lunatic asylum? The soldiers came to be for Azaña the *malditos* of "Don Juan" in Zorrilla, and he, like Don Juan, determined to keep them in subjection, confine them to their barracks, impose silence and discipline on them as soon as he became Minister of War, his oldest and perhaps his only aspiration in politics.

Generally speaking, the artist is not suited for political action. It is not always so; and Azaña himself was capable of action on occasions. But a hypertrophied aesthetic sensibility was to be always at odds in him with violence, and action is violence. Hence, the poetic strain is wont to be almost or completely lacking in the man of action. Let us turn our attention to the man of action in politics in relation to literature, since Azaña cultivated both rôles.

[1] Speech in the Cortes, Dec. 18th, 1932.

It is true to say that not a few men of action have distinguished themselves in literature and vice versa. But in general, this kind of person is proverbially unwilling to commit his thoughts to paper. And the higher the degree of action demanded from such a man by historical circumstances or the character of his mission, the less his inclination to express himself in writing. The fact that many politicians have been excellent, and some, like Disraeli, even prolific writers, means nothing. In a normal, well-organized and well-equipped nation, a man can be a great politician without being a man of action. And there are, of course, exceptions; the man of action with a many-sided personality, the genius with the soul of an artist. Such a man was Julius Caesar. But usually the man of action shrinks from literary expression. Most of them are orators, but not writers; and some, like Cromwell, express themselves with incredible obscurity and inaptness.

The founders of great political or religious movements have left no literature behind them. Neither Christ, nor Mahomet, nor Socrates, nor Pythagoras, nor Cromwell, nor Napoleon, stayed to write.

It is in Napoleon, the lover of politics and the hater of music, that the psychological attributes of the man of action are most faithfully, though perhaps at times exaggeratedly, portrayed.

Be that as it may, Azaña's sensitiveness obviously made him a weak politician, often fleeing from reality, crushed by the same thing which spurs on to action the man who can take the lead in violent situations. The following anecdote is significant. Azaña is speaking to the citizens of Valladolid: "A few days ago—and this is a tale of your own country—I received an impression of the Spanish character which delighted me. I was crossing a town in Castile. It was a feast day or market day—the *plaza* was full of people. When the word went round that the Prime Minister was passing, what a to-do! The crowd surged round the car, shouted, waved, so that we could hardly move. Ah! But all this, though flattering, can be irksome at times; so we had to leave the *plaza*. And there, on the corner, was a magnificent man, tall, dark, lean, who must have been, I suppose, a tanner, for he had an enormous leather apron which fell from his shoulders to his ankles. Leaning lightly against a stone seat, he saw me pass. I was on foot. He recognized me, threw me a glance of sublime disdain and did not move. Since then, I have had for this man such an admiration that I say: this is the man I would choose out of all the inhabitants of Castile. The Prime Minister passes and he is there with his

310

leather apron, perhaps with his hunger, and with his Olympian gesture, this man of Castile says: 'We two are equals'."[1]

But this "magnificent man" was certainly only a figment of Azaña's literary imagination. He was probably, as someone pointed out afterwards, a Carlist or a Monarchist, who for his insolence and discourtesy deserved anything but glorification.

So long as the conflict was confined to the parliamentary arena, Azaña triumphed over himself and the others. He had no enemies on the platform of the Ateneo, nor was he to have enemies in the Cortes. He conquered everyone by the spoken word. But in the realm of action he was discomfited by a septuagenarian Lerroux, and what was more serious, with Azaña the Republic fell. It little matters what methods the Radical politician used in order to supersede Azaña in the leadership of the Republic; a politician has to reckon with such methods, let alone the leader of a revolution.

I said before that Azaña was the Republic, the Republic of April 14th, the Republic which, in his own words, "began or came into the world with a low elevation", by which he meant "the trajectory which the Republican policy of reform and social transformation had to follow". And this Republic with the "low elevation" was the only one which Azaña, the hero of parliamentarianism, could embody. Now, at that moment Azaña eloquently expressed the feelings and desire of nine-tenths of the Spanish democrats, whose knowledge of history and political point of view were, for the most part, the same as his. And when, after the counter-revolution had triumphed, democratic opinion changed as to what ought to be done once the Republic had been reconquered, Azaña changed too. But the man of letters, assaulted by violent reality, refused combat, and allowed himself to be immured in the prison of the Presidency of the Republic. With the dreadful *crescendo* of civil war, the little that remained in Azaña of the man of action was extinguished. His political morale was shaken. Conflict, which he understood ill or not at all, separated him spiritually and decisively from public life.

But Azaña believed in the end that he had learnt something; and what Azaña thought he had learnt was precious.

It should be remarked that Azaña, like the Republic with which his name will always be linked in history, constituted a complete experiment, a whole political life, a life that began on April 14th when the Spanish people realized for the first time

[1] Speech at Valladolid, Nov. 14th, 1932.

that he existed, and ended with the Republic. A colossal experiment for anyone who desires and is able to understand it, and one that therefore deserves to be studied.

If by temperament, as we have seen, Azaña was no revolutionary, his philosophy made him even less so. He was a Hegelian, an idealist, who recognized in the State "the highest conception of the human mind in the political order, our guide and our mentor and the moral entity to which we must offer up our work, nor must we have or desire to have other entities to which to sacrifice and surrender ourselves."[1] This idealism led Azaña to conceive a Republic founded, not on this or that class, but on a moral idea, an idea that would be common to all citizens who accepted the régime and who ought to see in it the instrument which should restore the ethical values of the Spanish spirit. Azaña located the Republic in that zone "where reason and experience incubate wisdom".[2] "The Republic is much more than a Constitution; it is much more than a juridical structure. The Republic is a moral value, an idea. . . ."[3]

And since the Republic was the instrument of the realization of the "universal spirit" in the State, "with its aim fixed on heights overtopping the highest peaks of all the parties and all the divisions of Spanish society",[4] the important thing, thought Azaña, was to endow it with moral strength, to construct for it a moral axle of steel so that it should be indestructible. The Republic could only take root and become everlasting through its ethical values. Hence, Azaña was not so much afraid that the régime would perish at the hands of the Monarchists as that it would become corrupt. "If the Republic founders, but founders with its prestige, its reputation and its integrity unimpaired, it will be reborn with more violence, more force and more authority; but if the Republic becomes corrupt, what hope can the Spanish people have of its redemption?"[5]

A Republican politician, if he was to be loyal to this way of thinking and feeling, had to use the most scrupulous honesty in inter-party relations, in the working of the functions of the State, in administration.

The moral sense of the Republic asserted itself in civil liberty, in the sovereignty of the people, in a Parliament founded on universal suffrage. Liberty, elections. "In general elections,

[1] Speech at Valladolid, Nov. 14th, 1932.
[2] La Velada en Benicarló, p. 127.
[3] Speech at Bilbao, April 9th, 1933.
[4] Speech at Madrid, Feb. 11th, 1934.
[5] Speech in the Cortes, Oct. 2nd, 1933.

even those who do not recognize the Constitution have a right to be respected. Even the Communist who wants to blow up society; even the Monarchist who wants to blow up the Republic; even these—from the moment they enter the polling-booths, despite the fact that they do not recognize the Constitution, that they want to destroy it—have the right to be respected, protected, defended. . . ."[1]

Like Pi y Margall and the other apostles of the Republic of '73, Azaña repudiated victory won by coercion. "I prefer defeat after a fair fight to a triumph which might be disputed on the grounds that it was won by trickery."[2]

That is to say, Azaña denounced violence—any kind of violence—in the revolution. He refused to use the weapon of governmental coercion, the only weapon democracy possessed in Spain, against the economic coercion, thus declared inviolable, of the enemies of the people. He started from the false assumption, based on his integralist theory of the State, that property and wealth were not a decisive political category in a nation which was divided by social inequalities, as no other in Europe, into two diametrically opposed worlds. "I absolutely refuse", he said "to delimit political frontiers, the frontiers of political opinions, of party conflicts; I absolutely refuse to place these political frontiers in the same order as economic frontiers. I absolutely refuse, even though it may be an historical error."[3]

It was this historical error which gave birth to Azaña's Utopia, whose basis was the desire to build a State at variance with society.

Yet Azaña was not blind to the fact that "every régime needs a social class to support it".[4] And this social class could not be other than an economic class, a multitude of new proprietors, individual or collective. But Azaña's suspicion that every régime requires a social class to support it and that, therefore, the system of property constitutes the basis of political institutions, warred with his irrational and emotional idealism. It warred and was defeated. It was not that he was not aware of the facts; he knew very well that "a revolution, in order to be successful, must change the economic basis of power".[5] Yet his philosophic idealism made him incapable of placing what was urgent—that is, the social revolution, the transformation of the structure of property—before what was less urgent, all those political and

[1] Speech in the Cortes, Oct. 2nd, 1933.
[2] Speech at Madrid, Feb. 14th, 1933.
[3] Ibid., Feb. 11th, 1934.
[4] Speech at Santander, Sept. 3rd, 1932.
[5] *Tres generaciones del Atenéo. Ensayo.*

moral problems which in the last analysis have their roots in economic conditions. "If you will pardon my frankness, in me politics have the predominance over economics, and moral points of view over statistical data."[1] Here, as usual, Azaña reveals himself as more the slave of his temperament than of his intelligence.

The preponderance of moral and purely political values in Azaña's psychology hid from his discernment the true dimensions of the national deformity. For him the Spanish deformity was moral in character. And it must be admitted, in all justice, that the majority of Spaniards of his time concurred in this aberration—an aberration fostered in no small measure by the official Republican version of the history of Spain. It must not be forgotten that Spanish democracy in 1931 was still living in the political atmosphere of the nineteenth century. It was an orthodox Liberal democracy which included the workers' parties and which accepted as an article of faith, without criticism, the history of Spain as it was written by the Liberals of the eighteenth and nineteenth centuries. Azaña was conscious of this and wrote of it with a touch of reproach: "Spain is a sick nation, whose malady is to know its own history but ill, and not sifted by criticism; and Republicanism, as a member of the Spanish body, is not exempt from this sickness." Here I must confess that I have not found in Azaña's work any original observation, anything which could openly clash with the philosophy of history as expressed by the Liberals of the past century. Azaña reacted to Spanish problems—regionalism, the Church, militarism, property—with greater elegance per-haps, but from the same point of view as the heterodox movement from which he proceeded. If he had been guided by a philosophy of the history of his country different from that elaborated by the nineteenth century Liberals, he would have grappled with the problems he had to solve in another spirit and by other methods. Neither in his definition of those problems nor in his manner of dealing with them, did Azaña display any tendency to dissent from the Liberal tradition.

For a politician so fundamentally sceptical as Azaña, a contempt of economics and statistics was at once salutary and harmful. Salutary for him, at first, because it concealed from him the true profundity of the nation's disequilibrium. Thanks to this, he could dream that agrarian reform was a revolution and that the Republic, already in May 1933, had accomplished

[1] Speech at Madrid, Oct. 16th, 1933.

"profound, capital, transcendental reforms". Thanks to this he was ignorant of the capital part Spanish banking was playing in the maintenance and accentuation of the Spanish deformity. This problem—the second problem of our time in Spain—did not exist for Azaña. His conception of history and politics, by concealing from him the totality of the Spanish tragedy, fed his optimism, his faith in his work, and prevented him being overwhelmed by the reality. But all this was at the expense of realism. This was the harmful side of a policy which aspired to set the nation right without admitting the primacy of economics and statistics. If Azaña, instead of believing that "Spain's greatest ill was the lack of moral vigour, the moral weakness of the public spirit" (said at a time when the nation was standing on its feet and supporting him as never any other politician was supported), had attributed the Spanish infirmity to the disequilibrium of the classes, to the iniquitous distribution of wealth—without equal in Europe, let us not forget—he would have been dismayed at what the revolution demanded of him. He would then have perceived that words and deeds are not, unfortunately, the same thing in politics.

The sweeping nature of the change which Spain required, not indeed so that she could elbow her way to the front among the more advanced nations, but simply to prevent herself from being smashed to pieces, obviously could not be brought about by parliamentary methods. How to disarm the agrarian-financial oligarchy (for this had to be attempted before the opportunity was lost), while leaving it a free hand in economics and politics—this was the blind alley into which the Republic had strayed. But Azaña discovered no other alternative than liberal government and the Cortes as the instrument of change. "Dictatorship? Not on any account. Universal suffrage, free speech, governmental responsibility, legislative chamber, constitutional powers—beyond this, nothing."[1] Dictatorship terrified him. "No; the question was once asked (referring to Lenin), 'Liberty, what for?' . . . and every time I remembered or heard that phrase and the Liberal thesis has been impugned, I also asked myself, 'Dictatorship, what for? To what end? For whose benefit?'"[2]

Let Azaña supply the answer himself. "This plan", he said of the law on rural leases, which affected 50 per cent of rural property in Spain, "has been before Parliament since the month of April, and when a plan of such magnitude, submitted

[1] Speech in the Cortes, Sept. 6th, 1933.
[2] Ibid.

315

to Parliament in the month of April, is still at Article 16 by the end of August, I do not think, Señor Royo Villanova, that it can truthfully be said that we are acting with precipitancy—quite the contrary."[1] Quite the contrary, in fact.

And a week later: "The Commission, in the exercise of its free judgment, has not been able, or has not desired, to draw up a text which will satisfy the agrarian group; and in view of this, the agrarian group has submitted a hundred amendments to Article 16 which we were considering a week ago; and not only has it submitted a hundred amendments to Article 16, but I do not know how many hundred amendments to Article 17. [A deputy: Two hundred thousand.]"[2]

In January 1934 Azaña pronounced the most energetic condemnation of his own policy: "Under cover of the liberal Constitution of the Republic and its very liberal laws, the enemies of the Republic begin to employ against it the very juridical and legal weapons with which the régime has armed itself, and all those elements which were removed by the popular movement of 1931, men who did not even appear in the elections of that year to exercise their electoral rights, now think themselves masters of the situation and, strengthened by the complacency of the authorities and by the buying of votes, set themselves to reconquer the power they lost in '31."[3]

There is no need to say that in those days, at the beginning of 1934, the counter-revolution was already in power, lopping off the work of the Republic, persecuting Republicans, driving the proletariat to desperation. In Azaña's mind a crisis had been developing. A man "tortured by his critical spirit", there always lodged in the depths of his mind a vague scepticism which prevented him from employing the iron hand in Spanish affairs. Doubt, vacillation or misgiving, which his intellectual honesty led him to confess in public: "And when I began work in collaboration with those dear friends and with hundreds of other colleagues, we thought that a Spain and a régime were being formed in tune with the dictates of our own reason. Our own reason! . . . Which does not exclude the fact that this same reason cast doubts at times on the very postulates which formed the basis of our endeavour. But in politics we must leave behind us all those inner promptings of criticism and appear before the multitude, like the tragedian of old, in a mask of bronze."[4]

[1] Speech in the Cortes, Aug, 25th, 1933.
[2] Ibid., Aug. 30th, 1933.
[3] Speech at Barcelona, Jan. 7th, 1934.
[4] Impromptu in *El Sitio*, Bilbao, April 9th, 1933.

In failure, the vein of scepticism in Azaña swelled and threatened to burst. The *fin de siécle* pessimism which he thought he had cast off broke out again in him like a rash, and he relapsed, as it were, into the old despair. Seeking the cause of his failure, he could not find it in himself, but in the mass of the nation. He thought the Spaniard was ungovernable and, though he did not say so in public, he did not hide his opinion from his friends.

Turning his eyes to the past, he recalled the fugitive nature of all attempts at regeneration: ". . . and in the dark days, days almost of despair, I asked myself whether, in view of the future that lay ahead, in view of what I saw around me, in view of the latent danger beginning to stir under my hands, we should not be staging once more the impossible drama of the regeneration of Spanish political life."[1]

Yet Azaña was incapable of perceiving that the root of his personal failure and the failure of the Republic lay in the régime itself, in the mere fact of attempting to carry out a revolution in a system of liberty. He called this "Spanish originality"; and original it certainly was—a foolish and ruinous originality. As foolish and ruinous as would be a dictatorship today in England or France, which would lead to civil war in those countries as automatically as liberty leads to civil war in Spain.

"The question is", Azaña asks himself again, "whether, after having tried everything here, from violence to highway robbery enthroned in the Government, the moment has not arrived to allow Spanish originality full rein, to allow Spaniards to grow, to prosper, to work, to quarrel among themselves, under a régime which revolves between two distinct and well-defined poles—power and liberty?"[2]

Every nation, when it remakes its institutions, needs a government with plenary powers directed by a single man. And though Azaña was persuaded that everything had been tried in Spain, this kind of Government was certainly as yet unknown to Spaniards. Spain had only known reactionary dictatorships, theocratic or oligarchic absolute régimes, or anti-democratic Republican dictatorships like Castelar's. Spain has never had a Long Parliament—twenty years of revolutionary dictatorship—like England; nor an absolute régime like the one which lasted fifteen years under Bonaparte and consolidated the Revolution. The Directory in France and the Presbyterians in England

[1] Speech at Madrid, Oct. 16th, 1933.
[2] Ibid.

would have cleared the path for the Restoration fifteen and twenty years respectively before this actually happened, had not the progressive dictatorships of Napoleon and Cromwell radically prevented it. Reaction finally returned to power in England and France; but by the time it returned, the revolution had been carried out root and branch and it was indestructible. The twenty or fifteen years of absolute revolutionary command had created a new tradition. The middle class was omnipotent. Charles II's government in England and Louis XVIII's in France were a futile and doleful attempt to resuscitate a dead past. They were governments at loggerheads with society and they fell, in England, with the "Glorious Revolution", and in France, with the Revolution of July. But in Spain, because neither in the nineteenth nor in the twentieth centuries had there been a democratic régime with plenary powers, the State which was at loggerheads with society was not the State of the counter-revolution, as in England and France, but the parliamentary State of the revolution, whose average life was two years. And when the counter-revolution establishes itself in Spain, it remains in power for an eternity—ten years under Ferdinand VII, Narváez, O'Donnell, Primo de Rivera and probably Franco; and the Restoration of Cánovas lasted fifty years!

Such a situation showed only too clearly how catastrophic was the Republican policy, as defined and practised by Azaña, in preferring "defeat [in the elections] after a fair fight to a triumph which might be disputed on the grounds that it was won by trickery". As if the triumph of the Right in Spain meant merely a change of government! Apart from which, Azaña's statement was already a concession to the enemy in that it implied that the Spanish oligarchy could win elections in a "fair fight".

Spain, therefore, has never known that democratic government with more or less absolute powers which a great nation in process of transformation cannot do without. Even England, where more than in any other country liberty is a constant, could not do without such a government; England, whose love of liberty, as the great Hume says, has always prevailed over all precedents and even over all political reasoning. It is precisely because Spaniards persist in disregarding this natural law of history and politics that all their present sufferings have come upon them. For it is practically impossible for democratic reforms to take root and grow in the two years which are the customary life of a democratic parliamentary government in

Spain. Society has no time to assimilate them; and as the counter-revolution is in power for an infinitely longer period, the rivers of blood, the heroic sacrifices of the people, the abundance of energy and wealth consumed in the struggle for liberty and progress, are bound to be, if not entirely without fruit, at any rate quite out of proportion to what the revolution accomplishes.

Not the least depressing aspect of the case was the fact that under the second Republic an attempt could have been made to install such a régime, but the opportunity was allowed to slip past. At one moment, extraordinary power was concentrated in the person of Azaña. But who can explain it better than he? "I held in my hands, gentlemen, power such as has been given to few in this country in modern times; for I had a Government permeated through and through with my thought and my work, a Government that had been submitted to all tests and that never failed. I had almost plenary powers; in fact, until the Constitution had been adopted, I might omit the 'almost'."[1] That Azaña should be blind to the priceless advantages of that exceptional moment and to what his extraordinary authority committed him, did not denote prudence. But it was certainly not his fault that his nature lacked inner harmony. His delicate moral scruples may have honoured the citizen, but they did not excuse the weakness of the politician. In the hands of the intellectual, power broke like a reed, a phenomenon which Azaña himself analysed in these words: "Everything is limited, temporal, cut to man's measure; and nothing so much as power. This conviction acts like an invisible brake in the depths of my consciousness. I do not perceive its presence, yet it moderates all my actions—the lasting effect of the intellectual and moral mould in which I was first cast".[2]

Moreover the same thing was happening to Azaña as happened to most of the Spanish Republicans; he systematically identified Liberalism and democracy with the representative régime, the parliamentary régime. One reason the more why he should repudiate the personal use of power. He doubtless held that a government with plenary powers, whether conceded or arrogated, was incompatible with the exercise of a Liberal policy. Yet did not religious toleration, the chief tenet of Liberalism, triumph in England with Cromwell? "Under Cromwell", wrote a French Liberal historian, "everyone freely professed his own belief; papists alone were not tolerated, although

[1] Speech in the Cortes, Oct. 3rd, 1933.
[2] *La Velada en Benicarló*, p. 77.

even they in Ireland enjoyed more liberty than before".[1] And was not this same absolute régime, which is imposed on every revolution by historical and biological necessity, the régime of the "demos" or people, personified in one of its men—was not this a democracy?

When Azaña exclaimed in the Cortes, repeating in another form an observation made by Ruiz Zorrilla (for we are still in the nineteenth century): "We are fortunately far removed from any Caesar",[2] he did not perceive that he was celebrating his personal calamity and that of the Republic. Or did Azaña fear absolute power in a democracy because it could corrupt? But a parliamentary Republic was not free from this contingency, as witness the case of France, and of Spain under Lerroux. On the other hand, "the administration of Cromwell was honest, economical, judicious, and permitted no sinecures".[3] It depends, in short, on who exercises power, which indeed corrupts a Heliogabalus, but not an Antoninus Pius, or a Marcus Aurelius, or a Trajan. And I am not going to continue stressing the need for what is not, perhaps unfortunately, something which can be accepted or rejected at will, but a historical necessity, since Azaña himself, as we shall finally see, ended by calling for a Spanish Trajan, if one had existed.

But though he was not slow in perceiving it, he was over-reluctant to confess it. For Azaña, like the good faint-heart and the good Liberal that he was, was terrified of action, whether he or another was called upon to initiate it. Thus, when he turned on those—his friends and the people—who were urging him to establish a dictatorship, he did it with the viciousness of one who has a presentiment that he is about to be put to the test on a subject he does not like. To those Spaniards who disowned the sterile and suicidal methods of parliamentary procedure (sterile and suicidal for Spain, that is), he retorted that they had the souls of slaves, that there was in them an irrepressible servility, a longing to be ordered about and treated like dogs. He did not want to understand.

"There is", said Azaña, "an intimacy, an ultimate fibre,

---

[1] Armand Carrel, *History of the Counter-revolution in England*, Bohn's Classics, p. 43. This notable French historian and journalist was a member of the Foreign Liberalist Legion which went to the Franco-Spanish frontier to help the Spanish Liberals against the forces of the Duc d'Angoulême in March, 1823. Carrel was a fervid constitutionalist and the most brilliant personification of the political Press of France in his time.

[2] Speech in the Cortes, July 6th, 1933.

[3] Carrel, vid., p. 43.

where the very heart-beat of our moral life resides, a sanctuary which no one may profane, and which I cannot sacrifice either to the Republic or the revolution".[1] A confession which finally reveals Azaña to us. Circumstances—in which he played his part—made of him the political hero of a nation in its death-throes. Yet Spain could only be saved by a really great man, who would surrender his whole being with sublime passion; a hero who would give himself entirely to the people, to the country, to the highest and noblest cause that can take possession of a man.

Nevertheless, in some ways Azaña was not the same man in 1935 as he was in 1932. He had seen the enemies of the Republic in power, thanks to liberty. Temperamentally, of course, he had not changed; at his age, men do not change. But perhaps his intelligence accused him. Now he declared: "the Republic takes precedence of the Constitution and the revolution takes precedence of the Republic."[2] Was he then thinking of exercising or recommending a dictatorship if he returned to power? Let us hear what he has to say: "Within the Republican régime, sheltering behind the Republican Constitution, invoking the liberty which they (the reactionaries) want to break in pieces, are we going to let them succeed? No Republican responsible for the defence of the régime could endure such a situation as that which they have created for us".[3] ". . . I have submitted many times to satisfying the public conscience, knowing that in my heart I would be justified in doing otherwise".[4] "But now, my friends, things are not the same, for now this personal justification which some of us have been able to reserve in the depths of our conscience is already a universal justification, and you all share in it, and what once I could not do because I was prevented by a too rigid conception of duty, now I can do with the support of public opinion".[5]

Azaña's attitude was dictated at that moment not only by the promptings of his intelligence, but also by the general disillusionment which the parliamentary régime had inspired in the people. He was trying to justify and excuse himself to his own colleagues: "My duty, as the leader responsible for directing policy, was to serve the Constitution loyally in all its aspects, the dangerous and exaggerated, as well as

[1] Speech at Madrid, April 3rd, 1934.
[2] Ibid.
[3] Ibid.
[4] Ibid., Feb. 16th, 1934.
[5] Ibid., April 16th, 1934.

what was workable. . . . They gave me a parliamentary régime; well, they shall have their Parliament and nothing else ".[1]

But the inner struggle in the soul of the man who feared action did not abate. Almost every word that Azaña uttered these days was an excuse for or an explanation of his liberal, generous and utopian policy. Hedged in by the infallible instinct of the people, Azaña began to refine the argument. He did not think that "anyone could pretend that any political régime could be a normal, perennial and lasting thing, if the responsibility of the man at the helm, his political orientation, his rendering of accounts, were suppressed and if, in addition, the voting of taxes was suppressed ".[2] The most he would compromise on was the reform of Parliament which "could have been a difficulty, an embarrassment to the Republic, an obstacle in its path ".[3]

On the other hand, Azaña was still, in 1935, the hope of the Republican masses. That is to say, he had returned to that rôle with extraordinary energy and thoroughness. The October revolution of the previous year, which I shall discuss later, though not barren of results, had nevertheless showed the proletariat that they could not conquer by themselves, that their victory was inseparable from the victory of Spanish democracy as a whole. Azaña, on the other hand, had suffered great apprehension, had passed through great dangers, had feared that he would be made an example. The gusts of violence, cruelty and corruption which had lashed the country from end to end like a devastating sirocco, had alarmed the gentle and peaceable man. Spanish policy was already irrevocably centred in civil war. And no one else had come forward to take the place of Azaña, who was still, as I have said, the voice of democracy and the Word of the Republic; although it was now becoming more difficult every moment to be only the Word, the Word and nothing more—and not the mailed fist of the Republic.

The encouragement and enthusiasm of the people restored to Azaña all his polemical faculties, all his eloquence; and his politician's soul kindled once more in the presence of the vast multitude. He spoke at Baracaldo and Mestalla before huge crowds. His Republican following in the country urged and compelled him to a great endeavour. In the suburbs of Madrid, Azaña spoke on October 20th to half a million people, gathered together from the four corners of Spain; 500,000 people,

[1] Speech at Madrid, April 3rd, 1934.    [2] Ibid.    [3] Ibid.

congregated *"entre Goya y la Bombilla"* on the river Manzanares, whose narrow stream flowed at Azaña's feet like another Rubicon. And did anyone suppose that all this mass of humanity, surfeited with words, had come to hear a speech? They came to look for a man; to invent one, if they could not find one. And what had Azaña to offer them? One more promise of energy: "The triumph of the Republic cannot be an agreed or negotiated triumph; it must be a total triumph, with banners unfurled, with the victory trumpets sounding, with all our enemies facing us, not around us and behind us. Only by triumphing thus can the Republic raise up Spain."

On February 16th, 1936, the Republic triumphed, thanks to the bloody sacrifices of the people in October 1934. But Azaña did nothing. He became President of the Republic and Spanish democracy remained in the street, bereft of its head, without a national leader, drifting helplessly. Before, at least, there had been a voice which united it and a person in whom it had hoped. The voice of Azaña was silent. Mute, fantastic, unreal, Azaña, behind the stones of the Alcázar of the Bourbons, was the last guarantee that the Republic would be conservative, parliamentary and liberal to the end.

In 1937 the President of the Republic was besieged at Barcelona by a cordon of demented anarchists. If we are to believe him, Azaña continued imperturbably to write or revise *La Velada en Benicarló*, the political testament of a man who was born for literature and polite intercourse; perhaps also for politics in a balanced nation; a man who entered the Republic with a dramatic play about a civil war in which the leader of the revolution lays the crown at the feet of the conquered princess.[1] That other civil war, in which Spaniards were inflamed with fury, made the romantic element in high places in the Government look unreal. Nor was there even a princess in the monarchist camp to offer anything to.

Azaña awoke to a reality which he found unendurable, the reality which palpitates in *La Velada en Benicarló*, a dialogue through which there runs, among the exculpatory griefs, a dolorous lament. In this cruellest of struggles, whose fury spread to the Presidential steps, Azaña was a finished man. Perhaps he repeated to himself Danton's *de profundis*: "How much better to be a poor fisherman than to intermeddle in the government of men!"

[1] An allusion to *La Corona*, a play written by Azaña and produced at the *Teatro Español* of Madrid in the early days of the Republic.

But apart from recording his inner torture, Azaña had still something explicit to say in *La Velada en Benicarló*; among other things—looking at the civil war from the Republican point of view—that "impotence to organize State warfare, State discipline, springs from a monstrous conception of popular sovereignty".

"I have no place in public life", he concludes. "It is not disillusionment; I had nothing to be disillusioned about. I realize that I was born out of my time. Men like me come either too soon or too late." And again: "Among the innumerable cases of politicians who have had great ambitions, I find only two kinds that are worthy of respect and these are headed by Pericles and Trajan. . . . The need is for a great man. . . . Useless to look for him in the environs of Hispalis. If such a man there was, I would offer myself as his secretary to draw up his proclamations in that halting Latin which we Spaniards write."

Too late did Azaña turn his eyes to Caesarism, to Trajan, and too late did the vanquished politician react against the Word.

It was not Azaña's fault that he was not born to be a great man, great in proportion to the Spain he was called upon by destiny to lead. He deceived no one, except in so far as he deceived himself. All he did was open and above-board. He knew himself weak and timorous before the great question of power, like another Salmerón.

The tragedy was not, therefore, new, though the occasion may have been—and, in fact, certainly was. Neither in the nineteenth century, nor in the days of Espartero, nor in Costa's epoch much later, was a man offered a more perfect opportunity to change the trajectory of the modern history of Spain. As we know, the Spanish tragedy at the end of the nineteenth and the beginning of the twentieth century lay in the general prostration, the weakness of the nation's pulse, the public apathy. Spain was growing sceptical. Her infirmity was characterized, among other symptoms, by a horror of ideas, or ideophobia, as Unamuno called it. The people as a political entity did not exist; and the most thorny task of the politician was to get the masses to move, if he ever took any notice of them.

In contrast, the characteristic feature of the Spain of the second Republic was a passion for politics, a desire to improve, a tenacious determination to get somewhere. It was no longer necessary for the reformer to go in search of the people, for the people now went in search of the reformer. They did not find him in Azaña, as we have seen.

## CHAPTER VII

## THE REFORM OF THE ARMY

EXPERIENCE SHOWS THAT [it can be established as a general rule that every nation ruled by the Army is a nation which is militarily weak and, as likely as not, defenceless. As an example of this apophthegm, it could be seen that, when the military dictatorship and the monarchy fell, Spain lacked an Army. Nevertheless, or because of this, the number of officers far exceeded the needs of the nation. There were more than 800 generals on the active or reserved list, and 21,000 officers: almost as many as the German Army had in 1914. There was one officer to every six men.

Azaña found infantry regiments consisting of eighty men and cavalry regiments without horses.

As regards the artillery, the situation could not have been more deplorable. The Spanish Army's field batteries consisted of 75-mm. French guns acquired in 1909 and improved later. In the Moroccan war, the Moors used guns, taken from the French, which had a range of 14 kilometres; the Spanish artillery was hopelessly outranged. Heavy artillery hardly existed, and even so there was not enough ammunition. The rifles in use were of such poor quality that they could not be fired continuously for twenty-four hours.

For all practical purposes the Spanish Army had no air support. The Government possessed a few hundred reconnaissance aircraft, and that was as far as Spanish air power went. There were practically no fighter aircraft and only one bomber.

To sum up, there were no cannon, no rifles and no munitions.[1]

Moreover Spain had eight or ten Captains-General, who tacitly inherited in their various regions the mission of the old viceroys; the Captain-General came to represent the Crown by use and custom, and being above the law, took precedence over the civil and legal authorities, interfered in politics and intervened in social conflicts. As far as justice was concerned, a *Consejo Supremo de Guerra y Marina* usurped the functions of

[1] Azaña, speech in the Cortes, Dec. 2nd, 1931.

325

the civil jurisdiction in a multitude of cases which were undoubtedly within the competence of the civil authorities.

Finally, the Army officer enjoyed extraordinary privileges; he travelled at reduced rates, he paid approximately half the taxes which other citizens paid.

As I said in the previous chapter, Azaña was justly reputed to be well informed on military matters and the Revolutionary Committee instructed him to draw up a report on the reforms to be introduced into the Army. As a result of Azaña's activities, some thirty decrees were issued by him as Minister of War on the fall of the monarchy, which the Republican Cortes converted in due course into laws. Let us see what these military reforms consisted of.

The Captains-General were abolished. The *Consejo Supremo de Guerra y Marina* also disappeared and everything pertaining to justice was separated from the Ministry of War, a special court being created in the *Tribunal Supremo de Justicia* to deal with military offences.

The Army consisted of sixteen divisions, which Azaña reduced to eight. The rank of Lieutenant-General was abolished, seventeen Lt.-Generals disappearing from the army register, leaving four on the list until the category became extinct. There had been more than a hundred Brigadier-Generals; there remained few more than forty.

In Morocco, the military forces were divided into four commands, each under a general, with its military headquarters and other services. Azaña reduced them to two, for the moment, with the intention of cutting them down still further in the future.

As regards the kind of army in the Spanish African possessions, Azaña's idea was to establish a special force of volunteers to replace the conscript troops from the Peninsula.

The most spectacular plans for retrenchment referred, of course, to the officers' cadres in general. On April 25th, 1931, a decree was issued giving officers the option of voluntary retirement on full pay. Such was the timidity of the Republicans and the Monarchists' constitutional dislike of any kind of change, that both thought this proposal revolutionary. Eleven thousand officers accepted in due course the tempting benefits of the decree of April 25th, and 10,000 elected to stay in the Army.

Azaña achieved what France did after the Napoleonic wars and what is usually done in every country after a war—he put superfluous officers on the retired list. This was but common sense, but nobody had dared to take this step in Spain after the colonial or African wars, because it diminished the Army and the Army only wanted to grow. Hence, the initiative appeared to the Republicans advantageous, but risky. And to a certain extent, it certainly was. But the reform of the Army was so bound up with the fate of the revolution that, as usual, the one depended on the character the other was to assume. The mistake the Republic made was in keeping strictly to the technical side of the affair, side-stepping the political aspect which in a revolutionary situation was of paramount importance. Nothing perhaps will cause greater astonishment to future generations, far removed from the singular atmosphere in which the second Spanish Republic was born, than the blindness of its leaders on the subject of the Army.

When there is social violence, as there is in every revolutionary situation—that is to say, every situation in which civil society is passing through a crisis, as had been the case with Spanish society since 1810—the Army holds in its hands the fate of the country; brute force decides. Hence, the first care of any revolutionary or new régime should be to create its own army. Until the new society has arisen and the new civil state or moral force, acquiring solidity, can later by its mere authority confine the armed forces to their strict mission of defending the national territory, the Army is the key to the revolution. A revolutionary régime which leaves the armed forces in the hands of its enemies exposes itself, therefore, to grave reverses.

Practice has established that soldiers are not required to owe political allegiance, but this only holds good when civil society is on so firm a basis that the Army cannot change the form of government. Only then, here as elsewhere, is the path open to toleration. In France, the Dumouriez and the Lafayettes disappeared at the outset of the revolution. The same thing happened in England. The revolution did not tolerate doubtful generals; it eliminated Essex and Manchester and founded its own armed force, the New Model Army. For in such crises, it is unavoidable that the Army should be political. Necessity decrees that until the revolution has cemented the new social relationship or created the new moral and political balance of society, the Army should have a political conscience and concur with its rulers in fundamentals. The Army officers, from the highest ranks to the lowest, must merge their policy with the policy of the Government. Hence the justification for political commissars, who make their appearance in every genuine revolution. In the French Revolution, they were delegates of the Convention who kept their eye on the officers; in the English Revolution, these commissars had already acquired fame as "agitators", a corruption of the word "adjutators"; the Russian Revolution also could not do without the political commissar. And the constant reappearance in history of this personage corroborates the need for him, though the system is not without its disadvantages. In any case, the political commissar is not a Russian invention.

Nevertheless Azaña's reforms did not include a decision to found a Republican Army which would be imbued morally and politically with the ideas of the new Government. The Army of the monarchy was left intact, though with some technical improvements. The result was that many of the officers who sent in their papers under the law of voluntary retirement were Republicans. The Liberal officers, little enamoured of life in barracks and of a profession so often adverse to independence of mind and freedom of opinion, were bound to feel, more than the Monarchist, absolutist and militaristic type of officer, the oppression of Army life and Army regulations. To officers with Republican sympathies, therefore, the opportunity which the Republic offered to all officers without distinction, of leaving the Army without loss of pay, was a tempting promise of personal emancipation. They would be able to return to civil life, where they could breathe without the tabus or the straitjacket of discipline and the military codes. In contrast, the Monarchist officers, martinets, enjoying their commands, scrupulously observing the military hierarchies, chose to remain in the Army. The fact that they hated the new régime was in itself a sufficient reason why they should continue their military career.

Consequently, if the decree permitting the voluntary retirement of officers exercised any kind of selection, this consisted in eliminating from the Army not a few staunch supporters of the Republic and democracy and leaving in a dominant position in the garrisons numbers of officers who were enemies of the new political movement. As has already been stated, about 11,000 officers accepted the benefits of retirement; some 10,000 kept their commands. Events were soon to prove that of these 10,000 officers, the immense majority were hostile to the Republic. The Republican officers in the Army of the Republic were in a minority compared with the officers who were either indifferent or fanatically hostile to the régime. The Republic could count on some 3,000 loyal officers; it found itself menaced by 7,000.

328

The most conspicuous and brilliant generals of the Republic were almost all Monarchist, absolutist or neutral in politics. And so much was done, and rashly done, to favour these Army chiefs that toleration took on the character of protection. The Army was delivered up to them; they were given a free hand to conspire against the régime. General Goded, renowned Monarchist conspirator and typical *coup d'étatist* General, was appointed by the Republic to be Chief of the Central General Staff. Like Goded, the Francos, the Molas, the Cabanellas, continued to command units or to train the corps of officers· in the Academies.

This military policy, unique in the history of revolutions, put the Republican officers in a position which was insufferable from every point of view. As a result of it, the Army of the Republic was now more out-and-out Monarchist or hostile to all reform than the Army of the monarchy had been. Under the monarchy, the Republican officers had mingled with the Monarchist officers in their quarters and been respected because they were numerous. But under the Republic, they had to put up with the perpetual insults and interminable taunts of their fellow officers. The political atmosphere of the barracks had become too strained for a Republican officer. And the Republican soldier, usually in an impotent minority locally, had to stand by helplessly while the régime was held up to derision.

All this gave rise to violent personal encounters in which the Republicans came off worst. A lamentable incident, in which the protagonists were Monarchist and Republican officers, made plain to the nation the discord which was undermining the reformed Army.

The Minister of War decided that the cadets of the military Academies should carry out tactical exercises lasting some days in the *Campamento de Carabanchel* near Madrid. The Madrid garrison was invited to attend the manœuvres, the idea being that different Army corps should get to know each other and fraternize. On June 27th, 1932, after the manœuvres, the officers who were directing them met their fellow officers and guests at breakfast. After breakfast the generals said a few words. The General commanding the 1st Infantry Brigade alluded in his speech to the morale of the Army, which he deplored, and ended with a "*Viva España*", without acclaiming the Republic. Following on his speech, the Divisional Commander laid stress on the morale of the officers and commented on some remarks made by the Minister of War. He too ended with a "*Viva España*", passing over the Republic in silence.

Lastly, the General in command of the Central General Staff, Goded, added a few more words to the act. But Mangada, a Republican Lt.-Colonel, could not contain his anger over what was really a display of hostility to the Republic on the part of the Army chiefs and proceeded to heap reproaches on them. The generals replied with equal violence; the others joined in, the clamour grew louder every moment, and Mangada, beset on all sides by the anti-Republican officers, was shouted down. As was to be expected, this Republican officer was arrested and sentenced to be detained in a fortress on a charge of disrespect and insolence to his superiors. Azaña dismissed the generals.

It was clear that Monarchists and Republicans could not live together and that when incidents occurred, as they were fatally bound to do, the Republicans got the worst of it.

Professionally and technically, the Army which Azaña organized was superior to that of the monarchy. But the advantage was theoretical. The chief factor in an Army is morale, and the coexistence of a dominant Monarchist and a subordinate Republican body of officers could not but demoralize the Army in general. Such a situation destroyed what had been effected by the technical reforms. Spain continued to be without an Army, in spite of the efforts of the Minister of War.

How could Azaña side-step the political aspect of military reform, which was the essential factor in a revolutionary situation? The Republic needed a popular Army of its own, reliable and unreservedly loyal. We have already seen that the reforms produced exactly the opposite. Certainly, the rank and file were better treated by the Government, and Azaña even proposed to make them eligible for commissions by admitting them to the Academies—a distant plan which the Republic was not to have time to put into execution. And even if Azaña did indeed propose to reserve the greater number of vacant places in the Academies for the rank and file, the classes that were now finishing their courses would have to be used first and as there were too many officers already, it would be long, much too long, if ever, before non-commissioned officers could hope to predominate in the higher ranks.

The Republic neglected the political side of military reform, even going so far as to boast about it. "No one was asked what his politics were," said Azaña; and he added: ". . . and if anyone told me at any time that 'he distrusted So-and-So' (probably a Monarchist), I hastened to put that person in a position of responsibility; for I have observed that nothing has

330

such a tremendous effect as to confront a person with his own responsibility when he starts talking rashly. For as soon as he is in command, he forgets his imprudent words because they weigh on the consciousness of his own responsibility." This was to misjudge completely the anti-democratic generals and the oligarchy which was egging them on against the Republic.

As was, unfortunately, demonstrated beyond repair, Azaña carried his complaisance towards the enemy to highly dangerous extremes. By an ingenious sophistry, which only an intellectual could have evolved, he concluded apparently by convincing himself that Monarchist officers were what the Republic needed: "Anyone who wants to walk out of the Army," he explained, "for any reason whatever—political, personal or professional— can find the door open. This has its compensations; for anyone who remains, doubly accepts his military duties; he accepts them when he leaves the Academy, he accepts them when he takes the regimental oath, but he accepts them anew when the Republic says to him: If this régime does not please or suit you, you can walk out. Ah! you want to stay? Then you are taking your oath over again and binding yourself doubly by not accepting the option the Republic is offering you. In this way, I think it is morally more valuable to have in the Army an officer who is there because he wants to be, than one who remains because I have told him to stay."[1]

Those who warned Azaña against such conciliatory methods and deplored his confidence in men and institutions not worthy of trust, encountered a man whose mind was made up: "Those whom we must be on our guard against", he said, "are those who exploit the opinion and reputation of the Army; who, now in support of, and now as a threat against the Republic, keep alive the myth of the menace of the soldier and the sword. Believe me, gentlemen, this myth does not exist."[2]

It was not, however, a myth or a wraith, but a flesh-and-blood peril, an irremediable danger—not only because political passions in the Army ran high, but also because the social roots of the *pronunciamientos* were still untouched and the Republic did nothing to extirpate them. With this, we will leave this subject. But I must add one word more—how could the Monarchist and traditionalist Army chiefs be expected to remain quiescent when they had been told that in future the greatest number of places in the military Academies were to be reserved for sergeants?

[1] Speech in the Cortes, June 28th, 1932.     [2] Ibid., Dec. 2nd, 1931.

Azaña blundered; but he was not the only one. His policy reflected the imprudent middle line which the Republic as a whole had adopted. And if I point out these errors, it is naturally not because I have any prejudice against the reorganizer of the Army, but with the idea of putting things in their right perspective. Only thus can we learn anything from history.

It is well known that the Army in Spain enjoyed a pernicious ascendancy, a situation which, while it denoted the omnipotence of the military, indicated the weakness of the Spanish civil State. This preponderance of the Army dated from the nineteenth century, as I explained at the beginning of this work; and it led, among other things, to the unjustifiable pride of most of the officer class. Every reader of history is familiar with this phenomenon. Gibbon remarked of the Roman Praetorian Guards that "their pride was nourished by the sense of their irresistible weight" in the face of the weakness of the civil government (Gibbon, Bk. I, chap. v).

That the responsibility was not the Army's was a truth which, though it might escape more simple minds, was not lost on a man of Azaña's brains. "The Army in Spain", he observed, "has assumed the political preponderance which you all know, not through its own fault, nor by virtue of the military function as such or even of the personal merits of soldiers—for we are all hewn from the same quarry—but because of the lack of solidity of Spanish society, whereby, when the organisms of the *ancien régime* were eradicated and the authorities which maintained discipline impaired, the Army remained the only force in existence, the only executive and authoritative expedient to which the weak parliamentary Governments of the past century could resort in order to enforce obedience and even to restore themselves to power."[1]

No doubt this reasoning of Azaña's represents a considerable improvement on the vulgar judgment of the military problem in Spain. But it seems to me incomplete; perhaps because Azaña could not give it full rein in Parliament, or perhaps because he did not see the question in all its true profundity. For after this display of originality and good sense, he exclaims: "All this has ended." A crass error! All this had *not* ended, and we shall see why.

I must now take up the thread where I left it in Chapter IV of Book One. Not only in Spain, but everywhere else, the Army enters upon the political scene as the handmaid of revolution.

[1] Speech in the Cortes, Dec. 2nd, 1931.

If the revolution succeeds in its double purpose of destroying the old institutions and erecting new ones, the Army leaves the political stage under the same law as governed its entry. But if the revolution succeeds in its first task of liquidating the old institutions and fails in the task of raising up new ones, the Army remains in politics and becomes the arbiter of public life. Let us take a classic example. In Rome, the Army invaded political life with Marius (Mommsen, Bk. IV, ch. iv) and continued to take a hand in civil strife until Caesar founded the absolute monarchy, that is, until Rome had new civil institutions; and even then, because the ills of Italy as diagnosed by Pliny[1] were incurable, and because the Army had preserved the semblance of the popular power, it continued to weigh in Roman politics, though less under Augustus than under other emperors, thanks to the political genius of Caesar's adopted son.

The nineteenth century in Spain reproduces the case of Rome in modern history with a fidelity without equal in any other nation, though with reservations which will be noted. In Spain, the Liberal revolution destroyed the absolute monarchy, without creating in the structure of property the bases of a limited monarchy or of a republic secured on universal suffrage, régimes which are fundamentally analogous in so far as they are founded on the sovereignty of the people. (There is no need to emphasize that constitutional monarchy today usually has more in common with democracy and with a republic than with the classical monarchy, as anyone who is interested in political science knows.) The case of Rome in the final phase of the Republic is the same as Spain in this respect, though in the inverse direction. In Spain, the republic (or the monarchy based on universal suffrage) made its appearance in a country of millionaires and beggars, without a middle class. In the same social situation in which the Liberal or Republican State drew its first breath in Spain, the Roman Republic died (Mommsen, Bk. V, ch. xi). The Roman Republic succumbed for the same reasons as the monarchy or republic based on universal suffrage succumbed in Spain.

When the Roman Republic came into being—a popular régime tempered by a responsible aristocracy—the land was fairly equitably divided; but when, through the destruction of the small holdings by the accumulation of agrarian property, Italy became a nation of millionaires and beggars, the Republic lost its support in society. Absolute monarchy was inevitable (Mommsen, Bk. V, ch. vi).

[1] Verumque confitentibus, latifundia perdidere Italian (*Hist. Nat.*).

The Spanish absolute monarchy did not fall, like the Roman Republic, because it lacked a social base; it fell because it was overthrown by the Liberal ideas and winds blowing from France. But on the existing semi-feudal foundations of agrarian property, the Spanish Liberals proposed to build precisely that republican State which Rome had not been able to preserve in similar social conditions, and which provoked there the change of the Constitution which favoured absolutism, contrary to the will of Caesar who had no desire to be a tyrant (Mommsen, Bk. V, ch. xi).

The nineteenth-century Liberals in Spain, especially the economists, knew that they could not establish a democracy, either monarchical (with a liberal and limited monarchy) or republican, in a nation of social extremes. They wanted, therefore, to create a middle class in the rural areas by appropriating the lands of the Church. But they did not expropriate the aristocracy who were far richer in landed property than the Church, and the lands of the clergy became concentrated in a few hands or were parcelled out too minutely. The failure of the Liberals was obvious; they did not create a middle class. The most impious social inequality continued to reign in Spain. The result was that the civil institutions of Liberalism were hopelessly weak. The absolute monarchy, on the other hand, could not survive because it ran counter to the ideas of the epoch, the spirit of rebellion, the tendency towards equality, the sentiment of popular sovereignty. These ideas, this spirit, this sentiment, favoured limited monarchy or a republic; but, in its turn, the structure of agrarian property favoured absolute monarchy. In short, neither limited monarchy nor the republic could take root.

In my view, this is why Spain has had no civil institutions, or only very weak ones, since the eighteenth century. This is why the Army has subjugated civil society. This is why, finally, a civil war, which has lasted up till now for 130 years, is destroying the nation.

The fact is that the Army does not always exceed its functions through the lack of resistance to the impetus of its own force; often in Spain, civil society itself expressly invites its intervention. The oligarchy needs it to maintain society without a State; the Liberals, to maintain the State without society. And in the last instance, the Army is the State—such State as exists in Spain.[1]

---

[1] This situation is not, in its essentials, peculiar to Spain in our days. The Army is the State in every country which is dominated by a landed oligarchy or aristocracy, and in which universal suffrage has been introduced—as, for example, in Central Europe (Hungary), Poland, the Balkans before the second World War and Latin America.

Azaña, as we have seen, felt the lack of solidity of civil society in Spain, but did not indicate what was the ultimate reason of the phenomenon. What motives had he to say *à propos* of the *pronunciamientos*: All this has ended? Had all this indeed ended, when Spain was still in the year 1810 as far as the structure of society was concerned, or rather, when she was even worse off, since there was now greater inequality than when the peasants possessed their common lands and *bienes de propios* ?

No change had come about in Spain since the nineteenth century which could lead one to think that the era of the *pronunciamientos* had passed. On the contrary, in proportion as the landed oligarchy increased its economic power, inequality became more pronounced, because the agrarian proletariat grew in numbers. To a certain extent Cánovas removed the Army from the political stage and the Restoration State warded off this menace for fifty years. But all this was, by and large, at the expense of the Restoration régime itself and had tragic consequences for the monarchy. For as the oligarchy needed the Army to sustain an iniquitous Government, it did not reduce or discipline it, but kept it within bounds by engaging it far from the Peninsula in foreign adventures and corrupting it—a policy which destroyed the monarchy and deprived the oligarchy (the victim, in the end, of the armed forces) of political power.

Only the establishment of civil institutions on a solid foundation could relegate the Army to its specific function; but this entailed the birth of new classes of proprietors and the diminution of social inequality. The Restoration State was weak because it did not rest on the national will but on caciquism and the Civil Guard. It was a parliamentary dictatorship, not a liberal régime. Absolute monarchy gave way, not to a liberal monarchy, but to an absolute oligarchy under a pseudo-constitutional king. Having decided to maintain social inequality, the oligarchy staged this farce in order to keep itself going. But the Government lacked moral authority and the support of the citizens, the only defenders of a State against institutions which, like the Army, are capable of supplanting the civil power.

In spite of Azaña's illusions, the Republican State was, if anything, weaker than the Restoration State because, without having modified the structure of property, it did not disguise the Liberal political institutions with artificial defences. It claimed to represent without dissimulation a political democracy, when economic democracy was non-existent in the nation. This was the cause of its principal weakness. The middle class, by

335

itself, could not sustain it. The proletariat—"anarchist", for the most part—repudiated it. The Socialists supported it without enthusiasm. And the oligarchy, alive and full of vigour, fought it tooth and nail. It mattered little that millions of Spaniards should have proclaimed the Republic and that millions more would rise in its defence in the hour of peril. One thing had nothing to do with the other. The Republic was above the Republican State. The Republic meant hope for the people; and the death of the Republic at the hands of the oligarchy and the Army meant the death of the people. But the Liberal and Republican State, timid and conservative as it was, attracted but few Spaniards.

While Azaña was speaking in the manner we have seen, everything was, in short, as it had been in the nineteenth century. The Republic had not been able to set up new civil institutions, nor did there seem any likelihood that it would ever do so, because the revolution frightened the middle classes which headed the régime. Nor was the revolution possible without a revolutionary Army. In point of fact, to renounce the project of creating a popular Army was to renounce the revolution. In the meanwhile, the oligarchy defended its rights and the generals conspired—all very much in the fashion of the nineteenth century. And six months after Azaña had announced that all that had ended and that the menace of the sword was a non-existent myth, the first military rising under the Republic took place, General Sanjurjo's *pronunciamiento*.

CHAPTER VIII

## THE AGRARIAN LAWS

IT GOES WITHOUT saying that the problem of the land is the great Spanish question of our time. It is more; agrarian problem or agrarian question are concepts which do not express, for Spain, the immense background of the subject, nor its real amplitude or profundity, as the reader has seen in another chapter. Yet the Republic did not put its heart into this most vital of all questions. Agrarian reform was the name given to what, if it was to represent anything in the history of Spain, should have been a sweeping revolution. Having despatched the Constitution, the head of the Government requested the deputies to "make one sacrifice more and to prepare themselves to discuss the Budget, alternately with the agrarian law or some other project". And if one includes agrarian reform among the problems which demand urgent study, it is not by reason of its importance for the national destiny, but for its connection with public order; ". . . because there is pending in Andalusia and in other regions of Spain a very grave problem—the preservation of order and the maintenance of the people's lives which are menaced by hunger and social disorder. And it is the Republic's duty to apply, with all the haste the occasion demands, the immediate remedy to this social menace".[1]

The necessary vigilance towards this overwhelmingly important aspect of the revolution was not forthcoming. It was lacking among the middle class, the representatives of philosophical Republicanism, which moulded the régime on the basis of its transcendental Liberalism, ignoring the economic factor. In *petit bourgeois* centres, in Parliament, in the clubs and cafés, politics, personal affairs and anti-clericalism were debated with fervour. Outside the workers' parties, the land problem attracted the attention of only a few people with special interests in the matter; it never came to constitute in politics a national aspiration or primordial preoccupation of all the parties of the régime. It did not even merit a speech from the leader of the Republic.[2]

What was then, in the judgment of the Republicans, Spain's chief problem? Without doubt, the clerical problem—and in the second Republic there was no controversy more envenomed or one which more engrossed Parliament or the Republican philosophers. This theme is elaborated later on in this work, but I thought an allusion here was necessary, in this connection, to show how the anti-clericalists missed the mark.

They forgot—perhaps through misreading history, as Azaña thought, perhaps through reading no history at all—a fact of some importance; they forgot that the Church owed such riches as she possessed in 1931 and the recovery of her political influence with the monarchy of the Restoration, to the landed oligarchy. It is interesting to recall that the Church in 1874 was an institution which had been diminished and impaired in a very high degree by the Liberal revolution. For several years during the nineteenth century, there were no religious orders in Spain.[3]

[1] Azaña, speech at Madrid, July 17th, 1931.

[2] A speech on the agrarian question can be looked for in vain in the three thick volumes of Azaña's political speeches: *Una politica* and *En el Poder y en la Oposición* (2 vols.) Madrid, 1932 and 1934.

[3] According to Azaña, the absence of religious orders lasted for thirty odd years (Speech on Art. 26 of the Constitution, Oct. 13th, 1931). But it cannot

The Church lost, besides her landed property, the civil war. How was she to succeed in rehabilitating herself? It was the new landed oligarchy which, finally rising to political power after the downfall of the first Republic, facilitated and assisted the return, expansion, and material progress of the religious orders. And this political and economic apogee of the Church naturally aroused the violent anti-clericalism of the commencement of the present century.

I have already stated why and how this symbiosis came into being, this association of interests, previously contradictory and conflicting, of the new landed State and the Church. The grain and olive oligarchy needed the support of the spiritual arm to defend its iniquitous Government, founded on the odious distribution of landed property. Whilst it coveted the lands of the religious communities and the municipalities, this middle class waged war against the friars; but no sooner did it take over the management of the national wealth than it saw itself forced, in order to preserve its existence, to join hands with the Church against the people. The Church, in her turn, needed the new rich, now reactionary and conservative, to defend herself against the Republican neo-Liberalism and the laicizing tendency of the end of the century, and to retrieve her economic position, since she had remained without fortune; she stooped to bless the indefensible régime of landed property which arose out of the disentailing reform. The fatal absence of moral authority in the new Government did the rest in favour of the Church, which *ipso facto* resulted in her acquiring a position of impregnable power.

There is no doubt that the Church would not have recovered her political and economic vigour—as she did recover it, with interest—had she not entered, haltingly, the service of the new landed oligarchy. On this point, a few more words may be said.

Let us reiterate that, during the régime of the Restoration, as opposed to the first half of the nineteenth century, the Church owed her social strength to the fact that she had consented, after her defeat in the civil wars, to ally herself with the same social class which had expropriated both her and the people. Azaña touches briefly on this phenomenon when he says of the new oligarchy "that having initiated a liberal and parliamentary

---

be so many, at least consecutively, as the text of the Concordat on 1851 shows. In all probability, the dissolution only lasted in complete form from 1836 to that date, or a period of fifteen years. In any case, it is certain that for a considerable lapse of time the regular clergy in Spain disappeared. The friars were, as it were, a thing of the past.

revolution with a violent impulse towards radicalism and anti-clericalism, the same social class, perhaps the descendants of those collaborators of Mendizábal and the men who broke the entails in '36—these same men, after the process which I have just described, are those who brought to Spain tyranny, dictatorship and despotism, and in this evolution is comprised the political history of our country during the past century".[1]

*To place the clerical question, in order of urgency and importance, before the land problem, was, therefore, a manifest absurdity, dangerous in its double-edgedness, which, as we shall see later, was to cause the ruin of the Republic.*

From all the evidence, the Republic found a Spain that was sick beyond recovery, ungovernable, morally and politically in dissolution, although this was not apparent from a superficial glance. And this was due, in a final analysis, to the fact that in Castile, Andalusia and Galicia, economic conditions prevailed which rendered impossible the acclimatization of a system of political liberty and the organization of a State on the pillars of popular sovereignty. And in order to set the nation on the path to regeneration and moral equilibrium, it was necessary, as a preliminary and indispensable step, to solve the four questions to which the major weight of the agrarian problem can be reduced, namely: to facilitate access to property for the numerous landless proletariat from the regions of the latifundia; to abolish or change the system of short-term leases, legal sign of insupportable servitude which, as is known, affects in Castile a very high percentage of agrarian property; to undertake the reform of the Galician and Castilian smallholdings; and to cancel or redeem in some manner the Galician leases (*foros*). This was a tremendous work, calling for much expenditure of time and effort, particularly so for a middle class lacking the necessary impetus—but to leave things as they were in Spain was to abandon all hope of peace. The truth is that the true character of the Spanish national crisis was not appreciated in 1931, nor does it seem to be appreciated even yet. At the same time something was done: some decrees were promulgated and there was an attempt at agrarian reform, and this is what claims our attention now.

In the first months of the Republic, certain belated and elementary reforms were introduced into agriculture—mixed juries or arbitral commissions to adjust class conflicts; a law to cover workmen's compensation; the enforced cultivation of derelict land; a law relating to municipalities, with the object

[1] Speech on Oct. 13th, 1931.

339

of preventing the hiring of labour from other districts if any labourers were unemployed in the locality. Wages were fixed at a minimum of 5·50 pesetas a day for an ordinary day's work and 11 pesetas during the harvest, which meant a raise of 40 or 50 per cent. Lastly, the eight-hour day and workers' pensions were extended to agriculture. Most of these regulations had been in force for some time—and were more or less observed—in industry; in Spain, it will be remembered, no legislation had dealt with agriculture since the agrarian oligarchy took over the reins of government.

Special mention should be made of the most important innovation imposed on agriculture by decree, that relating to leases, a precept which had revolutionary consequences in Catalonia. The powers of the landowners were drastically curtailed (decree of April 29th, 1931) by fixing a limit to the arbitrary powers with which they had always treated their tenants; they were forbidden to evict them while a special law was being drafted to regulate this aspect of property. Another regulation conceded the tenants the immediate right to propose the revision of contracts and the reduction of rents.

Of course the Government's regulations were not complied with or respected in all quarters. But a rise in daily wages in Andalusia was sufficient to excite a favourable repercussion in the textile industries, timber-yards, etc.—incontrovertible evidence of the solidarity of interests between the Castilian and Andalusian peasants, on the one hand, and the industrial capitalists of Catalonia and Vasconia, on the other. In spite of which, neither in Catalonia nor in Vasconia do the nationalists understand, it seems, such an identity of interests. It is incontestable that the moderate reforms introduced into agriculture by the Republic prevented the industrial crisis from taking a more fatal course.

Let us now pass on to study agrarian reform, properly so-called.[1] By tradition, the latifundia were regarded as the major factor perturbing rural economic life. Agrarian reform having been conceived as the proposal to divide up certain large estates, to solve the problem of social order and combat unemployment, the law of September 1932 confined it to the regions of Andalusia, Estremadura, Ciudad Real, Toledo, Albacete and Salamanca. In these latitudes the law confirmed the occupation, already carried out by the peasants, of certain estates, and accepted in principle the temporary occupation of others while expropriation was being carried through.

[1] Unless other sources are quoted, it is understood that the data are taken from *La Reforma Agraria en España*, Instituto de Reforma Agraria. Valencia, 1937.

An Institute of Agrarian Reform, represented in the provincial capitals by provincial *Juntas*, was to be the organ for executing the transformation.

The initial work of the Institute consisted in compiling an inventory of estates earmarked for expropriation and a census of peasants suitable for settling on them. While the expropriation was proceeding, the peasants were to occupy estates selected from among those listed in the inventory. The Institute was to pay the owners a rental of not less than 4 per cent of the value of the estate; but if after a period of nine years the expropriation had not been completed, the temporary occupation was to lapse. The occupied lands would earn, then, rent for the owner and, once expropriated, would become the property of the State, which would carry out all the expropriations subject to indemnification in public bonds.

The State, therefore, became the landlord and ceded the lands in its ownership to the peasants. It transmitted to the new usufructuaries only the beneficial occupation and in no case the freehold, for fear that the peasants might sell the estates and the latifundia would reproduce themselves or some other situation would arise as pernicious as those it was trying to remedy.

The events of August 10th, 1932, resulted in a change of heart towards the dogmatic design of giving financial compensation to the expropriated landowners. The Cortes, confronted with the military insurrection and suspecting the hand of the aristocracy behind the plot, as I have related, rounded off the Agrarian Law which was being debated at the time with an *addendum* which deprived the nobility, without compensation, of their cultivable rural patrimony. This document dispossessed them of 383,062 hectares. In order to observe the Constitution, which prohibited the confiscation of property, the Government based its action on Article 44 which authorized it to expropriate *ad libitum* for reasons of public utility.

The unrestrained hostility of the great landowners towards an agrarian reform which undertook, before the events of August, not to expropriate them without due compensation, can be explained, in part, by the circumstance that the indemnities were to be calculated on the basis of the net taxable profit declared—the basis, in its turn, of the land tax. As is well known, the great landowners had been paying taxes, from time immemorial, which were much lower than the real value of their estates; they were going to be paid, then, less than what these estates were worth. The solemn promise of compensation did nothing to pacify them.

We already have some idea of the tendency and scope of the agrarian reform approved by the Cortes. It was a compromise law, worthy of the shortcomings of a Parliament which installed Alcalá Zamora, the landowner, as President of the Republic. The Socialists accepted the agrarian reform, as they accepted so many other things; they had to proceed cautiously so as not to imperil the Republic, even though the Republic were to collapse. The workers' parties had always thought the Agrarian Law inadequate and mistaken. In the dawn of the Republic, the Socialist Party had proposed to the Republicans a plan to transform landed property which was unanimously rejected.[1]

Partly owing to the itch for moderation, partly out of party interest, from the first hour there arose between the Republican middle class and the proletariat a conflict which was to contribute in a large measure to the sterilization of agrarian reform. And with this introduction, we will go on to a rapid analysis of the factors which conspired against the accomplishment of the land revolution under the Government's patronage. One of these factors, and not the most trifling, has already been mentioned—the indifference of all those Spaniards who had no stake in the land problem.

The failure of the reform can be set down also to the fact that a change in agrarian property was being attempted without modifying the Spanish financial system; apart from which, on the question of credits, the Agrarian Law laid on the shoulders of the peasant burdens which would eventually weigh heavily on him.

The cost of financing the reform fell, in principle, on the State. Every year the Cabinet were to set aside in the Budget the sums they would need to continue settling the peasants on the land. As an organ for financing the scheme, a National Agrarian Bank was founded and endowed by the State, for a beginning, with 50 million pesetas. A similar sum was promised by the legislature in five successive annual grants, starting with the second year of the foundation of the bank. In short, the administration and, later, the financing of the agrarian reform was handed over to the private banks, since the Agrarian Bank would be constituted of representatives of the Bank of Spain, the Mortgage Bank (*Banco Hipotecario*), the *Consejo Superior Bancario*, the *Instituto Nacional de Previsión* and the *Cajas de Ahorro*. The Board of this Agrarian Bank was to consist of the Governor

[1] There were even Republican deputies who called the agrarian reform a Socialist measure. "If anyone here opposes the Agrarian Law, it is the Socialist group," said Azaña in the Cortes on July 19th, 1932.

of the *Banco Exterior de España* and four representatives appointed by the firms, or groups of firms, which had taken up shares to the value of at least 5 million pesetas. The State was represented by a certain number of public officials.

The destiny of agrarian reform came to depend on Spanish financial capitalism, above all, on the Bank of Spain, the rusty axle of that capitalism. The Bank of Spain was managed and directed, in matters of political finance, by the nobility and those bankers who had recently been incorporated into the aristocracy. On its Board there sat a numerous and appropriate delegation of absentee grandees, presided over by the un-impressive effigy of the Duke of Alba. To this landed nobility, expropriated in the twinkling of an eye by the events of August, the Republic entrusted, in practice, the financial salvation of agrarian reform!

No clear-minded politician would admit the possibility of carrying out an effective revolution in agriculture, or in any other branch of economics, without changing the Spanish financial system, beginning by eliminating from the Bank of Spain the pernicious influence of the landed oligarchy. In the most favourable event, an Agrarian Bank run, as all the Spanish financial institutions are run, by private banking, would lead to the institution of a type of agrarian credit genuinely oligarchic in conception. The credit weapon having been delivered over to this primitive financial capitalism—the pertinacious enemy of all official banking—the peasants who had benefited by agrarian reform would remain, bound hand and foot, at the very mercy of the expropriated landlords; they would obtain credits, if they did obtain them, by mortgaging their farms on the edge of a precarious or non-existent solvency; they would pledge their future to wealthy persons or firms, thus remaining permanently in bondage to the rich and the *caciques*—in short, they would never be able to lift up their heads, crushed by mortgages and enslaved by debts.

It is clear that the preceding considerations imply the almost Panglossian assumption that agrarian reform would pursue its course in a stabilized Republic, an inconceivable thing in the fatally revolutionary state of Spanish society.

Agrarian reform should have been conceived on a purely political criterion, like that which was applied to the expropriation of the grandees' estates. Finding Spain subjugated by a landed class, the Republic's mission was to destroy that class at the root of its social power. It was not agricultural unemployment, nor rural penury, nor even the latifundia, however

343

scandalous these might appear, which were the most urgent problems confronting the Government. The key question was eminently political—either the Republic annihilated the oligarchy of the dry land, or the oligarchy of the dry land annihilated the Republic. And from this elevated point of view, all the national problems could wait or be deferred, except the agrarian and the financial. The latifundia were no more than an aspect, and not the most complicated aspect, of the general basic problem of the land in Spain. No legislator could ignore the profundity of the national problem created by the smallholdings. The poverty-stricken smallholder of Castile or Galicia, devoured by usury; the short-term leaseholder of Castile who has to pay the rent in cash, be the year good or bad, and is as much a victim of the moneylender as the small landowner; those multitudes of peasants who are entirely ignorant of the amenities of life, who can hardly breathe under an insufferable economic and political oppression which never lifts, who neither protest nor agitate and who form the miserable retinue of the oligarchy, humble and silent tributaries of the *caciques* and the great landowners, do they not denote a reality more sinister and disquieting than the landless, revolutionary and discontented masses of the South? After all, Andalusia is alive; the proletariat in those regions aspires to something—to property, a better society, emancipation. But the Castilian and Galician rural areas, ravaged by social suffering peculiarly their own, are totally devoid of a spark of social consciousness. Neither Castile nor Galicia assaulted the Government with a spectacular, clamorous and immediate problem, but this, far from being a motive for tranquillity or satisfaction, should have aroused the Republic to serious alarm.

However satisfactory the number of peasants settled on the land in the regions of the latifundia, the cause of reform in Spain would be little advanced if the system of land tenure in Castile or Galicia was left intact.

The important problem of short-term leases remained unsolved. Though for the moment, as we saw, the provisional Government put a check on the landowners and supported the reduction of rents, in this sphere, nevertheless the abusive character of property was maintained. There was need to abolish this class of lease, commuting it perhaps into an emphyteusis or converting it into an *aparcería* or share-cropping contract (which would have had the effect of the owner interesting himself in agriculture). However, while waiting for Parliament to discuss and approve a final law on leases, nothing practical was done. On

344

the contrary, as will be seen, the law on leases which was passed by the Cortes at the dictation of the oligarchy in the counter-revolutionary period put an end to the few long-term leases remaining in Castile.

In the Agrarian Law allusion was made to the ancient common lands and *bienes de propio* or rented lands belonging to the communes, which were the basis in other days of the people's rural economy, and it was left to the future action of the Cortes to redeem them and provide for their restitution to the people. Nothing further was heard of this project—the counter-revolution stifled it, as it stifled everything else.

Finally, the Republic sidetracked in the same way the endemic problem of the Galician *foros*. The ancient aspiration of the north-western peasant to free himself from this servitude was once more betrayed.

Naturally the principal reasons for the failure of agrarian reform are strictly political and social. It is an error to suppose that there were not enough technicians. It must not be forgotten that in view of social conditions in the Spanish rural areas, it was a very difficult enterprise to open the way to reforms in a system of political liberty. With the country torn from the first moment, as was natural and human, by a bitter conflict between the indigent proletariat and the great landowners, there was no method of giving effect to any planned reform, as any of this kind must be. The Government's ideas and projects, whether moderate or not, perished, trampled under foot by the ideas and aspirations of the peasants. No sooner had the Republic emerged, than the regions of the large estates, especially, were inevitably swept by collective outbursts of impatience. And the labourer would not now be content with anything less than absolute ownership of the land and the total elimination of the landowners.[1] Absolute ownership of the land—very well! But in what form? Private or collective ownership? And where communal farming was imposed, generally over the whole of the unirrigated land, what was to be the method of procedure? Collective or by families? These were insuperable obstacles for a Government rendered impotent by party strife.

And yet since the first World War, certain agrarian reforms had been accomplished in Europe to the satisfaction of the peasants. Now it must be recorded that those reforms did not come up against insoluble difficulties; first, because they were carried through by the landed oligarchies—more intelligent, it seems, than the Spanish oligarchy—who were frightened of

[1] Vide C. Bernaldo de Quirós in *Leviathan*, April 1936.

Bolshevism which was clamouring outside the door. These oligarchies were running the country virtually under a dictatorship, except in Czechoslovakia. And secondly, because the mass of landless peasants was in each one of these countries much less numerous than in Spain. The case of Spain, in the domain of agriculture, is unique in the West. Neither in Central nor in Eastern Europe did it happen that there were 2, 2½, or 3 million agricultural labourers hemmed in by the large estates, paid a starvation wage, in tragic mutual competition thanks to the superabundance of manual labour. In no Eastern country was, or is, the mass of agricultural labourers so multitudinous as in Spain, a landless proletariat like that of the worst days of Rome, a people for the most part of the year without work, that is, without bread.[1]

An agrarian reform imposed on Spain by the oligarchy of the Restoration or by the dictatorship of General Primo de Rivera, that is, by the Conservatives, would have worked smoothly, as did the agrarian reforms in the nations of Central and Eastern Europe. There would not have been created in the rural areas of Spain an anarchical and hopelessly confused situation. For the subversive force of the rebellious landowners, using the proletariat itself to strangle reforms, cannot be ignored.

Nothing of what happened in the sphere of agriculture was incongruous. The only incomprehensible thing was the incalculable incapacity of the Republican actors to perceive the true temper of the drama in which they played the chief parts—a frequent occurrence in history.

Turning from the general to the particular, agrarian reform in Spain was compromised in action by the discrepancy between the individualistic trend—the dogma of the Republicans—and the proposal to organize the new work of cultivation collectively—the criterion of the proletarian parties. The bogy of Com-

[1] Only in Hungary did the social problem of the land present the same features as in Spain. Most of the cultivable land belonged, before the second World War, to an oligarchy. Those peasants who possessed any property possessed diminutive parcels of land, as in Spanish Galicia. The problem was the same as in Spain: latifundia and minifundia, with a poverty-stricken peasantry. Yet Hungary had only 8 million inhabitants—in absolute terms the population affected was therefore much less than in Spain.

In Eastern Europe—always excepting Russia—the question assumes a different aspect than in Hungary or Spain. Great landowners do not abound since the reforms were imposed. In Eastern Europe, the burning question, as in Spanish Galicia, is overpopulation. The normal farm in Eastern Europe is usually 1¼ hectares, and in the poorer regions not even one hectare. In the Balkan and Polish villages, each family consists, in general, of four or five adults and the farm gives work to two, at the most.

346

munism or Socialism which terrified the Republican *intelligentsia* as much as the dukes, and the more justifiable fear of alarming the capitalist nations, rose up to prevent collectivist solutions, even though these were for geographical and technical reasons the only advisable ones in many cases.

If the Spanish revolution, entrusted to political parties which history has shown have never agreed in cases like this, had come about in different circumstances, its end would have been different. The individualistic or family system or the collective system were not, in a closed question such as was made of them, the solution, either from a technical or a political point of view. Agrarian reform could have made use of both methods of development. What was needed, before all, was a reform, whatever its nature, which would deprive the oligarchy of its exorbitant economic power. This political conception of agrarian reform was lacking. The worst solution would have been better than no solution at all.

However, supposing that everything had fallen out as the Institute desired and that agrarian reform as framed by Parliament had been effected during the Republican-Socialist Coalition, what would have happened if this Government fell? Could any intelligent person be so ingenuous as to expect that the oligarchy, on regaining power, would respect the work of the Republic? It is not enough to legislate or to set in motion a social and political change, but this must be defended and preserved against the ineluctable reaction of carping criticism and prejudiced interests. The Republic ought not to have permitted, still less facilitated by means of parliamentary liberty, the return of the oligarchy to power.

Such is the history of agrarian reform in the period 1931–3. The counter-revolution, triumphing in the elections of November 1933, abrogated all the decrees favouring the peasants. But in February 1936 democracy organized in the Popular Front returned to power. Agrarian reform or revolution enters then upon a second phase which I will summarize here. However violent and turbulent the land situation had been in the first two years of the Republic, it was more so afterwards as a result of the policy of revenge and persecution pursued by the Agrarians and Radicals in the Government. Civil war was then a trifle less than irremediable and events moved inexorably and obstinately in that direction.

At that moment, the Government of the Popular Front placed in the hands of the ploughmen (*yunteros*) of the provinces of Cáceres and Badajoz (decree of March 3rd) the lands which they had formerly tilled for the landowners. A few days afterwards another decree extended the benefits of this measure to the ploughmen of the neighbouring provinces.

A few weeks later (decree of March 20th) agrarian reform received an energetic impetus and, to a certain extent, a new orientation. According to the law of September 1932, the Institute, with an eye to expropriations, had gained control, by a methodical and meticulous inventory of estates suitable for expropriation, over the majority of properties included under the designation of latifundia. The new decree of the Popular Front declared suitable for expropriation, for reasons of social utility, all those landed properties situated within a municipality and even those covering several districts, which were capable of contributing to the solution of the "agrarian problem". While it was being considered in each case whether expropriation was opportune, the question of temporary occupation was decided. The decree took moral refuge in Article 44 of the Constitution, but maintained the principle of compensation for expropriation and reserved to the proprietor the direct ownership of the estates while the occupation lasted.

The third stage in agrarian reform opened with the military insurrection of July 1936. The Popular Front Government agreed (decree of August 7th) to suspend the payment of rents to the owners of the occupied estates. By a decree on the following day, the Institute and, by delegation, the municipal authorities, were authorized to take over all the rural estates and adjoining farm buildings which had been abandoned by the owners or usufructuaries. This measure was an attempt, not so much to punish a revolt—that came later—as to sustain agricultural production.

Almost immediately the decree-law of August 16th established the principle of ownership by the small leaseholders and share-croppers who were entitled to own the farms which they culti-vated, provided they had paid rent for them for a minimum period of six years. Under this decree they were permitted, by unilateral decision and without taking into account the owners' wishes, to commute the lease or *aparcería* into outright ownership. The peasant could take possession of the land, either by purchase in instalments or by conveyance on payment of a quit-rent (*censo reservativo*) redeemable at any time.

In the autumn (decree of October 1936) the Government introduced expropriation in favour of the State, without com-pensation, of all the rural estates whose owners had taken part in the rising against the régime. The task of determining who were the enemies of the Republic was entrusted to *Juntas* formed by the municipal governments, the Popular Front committees and representatives of trade unions and groups of manual workers and leaseholders. The accused person had the right of appeal to the Ministry of Agriculture.

Expropriated lands belonging to the enemies of the Republic which had been cultivated by the owners under their own direction, or managed by agents or stewards, were handed over for the use and enjoyment of the landless peasants and farmers of the district in which they were situated and, where possible, of the adjoining districts. Usufruct in perpetuity was granted to the farmers' unions, who were permitted to cultivate the farms collectively or individually, by agreement of the majority.

Lands belonging to the enemies of the Republic which had been cultivated, through leases or on a share-cropping basis, by small farmers, passed to the latter in perpetual usufruct.

The decree gave preference in both cases to volunteers in the Republican Army and people's militias who were registered in the municipality where they resided as agricultural workers. The ex-leaseholders were permitted to amalgamate their lots and establish collective cultivation. The next of kin of those who fell in the war under the Republican flag, and the next of kin of the disabled, were to be granted other plots of land by the State. Finally the decree was ordered to apply to all the territory under Republican jurisdiction and it was announced that it would be put into force in the provinces occupied by the rebels, as and when these were reconquered.

By virtue of the decrees passed in the third phase of agrarian reform, the State took under its control, between March 1936 and May 1937, 3,856,020 hectares of land. True, these expropriations were in a great measure purely nominal or theoretical since the estates situated in the zones under Fascist domination were included. In one year, from February 1936 to February 1937, the Institute granted credits to the value of 72,464,398·81 pesetas.

To sum up, agrarian reform, beginning feebly, experienced a natural process of radicalization and became a revolution when the rebellious oligarchy broke the narrow legalistic frame in which the incautious Republic of the constituent period had persisted in confining it. But the revolution came late. The Republic had abandoned to the enemy the initiative both at home and abroad, and the distressed regions, those most in need of agrarian revolution, did not know the moving and dramatic experience of the land emancipated from its masters.

In the area ruled by the Popular Front there were vacillations and blunders during the cruel struggle, but there were continual deeds of collective heroism in cultivating the land that raised the peasant to the moral eminence of the best soldiers of the Republic and of the people's cause.

For all kinds of reasons, the civil war shifted the centre of gravity of Republican policy to the land. Perhaps it was recognized at last that if more attention had been paid to the agrarian question, the tragedy might have been averted.

## THE AGRARIAN REVOLUTION IN CATALONIA

The Catalan agrarian problem, which is *sui generis*, took a tumultuous turn on the advent of the Republic. The conflict developed into a considerable agrarian revolution.

We know that Catalonia is a rich region, the most prosperous of Spain, and that the leaseholders implanted there the social problem of the land. A trifling problem, if we compare it with the Castilian, Andalusian or the Galician problems. But the Catalan leaseholder does not feel satisfied, like the Basque share-cropper or the small landowner of the Levante, both inhabitants of the other two socially sound regions of the Peninsula. Consequently the regulations relating to leaseholders profoundly affected the Catalan share-croppers, *rabassaires* and leaseholders.

The class struggle in Catalonia has two poles; the eagerness of the landowner to convert the old long-term leases into shorter contracts, and the aspiration of the leaseholder to own property, a desire largely due to the feeling of insecurity felt by him at the owner's tendency to reduce the period of the leases. There can be no doubt that, if they were permitted, the Catalan landlords would insist on the short-term lease which impoverishes Castile. Since the end of the last century, the *rabassaires* have been evicted with alarming frequency and in many cases the contracts of *rabassa morta*, which almost constitute an emphyteusis, have been converted into simple leases. These are the main lines of the rural conflict in Catalonia.

The proclamation of the Republic in Spain, while it promised social justice, introduced a natural tension into the Catalan land problem. The share-croppers and leaseholders, who had not till then formed groups of resistance, began to organize themselves into unions, like the *rabassaires*, in order to defend and augment their rights.

As I have just said, the decrees suspending the eviction of tenants, revising contracts and reducing rents, were received by the leaseholders and *rabassaires* of Catalonia with lively interest. No fewer than 29,971 petitions for revision were presented in Lérida, Gerona and Barcelona. The Catalan rural areas were in an obvious crisis and, while judgment was being given in the courts on the demands for revision, the peasants, with those from the other regions mentioned, decided to hasten the reforms by diminishing the proportion of the produce which the owners had been wont to receive. The rioting was so serious that at times the authorities had to use force.

The affair naturally devolved upon the Government of the *Generalidad* and called for instant action. The Catalan authorities, as a first step, summoned to the *Generalidad* in September 1931 the representatives of the *rabassaires* and the landowners. These negotiations resulted in a temporary agreement, in virtue of which an important concession was made in the rent; the *rabassaire* who was paying half the crop was to pay a third, and the others in equal proportion. The agreement was to lapse at the end of the year and affected only the *rabassaires*.

But the peasants were not content, apparently, with less than the whole product of their labour; moreover, they wanted the land. Meanwhile the division of the crops continued after the end of 1931, and at times some of the *rabassaires* kept back the whole of the produce. As may be imagined, the conflict grew steadily more embittered.

On the 14th April, 1933, the *rabassaires* commemorated the anniversary of the Republic by marching in a crowd on Barcelona to exact from the Government of the *Generalidad* a final solution of the dispute. The *Generalidad* replied two months later with another postponement, though they decreed that the discontented leaseholders, that is, those who were at strife with the owners (Law of Conflicts) should pay half the rent agreed.

Finally, at the end of that year, the autonomous Government submitted to the Catalan Parliament a draft law that promised to settle the problem. This was the afterwards famous *Ley de Contratos de Cultivo*, promulgated in April 1934.

The peasants had triumphed. The contract of *rabassa morta* was to be considered as an emphyteusis. The worker was to possess the land while he cultivated it; the taxes were to be paid by the owner; the lease was to have a family character, the land being no longer leased except to the family and subleases being prohibited; no lease was to be drawn up for less than six years; if the leaseholder did not announce to the owner his intention of terminating the contract six months before the date of expiry, it was to be taken as continued; only in the case where the owner and his family undertook to cultivate the land could the lease be terminated at the end of the stipulated time, but such decision had to be communicated to the leaseholder two years before the expiry of the contract; in such a case, the leaseholder was entitled to compensation for any improvements made on the estate and a sum equivalent to a year's rent for every six years that the contract had lasted.

The right to cultivate the land was declared hereditary, in case of death, in favour of the descendants of the leaseholder. The rent could not exceed 4 per cent of the value of the land, which the leaseholder could buy when he had cultivated it for eighteen years, by a single payment or by instalments.

The *Ley de Contratos de Cultivo*, revolutionary in any light, although not exempt from conservative sentiment, met with the approval of the leaseholders. Quite a few who were in a position to buy the land were automatically converted into owners. Others would be in a few years' time. All of them enjoyed the usufruct in security and were protected from the whims of the landlords.

The landlords resisted this revolution, which would oblige them to cultivate the land if they did not wish to lose their property, giving occasion, as we shall see, to one of the most resounding events of the second Republic and the most fraught with consequences.

## CHAPTER IX

## THE UNITY OF SPAIN

The reader has found in the course of this work more than one allusion to Catalan and Basque nationalisms, but we have not yet analysed these phenomena, which are of cardinal importance and cannot be set aside. Now is the time to study them, since without a detailed explanation of these problems no complete picture of modern Spain can be formed. But at the same time, nationalism and political regionalism would be extremely difficult to understand without any notion of their remote antecedents, that is, without taking into account the peculiar characteristics of Spanish national unity. I shall devote this chapter, therefore, to national unity in general, with special mention of the place occupied in it by Portugal and Catalonia. A necessary parenthesis in the study of the second Republic, it will also serve as the indispensable preamble to the two following chapters.

It is important to remember, firstly, that the political unification of Spain, initiated by the Carthaginians, continued by the Romans and completed by the Visigoth monarchy, was destroyed by the Moslem occupation, which lasted to a greater or lesser extent from A.D. 711 to 1492; secondly, that when the Reconquista was ended—which left as a legacy to the Peninsula a kind of political instability unknown to the rest of Europe—the peninsular State did not reappear. The cause of this obviously retrograde state of affairs lay, in my view, in the dispersion of military and political power occasioned in the Middle Ages by the independent struggle of the great military leaders with the Saracens. The division of Spain into multiple mediaeval kingdoms can only be explained by the exceptional conditions created by the Reconquista in Spain. The feudal principle, which was excessively weak in Spain, did not bind the chief nobles to the Crown so strongly as in other countries; and disloyalty and ambition conspired together to make those who in other nations would not have exceeded the rank of dukes or counts owing fealty to the monarchy, turn their title into an hereditary one, like Count Fernán González (the first step towards the foundation of a *monarchy*) or set themselves up without further preamble as princes, like Alfonzo Henríquez of Portugal, or the primitive warrior who changed the obscure *senorío* of Pamplona into an independent monarchy.

The continuous tendency towards disintegration which appeared in Spain between 905 and 1036—the period when the petty kingdoms of the Reconquista were being formed—cannot be explained, in my opinion, save in the light of the warlike anarchy to which I have referred. This is confirmed by the appearance, later on, of the independent kingdom of Portugal, whose founder also based his right to the Crown on the power which he acquired as independent leader in his victorious campaigns against the Moors.[1] Had not their autonomy as warriors and their independent intervention in Cordova given the Counts of Castile a similar sovereign personality? In the ninth century, this region owed its very name *Castella* (*castillos*, or castles) to war.

It can be readily understood that the independence of the territory wrested from the Moors in centuries or moments of great anarchy was associated in the mind of the leader of the region with the idea of political independence for himself, for the liberator. The unwonted military independence of the nobles

---

[1] "There is no geographical or ethnological reason why the part of the Iberian Peninsula called Portugal should have formed an independent kingdom more than León or Castile. It was the greatness of one man which made it an 'independent country'" (Morse Stephens, "Portugal", in *The Story of the Nations*, p. 59).

led, therefore, to the independence of their dominions, and it was in this way that the kingdoms of Navarre (905), Castile (1029) and Portugal (1143) came into being.[1]

The Portuguese, Castilian and Navarrese nations—the kingdoms of the Reconquista—owed their origin to the same cause, according to the point of view I have just explained. But the kingdom of Aragon had a different origin; it was created in 1035, out of a modest *condado*, by Sancho el Mayor of Navarre, when he was at the point of death, for his son Ramiro. In this kingdom of Aragon was afterwards incorporated the Catalan nation, which was also not the political fruit of the fatal accident of the Reconquista.

Clearly, the independent Portuguese State was not founded on a biological reason[2] but on historical events, like the Reconquista, foreign intervention, the geographical discoveries. The two first have already been dealt with. As regards the last, there is no doubt that the geographical discoveries of the Portuguese endowed Portugal with a personality which accentuated her

[1] It is interesting to note that, although the kingdom of Castile came into being in 1035 through its elevation from a *condado* to a monarchy when Sancho el Mayor of Navarre left these states to his son Fernando, in 1029 Bermudo III of León had conceded the title of king to the Count of Castile. That is to say, the kingdom already existed.

[2] The independence of Portugal was due, in the first place, as I have pointed out, to the circumstance of the Reconquista. But without the collaboration of the Pope and the German Emperor, Alfonso Henríquez would probably not have been able to found the Portuguese Monarchy. The Emperor was an ally of the Pope, and Rome favoured the universal Catholic Monarchy. The Roman-Germanic policy had received a check in Spain with the resistance of Alfonso VI (1073–1109), who not only denied, in the face of the claims of the Lateran Palace, that Spain was the patrimony of St. Peter, but also took the title of Emperor, which his father had already used. Alfonso VII (1126–57) continued to assert with even greater emphasis the Imperial character of the Crown of León, and perhaps the fear that there might arise in the Peninsula an Imperial rival of the Holy Roman Empire induced the Church and the German Emperor to procure the political division of Spain.

While the external stimulus which I have just referred to was important to the gestation of Portugal's independence, the military and diplomatic intervention of England from the fourteenth century onwards was decisive to its consolidation. Wellington's reflection: "If I hold Portugal, France cannot hold Spain and will not hold her" was already the maxim of English politicians in an epoch when the historic Anglo-French conflict was reaching its greatest intensity. England not only needed Portugal to carry on her struggle with France; she needed her also in order to weaken the power of Castile. Hence, in its beginnings as in its consolidation, the independence of Portugal was largely, if not entirely, the offspring of the policy of the *Balance of Power*. Incidentally, nothing can be more fruitless than to dream of the unity of Spain, so long as no other method of ensuring international equilibrium flourishes. Meanwhile, to talk of the reunion of Portugal and Castile is pure waste of breath.

political independence; but these feats did not denote a genius distinct from that of Castile, which also produced explorers of equal stature. The sea-voyages of the Portuguese, which lent such emphasis to the independence of Portugal, were the result, in their turn, of the separation. Portugal, with her extended coastline and her shallow hinterland, had to sail the seas or condemn herself to a life which was morally and economically poor, the sort of life she leads today. Before the discovery of America, Portugal was already striving, with an anxiety that bordered on anguish, to increase her vital space, which could only be maritime if she persisted in maintaining frontiers with Castile.

In the fifteenth century the whole of Spain burned with the desire for political unification. Alongside this feeling, there flourished the centralizing principle of the monarchy, which was favoured by the decadence of the Cortes and the municipal régime. The legal unification of Castile came about, "as often as not", through the petition of the *procuradores* or municipal deputies; and when Ferdinand the Catholic modified the political constitution of Catalonia, the *concelleres* could not enlist public opinion on their side to oppose the prince, "an obvious proof", we are told, "that the ancient love of independence had been lost and that the people were dominated by the prestige of the royal authority and by the absolutist ideas of the epoch". We are faced with the reaction of the Renaissance throughout the whole of Europe against the disintegration of power in the Middle Ages. Under Henry VII, England riveted her political unity; France did the same under Louis XI. In the Iberian Peninsula, Ferdinand the Catholic was the perfect counterpart of these two princes. Spain also was striving, with nervous persistence, to found a State common to all her peoples. At that moment, all the Spanish kingdoms ardently desired unity, and no foreign nation could gainsay this desire. Spain was sovereign to an extent she had never been before, and as she was never again to be after the sixteenth century.

Portugal was as ardent as Aragon and Castile in pressing for union. But the incorporation of Portugal in the new State came to nothing, though this was not due to any profound reason. Union at that time depended on the matrimonial alliances of royalty, and only the fact that death carried off the Castilian-Portuguese princes who were successive candidates to the throne of Spain, prevented these lofty projects from bearing fruit.

Portugal remained, as we know, outside the Spanish State, though there continued during the sixteenth century that deep-seated cultural intimacy which had wedded her to Castile through the bond of a bilingual poetry from the middle of the previous century. Union, though frustrated, was always just below the surface, and it was eventually to be realized. In 1580, it became an accomplished fact. Philip II was king of all the *Spaniards.* (The Portuguese had been protesting since the days of Ferdinand the Catholic against the use of the title of King of Spain by the Spanish monarchs, refusing to admit that the latter had any right to adopt this name when they were not also kings of Portugal.)

During the sixteenth century the expansion of Castile in the Peninsula did not rest on force; it had a moral basis, and its predominance was also moral. It should not be ignored that Castile was the largest kingdom in the Peninsula, recently expanded by the incorporation of Granada and Navarre, master of the West Indies, the richest, the most populous, and the most advanced socially; which was why there never occurred there those risings of the serfs which stained the Galician and Aragonese-Catalan lands with blood.

The modern Spanish State's idea of unity was, above all, religious homogeneity (the only organism common to all the kingdoms was the Inquisition), and all other kinds of differences —political, cultural, etc.—were met with exceptional tolerance. The Catholic Monarchy did not complete the edifice of unity with the use of force, though the multiform intervention of the State would not have been a bad thing in those territories and regions where primitive customs and cultures survived. Though the structure of unity was only half completed, it yet managed to survive for 170 years.

The incorporation of Portugal reveals to us why such a loosely-knit political unity was able to sustain itself. The apogee of Spanish power acted like a centripetal force, strengthening the natural propensity of the various regions of the Peninsula to constitute a single State.

In 1580 Spain reached the highest point of her historical meridian. Outside the Peninsula, the dominions of Philip II comprised the Balearic and Canary Islands, Roussillon, Naples, Sicily, Milan, Sardinia, Flanders, the Low Countries, Franche Comté, the North African *plazas*; in America, Mexico, Peru, New Granada, Chile, the provinces of Paraguay and La Plata and all the islands today called the West Indies; in the Pacific, the Philippines. At this time, the Spanish monarchy was the most powerful in the world—its military and diplomatic strength irresistible. Portugal, on the other hand, was declining; and she perceived, perhaps, the error of separation which was, in reality, no one's fault. Portugal accepted Philip II as king in the Cortes of Thomar (April 1581). Neither Philip II's indisputable right to the Portuguese Crown, nor the military position which opened up to him the physical road to the throne, explained the union which owed its success and the fact that it endured for sixty years to deeper motives.

Catalonia, whose institutions the Crown left, in substance, intact, became "Castilianized" (se castellaniza)[1] for the same reason as facilitated the rapprochement of Portugal—the irresistible moral pressure of the Spanish national idiom prevailing in the two hemispheres. This factor was allied with other, decisive, ones which divested Catalonia of power; the discovery of America, which directed mercantile activity westwards; the conquests of the Turks in Asia Minor, which interrupted Catalan commerce with the seaports of the Levant; Turkish and Arab piracy, which rendered shipping unsafe in the Mediterranean; and the religious question, which deprived Barcelona of a considerable amount of capital in the hands of orthodox and converted Jews. It was these accidents which dealt Catalonia the blow which ushered in her decadence and almost effaced her personality. For the most part, therefore, the decline of Catalonia had its roots in economic ruin.

[1] This is not the most exact word to describe the supplanting of the Catalan language in the great centres of population of the principality by the idiom spoken by the majority of Spaniards. Instead of se castellaniza, we should say se españoliza. For the language which is spoken throughout the Peninsula, a supra-regional language, is not, strictly speaking, Castilian, but another language which, though built up on the Castilian dialect, is yet distinct from it. The "Romance language which resulted in Castile through the progressive corruption of Latin" was far from being the language of culture which was "composed and built up on the corruption of the Castilian dialect by the most cultured men of all the regions of Spain". Like the other regions, Catalonia contributed to the formation of that national language, Spanish, which, by spreading to the north-east of Spain, at the expense of the Catalan language hastened the process of making Catalonia Spanish. Castilian properly so-called continued to be a dialect like any other, and did not cross the borders of Old Castile. Nevertheless, I have written se castellanizó and not e españolizó, taking into account the fact that Catalonia is a region of Spain, a Spanish region, and would be so even if only Catalan was spoken there. The latter expression is only valid, therefore, as a suitable way of defining the linguistic event. When Spanish spread through the Catalan cities, Catalonia did not, in short, receive a foreign language, but the national speech of Spain which belonged as much to her as to the other regions and was fashioned by all the cultured minds of the Peninsula; by the Valencian Vives, as well as the Portuguese Gil Vicente, by the Andalusian Herrera as well as the Catalan Boscán. (See the excellent and erudite study Castellano, español, idioma nacional, by Amado Alonso, Buenos Aires.)

I pointed out earlier on the difference of origin between the kingdoms of Navarre, Castile and Portugal on the one hand, and Aragon and Catalonia on the other. The former were brought to birth by the Reconquista and owed their existence to an accident, though one with far-reaching consequences. The latter were mediaeval creations, to the extent that only in Aragon and Catalonia did a perfect feudalism, on European lines, flourish; in the rest of Spain, feudalism was incomplete and weak.

Catalonia properly so-called did not owe her national personality to the struggle with the Moors, though she had to wage war on them in common with the other Spanish regions; that is, even if there had been no Arab invasion, it must be supposed that the Catalan nation would have arisen, as indeed it did arise out of feudalism. A typical feudal creation, Catalonia, the *Marca Hispánica* of the Carlovingian Empire, definitely revealed herself as a feudal nation in the *Usatges*, the codification of characteristically feudal customs carried out by Ramón Berenguer I (1035–76). Here the historian comes to our aid. "As an essentially feudal State, Catalonia had no centralizing political power like that of Castile. The Counts of Barcelona did not exercise over the other feudal lords of the ancient *Marca Hispánica* sovereignty other than that proceeding from the feudal relationship, with the payment of homage, which the *Usatges* prescribed should be made in writing."

From the eleventh century onwards, Catalonia was, therefore a nation, and a nation sprung from feudalism, not from the Reconquista, with a mediaeval republic, Barcelona, as its head. We now find, when confronted with the powerful personality of Barcelona in the Middle Ages, that even if the unity of the Spanish State in the eighth century had not been broken, this city—which was much more than a city in the modern sense —would have been, in any case, a political exception in the Peninsula. Now, though this seems to have been its irrevocable destiny in the Middle Ages, a different fate awaited Catalonia under the Renaissance, for when the modern State was born, this region could not escape its status as a *Spanish* nation, recognized as such from remote antiquity and emphasized by Charlemagne. A feudal and mediaeval creation, the political constitution of Catalonia was bound to change, when Spain came to be ruled by the new monarchy.

The idea that the Austrian Hapsburgs, a foreign dynasty introduced the centralizing régime into Spain is, of course absurd. In the first place, no such *Austrian* dynasty existed. Psychologically Charles V (Charles I of Spain), as the inheritor of the moral personality of his mother, Joanna the Mad, without a single personal trait that recalled his father, the frivolous Philip the Handsome, was a profoundly Spanish character.[1] There is no need to speak of Philip II, since he was the son of "so Spanish" a father and of a Portuguese mother. Moreover, or above all, Charles V, in his Caesarian policy in Spain, was merely continuing the work of the Catholic sovereigns though without the necessary continuity and energy since he was absent most of the time. And Philip II continued the policy of his father, even in the Protestant question. (It has been maintained that because there was a time when Charles V was seeking reconciliation with the Lutherans and when he kept up a correspondence with Erasmus, Philip II, the irreconcilable enemy of dissent, followed a policy completely at variance with his father's, though what he did was to develop it. Charles V's "decisive stand in favour of Catholicism and against the Reformation, his support of the Great Council—in a word, his whole anti-Reformation policy" are forgotten. Forgotten also are the draconian instructions which he issued to Philip II from the monastery of Yuste against the Protestants of Valladolid and Seville.)

From the thirteenth century onwards absolute monarchy continued to make progress, urged forward by the resurrection of Roman Law; and the organic unity of Spain was a need of the epoch, imposed, as we have seen, by the reaction against the mediaeval order and also by the necessity of surviving in a world where the divided nations succumbed to the youthful appetite of the united ones. The precarious unification and centralization carried out by the Catholic sovereigns and continued by Charles V and Philip II, probably saved Spain from the tragic destiny to which political disunity condemned other nations. And the nineteenth century—which still continues in Spain—has been unjustly severe to the classical Spanish monarchy. This severity is due to the false assumption that fifteenth-century Spain was a nation which had developed biologically, so to speak, with no untoward accident, step by step, faithful to the cycle of the ages, like a normal being. But

[1] Cristobal de Villalón, a contemporary of Charles V, emphasized in his *Gramática Castellana* (Amberes, 1558) that the Emperor "prided himself on being Spanish". "We find", he adds, "that when His Majesty conquered the Lansgraf and the Duke of Saxony at the river Albis, all the lords and princes of Germany came to do homage and ask his pardon. And all spoke in Spanish, thinking to do him pleasure."

we cannot judge the revolution which the Catholic sovereigns brought to a head without bearing in mind that Spain emerged from the Middle Ages sick almost to death, so divided and ungovernable that, as far as human reason could foretell, no remedy was possible. Spain was condemned to devour herself in intestine conflict, to disappear in a chaos of strife between social classes, between races and between religions. If we lose sight of this fact, we shall err gravely in our interpretation of the modern history of Spain. There seemed to be no way out, and in the coherent, the natural course of events, there was no way out. The accession to the national throne of Ferdinand and Isabella was, therefore, a providential event; and the more we study it, the more portentous does it appear. There was, in fact, something prodigious in the union of these two great statesmen, who together—for they were complementary—made up a personality as striking as that of Julius Caesar, though inferior to him in general culture. (Ferdinand had passed his youth following his father to the Catalan wars and was practically illiterate. Mariana draws attention to the fact that he could hardly sign his name.)

These two certainly saved Spain, as Caesar saved Rome; and it was due to them that Spain was able to carry on, even with a certain splendour, for another three centuries. The assumption that in the sixteenth century a foreign element was introduced into Spanish history "which cut short the normal development of the Spaniard and placed him, with all his energies and greatness, at the service of a dynasty which served, in its turn, an imperialist and Catholic idea" is absurd, for it necessarily eliminates the real nature of mediaeval Spain which impelled the nation in that direction.

Moreover absolute monarchy did not take on in Spain, as it did in England under Henry VIII, the character of a despotic and tyrannical power.

It is important, therefore, to ask what the critics who reject the Catholic sovereigns and their absolutist and centralizing policy conceive sixteenth-century Spain should have been? What was the alternative? Apparently, a policy which would have enabled the Spanish cities to organize themselves in a régime similar to that of the Italian Republics. But this was impossible in the Spain of the fifteenth and sixteenth centuries (in the first place, it did not appeal to the people), and would have proved fatal to Spain. It is enough to read the jeremiads of Machiavelli on the tragedy of a disunited Italy, rent by invasions, the battlefield of all the armies of Europe, the victim of the heartless intrigues of international diplomacy, to see why this great Italian patriot regarded the Spanish monarchy as an edifying and exemplary régime.

Nevertheless, as I have pointed out, the organic unity· of Spain made little progress in the 150 years of Spanish might. Not in vain had the Middle Ages in Spain left their mark on the national soul, a mark more pronounced than in other nations, because mediaeval sentiments and values developed to an unwonted degree in the Peninsula. The policy of the Spanish State in the sixteenth century was purely mediaeval, not Renaissance, in its ultimate aspirations—like the Spanish culture, like everything in Spain. The aim was to perpetuate the Middle Ages, not only in Spain, but in the whole of Europe. And that had two important consequences; one, that the nation directed its interests and force outwards, neglecting itself, and the other, that the State disinterested itself in the work of organic unity, because, thinking along mediaeval lines, it did not find the matter urgent, as, for example, the French State did. And as the various regions reasoned in similar terms, they defended the mediaeval particularist tradition with peculiar tenacity.

The Renaissance had favoured the *rapprochement* of the Spanish peoples and, in proportion as it penetrated into Spain, it facilitated the policy of the Catholic sovereigns and of Charles V. The rising of the *Comuneros* in 1520 was a mediaeval revolution both in style and background, which ought to have broken out against Ferdinand and Isabella, but was postponed, thanks to the good government and popular prestige of these sovereigns. It actually broke out when the disorder and licentiousness of Charles V's Flemish followers offered a plausible and patriotic pretext to the aggrieved classes, the greater and lesser nobility, the clergy and the municipal aristocracy.

Although in their religious policy Charles V and Philip II continued the work of the Catholic sovereigns (for, when all is said and done, the anti-Reformation policy of the former "took its inspiration from the feelings and tendencies of Spaniards" as much as Ferdinand and Isabella's policy had done), it is equally certain that Charles V did not direct with a firm hand or pursue with the required energy the work of nation-building which his maternal grandparents had undertaken. Strictly speaking, the thirty odd years of the reign of Charles V were lost years for Spain, since he was absent for about twenty-three of them, and on one occasion did not show his face in Spain for almost fifteen years.

The nation which the centralizing monarchy had begun to raise, a nation whose outlines had already been filled in during the three centuries of political administrative and linguistic unity under the Visigoth régime, was still, therefore, waiting to be made. Yet in the sixteenth century the work already admitted of no delay, for in most of the Spanish villages the people still lived as their ancestors the Iberians had done. No one appreciated this better than Charles V and the members of his suite, whose first contact with Spain "was sufficiently depressing". A modern essayist has given us a highly picturesque and interesting account of the entry of the young prince into the Peninsula.

Charles and his Court landed on an Asturian beach in September 1517. "The men of that region", says this author, "were pure *hidalgos*, proud of their lineage which went back to the remote days of the expulsion of the Moors. But they wore rough woollen doublets, lived in miserable hovels, had neither shoes nor hose, and looked ferocious with their long, unkempt beards. The women went about dishevelled and bare-legged; some had their legs wrapped in cloths instead of stockings. The food was scanty and bad; the beds, consisting of benches with a bundle of straw, still worse. The travellers, therefore, hurried south with all speed, so as to reach Valladolid, where the seat of government was, as soon as possible. The King, with the most important members of his suite, went through hamlets and villages which looked as if God had abandoned them—Colunga, Ribadesella, Llanes, Colombres, Treceño, Cabuérniga, Los Tojos, Ampudia—the inhospitable mountain districts of Asturias and Cantabria. At Cabuérniga they lodged in dwellings whose walls were hung with bearskins, and where there was no furniture. At Los Tojos they had to spend the night in tents, because the houses were full of goats and pigs, cows and horses, as well as human beings. Near Revenga the road ran through the country of the cave-dwellers, a species of troglodytes, who lived in holes in the ground, to the great astonishment of the Flemish gentlemen."

This backwardness could not look for redress to Philip II, who though he hardly ever left Spain, continued to be absorbed more by the progress of the world, which he hoped to rule, than by the progress of his country, to which, nevertheless, he paid more attention than his father did.

Philip II did not push on with the work of centralization begun by the Catholic sovereigns. During his reign, Spain turned back completely to the Middle Ages. For Philip II's ideals were those of his great-grandmother, Isabella the Catholic, who belonged to the Middle Ages, as did her spiritual advisers, Torquemada and Cardinal Jiménez de Cisneros, though the mediaevalism of the latter was not untouched by the light of the Renaissance. In the *diarchy* or dual government, in which Ferdinand had personified the *raison d'état* and scepticism of the Renaissance, Isabella represented, with at most a slight tinge of humanism, those same mediaeval ideals which Philip II defended. Now, nothing survived of the Renaissance monarchy but its power, a power which was to be dedicated to the service of God "though the country perish"—Philip II's unstatesman-like formula, which Isabella had enunciated in similar terms a century before, and which was very different from any that Ferdinand the Catholic would have employed.

Philip II allowed the mediaeval political organization, which was not affected by the reforms of his predecessors, to remain in the various regions. Rather than abolish feudal privileges, he upheld them, even when the people clamoured for their abolition, as happened in the case of the despotic judicial tribunal of the *Veinte* at Saragossa, which was set up at the beginning of the twelfth century and which, even in 1589, sentenced two men to the gallows without the form of a trial. True, the institution of the *Justicia Mayor* of Aragon lost its independence during the reign of Philip II, but this would not have happened without the disturbances due to the presence of Antonio Pérez, the King's Secretary, who, a fugitive and a rebel, took refuge in Saragossa. It was never Philip II's intention to abrogate this *fuero* which was, for the rest, of unmistakably mediaeval cast, since the function of the *Justicia* consisted in watching over the safety of the nobles. The fact is that, during the Middle Ages, especially in Aragon and Catalonia, liberty had a very restricted meaning; it was the privilege of a minority, compatible with the most outrageous oppression of the serfs. Hence, the egalitarian action of the absolute monarchy guaranteed the popularity of the prince and the triumph of the régime.

As we have seen, Philip II made no essential change in the political constitution of Catalonia.

In Portugal, he scrupulously respected the principle of autonomy. The members of the supplanted dynasty—except Don Antonio, the Prior of Crato—continued to reside in the country, to enjoy absolute freedom of movement, and to receive liberal treatment, even to the extent of being allowed to retain the Portuguese Court. As far as any possible offence to the national sentiments of the Portuguese was concerned, the change of régime was reflected only in the presence of a Viceroy, a small detachment of Spanish troops and a few trifling taxes. The public offices continued to be filled by Portuguese. On no occasion did Philip II attempt to use the army and navy of Portugal in campaigns which did not directly concern that nation. Portugal administered her revenues without the intervention of the Crown. The colonies remained under the government and administration of the Portuguese.

In short, Portugal had no cause to complain of Philip II, whose policy erred, if anything, on the side of timidity, a failing to which this king, as we know, was excessively addicted, except where religious matters were concerned.

It has been said that Philip II did not extract from the union with Portugal all the advantage it promised for Spanish interests, and that he ought to have moved the Court to Lisbon. There may be some foundation for the first reproach; there is none for the second. From time immemorial the Portuguese had been educated by their ruling classes in hatred for Castile (and the Castilians, stupidly, in contempt for Portugal); and the union called, therefore, for a very light touch on the part of Spaniards. Philip II, realizing this, was careful to take no steps that might wound the hyper-sensitiveness of the Portuguese.

The fusion of both States, as yet restricted in range, did not prejudice the interests of Portugal—quite the contrary. Philip II gave a new impetus to Spanish commerce by abolishing the fiscal frontiers between the two kingdoms; he planned to make the river Tagus navigable from Toledo to Lisbon; he waged war on mendicity, with appreciable results; he improved public administration and completed the revision of the Portuguese legal code, recasting it in a connected whole.

Under his reign, Portugal continued to enjoy the benefits of union with none of the disadvantages. But after the defeat of the Invincible Armada in 1588, Spain began to slide down the slope which led to her military and political eclipse, and what prestige and success had knit together, failure and penury were to sever.

So long as Spain maintained her relevant position in war and diplomacy, the acute diversity of regional policies and administrations, that is, the weak penetration of the idea of national unity, did not seriously worry the monarchy. But the rapid decline of Spanish power in Europe suddenly brought to the forefront the problem of the effective unity of the nation.

Spain was constantly at war with France, a uniform power, based on a strong centralized government. The vastness of the Spanish possessions everywhere—all of them coveted by young

States desirous of increasing their wealth and power—imposed on Spain willy-nilly a war without truce. Since the union of the Crowns of Aragon and Castile, Aragonese-Catalan policy in the Mediterranean in the past had already complicated Castile's task in the wars by forcing her to reconquer or keep a guard on the territories of Naples, Sicily, Sardinia and Roussillon; while the traditional rivalry of Aragon and Catalonia with France forced the Catholic sovereigns to seek alliances in the north and centre of Europe. Hence, the marriage of Joanna, the daughter of Ferdinand and Isabella, to the Archduke of Austria, Philip the Handsome. The territories which the Hapsburgs and Burgundians brought into the new combination of States made the intervention of Spain in the continental wars more than ever unavoidable. There was certainly nothing capricious in the direction taken by Spanish interests, though it might be true to say that, when the Imperial Crown of Germany devolved upon Charles I of Spain, a new factor arose to multiply Spanish comitments in Europe. But the most important fact was that, once the union of Aragon and Castile had been consummated, French imperialism dragged Spain into the alliance with the northern countries and Central Europe, and vice versa.

The interminable wars in which Spain found herself involved in the fifteenth, sixteenth and seventeenth centuries originated, therefore, either in the need to preserve the heritage of the Crown of Aragon in the Mediterranean and France, or in the imperialistic designs of Ferdinand the Catholic (shared equally by Isabella in a national sense), or in the defence of anti-Reformation religious ideals. These wars, added to the hazards and labours of the discovery and colonization of the West Indies, rapidly exhausted the energies of Spain, and particularly those of Castile. But we are not, as has been supposed, confronted by enterprises and adventures which Castile, in pursuit of a policy and ideals peculiar to herself, imposed on the rest of Spain.

We have already seen how the interests of the Crown of Aragon and Catalonia diverted the strength of Castile into the Mediterranean and continental whirlpool. As regards the wars of religion, the Basques, the Aragonese, the Catalans and the Portuguese were as ardent in their militant championship of the Catholic Church as were the Castilians. The defence of Catholicism was a nation-wide ideal.

In spite of this, the existence of local privileges and individualisms, due to a regional organization on mediaeval lines, threw almost all the burden on Castile. No other region contributed a fair and just proportion of men and money to the wars which were overshadowing the Spanish State; as if it were Castile who was always seeking the wars and as if only a purely Castilian or dynastic interest was involved in them. The Catalans systematically resisted any attempt to tax them, refused to allow the King of Spain's troops to enter Catalan territory, professed to disinterest themselves in the struggle with France (so long as Catalonia was not invaded) and tolerated the functionaries of the Crown with a very bad grace. The Basques and the Aragonese adopted the same tone. Vizcaya, Navarre, Aragon, Catalonia, Valencia, Majorca, showed themselves, through their organs of government, through their Cortes, their Councils, their *Diputaciones*, their *Juntas*, exceedingly sensitive to anything which would diminish the mediaeval tradition of independence, already anachronistic and untenable.

This absence of solidarity among peoples whose moral, political and economic interests were, whether they desired it or not, closely entwined, revealed itself at its crudest when the critical situation of Spain in Europe and the bankruptcy of the nation forced the rulers to adopt heroic measures. In those conditions, it was impossible for the Spanish State to confront its innumerable and powerful enemies abroad; and there were not lacking those who, in pondering the causes of Spain's weakness, attributed it chiefly to the atavistic mediaevalism (which in some cases amounted to the primitiveness of savages) in which certain regions lived and had their being. It was discovered that, as far as national unity was concerned, everything was still to do; and it was agreed that a new and decisive impetus to the work of unification was urgently needed.

The principal author of this policy was the Conde-duque de Olivares, dictator under Philip IV (1621–65). Olivares realized better than anyone the disastrous results of the mutual isolation and ignorance in which the provinces of the monarchy lived. And, in fact, it was deplorable that each region should look upon other Spaniards as foreigners. Moreover Olivares attributed the major part of France's diplomatic and military victories to her energetic centralization. He perceived, no doubt, that he was fighting Richelieu (whom he admired and desired to imitate) in conditions of manifest inferiority. The Spanish dictator would have liked to do in Spain what his rival did in France. But the France of Richelieu was on the crest of the wave, while Spain, since the last ten years of the reign of Philip II, had been rapidly sinking into the trough.

Olivares' idea was to make an end of all regional autonomies, combining a show of force with diplomacy. This was the advice he gave Philip IV in the *Memoria* he submitted to him in 1621. In this document the favourite made specific proposals for multiplying and stressing the relations between the peoples of the Peninsula, so that they might know and respect each other and cease to regard one another with suspicion. It was essential, he said, that Catalans, Castilians, Aragonese, Portuguese, Basques, etc., should all share in the functions of the State. Catalans must be attracted to Castile, and the doors of Catalonia must be opened to Castilians. Olivares' aspiration was, in short, to fuse the nations of the Peninsula into one great Spanish community, each one of whose component parts should be conscious of the reality of overriding Spanish interests common to all the regions. In the same document Olivares elaborated this policy with reference to Portugal. The King ought to pay more frequent visits to the Portuguese, give them offices and honours in Castile, choose from among their upper classes Army chiefs, Palace officials, Viceroys, Ambassadors. At the same time he ought to employ a certain number of Castilians in Portugal.

Olivares hastened to put his theories on national unity into practice and sent the Marqués de Castel-Rodrigo to Portugal to carry out his views. Representatives of the Portuguese nobility, clergy and cities arrived at Madrid to begin negotiations. There was talk of establishing the Cortes of Portugal and Castile. The Council of Castile which dealt with the problems of the two kingdoms was to be replaced by another council, under the presidency of a Portuguese, the Archbishop of Evora.

In seventeenth-century Spain, the attempt to achieve the political and administrative centralization of the Peninsula was, however, a needlessly hazardous proceeding. The favourable moment for this policy had passed. Philip IV inspired neither the devotion nor the fear which the Catholic sovereigns, Charles V and Philip II, had successively inspired. Olivares was, not to mince words, a tyrant and his Government intolerably unjust; and his foreign policy, which persisted in pursuing objectives that no longer interested the people, had the defect of being ruinous from a short-term point of view, besides being outmoded and unpopular.

At that moment the monarchy lacked the moral and material force to preserve the political unity of the Peninsula and, given the disasters abroad and the formidable discontent at home, the only suitable policy would have been to discover a method to avoid disturbing the insecure bonds uniting Portugal and Catalonia with the national State. To maintain the existing unity, not to accentuate it, would already have been a triumph for the Government. But to bring up the question of local autonomies (though there was much in them that was abusive), when the moral and physical authority of the State was touching its nadir, was obviously to stimulate the centrifugal impulse which had been encouraged by defeat abroad and misgovernment at home.

It was, in short, the only moment since the days of the Catholic sovereigns when [elementary prudence counselled the renunciation of the policy of centralization. But this very situation— defeat in the wars, national bankruptcy, disorder at home— which diminished the ascendancy of the central monarchy over the provinces, incited the Government of Philip IV to violate those privileges which prevented the King from obtaining men and money to defend the country.

Catalonia's rebellion in 1640 and the cruel twelve-years' civil war to which it led—during which the Catalans tried to set up an independent Republic and afterwards elected to become subjects of Louis XIII of France, a step they immediately regretted—this war, I repeat, had its immediate cause, not in the defence of local privileges, but in the ineptitude and intemperance of the central Government. The Catalan peasants rose to the cry of "*Visca 'l rei i muyra lo mal govern!*" (Long live the King and death to the bad Government!). In principle, therefore, Catalonia rebelled, not as a nation, but as a province of the Spanish monarchy. And when we consider the grievances (not all of them avoidable) which the Catalans suffered from the time when the King's troops encamped on their territory on their way to France until the rising became general, we can certainly find grounds to justify their conduct. Any other province would have reacted in similar circumstances, if not with equal violence, at least in the same way. Catalonia could bear no more.

In the dispute over the *fueros*, historical reason was on the side of the monarchy, but this advantage was more than offset by the obvious untimeliness of Olivares' attempt at centralization, aggravated by the dictatorial haughtiness with which it was introduced. Nor was the *fuerista* spirit now so intransigent that it would have excluded an agreement on the principal matters at issue. Before the rising the Catalans had made a prodigious effort in the war of Roussillon, in which they gave everything, men and money, with a generosity that made possible the first victories over the French. Afterwards Catalan troops were to fight against the separatists, their compatriots, under the royal banners. And even when the civil war had begun, the Catalans did not forget to dispatch an emissary to the Court,

368

begging the King to confirm, as usual, the election of the new *concelleres*—no doubt so as to put on record that they were at war with the Government but not with the State, just as the villagers had shouted: "Long live the King and death to the bad Government!"

These and other highly significant incidents tend to show that separatism was an offshoot of govermental imprudence. Olivares placed undue reliance on force; not only did he not fear the insurrection, but he was even prepared to welcome it as a pretext for suppressing the *fueros*—a perverse policy of reprisals which led him in Portugal and Catalonia to abuse a force which the Spanish State did not possess and which destroyed in the bud any fruit which the negotiations on unity might have borne.

The Catalans showed themselves even more favourably disposed to the monarchy than the Portuguese. But in Portugal itself, the power of the Crown had struck roots. The centralist party (to give it another name than "Spanish party") was very strong there. It included "many grandees and important persons of the kingdom", among them the Archbishop of Braga, the Marques de Villarreal, the Duque de Caminha, the Conde de Valde Reys, the Conde de Castañeira, the Conde de Armamar, General Francisco de Mello, Commander of the Spanish army in Flanders. Already the fact that though Spain and her monarchy had sunk so low, there should be Portuguese nobles, clergy and citizens ready to discuss with Olivares the question of the organized unity of both kingdoms, pointed to a state of affairs which, carefully handled in more opportune times, would have led to fusion being achieved, at least within certain limits.

Doña Margarita of Savoy, Duchess of Mantua, a woman of extraordinary intelligence and great tact, who had so discreetly filled the rôle of Vicereine in Lisbon, understood the position of Portugal as few people did; and her conviction, which she expressed to Philip IV, was that "the loss of the Portuguese Crown was attributable solely to that man (Olivares) and his followers and friends".

The impulse which estranged both Portugal and Catalonia from the Spanish State in 1640 was one and the same, provoked by the odious government of Olivares. But in the Portuguese protest there was from the beginning a separatist urge, which the Catalans did not feel. For Portugal had preserved her own dynasty (which had been lying low, awaiting the opportunity to return to the throne) and counted, moreover, on what had always saved her—or ruined her, according to different points of view—the help of foreign troops (French, Dutch, and English);

while Catalonia, who could not exist now as a mediaeval Republic, soon found herself faced with the disquieting alternative of becoming French, and France was more centralist than Castile. Besides which, there was an anti-French tradition in Catalonia which was not slow in flowering; the towns ended by opening their gates to the troops of Philip IV and shutting them to the French.

The result was, therefore, that the Catalan insurrection of 1640 was not, in its inception, a separatist movement, but a reaction against misgovernment, and misgovernment also meant, as I have pointed out, the attempt to abolish autonomy at that instant and by such and such warlike and pseudo-diplomatic proceedings. The seventeenth century revealed anew the character of the Catalan tradition within the Spanish State. Catalonia has never been separatist, except as a reaction against an intolerable government or under the spur of the disintegration of the State. The mere threat to her *fueros* had never made warriors of the industrious Catalans.

Philip IV did not abuse his military victory over the separatists and, save for some precautionary measures, left the principality in the enjoyment of its ancient privileges; which was to add to the error of provoking civil war, the error of not taking advantage of its logical consequences. But Catalonia was not a static entity, insensible to the passage of time; and within Catalan society there fermented a social revolution which was pertinaciously working against the particularist tendencies inherited from the Middle Ages. This imponderable was not the least of the threats which fed the mistrust of the *fueristas*, who represented reaction, or rather, that attitude of surprised alarm which is common to all societies menaced by the simple passing of the days. The out-and-out decadence of the autonomous institutions, in Catalonia and outside Catalonia, presaged their end and weakened the hold of traditionalism. The most dangerous enemies of this traditionalism, which appeared to be liberal and was, as I say, reactionary at bottom, were the new social classes of the Catalan region itself which emerged as a challenge to privileges of all kinds. Catalonia's final position as a province of the Spanish monarchy eliminated the possibility of her remaining indefinitely under the national State with institutions that pre-dated political unity. The King could not be sovereign while in Catalonia another sovereignty disputed his prerogatives. Either he was also king of the Catalans, or he was not king at all. Either Catalonia broke away and, in that case, it might be possible for her to exist fully as a nation, or, if secession was impossible, she would have to agree to yield as much of her nationhood as was incompatible with the unity of the State.

This was the problem, however much Philip IV tried to obviate it; and the problem came to a head, naturally, with the disappearance of the *fueros*, the inexorable corollary of the fact that Catalonia had to continue to be Spanish because history so ordained. As we shall see later, the regionalists were quick to grasp this reality, and the long and the short of it was that local privileges died a natural death.

Inasmuch as the question of the *fueros* did not depend solely on the will of the monarch, Philip IV, by respecting them, kept the conflict alive for his successors. The constitutional anarchy was prolonged for another fifty years, but as soon as a new crisis of the State arose, the problem of the survival or disappearance of the ancient privileges came to the forefront again. During the years 1707–16, Philip V at last put into practice the designs of Olivares. We must now see how this came about.

The causes of the War of the Spanish Succession at the beginning of the eighteenth century are well known. Charles II of Spain died without issue, and the Hapsburgs and the Bourbons each put forward a claimant to his throne, the Archduke Charles, son of the Emperor, and the Duke of Anjou, grandson of Louis XIV. The dispute lasted for nine years, and in the course of it it became clear that Catalonia, Aragon and Valencia, that is, the provinces of the ancient Crown of Aragon, enthusiastically supported the Austrian candidate, while Castile no less fervently supported the Duke of Anjou. Let us try to explain this curious and suggestive phenomenon.

The fact that Castile rejected the Archduke can be readily understood, since "the misgovernment of Philip III and Philip IV, the levity of the Queen Regent, the nullity of Charles II and the avarice of his wife Doña Mariana, had made the name of German odious". In the course of the war, the adherence of Castile to the Bourbon was assured by the alliance of the Austrian claimant with Holland and England, both of them Protestant and *heretic* nations. The reactionaries, therefore, embraced wholeheartedly the party of Philip V, and as the Bourbons counted beforehand on the sympathy of the Liberals, who were already admirers of France, hardly one heart, outside Catalonia, Aragon and Valencia, beat for the son of the Emperor.

Why did the provinces which had belonged to the Crown of Aragon choose the Austrian in preference to the Frenchman? Did they fear for their *fueros*, in view of the reputed liking of the

Bourbons for a centralized monarchy? This does not appear to have been the principal reason for the hostility of these provinces to the new monarch, since Philip V, when he visited Barcelona in 1702, did not give the impression that he meant to abrogate local privileges. His contact with the Catalan Cortes was not marked by cordiality, but this had been the case with former monarchs; and it was perhaps to quieten Catalan fears on this score that the Bourbon king granted Catalonia new privileges, which the Barcelonians later rejected, making a public bonfire of the charters. For the rest, Catalonia had suffered as much as Castile from the confusion of Charles II's reign and was not going to shed any tears over his passing.

I think that the chief motive for the attitude of the Aragonese, Catalans and Valencians was the traditional dislike of the subjects of the Crown of Aragon for the neighbouring power. This inveterate hatred—today, no doubt, quenched—was then intensified by recent events which were still very much alive in the minds of all Catalans. In the last twenty years of the seventeenth century the Franco-Spanish war had been waged, on Spanish soil, in Catalonia, where terrific struggles had taken place and where Barcelona had heroically endured a fifty-two-day siege. The weapons with which the Catalans had fought the French were still smoking when Louis XIV dispatched his grandson to the throne of Spain.

The truth is that Catalonia, who, in an ecstasy of despair, had enfeoffed herself to France in 1640, reaffirmed her Spanish destiny by her actions in the war of the dynasties. That former moment of weakness was, therefore, something that she did not wish to be reminded of, and in the centralization decreed by the victorious monarch, Philip V, we cannot but see, in the last analysis, the irrevocable consequence of Catalonia's reaffirmation of her Spanish status.

It is possible that the francophobia of the provinces which rose in support of the Austrian Archduke influenced Philip V when he decreed the abolition of the *fueros*. But there is no doubt that, in so decreeing, the new king was acting like a prince of his time and not like an aggrieved Frenchman. In 1707 he had already abolished the privileges of Aragon and Valencia, basing his action on other *fueros*, those belonging to the sovereignty of the Crown, to which is reserved, in the words of the Royal Decree, "the passing and annulment of laws which, *in view of the inconstancy of the times and the mutability of customs*, We might well alter, even without the grave and well-founded motives and circumstances which today make such a course advisable".

The King deferred modification of the Catalan institutions until the end of the war. In 1714 he dissolved the *Consejo de Ciento*, the *Diputación general* and the military or noble *Brazo*, replacing them by a *Real Junta Superior de Justicia y Gobierno* consisting of six Catalan citizens. The reforms were completed by the *Nueva Planta* decree (January 1716) which abolished the remaining political privileges. The Viceroys disappeared and were replaced by the Captains-General.

Nevertheless centralization was very far from being general and absolute. Catalonia kept the greater part of her penal laws, while her civil and commercial laws, her monetary and taxation systems, her exemption from military service, and other no less individual *fueros* remained intact. Only in the administration of justice did the King insist on the use of the Spanish tongue.

Political and criminal repression in Catalonia, on the other hand, took on a draconian severity. Among other unpopular measures, which are still resented by the Catalans, Philip V ordered the University of Barcelona to be transferred to the provincial town of Cervera, apparently with the object of avoiding the disturbances of students in the capital.

In general, autonomy, already very languid, as I have said before, was much less vigorous in practice than in law. For this reason, the consigning of the Cortes of Valencia and Aragon to the archives of history met with no obstacle. In 1709 the deputies of these ancient provinces mingled with the deputies of Castile in the Cortes of Madrid, and in 1724 the Catalan cities also sent their representatives for the first time, by royal privilege.

In reality Philip V confined himself to enforcing a political unity which Catalonia could not for long reject without hurt to herself. In this way Catalonia was finally compelled to assume the full responsibilities of her Spanish mission. If her mediaeval privileges were curtailed, she was not now excluded from other benefits. For more than one reason (not all of them comprehensible to us), the subjects of the Crown of Aragon had been refused a share in the trade with America. Philip V raised this absurd embargo. In 1720 regulations were laid down for the exportation of Catalan manufactures to Spanish America. The decrees of the new monarch resolved themselves into greater liberty of movement for the Catalan *bourgeoisie* and a check on the power of the nobility. In this way the democratic revolution begun centuries before was brought to a head. It was Philip V who abolished the barbarous power of life and death which the nobles in Aragon exercised over their serfs. The absolute monarchy, in the person of Charles V, had authorized the people to use the sword to defend themselves against the nobles. The grandson of Louis XIV was now forbidding the nobility to arm themselves with this symbol of sovereignty and class power.

With the new reforms, Catalonia lost her political autonomy, but retained her cultural and juridical autonomy. The Crown did not propose a policy of assimilation, and the differential factor, in its most noble and substantial aspect, was recognized. For the rest, as I said before, neither in Catalonia nor in the other regions affected by the change did centralization stifle any vital fount of genius peculiar to any of them.

Philip V laid the foundation-stone of the new Catalonia, of the modern Catalan *bourgeoisie*. In so far as this metamorphosis was due to the monarch, the Catalan *bourgeoisie* was in debt to him and his successors, Ferdinand VI and Charles III, for its place of authority in the economic world of Spain at the end of the eighteenth century, the beginning of the Catalan renaissance, to which Catalonia owes, first, her mercantile and industrial wealth and next, the revival of her language and culture.

CHAPTER X

## CATALAN NATIONALISM

THOSE SPANIARDS WHO, when the unfortunate Charles II was on his death-bed, thought that only a change of dynasty could save the nation, and who consequently supported the Duke of Anjou in the hope of obtaining radical reforms, were not mistaken. Though the dynastic and imperialistic policy of Louix XIV brought unforgettable disasters to Spain abroad, the first three Bourbons to sit on the Spanish throne were acceptable kings and most of their Ministers—almost all of them of humble origin—have left an illustrious name in the history of Spain.

The reforms were quickly reflected in the volume of the population, which had been progressively declining since the sixteenth century, until at the close of the seventeenth century it was reduced to 5,700,000 inhabitants. Under Philip V the contrary process had already begun, and at the end of the eighteenth century, in 1789, Spain had almost doubled her population, which had now reached the figure of 10,541,221. This presupposed an increase in economic activities, and, in fact, the monarchy of enlightened despotism realized its most fruitful effort in this domain. The *Sociedades Económicas de Amigos del País* (Economic Societies of Friends of the Country), founded half-way through the century, effectively helped to interest the nation in questions which until then had excited a minimum of curiosity among Spaniards. Commercial companies were founded to exploit the wealth and markets of Spanish America. Industries, especially the textile industries, were actively supported. It was here, in the textile industry, that the encouragement and protection of the nation's labour left their most permanent mark; so much so that, if only by reference to this branch of production, we could speak of the industrial renaissance of Spain. This was made possible by a concerted lowering of taxation, the importation without customs dues of all machinery, the annulment of the prohibitive and restrictive laws of the sixteenth and seventeenth centuries which manacled industry and restricted the weavers' liberty to instal as many workshops as they could and to vary their fabrics at will; in other words, the abolition of the ancient laws of the guilds and complete liberty for the textile industries. Most of these decrees were passed in the reign of Charles III (1759–88).

At the same time the rulers of the eighteenth century were interested in encouraging the cultivation of cotton in the Spanish Indies. The Governors were urged to promote this class of production and exhorted to set aside for it the most suitable land, even by parcelling it out, as in Puerto Rico in 1778.

None of the hindrances and historical accidents which since the fifteenth century, had deprived Catalonia of her economic personality and, with it, one of the most salient features of her genius—the spontaneous aptitude for industry and commerce—now existed. On the contrary, the creative vein of this rich and industrious region was now, in the eighteenth century, being stimulated, flattered and protected.

It should be noted that no Spanish region derived more benefit from the industrial policy of the first Bourbons than Catalonia. Unparalleled economic privileges were reserved for the Catalans, and where the importation of cotton from the Spanish possessions in America was concerned, they had exclusive rights which amounted practically to a monopoly. The *Cedulario Índico* of the *Archivo Histórico Nacional* contained copious proofs of the favours dispensed to the Catalans by the Ministers of Ferdinand VI and Charles III. In 1752, for example, the factories of the principality of Catalonia were granted in general "complete exemption from all customs duties on all cotton imported from America".

Favoured by natural conditions and official protection, the great industrial tradition of Catalonia was being reborn. The Catalans rapidly acquired undisputed hegemony of the cotton industry of Spain. In fact, Catalonia was the only region of Spain which carried out its industrial revolution, becoming in the nineteenth century a miniature Lancashire. In 1792 the looms of Barcelona employed 80,000 operatives. Reus, with its seventy-two factories and workshops, was the second textile city of the principality, and Arenis de Mar, Mataró, Vich, Martorell, Gerona, La Riba, Sabadell equally foreshadowed the future industrial power of Catalonia and the incalculable part her *bourgeoisie* was to play in Spanish politics.

Naturally the Catalan industrial revolution, which began in the eighteenth century and continued during the nineteenth and the first twenty years of the twentieth centuries, was accompanied by considerable political and spiritual consequences. The first offspring of the change was nationalism, a sentiment that no social class in any epoch has felt so profoundly as the *bourgeoisie* of the nineteenth century.

Prompted by the budding spirit of nationalism, the intellectuals began to delve into the Catalan Middle Ages, seeking in past greatness and ancient glories the soul of Catalonia's buried nationality. Scholars began to extract from mediaeval chronicles and parchments the ingredients for the reconstruction of the literary and historical personality of Catalonia, the most important being, of course, the language. These were the origins of cultural Catalanism. Perhaps its earliest manifestations, at the end of the eighteenth and the beginning of the nineteenth centuries, were the *Sociedad Económica de Amigos del País* at Barcelona, and the historical works of Capmany.

With his *Memorias de Barcelona*, his *Práctica y Estilo de celebrar Cortes en Aragón, Cataluña y Valencia*, his *Historia de la Marina Catalana en la Edad Media*, Capmany revealed to his compatriots, without as yet any political premeditation, the past splendour of Catalonia. Yet the spirit of nationalism underlying these historical works already indicated the confused desire for regeneration which filled the Catalan burghers.

In 1833 the Catalan poet Buenaventura Carlos Aribau published an "Ode to the Fatherland", which is generally considered to be the first lyrical expression of Catalanism. Aribau wrote these romantic verses in Madrid, in the uncertain, maimed Catalan dialect which survived the "Castilianization"; it was symptomatic that they were published in a Barcelona periodical which flaunted the progressive and bourgeois title of *El Vapor*. Romanticism, with its nostalgia for local customs and traditions, here appears in intimate alliance with the machine, and reveals the origins, at once economic and ideal, of the Catalanist phenomenon, the child of a revolutionary and positivist epoch. In my view, this, and no other, is the significance of Aribau's poetic-patriotic venture.

The Catalan literary renaissance dawned, about 1840, with the learned Rubió y Ors. The language began to revive as an instrument of culture. The tentative linguistic approaches of the first Catalan romantics at the end of the eighteenth century became, in the *Gayter del Lobregat* of Rubió y Ors, a determined and conscious attempt to restore to the Catalan language its ancient nobility and richness.

In 1858 Antonio Bofarull published an anthology of young poets: *Los Trovadores nous*.

In the following year Milá y Fontanals rescued from the dust of oblivion the *joch florals* (floral games) or mediaeval poetic contests, and the Barcelona Municipality restored another of the Catalan intellectual traditions with marked success.

In 1860 the first newspaper was printed in Catalan, *Un troç de paper*, and the first literary review, *Lo Gay Saber*.

At the same time the Catalan language, refined and enriched with every successive endeavour, was finding its way into the theatre and a constellation of new playwrights, preceded by Federico Soler, were bringing onto the stage strongly realistic presentations of Catalan life and history, in both comic and tragic vein. Jacinto Verdaguer, Guimerá, Rusiñol, and others less renowned, kept the new Catalan theatre at a high pitch of enthusiasm for several decades.

Judged in any light, the Catalan *bourgeois* revolution had much to its credit in the reconstruction of the language, in philology, in poetry and in the theatre, that is, in literature. But Catalonia's self-assertion in literature was not exempt at times from a certain puerile and unjust flavour of emulation. The new Catalan cultural movement disinterested itself daily more and more in "Spanish" culture, which the more radical Catalanists treated in most cases with the indifference of *nouveaux riches*. Catalan centres of literary and historical research had no contact at all with corresponding societies in the rest of Spain. Catalonia tended to make the archives of the Crown of Aragon her spiritual refuge, and from these archives a biased erudition resurrected more than one frightful mummy, especially in matters relating to history.

It was essential that if cultural Catalanism was to be a genuine enrichment of Spanish culture, Spanish[1] ought not be allowed to fall into desuetude in Catalonia. If the renascent Catalan language was going to compete with the idiom of Cervantes, with the language of all Spaniards, it was obvious that its resurrection at the expense of Spanish in a region where the latter had found many noble exponents, would impoverish the national culture. Catalan culture ought to add to the whole, not subtract from it.

There was an obvious risk that Catalanism would not manifest itself solely in the cultural area but would spread to the political battleground, that is, that in the sphere of the State also the Catalan *bourgeoisie* would try to exhume the mediaeval institutions of Catalonia. The lucubrations of a precocious nationalist Press soon made it clear that the peril existed. The history of the Peninsula, so the tale ran, was one long proof of Catalan superiority stifled by Castilian imperialism. Castile was represented as the secular oppressor and Catalonia as the victim, oppressed for centuries by Castile—a strange way of interpreting history and a political optical illusion which was to lead the Catalanists to pose their problem in a false light. According to this theory, San Vicente Ferrer, a Valencian, who to all intents and purposes placed Don Fernando de Antequera on the throne of Aragon, Juan II of Aragon and Ferdinand the Catholic (the first reformers of the mediaeval political constitution of Catalonia) were imperialist Castilians. With equal lack of understanding, the universal revolution of the Renaissance which brought to birth, not only in Spain, but in the whole of Europe, a unifying monarchy, was ignored. If Catalonia was anyone's victim, she was the victim of historical circumstances, not of Castile; and her conflict, if it existed, was not a conflict with Castile—a heterogeneous entity, made up of antagonistic social classes—but with history. The Catalanists were attacking a Castilian phantom, like Don Quixote fighting windmills in the belief that they were giants.

However, the best intellects among the Catalanists did not think along these lines, nor was such a frivolous interpretation of Spanish history taken seriously; but these unfortunate ideas prepared the ground for the tremendous political complication of the twentieth century.

The political drama did not begin till the latter end of the nineteenth century, and in its gestation there entered a number of factors which must be minutely analysed if we want to understand the Catalan problem in its present phase.

[1] See previous chapter for note on the national idiom.

In the nineteenth century the ideas of the epoch were not favourable to the task of finding an adequate place for Catalonia within the new political constitution of Spain. The Liberals who directed the constitutional revolution in Madrid did not halt at barriers but rushed on the work of centralization to an extent that was quite ill-advised, particularly as regards Catalonia. From 1822–45 the Catalans witnessed the disappearance, as if by magic, of the remnants of their autonomy. The *liberties* left to them by Philip V vanished and Catalonia was reduced to four provinces of the Spanish State under an equal number of Governors.

The speed with which the last vestiges of Catalan autonomy were suppressed in Madrid and the celerity with which the constitution of liberty, equality and fraternity was applied, point by point, to this region (when Catalonia, under the stimulus of similar principles, was preparing her rebirth as a nation), betrayed an erroneous view of the historical position of Catalonia in the Peninsula; and here dwelt one of the principal causes of the imminent collision between the national State and the Catalans. The Madrid politicians had forgotten that to impose on Catalonia uniformity with other regions or peoples of Spain was not possible without doing her great violence and sterilizing her genius. The difficulty of appreciating this must have been unsurmountable to nineteenth-century Spanish politicians. No doubt the widespread decadence of Catalonia and her conformism in the eighteenth century had created the illusion in the mind of the Liberal legislator and of the absolute monarch that she was now, or had always been, a mere province of the monarchy. Granted the immanence of Catalan nationality, the mission of the Spanish statesman—Catalan and non-Catalan—was to discover a special régime into which Catalonia could fit without detriment to national unity.

For Catalonia was a nation, but the Catalans were Spaniards. Thus did the founders of political Catalanism themselves conceive the situation. Valentín Almirall remarks: "Catalonia is part of the Peninsula, since she is separated from France by the barrier of the Pyrenees; and therefore, geographically speaking, Catalonia must be Spanish. Moreover, the relations which she has maintained for centuries with the other Spanish regions have created bonds of interest and mutual affection which it would be almost impossible to break. The manufacturing industry of Catalonia is almost the only one existing in the nation and finds its natural market in the Spanish agricultural districts which in turn supply Catalonia with what she does not produce and use her as an outlet for surplus products.

"The affection which unites the different regions of Spain is so deep-seated, and so strong the reciprocity of interests, that these sentiments have never been diminished or destroyed either by the measures dictated by the central Government, of which the Catalans, like other Spaniards, have been victims, or by the passing rivalries which the mania for unification in the interests of the centre has sometimes succeeded in arousing in these regions.

"The Catalans are, therefore, as Spanish, generally speaking, as the inhabitants of the other regions of Spain, and this not only out of sentiment but at the dictates of reason. Given our geographical situation and our historical antecedents, we cannot be anything else but Spaniards."[1]

These two incontrovertible facts—the existence of a Catalan nation and the reality of her historic Spanish destiny—contain the elements of a constitutional conflict of extraordinary originality—a vital and complicated drama. The problem has no equivalent outside Spain; and those Catalans who consider themselves an oppressed minority (with evident injustice to the personality of Catalonia), like those who compare the vicissitudes of their nation with those of other modern nations, fall into the error of not recognizing the singularity of the Catalan case in Europe or—what is equally important—in Spain. Catalonia in Spain, as Almirall tacitly says, is something very different from the Ukraine in Poland, from Croatia in Yugoslavia, from Scotland or Wales in the United Kingdom, or even Ireland when she was under English domination. The difference is so palpable that it is not necessary to discuss it further.

Almirall's thesis can be completed by pointing out that the geographical, ethnical, moral and economic unity of the Iberian Peninsula is so precise and perfect that political unity cannot be disturbed without portentous consequences to all the Spanish peoples. Spain is an entity formed by a fraternity of multiple material and spiritual interests, common to all her peoples; and this entity does not allow of secessions save at the price of enormous damage to those breaking away and those remaining.

Political Catalanism seemed, at its birth, to be well aware of these axioms, and it must be said to its credit that its most outstanding leaders never ignored them.

That is to say that, in a Spain blessed with good government and with an adequate knowledge of her past, the task of fitting Catalonia into the national framework without loss of her

[1] *L'Espagne telle qu'elle est.* Paris, 1887.

personality would have been relatively feasible. But in nineteenth-century Spain, who could tell what he was about? It is not surprising, therefore, that in conditions so little favourable to the systematic reorganization of the nation, the Catalan problem should have become distorted in Madrid and Barcelona.

Political Catalanism had for protagonists two quite distinct social movements. The Catalan industrial revolution gave birth to *bourgeois* Liberal nationalism, which in Catalonia was supported by a middle class endowed with a vigour that the moral Liberalism of Madrid lacked. (In Castile, Liberalism was a phenomenon, a reflex, as we know, from outside; not the creation of the industrial and mercantile *bourgeoisie*, which did not exist there. Hence its eminently moral, non-economic character, which is nowhere more apparent than in the name *serviles* (lackeys), given by the Madrid Liberals at the beginning of the century to the enemies of the Constitution.)

The march of political Catalanism began at the moment when the Catalan *bourgeoisie* celebrated its coming-of-age, so to speak, as a class. The definitive formation of this capitalist social class in Catalonia coincided inevitably with the accession to power of the Castilian-Andalusian landed oligarchy which had just founded in Madrid the agrarian State of the Restoration. The decisive factors in the new Castilian-Catalan dissidence (an inadequate but intelligible way of describing the conflict) began to take effect, and political Catalanism, whose ruling class was the *bourgeoisie*, must be considered, in its most serious aspect, as the product of the historic rivalry between the industrial interests predominating in Catalonia and the agrarian interests prevailing in the rest of Spain.

The founder of *bourgeois* political Catalanism was Valentin Almirall. Almost the whole of Almirall's political work, both written and empirical, is comprised, chronologically, in the eighties of the nineteenth century. In 1879 this restless organizer launched the first political newspaper in the Catalan language, the *Diari Català*; in 1881 he published *España tal cual es*; in 1882 he founded the first Catalanist political society, the *Centre Català*; in 1885 he submitted to the Crown a document drawing attention to the moral and material interests of Catalonia; in 1886 he brought out his doctrinal work *Lo Catalanismo*.

*España tal cual es* contained the essence of political Catalanism, for in this book the Catalan *bourgeoisie* made for the first time a reasoned statement of its incompatibility with the Castilian-Andalusian oligarchy. Almirall set down in black and white

381

one of the most exact and implacable descriptions ever written of the Restoration oligarchy, its methods of government, its representative personalities, the political atmosphere of Spain.

From the first moment of its entry on the scene, *bourgeois* Catalanism was moved by two ambitions, an affirmative one where Catalonia was concerned, consisting of the desire to take over the regional government; and a negative one where Madrid was concerned, to put a distance between Catalonia and a sickly nation subjugated by the agrarians. In short, the Catalan *bourgeoisie* was posing the question of its total emancipation. Its Catalanism was the romantic and positivist revolutionary nationalism of the epoch, driven to extremes by the *mal govern* or bad government of the oligarchy.

Another Catalanist social movement had to be reckoned with—the peasant movement, Catalanist because it was traditionalist, and ultramontane. While the Catalan *bourgeoisie* sought in the past the roots of the liberty it needed to emancipate itself as a class, rural ultramontanism also repaired to the mediaeval springs in pursuit of a justification for its present existence, menaced by the Liberal revolution.

The most eminent leader of traditionalist Catalanism was the famous Bishop of Vich, Torras y Bages, author of *Tradicio Catalana*, the doctrinal body of this movement. It hardly seems necessary to point out that these ultra-Catholic Catalanists were an echo of Carlism. When Carlism was defeated by the central oligarchy, the Catalan traditionalists, like the Basques, renounced universal absolutism, or the idea of imposing on all Spaniards an absolute king under the thumb of the clergy, in favour of regional tradition. This *volte-face* was logical. Once the Carlist hope had vanished and an anti-Carlist, Liberal Government was set up in Madrid (though its Liberalism was that of the oligarchy), nothing was more natural than that the Catalan ecclesiastics, or many of them, who had fought for Don Carlos not less fanatically than the Basque clergy, should take refuge politically in regionalism. And in politics the countryside thought as the Church thought. It will be remembered that in the Carlist war, the Catalan cities had supported Isabel II and the rural districts the Pretender—as everywhere in Spain where Carlism had been able to keep itself in being as a military force thanks to the geographical conditions of the country. Clerical traditionalism and *bourgeois* Liberalism continued to be at loggerheads in Catalonia, though the acrimony of the conflict was somewhat mitigated by the need to wage war on the common enemy, the Government of Madrid, which was unacceptable

382

to the former Catalan Carlists for reasons we are already familiar with, and no less energetically repudiated by the new capitalists on the grounds we have just stated. This made possible within certain limits the co-existence of traditionalism and *bourgeois* Liberalism in Catalonia, unlike the state of affairs in the Basque country where the Basque *bourgeoisie* was not nationalist or regionalist, no doubt because of the fact that industry had not so strong a hold there as in Catalonia, that the industrialization of Vizcaya had started later, and that Basque capitalism was chiefly financial, the greater part of the capital being distributed throughout Spain. But although traditionalist Catalanism had some importance at first, it was the industrial *bourgeoisie* of the cities which nourished and directed the Catalanist political movement.

Catalan nationalism, an essentially *bourgeois* ideal, as emotional as only the Catalan middle class can be, did not enlist in its ranks the proletariat who were oppressed in the factories by that same social class which, when it demanded a free Catalonia, meant, as later events will show, only its own freedom as a class *vis-à-vis* the other social classes, whether Catalan or no. The nationalist oriflamme of the *bourgeoisie* was regarded with deep suspicion by the proletariat which followed, first, Pi y Margall with his anarchist federalism and, later, Lerroux, radical, anti-clerical and *españolista* in the service of the central oligarchy.

The Catalan *haute bourgeoisie* made a mistake then that was fatal to its cause from the historical point of view. This social class was born without driving force and ambition as Spaniards, lacking the universalist spirit. Catalanism, if it was not to be an unattainable ideal, ought to have been the beginning of, or prelude to, a great Catalan movement for the regeneration of Spain, and, for this, the Catalan *bourgeoisie* would not have lacked connections and support outside Catalonia. In every region of Spain there existed, as we know, the shadow of an industrial and mercantile middle class, without sufficient power to overthrow the oligarchy, but still the natural ally and potential instrument of Catalan capitalism. Only from Catalonia could the regenerating energy radiate which would make Spain a better nation. And this was understood by many Spaniards, not necessarily Liberals, among them Menéndez Pelayo, who saw in Barcelona "the great Mediterranean metropolis, erstwhile mistress of the Latin sea *dives opum studiisque asperrima belli*, destined perhaps by God to be the head and heart of regenerated Spain".[1]

But Catalanism confined its activities to carrying out in Catalonia a work which was in many ways admirable in the

[1] *Estudios de critica literaria*, 5th Series, p. 68.

sphere of culture and regional administration; but its good effects hardly extended beyond the Catalan provinces. The results of Catalanism were, as we shall see, unmistakably tragic for Spanish politics. Catalonia ended by becoming an irresistible agent of anarchy, of civil war, and, in no small measure, of corruption of the national policy. It simply happened that Catalan nationalism did not merge into imperialism, that it had no eyes for the infinite possibilities opening out to it in the Peninsula. Instead, Catalanism remained on the defensive, faint-hearted, terrified of Spain, from whom it tried to detach itself or to flee, when its mission was to breathe new life into her. When hostilities broke out with the centralist oligarchy, the Catalan *bourgeoisie*, instead of advancing, so to speak, on the enemy positions, dug itself in in its vulnerable provincial citadel, where it was soon beset by the two social forces which were its historic enemies—the great landowners of the South and the proletariat of Catalonia. In other words, the Catalan revolution could not stay on the line of the Ebro without failing politically and leaving the Spanish revolution incomplete. And, in fact, by falling back on a provincial nationalism, the *bourgeoisie* of Barcelona deprived the Spanish revolution of its most valuable instrument of construction, threw the public life of the nation into inextricable confusion and wasted in a sterile battle which lasted fifty years the splendid energies of the Catalan people and the energies of others as well.

We shall now see how this fruitless struggle began and developed.

Under the inspiration of the indefatigable Enrique Prat de la Riba, Catalanism, in its double cultural and political aspect, developed with surprising energy. Prat soon had a dynamic and eloquent collaborator in Francisco Cambó, then in his first youth. Both represented the *haute bourgeoisie* which, originally organized in the *Lliga de Catalunya* (1887), as distinct from the *petite bourgeoisie*, assembled all the elements of political Catalanism at the beginning of the twentieth century in a powerful party, the *Lliga Regionalista* (1900).

In Almirall, political Catalanism had not yet found the formula of its ultimate realization. Almirall's views on this head were diffuse, vacillating and, above all, conciliatory. His ideal was integration, "harmony between the generalizing spirit of Castile and the analytical character of the regions constituting the ancient Aragonese confederation, so as to produce the synthesis of a new organization of the State". This was bad literature, doubtful scientific truth, but as a policy, not so bad.

Prat de la Riba, for his part, elaborated a theory of Catalanism which advocated less political interpenetration with the rest of Spain. Prat was the great impresario of Catalan nationalism, a creative temperament, in which the intellectual and man of action balanced one another; but his talents were those of an organizer rather than a philosopher.

As soon as the ideal of the Catalan *bourgeoisie* became articulate and laboured to bring forth tangible concepts, the history of Spanish political thought was enriched by a truly *ridiculus mus*. Catalanism resolved itself into an ingenuous aspiration to re-unite the ancient Catalan-speaking territories into a federation loosely bound to an Iberian State, which would obviously include Portugal. This was Pi y Margall's federalism, though without its Socialist elements which naturally filled the Catalan *bourgeoisie* with alarm. The *bourgeoisie* regarded Pi as a doctrinaire, "a man who had bent all the force of his character to sustaining a thing so fragile as a little pamphlet by Proudhon". Proudhon ("property is robbery") had no place in Catalanism. Nevertheless, though it indulged in no Socialist or Anarchist flights of fancy, the federalism of Prat de la Riba was no less remote from the realms of Utopia than the federalism of Pi y Margall. The idea of annexing French provinces which once spoke Catalan, or an idiom of which Catalan is a dialect, was impracticable in the extreme. The reincorporation of Portugal into the body of Spain could also not be taken seriously. In short, the federation of the peoples who had lived together under the Aragonese Crown in Spain was not a feasible project. It was in failing to perceive this, in not discerning that Spain was struggling in a centrifugal crisis, of which Catalan nationalism was itself, in part, a symbol, that the roots of the *Iberista* delusion lay.

Iberian federalism has always been either the spring-board of demagogues hoping by some such grandiose proposal to escape from disagreeable present reality, or the speculation of muddled minds, of philosophers without a notion of Spain's real situation at home and abroad, or else the contrivance of wide-awake separatists ingeniously proposing the dislocation of what remains of the Spanish nation as the necessary preamble to the spontaneous future union of all the peoples of Spain.

The question needs clarifying. The federal idea is synonymous, I repeat, with approximation or union. To bear fruit and to be genuine, it must flow from prosperity and sympathy. Yet in Spain, it was born of desperation and antipathy. There could not, therefore, be a federal conscience in the Iberian Peninsula;

it did not exist, nor had it ever existed, least of all in any part of the discontented regions.

Various peoples, provinces or nations are mutually attracted by the magnet of a latent joint mission, feeling perhaps that in separation lies individual frustration. Or perhaps the greatness of one of them attracts the others to the shelter of its strength and prestige. That is to say, federalism is a centripetal movement, an integrating power whose motive force is sympathy. It is obviously the opposite of separatism, which originates in incompatibility or the disharmony that breeds antipathy. Federalism and separatism are mutually exclusive movements. It is impossible to feel repugnance for present union while at the same time professing a love for future federation. Hence, when national unity is broken, it is broken perhaps for all time, as in the case of Portugal.

The position of Spain in the nineteenth century and during the early years of the twentieth century was quite different from her position at the end of the fifteenth century, which facilitated the union of the kingdoms of Castile and Aragon and made possible the union of both Crowns, fused into one, with the Crown of Portugal in the last years of the sixteenth century. At the beginning of the nineteenth century we find a conglomeration of factors conspiring in favour of the dispersion of the Spanish peoples which still remained united and the maintenance of Portugal's separation. With the simulacrum of a Liberal revolution which began with the Cortes of Cadiz, the process of the nation's disintegration began. The reason for this is obvious and has already been explained in the early pages of this work. The philosophic Liberalism which destroyed the eighteenth-century State in Spain was strong enough to wound the old Spain and to overthrow her institutions; but outside Catalonia there was no *bourgeoisie*, and because this instrument of the Spanish revolution was lacking, the institutions which fell were not replaced by others capable of exercising an integrating authority. In France, the contest between the centrifugal tendency inevitable in any overthrow of the State and *bourgeois* nationalism, turned out to the advantage of unity because the French *bourgeoisie* was a powerful class and lost no time in setting up a new State, thanks to Napoleon. In contrast, between 1808 and 1874 Spain might be said to have had no State. Anything constructive in Spanish politics during that period was fugitive and unstable. The germs of constitutional decay were undermining, day by day, during the whole of this time, the foundations of the incomplete unity of the nation.

The progressive dislocation culminated in the cantonalism of the first Republic.

The new institutions founded in 1874 by the landed oligarchy were distinguished chiefly by their anti-vitalism. The oligarchy brought with it neither of the two virtues which had power to interrupt the process of the fragmentation of the nation—neither the creative dynamism of the triumphant *bourgeoisie* in Europe and in Catalonia, nor the necessary moral ascendancy which enables a régime to exercise a cohesive effect on the peoples under it. It was not that Spain was making no progress. During the reign of Alfonso XIII, the national wealth notably increased, thanks partly to Spain's neutrality during the first World War; and even the general level of education was higher. But this was an unbalanced prosperity, a false dynamism. The increase in the national wealth did not make Spain a more prosperous country, for "the prosperity of States", says Sismondi, "does not depend upon the sum total of wealth, but upon its distribution".

The government of the great landed proprietors of Andalusia and Castile was of such a disintegrating nature that not only did it dismember Spain by its acts, but it also stimulated the process of dismemberment by its verbal defeatism. Cánovas' phrase will be remembered: "**They are Spaniards who cannot be anything else.**" That is to say, anyone who thought he could be something else than a Spaniard—a Basque, a Catalan, a Galician, a Valencian—was invited, if he was not very intelligent, to try to protect himself with the shield of a new nationality.

The dissolution of all the ties which united the Spanish peoples proceeded apace, therefore, under the absolute oligarchy. It lost in extension, by comparison with the disintegration of the first Republic, but it gained in profundity. Mutual dislike grew, and such a sentiment naturally could not be the basis of a federal alliance. No spontaneous alliance can be formed on the ruins of a unity broken by repulsion. On the contrary, the obvious reaction is a resentful enmity, or perhaps, for some time at least, a continuous tension. For a long time England had no more irreconcilable opponent than the United States, Castile no bitterer adversary than Portugal, nor Spain than the American Spanish-speaking republics.

But let us return to the Catalans.

Political Catalanism had one intrinsic, absolute meaning, deriving from the circumstance that Catalonia was a nation; and another extrinsic, relative meaning, arising out of the fact that Catalonia was carrying out her industrial revolution in a

Spain which was tied to the old economy and governed by an agrarian oligarchy. The Catalan *haute bourgeoisie* scrupulously called itself regionalist, not nationalist, without thereby ceasing to think of Catalonia as a nation. This attitude was dictated by the economic interests of Catalan capitalism, since 95 per cent of Catalan manufactured goods were absorbed by the Spanish market and, moreover, without high tariffs Catalan industry could not subsist. These two realities were the ballast in the ship of *bourgeois* Catalanism, which could not be thrown overboard. The Catalan *bourgeoisie* was forced to adopt a cautious attitude towards regionalism mainly because of the economic factor. It was not without significance that the centralist oligarchy negotiated the commercial treaties and held the key to tariff policy. But the Catalan capitalists' predisposition to compromise with the central Government was not due solely to this. The class struggle, the revolutionary agitation of the Barcelona proletariat very soon made it clear to the Catalan *bourgeoisie* that its status as a conservative class forbade it to indulge in separatist extremism. Without the help of the central Government, the capitalists of Catalonia could not defend themselves against the working class.

But the Catalan *petite bourgeoisie*—the intellectuals, the functionaries, the shopkeepers—was not constrained by any such economic considerations, and it was to this sector that the separatist elements were drawn as if by a magnet.

The importance of the economic factor was decisive, therefore, not only in the gestation, but in the whole development of Catalanism. The first to recognize this was the Catalan *bourgeoisie*, which was mainly intent upon exploiting Catalanism to its own advantage, as a means of wresting economic concessions from the oligarchic Government.

Cánovas had initiated his high tariff policy for the protection of industry, hoping that in this way he would disarm separatism —a form of compromise between the new régime and an irrepressible section of Spanish society.

Spanish industry, which was concentrated, as we know, in Catalonia and Vizcaya, prospered considerably under the tariff reform of 1892; and though the traders and exporters protested, the Castilian wheat-farmers and the Basque and Catalan industrialists hailed the change with loud jubilation. In this respect, the interests of the oligarchy coincided with those of the industrial *bourgeoisie*.

As we saw in Chapter V of Book Two, the explanation of this concordance of views lay in the fact that neither Spanish industry nor the wheat-farmers were dependent on exports. Thanks to protectionism, the wheat-growers sold their products in Spain at 46 pesetas the quintal, when the price per quintal in the world market was 16 pesetas. In the same way, the iron-masters in Spain sold their girders at 930 pesetas a ton, when the French iron-masters were offering them on the other side of the frontier at 430 pesetas. Spaniards were buying Spanish steel plates at 550 pesetas a ton, while British ones could be had for 250 pesetas.

The protection of industry did not affect the interests of the monopolizers of power in Madrid. They were not exporters and were not concerned with the development of commerce. Manufactured articles which Spain had to import from England, France, Germany and the United States were paid for in gold at a premium of 21·50 per cent; for Spanish tariffs led to corresponding tariffs in other countries. A good part of the goods acquired abroad was not paid for with agricultural products or raw materials, and Spain was always in a state of more or less open commercial warfare with the rest of the world.

The idea of the Restoration politicians was to keep Catalanism at bay by protecting industry, whose future undoubtedly lay in their hands. Cánovas and his successors played this card well from their point of view, for the Catalan *bourgeoisie*, besides being afraid of its proletariat, never had enough courage to face the social and economic consequences of a revolutionary rupture with the landed oligarchy. The Catalan *bourgeoisie*, in its turn, gambled on its political power in Catalonia and, in order to obtain the economic support it desired, persistently from the beginning of the nineteenth century posed as separatist, whenever it thought it opportune to do so, threatening to sever Catalonia from Spain. Both policies were despicable and were to have grave consequences for the whole of Spain.

Unlimited protectionism did not mean, therefore, that the oligarchy desired to foster industry, but only that it was trying to appease the Catalan and Basque industrialists. The result was that, outside Catalonia and Vizcaya, hardly any industries sprang up. Castile, Andalusia, Estremadura, Galicia, Aragon, etc., were not industrialized. Catalan industry grew with protection, and in proportion as Catalonia became industrialized, the difference between this region and the others became more marked and separatism took on greater significance.

The new tariffs of 1892 soon led to a considerable increase in the consumption of foreign raw materials, chemical products and coal by Catalan industry.

The year 1892 is an important landmark in the history of

Catalanism. It was also the year of the *Bases de Manresa*, a document in which the Catalan *bourgeoisie* laid claim to no less than the independence of Catalonia. In 1892 the first bomb exploded in Barcelona, as I have pointed out elsewhere. Catalan nationalism was entering upon its Iron Age, an epoch dominated by terrorism (described in Chapters VII and XI of Book Two), corruption, and gathering clouds.

In reality, it was some time before the Catalan *bourgeoisie* began to be really anxious about the disorders, the interminable strikes, the affrays. It thought that the more patent the incompetence of the Government, the nearer Catalonia would be to realizing her aspirations. The Catalans intended to use the general chaos as a weapon against the central Government. Thus, in September 1905, we find the Barcelona Municipality discussing the advantage of pointing out to foreign Consuls that only the Government was responsible for the chaos in Barcelona. A corollary of the lack of a sense of responsibility of which Catalan capitalism had given proofs since the end of the nineteenth century was that Catalonia lost her ruling class.

Every national catastrophe brought new levies of burghers into the ranks of Catalanism and made the movement more turbulent and nationalist. The disaster of 1898—the loss of Cuba, Puerto Rico and the Philippines—enriched the Catalanist movement with "considerable new elements, particularly from industry and commerce."

Nevertheless, the Catalan *bourgeoisie*, which had been loudly proclaiming from the house-tops its ideal of self-determination, was deaf to the clamour of the Cuban autonomists and did not conceal its adhesion to the policy of force practised by the oligarchy in that island; probably because Cuba was a market for Catalan goods.

The twentieth century opened with the Catalan *bourgeoisie* in open rebellion against the State. By decision of the *Lliga Regionalista* Barcelona took no part in the coronation festivities of Alfonso XIII. In the municipal elections of November 1905, the Catalanists obtained the majority of seats in the Catalan capital. Catalan nationalism seemed destined within a very short space of time to enforce its claims, whatever they were. The Catalan *bourgeoisie* was the richest in Spain and the *Lliga* had young, combative leaders, well prepared for the fight. Moreover at that moment Catalanism was fortified by a symptomatic alliance. The only focus of real opposition to the oligarchic form of government in Madrid was centred in Barcelona. The Republicans hastened to the Catalan capital in search of the Republic. There came the Andalusian Salmerón and there was founded the *Solidaridad Catalana* movement (February 1906) which included all the Republican parties of Catalonia, except the Radical Party under Alejandro Lerroux.

But Republicanism had no large following in Spain and the *Lliga* was too dependent on its regionalist programme. Outside Catalonia, the *Solidaridad* awoke no great sympathy or support. In Catalonia itself there was a not inconsiderable section of the public which saw in the *Solidaridad* an anti-Spanish movement. It was the loquacious and emotional politicians of the *Lliga* (of whom the most representative was Puig y Cadafalch) who aroused these suspicions—those loudspeakers of a strident nationalism which made many Spaniards who were sincerely disposed to sympathize with the discontent of the Catalan burghers tremble for the unity of Spain.

Catalonia split into two bodies of opinion: the *solidarios* and the *antisolidarios*. The centralist oligarchy exploited the reaction provoked by the Catalanists between an important nucleus of Catalonia's middle class (a middle class with many non-Catalan elements, no doubt) and the proletariat of Barcelona (always ready to take up arms against its *bourgeoisie*), and sent Lerroux on an official mission to the Catalan capital, with instructions to organize war in the street against *separatism*.

From the first day, the struggle between *solidarios* and *antisolidarios* was stained by violence. Salmerón and Cambó were the victims of an attack which nearly cost the latter his life. This execrable deed could not but advance the cause of *Solidaridad*, and in the subsequent elections the *Lliga* and its Republican allies captured 41 out of the 44 seats which made up the Catalan provinces.

For many years both groups were to compete, with varying success and in an atmosphere of civil war, for the favour of the Catalan public.

With the untimely death of Prat de la Riba, the *Lliga* found in Francisco de Asís Cambó its most intelligent leader. Cambó, a business man, the perfect champion of his social class, was at once the guide of Catalan capitalism and the instrument of its despotic interests. At the beginning of the century the *Lliga* passed for a Republican movement. But the revolution of 1909 in Barcelona (described in Chapter XI of Book Two) alarmed the Catalan *bourgeoisie* and the *Lliga* became reconciled with the monarchy. On December 20th, 1911, Cambó declared at Saragossa: "I accept the monarchy of Alfonso XIII."

This inconsistency of policy, induced by the contradictory

reactions of powerful capitalist interests, was prejudicial to Catalanism. The *Lliga* had no clear political line which would allow its true aspirations to be deduced. It may well be that, if Catalanism·had confined itself to an autonomist policy that was both moderate and effective, it would not have conjured up the suspicions that made it unpopular, off and on, throughout Spain and helped to maintain the oligarchy in power for fifty years.

A Catalanism that recognized its historical responsibilities would have concentrated its efforts on achieving a special régime for Catalonia, but in line with the rest of Spain, with integration as its prime motive. In the cultural sphere, Catalanism was entitled to full autonomy, which was presumably not incompatible with the cultivation of other Spanish cultural values; but in the realm of politics, it ought to have been satisfied with a sufficient measure of autonomous activity to awaken and canalize regional energies, without ignoring the fact that Catalonia's ultimate responsibility was bound to be a Spanish responsibility, the responsibility of the nation as a whole. In any case, that is, in my view, the lesson of experience.

The Catalanist philosophers, however, exercised a very different influence on Catalan public opinion, for they educated the middle class in the belief that Catalonia should and could become a nation again, as she was in the Middle Ages. From the historical angle, this solution would appear undoubtedly retrograde, for it was equivalent to reversing a long process which could not be condemned without implicitly condemning the natural order of things. Moreover the structure of modern society, the convulsions of class warfare, the innate tendency of the property-owning classes to seek abroad, in moments of crisis for their interests, help which would endanger the independence of the nation or the conception of that independence—all this foretold a hazardous existence for autonomy.

On the other hand, the frivolous federalism in whose name Barcelona was encouraging in other regions nationalist movements and sects which ought to have been restrained rather than stimulated, was pernicious in the highest degree. Already, on its own account, the irresistible current of Catalan nationalism was serving as a spur, in particular to Basque nationalism; and besides this reflex action, *bourgeois* Catalanism was deliberately engaging in other, direct, action by convening at Barcelona, and noisily regaling, detached elements of the regionalist and separaties parties of Galicia and the Basque Provinces.

The Catalanists were rashly confounding their case with that of a *galleguismo* with which they had nothing in common save the lyrical inspiration of its founders and the disintegration of the Spanish State. Though distinguished by their rich folklore, the Galician people did not feel the urgent need for a political canon different from that of the majority of Spaniards. In vain had ardent *galleguistas* endeavoured to awaken in their fellow countrymen the feeling of an oppressed nationality. Brañas had published in 1889 *El Regionalismo*. Pondal, Murguía, Barcia and others had also dedicated themselves to the task of creating a regionalist political movement; but the only fruit of their labours in Galicia was a corresponding cultural movement of limited dimensions which threw up a few newspapers with a modest circulation, some centres of recreation and the *Irmandades da Fala*.

Both on account of its origins and its foreseeable consequences, Basque nationalism, the theme of the following chapter, must be included in another category.

As we consider the matter, little by little the vast differences between mild and lyrical *galleguismo*, eruptive and irreconcilable *vasquismo* and *bourgeois* and hectoring *catalanismo* become clear. Basque nationalism was separatist and anti-Liberal, as opposed to Galician regionalism and Catalan nationalism. The Catalan *bourgeoisie* was not sincere in its separatist pose. It did not *feel* separatism. For the rest, the copious interests of Catalan capitalism reacted strongly against the tendencies of the secessionists. For those in the secret, the nationalist extremism of the *Lliga* was always a stupendous *bluff*, and its adventitious separatism—peculiar to the capitalists who wanted to turn it to their own advantage—was dangerous *blackmail*.

The Catalan *petite bourgeoisie*, not being under the compulsion of economic considerations, could, with a certain amount of conviction, boast of being separatist, but there was much intellectual truculence in its attitude and also not a little *personal blackmail* on occasions.

It can be definitely said, therefore, that the separatists hardly counted in Catalanism. They have never counted. The convinced separatist has always been the exception in the Catalanist movement and time has taught us that his actions and words are best not taken seriously.

But where Basque nationalism is concerned, the partisans of the policy of preserving fundamental connections of any sort with the rest of Spain are the exception.

Clearly, it would be rash to regard the other regionalist and nationalist movements as equivalent to Catalanism. Neither in their roots, nor in their terminations, nor in their ultimate consequences, could they be compared.

The support of the Spanish parties of the Left for the autonomist movements was largely opportunist. The Republicans demanded autonomy for Catalonia in order to win over this region for the Republican cause, just as the Bolshevists proclaimed the right of nationalities to secede in the hope of attracting the peoples oppressed by Czarism. Moreover the political uniformity of the nation, the dogma of the nineteenth-century constitutionalists, was a principle which appealed less and less to the democratic organizations, all the more so as the oligarchy revealed itself as centralist *à outrance*.

To a greater or lesser extent the working-class parties also adhered to the autonomist principle, for these and other reasons. From the doctrinal point of view, the anarcho-syndicalists approved of federalism as a doctrine consistent with their mistrust of the State and their desire to divide and subdivide the political power. The Socialist Party declared themselves explicitly autonomist in their programme. In this, as in other things, the workers' movement had a prejudice in favour of Liberalism. The autonomism of the Socialists was a concession to the regional middle class or nationalist *bourgeoisie*. Nationalism had no appeal for the proletariat, perhaps because it was contrary to their interests. Hence the indifference with which Marx and Engels heard the laments of nationalities aspiring to emancipate themselves. Marxism disapproved of the birth of new States; Marxist doctrine was opposed to the institutional political progress of the regions and nationalities comprised in the great States. If Marxist philosophers supported the separation of Poland, they did so with the sole idea of weakening Czarism. It can be taken for granted that an increase in the political power of national or regional *bourgeoisies* contradicts the internationalist ideal of the proletariat, save in those cases where political tactics make it desirable. Some years ago Stalin wrote:

"In the middle of the nineteenth century Marx was in favour of the separation of Russian Poland; and he was right, for it was then a question of emancipating a higher culture from a lower culture that was destroying it.

"At the end of the nineteenth century the Polish Marxists were already declaring against the separation of Poland; and they too were right, for during the fifty years that elapsed profound changes had taken place, bringing Russia and Poland closer economically and culturally".[1]

[1] Stalin, *Marxism and the National Question*, 1913.

In fact no one fought the principle of self-determination with greater ardour than Rosa Luxembourg, the Polish Socialist, and this while Czarism was still alive.

To sum up, the duty of the working-class, according to Marxism, is to fight conscientiously and indefatigably against the nationalist delusion, wherever it proceeds from.

In quoting these examples I do not propose to compare the problem of nationalities in Spain and Russia, since in both countries its scope and importance vary and it is dangerous to generalize on the subject. In both nations there are historical and political circumstances (relating to both foreign and domestic policy) which set their own stamp on the problem. The most liberal attitude towards regional or national particularism would have to admit "that autonomy or separation is not always and everywhere necessarily beneficial to a nation".

In Spain the progressive disintegration of the institutions, the growing stimulus the Catalans were receiving from non-Catalan liberal opinion, the support given them in Parliament by the opposition groups, the state of endemic anarchy which was convulsing Barcelona, finally forced the politicians of the *turno* to pay some attention to the claims of the *Lliga*. On March 25th, 1912, the draft law of *Mancomunidad*, the work of Cambó and Corominas, was read in the Chamber of Deputies. For two long years Parliament fiercely debated the Catalan question, and on December 18th, 1914, a Royal Decree was passed, granting the Catalan provinces the right to act together in political-administrative matters within their competence.

This, however, did not go far enough. The *Mancomunidad* did not satisfy the political ambitions of Catalanism, and in 1915 Cambó returned to the charge, raising the question of "Catalonia's suit for complete sovereignty".

The crisis which filled the next years with drama has been minutely described in Chapter IX of Book Two. There the reader will find the history of the Parliamentary Assembly (July 1917) convened by the Catalan *bourgeoisie*; the formation of the first Coalition Government, which included Juan Ventosa of the *Lliga* and Felipe Rodés of the Catalan Nationalist Party; the formation of Maura's National Government (March 1918) in which Cambó and Ventosa became Ministers; the visits of the *Lliga* politicians to the Levante, Andalusia and Galicia with the object of founding related parties; the personal and political quarrel originating in the clash of economic interests between Cambó and Alba, a quarrel that brought down Maura's

National Government; the presence of Alba in the succeeding Ministry where he tried, as Finance Minister, to carry out a tax and tariff policy that struck terror into the hearts of the Catalan industrialists.

We also saw how, when the politicians of the *Lliga* were absent from the Government, Catalanism gained in virulence; how the social convulsions in Barcelona, the strikes, the terrorism, forced the Catalan capitalists to come to terms with Madrid. ("Towards Concord" was the title of the book which Cambó wrote shortly afterwards.)

The Catalan *bourgeoisie* was naturally alarmed by the rapid disintegration of the State; the *Lliga's* policy, as will be remembered, now had no other aim than to prop up the monarchy and salvage the remnants of the Restoration régime. Questioned about their views on the monarchical institution, Cambó and Ventosa replied: "Monarchy? Republic? Catalonia!" The truth was that the *Lliga*, in whose calculations Catalanism already occupied a subsidiary place, could not declare itself in favour of the monarchy without alienating its Republican allies in all parts of Spain and decreeing its own dissolution; but to declare for the Republic would have made an enemy of the King and of the Conservative politicians in Madrid, from whom the Catalan capitalists were hoping for great favours in those difficult times.

The unity of Catalanism was, therefore, shattered. Already in 1918 Cambó had denounced separatism in Parliament, at a time when the *petite bourgeoisie* in the person of Maciá was dilating upon the subject in terms of extreme radicalism. Further, while the *Lliga* was being converted to moderatism, the Catalan *petite bourgeoisie* was sounding Clemenceau with a view to procuring political support abroad, an approach which the Tiger cut short with a brusque gesture: "Pas d'histoires, Messieurs."

The unity of Catalanism was, I repeat, broken; and later events were to complete the separation of the two social classes which made up the *Lliga*. When the great industrialists sacrificed the Catalanist ideal to their immediate and pressing class interests, the leadership of Catalanism passed to the *petite bourgeoisie*.

In 1922 *Acció Catalana* came into being, founded by two intellectuals, Rovira y Virgili and Nicolau d'Olwer. *Acció Catalana* was mainly composed of professors and intellectuals, University dons and bureaucrats, with no foothold in reality; and its bent was separatist, though some did not dare to say so and even denied it. Almost at the same time *Estat Catalá* was formed under the leadership of a soldier, Colonel Francisco Maciá. *Estat Catalá* attracted, in general, another class of people, the black-coated workers; the typical member of this organization was the *dependiente de comercio*.

It hardly needs to be said that *Acció Catalana* and *Estat Catalá* were two groups with such a small following that to apply the name of party to them would be excessively flattering.

Primo de Rivera's dictatorship proscribed all political manifestations of Catalanism, though it did not persecute the leaders, some of whom, however, like Maciá, went into voluntary exile and took up residence in France and Belgium. The *Lliga* temporized with the new régime, which the Catalan industrialists had favoured before it was established; though they felt they had been cheated because Primo had promised before the *coup d'état* to give satisfaction to the autonomists.

During the dictatorship, Catalanism achieved visible progress in the cultural sphere. With the curtailment of their political liberty, the Catalan nationalists devoted themselves more systematically and assiduously to their national culture: which did not mean that *Acció Catalana* ceased to feed the Catalanist political flame or that Maciá resigned himself beyond the Pyrenees to the passive rôle of the exile. The former went on waging a clandestine political war, and the Colonel's one desire was to liberate Catalonia with an improvised and weaponless army which he formed in France.

As always happens in such cases, it was inevitable that the fervour of the Catalans for their language and their flag should be tried in the furnace and emerge stronger than ever. But with the disappearance of the dictatorship and the subsequent fall of the monarchy, Catalan nationalism did not come out into the open as the irreducible separatist movement which eight years of despotism might have been expected to engender. A silent and profound revolution had taken place in Catalan politics. The new Catalan political parties, led by the radical lower middle class, had a common interest in social questions. There was a numerous *Unión de Rabassaires*, a peasant party; a party of the Catalan Left *(Esquerra)*; a Catalan Socialist party, led by Campalans; and other groups not worth mentioning. Moreover, *Acció Catalana* and *Estat Catalá* were still in existence.

As I have just said, the new Catalanist parties of the Left emphasized, at the expense of nationalism, their character as political forces bent on transforming Catalonia from the social point of view. They were more forthright on the social question

397

than the *petite bourgeoisie* of *Acció Catalana*, and their Catalanist ideal was more temperate. The radical lower middle class sought their following in the only possible place—among the urban proletariat and the peasants. It was only thus that the *petite bourgeoisie* could aspire to direct Catalan policy; if it relied on its own strength, it could not hope to compete with the *Lliga* or with the non-Catalanist proletariat. The *Esquerra* (about which we shall say a word later on) created for itself, with its social programme, a political future; but it owed its triumph to the working class and the peasants and thus became from the outset dependent, in politics and in the Government, on the workers.

The *Esquerra de Catalunya* was the name of the coalition of parties which hastened to unite on the eve of the municipal elections of April 1931 which overthrew the monarchy. *Acció Catalana* was not a party to this coalition, but *Estat Català* was. The leaders of the *Esquerra* not only displayed working-class sympathies in their policy, but some of them, principally Luis Companys, had long maintained a close personal relationship with the workers' and peasants' organizations of Catalonia. In addition the coalition of Left parties was frankly Republican. For all these reasons, the lower middle class and the proletariat put their trust in the *Esquerra ;* and so unanimously and resolutely did they support the movement that it won a victory which surprised no one more than its leaders, who had taken it for granted, in spite of the unpopularity of the *Lliga*, that the powerful organization of the upper middle class would win the election.

*Acció Catalana* went to the polling booths as a separatist party, but found no support among the public—a striking proof that extreme nationalism did not appeal to Catalans and also that Catalanism without what might be called its *social content* attracted no followers. The political movement was dominated then by the class struggle. We shall have a better understanding, perhaps, of the new situation in the internal politics of Catalonia, if we note that the partisans of *Acció Catalana*, who were above all nationalists, regarded the *Lliga* with resentment, as a renegade party, while the members of the *Esquerra* contemptuously called the Catalanists of *Acció senyorets* (*señoritos*), with the accent on their social position.

The advent of the Republic and the predominance of the political forces of the Left in Catalan politics foreshadowed a solution of the Catalan problem. The social classes—lower

398

middle class and proletariat—which had taken over the reins of government in Madrid were the exact counterpart of the social classes which were preparing to govern in Barcelona. The Republic was guaranteeing to all Spaniards political liberty, a more decorous use of power, justice, etc. Hence, in so far as Catalanism had been a protest against *mal govern*, or misgovernment, it now lost its *raison d'être*. Nevertheless the *Esquerra* was pressing the Republic to grant autonomy, on the grounds that, in accordance with a mode of thought which is familiar to us, Catalonia would not be completely free until she had her *Estatuto*. The Constituent Cortes in accordance with another mode of thought equally familiar to us, sympathized with the impatience of the Catalans, and, anxious to assure Catalonia's enthusiastic support for the new régime, devoted itself eagerly to the task of founding (on paper) a national State "integrated (Article 8 of the Constitution) by associated provincial *Municipios* and autonomously constituted regions".

When the Constitution was promulgated in December 1931, the Catalan provinces, taking Article 11 as their authority, agreed to organize themselves into an autonomous region to form an administrative political nucleus within the Spanish State and, under the terms of Article 12, they submitted a draft statute to the Cortes for examination and approval.

For several months, in sessions that were sometimes stormy, the deputies analysed, discussed and amended the Catalan document; and Catalonia's Statute of Autonomy was converted into law in September 1932, thanks probably to Azaña's logical genius.

Catalonia was henceforth to have her own Government called the *Generalidad* (as in the Middle Ages) and her own Parliament. In the political order, Catalan autonomy went farther than that, for example, of Scotland and Wales.

The Catalans (or, to be more exact, the Catalans of the Left) declared themselves satisfied and were loud in their praise of the Republic, Azaña, and Alcalá Zamora.

The Statute did not satisfy the *Lliga*, chiefly because it was going to put the *Esquerra* on the map; and in the hands of these parties it promised to be a subversive instrument. The separatist lower middle class was also disillusioned with the Statute, for the measure of autonomy granted fell short of what it had hoped for. We thus find inside Catalonia two considerable forces, the capitalists and the intelligentsia, mistrustful of and hostile to the Statute.

Outside Catalonia there were equally important elements which did not accept Catalan autonomy; the oligarchy, in full enjoyment of its social power; the Army, which was the same as under the monarchy; and most of the middle class in general, which was hard to convince that autonomy was not a step towards separation.

Catalan autonomy, let me repeat, was a historical necessity which could not be bypassed or endlessly deferred. From the end of the eighteenth century onwards, as we saw, important events were taking place in Catalonia which enjoined the setting up of a particular régime for this region. The Statute granted by the Republic had had an interesting antecedent in the work carried out in 1919 by an extra-Parliamentary Commission consisting of Don Antonio Maura, Sánchez Toca, Rodrígañez, Ruiz Jiménez and Alcalá Zamora. These politicians of the monarchy gave their verdict at the time for a system of autonomy which would have its point of departure in the municipality and consist of a regional *Diputación,* an Executive responsible to the latter and a Governor-General with wide powers. This project remained on paper, but it bore witness to the fact that before the rise of the Republic the idea of the Statute had gained much ground.

Now it is very doubtful whether a Catalan Government and Parliament were the most advisable shape for Catalan autonomy to take. Since Home Rule was bound to be a bone of contention in a Catalonia tragically divided by the clash of class interests, autonomy—if it was to consolidate itself—ought perhaps to have laid more stress on its cultural than its political side. For "in every nation there are, on the one hand, factors which have a disintegrating effect, such as political and economic interests, and, on the other, factors which unify, and foremost among these is culture".

What could have been foreseen, afterwards came to pass; the stability of Catalan autonomy was to be in inverse ratio to its political-administrative extension. The more power the Government and Parliament of Catalonia enjoyed in this domain, the greater were the probabilities that the Statute would not take root. The greatest threat to the new autonomous régime was a possible conspiracy of the non-Catalan and Catalan forces which were hostile to the new political organization. For the first two years autonomy functioned without insuperable difficulties, but when the *Lliga* withdrew from the Catalan Parliament as a protest against the *Ley de Contratos de Cultivo,* it dealt the first serious blow to the experiment in autonomy.

The agrarian programme of the *Esquerra* finally persuaded the *Lliga* that so much liberty was not suitable for Catalonia—whether this was legal or not. And when in 1934 Lerroux's Government and the *C.E.D.A.* suspended the Statute and imprisoned the Government of the *Generalidad* (as will be described in another chapter), the men of the *Lliga* hastened to replace the *Esquerra* politicians as the leaders of Catalonia. The *Lliga*, defeated in the elections, received from the central Government the power which the Catalan people had refused it.

The Statute of Autonomy had met with the same fate as the other Republican reforms. The Catalanists thought, no doubt, that the new Catalan institutions would protect Catalonia against the intrusion of the central Government. It was soon apparent that they were under a delusion. Catalonia's freedom did not depend on her institutions, but on the general state of affairs in Spain.

I have already pointed out that a revolution which begins by dispersing its powers or dividing its energies cannot be successful. It is, therefore, natural that all revolutions worthy of the name should display in common an energetic unifying and centralizing intention. It will be remembered that the French Convention made centralism its dogma and put down federalism with a heavy hand. The policy of the nineteenth-century Spanish Liberals was also centralist in tendency. Nor did the Bolshevist revolution in Russia, in spite of its anti-*bourgeois* character, violate this general historical law; on the contrary, it obeyed it more rigorously, in political and economic matters, than did the *bourgeois* philosophers—a fact that can be explained perhaps by the sweeping nature of the Russian revolution, which penetrated more deeply into the economic subsoil than the revolution of the *bourgeoisie*. The greater the sweep of the reforms, the greater the need for the concentration of power.

Under the formal semblance of federalism, an intense centralization was the order of the day in Russia from the first hours of the Soviet State. The Soviet system conceded a *de facto* cultural autonomy, but not political autonomy. Though the Constitution allows the right of secession to every region or republic of the U.S.S.R., it is obvious that this right exists merely on paper. In everything that matters, in the political and economic sphere, the authority lies with the central Government. For example, no Republic has an independent budget, and in anything connected with finance and credit, the local government is at the mercy of the central Government; the boundaries of the division of the U.S.S.R. into economic regions do not coincide with the boundaries of the division into nations or political regions, and the direction of economic affairs is entrusted to supreme central bodies with sweeping powers, without which planning would be impossible. But the decisive factor in the Soviet régime is this; that the ruling party in all the Republics, the Communist Party, is rigidly centralized in Moscow. Hence, the power conceded by successive Constitutions to the local organs of administration lacks effectiveness against the real Government of the U.S.S.R. which may be more exactly defined as, not the Communist Party, but the Political Bureau of the Communist Party, or, to push realism still farther, not the Political Bureau of the Communist Party, but the Secretariat of the Party.

We can conclude, with Sir John Maynard, that effective autonomy in the Soviet Union has no great depth or extension, except in cultural and linguistic affairs. "I arrive", writes this excellent guide to Soviet Russia, "at these paradoxical conclusions: that the constitution gives little or nothing in the way of actual power to the constituent bodies which are parties to the federation: that the political system is one of intense centralization, particularly in the vital sphere of finance: that the concessions to local language and culture give a very large part of what national feeling most desires. . . ."[1]

Among other things, a revolution is an act whereby a nation affirms the right to continue its existence as such, and this right hardly accords with the right of peoples to arrange their destinies freely. Moreover a region, urged by the past, may desire autonomy or separation for reasons which the revolution renders null and void. Let a nation in general be given a collective ideal, a national ideal; let it begin its own regeneration; let revolution instil into it a dynamism capable of absorbing the attention and energies and awakening the enthusiasm of all the peoples constituting that nation—will the discontented regions think and feel as they did under the old régime?

When a revolution begins with the grant of autonomies, it may be taken for granted that the failure of both is inevitable.

If the autonomist policy of the Spanish Republicans (in the generic sense of the word) had been confined to the Catalan case, matters would not have been so serious. But the Republic offered autonomy to as many regions as demanded it.

[1] *The Russian Peasant; and other Studies*, p. 400. Gollancz.

The Constitution of 1931 laid down (Article 12) that the Cortes should approve any Statute not violating that Constitution in any way, which had been put forward by a number of municipalities comprising two-thirds of the electors of the region, and which had been subsequently accepted by two-thirds of the electors inscribed in the regional census.

Given the situation of the Republic in Spain—attacked by the centrifugal disease which had been engendered by an abortive revolution and by half a century of oppression and misgovernment—it was to be expected that the regions where any particularist sentiment existed would be prompt to cast two-thirds of their votes in favour of the Statute. The Republic was inviting the regions to place in the Statute that ingenuous faith which the Republican section of the nation placed in the Constitution. A sick nation, like a sick person, would hasten to try the therapeutic virtues of any remedies available, and in time (unless the Republic succumbed in the meanwhile) regionalism would make converts in some regions and add to its followers in others, simply because the Statute would be the only solution which had not yet been tried there.

Once the right to autonomy had been inserted as a general principle in the Constitution, it was obvious that the Republic could not refuse it, without denying its own law, to any regionalist movement, whatever its nature, which obtained the necessary two-thirds of the regional votes in favour of the Statute. It was a flagrant inconsistency, therefore, on the part of the Republicans to try to make an exception of the Basques because their party was Catholic, Conservative, and well known for its separatist views.

Basque nationalism was a problem, not only for the Republic, but for Spain, because liberty exacerbated it as much as repression. But where the problem did not exist, the Republic went about, perhaps, to create it. It was evident that the Republic was creating a new interest and that round this new interest illusions and appetites were congregating and daily demanding satisfaction with greater impatience and force. Thus, Basque nationalism was to succeed, after the grant of autonomy, in infecting persons who had been lifelong adherents of internationalism, but who were now corrupted politically by the power which autonomy had placed in their hands; while on the lips of old Socialists was heard the strange and hitherto undreamt-of phrase that they were Basques first and Socialists afterwards.

Thanks to the liberality of the Republicans, the Galician

regionalists converted themselves into a political organization which claimed comparison, in the realm of politics, with the ancient and vigorous political nationality of Catalonia.

Valencian regionalism, for its part, was quick to hoist its flag, as a challenge to the Republic that in this region too there were old traditions and customs.

In Andalusia also, a group of Cordovans and men from Seville unfurled a regional flag, as the expression of their claims to the establishment of yet another small State.

In Aragon, certain circles thought it their patriotic duty to insist that their region should not be passed over in the share-out of liberties, and proclaimed their aspiration to equality with Catalonia, Galicia, the Basque Provinces, Andalusia and Valencia.

Just after the Statute had been granted to Catalonia, a picturesque incident occurred which revealed to the Cortes the absurdity of the autonomous policy embodied in the Constitution. In November 1932 Señor Marraco, an Aragonese, asked the Minister of Public Works to defer certain measures until the Government of Aragon had been formed. Marraco's action made it clear that the situation as regards the Constitution had a fluidity that boded no good to the Republic. It was obvious that the constituent period would never come to an end, since there would always be some region which was absorbed in the internal struggle for autonomy, that is, for the regional constitution.

No one would deny the geographical diversity of Spain or the variety of her local customs and traditions. But apart from the fact that no great nation consists of a single people, race, or body of traditions, it is obvious that neither geographical nor ethnical characteristics, nor the existence of a dialect or primitive language, nor the anachronistic perpetuation of various mediaeval *fueros*, nor a peculiar method of dancing or extracting sounds from curious musical instruments, can be accepted as a basis for the right to set up a State or to found particular political institutions.

The wholesale granting of autonomy prevented the consolidation of the Republic and played a greater part than might appear in its tragic destiny. Azaña (as we shall see later) had to confess that this was true.

And this reality, which at the time was obscured by the fog of enthusiasm and inexperience, today might inspire every intelligent Republican to paraphrase with approval the words of Stalin as follows: It must not be forgotten that, side by side with the right of nations or regions to self-determination, there exists the right of the popular Republic to consolidate its power. And the latter right takes precedence over the right of self-determination. There are occasions when the right of self-determination finds itself in conflict with the other and higher right, the right of the triumphant Republic to consolidate its power. In such cases—this must be said without hesitation—the right of self-determination must not and cannot be an obstacle to the Republic's exercise of its right to exist. The former must yield to the latter.

CHAPTER XI

# BASQUE NATIONALISM

LITTLE OR NOTHING is known for certain of the origins of the Basques. And as in this particular there is no generally admitted hypothesis, the best we can do here is to ignore the theories in circulation.

The Basque race has lived for centuries on both slopes of the Pyrenees, most of them on the Spanish side. But investigations carried out in 1834 showed that pure-blooded Basques in the provinces of Vizcaya, Guipuzcoa and Alava accounted for less than a third of the population; and Broca discovered among the French Basques a brachycephalic appearance which does not exist among the Spanish Basques.

What is beyond a doubt, on the historical plane, is the extraordinary influence of this people on the destinies of Spain.

As the Reconquista proceeded, Castile was repopulated with "many colonies of Basques". As a result, a considerable proportion of Basque blood flows through the veins of the Castilian people. In fact the name García, a name as common in Spain as Dupont is in France or Smith in England, is of Basque origin.

With Ferdinand I (1035–65), son of Sancho el Mayor of Navarre, Castile as a kingdom was born under the domination of a Basque dynasty. Later Alfonso the Wise founded Puerto de Santa María and repeopled other Andalusian cities with Cantabrians and Basques.

Juan Sebastian Elcano, who, without detracting from the merits of Magellan, brought Spain the glory of being the first nation to have circumnavigated the globe, was a Basque.

Saint Ignatius Loyola, whose influence on the history of Spain and of Europe needs no emphasis, was a Basque.

Unamuno, the most genuine Spanish philosopher since the seventeenth century, was a Basque.

The point I want to make is that, for some profound moral reason, all the great Basque qualities combine, in the same way, to make typical Spaniards. In fact, racially, Castilians and Basques have long presented "special ethnical affinities".[1]

In all the Spanish national enterprises, Basques played an outstanding part. They took a hand in the Reconquista, and it was with the help of their fleets that San Fernando conquered Seville. They contributed with success to the American epic, as is shown by the fact that the territories forming the province of Río de la Plata were given the name of "Nueva Vizcaya". Two Basque fleets of ten galleons each figured in the "Invincible" Armada which Philip II sent against England; one from Vizcaya under the command of Juan Martínez de Ricalde, the other from Guipuzcoa under Miguel de Oquendo. (In this enterprise the Basques sent more ships than Castile, which only contributed fourteen galleons.)

Finally, in modern times Churruca, another Basque, won immortality facing Nelson at Trafalgar.

Until the end of the nineteenth century the Basque combined his local loyalties with his passion for what was universally Spanish.

Until the nineteenth century the Basque people as a whole lived politically and socially amid individual institutions, with their provincial *Juntas*, their parochial democracy and their Tree of Guernica, symbol of the rustic and primitive liberty they enjoyed. They were essentially a rural and patriarchial people. There were, of course, Basques who sailed the seven seas and others who showed marked aptitude for business and banking—but these were in a minority. The immense majority of the Basques—in Vizcaya, Guipuzcoa, Alava and Navarre—were misoneist peasants, fanatically religious, making a point of opposing everything new. They kept up prehistoric customs; the *espata danza* has been identified as a derivation of the *Tripudium* of the Iberians; and the palaeolithic language they spoke kept alive among them an association of ideas which was impermeable to progress; the root of such current words as plough, knife, axe, is *aiz*, which means stone.

The Tree of Guernica, the civil monument which the Basques

[1] Menéndez Pidal, *La España del Cid*, Chap. II, sub. 6, p. 67.

take from Nature as the emblem of their liberty, is not an exclusively Basque symbol; rather does it perpetuate a prehistoric custom common to innumerable peoples. In the pastoral *cantons* of Switzerland, the peasants thresh out their problems of government (or did until quite recently) under a leafy oak-tree.[1]

Naturally this Basque rural population, intimately attached to the remote past, to its antique myths, with the same or with new names, fought the Liberal revolution tooth and nail. The history of this reaction is the history of Carlism, a movement which we have studied elsewhere. Let us recall that the Basque countryside was Carlist and the Basque city Liberal. Let us also recall that the Carlists were fighting for the Inquisition and for the government of the Church. They had already fought against Ferdinand VII who was too Liberal in their eyes. It is a mistake to think that they were fighting for the Basque *fueros*. That would mean that Carlism was fighting on the defensive, a theory which has no basis in reality. The Carlists of the Basque Provinces and Navarre were trying in 1833 to impose on Spain a given political régime, an ultramontane State, an aspiration which, though subsequently abandoned by the majority of Basques in Vizcaya and Guipuzcoa, still persists in Navarre. The Carlists were not fighting for their local liberties, *fueros* or political privileges, but in order to deprive other Spaniards of liberty, to impose absolutism on the whole of Spain.

There is abundant documentary proof that the *fueros* were not the cause of the civil war of 1833. In the first place the proclamation issued by the *padres de provincia* of Bilbao does not make the slightest mention of the *fueros*, but calls upon the citizens of Bilbao to unite against "an anti-religious and anti-monarchical faction". Moreover, we have the invaluable personal testimony of Henningsen, the careful annotator of everything that happened in the Carlist campaign. He writes in his Memoirs, already quoted in this work: "When the King (Don Carlos) reviewed the Carlist army, after the battalions of Navarre and Castile had been deafening the air with their shouts of *Viva Carlos Quinto! Viva Nuestro Rey!*, those of the Basque Provinces, although much more clamorous as he passed, instantly changed the cry to *Viva Nuestro Señor!*, 'Long live our Lord!', or modifying it to *Viva el Rey, nuestro Señor!* 'Long live the King, our Lord!' Founding their ideas, most probably, on this and similar circumstances, the journalists have long gravely told the public that the insurgents fight with such determination

[1] Rousseau, *Du Contrat Social*, Bk. IV. Chap. I.

and success, not for the cause of Charles V, or from any feeling approaching to royalism, but for their own rights and *fueros*. This certainly seems highly plausible and probable; yet, in fact, with the immense majority, this neither seems an additional incentive to their zeal, nor appears even to have struck them at all, although the provinces were certainly on the point of having the privileges curtailed. Of those now carrying arms, not one in twenty knows even the signification of the word *fueros*, although it may be familiar to his ear. When I was anxious to obtain some information on this subject, I interrogated the soldiers many times before I could obtain an answer in the least satisfactory; and on asking what they were fighting for, they invariably replied, 'For Charles V', or, 'For the King!'. I do not mean to say that it is always either a reasoned opinion they hold in favour of the prince for whom they are fighting, or a reasoned affection towards him, any more than is to be met with amongst the masses of all parties" (Vol. 1, pp. 70 and 71).

This point is of superlative importance, because Basque nationalism now poses as, and probably is, a Liberal movement, claiming always to have been Liberal and boasting of its love of liberty. On May 27th, 1932, Azaña, either because it suited his policy of the moment, or because he sincerely believed it, advanced the absurd theory in the Cortes that "the regions which had adhered to the despotic cause of Don Carlos were absolutely indifferent to the dynastic problem, because what mattered to the Basques was not Don Carlos, but their *fueros*".

As we have just seen, the truth is quite otherwise. But the Basque nationalists were delighted with Azaña's theory, since it fortified the party's position in its present struggle for the wide measure of autonomy pursued by some or the independence pursued by others. Thus on September 25th, 1942, José Antonio Aguirre recalled, in the Spanish Republican Centre of Buenos Aires, that "Azaña had declared in a plenary session of Parliament, speaking of the Basques in their first civil war, and answering the charge that they had fought for absolutism: "No, they said that, but it is not true; you fought for liberty". Aguirre adds: "We loudly applauded that man who did us justice."

Azaña was neither doing justice to the Basques, nor was his version of the Carlist rising anything but a careless improvization or a political weapon. But when we remember that there were Basque Liberals fighting Basque Carlists, and when we ask ourselves why the former were fighting, the fraud is exposed, for the love of their *fueros* burned almost as strongly in the breast of the Basque Liberals as in that of the Carlists.

For one reason or another, the question of the *fueros* did not enter into the calculations of either Basque Liberals or Basque Carlists.

Nevertheless the Liberal revolution, by its very nature, and in the name of liberty, equality and fraternity, was opposed, as I said in the previous chapter, to the continuance of regional privileges. Liberalism came to destroy the institutions of the Middle Ages, and the privileges of the Basques were as mediaeval as the privileges of the Church and of the nobles; the *fueros* were as much a part of the Middle Ages as the Inquisition. The Basque *fueros* lost their *raison d'être*, once the new Constitution had liberated all Spaniards from the tyranny of the Crown and of the nobility, to combat which these local privileges had been born, or were confirmed or recognized. The *fueros* found themselves, therefore, in conflict with the new age which, moreover, favoured the principle of great nationalities, the idea of equality and the criterion of the unity of the law. But on the other hand, the Liberal revolution had also been engendered by romanticism, and romanticism encouraged the local and the typical. Hence the strong romantic character of Carlism, champion of undiluted traditionalism.

Another proof that the first Carlist war was not concerned with a subsidiary question like that of the future of the *fueros*, but with the great problem of the common destiny of Spaniards under a Liberal constitution or an absolute monarchy, may be found in the case of Portugal. In Portugal there was no problem of *fueros*; yet a similar conflict arose there, and Liberals and *Miguelistas* unleashed a civil war equivalent in form and background to the Spanish civil war.

For a host of reasons, the triumph of Liberal arms in Spain involved the curtailment of political privileges in the Basque Provinces and Navarre. Spain could not cut loose, or progress, with her economy strangled and her laws dispersed. The fiscal frontier between Castile and the Basque Provinces was on the Ebro at Miranda. Everything, inside and outside the Basque country, conspired to fetter commerce. It was, moreover, the hour when those nations which had not yet achieved political unity were making a final bid for it. France was consolidating her political unity; Germany and Italy were pursuing it with obsession. Such an intelligent traveller, and one so enamoured of Spanish local customs and traditions as Richard Ford, wrote in 1845, after having traversed the Peninsula from end to end:

409

"Sooner or later, however, the Basque *fueros* must be abolished whenever a really strong Government can be formed" (Handbook, Vol. II, p. 923).

Apart from the fact that, as has been said, the centralizing current of the nineteenth century was at odds with local political privileges (which were founded, and in the case of the ancient Basque political usages, confirmed by the weak mediaeval State), there were in Spain special reasons conspiring against the continuance of the Basque *fueros*. In Madrid a Liberal Government could enjoy no security while the Carlists in the Basque Provinces and Navarre were masters of the Franco-Spanish frontier. There they received their flow of armaments; there they carried on an active contraband trade which considerably diminished the nation's revenue. The Government's jurisdiction hardly extended beyond the Ebro; and in order to disarm the absolutist movement and put an end to the civil war, Liberal Spain was forced to extend her power sooner or later to the Pyrenean frontier and make an end of a situation which allowed the Carlists to maintain an army on a permanent war footing, to plot attacks on Liberal institutions and to keep alive the dream of setting up in Madrid a theocratic and rural State, the Government of the countryside and the Church.

When the first Carlist war ended in January 1839, the question of the *fueros* was put forward at the peace negotiations of Vergara. The Carlists, though defeated, endeavoured to save their cause from total disaster. They renounced for the moment their plan to enthrone Don Carlos and absolutism in Spain, in order to concentrate on the defence of the *fueros*, which were the guarantee of their freedom of movement and, therefore, of their future power.

With the Basque country and Navarre occupied by the Liberal army, the provincial privileges were suspended in actual fact. The Carlists demanded their reinstatement at Vergara; and Espartero promised in writing that he would use his influence to urge the Government to fulfil their promise and propose to the Cortes that the Basque rural liberties should be confirmed, subject to certain modifications. That was as far as Espartero would go.

The Cortes of 1839, with a Liberal majority and revolutionary, or—as we should say today—Left leanings, unanimously resolved in October that the *fueros* should be respected "so long as they appeared compatible with the constitutional unity of the country" and that, after consulting the regional Parliament, those changes which the interests of Spain and the well-being of the provinces required, should be introduced.

These changes were established by the law of October 25th 1839, a law (according to the Basque nationalist Señor Aranzadi) imposed by a foreign State; as if the Spanish State was not the State of the Basques, who had never constituted a political unit, still less a State unit.[1]

---

[1] In the eighth century, Vizcaya already appears, though obscurely, subordinated to the duchy of Cantabria, ruled by Alfonso I (739–57). Later on Vizcaya became a county under the protection of the King of Navarre. Still later, it passed under Castilian suzerainty, being finally incorporated with Castile, by inheritance, in 1376. Alava had Castilian Counts in the ninth and tenth centuries. In 1035 it was incorporated with Navarre under García, son of Sancho el Mayor. In the reign of Alfonso VIII, Alava again came under the sovereignty of Castile. The representation of the central power devolved first upon the Counts and afterwards upon the chief provincial Governors of Castile. In the eleventh century we find Guipuzcoa governed by Counts delegates of the King of Navarre; but in the time of Alfonso VI and the Cid, it owed allegiance to the Castilian monarchy. Its next stage was self-goverment under the sovereignty of Navarre, when important *fueros* were granted by the Crown. But in 1200 it submitted to the overlordship of Alfonso VIII, to remain subsequently under the authority of the kings of Castile.

It should be noted that the political privileges of the Basques of these three provinces were established by the perpetuation of customs which were respected by the kings of Castile and Navarre and by new *fueros* granted by these monarchs in use in the whole of Spain. The Basques were no freer in the Middle Ages than other Spaniards, their régime, with its *pase foral* or power of opposing the abusive acts of the *corregidores*, corresponding to that of the *behetrías* called *de mar a mar*, or towns which were free to choose their own overlord and were widely scattered throughout the Peninsula. The statement that the Basques in the Middle Ages had an autonomous government, while the remaining Spaniards were living in feudal slavery, is fundamentally untrue. The municipal autonomy of the Basque cities and villages was also enjoyed by innumerable cities and villages outside these provinces. Spain was a hive of mediaeval republics. This certainly made the Spanish State an excessively weak and poor institution. But the State was one and the same for Castile and the Basque provinces, or, alternatively, for any of those provinces and Navarre or Aragon. Nevertheless, Navarre never had sovereignty, like Castile, over the whole region.

There was never a Basque State or a Basque nation, since the individuals of this race were never united by a system of fixed and general institutions common to all of them, and depended on various States, though some provinces had at times joint assemblies. The general *Juntas* of Alava and Vizcaya did not appear in Guipuzcoa, whose first organ of provincial government dated only from the fifteenth century and derived from the general *Hermandad* of the province, an institution of Castilian origin. In Vizcaya, the towns were subject in the Middle Ages to Castilian law, while the rural districts obeyed a traditional law which was never written down till the fifteenth century, and then only in part. In the towns of Vizcaya the *señores* appointed the mayors and public functionaries. The countryside was democratic; but in Alava, in contrast, real democracy was unknown until the kings of Castile and Navarre introduced the municipalities and *fueros* which favoured the common people,

Though mutilated, the *fueros* survived the above-mentioned law and the question remained a running sore.

To the list of grievances which the Carlists already had against the Liberal State was now added, for the first time, another one about the recovery of the *fueros*. In that moment the real battle for the *fueros* began, though the Carlist rebellion did not lose its general and deep-seated political character.

Soon the conspiracies began again in the north, and this time the Carlists were not the only conspirators—they were joined by certain Basque Liberals, opponents of the political situation reigning in Madrid.

In 1841 there occurred the insurrection against Espartero. The movement had wide ramifications in the Basque Provinces and Navarre, although Don Carlos had ordered the Basques to refrain from trying to overthrow the Regent. Once more it was clear that Basque privileges would continue to be a menace to whatever Liberal Government ruled in Madrid, since any ambitious *caudillo* could count beforehand in the north on the support of forces ever ready to rise and well supplied with arms.

General O'Donnell rose at Pamplona and General Montes de Oca in Guipuzcoa. The *pronunciamiento* failed; and as soon as his hands were free, Espartero rushed to Vitoria, and immediately on arrival drew up a decree abolishing the whole of the Basque *fueros* with a stroke of the pen.

By this decree of October 29th, 1841, which increased the severity of the law passed by the Cortes two years previously, Vizcaya and Guipuzcoa were deprived of the special magistrate who until then had acted as Crown adviser in the local parliaments; Civil Governors were appointed, as in the rest of Spain; the powers of the local parliaments were transferred to the *Diputaciones provinciales*, in accordance with the Constitution; the municipalities and law courts were brought into line with others throughout Spain; the fiscal frontier of the Ebro disappeared; Spanish customs duties, which up till then had been effectively levied only in the ports of San Sebastian and Pasajes, were to be enforced along the whole land and sea frontier with France; those provinces which were formerly obliged to provide for the defence of their own territory were to be subject to military service.

who had been excluded from the *Cofradía de Arriaga* in which only the nobles and clergy were represented.

Still fewer political and other ties existed between the individual institutions of the Basques of Navarre and those of the Basque Provinces.

Nevertheless both the law of October 25th, 1839, and the decree of October 29th, 1841, had an ephemeral life, like the political situations which dictated them. Espartero and the progressives fell from power in 1843, and from that year to 1868, if ·we except the two progressive years 1854–6, Spain was governed by the absolutist reaction, with Narváez and Bravo Murillo as representative figures. The names of Nocedal, Arrazola, Bravo Murillo, González Bravo set the tone for the period. Father Fulgencio, confessor of Don Francisco de Asís, the King Consort; Father Claret, confessor of Isabel II; Sor Patrocinio, Fray Cirilo de la Alameda, ex-adviser of Don Carlos, ruled at the Palace. That meant, as we saw in Chapter VIII of Book One, that Carlism had no need to resort to arms; it had assumed the reins of government by peaceful methods. The centralizing laws were not carried out, for the governing reaction approved of the *fueros*, and the Church—which was the Carlists' chief concern—had recovered her ancient influence over public life.

When Cabrera returned to Spain in 1848, some skirmishes took place in Catalonia; in 1860 General Ortega, Captain-General of the Balearic Islands, landed on the Catalan coast to lead a Carlist rising which failed. Except for these not very serious alarms, Carlism remained quiescent during this period. Its theme continued to be *God, Fatherland and King*—the national fatherland, not the Basque fatherland, and an absolute king for all Spaniards. The *fueros* continued to occupy a secondary place in the Carlist creed.

In 1869 the second Carlist war—the answer to the anti-clerical Constitution of that year—broke out. The coronation of Amadeo of Savoy stirred up the Carlists to fresh wrath; not only because he was a Liberal king, but also because he was a member of the House of Savoy, a dynasty which, in the opinion of the ultramontanes, had usurped the temporal power of the Church of Rome. Amadeo fell, and was followed by the federal Republic, the future Constitution of which (also federal) was discussed in the Cortes. If, as has been said, the Carlists were fighting for the *fueros*, what sense was there in their rising against the federal Republic? They repudiated the federal Republic because it was anti-clerical; and they continued to place the principle of *national* absolutism before the principle of *regional* liberties.

The second Carlist war was, in substance, an exact copy of the first. Carlism was fighting for a Spanish national ideal; it was the party of *imperialism ;* it wanted to conquer Spain.

The *fueros* or privileges which in practice existed, served the Carlists as instruments to conspire and arm.

But the Carlists lost the second civil war, too. They knew before starting it that they were gambling with the *fueros*, but they were prepared to sacrifice them, if this was the price of imposing their ultramontane ideal on the whole of Spain.

When Alfonso XII began to reign, he addressed a proclamation to the rebellious provinces of the north (Jan. 22nd, 1875). "Before opening the battle, I offer you peace," he said. The King promised a general amnesty and confirmation of the *fueros*. The Carlists rejected his offer. Can anyone still maintain that they were fighting for the *fueros*? They themselves made their position clear. They were fighting "against a numerically insignificant faction which had imposed on Spain a series of atheistic and anarchic Governments beginning with the Cortes of 1810 and ending with the Republic of 1873".

As I said, every Carlist knew that the provincial privileges were the price they would pay if they failed in their attempt to establish absolute monarchy in Spain. They could not be surprised, therefore, if Alfonso XII proclaimed in Somorrostro in March 1876 the abolition of the Basque *fueros*.

After this, Cánovas del Castillo revived the law of October 1839, and the precepts of the new Constitution were also applied to the Basque Provinces. Cánovas maintained that it was unjust for some provinces to enjoy privileges which the others did not, especially as these provinces were in a state of permanent rebellion. In the Cortes, and at conferences with the representatives of Vizcaya, Guipuzcoa and Alava, Cánovas declined to discuss anything but certain fiscal and administrative concessions to be granted to these provinces on condition that they allowed other Spaniards to live in peace. The new régime for the Basque Provinces was defined by the law of July 1876. The Basques refused to accept it. Cánovas received a Basque delegation which came to ask him to withdraw the law. The Prime Minister refused to budge. The law was passed; but the local governments would not co-operate with the new authorities. The Basque Provinces were in a state of ferment, but the Army of occupation prevented them from rising. The extraordinary *juntas* of representatives from the three provinces were prohibited; the *Diputaciones forales* were abolished and replaced by *Diputaciones provinciales* elected by the Civil Governor (April–December 1877).

Faced with the implacable State founded by the new oligarchy, the Basques ended by agreeing to negotiate in conditions acceptable to the central Government.

The *Diputaciones provinciales* soon became the last-ditch defenders of the Basque privileges. The Carlists' ideal had been to impose on Spain a given political régime. Defeated in this design, they tried to save the *fueros*, with equal lack of success. The Carlists were fanatics, not inclined by nature to conciliation or compromise. It was the Basque Liberals, with their great influence in the *Diputaciones provinciales*, who took upon themselves the task of defending the remnants of ancient local liberty. Now, these Liberals were speaking in the name of the city *bourgeoisie* (which had always, since the Middle Ages, held aloof from the intolerance of the rural districts), and they concentrated their efforts on concessions of an economic nature. Basque privileges were reduced, therefore, to economic advantages. The Basques were allowed to administer their own taxation system, paying the national State an agreed sum corresponding to the resources of the region; though the result was that the Basque Provinces paid, in practice, less than they ought. Other administrative *fueros* were also reserved to them, and their ancient civil codes of law were likewise respected.

This solution, which was so little in tune with tradition, provoked a profound crisis in the Carlist movement. In Vizcaya and Guipuzcoa, Carlism was converted into regionalist nationalism, while in Alava and Navarre it conserved its character as a Spanish national traditionalist movement.

The causes of this political differentiation must be sought in various historical and geographical factors. Basque nationalism is a social product of Vizcaya, of the Vizcayan countryside. Geographical and economic circumstances place Vizcaya in a special position, especially in respect to Alava and Navarre. The sea, the proximity to large-scale industry, the nature of the villages, the legal tradition, the strong Liberalism of Bilbao conspire together to create the nationalist complex in the Vizcayan Carlist, a complex which is not met with in Alava and Navarre. The peasant of Vizcaya, a province where the *caseríos*, or isolated farmhouses, are very widely scattered, lives a more isolated life, is more parochial than the peasants of Alava or Navarre. The Basque from Navarre and Alava has no contact with the sea, nor does any industry flourish in these two provinces.

At the close of the nineteenth century the Vizcayan and, to a less extent, the Guipuzcoan Basque (especially the peasant) adopted a local nationalism bounded by a narrow horizon. He desired to found a Basque nation with its own State, to unite all Basques under the banner of race and, consequently, to break with the rest of the Spanish community. This doctrine had its apostle—Sabino Arana y Goiri, the virtual founder of the *Partido Nacionalista de Euzkadi* (Basque Nationalist Party). Like Carlism, from which it sprang, Basque nationalism was more than a political movement; it was almost a religion. Its text was *Jaungoikua eta Legi Zarra* (God and the Old Laws). Sabino Arana devised a new setting for nationalism and religion: *Todo para Euzkadi y Euzkadi para Dios*—All for Euzkadi and Euzkadi for God. That is, apparently, the Basque was to give up everything for Euzkadi and Euzkadi was only to exist for God.

For the Basque nationalists, Sabino Arana was a hero, a myth, the Messiah of the race, who died to redeem God's chosen people. Arana suffered imprisonment for his separatist activities. He created a nation-wide uproar in May 1903, when, from his prison cell, he congratulated the President of the United States on the independence of Cuba. His term in gaol did not last longer than five months, which in Spain is small title to a martyr's crown. He died the year he was set at liberty at Pedernales.

It is possible that if Catalan separatism had never existed, Basque separatism would not have seen the light of day. Sabino Arana was a student at the University of Barcelona when Catalan nationalism was at its liveliest, and he returned thence to Vizcaya with the ideas which he incorporated into a booklet, *Vizcaya por su Independencia*.

Once the Basque Nationalist Party, founded in 1906, was on the march, the intellectuals of the movement set about defining its character. Of the "God, Fatherland and King" of the Carlists, only God remained. The greater fatherland, the nation, had contracted, like another *peau de chagrin*, into Euzkadi, the fatherland of the Basques alone. The King was dropped from the nationalist creed. The *vizcaitarras* (as they were called) or Basque nationalists were as fervent Catholics as the Carlists; but it was not the first time that Catholicism and Christianity seemed to represent different things.

For, above all, Basque nationalism was a party founded on race. The nationalists were fighting for political independence in the name of racial values. The powerful impulse behind Basque nationalism was "racial yearnings" (Aguirre). The aim of nationalism was "to recover all our racial characteristics" (Aranzadi). Finally, the Basque race, if it was to fulfil its racial destiny, needed a Basque State.

The Basque nationalists would naturally not have taken up a moral position like this, had they not been convinced that theirs was a superior race. This conviction breathes through all their acts and through their interpretation of history. The Basques are a superior race; and, therefore, the best, the most intelligent, the most active, the most hard-working, the most cultivated. They are, moreover, the most noble, the most pure-blooded. In the Basques, Spanish pride soars to giddy heights, and the nationalists, by turning it into racial channels, often fall into childish vaingloriousness when comparing their own people with others.

Basque nationalism was bound to stir up the ancient xenophobia of the peasant with its racial creed; and at a time when it was boasting of its stainless Catholicism, it was in open collision with the essence of Christianity, which is, surely, charity. The non-Basque Spaniards living and working in the Basque Provinces were regarded with singular disdain by the nationalists, who rejected them as members of an inferior race, calling them *maquetos*.

At the beginning of the present century the Basque Nationalist Party was probably the only racial movement in Europe. The *vizcaitarras* could be seen using the oriental swastika, the racial emblem.

Basque nationalism was opposed to class warfare and founded *Solidaridad de Obreros Vascos* in opposition to the Socialist trade unions. The Basque nationalists had their para-military organization, the *mendigoixales*.

The political-social strength of the Basque nationalists resided chiefly in the country districts, though they have never been without a minority of industrialists and bankers, among whom Don Ramón de la Sota y Llano was outstanding. But because Basque nationalism was a Catholic and reactionary force, favouring a workers' movement opposed to class warfare, the capitalists looked upon it from the beginning with a friendly eye. Though they did not belong to the Nationalist Party, the capitalists were interested in the progress of nationalism and of *Solidaridad de Obreros Vascos*, since the nationalist movement was a rampart defending the propertied classes and the Church against the Socialist movement which was very strong in Vizcaya.

Sabino Arana had no great difficulty in laying the foundation-stone of the nationalist edifice, and his successors went ahead with the work with astonishing speed. In the rural districts of Vizcaya and Guipuzcoa, the nationalists could count on a vast number of Basques who were predisposed to accept the new ideology. By cultivating traditions and old customs, by using a few words of the local idiom (the only ones they knew), the nationalist leaders were fighting the other non-nationalist reactionary parties on favourable ground. There was, moreover, in the appeal of the nationalist leaders a warmth which the other conservative parties lacked. With their glib use of the language, their racy jests and use of "local colour", their condemnation of everything that was not Basque, the nationalists aroused in the rural districts feelings and passions which neither Socialists nor Monarchists knew how to, or wanted to exploit.

In these provinces Carlism or traditionalism, represented by mature and *respectable* persons, retreated before youth, which enlisted in the nationalist movement. One of the first of the young men to join the Basque Nationalist Party was a powerful writer (in the Spanish tongue, naturally) called Tomás Meabe. But because he was a man of great intellect and of wide human horizons, Meabe saw the error of his ways and broke off his connection with the nationalists. When Sabino Arana heard that Meabe had left the Party, he exclaimed: "I would let my right arm be cut off, if only this were not true!"

For the Basque peasant—the Carlist of yesterday—the nationalists were not only Catholics and traditionalists; they offered in addition a "national" ideal which was to save everything he loved.

In the villages, recruits to nationalism were in an immense majority. But the great cities continued to be Liberal, seeing in nationalism an anti-Liberal movement, fanatical and clerical, a genuine ramification of the Carlism against which they had always fought.

To sum up, Basque nationalism owed its strength to its energetic appeal to the soul of the Basque peasant, to its character as a conservative and anti-socialist political organization, and, last but not least, to the weakness, incompetence and corruption of the oligarchic State. This last justified the nationalist protest, and no doubt, as we have seen, inevitably fostered secessionism, in the Basque Provinces as well as in Catalonia.

However, the Basque nationalists were not always just over what they called, throwing up their hands in despair, "That Spain . . .!" For, after all, Spain had been the victim of the policy followed at home and abroad in the sixteenth century. Spain was ruined in the struggle against the Reformation. From this springs all the confusion of modern Spain. But the part played by the Basques in the creation of the religious Empire which destroyed Castile was immense and decisive. Saint Ignatius Loyola was, I repeat, a Basque; and the Society of Jesus, the militia of the Counter-Reformation, was a product of the Basque country. The majority, perhaps, of the eminent theologians who, at the Council of Trent, launched Spain on the path of economic and political annihilation, were Basques. From the Basque Provinces, then, came the idea of saving Rome, even if that meant the end or destruction of Spain.

Now the Basques who contributed so much to despatching Spain on her overhard enterprise, which seems so mistaken to us today (though it should not appear so to those ardent Catholics, the Basque nationalists), did not contribute in equal measure to the burdens of the adventure. They paid practically no taxes to the national State until the nineteenth century; and even then, Castile, poor, without industry, without commerce, paid in taxation double what the three Basque Provinces did. The Basques, moreover, free from military service on land (though they were always to be found in the thick of naval combats) held aloof from the religious wars into which their theologians had plunged Spain. While Castile was sending her infantry regiments into battle and spending her last *maravedí* for the policy of St. Ignatius Loyola, the Basques were cultivating their fields and putting their economic life in order. Small wonder, in the end, if the Basque Provinces were a habitable, ordered, more equalitarian and better administered country, and Castile lay in ruins, subjected to a corrupt oligarchy.

The Basque nationalists' plan to found a society based exclusively on the ties of blood, such as existed before the dawn of civilization and the State, must be repugnant to any liberal mind. It is symptomatic that no outstanding Basque intellectual belongs to this party. Since its foundation, its political leadership has been carried on by lawyers and its cultural leadership by the parish priests. The rôle of the Basque priests and friars in the moral and literary development of secessionism is notable from a political point of view, though intellectually it is characterized by its poverty. Just as the Society of Jesus and the lower ranks of the clergy were the *deus ex machina* in the separation of Portugal in the seventeenth century, so in this case, the noumenon behind Basque separatism is the clergy.

In this age of universalism, when man is striving to eliminate frontiers and sovereignties which are contrary to the interests of the human race, Basque nationalism, although from the social standpoint it has become very liberal, is reactionary and anachronistic. In these present days, when we are seeking a universal language, trying to unite the most widely separated peoples and struggling to put an end to racial conflicts and differences, the Basque nationalists, for political ends, strain every nerve to propagate the *éuscaro* or Basque language, which is now only general in the rural districts. The Basque language is a tongue without a literary tradition, without written documents prior to the fifteenth century; it is, if I may say so without offence, the language of a primitive culture, and by giving it a new lease of life the Basque nationalist leaders (the majority of whom did not speak it and have only now begun to learn it) are engaged in introducing a new source of confusion in the relations between peoples, especially between the Spanish peoples. They want to extend its use at the expense of the Spanish idiom, the vehicle of a higher culture and a language which has received not a small part of its lustre from the Basques themselves; in fact Hernando de Herrera, in the sixteenth century, places Bilbao and Bermeo among the populations of Spain which speak it best.

There is no doubt that Basque nationalism, though some of its leaders think otherwise, is a retrograde step, which can perhaps be explained by a moral factor of very frequent occurrence in the gestation of movements of this kind. This moral factor is resentment. In my view it is evident that the victory of the towns over the country in the two Carlist wars sowed the seeds of present-day nationalism in the minds of the peasants of Vizcaya and Guipuzcoa who were Carlists to a man. These peasants, who had been twice repulsed before Bilbao after having twice besieged it, and who had seen the moral leadership of the region pass to the cities, and to cities which contained a majority of non-Basque citizens, had ended by giving way to an understandable frustration-complex. Impotent to impose their absolutist ideal on Spain, not even on the principal cities of their own region, they had reacted by turning to racialism and separatism. That the Carlist from Alava and Navarre was not affected by a similar aberration confirms this idea, in my view; since neither in Alava nor in Navarre are there great cities, or any Liberal tendency of importance.

The existence of heavy industry, the last word in modernity, in the proximity of the primitive rural districts, must also have helped to exacerbate Basque racialism. The birth of large-scale industry and its unbridled development in Vizcaya runs parallel to the birth and swift development of Basque nationalism. What bearing one phenomenon has in detail on the operation of the other—the economic difficulties of Vizcaya during the last fifteen years—I do not propose to enquire. But the example

420

of Germany proves, in my opinion, that the rapid industrialization of a primitive-souled, romantic nation can engender, or accentuate, a "superior race" complex and imperialism. The imperialistic impulse of Basque nationalism is shown by its claim to extend the frontiers of Vasconia to the north-east and south, beyond the present boundary of the Basque Provinces. The nationalists aspire to create a Greater Basque Reich by extending the jurisdiction of the Basque State to all the territories where there are communities of their race.

We already know the origin and initial stages of Basque nationalism. It might be well now to give an account of the principal events which make up the history of this movement from the foundation of the Party to the civil war of 1936.

In July 1917 the Basque *Diputaciones* met at Vitoria and agreed to demand a régime of far-reaching autonomy. This decision was confirmed by the assembly of municipal governments held at Guernica on August 10th of the same year. In the following October the presidents of the three *Diputaciones* waited upon Alfonso XIII in order to crave the King's assent to the autonomous régime.

In September 1918 a Basque Cultural Congress, summoned for obvious political ends, was held at Oñate.

In October of the same year the Basque nationalists appealed to the President of the United States for his support in their cause.

Under Primo de Rivera's dictatorship, the Basque nationalists adopted a submissive attitude. The social strife and public violence which preceded the military *coup d'état* in 1923 had made the Basque nationalists, as a clerical and conservative party, an ally of the dictatorship. "Have you ever seen", asked Indalecio Prieto at the end of that régime, "a more grievous spectacle than the abjectness of the Basque authorities and public corporations during these last six years? Surely a record in ignominy and political meanness! When have the remnants of the Basque autonomous tradition suffered more serious damage than during these last years? When has the hope of a resurrection of the country's aspirations been more completely damned than in these six years? Yet the *chistularis*, who represent what is most idyllic in the Basque tradition, have gone to the grotesque cavalcades, the carnivals, organized by the dictator in Madrid; the *miqueletes*, emblem of the rags of Basque sovereignty, have formed part of them, to provide a guard of honour for the man who outraged the Basque language, prohibited its teaching, and derided at every moment and with morbid pleasure, the country's traditions."[1]

When the monarchy fell, the Republican parties were reluctant to grant autonomy to the Basque movement because they thought, as I said before, that the Nationalist Party predominating there was a reactionary, fanatical and Catholic movement, of which the Republic had to beware. For their part, the Basque nationalists at that time only hoped for the satisfaction of their aspirations from the oligarchic and capitalist parties.

In the municipal elections of April 1931, just before the proclamation of the Republic, the Basque Nationalist Party went to the polls independently of the other political parties, the Republicans and the Monarchists. The Republican and workers' parties were successful in the Basque capitals and the nationalists triumphed in the villages, except in Navarre and part of Alava, where the coalition of Monarchists and Carlists was victorious.

With the Republic under way, the Nationalist Party opened its campaign for autonomy by seeking support among the Carlist and oligarchic forces. A Basque-Navarrese group, composed of Basque nationalists and Carlists, appeared in the Cortes. In close collaboration with the Carlists, the nationalists endeavoured to secure their co-operation in the task of obtaining the Statute of Autonomy. Both parties, branches of the same political tree, endeavoured to maintain and consolidate the alliance, and, to this end, drew up a pact, the Statute of Estella, which failed because the Carlists would not compromise with the autonomism of the Basque nationalists which to them was disguised separatism.

On November 5th, 1933, the plebiscite provided for under the Constitution of the Republic, whereby a region might aspire to autonomy, took place in the Basque Provinces. The result was a resounding victory for the autonomist cause; for it was not only the Basque nationalists who demanded the Statute, but also a great number of citizens domiciled in the region who, though not supporting separatism, yet thought it advisable or necessary to try the experiment of politically reorganizing the national State. Many Republicans considered that autonomy might be the solution of an old and bitter struggle, and thought that since the Constitution allowed it, it merited a trial. The policy of the Castilian-Andalusian oligarchy was

[1] Speech at *El Sitio*, Bilbao, May 3rd, 1930.

opposed to regional liberties—as it was opposed to all liberties—
and Republicans of all kinds saw in regional autonomy, as I
said before, a satisfactory alternative which was preferable to
the use of force against the nationalist movements of the Basque
Provinces and Catalonia.

In the elections of November 1933, when the counter-
revolution triumphed, the Basque nationalists again stood as
an independent party and obtained the majority of votes
throughout the Basque country.

The nationalists still thought that if the Statute was granted
by the Cortes, they would owe it to the reactionary parties.
In fact no sooner had the new Parliament begun its sessions,
with an oligarchic and Lerrouxist majority, than the Basque
minority presented its draft Statute to the Chamber. A Parliamentary Committee was thereupon appointed to report on the
Basque document and submit their findings to the Cortes. But
in the course of two stormy sessions, the nationalists were
forced to conclude that the parties of reaction were violently
opposed to granting autonomy to the Basque Provinces.

Then began the mutual drawing together of the Basque
nationalists and the Republican and workers' parties. The
Left parties, in a minority in Parliament, abandoned their
attitude of opposition to Basque autonomy and now supported
the Basque nationalist deputies, because in this way they were
weakening the Parliament and the Government of the counter-
revolution.

The Cortes of 1933 dropped the question of the Basque Statute.

When the Popular Front triumphed in the elections of
February 1936 (in which the Basque nationalists again stood
as an independent party), another Parliamentary Committee
was appointed to give special attention to the Basque Statute.
This Committee was constantly hampered by the obstructive
tactics of the Right, implacably pursued under the leadership
of Calvo Sotelo.

The violent workings of politics in a nation on the verge of
civil war made it certain that the more energetically the oligarchy
opposed the Basque Statute, the more sympathy it would awaken
among the parties of the Left.

At the beginning of July 1936 the final text of the Statute
had already been drawn up by the Parliamentary Committee
and approved by a majority composed of all the parties of the
Left and the Catalan parties of the Right. But on July 18th
the civil war broke out and as the sessions of the Cortes were
suspended, the deputies had no immediate opportunity of

approving the Basque Statute and converting it into law, which was only finally done on October 1st.

At the outset of the civil war, the Basque Nationalist Party—Catholic, conservative and anti-Socialist—found itself in an extremely delicate position. Its exalted Catholicism—the Catholicism of the Carlists—its respect for private property and its fear of revolution impelled the Basque nationalist leaders and their followers towards Franco's faction. But at that moment, the Basque nationalists did not regard themselves as either Republicans or Monarchists, Catholics or atheists; they regarded themselves as Basques.

On the other hand, there were influential Republican and Socialist politicians who thought that to win over the Basque nationalists to the Republican cause in the civil war would be of incalculable benefit to the régime. From July to October the negotiations between the Republicans and the Basque nationalists went on unceasingly. In the end autonomy was conceded. Shortly afterwards the Basque municipal representatives met at Guernica and elected José Antonio Aguirre to be President of the Autonomous Government.

## CHAPTER XII

# THE REPUBLIC AND THE CHURCH

"If anything of a national character is to be constructed in Spain," wrote Angel Ganivet, "it must be built on the foundations of tradition. This is but logical and right; for having ruined ourselves in the defence of Catholicism, there could be no greater affront than to betray our fathers and add to the sadness of a defeat, which is perhaps transitory, the humiliation of submitting to the influence of our conquerors' ideas. . . ."[1]

I confess that this sentimental defence of traditionalism does not strike me as very convincing. To have ruined oneself for an idea, far from being a reason for persevering in its defence, is a bitter experience which should put any nation with an instinct for self-preservation on its guard against that idea. Something like this happened in Spain. What Ganivet really means to say is that, in the case of Spain, philosophy has to make concessions to politics, to yield to political necessity.

[1] *Idearium español*, p. 29.

We have here, to all appearances, a traditionalist and Catholic Ganivet, calling the attention of the political reformer to the danger of building on a foundation which does not accord with the religious tradition of Spain. But he is not a Catholic, as constantly transpires in his *Epistolario*, where he ends by confessing without beating about the bush: "This is why I, without being a Catholic . . ."[1] Nevertheless both attitudes are perfectly consistent in a mind preoccupied, perhaps tormented, by the Spanish tragedy. In the *Idearium*, Ganivet is adopting an attitude foreign to his own convictions and his personal interest—the attitude of the politician who is responsible to the nation; he is expounding a Spanish *idearium*, a guide for someone in a responsible position who has to solve the problems of Spain. The *Epistolario*, on the other hand, contains the intimate, private and individual views of Ganivet, a great Spaniard who realizes that in Spain's present state, only a policy of prudence towards certain problems can save the nation.

Ganivet thought that "Spain and her religious ideal are one" and that to attempt to "de-Catholicize" her was a waste of time. But this was the very reason why there was no need to fear opposition; on the contrary, it would be a good thing if there existed other confessions which would "stimulate and revive genuinely national energies, now dormant and as if mummified". In her own interest, he continued, the Catholic Church ought to encourage schism. With this idea in his mind, he inserted in the *Idearium* the story of the man who, travelling in a sleigh with his five sons, was attacked by hungry wolves, and saw no way of escape but to throw them the youngest child; and while the wolves were quarrelling over their prey, the man sped on his way with his four remaining sons unhurt. And he concludes: "Spain ought to act like that barbarous but loving father. . . . Some sentimentalists would immediately say that the expedient is too brutal; but faced with the spiritual ruin of Spain, we must have stones in place of hearts and throw a million Spaniards, if need be, to the wolves, if we do not want to be all thrown to the swine."

Ganivet wrote all this in 1896, in the presence, as he tells us, of the spiritual ruin of Spain. The prostration or moral debility of the Spanish people coincided at that time with a certain material advance; the disaster overseas had not yet occurred, nor had Basque nationalism arisen, while Catalan

---

[1] *Epistolario*, p. 274. Madrid, 1904. An interesting study on the ideas and personality of Angel Ganivet will be found in *The Soul of Spain*, by Havelock Ellis. London, 1908.

nationalism had not assumed the violent character it suddenly took from '98 onwards. The political disintegration of Spain was checked outwardly by the iron police-*cacique* system of the Restoration. Today the ruin of Spain is not only spiritual, but also political and physical, absolute and complete. Today we are writing in the light of a terrible, unheard-of, unprecedented experience. And we know, among other things of the gravest import, that the social and political development of Spain has been violently upset at two critical phases of her history—in 1823 and 1936—by foreign interference. The precariousness of the national independence, the scant freedom of movement of the revolution—more urgent now than ever—oblige Spanish democracy to conserve its energies and not to create for itself more enemies inside and outside Spain than those which are really unavoidable and can be overcome.

In the spiritual domain the problem still lies in establishing liberty of conscience and preventing the Church from becoming a State within a State. But a century and a half of anti-clericalism bears witness to the failure of Spanish Liberal policy in what is precisely the pivotal point of its doctrine. Spanish Liberalism has lost its battle with the Catholic Church in the political field, and in recognizing this fact (if, indeed, Liberals can get as far as recognizing it) there can be no question of apostasy. An army which surrenders does not pass over to the enemy. A reflection which brings us back to Ganivet's story, though in an inverse sense. The question was whether the Spanish Republic would not find it too brutal an expedient to throw to the wolves its youngest child, in this case the religious question considered as the fundamental Spanish problem. Faced with the total collapse of Spain, the Spanish Liberals should have hardened their hearts as advised by the author of the *Idearium*, and patriotically admitted that they had been mistaken in the diagnosis of the national disease. They were not asked to capitulate ignominiously, which was not necessary; and besides, nothing is ever gained by dishonour. All that was required was an acknowledgment that the philosophic Liberals had failed in Spain by presenting the religious question in a false light and that therefore they should revise their political tactics. The fact that the Church now had more political influence and wealth than it had about the middle of the past century, proved beyond a peradventure that Liberalism had been routed in its struggle with clericalism.

In fact, half-way through the nineteenth century, the Church in Spain was poor and had suffered much from expropriation.

As a contemporary observer remarked: canons and Church dignitaries were reduced to absolute want and it was not rare to find them soliciting public charity. There were no religious orders; and convents were used as barracks or schools or turned into art museums like that of the Carmelites at Valencia, when they were not used for bull-fights as in Malaga. Any Spaniards who counted individually were Liberals—more or less moderate or ultra-radical. The aristocracy, the landowners, the *bourgeoisie*, the Army, boasted of their Liberalism. Anti-clericalism and culture were *à la mode* in the drawing-rooms. The Church found herself forsaken, save in the north, divorced from the State and the ruling class, her traditional popularity beginning to turn into hatred. The Spanish clergy pinned all its hopes then on Rome, on a Concordat, on foreign help.

Things changed radically with the Restoration régime, as I have said more than once in these pages. Spain filled up again with convents and religious communities, as if the Cortes of Cadiz, the disentailing of the estates and the Liberal revolution had never been. Of all that Liberalism had won in a century of bitter struggle, there only remained what society had been able to digest—nothing more. The spirit, if not the letter, of toleration had gained ground in the great urban centres, but the rural clergy were still Carlist. And however much toleration was written into the Constitution, it would never penetrate into the inert, depopulated and rural provinces, or—which was the same thing—into the viscera of the nation. In 1931 the Cardinal-Primate of Spain was a typical mediaeval archbishop.

Was it worth while aiming at becoming politically another Belgium or France? asks Ganivet. This was another question. Ganivet's opinion was that Spain was better off as she was, as she used to be in 1896. Many Spaniards will certainly not agree with him. But the point I want to emphasize—and it is a point I have stressed before—is that toleration must be regarded as the corollary of a civil environment which is more powerful than a Church or Churches; that it does not spring, as Ganivet supposed, from a plurality of religions in the same nation, which, if they are sufficiently powerful numerically, lead not to peace and harmony but—where the civil power lacks vigour—to civil war, as happened in sixteenth-century France and seventeenth-century England.

Once they had expropriated the Church, the Spanish Liberals dissociated the economic and religious factors at their convenience. By depriving the Church of her lands, they thought they had got the best of her; and the Church did indeed remain subdued for some time, until a change of policy and the adoption of other tactics restored all her ancient wealth and more, though a different kind of wealth. The Church owed her material resurrection in Spain (for spiritually she never recovered) to fifty years of oligarchic protection; and the protecting oligarchy owed its whole existence to its monopoly of land and banking, to its possession of the national wealth. The most dangerous enemy of the Republic was not to be, therefore, the Church, but her supporting base, the agrarian-financial oligarchy. Yet the Republican and workers' parties reserved their thunder for the clergy and the religious orders. Thus, democratic opinion relegated to a subordinate place those "other and more deadly communities of frock-coated friars, under whose influence [as Costa said] Spain has degenerated into a conglomeration of slaves, with a cruelly ironic democratic Constitution".

The "frock-coated friars" had saved themselves, and in doing so, had also saved the real friars. The oligarchy, whose only god was Mammon, was incalculably strengthened, at a critical moment for its vast property, by becoming the spokesman of the Church's cause and having the Church herself on its side. Even the ancients understood how important it is in civil strife to fight under the banner of religion.

In the light of subsequent events, did the Republic in 1931 deal with the ecclesiastical question in the best way? It must be admitted that neither the political situation, nor the general atmosphere, nor the state of public enlightenment, nor the system of government adopted by the Republic, admitted of a solution different from that actually adopted, however absurd this may appear to us today. The doctrinal and political bias most attuned to popular opinion prevailed. In Spain, as in other countries, the people take their tone from the middle class. And the Spanish middle class, which was clearly obsessed by the clerical or religious problem, easily persuaded the proletariat, for reasons which will be explained later, that this problem was the key to public happiness or misery. The conduct of the Church and the ignorance of the common people conspired together to create this illusion in the popular mind.

These factors deserve special attention. First, the attitude of the middle-class intellectuals, the only social stratum in the Spanish social structure for which a religious problem existed. This enlightened section of the middle class, which would be hard to cement into a homogeneous body, had its own kind of religion—pantheistic humanism, or Erasmianism or its offspring Krausism, or a Voltairian deism, or simply agnosticism with a marked militant anti-Catholic bias. This nucleus, whose moral and intellectual authority was considerable, was opposed to the Catholic tradition of Spain and to present-day official Catholicism on conscientious grounds. Unorthodox Spaniards of this class considered "that the religious problem, with its outward aspect, the ecclesiastical problem, was the most intimate, the most profound problem in the life of Spain", and seized the opportunity of discussing such a lofty subject in the Constituent Cortes to render (amid loud and prolonged applause) "a tribute of respect and the homage of our vindication" to the Jews who had been expelled by the Catholic sovereigns in the fifteenth century.

However, as always in Spain, the Protestant religion and other positive religions hardly existed. So scattered were the unorthodox of the Protestant sects which vegetated obscurely in Spain, that Azaña, when he was a Minister of the Republic, did not know if there was one Protestant Church, or many, or where they were.[1] What characterizes the unorthodox in general, whatever their intimate beliefs (which nobody knows for certain) and the profundity of their faith, is their belief in toleration. Their ideal, therefore, is the secularization of the State and liberty of conscience. A lay Republic on the French model is what they aspire to; and for the true unorthodox, that is, for those who have a religious faith, this aspiration means that merely political values must give way to spiritual values.

This was the religious and anti-clerical attitude—an attitude with a visible streak of idealism—of a small section of the Republican middle class. But not all the middle class intelligentsia were Erasmianists or Krausists, nor had they a religious attitude to oppose to the Catholic Church; for some of them, the political aspect, State policy, political sentiment based on Hegelism, came first, as in the case of Azaña, whose attitude we shall analyse later.

Nevertheless, in one way or another, the middle-class intelligentsia displayed complete unanimity in regarding the secularization of public life as a pressing necessity.

Then there was another, essentially different, anti-clerical attitude—that of the proletariat. The anti-clericalism of the

---

[1] "There is a Protestant Church in Spain—or there may be many, for all I know—with its bishops and its faithful; and the State absolutely ignores the Spanish Protestant Church." (Speech on Art. 26 of the Constitution.)

middle class had either a religious or a political root. The anti-clericalism of the masses, of the common people, was neither religious nor political, but social. The Spanish people had drifted apart from the Church for other reasons than those of the unorthodox. We have here a profound historical tragedy which cannot be attributed to modern revolutionary currents; for Spain, in innumerable aspects, is Ireland on a large scale; and in Spain the common people would have continued to be Catholic in spite of modern ideas, as they continued to be in Ireland, had not the Church expelled them from her bosom. Whether that is a good thing for the proletariat or for Spain is another matter. What must be noted here is that the reason why the people are *against* the Church after having been *for* her, and are not merely indifferent to her as in other nations, is plainly not an external, philosophic reason, but an intimately Spanish reason arising out of the fact that the Church in Spain has fallen into a rigid attitude as an oppressing *class*. Since then the Spanish people have learnt to be anti-clerical, taking their cue from the Liberal middle class, to which they formerly turned a deaf ear. For about the middle of the past century the poorer classes were profoundly religious, "loyal and religious at heart" (Ford, I, p. 65). Today, in everything appertaining to the Church, a state of affairs exists which is at the opposite end of the pole to the Spanish tradition. In the fifteenth, sixteenth and seventeenth centuries—up to the nineteenth century in fact—the people followed the lead of the Church against the unorthodox and the rich and even against the Government. During the reign of Charles III the Jesuits could still incite the people to rebel against the Government and overthrow a Minister by stirring up popular opinion against him. The persecution of Jews and Moors by the people and the Church in the fifteenth, sixteenth and seventeenth centuries did not originate merely in hatred of heresy, but, to a great extent, in the fact that their standard of living was higher than that of most Spaniards and that not a few were wealthy. But now the people sided with the free-thinkers against a Church allied with the rich; and there can be no doubt that the major responsibility for this revolution in popular feeling lay at the door of the Church. For it is the Church which has changed. The unorthodox Spaniards, though numerically greater, and the Spanish people are the same as they were in the sixteenth century; but the Church is not the same.

The neo-Catholicism of the middle of the last century, which came upon the scene with the new oligarchy, initiated the unhappy class policy, the championship *à outrance* of an unjust system of property, which was sealed by the compromise with the great landowners in the Restoration State. As a result, the Church was to condemn every protest by the disinherited and support every repressive measure by the oligarchic Government. Woe to the priest who dared to denounce the rich from his pulpit! On him would fall the heavy hand of the bishop. So degenerate had the ecclesiastic hierarchy become that it could find no better remedy for the struggle between the classes than the reinforcement of the police and an increased severity in the laws; like that Bishop of Salamanca who in 1892, during the events at Jerez, demanded of the Senate a more rigorous Penal Code. What hope could the Church have, when she behaved like this, that the proletariat would listen to her other voice calling them to prayer; what hope of a doctrine which took advantage of the poor? Pulpits and pastorals resounded with systematic denunciation of the people's protests, while the most heartless exploitation was encouraged by an ominous silence. The Church raised her workers' trade unions in the service of the capitalists, without, however, much success; and during the social struggles it was not a rare thing—however incredible this may seem—for the Church to entrust the defence of capitalist interests, already apparently coupled with those of religion, to the pistol of the hired gunman. Oligarchy and Church had merged into one. Only the eye of a lynx could at times distinguish between the bishop and the police officer. Both were instruments of a vile policy. And the people reserved, perhaps, their bitterest resentment for the clergy, firstly, because the violence of the State offended their sensibilities less than the Church's lack of charity; and secondly, because the middle classes indicted the Church as the fount of all ills, past and present, in Spain, a thesis to which the class policy of the clergy lent colour in the eyes of the proletariat. ". . . and if a single lamb should die through his (the bishop's) neglect, without the Sacraments, or should perish of hunger, he will be called to account", wrote Father Nieremberg.[1] And so it was; the people called the Church to account for having abandoned them.

The burning of churches is frequently ascribed to the anarchists, and foreign pens, usually so apt to idealize Spanish anarchism, endeavour to descry in the aggressiveness of the Spanish people towards the Church an outraged religious

[1] *Epistolario*, Clásicos castellanos, p. 76.

feeling. Anarchism, we are told, may be defined as the Spanish Protestant heresy; and the hatred of the anarchist for the Church may be interpreted as the reaction of an intensely religious people which perceives that it has been abandoned and betrayed. But the position seems to me more simple; in my view there is no need to look for a theological or esoteric explanation for something which is transparently social in character. The Catholic Church in Spain—the high dignitaries and some of the religious orders—has betrayed the essence of religion by exaggerating the importance of this world's goods; she has valued money and business too highly, and when she has had to take a stand on the social question—and who has not had to, in Spain?—she has pronounced judgment against the poor. The cupidity of the clergy alone would have provoked a reform movement in Spain, if Spain had been living in a religious age. But as this was not the case, the tendency among those whom the Church had defrauded was not to purify her, but to destroy her. For their part, the simple-minded people, who found fault with the religion of their forefathers for not being sufficiently egalitarian and democratic, and rightly (though this scandalized the learned) saw in the Gospel a social doctrine and in Christ something like the harbinger of agrarian reform, were encouraged to turn away from the altars by the conviction that the Church which blocked their progress in every direction was the only thing that separated them from Christianity.

But was not the same thing occurring everywhere? No. Even those who most firmly believe that "the banner of the Church has very seldom been seen on the side of the people" (Gibbon, III), will readily perceive the difference which, in social matters, separates the Belgian, French, and especially the German and English Catholics, from the Spanish clergy. The English Churches champion the people's cause with a zeal which would alarm the Spanish bishops. The right of the working classes to rebel when the necessaries of life are lacking is a principle that is often recalled by the English priesthood. And at this very hour the Church of England is persisting in leading the movement towards political and economic regeneration, not without misgivings on the part of the Conservatives. A Church which behaves in this way may not make converts in a sceptical age, but socially it will be a popular Church.

The secret of such a laudable attitude does not lie in the fact that the Church of England is a Protestant Church.

Catholicism is as popular in Belgium as Anglicanism is in England, because it directs its social policy, if not towards emancipation, at any rate towards the defence of a decent standard of living for the oppressed. And even in France the Catholic Church has found in a bland neutrality towards the daily incidents of class warfare, a clever expedient whereby it neither annoys the rich nor incurs the hatred of the exploited. Finally in Germany, before the advent of Hitler, a large working-class body—more than a million strong—which served in the ranks of the Christian trade unions, was proof of the fact that the Catholic Church, like the other Churches, was not indifferent, much less hostile, to the social interests of the workers.

Certainly the relative equilibrium of society, in these and other nations, has favoured the position of the Church as a popular institution. The clergy can incline to the side of justice without running the risk of encouraging revolution or of losing the support of the propertied classes. The social structure in England, for example, of which the backbone is a numerous middle class, relieves the Church of the hazardous duty of pronouncing judgment in a war between millionaires and beggars. Such is not the case in Spain. Society is divided, as we so well know, into two extreme factions and there is no place for the social neutrality of an institution like the Church. So opposed are the interests of the people and of the oligarchy, that there is no choice between either supporting the people against the oligarchy or the oligarchy against the people. Towards the close of the nineteenth century the Catholic Church in Spain was faced with the choice of being either a poor, but morally healthy, Church, or a rich, but unpopular and corrupt Church. She chose the second course.

But it is important to point out (and this fully confirms my thesis) that in those regions of Spain where the social question appeared less harsh owing to the fact that inequalities were less glaring, the clergy continued to enjoy the support of the lower classes. This was the case in the Basque Provinces, in Navarre, in the rural districts of Galicia, the Levante and Catalonia, and to a great extent, of Old Castile. In the regions where the land is reasonably divided up, poverty is universal, as in Galicia, or a tolerable standard of living is the general rule. The local clergy had not to pronounce on a basic social conflict or opt for one of two antagonistic groups as in the regions of the great estates. Or if they found themselves obliged to take sides in a social quarrel, such as that of the Galician *foros*, they supported the cause of the discontented *foreros*. In dealing with anti-clerical violence, therefore, geography shows us the reason for the anger of the people with the Church; it is a manifestation of the class struggle in which popular feeling is bitterest in places where the contrast between wealth and poverty is most repulsive and which vents itself on the Church as the champion of inequality. I think it may be taken as axiomatic that if property had been divided up over the whole of Spain as it is in the north, the Church would have enjoyed, if not the fanatical enthusiasm which distinguishes Navarre, at least the popular respect on which the clergy prided themselves in the Basque Provinces.

It should be remarked, therefore, that, in spite of her disastrous policy, the Church has not altogether lost her old standing with the people, for, as I have just said, she is deeply rooted in the heart of entire regions where there is an egalitarian rural society. She reigns supreme in the provinces to the north of the Tagus and the Ebro and some regions can still raise an army of visionaries, ready to die for their religion as they died in the sixteenth and seventeenth centuries, such as could not be found in any other country of the Western world today. The religious sentiment grows fainter and weaker the nearer we approach to the great modern cities, of which there are few in Spain. Here the Church exchanges the support of the people for that of the oligarchy and a considerable section of the middle class. It is superfluous to point out that, both in the country districts and the cities, the so-called weaker sex becomes the stronger sex, so highly praised in the Bible, where the Church is concerned; it forms the religious contingent which is courted by the clergy with the most success. In general, the feminine portion of the proletariat have turned their backs on the Church, partly because in the workers' homes the husband gives the orders, and partly because the working-class woman experiences at every turn the consequences of a social order which the Spanish Church proclaims to be perfect. But the middle-class woman, from whom the class struggle has not torn the veil of superstition, is a force which is directed from the confessional. The wives of anti-clericals are not always an exception; nor is it rare to find the images of the Catholic faith in anti-clerical homes—which the malicious might perhaps interpret as husbandly weakness or the ingenuous as proof of a tolerant mind. How often does the freethinker go to Mass on Sundays "in order to avoid a scene with his wife", like Campoamor!

434

All this shows how delicate was the clerical problem, the most brittle with which the Spanish democrats had to deal.

Before starting to examine the ecclesiastical question under the Republic, it would not be out of place to say a few words and give a few figures about the personnel and property of the Church and the religious orders in 1931.

There has always been wide-spread confusion on this subject, since the true facts have been concealed from the public and even from the Government of the day. Above all, the calculation of the wealth of the clergy has had to be left to conjecture. The truth is that, before the Republic, there was no trustworthy official census either of Church property or of the numbers of the clergy. The first Minister of Justice in the new régime had to compile a census by telegraphic orders. The data collected then by this Department of State were, therefore, the most reliable and, though incomplete, afford us the best guide.

Thirty-five thousand men, among them archbishops, bishops, abbots, dignitaries, canons, parish priests and deacons, were dependent on the Budget for Public Worship and the Clergy.

According to information collected by the registrars of property, Church property amounted to 11,921 rural estates, 7,828 urban estates and 4,192 *censos* or leases. The declared values amounted to 76 million and the proved values to 85 million pesetas.

On the basis of the foregoing data, the experts pointed out that declared values are always low, especially as regards immovable property; that a minimum of 30 per cent can be added to them; that the immense majority of the estates had been valued in accordance with the tax rating and not the surveyor's measurements, without the corresponding surcharge having been added; that 265 rural properties and 398 urban properties had never been valued; that many *censos* payable in grain and others, whose capital value was not evident, as well as the numbers of masses said, were not computed; that these were the registered properties, but the value of those not registered, calculated by the tax rating or cadastral survey, amounted to about 20 per cent more than that already fixed, or a total of 129 million pesetas.

To these observations the Minister added that the income from *patronatos* depending on the Crown amounted to 20 million and that the income from chaplaincies and from transferable securities representing ecclesiastical reserve funds and deposits was unknown.

As regards the religious orders and congregations, about which there has never been any exact information, the Government was able to draw up a statement giving the number of convents as 2,919 (with the exception of seven or eight dioceses which had not yet made their return), the number of monasteries as 763; the number of nuns 36,569, and the number of monks 8,396.

The ecclesiastical community, as far as could be ascertained, comprised 35,000 clergy and 44,965 monks and nuns—a total of 79,965. Taking into account the fact that the figures relating to the religious orders are not entirely reliable, the total number of clergy, monks and nuns at the advent of the Republic may be put at more than 80,000 souls, a figure which can be confirmed by the statistics circulated in more or less official publications.

The anti-clericals have let their imagination run riot on the subject of the property belonging to the religious orders. But unfortunately, in many cases, reality has outstripped imagination. The year the Republic came into being, the Minister of Justice had not had time to prepare a register of the property of the religious orders, but he had completed a census relating to Madrid and its province, from which it could unquestionably be seen that the monks possessed considerable wealth. The urban properties of Madrid were worth 54 million and the value of the rural properties had been fixed by cadastral survey at 112 million pesetas. From this sample, which only refers to property registered in Madrid, it can be readily imagined what monastic property over the whole of Spain was worth.

Moreover there was an impenetrable jungle, a region where the revenue officials could not penetrate to assess the property of the religious orders; I refer to industry and banking. The total wealth of the Spanish religious orders in the financial and capitalist world has never been known, nor will it ever be known. But there is no doubt that it was prodigious—a crying scandal in a country where two-thirds of the population were suffering from endemic malnutrition. With the usual reserve, I append as a footnote a list of the directorships held in 1934 by Don Valentín Ruiz Senén, the powerful business-manager of the Society of Jesus.[1] The economic power of the Jesuits is clearly shown here, however much the personal interests of Señor Ruiz Senén might be merged in those of his masters.

[1] Chairman of Hidráulica Santillana; Gas, Madrid; Duro Felguera; Compañía Madrileña de Transvias; Hutchinson, Industrias del Caucho; Energía e Industrias Aragonesas; Gran Empresa Sagarra; Fomento de la Propiedad; Cooperativa Electra de Langreo. Vice-Chairman of Saltos

This ubiquitous company director was rescued by the Jesuits from an obscure corner of a Madrid notary's office and elevated to the heights of finance and industry where, with a sagacity worthy of more reputable clients, he was a living witness to the skill of the Jesuits, not maybe in saving the Catholic Church as they saved it perhaps in other times, but in choosing men of straw and in playing a dominant rôle in the despised business affairs of this vale of tears.

With these prefatory remarks, we are now going to broach the subject, not of the Jesuits, but of the wider problem of the Church as a whole, as it presented itself to the Republic and as the latter attempted to deal with it.

The problems of the relations of the Church with the Republican State and of the position to be assigned to the Church in Spanish society was certainly one of the most polemical. A Constituent Chamber could not discuss it without a brawl or settle it to the complete satisfaction of any of the interested parties. The brawl was inevitable, partly because of the publicity of the proceedings and partly because of the eminence of a platform where philosophic eloquence could triumph only to the detriment of the art of governing. It was there that Azaña threw a bomb which he had been patiently manufacturing during his studies at the Ateneo: "Spain has ceased to be Catholic!"

An affair of this calibre, therefore, cannot be patched up in Parliament, by stringing together emendations in a haphazard way, without producing something as unreal as Don Quixote's *baciyelmo* or barber's bowl helmet. Cortes and Ministers had to use their heads more than their hearts.

No sooner had the nimble ship of the Republic spread her sails than she ran into the first squall—a violent pastoral from

del Alberche; Compañía Telefónica Nacional de España; Ferro-carril y Minas de Burgos; Cementos Portland; Agencia Telegráfica Fabra; Fuerzas Hidroelectricas de Andorra; Consejero de Industrial Química de Zaragoza; Banco de Credito Industrial; Accumulador Tudor; CHADE; Banco Urquijo; Sociedad Productora de Fuerzas Motrices; Standard Eléctrica; Banco del Oeste de España; Ferrocarriles del Norte; Ferrocarril de Carreño; Ferrocarril Central de Aragón; Banco Urquijo Vascongado; Sociedad Española de Fabricación de Automoviles; Banco Urquijo de Guipuzcoa; Gran Hotel de Zaragoza; Hidroeléctrica del Oeste de España; Distribuidora Eléctrica de las dos Castillas; Unión Electrica Madrileña; Eléctrica de Castilla; Compania Auxiliar de Ferrocarriles; Establecientos Gaillard; Electrodo; Obras y Construcciones Ormaeche; Banco Urquijo Catalan; Banco Hipotecario de España; Banco Minero Industrial de Asturias; Compañía Aragonesa de Minas; Union Radio. (From the *Anuario Financiero*, by Guillermo Ibánez, 1933–4.)

the Cardinal-Primate. His Eminence Don Pedro Segura, Cardinal-Archbishop of Toledo, was a good example of a thirteenth-century churchman, and a glaring anachronism in 1931, even in Spain. It was not surprising, therefore, that he should see in the Republic and in universal suffrage the end of the Middle Ages and of everything he considered respectable. In vain did the new régime appoint the Catholic Señor Semprún to be Civil Governor of Toledo. For the Primate, Republican and Catholic were two irreconcilables and Semprún did not succeed in establishing with the archiepiscopal palace those peaceful and harmonious relations which the Spanish hierarchy, in a collective declaration, had expressed the pious hope of establishing with the Republic—a policy which reflected the cautious waiting policy of the Vatican, as well as the moderate and liberal view of the most illustrious ecclesiastic of the hour, Cardinal Vidal y Barraquer, Archbishop of Tarragona.

Segura owed his eminent position to Alfonso XIII who discovered him when he was Bishop of Coria in Estremadura, engaged in comforting the almost less than human inhabitants of the Hurdes. The King saw in him a person already ripe for canonization, a type which the Church no longer produces, a man whose piety seemed eccentric to modern eyes, who thought a bath was the invention of the heathen, if not of the devil himself, and who wore the hair-shirt like a monk of old. On a frivolous libertine like Alfonso, the fanaticism and the peculiar asceticism of this ecclesiastic, who was as uncompromising towards the temptations of modern society as he was humble before the institution of the monarchy, made a great impression. Six years later Segura was translated to the ancient see of Toledo, like another Don Rodrigo eager to set out for a *Navas de Tolosa* in a crusade against the Republican infidel, Semprún or no Semprún in the Civil Governorship. The Primate said farewell to Alfonso XIII in his pastoral in the doleful accents of a Jeremiah, practically prophesying that the coming of the Republic meant the end of the world. Obviously his position as head of the Church was already untenable and he had to leave Spain; but he was back again shortly, breathing fire and slaughter, and the Minister of the Interior, Don Miguel Maura, whose Catholicism had unfortunately not impressed the hirsute Cardinal, ordered him to be arrested and escorted to the frontier by two Civil Guards, an unheard-of misadventure for a prince of the Church.

The conduct of the Primate, who was supported by the Bishop of Vitoria, alarmed the Holy See. The Vatican, with its proverbial opportunism, was bound to disapprove of anything which helped to aggravate the position of the Church at an adverse moment for her privileges in Spain. Rome and the Spanish hierarchy made it plain that they did not countenance the extremist methods of that sector of Catholicism which was most hostile to the Republic. And Monsignor Tedeschini, the Papal legate at Madrid, a politician of the school of Don Sturzo and an accredited diplomatist, brought a delicate situation to a successful issue with the supersession of the Cardinal of Toledo —a solution which was confirmed by the Pope. The outcome was considered by the Spanish Government as a victory for the Republic and for Spain, "because that sector, more political than religious, which conceals its political bellicosity under the cloak of religion—that sector has been vanquished, and vanquished by the justification of our conduct, expressly made by the Holy Father himself".

The disturbances of May 1931, provoked by the Monarchists and accompanied by the destruction by fire of some eighty churches and convents and damage to several others, seriously impaired the relations between the Republic and the Church.

Among the events which proved fatal to the second Republic and to Spain, we must include the frequent burning of churches and monasteries, of which it would not perhaps be an exaggeration to say that those who set fire to them, set fire, intentionally or unintentionally, to the Republic. It is deplorable that there should be Spaniards who could think that the Church would be harmed by this kind of licence, when nothing could strengthen her position as a conservative institution more than the pyromania of anarchists. Pablo Iglesias, the Socialist leader, had already pointed this out; but the convents went on burning—perhaps for this very reason. When all is said and done, Spain was a political Sodom, full of dark lurking-places, a wide field of manœuvre for the "clients of the aristocracy". And though it must be admitted that the people had no reason to love the clergy and were driven by their undisciplined feelings to attack them in their persons and their temples, the fact cannot be overlooked that these disturbances suited the book of the oligarchy and of the Church herself. It is not always clear from the circumstances in which the burning of religious edifices under the second Republic took place, from what murky hiding-place the incendiaries issued, much less from what remote distances the incitements to vandalism proceeded. But a faint light penetrates these clouds; and that is, that no one took the burning of convents in Spain greatly to heart. No one offered to protect them; and even when, as could be proved, shots were fired from inside, it appeared as if a deliberate policy was being followed of letting the wrath of the people expend itself on the sanctuaries. Certainly no one raised a finger to defend them, while an assault on a bank conjured up the presence of the police and of worthy, law-abiding citizens with miraculous speed. No doubt the Republicans were convinced, whether they admitted it or not, that all the convents in Spain were not worth the life of a single Republican; and the clergy were no less persuaded that the overthrow of the Republic was well worth the sacrifice of a few hundred chapels. The democratic parties saw in the conflagrations a moral argument against the Church, which had alienated popular sympathy, while the Conservatives saluted the disasters as the most effective and resounding propaganda against a régime which, according to them, was incapable of maintaining the standards of civilized life.

In May 1931 the vigour which the Republic derived from popular support, a vigour which carried everything before it, prevented the clash with the Church from destroying the possibilities of an understanding between the clergy and the nascent State. The Church was persuaded of her momentary weakness, and, confident of being able to reach a Concordat or at least a *modus vivendi*, the Vatican adopted a waiting policy and advised the faithful in Spain to keep calm. The oligarchy gave no sign of life. Neither the expulsion of Cardinal Segura, nor the burning of convents, caused it any loss of sleep. Nor did it even rebel against the solution which was subsequently applied to the religious question by way of the Constitution, violently opposed though it was to the privileges of Catholics. To be sure, the oligarchy had its religion—like Louis XV it believed in the devil. And it was keeping Sanjurjo and his aristocratic cavalry officers in reserve against the time when the law of agrarian reform was about to become law. The oligarchy knew no cause nobler than that of property. As far as it was concerned, all the churches in Spain could be burned to the ground. Neither in May, nor afterwards when the attacks on the convents were renewed, was a single Catholic seen to risk his skin in saving them or to empty a bucket of water on the flames. The ruling classes in Spain were not exactly of the stuff of which religious martyrs are made.

Here we should say a word about the misguidedness and inconsequence of the Republic's policy in this domain. I shall try in passing to reduce the religious question to what I think

440

are its true proportions within the circumference of the Spanish national revolution. To my mind, the anti-clericalists have attributed to this problem a far greater importance than it has for the popular interest, though it is to some extent understandable that Liberal professors and philosophers should discover in the Church the greatest obstacle to the regeneration of Spain; they were led astray by their idealistic conception of history and their daily encounters with Catholics in the course of their profession and sometimes also in private life. But this was an error of perspective which repeatedly resulted in the Republican car sinking in a quagmire and being put out of action, every time democracy triumphed in Spain.

In this domain the failure of the Republicans was beyond doubt. Their aim was that the Church should present no hindrance to the growth and prosperity of Republican democracy; yet Republican democracy received its death-blow from the policy it followed with regard to the Church. Azaña and his colleagues were afraid of this; yet in 1931 the Republic appeared stronger than it actually was and the Church more defenceless than was really the case. "Do you believe", Azaña asked Parliament, "that a policy based on what I have just said, on that conception of the Spanish State and of Spanish history, would lead the Republic into some blind alley where its enemies could cut its throat with impunity? You do not believe it. Then I, with this guarantee, will now pass on to the texts under discussion."[1]

The realization that the clergy were a danger to democracy inspired, in substance, the Republican policy. It was a defensive policy, which could not be altogether without its aggressive side, since it had to break with a situation which was impossible, not so much for a lay State, as for any State that was jealous of its prerogatives. The inevitable frustration arose, as we shall see, from the fact that, things being as they were, the Republic with more enthusiasm than logic made a free gift to the Church of powerful elements of resistance over and above those already inherent in it.

As we know, Azaña revealed himself to Parliament in the debate on Article 26 of the Constitution as an ingenious politician of unusual talent. Here he was on firm ground as a philosopher, for as Renan has said: "Those who leave the sanctuary are more deadly in their blows than those who have never entered it." The axiom was welcome to the orator, and he was not slow to seize the occasion to demonstrate its meaning. Nevertheless

[1] Speech on Art. 26, Sept. 13th, 1931.

Azaña was not seeking revenge. What mattered to him was, quite simply, the defence of the State. As a Liberal, he wanted to respect liberty of conscience "without excepting liberty of the Christian conscience; but on the other hand, we must, in duty bound, look to the safety of the Republic and the State. These two principles clash; hence the tragedy, which like all true and great dramas, has no solution." What was to be done, then? "What we must do", he replied, "is to take our stand on a higher plane than these two conflicting principles and this stand, for us laymen, servants of the State and political rulers of the Republic, cannot be other than the principle of the safety of the State." "As for the religious orders, we must proscribe them because they are a danger to the Republic." But before, he had warned his hearers that "in our campaign of reform of Spanish religious institutions, we must stop short of the point where our surgical operations would be harmful or dangerous. Imagine, gentlemen, that we are going to carry out a surgical operation on a patient who has not been anaesthetized and that in his pain he struggles, and his struggles complicate the operation so that perhaps it takes a fatal turn—I don't quite know for whom, but fatal for someone".[1]

It is obvious that the Republic did not feel as if it was being poisoned by a religious problem. The Chamber, and Azaña as its spokesman, envisaged the question in general in the light of the security of the régime, with the avowed intention of denying their political principles if the peace of the nation and the interest of the State so required. That was to be the criterion which actuated the majority. The revolution rested, they thought, on depriving the Church of political power, and once this had been successfully accomplished, Spain would be a different country. "The most intimate, most profound problem in Spanish life (according to the Liberal middle class) would have been solved."

But whence does the Church derive her political power? This was the first question to be considered, and if the Republic was not to start from a false premiss, it had to be answered accurately. In my view, not so much from her union with the State, as from the ends that the State pursues. If the State uses the Church as an instrument of oppression, a class instrument, it will give her power to oppress, as has been the case in Spain since the Restoration. But the politicians of the Republic thought that to separate the Church from the State was to carry out the revolution, for in their view the Church "because of this union, used

[1] Speech on Art. 26, Sept. 13th, 1931.

the political power given her by the State and the uniting of her organs with those of the State, to scourge the conscience of dissenters". Experience has proved this thesis to be false. In England there is an Established Church; but this does not lead to the scourging of dissenting consciences, nor does it invest the Church with more political power than can be reasonably expected in a nation where civil society is supreme. The influence of the Spanish Church in the sixteenth century was not the outcome of the union of Church and State, but sprang from the fact that the State adopted as the national policy what was then considered to be best suited to the interests of Spain, namely, to take the Catholic cause everywhere under its patronage. Everything depends on the character of the State. But was the Republican State going to be the same State as Spain had under Philip II or as she endured under Cánovas? To sum up, the greatest toleration and the soundest civil institutions can exist in a nation where Church and State are united, as in England, while the crudest intolerance and almost total absence of civil institutions are found in a country like Portugal, where the Church is separated from the State.

The Church, whether disestablished or not, will always be an uncoercible *political* power, like the Army, wherever the State, because of its lack of correspondence with society, is weak.

In Article 26 of the Constitution, the Spanish Republic introduced the separation of Church and State. Irrefutable arguments, based on Liberal principles, were brought forward in profusion in support of this change; but there were not, perhaps, so many political reasons in its favour. Nor, above all, was there any reason to attribute to it effects which it could not have on the progress of the nation. Spain, which many Republicans thought would rise to the level of France once Church and State were separated, descended in reality to the same level as Portugal. The only difference this change would establish between Spain of the monarchy and Spain of the Republic would be that the State Budget would be reduced by the sum of 60 million pesetas formerly paid to the secular clergy; and even this never actually materialized. Finally, the separation of Church and State may have been either good or bad, a mistake or a success, from the point of view of principles; but from the point of view of the revolution, it settled nothing fundamental in itself. Civil society would continue to be subjugated by the Church, unless, I repeat, a strong civil society and a State to correspond were born—a solution which was linked up with

443

the transformation of property and of which there was not a glimmer anywhere.

Moreover it goes without saying that by suppressing the Budget for Public Worship and the Clergy, the Republic was helping to cement still more firmly the alliance of the Church with the oligarchy, an alliance which, as events showed, was a veritable menace to democracy, since the oligarchy continued in the full enjoyment of its extraordinary social power. If in the nineteenth century the Church, finding herself despoiled of her property, had sought the support of the rich, in exchange for which she had to countenance whatever atrocities they committed, what would she not do now? To what lengths would the priests not go to curry favour with the oligarchy (up till then, the religious orders had carried off the palm for complicity), in order to live? For the faithful would not support the secular clergy; and it was for this very reason that, during the past century, the Liberals had respected the Budget for Public Worship and the Clergy. Without the economic support of the State, the Church had a hard struggle to maintain her existence; and it was with the aim of reducing her considerable deficit that a State grant was originally voted in the nineteenth century and kept in being. The Budget for Public Worship and the Clergy was intended, therefore, to supplement the lack of generosity or lack of means of Spanish Catholics (I have already pointed out that in the nineteenth century the people continued their membership of the Church, but the wealthy classes were flirting with Liberalism and anti-clericalism). It is not, therefore, true to say that in the nineteenth century an attempt was made with the Budget for Public Worship to compensate the Church for the capital which had been expropriated in the process of disentailing the estates.[1]

For the rest, it was vital for the revolution that the religious question should not cut across the problem of property. The Republic had not sufficient strength to take on both the oligarchy and the Church together; and what was worse, there was no intention of quarrelling violently with the monopolizers of wealth. The directors of Republican policy, who were so meticulous when it was a question of curbing the Church, did not show themselves so exacting with the "frock-coated friars". When the Ministerial crisis of December 1931 occurred, Indalecio Prieto ceased to be Minister of Finance at the request of the Bank of Spain which under the Republic, as under the monarchy, proved to be more powerful than the Church, since it was not

[1] F. de los Rios, ibid.

till much later that the Church was able to overthrow any Republican Minister. We shall have to return to this later.

Article 26 of the Constitution was debated with acrimonious and sterile bickerings and finally passed by 178 votes to 59, in a House composed of 470 deputies, that is, without that unanimity and force which were needed to carry out the policy it outlined. It estranged the Republic from· a minority of progressive Catholics, who had been stimulated by the régime, and who could to some extent have breathed new life into a soulless Church. The historic middle class, the business men and industrialists, whose support was vital to the Republic against the formidable landowners and the absentee aristocracy, saw in the religious policy a proof of demagogy. The Church, without reason but with success, declared that she was being persecuted; her political parties raised the standard of constitutional reform . . . already an augury of civil war . . . before anything practical had been done with regard to property and with an Army officered almost entirely by anti-democrats. The only benefit that resulted from Article 26 was the exit of Alcalá Zamora from the Government; but this advantage was thrown away when the same Cortes raised Don Niceto, the enemy of the Constitution, to the Presidency of the Republic whence he set about destroying the régime through his obsession to have this controversial Article annulled.

It may be appropriate here to give the essence of the famous Article 26. I think I have already said enough about the separation of Church and State. The rest provided for the dissolution of the Society of Jesus and the nationalization of Jesuit property. The other religious orders were to be the subject of a special law (subsequently promulgated) by which those which constituted a danger to the safety of the State were to be dissolved; they were forbidden to acquire and hold any property other than that appropriate to their purposes; they were not to engage in industry, commerce or teaching; they had to pay taxes and to render accounts to the State of the investment of their property.

Article 27 provided for liberty of worship.

With the Society of Jesus an absurd policy was adopted, the inevitable and obvious result of entrusting the revolution to the emendments and formulas of the lawyers. Here a deplorable *baciyelmo* was fabricated! For the dissolution of the Society left the Jesuits in Spain. It left them irritated and rebellious, and in a position to continue with private teaching and to have a finger in any plot that was being hatched against the Republic. So that though they were better treated by the Republic, not suffering persecution as they did under Charles III or at the hands of Pope Clement XIV, yet by adopting a vacillating and inept policy the Government exasperated them without bringing them into subjection. The Jesuits saved most of their property, which had been skilfully tied up through third-party nominees or could not be traced; the Government was only able to lay hands on about 200 million pesetas belonging to the Society.

In the same way the Republic showed itself more mild and benevolent towards everything touching the religious orders and communities than the nineteenth-century Liberals or the Portuguese Constitution of 1911 had been. It is permissible to emphasize that the Republican legislator had no wish to persecute, only to defend the State. "Let us guard ourselves", reiterated Azaña, "against pushing the situation to extremes by making a show of persecution, which is not in our minds or our laws, in order to prove a legend which cannot but harm us." The only reproach that can justly be levelled against Republican policy is that of incongruity and contradiction. A policy which ought to have protected the State was transformed by legislative mildness and disorder into a major threat to the interests of the régime, a menace to its very existence. This concludes our survey of the solution of the Jesuit problem. For the same thing happened with the other orders and congregations. The latter were not even dissolved; they were allowed to remain in Spain as they were. But they were not permitted to engage in industry or commerce or in teaching. On the other hand, the charitable and beneficent activities of the monks and nuns, especially of the nuns, were strictly limited. The secularization of public life eliminated nuns as nurses from the hospitals and asylums. What were the religious orders—ever on the increase and absorbing new elements—going to do? To think that a new Thebaid would arise, vegetating piously in cells and cloisters or watching the clouds sailing by the weathercock on the steeple, was to attribute to the religious orders a mysticism they did not feel. How were the twenty-four hours of the day going to be filled, but in conspiring against the Republic?

The Republic ought to have adopted exceptional measures to deal with the Church and the religious orders; it ought to have rectified the complaisant policy of the Restoration. Spain was not a social Paradise for the immense majority of Spaniards and the religious orders could not be allowed to continue living off the fat of the land. But the Republic was face to face with a problem which could not be answered by war with the Church. And the frequent lessons of history had shown, in Spain and elsewhere, that it was neither advisable nor befitting that the new régime should be forced into capitulation or into performing an act of penitence at some future Canossa, or that the Republic should take up arms once more against the half of Spain where the Church's banner waved. The interests of the Republic, which were those of the revolution (since events could not turn out as they did in France, still less in Russia), lay in coming to an immediate compromise with the Church and passing on to other problems, less metaphysical perhaps, but more fundamental. In 1931 the Republic had not yet revealed its weakness and was in a strong position to deal with the Church—a position which it never subsequently regained. But an exaggerated estimate of the strength of the new régime eliminated compromise as a working hypothesis. The idea was not to parley with the Church, but to impose a solution from without—a solution which, owing to the fact that it was imposed by force, was not a solution at all. The policy of the Constituent Cortes was to confront the Church with a juridical *fait accompli* in such a way that she would later submit to a *modus vivendi* on the basis of the separation of Church and State, the secularization of public life, lay education, the dissolution of the Society of Jesus, and the reduction of the other religious orders to merely contemplative orders—a more extensive policy than France had pursued during the agitated period between the laws of Jules Ferry and the *entente* of 1924. Discussion took place on these lines; and it is fair to point out that, at the time, very few Republicans appeared to think them dangerous.

But the Spanish Republic had not had time, like France, to create a middle-class State, or had even begun to sketch out a plan for creating one. And the absence of a powerful and autonomous civil power kept the régime, in the realm of realities, in a position of inferiority *vis-à-vis* the Church. The Church was an effective force, deeply rooted in Spanish time and space, while the Republican parliamentary State was as yet but an aspiration.

Reviewing the course of events, it can clearly be seen that the quarrel with the Church, which arose, or was provoked, before an invulnerable civil State had been cemented, led the Republic into that dreaded alley where the cut-throats lay in wait. It was not that the Republic was a phantom, the insignificant child of fortuitous circumstances, without a basis in society. The Republic sprang from the womb of the people; it was the

447

longed-for offspring of the cities, whose birth was greeted with obvious pleasure by many different sectors of society. Many Catholics were Republicans and many Republicans were Catholics. But this very fact bore witness that Republican society, the nursery of social classes which looked to the Republic for wellbeing or happiness, urgently needed a State which would satisfy their desires, the higher and cohesive social entity which would correspond to the vast political entity forged from below, in the mass of the people, by a common feeling of hostility to the monarchy, which was also hostility to the oligarchy. The pillars of the State are the social classes, and the social classes are economic strata. This was the terrain to which the Government should first have turned their attention, if they desired to build a State strong enough to impose conditions on the Church in the only task which could have borne fruit, the task of splitting up the landed and financial oligarchy and with the fragments making the new social class, or classes, as a foundation for the régime. To open proceedings by declaring war on the Church was equivalent to a man starting to build a house by first putting on the roof; it was to pose a problem to which—until such a State had been created—there was no answer, or an answer that was unfavourable in every light to the Republic. By placing the clerical question, the rupture with the Church, before the economic transformation of the nation, the Republican State remained a fiction and the Republic ended by losing its standing with all sections of society; the proletariat were to withdraw their support from the régime and hoist the standard of a defrauded economic class, and a good part of the middle class were to do the same, alienated by the outrage done to their religious feelings. And as soon as the Republic disintegrated in the minds of the society which brought it forth, the phantom-State of democracy crashed in ruins.

There were other considerations to be borne in mind by the Republicans, for whom it was important to see whether the play of political forces, inside and outside Spain, would allow the Republic to take off the gloves when dealing with the Church or not to deal with her at all. "It was safe to say", wrote a Catholic, "that the Holy See would be magnanimous if the spiritual peace of Spaniards was thereby advanced." This was a clear, unsolicited testimonial to the Republic's firm diplomatic position in 1931 where Rome was concerned. The Vatican had recommended the heads of the Spanish Church to adopt a tolerant attitude towards the new régime and such a policy perhaps afforded the Republic an opportunity to solve the problem of

448

the Church on a permanent basis. The other alternative—to conclude the framing of the Constitution while the Church was in rebellion meant that the constituent period would be prolonged indefinitely and the religious question, that most delicate of problems, would remain outstanding, and as envenomed as ever. It was easy to conjecture that an understanding with Rome, which the powerful Republic of 1931 could have concluded without dishonour, would have cut the ground from under the feet of the monarchist Catholics and the Carlists, leaving them without outside support; would have divided the Catholics and would have deprived the oligarchs of their religious rallying-cry and partly disarmed that indomitable faction, who were intent upon avenging their political humiliation by exploiting religion.

For it mattered little that the conscience of the deputies should rest on the certitude that no citizen was being persecuted for his religious opinions; politically, the opinion of the Church counted for more than the legislator's purity of intention. Nothing would have been gained by the Church declaring herself persecuted. And the agreement with Rome would have been an open proof that there was no persecution, without implying that the State was defenceless or that dissenting consciences would be outraged. Everything depended, I repeat, on the kind of State to be erected. Moreover, the reforms to be introduced in the relations of the Church with the State would have been viable; the new juridical status of the Church would have come into being with roots to strike deep into the ground. In contrast, what advantage was there in decreeing a vast transformation, if the Republic lacked means to carry it out? We shall follow the course of this experiment later with a cursory examination of what happened in the teaching profession.

When the Constitution was promulgated, the Spanish bishops issued another collective statement. This time it was to incite Catholics, in suitably discreet language, to disobey the civil authority. "The principles and precepts of the Constitution in religious matters", they said, "show no respect for freedom of worship or any recognition of the essential rights of the Church, which the dignity of the State requires in its own interests; moreover, inspired by a partisan spirit, they represent an act of hostility to these minimum requirements of the Church." After this, there could be little value in their subsequent protestations of fidelity to the constituted Power. The Church now pinned her hopes on counter-revolution, which need not be insurrectionary, since the parliamentary system guaranteed the speedy triumph of those interests which had been thwarted by the Republic. It was merely a question of devoting a few million pesetas to electoral propaganda—millions which the parties of the régime did not possess.

Already something had become apparent which almost all Spaniards had noted, except those who might have prevented it happening, those who were to be its first victims—I mean the fact that Alcalá Zamora, enemy of the Constitution, consented to occupy the highest office of the Republic, with the lofty ideal of assuring for himself life eternal beyond the Milky Way. For his religious faith, with its strain of oriental credulity, was genuine. In this Don Niceto differed from many oligarchs whose religion was pure cynicism, and would cheerfully have sacrificed his fortune, his political career, and—not so cheerfully, but not less resolutely—the Republic, if his unyielding conscience as a Catholic had required him to set aside his opinions as a politician. His ear was attentive to the voice of public opinion, which flattered his desire; and he desired nothing so much as to lop off that anti-clerical branch which, in his view, had been grafted by an eccentric hand onto the constitutional tree. The shipwreck of Article 26 cannot be fully understood unless we bear in mind the spiritual identification of the President of the Republic with the partisans of the revision of the Constitution.

Taking it clause by clause, what most alarmed the Church in the contents of Article 26 was probably not the secularization of the State. If everything had consisted in the separation of Church and State, the Catholics would have shown themselves more disposed to be accommodating. They had before their eyes the neighbouring example of Portugal, where, though Church and State were separated, they could witness the spectacle of the Cardinal-Primate Cerjeira and the Society of Jesus carrying on their reign from the political wings. Nor were the Catholics particularly disturbed by freedom of worship which, as was proved by the toleration of those Protestant Churches whose resting-place no one knew, had succeeded in becoming an established fact. But two extreme measures—the one, prohibiting the religious orders to teach and the other, bringing to an end religious demonstrations (a measure which abolished among other famous festivals, the Seville Holy Week celebrations), touched them on the raw. The churches remained open to everyone, but the Catholic Church was being expelled from the street, and this was a serious matter; for the silent and secluded divine services were not, perhaps, so important to the

Church as to be mistress, with her imperial ceremonial, of the street. It goes without saying that the innovation brought the Republic into conflict with highly spectacular and deeply-rooted traditions.

The other problem—a difficult and unanswerable one—which the Republic also introduced at the outset, was the secularization of education, a measure which led to the religious ;orders being forbidden to teach and to the removal, on a given day, of the crucifix from the educational centres—amid the indignation of the Catholics, the lukewarmness of the schismatics and the indifference of the people.

Azaña and his colleagues attributed too much importance to depriving the clergy of their teaching activities. Without denying a rational basis to the laicizing policy, it seems to me that the danger of leaving education in the hands of the priests was disproportionately exaggerated. I do not say that the danger did not exist; only that it was exaggerated. For example, Azaña believed that "Deusto, El Escorial, and the *bourgeois* middle class which has been educated in these surroundings and in the schools of the religious orders, produce, produced, and always will produce, whenever occasion arises, the General Staff of dictatorships and absolute monarchies in Spain".[1] But it should be noted that this accusation came from a Minister of the Republic, soon to be Prime Minister, an ex-pupil of the Augustinians, around whom were gathered, in the Republic, a multitude of fellow-countrymen educated by the Jesuits or by the monks. Azaña himself was not sure of his thesis, since shortly afterwards, on a more solemn occasion, he was accusing the social class "which with its violent straining after radicalism and anti-clericalism" had brought to a head the disentailing of the estates, of having "introduced into Spain tyranny, dictatorship and despotism".[2] In my view, there was more objectivity in this statement. Narváez, O'Donnell and the budding oligarchy belonged to the anti-clerical nineteenth century. And this oligarchy which, since the Restoration, had kept Spain under a parliamentary dictatorship "with a cruelly ironic democratic Constitution", was as anti-clerical as Mendizábal might have been. For did not Cánovas and Sagasta and Martínez Campos and General Weyler and Count Romanones and the Duke of Alba take offence if their Liberalism was questioned? It was not so much the fact, or rather, it was much less the fact that education was in the hands of the priests which

[1] Speech at Madrid, Sept. 14th, 1931.
[2] Speech in the Cortes on Art. 26.

was the cause of despotism, dictatorship or tyranny, as a particular grouping of classes which could only perpetuate itself by force and which the rich—pious and blasphemous alike—were not disposed to modify, whether they had been pupils of the Jesuits or of the Grand Orient.

In addition, 90 per cent of those Spaniards who had been educated in monasteries did not go to confession or hear Mass after their education was finished.[1] From which it can be gathered that it might perhaps suit the anti-clericals better to encourage education by the religious orders and even to pay for it out of their own pockets, if they were genuinely interested in collaborating with the Church in de-Catholicizing Spain.

But we must not exaggerate. Here was a serious problem which the Republic could not by-pass. Education in the hands of the religious orders would require the intervention of the Government, some kind of check. The State could not be indifferent when faced with anarchy in this domain. Fifty-seven per cent of the private teachers, lay and religious, had no professional qualifications. The Republic met the problem with a decree of May 1931, but the religious communities disapproved of it and it did not prosper—a proof that professional competence was of no moment to them. They naturally regarded education as a weapon in their hands, although, as we have seen, it was not as terrible as the anti-clericals imagined or as effective as the Church believed.

The Republic's most noble effort was concentrated in the field of education, and of this we shall speak later. But in the task of taking education out of the hands of the religious orders the new régime was doomed to run on the rocks for lack of real political power. The fate of the decree against unqualified teachers, which fell upon stony ground, already marked the opening round in a campaign of resistance which was all the more tenacious because it counted on strong support from inside the Republic. In this domain the Republic was committed to a task which was beyond its powers.

There were in Spain 500,000 children without schooling; 12 million Spaniards, 50 per cent of the population, belonged to that strange species of human beings, extinct in almost the whole Western world—the illiterate masses. The Republic undertook an onerous task, when it assumed the moral obligation to provide education, within a reasonable space of time, for all Spanish children and not a few adults. But by forbidding the religious orders to teach, the already enormous number of

[1] Vide *El problema religioso—social de España*, by Fr. Francisco Peiró. 1936.

children without schooling was going to be swelled, according to the Government's data, by 128,258 boys and 222,679 girls, or 350,937 pupils; and according to the Catholic Press which was, of course, interested in enlarging upon the error, 600,000. It might be of interest to recall that the common sense of the English and the firm structure of their State which, since the seventeenth century, had protected civil society from the ecclesiastical menace, had led them in 1870, when compulsory elementary education was the order of the day, to found schools in those places where there were no Church schools. And although there was a radical objection to Church schools—a point which is still being debated—the policy of the State was to deprive the Church gradually, as means permitted, of her educational function. And this is what has happened. The British Government has continued to extend its authority over education and to establish teaching centres which gradually superseded the Church schools.

The greatest obstacle encountered by the Republic in replacing the schools run by the religious orders was not so much material as political, though it was evident that the replacement of the monks was going to absorb many educational facilities which would otherwise have been available to the illiterate population, who had been hoping from time immemorial for a chance of education. For the 350,937 pupils of the friars and nuns, the Republic had to provide 5,951 more schools, without including those required in Madrid. The Government was complicating its own existence, especially when it was not going to make a success of what it set out to do, since an infinite number of schoolchildren would continue to be taught by the clergy, now in secular garb, and at times not even with that transformation.

Nevertheless the Azaña Government determined, in fulfilment of the Constitution and the *Ley de Confesiones y Congregaciones religiosas*, to complete the work of substitution. It has been said that there were no teachers; but this is not true. 7,000 were required and 20,000 citizens prepared to qualify. Half of these passed their examinations with flying colours. A more difficult problem was that of school premises. The Spanish public was called upon to collaborate in suppressing education by the priesthood, and while there were provinces like Alicante which rapidly provided 104 local schools out of the necessary 130, others like Vizcaya only agreed to provide 196 out of the 219 schools required to replace those run by the religious orders. The province of Guipuzcoa was asked to provide 355 schools; it promised only 56. In the Catholic regions *par excellence*, the local authorities refused to facilitate the work of the Republic in this sphere.[1]

Notwithstanding all this, the insuperable obstacle was political in character, since the State could have succeeded in overcoming the indolence or the hostility of the municipalities by providing the capital itself. The *Ley de Confesiones y Congregaciones*, promulgated on June 2nd, 1933, decreed that the replacement of denominational education should be effected in two stages, ending on October 1st and December 31st of the same year. This law, which was a corollary of the Constitution, was the immediate cause of that disorderly obstruction in the Cortes which dealt such a shrewd blow at the tender shoots of the Republican institutions. It was then that Azaña realized "that our Government and our Parliament are about to run into the most violent squall that any Parliament or any Government has ever had to weather. I mean Article 26 and the *Ley de Congregaciones*".[2] And there can be no doubt that the intimate persuasion that the ostentatious clamour of the obstructionists would not be frowned upon by the President of the Republic emboldened the parliamentary opposition—forerunner of the future electoral alliance between the dregs of Spanish society, Lerroux's masons and the oligarchy, against the Constitution and the essence of the Republican régime. In the end, the promoters of these obstructionist tactics began to be uneasy at the result of their own actions; the Cortes finally succeeded in negotiating the hurdle and the *Ley de Congregaciones* was passed. But only on condition that the Government recognized that its days were numbered. Alcalá Zamora, whose signature was indispensable before the Bill could become law, registered his protest rather than his dissent, by holding up the measure as long as was permissible under the Constitution. Azaña could count on a consistent parliamentary majority, and the President did not dare to take the responsibility for bringing down the Government. The hair-raising inconsistency of the Cortes in forcing the opening pace of the secularization policy while appointing a convinced Catholic to the highest office in the régime, accentuated the unequal character of the struggle between the Republic and the Church. The President was in a state of open warfare with the Constitution. So the Republican-Socialist coalition continued in power, but from that moment no Minister of Education was able to stay the course. Hardly

[1] Vide *Las órdenes religiosas y la Enseñanza*, by Rodolfo Llopis. Leviatán, July 1934.
[2] Speech at Barcelona, Jan. 7th, 1934.

had the *Ley de Congregaciones* been passed than Don Fernando de los Ríos ceased to be Minister of Education; and in the brief lapse of six months, no less than five Ministers filed through this Department. None of them was capable of giving effect to this law.[1] To such a pass do things come when a régime based on universal suffrage is expected to carry out a revolution!

And they were to come to an even worse pass. For the electoral triumph of the Catholics and the Radicals—the counter-revolution—adjourned *sine die* the replacement of the monks as teachers, closed the schools which had been opened by the Republic, ostracized Article 26 of the Constitution and gave the Church her anxiously awaited opportunity for a much-desired revenge. There was no longer any need for the President or the Catholic parties to revise the Constitution; by not observing it, it was already revised.

Here it might well be recalled that, when the religious question first came under review, Azaña had asked the Cortes: "Do you believe that a policy based on what I have just said . . . would lead the Republic into some blind alley where its enemies could cut its throat with impunity?" No one had believed it; not even Azaña himself at that time. But towards the close of the year 1933 the Republic was in that sinister alley. And now the democratic leader was asking himself what was the chief reason for the downfall of the régime. "Every time I review, in my mind's eye the annals of Parliament, and try to discover where the future of Republican policy was gambled away and where the capital question which has served to confuse us cut across our course, I am reminded inexorably of the *Ley de Congregaciones religiosas*, of Article 26 of the Constitution, of the secularizing policy, of the neutrality of education, of all the benefits, the hopes, the expectations of justice which derived from the principle enthroned in the Constitution of the Republic, against which all the visible and invisible manœuvres capable of raising up a reaction against us have been set in motion to see if they could wreck us and, in the end—let us confess it—they have wrecked us and we have gone to the bottom."

Azaña, an honest thinker, confesses his error, which was not his alone (it was personal only up to a certain point), but the error of a disorientated democracy. By seeking guarantees for the security of the Republic where the peril was not greatest, the régime was plunged into crisis, perhaps even sacrificed.

[1] The five Ministers were: Don Francisco Barnés, Don Domingo Barnés, Don Salvador de Madariaga and Senores Pareja Yébenes and Villalobos.

The origin of the error, in my view, lay in the fact that the Republic tried to solve the religious problem *unilaterally*. This brought in its train the classic conflict with the ecclesiastical power. The Republic brought a hornets' nest about its ears. The idea of negotiating with Rome had hardly any supporters in 1931. At the time when the régime might have made a good bargain, the *modus vivendi* was looked at askance and the idea of a Concordat regarded with horror. Three years later, a certain Pita Romero was approaching the Vatican and humiliating the Republic and Spain by seeking a compromise. He was sent by the President of the Republic, after the latter had made him Minister of Foreign Affairs for that purpose. The Spanish Republic was going, at last, to Canossa. But the Holy See was not then in a hurry (no one then was in a hurry for anything) for a Concordat. The Vatican was shuffling the cards, weighing up opportunities and prospects, and with its usual reticence was holding back from dealing with a régime in process of evolution, which would either fall into the hands of an exasperated proletariat, in which case the Church would lose any concessions she might have obtained, or would veer towards absolutism, when—as happened later under Franco—the Spanish State, a ridiculous entelechy dependent upon outside support, would surrender to Rome more completely than at any other period of its history.

CHAPTER XIII

## REFORMS IN EDUCATION, HEALTH, PUBLIC WORKS, FINANCE AND BANKING

As the heading shows, I am grouping in this chapter the rest of the questions which merited special attention from the first Republican Cabinets—aspects of public life and administration in which reforms were attempted or the style of the new régime was displayed in a markedly characteristic way. The reader will thus note, albeit in summary fashion, the other innovations introduced by the Republic in order to raise the cultural level of the nation, improve the public health, transform the economic situation and purify and bring order into the administration. In passing, I shall have to refer to some other problems which urgently claimed the Government's attention.

The Republic's most noble effort centred, without doubt,

on the educational question: and this honourable endeavour will withstand for all time the unenlightened criticism of those who, out of a sectarian spirit and for reasons of self-interest, portrayed the régime as devoid of all virtue and fruitfulness. The oligarchy, during its half-century of absolute dominion, and the dictatorship, during its eight years of destructiveness, were at one in bolstering up obscurantism with the assent of the Church. It is hard to believe—but it is a proved fact—that the ten *grupos escolares* which had been built in Madrid through the initiative of the Socialist municipal group before the dictatorship, remained hermetically closed until the advent of the Republic. In this, the dictatorship, which accorded University status to the principal colleges of the religious orders, bowed submissively to the wishes of the clergy. To their way of thinking, the fewer State schools there were, the better. In the last Budget of the old régime, 6½ million pesetas were set aside for building elementary schools, and even this meagre sum was not used. In contrast, the Republican Budget of 1933 allowed for 25 million to be spent on building schools and the Cortes authorized a loan of 400 million, spread over eight years, for this purpose. The Republic was on the way to endowing Spain with a sufficient number of schools. Here, as in no other sphere, the Republic stood for real revolution. The results of this policy, the most effective within the framework of the Republican proposals, made themselves felt immediately. In 1931, 40 per cent of the children of school age attended school; in 1932, 55 per cent— and had not reaction intervened, the ideal would have been attained which is embodied in Article 48 of the Constitution— compulsory elementary education.

The Republic created 7,000 schools in the year of its birth; 2,580 in 1932 and 3,990 in 1933. And these schools did not merely exist on paper, like agrarian reform, but functioned with obvious efficiency.

But it was not enough to multiply the number of schools; the children from the poorest homes had to be fed. The Republic, therefore, set up a great number of canteens in the elementary schools.

In addition to all this, the Government distributed 5,000 circulating libraries among the towns and provinces where they also brought the so-called Educational Missions with their theatre and art museum.

In some Departments of the Ministry of Education, the Republic raised the estimates by 800 per cent and the general budget of the Ministry increased by more than 100 million pesetas. The teachers' salaries, which represented 5,890,000 pesetas in the 1931 Budget, rose the following year to 38,283,000 pesetas. In general, the salaries of teachers rose by 50 per cent.

As regards secondary education, the Republic doubled the number of schools. And in all the teaching centres, from the kindergarten to the University, besides founding new institutions like the School of Arabic in the University of Granada, the new régime introduced capital reforms into methods of teaching, to keep pace with modern educational trends.

In short, educational reforms of all kinds were the most marked feature of the régime in the spiritual sphere. Education was, briefly, the religion of the Republic, a work of mercy which transcended even that of feeding the hungry. It seemed as if Spain was on the way to become, as it were, a *magistocracy*, an El Dorado for professors and teachers, who, from being the pariahs of society, were becoming its new aristocracy. The forces of reaction saw in these legions of lay teachers a kind of Republican and masonic clergy who threatened to oust the Catholic clergy from the spiritual governorship—hence the fury with which they fought the whole policy of the Ministry of Education, the intelligent with the unintelligent, the realizable with the utopian.

In the field of public health, the policy of the new régime was also brilliant in the extreme. For the first time, the health of Spaniards was given an important place in the Budget. The Republic made an admirable effort "to see whether it is possible that, as one can endeavour to dam the flow of rivers which are lost in the sea without benefit to Spain, so one can also staunch the bleeding to death of Spanish lives, which are lost unfruitfully in infancy or sometimes in maturity, through the barbarous penury and neglect in which the care of the person is held in Spain". With these noble words, Azaña announced the Republic's health programme; and the seriousness of the design was matched by the results.

The General Board of Health (*Dirección General de Sanidad*) became a sub-Secretariat and ended by becoming a small Ministry in practice, thanks to the zeal, enthusiasm and intelligence of the men who ran it. A multitude of rural health centres were created, which brought the aid of science to communities which lived at astronomical distances from hygiene. New clinics and a great profusion of new sanatoria, especially tuberculosis sanatoria, bore witness to the Republic's interest in alleviating the lot of the sick, only too numerous in a country where ignorance,

458

malnutrition and exhausting work conspire together to keep the rate of mortality at a frightening level.

In public health, the Republic accomplished a prodigious work, with scant means and little fuss.

The awakening of the vital energies of the Spanish people, so long repressed, guaranteed beforehand the issue of the new régime's health policy. The love of the masses' for water, fresh air and mountains only needed the political revolution of April 1931, with the immediate amelioration in working-class conditions of life, to expand in the desired direction. Within a few months of the advent of the Republic, the people evinced a great desire to travel and make holiday excursions to the marvellous ranges of mountains near big cities like Madrid. There is no doubt that the change of régime was accompanied—where it was not preceded—by a national rejuvenation. Spain was finding herself anew—she wanted to live, to work, to enjoy life, to create, to use to the full her inexhaustible moral forces. Youth was the keynote in politics and in the street, after half a century of subjugation by an oligarchy without youth and without faith, an oligarchy which was born old, respectable and conservative. Saturn, the democratic god, swallowed up blackcoated Youth with the high, starched collar.

On Sundays all Madrid repaired to the splendid *sierras* nearby and their romantic environs, and if the crowds were not more addicted to Alpine sports and excursions, it was due to the lack of communications which were everywhere inadequate to the new needs.

The eagerness for individual and collective regeneration due to the moral and economic stimulus of the people's Republic, was one of the most encouraging signs of the new era.

The Republic threw open to the people beautiful grounds which had before been reserved for the exclusive enjoyment of the rich. But neither the *Casa de Campo* nor the *Pardo* sufficed to contain the Madrid crowds. The Government applied itself to solving this problem, too. With the Railway Network—(*Enlaces ferroviarios*)—a modest name for a work of considerable importance—the Republic proposed to make Madrid a great modern capital.

This project sprang out of the extreme urgency of establishing rail communication between the north and south stations and was due to the initiative of Indalecio Prieto, Socialist Minister of Public Works. After consultation with the experts and concerns affected, the idea gained ground of enlarging the scope of the enterprise. A new station was to be constructed on the high

459

flat ground in north Madrid to connect up with the lines of the three old Madrid stations—south, north and west. In this way, railway connections would be established for travellers who did not wish to stay in the capital and who, on arriving in Madrid, would no longer have to cross the city to continue their journey northwards, if they came from the south, or southwards, if they came from the north; while the rolling-stock would be circulating for the greater part of the twenty-four hours and would never circulate empty. Another underground station in the centre of Madrid would absorb the travellers who were ending their journey. Thus, difficulties arising out of the fact that the principal railway stations were situated far from the centre of Madrid would be obviated, with a consequent cheapening of transport. The old stations, which it was impossible to enlarge, given their situation, would remain almost without traffic, semi-paralysed and doomed to disappear. This would facilitate the growth of the capital, with a reduction in the cost of living in Madrid— the highest in Spain—and would permit the expansion of the population in zones where now it is cramped and congested, thanks to the inadequacy of transport facilities.

Undoubtedly the realization of this great project for improving Madrid would result also in other benefits for the working classes and for commerce and industry, with notorious advantage to the aesthetic aspect of the capital. It would allow of a rapid and cheap railway service which would lessen the distance between Madrid and the Sierra del Guadarrama and, by facilitating it, would canalize the natural tendency of the city to develop towards the north; it would encourage industrial development in the area most propitious to industry—north-east of the capital.

The estimates for this work amounted to 163 million pesetas in 1933.

In the summer of this year, a major part of the undertakings had been contracted for, the tenders for the electrification of the lines from Madrid to Avila and from Madrid to Segovia had been opened—work was going ahead boldly and swiftly.

The Government, and the Minister of Public Works personally, counted on the approval of all the progressive elements of the nation. They were supported particularly by the Chambers of Commerce and Industry and the workers' organizations. But the agrarian-aristocratic oligarchy and certain railway companies unleashed a deplorable and base campaign against the Minister. Their powerful Press (as indeed it had an impeccable constitutional right to do) discovered unsuspected horrors in the work and denounced it as a criminal enterprise conceived by the French

General Staff in order to facilitate the transit of African troops. Once more it was clear that the oligarchy was incompatible with the interests of Spain. The confused babble of prejudiced interests did not succeed in disillusioning the people of Madrid, the experts or the Government: and when the oligarchy had exhausted the repertory of high treason and other grave accusations, which impressed nobody, it decided to damn the Railway Network by ridicule—perhaps the most effective way of doing it in Spain. The work on the *Paseo de Recoletos* was stigmatized in the anti-Republican Press with the most contemptuous and grotesque expressions—it was the *Sinplan* (Planless) Tunnel, the Simplon, etc.

The affair, however paltry it may appear, is important in the sequel. Again the baseness of the Spanish ruling class was reflected in a concrete problem. But again it was evident that a Government desirous of governing could count in Spain on the adherence of other classes of society—the proletariat, industry, commerce—if it had vision; and that this Government, if it was guided by a high and strongly anti-oligarchic ideal, could without great difficulty revive the historic solidarity of the progressive classes and isolate the agrarian oligarchy as a preliminary move towards destroying it.

The Republic's lively capacity for hard work was apparent also in the sphere of hydraulic works. The new régime opened the campaign with the work on the Cijara reservoir, in the province of Badajoz, whose object was to irrigate "very extensive plains" in a region of productive, but parched lands. Shortly afterwards they commenced operations, among others, on the Ortigosa reservoir in the province of Logroño—a work which was to yield immediate benefits.

The Republic found a sluggish and confused tradition in the planning and execution of hydraulic works, although, as all intelligent Spaniards agree, the resurgence of Spain depends on these operations. In 1902 work was begun with a meagre grant of 4 million pesetas, and by 1931 the estimates had risen to 640 million pesetas without any results worthy of the outlay.

Dams were built over all the big rivers, but with a parsimony quite out of keeping with the prime importance of the work. Funds were scarce, and the impetus and width of vision which a work such as that of giving water to the Spanish *páramos* should have called forth in the Government, were lacking. The undertakings were administered and carried on from 1926 onwards by Hydrographic Confederations, autonomous bodies, in many respects independent of the State, although the State provided them with capital and guaranteed the private loans negotiated by them. Nor did the Confederations have any real solidarity among themselves. Prieto reorganized them, changing their name to that of *Mancomunidades* (unions) a title which reflected the introduction of a closer co-operation between them—the necessity for which was apparent when, in 1932, the Guadalquivir Hydrographic Confederation possessed 9 million pesetas lying idle in its coffers, while other Confederations had to suspend work for lack of funds[1]

The Socialist Minister emphasized the interest of the State in co-operating with these organizations by submitting them to a control which had formerly been nominal, a policy which he also followed with the railway companies by creating State Commissariats to scrutinize their working.

And not only was greater cohesion forced upon the Confederations, both between each other and between themselves and the State, but hydraulic undertakings as a whole were co-ordinated within the framework of a national plan which had never before existed. Within the limited radius of the *Mancomunidad* of the Ebro, an official of extraordinary aptitude, Don Manuel Lorenzo Pardo, was doing valiant service. Prieto brought Señor Lorenzo Pardo to Madrid as his principal adviser and when the Centre of Hydrographic Studies was founded, recommended this admirable engineer as its head.

The Centre of Hydrographic Studies drew up a National Plan of Hydraulic Works. The Republic prepared to do things on a grand scale and instructed the experts to draw up what amounted to a plan of economic revolution of the Spanish rural areas, with the aim of ending the deficit in the trade balance. And the hydraulic works constituted only one part of the problem. The experts were to study also the needs of forestry and bear in mind the indispensable task of electrification. All this was interlocked with the social question, the solution of which depended upon agrarian reform. This transformation of Spanish agriculture was to cost the State 10,000 million pesetas, apportioned as follows: 5,000 million for hydraulic works, 1,250 for afforestation, 1,000 for electrification and 2,000 to compensate the owners of expropriated estates.

Naturally such a huge conception of what the new régime ought to offer Spain was no more than a dazzling chimera, since the ideal political régime which was alone capable of bringing it to perfection had yet to be forged. The parliamentary Republic,

[1] Prieto, speech in the Cortes, Nov. 30th, 1932.

harassed by social discontents, lacked the continuity necessary to consummate, and perhaps initiate, such a vast transformation of the national soil and economy. But though Spanish democracy sinned, as always, through excess of confidence, the intrinsic merit of the idea calls for our recognition—it indicates that the Republic would have saved Spain if it had first known how to save itself.

Prieto transmitted to his collaborators in the Ministry his contagious enthusiasm for irrigation and, both in the office and on the river banks, men laboured with unaccustomed faith. Within a few months the Minister had inspected all the most important works, visiting, after exhausting journeys, all the regions of Spain where work was in progress. And during one of these official visits, Prieto conceived, or adopted, the idea of completing the irrigation system of the Levante.

In the Spanish rural areas there is no drama to compare with that of the dry land of the south-east. From Alicante to Almería, except for the *huerta*, the scarcity of rain, whose appearance in Cartagena and Almería is regarded as a miracle, keeps the population in a state of the direst penury, although the soil is of excellent quality. Hence, the anarchists who invade the industrial centres from the eastern periphery. If there was a possibility of completing the eastern irrigation system from the south of Castellón to the province of Almería, Spain would have solved an oppressive social and economic problem. And in these zones the sterile land only waited for the water to blossom forth into tropical flora and reward the farmer with multiple crops.

The region contains 386,500 hectares suitable for irrigation, but only 241,000 have actually been irrigated. For the remaining 145,000, the eastern valley lacks surplus water, for its rivers have already been drawn off to a very large extent. Nevertheless Spanish technicians, who in this respect, as in all others (let this be noted by those who regard the Spaniard as an anti-mechanical Bœotian), have attained absolute efficiency, replied that the work was practicable. They brought forward a highly encouraging plan conceived by Señor Lorenzo Pardo. Not only could the lands of the Levante be irrigated, but also a good number of hectares in the arid Mancha.

The necessary capital for such a vast and civilizing work was calculated at 5,000 million pesetas, including 1,105 million for means of communication, dwelling-houses, granaries, etc. According to the experts the plan would take twenty-five years to carry out. That is, the State, out of its normal revenues and with the help of private capital, would have to find 200 million pesetas annually, a sum in no way beyond the resources of

Spain. And in exchange for this effort, how many economic, financial and social problems would be on the path to solution, if not solved outright! Spain could emancipate herself from the burden of importing products which her soil could produce in the quantities required by the consumer, such as wheat, maize, cotton, tobacco, timber, etc., besides permitting ample development of her agricultural exports.

Yet neither technical genius nor political enthusiasm sufficed to carry out an idea which required a stable political régime for its execution. A quarter of a century, almost a generation, was needed with democracy firmly in the saddle, a long and indispensable period of tranquillity and work, the classic truce to party strife which those Western countries which are prosperous today have enjoyed—and suffered—in one or other epoch of their history.

It was not necessary to launch out on the noble and high enterprise of regenerating the nation to observe that sordid private interests, more obstinate enemies in Spain than in any other country of all methods of good government, would only yield to reason based on force, imposed without weakening and with continuous pressure by the Government. As a case in point, while the Minister of Public Works was echoing the words of all reformers and reminding Spaniards that the lack of water constituted a factor of prime importance in the nation's fortunes, the dams and canals in certain Andalusian valleys, which, though completed, had not been utilized in the vicinity of the dry lands, bore witness to the unpatriotic rebellion of the landowners. Here there was abundant water, but the landlords refused to use it; they were not to be seduced into increasing or improving production, just as, at other times, they were content to leave the land desolate. The Republic proposed to break the landowners' resistance to using the stored water supplies in the Guadalmellato and Guadalcacín reservoirs; and the Cortes empowered the Government to act as a substitute for the individual where dereliction of duty was proved. A law for placing lands under irrigation was then passed and the State thereupon embarked upon undertakings of the greatest importance in the lower valley of the Guadalquivir.

The new régime showed its predilection for Public Works in the Budget figures, voting for that purpose about 1,000 million pesetas, 150 million of which were for water undertakings.

In finance, the conduct of the Socialist-Republicans was most respectful towards the interests of the moneyed classes and set itself to rectify the excesses, disorders and administrative intemperance of the dictatorship. Until December 1931, when he moved to Public Works owing to the exigencies of politics, the discharge of this office—there is no word that better fits the perils of the enterprise—devolved upon Indalecio Prieto, "because no one else wanted it", as he said himself. The revolutionary Committee, on constituting itself a provisional Government, had offered the Treasury successively to various Republican financial experts, but no one had the courage to shoulder this onerous burden. Even Azaña had to confess in public that if he accepted the War Office, it was because everyone else had refused it. And when we think, in the presence of this general avoidance of responsibility, that that was the training-school of citizens who were destined by history and the Spanish people to deliver Spain from the toils of a political and economic crisis that might prove mortal, certain philosophical reflections are inevitable. The men of the Republic recoiled with dismay from the deficit left by the monarchy—"it is the deficit which is going to save us", said Mirabeau—and were terror-stricken by the military problem—not a very brilliant state of mind in which to launch a revolution.

Prieto, then, accepted the Treasury and took up residence in "that barracks of a building, where (he confided to Parliament) I have spent the bitterest hours of my life".

The state of the Exchequer was indeed lamentable. The State owed the contractors 300 million pesetas for Public Works, a legacy from the dictatorship. Other heavy arrears at home weighed on the budding Republic. And in fact, foreign short-term debts amounting to £12,500,000 compromised the solvency of Spain and threatened Spanish international trade. As already stated, Spanish traders, hoping for the revaluation of the peseta and trusting to the promises of the dictatorship, had repeatedly doubled their operations, sure of liquidating them, in time, in better conditions. Hence, the Spanish export trade was getting into a perilous situation. The world financial crisis which, as we saw, coincided with the change of régime in Spain, put an end to the liberal flow of credits from foreign banks. The Republic faced up to the situation and liquidated the debt of £12,500,000. Spain met her foreign debts with exemplary probity. To do this, the Treasury concluded an agreement with the Bank of France, with gold bars as security. This was a simple and convenient transaction, at $3\frac{1}{2}$ per cent—a much better bargain than the Morgan loan negotiated by the dictatorship at $6\frac{3}{4}$ per cent, though without metallic security, which in the case of the Morgan loan (the dictatorship being opposed to the mobilization of gold) was replaced by the signatures of the Bank of Spain and the Spanish Government. The Republican Government could have sold the gold, which would have been more advantageous for them, but the fear of alarming the oligarchy and of diminishing the gold backing of the notes in circulation, at that time much deplenished, inclined them to negotiate the loan with the Bank of France.

This indicates how conservative was the Socialist-Republican policy in financial matters. The Republic found a margin of 400 million pesetas in the fiduciary issue, which on some days was almost entirely exhausted. The Coalition extended this margin in three years to 800 million. So that, as regards both the note issue and the preservation of gold stocks, the new régime held with surprising rigour to the policy of the financial oligarchy. In a country like Spain, where rates of interest are usurious and popular savings small, a discreet inflationary relaxation would have alleviated the situation of the middle and working classes.

In its policy towards the exchanges, the Republic also observed the utmost scrupulousness. Political vicissitudes forced the Government on various occasions to intervene in order to check the fall of the peseta. On May 11th, 1931, on the occasion of the burning of the convents and other disturbances, the Spanish currency collapsed, the peseta falling to more than sixty to the £ sterling. The Treasury checked the avalanche with little delay.

The new régime added no essential reform to the financial structure. The oligarchy continued to pay taxes at their own caprice and their evasions were allowed to go unchecked, even more so than under the Dictatorship. And even the dullest mind could see that, however radical the changes in the form of government, there could not be the least change in Spanish society so long as finance, taxation, the Budget, etc., preserved the same mould as under the oligarchic monarchy. Clearly Prieto felt uneasy in the rôle of a Socialist tending the economic health, not even of the *bourgeoisie*, but of the rapacious oligarchs; "but I did not feel", he confessed, "that I had either sufficient strength in myself to remedy this state of affairs or could count on the necessary help from others".

The new régime did nothing to cheapen money, in spite of the representations of commerce and industry. Such a step could not have been taken without embarking on some form of control of capital, and, besides, if the old financial structure

466

was to be respected, the economic and political crisis demanded the opposite of a cheap-money policy.

A tax on unearned income figured in the last Budget of the Republican-Socialist coalition; but the incidence of the tax was so insignificant as to make little difference in the State revenues. This tax, introduced in 1932, did not apply to incomes of less than 100,000 pesetas a year. Above 100,000 pesetas, the tax was 1 per cent, which rose to 7·70 per cent on incomes of a million or more a year. Azaña excused the triviality of the new tax by saying that "a tax of this magnitude must begin modestly and, whatever its future, time must pass before it can yield all that can be hoped of it".

As can be appreciated, the financial oligarchy did not suffer the least hurt in its privileges. The Republican middle class, led by functionaries and intellectuals, attested at each step its alternate disdain for, and orthodoxy in, financial matters. Azaña, for example, in opposition to Prieto, considered that the gold buried in the vaults of the Bank of Spain, like the famous treasure of the Nibelungs, should not be touched. Because "the gold reserves, whether large or small—and the larger the better—are always necessary to us; they are necessary to this Republic and to any Socialist Government that may come hereafter, for a sane, strong and, as far as possible, independent monetary policy."[1] Thus thought the leader of the Republic, already flung from power and enunciating from the Opposition a safe policy for the future. This "strong" monetary policy was the traditional policy of the financial oligarchs and the absentee landlords. If it had followed its own inclinations, the oligarchy would have nailed the people, not to the cross of '98, as Costa said but—in the words of Jennings Bryan—to a cross of gold. And the Republic's financial policy followed the pattern of the Restoration and the military dictatorship, which was the Age of Gold of the Spanish banks. The oligarchy's ideal was the gold standard, which means progressive deflation. Hence their love for gold bars. The idea of revaluation forced Calvo Sotelo to try to get a foreign loan in gold. The Republic did not abandon the policy of deflation, and, if it did not revalue the currency, it was because, fortunately, it could not, any more than the dictatorship could. But it insisted upon keeping the gold and in accumulating gold if possible, with a view to revaluation. No policy could have been more fatal to the public interest or to commerce and industry generally. As Keynes says: "Deflation is not desirable, because it effects, what is always harmful, a

[1] Speech in Madrid, Feb. 11th, 1934.

467

change in the existing Standard of Values, and redistributes wealth in a manner injurious, at the same time, to business and to social stability. Deflation involves a transference of wealth from the rest of the community to the *rentier* class and to all holders of titles to money; just as inflation involves the opposite. In particular, it involves a transference from all borrowers, that is to say from traders, manufacturers and farmers, to lenders, from the active to the inactive."[1]

Instead, mild inflation favours the worker and all active producers at the expense of creditors. During an inflationary phase, debts and interest on loans are paid with greater facility; and these benefits are also shared by the State. And though the rise in wages is certainly offset by the rise in prices, it is none the less the case that this is compensated for by the increase in the employed population, since forced unemployment is diminished. The working classes gain, for what determines the level of their prosperity is not the individual, but the family wage.

All this is quite elementary, but the Republic, on its bended knees before the banks, showed in this extremity a blind traditionalism which contrasted with the boldness with which it abolished the titles of nobility, curtailed the privileges of the Church and declared itself the enemy of historical tradition. Perhaps Anatole France was right when he said: "Dans tout État policé, la richesse est chose sacrée; dans les démocraties, elle est la seule chose sacrée."

But it was not because Republican timidity, very patent in all its decrees, came to a head in the financial question, that there occurred the collision with the Bank of Spain, the most retrograde institution in Spanish economic life. The Republican Law on the Regulation of Banking (*Ley de Ordenación Bancaria*) was an endeavour to curtail certain inadmissible faculties of the Bank of issue. It was imperative to impose on the central Bank a more intimate collaboration with the State and with the principal organisms of the national economy, and this was the aim of the new Law on the Regulation of Banking which provided that the profits made by the Bank out of the increase in the fiduciary issue should be subject to a special tax, divided between the Bank and the Treasury the losses incurred by intervention in the exchanges, and empowered the Treasury and the Bank to fix the rate of discount. In the end, the Government appointed three direct representatives of the State to the Board of the Bank of Spain and set up a board of inspectors, to be appointed from among Treasury officials, to supervise its accounts.

[1] Keynes, *Monetary Reform*, p. 143.

The Law on the Regulation of Banking did not reduce the Bank of issue to a mere appanage of the Treasury, taking its orders from that body, as does the Bank of England. The Bank of Spain continued to be managed by a Board appointed by the shareholders, a phenomenon without equal in countries where banking is progressive; and on this Board there continued to sit, in spite of an incongruity which good sense should have denounced, the landed and absentee nobility as well as bankers. The Bank of Spain did not lose, therefore, its most aggressive oligarchic character under the new law. Nevertheless—and partly for that reason—it declared war on the Socialist Minister of Finance and launched against him the customary Press campaign— Spain being a free country—to finance which the Board of the Bank secretly subsidized certain publications on condition that they held up the Government to ridicule. Extraordinary meetings of shareholders were summoned to pass protests against the policy of the Minister, which they denounced as little short of Bolshevism. The Minister saw closing upon him the vice of those powerful interests which were, it was clear, much stronger than the Liberal and parliamentary Republic. And though the disputed Law bore the mark of the whole Cabinet, the Bank made it a point of honour to drag down the Minister of Finance. In this situation, Prieto remarked to the journalists: "The Bank of Spain is accustomed to getting rid easily of Ministers of Finance under the monarchy; let us see (and this occasion will prove it) whether they can so easily get rid of Ministers who are in their way, under the Republic."

The conflict between the Bank and the first Republican Minister of Finance, whose policy would have seemed excessively conservative in the City of London, ended, as the reader knows, with the rout of the Minister. When the Cabinet was re-formed in December 1931, Azaña moved Prieto—who was literally expelled from the Treasury when its problems were just becoming clear to him—to the Ministry of Public works.

The financial oligarchy, fewer than twenty *caballeros* and four banks, had imposed its will once more on the Republic and on the nation. The touchstone of Republican policy was, naturally, how it would solve the land problem and the banking problem. The credit revolution was no less pressing than the agrarian revolution. It is an axiom of political economy that without credit there can be no trade (Jevons). And without trade, there is no *bourgeoisie*, and without a *bourgeoisie* there is no Liberal middle class, and without a middle class there is no Republic based on universal suffrage. But the second Republic, like the first, lacked bearings. Out of principle, it lost the opportunity of gaining the firm support of commerce and industry, of the limited middle or neutral class, for the new régime. Neither the merchant nor the manufacturer could visualize in the Republican system—the realization of the anti-clericalist's dream—any solid advantage which would tell them that this was the anti-oligarchic régime, the antithesis of the old régime in which the interest of the progressive classes was subordinated to the egoism of the great landowners, and the aristocrats and bankers associated with them. Every State practises class politics, and fosters, favours and nourishes certain interests, if not by actually injuring other interests, at least by relegating to the background those to which it is not tied by vital knots. The Republic did not have a class policy, which in its case would have been appropriate, in order to succour the historic middle class and the proletariat at the expense of the two-headed oligarchy. The new régime remained the prisoner of the oligarchies in the persons of certain of its most eminent politicians and there is nothing extraordinary in the fact that it was choked to death through the infidelity of those within, the corrupt Republicans, and the power of those outside. The Republic probably saved commerce from a grave collapse by liquidating the debts due to international banks; but the commercial community did not acquaint themselves with the facts, nor did this operation assume sufficient dimensions to enrol the "neutral" classes in enthusiastic defence of the new State. The commercial classes and the small industrialists, who were always complaining about the "feudalism" of the Bank of Spain, watched it triumph over the workers' Republic. The key of credit remained in the hands of the oligarchy of the "Twenty", 30 per cent of them titled nobility. In a word, the Republic did not create a genuine following among the Spanish middle class.

The moderate policy and scrupulous administration of the Republic showed to advantage in the Budget. The last Budget of the dictatorship had closed with a deficit of 924,499,160·81 pesetas. The Budget of 1931, administered, though not drawn up by the Republic, showed an excess of expenditure over revenue of 356 million in round figures. The following Budget, in 1932, closed with a deficit of 410,773,918·20 pesetas, but from this should be subtracted 300 million which was applied by the Republic during the financial year to pay the contractors the sums owing to them since 1930. In February 1933, Azaña could assure the Cortes that the financial situation was becoming

470

normal. The receipts had amounted to 4,409 million pesetas, as against the original estimate of 4,550 million. Expenditure has been 172 million less than the Budget estimate. There was a surplus of 111 million, which exceeded the original estimate by 31 million. It is true that from this surplus there fell to be deducted the revenue obtained by the issue of Government bonds. But here, again, the moderation and integrity of the Republican-Socialist Government in administrative affairs was thrown into relief. The dictatorship had issued Bonds to the value of 4,656,633,000 pesetas, or a yearly average of 776 million. The Republic found the internal Debt standing at 20,000 million and in three years increased it by 872 million, that is, at the rate of 290 million a year. But if we subtract the 300 million paid to the Public Works contractors, the Debt increased only by 572 million during the first three years of the Republic, that is, an average yearly increase of 190 million pesetas. The enormous difference between this yearly average of 190 million and the 776 million of the dictatorship should be noted.

Azaña could with justice contend that his Government had re-established the public finances and administered the Treasury with exemplary rigour.

The Budget for 1933 was introduced by the new Finance Minister, Don Jaime Carner, a Catalan banker. From an economic standpoint, it was a perfectly orthodox affair which only broke with tradition in the distribution of expenditure, now higher than ever, in the field of Public Works, Education, Health, etc. Reaction prevented this Budget from being brought to completion.

Even a person quite unaccustomed to gauging economic and financial movements in Spain would have been persuaded in the summer of 1933 that the Republic had won the battle for credit and confidence, both at home and abroad. The amount of the fiduciary issue, the quotations of public funds and of the peseta, the liquidation of the 1932 Budget, the repatriation of capital which had fled on the advent of the régime and the reappearance in the tills of the banks of money withdrawn from circulation, the continuous offers of more or less adventurous foreign capital—all testified in the economic and financial field to the solvency of the nation under the romantic Republic, as even its detractors had to admit. Neither the international crisis nor the depression which certain branches of industry experienced had undermined the eagerness for work and the desire for prosperity with which the Republic had infused Spanish society. The general rise in wages successfully offset the persistence of, and even a slight increase in unemployment. The acquisitive capacity of the masses rose ostensibly, with a bound, without a corresponding rise in prices. When the Republic appealed for public credits, its loans were subscribed with confident celerity and it was able to obtain the money more cheaply than at other times—a proof that there was an abundance of idle and stubborn capital which could have been invested in industrial shares. On the other hand, the banks did not conceal the fact that the money was over-flowing in their current accounts. Considerable stocks of gold made of Spain the fifth or sixth country in the world as regards metallic reserves. The money deposited in the *Cajas de Ahorro*, in the banks and in the Post Office Savings Bank, which amounted to 3,412,500,000 pesetas in 1930, rose to 3,571,600,000 pesetas in 1931, the year of the Republic, that is, it increased by 159,100,000 pesetas. In 1932 savings in Spain were, without doubt, greater than in the previous year, for "though the relative data were lacking in various banks of no mean importance", the figure was 3,476,500,000, which was already higher than the figure for 1930. Compared with the year 1928, Spanish savings had risen in 1931 and 1932 by 34 per cent.[1] And if anyone calculates that in the last months of the Azaña Government Spanish savings amounted to round about 3,500 million pesetas he would certainly not be guilty of hyperbole.

Such was the economic and financial situation on the eve of the fall of the Republican-Socialist Coalition. A satisfactory situation for one who was content to live in the immediate present. The Revolution had come into being when the peseta was in jeopardy; the peseta had been saved, but the Republic had cut its own throat.

CHAPTER XIV

## THE REPUBLIC AT THE CROSS-ROADS

THE REPUBLIC PERMITTED Azaña to cherish the hope "that in our country a profound transformation of society would be accomplished while sparing us the horrors of social revolution".[2] But at the outset, experience showed that such a smooth transformation was not possible in Spain. A clear-headed, patriotic ruling class would have seen in Azaña what he was in effect, or wanted to be—the dyke which would keep back the

[1] *España Bancaria*, Oct. 1933.
[2] Speech in the *Frontón Central* of Madrid, Feb. 14th, 1933.

flood of social discontent. The reforms which filtered through the social dam constructed by this Republican statesman, in collaboration with the Socialists, afforded the necessary outlet, without which the tidal wave of the people's sufferings would have engulfed everything. Nevertheless, the Conservative newspapers called Azaña "the monster", an illusion to a supposed measureless iniquity. With a plutocracy of that kidney, democracy could not be under any illusions. The Spanish reactionaries would only adapt themselves to a régime of iron and utter darkness, and their hatred for Liberalism and equity, which was on a par with their unbridled egoism, made the two-headed oligarchy incapable of seeing the solution which was, at bottom, the least opposed to their interests—typical blindness of a degenerate oligarchy.

During the first two years, Azaña's way of thinking was also that of the Socialists. They had a "common way of considering Republican policy, of regarding the Republic and of understanding how the Republic should be governed". Spanish Socialism, as has been pointed out and as we shall see again, occupied the place of a non-existent middle class in the new régime and practised the evolutionary and parliamentary policy of the European Socialist parties, the appendix of the Liberal middle class. But this Spanish Socialist policy, like that of Azaña, was impaired by an error of principle—that of not perceiving clearly that the survival in Spain of a semi-feudal class with all its pride and landed power, created an organic disequilibrium in Spanish society, impossible to readjust by a parliamentary compromise. Moreover, the modern proletariat can on occasions come to terms, however temporarily, with the *bourgeoisie*. But in Spain, 72 per cent of the producer class are peasants and the land is monopolized, in the regions where the oligarchy reigns, by about 10,000 landowners, and at their head 100 noble families, lords of the principal latifundia. Here there can be no compromise, as there could be none in seventeenth-century England or in eighteenth-century France; it is excluded by the seigneurial character of property and the psychology of the proprietors. Consequently, the humane intention of Azaña and the Socialists to "make a profound change in society while fleeing from the horrors of social revolution" took no count of realities in Spain. Horrors, or no horrors, the agrarian-aristocratic oligarchy could not be liquidated without grave disturbances which would certainly affect the stability of the peseta.

The elementary reforms carried out by the Republican-Socialist Coalition justified, perhaps, the irritation of the oligarchy

473

especially if we take into account their lack of intelligence. But there were certainly no grounds for any Republican, however conservative he may have felt, to join the chorus of the Monarchists. The Republic was not possible physically without the adherence of the popular classes, nor could a parliamentary democracy take root in Spain unless it had previously laid a foundation with revolution. This axiom, which is pure political biology, escaped the attention of a large section of the middle class and of many important Republican personalities; some fearful of alarming the wealthy classes, others without principles and only desirous of replacing in power those they had cut down. The worst danger for the Republic lay in these elements, dissenting from Azaña and the Socialists.

To call oneself Republican and Conservative might be, perhaps, consistent in France, where the Republic had followed the social revolution. Republican and Conservative, in Spain, implied a crass misconception. There could be no Conservatives in the Spanish Republic until the régime had been nationalized, that is, until democracy had taken root in society and had been accepted by all social classes. And this—we always return to the same point—presupposed revolution, the destruction, not necessarily of persons, but of the oligarchies which would never, so long as they lived, accept the popular Republic.

Azaña considered the presence of the Socialists in the Government one of the firmest guarantees of the stability of the Republic. By their numbers and their power, the Socialists were the natural and irreplaceable allies of the Republican middle class. Regarded in all lights, the Republican-Socialist coalition came to be the cornerstone of the régime. The Republicans could govern the Republic without the Socialists, but not against the Socialists, unless they were to seek support among the parties hostile to the régime. To dispense with the collaboration, either in the Government or outside the Government, of the reformist labour movement was a fundamental blunder, firstly, because it was equivalent to depriving the Republic, itself poor in middle-class elements, of a following which, by accepting the Liberal postulates of the régime, had made it possible and enabled it to progress; secondly, because the programme and reforming zeal of the Socialists ensured that the social bases which the Republic lacked at its birth would be created more or less swiftly; thirdly, because if the Socialists were excluded from the Republic, they would change from allies to antagonists of a régime which treated them no better than the monarchy did; fourthly, because they would join forces with the revolutionary proletariat which, without them, and still less with them in the Government, would never be a serious danger to the Republic; and fifthly, because the Republic, one of whose weaknesses was the lack of capable men, would lose the personal services in all branches of politics and administration, of a host of excellent citizens with a nucleus of government in every place.

If the second Spanish Republic lasted longer than the first, or took firmer root, it was in virtue of the contribution made by the proletariat, organized under the Socialist banner, to the constructive policy of the Liberal middle class. The first Republic came to a sudden end because the middle class could not count on a disciplined workers' movement capable of assisting them in the function of government. Thanks to Socialism, the frail plant of Republicanism could weather the storm better in 1931 than in 1873. This was the new fact in Spain. Nothing had substantially changed since the nineteenth century; but the presence in politics of a numerous working class, agreeing with the Liberal masses on the capital points of the Republican régime, was a providential fact, a happy augury, from the point of view of the Republicans, the Republic and the nation, of excellent things to come. The Republic was now possible in Spain, or at least less impossible than in the last century. But the *sine qua non* of the régime's existence was that Republicans and Socialists should march shoulder to shoulder, at any rate until the revolution of the middle class had been accomplished, a step in the general progress of Spain whose execution was as important to the proletariat as to the *bourgeoisie*. The originality of the Spanish Republic's position is patent compared with, say, the French Republic, which had consolidated itself without having to call on the working class for help, and even while it was waging a bitter war on the workers. In Spain, to do without the Socialists, *à la* Thiers, meant to nullify and tarnish a miraculous accomplishment of history, the bringing to birth out of nothing, through the labour and love of a group of printers, of what Spain most needed—a political centre, a middle force.

With this same point of view, or one which led to the same conclusions, Azaña held the Republican-Socialist alliance to be the keystone of the Republic. But we have already seen that there were plenty of unpardonably frivolous Republicans who disliked the régime's association with Socialism. As always, they thought that Spain was another France and that, because other Republics could dispense with the Socialists, they could do likewise in their country.

The Spanish Socialists conducted themselves unfailingly in the Government like a Republican party. Azaña himself went surety for them: "You—I say nothing about my own services—have fulfilled these commitments, these obligations, and you have never asked the Republicans in the Government for anything which the Republicans were not under an obligation to do before you asked for it."[1] And yet, I repeat, a good number of Republicans, including some from Azaña's party, were persuaded that the Republican-Socialist coalition was pernicious to the Republic. What a curious idea of history and of the realities of the national situation these Republicans had! The régime could have had no worse enemies.

For its part, as was *de rigueur*, the oligarchy chalked up to the debit side of the Republican-Socialist governmental alliance indescribable evils. The oligarchy was not ignorant of the fact that the Republic would be threatened by extinction if the Socialists and the Republicans were to separate. Conscious of what the Socialists represented in the Republic—and guided also by foreign examples which would have been fatal if applied to the Spanish case—it showed its hostility to the Azaña Government in a most impudent and premature anti-Marxism, as if Socialist policy in the Government was the very apex of revolution. But by imitating the language and conduct of European reactionaries, the oligarchy dug its own grave. It evidently did not know that if the Socialists were the pivot of the Republic, they were also the pivot of social order and tranquillity. For the second Spanish Republic, precisely because the Socialist workers' movement had sprung up, was so fused with the destiny of Spain that if this master column was overthrown, not only would the Republic collapse, but the whole edifice would crumble. Yet the reactionaries could look no farther than the seductive prospect of expelling the Socialists. In effect, the Republic could only be governed by the Republicans, as I have indicated, with the aid either of the Socialists or of the Monarchists. There would never be a Parliament with a sufficient middle-class majority to enable the Republicans to dispense with proletarian Ministers or proletarian votes. The exclusion of the Socialists would imply, then, that the Republic would have to be governed by one or several Republican parties, at the mercy of the oligarchy. And this was the situation which the enemies of the régime were trying to create, every day with greater hopes of success.

The Republicans who imagined that the exit of the Socialists

[1] Speech in the Cortes, Oct. 2nd, 1933.

from the Government would save the Republic (they had actually got as far as that) confronted Azaña's policy with a plan for broadening the basis on which the Republic rested, in a contradictory sense. They argued that it was necessary to incorporate into the Republic those social classes which opposed it so long as the Socialists were in power, but which would rally to its support the moment the coalition was disrupted. That is, it was necessary to expel—and, who knows?—even outlaw—a considerable and indispensable popular party in order to incorporate into the Republic the enemies of the Constitution and of social reform.

Since the constitutional Charter was promulgated, the broadening of the basis of the Republic inspired the policy of the President of the Republic, of certain Republicans without party, though of recognized personal authority, and of the Radical Republican Party. The reader will note that this party entered the Republic as part of the Republican alliance and the provisional Government. Lerroux enjoyed the strange privilege of dragging into the Republic, as into the monarchy, this rotten nucleus of democracy. No honest Republican ever trusted him, yet neither the old nor the new régime could dispense with this consummate demagogue. In this respect, the situation matched the abnormality of Spanish society, for, on the sovereignty of the people being decreed, a new instrument of corruption was introduced. Lerroux was a force in Spanish politics, as Catiline was a force in the Roman Republic, and this explains why, on the one hand, those who considered him an undesirable associate invited his co-operation in their deliberations and labours, and, on the other, why the forces of reaction courted his equivocal services. The political underworld was as active, if not more active, under the Republic as under the monarchy. And the services of Lerroux were as indispensable to a parliamentary Republic as they were to the monarchy of the Restoration, also parliamentary. Under the Republic, the danger was that the Radical Party would pass over to the monarchy, and under the monarchy, that it would work in earnest for the Republic. But the demagogic character of the organization led it inevitably to hinder the advent of the Republic under the monarchy, and to facilitate the restoration of the monarchy under the Republic. Lerroux hoped, then, that the Republic would be proclaimed so that he might set himself up as the preserver of the basic institutions of the monarchy.

The romantic and philanthropic Republican who, during

477

the past régime, had envisaged the Republic as a vestal, wearing the cap of liberty, all purity of line, innocence and civil piety, did not take into account the fact that a fraction of Republicanism was corrupt to the core. The Lerroux brand of Radicalism was the unavowable disease of the Republican Minerva. And the first act, perhaps, of a Republican dictatorship, as eulogized by Costa, would have been to extirpate this same disease; but the Republic having been delivered over to Parliament and universal suffrage, the evil could not but make rapid progress. We have consequently to note that among the immediate causes of the decease of the Republic was the moral and political corruption of one of its democratic organs. The ethical, not the political, element undermined the collaboration of the principal parties of the régime.

Because Lerroux was a force, he obtained two portfolios in the provisional Government for his party. But because he was a dubious force, these two portfolios were the Ministries of Foreign Affairs and Communications. The Radicals were put into those Departments which were least likely to evoke their famous weakness. The *whole* party became suspect, no doubt without justification.

It must be recalled here that in the Government crisis of October 1931, Alcalá Zamora and his colleague of the Republican-Liberal Right, Miguel Maura, left the Cabinet as a protest against Article 26 of the Constitution. The Radicals continued in the new Cabinet, under the leadership of Azaña. In December there occurred the anticipated Ministerial crisis arising out of the promulgation of the Constitution and the functioning of the new Presidential power, and it was agreed beforehand by all the Ministers and governing parties that, when this moment arrived, the Republican-Socialist coalition should continue in power. When this agreement was adopted, Azaña considered that the Government ought to continue to be formed of the same parties, to which Lerroux added: "And the same persons."

The President opened the consultations in the expected crisis of December and Azaña was charged with forming a Ministry. In the morning, Lerroux gave him *carte blanche* to form one at his own discretion; at nightfall, Azaña submitted to the Radical leader a list of names in the new Government. Lerroux then withdrew his support—it was not consistent with the continuance in office of the Socialists.[1] Clearly, a few hours'

[1] The explanation of the solution of the crisis can be seen in Azaña's speech to the Cortes, Feb. 3rd, 1933.

deliberation could not have provoked a change of heart on a fundamental question such as whether the Republic should be governed by Socialists and Republicans or by Republicans alone. Lerroux cancelled his agreement with Azaña and, in fact, with the Republic, because Azaña had included in the list of the new Government as Minister of Finance Don Jaime Carner, a Catalan who had not ceased to denounce the administrative corruptions of Lerrouxism in the Municipal Government of Barcelona under the old régime. For Lerroux, Carner was another moralizing Pertinax, an Argus who was going to watch over the Radical Ministers with his hundred eyes. The Radicals had already suffered for a year the prying eyes of the Socialists and of Azaña and they were not going to be confined to Ministries where there was less margin for profit, by such tiresome mentors of virtue. Probably, also, commitments of all kinds led the Radicals to change their policy; nor did their *amour propre* tolerate this well-merited but humiliating tutelage any longer. Such is the true explanation of the ominous conflict. Azaña advised Lerroux to form a Government himself, promising to support him and to obtain perhaps the co-operation of the Socialists. But Lerroux was not interested in governing in such conditions. He wanted to flee from his impertinent judges, to put such a distance between himself and them, that he could carry on his private policy of gangsterism without interference or contradiction. His ambition, presumably, was to be head of a Government, but with indulgent allies in the Chamber and sympathetic Ministers in the Cabinet. Naturally in the Republic this was unlikely. Only the oligarchy would lend itself, in exchange for a hand in the affairs of the Republic, to countenancing the excesses of Lerrouxism. A force engendered in society and politics by the oligarchy of the Restoration, the Radical Party returned to the service of the oligarchy under the Republic. Both held a common view of politics—moral laxity and the idea of power as an end in itself.

Freed from the discipline tacitly imposed on him by association with the Republicans of the Left and the Socialists, Lerroux, although tarred with the Conservative brush, recovered his ancient demagogic idiom. His house, always hospitable, became a channel of resentment and discontent. There, as in other times, the aristocrat and the incendiary, the atheist and the Catholic, held their rendezvous. He became the confidant and the protector of all the enemies of the Republic and threw his ample cloak round all the detractors of the Government. Spanish politics fled again from the clear light of Parliament to the murky darkness of the old witches' Sabbath. And under cover of these conspiracies, the monarchical-republican and Catholic-masonic coalition was being woven which was to fix the future course of the civil war.

Lerroux's anti-Socialism, as we have just seen, had been improvised in an instant of deceit to cover a personal question and a point of ethics. In a nation which is politically sick, this manœuvre is often employed; personal and other conflicts which it is not convenient to admit, turn, in public, into profound political divergencies and even into philosophical and dogmatic rivalries. But apart from glossing over his refusal to continue in the Government, anti-Marxism was the ladder by which Lerroux rose to power through the back door of the Republic—the only ladder which he could scale. With his new programme he sought outside the régime the assistance which was denied him within. From his parliamentary bench or from the public platform, he cajoled those who were by temperament hostile to democracy.

In July 1932 Lerroux spoke at Saragossa. He declared himself ready to collaborate with "men of the monarchy" He rallied all the voices of discontent, echoing the disgust of the military Monarchists, the wrath of the landlords, and—what was positively extraordinary in an anti-clerical of such crude antecedents—the uneasiness of the Catholics. And as he held in his hands the clues to certain activities which would threaten the Republic, he demanded that the Azaña Government should terminate or change its policy, a suggestion which, if complied with, would have meant the capitulation of the régime before a group of Monarchist conspirators.

His other hand—the left—Lerroux gave to the anarchists. The proletariat, he complained, were not being treated fairly. Azaña asked himself, with the uneasy curiosity of the disquieted statesman, what social legislation would satisfy the "dynamite" organizations, whose vital principle consisted in ignoring the State and whose philosophy lay in disobeying all its laws.

From all accounts, Lerroux would not have gone so far in his demand that Azaña and the Socialists should leave the Government, had he not found in the old Royal Palace more concurrence than disagreement.

The President also wanted to set the régime's policy on another course. He was obsessed with the reform of the Constitution and, as I said before, with the broadening of the basis of the Republic. He dreamed of bringing into the Republic other parties and other men, that is, the old parties and the

480

old "Box and Cox" foxes, among whom he counted himself. For this last reason, Alcalá Zamora, once invested with his high office, soon felt himself ill at ease with a Government of politicians of some force of character, who proposed to foster a standard of scrupulousness in the relations between the powers of the State. Unfortunately, the President of the Republic displayed an overwhelming bias for personal government. The ideal Republic of Alcalá Zamora would have been a monarchy without a king, but even this slight difference did not appear to prosper under his mandate, which gave him the opportunity of imitating Alfonso XIII and even of excelling him in tortuous devices. Don Niceto wanted not Ministers, but Government officials, obedient to his commands and pliable to his will. Obviously, Azaña and his Socialists could not help him, either with his design to revise the Constitution and the general policy of the Republic, or with his proposal to convert the Republic into a Presidential régime. But as Lerroux was opposed, for the reasons already set forth, to forming a Government based on the Constituent Cortes, there were no other Cabinets possible but those which Azaña could form. The President would have to dissolve the Chamber if he wanted a change of policy and this was a highly delicate matter—the only consideration which could restrain him—since, during his term of office, he could only dissolve the Cortes twice. In June 1933, Alcalá Zamora obstinately bent on getting rid of Azaña and the Socialists, provoked a Ministerial crisis. But the experiment showed that the parliamentary majority continued to support the Coalition.

However, the confidence of Parliament was not enough. The Government was frankly growing weaker through that slow process of attrition which is bound to overtake every Executive which governs with liberty in a state of civil war. Agrarian reform was at a standstill. The social laws, for the most part, were flouted by a turbulent landed class. A numerous body of Monarchist officers were carrying on an agitation in the Army. The monarchy prevailed even in the provinces, where partisan elections for a few thousand rural municipalities had been, as was to be expected, adverse to the Government. That part of the Press which was hostile to the régime kept up an unrestrained onslaught against the Republic, against the Ministerial coalition and its men, frequently in a grossly libellous vein. The insurrections of the Monarchists and the Anarchists, especially the events of Casas Viejas which so deeply wounded the humanitarian sentiments of the oligarchy; the crudeness of the class struggle, in spite of the moderation of the Socialist urban proletariat;[1] the volatility of the President of the Republic, an incalculable and depressing factor—all these insuperable obstacles and problems, cruelly abnormal as they were for a parliamentary democracy, tended to debilitate and finally bring to ruin a helpless Cabinet with very limited powers, in the use of which it was narrowly scrutinized by an irresponsible Opposition devoid of good faith and of the spirit of Republican collaboration.

Disillusion spread among the Socialists and among not a few of the Republicans of the Left, in whose spirit there sprang up a doubt as to whether such proceedings and such a system led anywhere. The disenchantment was greatest among the Socialists, who had sacrificed their principles and immolated their popularity in an experiment in government which they had not aspired to, and which seemed to them desolatingly sterile. And the fact that their moderation and patriotism were appreciated by practically nobody tempered the Liberal enthusiasm of the workers' leaders.

In two years of the Republic, the experiment of regenerating Spain by constitutional means had failed—that was all. The Liberal system had failed and the Republican-Socialist coalition had failed. This was the clearest lesson to be learned from the course of events. Azaña, an unrepentant Liberal, could not accept it; but in his own party, the idea of a régime of force was beginning to germinate—an idea which he, fearful of the unknown, suppressed with the precipitancy of one who ventures too near the brink of the abyss.

Socialists and Republicans had united to overthrow the monarchy and they continued in association to carry out a revolution from the seat of government. It was an alliance which could only endure if the dynamic spirit, offensive or defensive, was present. But in 1933 the offensive dynamism slackened, owing to the certitude among both Socialists and Republicans that they could advance no farther. The work of revolution had consisted in the promulgation of certain fundamental laws, and these, with the exception of certain laws completing

[1] Azaña was loud in his praise of the conduct of the proletariat: "Moreover, on this subject, it is opportune to affirm something else, and that is the exemplary conduct of great bodies of industrial workers who, knowing that it is not in the power of this, or any other Government to improvise a solution of their unemployment crisis, suffer with abnegation the scarcity and want of their limited circumstances, and give an example of social discipline and of obedience to the Government which is worthy of all praise and to be noted with applause." (Speech in the Cortes, Feb. 3rd, 1933.)

the Constitution, had been promulgated. And when it was clear that the laws which had been dictated with such frequency were not being observed, the mood of the Government turned to scepticism. The Socialists had adjusted their aspirations to those of the Republicans and the Republican bow had been stretched to its farthest extent; the Left *bourgeoisie* would never go farther than it had done, either in substance or in procedure.

The other kind of dynamism, the defensive, which might have united the Socialists and the Republicans of the Left and, indeed, was to unite them in exceptionally dramatic circumstances, never even came into play. The military rising of August 1932 was a fiasco and the probabilities of any other chimerical attempt triumphing appeared, and were, in fact, insignificant.

Azaña held, with good judgment, that numerical superiority in the Chamber had no value in itself. Republicans and Socialists had united to carry out something which had, within its limits, been realized. It was therefore fatal that, when the Republican car was held up at the cross-roads by interests which could not be overthrown by parliamentary methods, and when it was apparent that the Government had no idea, or proposal, or desire, or perhaps method for beginning the democratic revolution anew, a part of Socialist and even Republican opinion should have gone over to radicalism. The working-class and Socialist masses, and particularly youth, felt they had been cheated and fooled. No one could have been less satisfied than Socialist youth to persevere with the sacrifice of ideals and political positions among the proletariat, which is what the perpetual union of Republicans and Socialists would have meant. If this was to continue, the proletariat would end by supporting the Communists and the Anarchists, especially the Communists.

The voice and the gesture which were to rouse the Socialist Party to recover its liberty were those of youth. The old *cadres* of Spanish Socialism had to choose between the demands of youth, which had never been charged with frivolity or impatience, and the call of exhausted forces. But the appeal which the Republicans made to the Socialists to preserve the coalition was neither unanimous nor hearty. Most of them had been dazzled by the theory that a more conservative Republic would be more workable, a mirage which bears witness to the fact that the Republic of April 14th was too exhausted to create, whether for good or for ill.

Socialists and Republicans of the Left still regarded each other with affectionate intelligence, but with the melancholy disillusionment of the partners to a childless marriage. They dragged out their existence in power, hoping that the death of the Government would bring them their release, a much more pious solution for all concerned than a scandalous divorce.

## CHAPTER XV

## THE REACTION

IMMEDIATELY AFTER THE Ministerial crisis of June, Azaña had expressed to the Cortes his intention that teaching should be taken out of the hands of the religious orders by the following 1st October, and as regards the Law of Confessions and Congregations, he said: "we are going to fulfil it from A to Z, with all loyalty, with all rigour."[1] Lerroux then had the hardihood to declare, with the satisfaction of one who perceives a rift ahead, that the Law of Confessions would produce a Presidential crisis. There was no such Presidential crisis, but on September 11th the Azaña Government fell, because the President withdrew his confidence.

The last touch of the spur which induced the President of the Republic to take such a critical step was provided by the elections for the Tribunal of Constitutional Guarantees, the result of which was unfavourable to the parties of the régime. For the first time, Socialists and Republicans presented a disunited front to the electors.

On the 12th September, Lerroux formed a Cabinet of Radicals and began, before he had canvassed the confidence of Parliament, to undo the work of Azaña. On October 2nd the new Radical Cabinet appeared without a blush before the Cortes. In his Ministerial statement, Lerroux announced, among other significant items, that an amnesty would be declared for those indicted and sentenced for crimes against the régime, that is, for Monarchists and Anarchists. The Government, as was obvious beforehand, did not command enough votes to survive, and the President decided to dissolve the Chamber. A general election was fixed for the 19th November by another Government, headed by Lerroux's lieutenant, Diego Martínez Barrio, a less unpopular figure, with a special talent for arbitration. For

[1] Speech on June 20th, 1933.

reasons which are not clear, Martínez Barrio excited less misgivings among all the political parties than Lerroux. Elections presided over by him, they thought, would not be so scandalously manipulated as if Lerroux had managed them.

But further reflection shows that Martínez Barrio was more of a problem to democracy than his chief, although he did not appear to be, or to put it better, just because he did not appear to be. His political career, which had opened with a demagogic gesture—Lerroux's diffuse anarchism, but a less strident brand—was culminating now in an anxious desire for peace and order. Between Lerroux and Martínez Barrio there existed certain differences, due less to political divergencies than to personal idiosyncrasies. Lerroux had a streak of vulgarity which was lacking in Martínez Barrio, a refined Andalusian. Moreover, the man from Seville was free from the petty temptations which discredited other of his colleagues. A sober way of life enabled Martínez Barrio to live on little, and this little was forthcoming, before he became a professional politician, from his employment as printer and later from the ownership of a modest printing-press. Yet the new Prime Minister not only belonged to the Radical Party, but occupied the second place in its hierarchy. Martínez Barrio passed, with justice, for the best of Lerrouxism, but the best of Lerrouxism was nevertheless the worst of the Republic.

A legitimate ambition, not untinged, perhaps, with sincere patriotism, impelled the leader of the Seville Radicals to play a prominent rôle in his country's politics. But in the old way. Having formed his political opinions in the *milieu* of the Restoration political system in Seville, Martínez Barrio had assimilated from the oligarchy its negative and one-track view of the fundamental problems of Spain. For him, to govern was to maintain public order and to carry out elections. His programme as a whole was realized, as was Lerroux's, on the fall of the monarchy; he became automatically a preserver of whatever remained standing. His weakness now lay in appearing moderate and in forging for himself a reputation for respectability. And he would have abandoned the Radical Party if he had had the moral strength to adopt this or any other great decision. He would only shake off Lerroux if to support him would imply his political ruin. This last he was not prepared to stand. The greatest flaw, then, in the character of Martínez Barrio was his moral weakness—a fault which was almost a virtue in the Lerrouxist circle, where horror of the constructive, a sterile conception of government and the idea of politics as business between friends, reigned supreme.

Martínez Barrio had two qualities which were effective in opening to him a way in Spanish politics. He had a ready tongue and he was astute. But these gifts alone did not raise him an inch above the old politicians and the Republic had come to mean something to Spain.

In the months which preceded the historic November of the elections, Martínez Barrio had fought Azaña and the Socialists with indubitable success. His personal opposition in Parliament, with that of other "moderates", was one of the chief agents in breaking the Government. Martínez Barrio had skill and to spare for these sort of tactics, all the more so because his political integrity frequently did not come up to his personal rectitude. Thus, few derived more profit, at the expense of Azaña and his Ministry, from the crime of Casas Viejas; without reflecting where the interests of the Government ended and those of the Republic began. The same may be said as regards his conduct in parliamentary obstruction, which reached such a pitch that the régime was paralysed and the prestige of the Cortes considerably reduced. And, finally, Martínez Barrio was the author of that unfortunate and exaggerated phrase: "mud, blood, and tears" which, flung originally in Azaña's face, stuck to the Republic for ever, at least in the propaganda of its enemies. The monarchist Press printed it almost daily for months and it even circulated as a definition of the Republic by an authentic Republican.

In forming the Government which was to supervise the electoral contest, Martínez Barrio was to crown the campaign to destroy the Republic which had been begun by his party at the end of 1932. His conviction—held, no doubt, in all good faith—that the régime would overcome its troubles by adopting a more temperate policy, had the logical consequence of incapacitating him from protecting the Left against the foreseeable and fatal onslaught of the oligarchic *caciques*. And his lack of moral fibre, which made him another Pontius Pilate, guaranteed that, in most of the cases where democracy was at stake, the Government would not obstruct the most criminal encroachments of reaction. Martínez Barrio was subsequently to exclaim, perhaps to assuage the prickings of conscience: "My hands are clean!" Who could doubt it, since the speaker was so frequently washing them?

The tacit alliance between the Radicals and the Monarchists which had come into being during the parliamentary aggression against Azaña and the Socialists, developed into open collusion before the ballot-box. But let us first say a few words on the distribution of the political forces at the time of the ill-omened elections of November 1933.

It was already apparent that the double-faced oligarchy of the Restoration régime presented another appearance under the Republic. Now, instead of being double-faced, it was two-headed. *Renovación Española*, the party of the *caballeros* (an anachronism equivalent to the Cavalier Party in seventeenth-century England) was characterized by its unbreakable adhesion to the monarchical form of government and represented the highest peak of the social pyramid—the landowning aristocracy, with interests predominating in the southern regions of the latifundia and the olive and in high finance, and the financial oligarchy properly so-called. It was a *coup d'étatist* party, which aspired to destroy the Republic with violence, from the barracks. The insurrection of August 10th had been suppressed, but the insurrectionists did not despair of repeating the performance with better results. *Renovación Española*—so called presumably because it set its face against anything new—was opposed to the least compromise with the Republic.

Side by side with the party of the *caballeros*, the agrarian Popular Action Party (*Acción Popular Agraria*), the specific political organization of the great Castilian landlords and the Church, unfurled its banners.

Popular Action, attentive to the suggestions of Vatican diplomacy, did not put any stress upon forms of government, a problem which it would only have to face at a later stage of its struggle, its *Kampf*, when it held the Republican State in its hands. For the moment, it called itself neither Republican nor Monarchist. To declare itself Monarchist would close to it the doors of the Republic, which it proposed to transplant pacifically, without bloodshed; the bloodshed would come later, if it could not be avoided. On the other hand, if Popular Action were to raise the Republican standard, it would in all probability affright the bulk of its adherents. As we have seen, the policy of the great agrarian and Catholic party was equivocal in form, but its basis, by contrast, was as clear as day—Monarchists and Agrarian-Catholics were out to annihilate the Republic, each in their own way.

Before the November elections, Popular Action became the magnetic centre attracting a mass of small related parties, and this amalgamation called itself *Confederación Española de Derechas Autónomas* (Spanish Confederation of Autonomous Rights), *C.E.D.A.* The *C.E.D.A.* was in its turn the pivot of the anti-Republican electoral coalition, which included a small agrarian party formed by the owners of medium-sized estates in Castile, the Traditionalist Party (*Comunión Tradicionalista*) or traditional Carlists, *Renovación Española*, etc. *Cedists* and Monarchists presented a united front, then, to the electors, that is to say, the oligarchy constituted once again a single *bloc* and subscribed, for reasons that are readily understood, to Catholic extremism. The cry of alarm went up that Religion and Property were in peril.

The Radicals appeared as politically expedient friends of the Right *bloc*, all the more necessary as they were in power.

The November elections were to Monarchists and Republicans what Waterloo was to Wellington and Napoleon; and therefore they merit more than a few words.

The oligarchy, if it had not rehabilitated itself, had at least repaired its fortunes. Confident in its intrinsic strength, in its influence and its wealth and, what is more, confident in the help it could depend on, whether open or subterranean, in the high places of the régime, it took the field, full of confidence and determined to win. The muster of financial power in its propaganda was overwhelming from the first hour. The aristocracy, the bankers, the landlords, the Church, poured forth copious funds with rare disinterestedness, which even their own egoism did not arouse in them at other times. The Right *bloc* indulged in extremes of language which ill became those classes of society which, among other privileges inaccessible to the majority, had enjoyed a secondary school and University education. This wild provocation resulted in the electoral battle degenerating into a slanging-match. In this tempestuous moment, Spain proved that a nation can possess an opulent oligarchy and yet lack a Conservative class. The kernel of reactionary propaganda was an implacable anti-Marxism; as if the Spanish Socialists had practised in the Government—in which they had only participated with many misgivings—or had promised to practise a class policy, and as if there had been in the Parliament which had been dissolved a numerous and menacing Communist Opposition. The anti-Marxism of the oligarchy was Fascism, but so artificially engendered that it had recourse to the demagogic expedient of painting in its speeches and handbills a Spain in ruins, demolished by the pickaxe of Azaña and the Socialists. The object was to create the psychological basis for Fascism which was created in other countries, now by the occupation of the factories by the workers, now by the presence in Parliament of a hundred or so Marxist deputies. But none of this had happened in Spain.

In all propaganda, we have certainly to discount a margin of hyperbole; but in the electoral campaign of November, the Spanish reactionaries were seized by suicidal hysteria. If they were to be believed, there was no money in the banks because the Socialists had swept away the last farthing; the .Catholics were suffering a persecution only comparable to what was inflicted on them by Nero and Diocletian; the family would rapidly disappear, thanks to the Republican laws; the country-side would be devastated by Bolshevist hordes; national independence would perish, because Azaña had destroyed the Army. In short, there was no social plague which the Republican-Socialist coalition had not inflicted on Spain. Thus did certain social classes, who still enjoyed privileges and incomes which had been abolished in the rest of Europe, talk to ignorant and fanatical audiences. And it can be imagined that, by dint of repeating and listening to this kind of propaganda, speakers and audiences ended by believing these perfidious and hair-raising flights of fancy.

What most roused the Catholics—the anti-clericalism of the Republican laws—was not in any case the specific work of the Socialists, but of the Republican parties, like the Radical Party, a masonic party which now appeared arm in arm with the politicians of the Church—proof that religion was less important to the oligarchy than property.

The Socialists and Republicans of the Left fought in a manifestly inferior position. They had no money for propaganda to oppose the avalanche of gold which flowed from the *salons* and the banks. They could expect no justice from the Government, still less the favour they merited in this hour of the Republic's deadly peril. In addition, for the reasons set out in the preceding chapter, the parties of the Left did not maintain a united front. The resistance of the rich to every attempt at reform and the Republicans' lack of energy in imposing such reforms, con-strained an exasperated proletariat to measure their strength as a class in the electoral struggle.

The elections took place in an atmosphere of civil war, a slant imposed on the struggle by its character of finality, given the destructive fury of the Conservative programme. The electoral alliance of Monarchists, Catholics and Radical Masons, so care-fully concealed in the first ballot, was open and cynical in the second. In some provinces, such as Cordova, the Catholics, who had partnered the Monarchists in the first ballot, deserted them in the second and threw in their lot with the Radicals. The Martínez Barrio Government made a pact with the

Right *bloc*, as was subsequently proved by letters which were published in the Seville *ABC* and the Madrid *Informaciones*. The general idea was for all the political parties, except the Republicans of the Left, to join forces against Socialism. A handful of Republican Conservatives from Miguel Maura's party also stood as candidates with the Monarchists.

In their outward form, the elections were a faithful copy of elections under the monarchy. But now the oligarchic parties came up against difficulties which they had not experienced under the old régime and which helped to intensify their methods of combat. The Right encountered in 1933 an unsubmissive agricultural proletariat. The peasants wanted to vote for representatives of their own class, even at the risk of losing their poor wages, the strip of land they rented and, in many cases also, the hovel they took refuge in with their children. But, as was natural, there were innumerable cases where the proletariat, especially in the villages, yielded to the pressure of the landlords. But what did it matter if they voted, where they could, for the Left, if in the end the Right managed to get enough votes to win the election! The provinces had been delivered over to fifty or so Lerrouxist governors, personnel for the most part of the Monarchist parties and the *Union Patriotica* of Primo de Rivera, and it was a foregone conclusion that the Republic would lose the elections there.

There were many towns where the appearance of an Opposition candidate was impossible, owing to the violence with which the fight was waged on behalf of the Government candidates. Fernando de los Ríos, ex-Minister and Socialist candidate for Granada, was welcomed in Huéjar with an unexpected volley in the heart of the village from a dozen gunmen who had been armed for the purpose of the elections by the *cacique*. In Jerez del Marquesado, another place in the same province, the Socialist ex-Minister could not pass, because it was ascertained that certain gunmen in the pay of the Right had been posted in the neighbourhood to head him off at all costs.

The elections were such that Botella Asensi, Minister of Justice in the Government that presided over them and arranged them, hastened to hand in his resignation and made it known to the Press that his attitude was dictated by the illegality of the results.

Thus, with the November victory, the Radicals and the Ultramontanes came into power. The Left was routed because circumstances and the Government had decided that it should not win. Before the revolution had even taken place, the hour had struck for the counter-revolution which the régime had taken no thought to render impossible; and, as a consequence, Spain was now rushing headlong down the slope to civil war. With greater justification than Louis XV, Azaña could have said: "Après moi, le déluge!"

A deficient knowledge of history, the lack of a great political leader or real men of action, the weak civic pulse of the parties of the régime, the corruption of one of the largest Republican groups—these were, in my opinion, the reasons why the Republic failed. To ascribe the failure to the electoral law, the women's suffrage, the abstention of the Anarchists, or other subsidiary and adventitious happenings, would be to misunderstand the whole historical profundity of the tragedy.

The composition of the new Parliament confronted the popular Republic with a hostile majority. The Republican parties of the Left had been all but annihilated and Azaña obtained a seat in Parliament, in the second ballot, thanks to the generous solidarity of the Socialists. The parliamentary forces of any considerable size were: the Right *bloc* with 212 seats, the Radicals with a hundred or so and the Socialists with about sixty. But Lerroux, who formed his second Cabinet in December, found that the anomalous political geometry of the Chamber presented no problem. He would never have been able to govern in his own way with a Republican Cortes and he had decided beforehand to lean on reaction. Once the position in Parliament became clear, Martínez Barrio left the Radical Party with a group of penitent stragglers. But he was too late. The Republic was already being besieged by the oligarchy.

The Government of Lerroux soon fell, owing to a certain faithlessness on his part in amnestying the insurrectionists of August 10th. Alcalá Zamora promulgated the decree, but, finding it not to his taste, sent a message to the Cortes expressing reserves and legal scruples which meant a declaration of lack of confidence in the Government.

Lerroux was succeeded in the Premiership by a Señor Samper, a Valencian autonomist, a contumacious lawyer, a typical personage of the municipal courts, the worst possible man to direct the destinies of Spain at a time of profound public agitation. But the insignificant figure of Samper satisfied the President of the Republic, who had found that even Lerroux had too much character. Don Niceto, free now from restraint, revealed his passion for Presidential rule and authorized a Cabinet of nonentities, mere ciphers, obscure persons whom

491

he drew from a well-deserved anonymity so that, grateful for the Presidential favour, they would carry out his suspect policy.

The Samper Ministry, which was to remain in power for almost a year, was the authentic Government of the classic Restoration, another Cabinet of the Cabal. It is worth while for the reader to make the acquaintance of some of its Ministers.

The Agrarian Party threw up a choleric Señor Cid, whose pleasure it was from the first moment to make life impossible for the officials in the Ministry of Communications. He said there were soviets in Communications. Cid was a Monarchist, with an enormous head stuffed with tyrannical ideas and better qualified to be a bishop in the despotic Spanish hierarchy than a Minister.

Count Romanones pointed out to Lerroux that Salazar Alonso "would be a useful man in the Government", and this insignificant person was put into the Ministry of Police. But Salazar Alonso, a typical Radical, hastened to create for himself with all speed a reputation for being anti-Marxist, and his appointment, besides receiving the oligarchy's stamp of approval, foreshadowed that war would be declared on the proletariat in terms hitherto unknown even during the electoral period.

In such a fantastic Arabian Nights entertainment as Madrid was under Alcalá Zamora and Lerrouxism, Señor Marraco, that quintessence of mulishness and ineptitude, could not fail to put in an appearance as Minister of Finance, quack doctor to the Treasury.

For the Ministry of Labour, Samper chose a Catalan poet, Estadella. Estadella used to reply in alexandrines to the remonstrances addressed to him by his friends and acquaintances among the deputies.

The War Office was taken over by a lawyer, Hidalgo, founder and backer of the Communist publishing firm *Cenit*. Hidalgo reinstated in the Army, and took as his advisers, the Monarchist generals.

It is not extraordinary that, confronted with such a Government, Azaña should have cried one day: "I prefer the King and his Ministers!"

In fact, from December 1933, the nation fell under a dictatorship of the Monarchist-Catholic-Agrarian parliamentary majority. The freedom of the Press was purely theoretical. On the slightest pretext, and sometimes without a pretext, the Opposition papers were confiscated. In less than a year *El Socialista* suffered more than a hundred confiscations and three fines of 5,000 pesetas. *Avance* of Oviedo met with the same adverse fate, like the rest of the workers' Press; and Republican newspapers, or newspapers which did not always accept the situation with complacency, such as *El Liberal*, *La Voz* and *El Sol* of Madrid, also suffered, though lightly, from police persecution and economic reprisals.

The provincial Radical Committees made themselves masters of the municipal governments. At the suggestion of any petty Lerrouxist, Salazar Alonso ordered the dismissal of Socialist or Left Republican mayors and councillors. By September 1934, barely half a dozen Republican-Socialist municipalities remained in being. Nor were the Conservative-Republican councillors respected in their posts. Even Martínez Barrio's self-styled democrats lost their representation in the public Corporations. And it was not entirely correct to say that the Republican parties passed out of existence; rather were they throttled by the Government.

The counter-revolution made its presence felt immediately, with unheard-of severity, in the rural areas. Perhaps it was here that the agrarian oligarchy had most to avenge. Under the amnesty, the grandees received back the lands which had been expropriated. Subsequently, by the decree of February 11th, 1934, the peasants on the estates given over to intensive cultivation were evicted, which meant the lightning dispossession of 28,000 peasants, 18,000 of them in Estremadura. By a circular dated the 16th of the same month, the revision of rents on the rural estates was suspended and the owners were again left free to eject any leaseholders whom they did not find satisfactory. Finally, a decree of May 28th abrogated whatever laws the Republic had passed regarding hours of work, wages and location of labour in the rural areas. Wages fell by 50 per cent and there were places where the peasants did not even work for wages, but for maintenance, that is, for a dish of *gazpacho* and a crust of bread. The boundless egoism of the landowners reigned over the countryside again, this time with an added spirit of vengeance to make it more vicious. Not a few landlords began again to leave their estates uncultivated, and it is a fact which perfectly illustrates the situation, that the workless peasant was dismissed with a phrase as brutal as it was worthy of such an oligarchy: "Go and eat the Republic!" he was told.

Apart from accentuating the general misery in the country districts, all these regulations and abuses gave a terrible impulse to rural anarchy. Agrarian reform, with the modest hope it represented, was already a lost cause.

493

Another infamous measure was the annulment of the *Ley de puesta en riego* (Irrigation Law), which had given rise to such important works in the valley of the Betis.

The Monarchist officers, on the other hand, who had risen against the Republic on August 10th, were allowed to re-enter the Army (as if Azaña had not left in it enough enemies of the régime!), and these gentlemen were entitled, under the law of amnesty, to draw the pay which they had lost while they were in exile or prison.

In the Ministry of Education, the supplies voted were reduced with symptomatic haste. The grant for elementary education fell by 13 million pesetas ; the 200,000 pesetas for the Teaching Missions disappeared and the iniquitous oligarchy, which prided itself on its piety, noted without a qualm (if indeed the suggestion did not come from it) that the 125,000 pesetas destined by the Republic to feed some thousands of pauper children in the schools, were also withdrawn.

But in exchange, the Budget for Religion and the Clergy was partly re-established; and the authors of the Constitution saw with startled surprise that the new Minister of Foreign Affairs, authorized by the President of the Republic, was going to Rome to negotiate a Concordat in defiance of the law, ignoring the Cortes and gravely troubling Liberal opinion.

The counter-revolutionary tendency of the Government, which was feverishly engaged in uprooting, destroying and mutilating the work of the Republic, grew more complicated as it grew more pronounced, thanks to the incredible inefficiency of the Ministers. That there would be extensive and bitter controversies no one could doubt, since of thirteen Ministers— a number which might have warned the superstitious of what would befall—eleven were lawyers, besides which, the President of the Republic and the Speaker of the Cortes also belonged to this contentious profession. Conflicts which might have been easily solved became so embroiled that no pacific solution could be found.

We have already seen that, since the fateful November elections, the peasants were living in total want, dependent on the will of the landowners. They went to the leaders of their trade unions for protection and, with even less hope of success, to the authorities for justice. In the trade-union offices they were advised to keep calm and have patience, in the hope of better days. In the Ministries or Town Halls, they were naturally not even listened to. And then desperation, always a fatal counsellor, led the peasants to declare a general peaceful strike just before the harvest. They hoped to call the Government's attention to their miserable plight. The strike was declared by the *Federación Nacional de Trabajadores de la Tierra* (National Federation of Landworkers) in accordance with the usual democratic trade-union practice, after a referendum which resulted in 70,000 votes being cast in favour of the strike and 350 against. This act of protest transgressed no law. Within the period prescribed by the official texts, the peasants presented in writing formal notice of the strike, stressing the fact that it was to be a peaceful one. The Government could have avoided it, seeing the smallness and justice of the peasants' claims and the fact that they were predisposed to compromise, without the least hint of a threat. But as soon as a conflict arose, whatever its nature, Salazar Alonso, the Minister of Police, became the only Minister in the Samper Government. From the first instant, the Minister of Agriculture and the Minister of Labour disinterested themselves in the problem of the rural areas, or they were supplanted by the Minister of the Interior, who had no doubt at all that the strike was revolutionary in character. The landlords, the *caciques* and police forces, mobilized as if for war, fell upon the strikers as if they had to stamp out an agrarian insurrection. The peasants were treated like rebels. An absurd wave of governmental terrorism broke over the fields of Castile, Estremadura and Andalusia. All the *Casas del Pueblo* in the villages were closed and thousands of those outcasts, whose painful mission it is in Spain, as Costa said, to turn stones into bread, were cast into gaol. In all, some 8,000 strikers of both sexes were imprisoned, and not a few, as was customary, were brutally beaten in the police stations, without consideration of age or sex.

A peaceful strike which, even if it had been begun, could have been solved with surprising simplicity if the Government had wished, plunged the peasant population into the most tragic desolation.

Because the Government, conscious perhaps of its weakness, persisted in putting down with a heavy hand anything that promoted strife, Saragossa endured for several months the tremendous effects of a general strike which ended by reaching epic dimensions. In December 1933, shortly after the formation of the second Lerroux Government, the Anarchists had thrown themselves into the revolution *against Fascism*, impatient, perhaps, that it should be realized that their persistent hostility to Azaña and the Socialists had not yielded to a predilection for a Cabinet of Radicals and Monarchists. The Anarchists began to perceive

495

the consequences of the change of régime—which had not occurred else—in labour conditions, but the moment chosen could not have been less propitious to a proletarian insurrection. Now, as before, only a visionary or an *agent provocateur* would have counselled a proletarian revolt. In a word, the movement was naturally abortive, and the Government imprisoned a host of workers, especially in Saragossa where the rising had taken a more violent turn. But the treatment meted out to the Government prisoners and detainees in the prison of the Aragonese capital moved the *C.N.T.* to decree a twenty-four-hour strike as a protest. A great number of employers, however, especially in commerce, listened to the suggestions of the authorities and refused to reinstate the strikers. Whereupon the strike went on indefinitely and the whole economic life of Saragossa suffered a mortal blow. The spectre of hunger took up its abode in the homes of the workers, not sparing the children who, at the last moment when the economic resistance of the strikers was at its lowest ebb, were received into the houses of workers in other capitals.

After two months of the strike, the whole of Saragossa, the poor and humble part of Saragossa, presented a horrifying spectacle of distress. Every day, at the shop doors and in the street markets, heart-rending scenes were enacted. The village women who brought their vegetables and garden produce to market, gave them to the starving mothers who roamed from place to place, begging not alms, but solidarity. Many modest tradesmen were ruined and innumerable homes destroyed. But neither the Government nor the Conservative classes were moved to pity.

The same thing occurred with another strike, that of the metalworkers of Madrid. The Madrid metalworkers claimed the forty-four hour week which had been granted to members of their craft in Valencia, Saragossa and Barcelona. The employers—to be precise, the small employers only—opposed the concession. The Minister of Labour found himself, as usual, unable to do anything, and the Minister of the Interior urged the owners of the factories to resist, which they did *au pied de la lettre* in spite of losses occasioned by their intransigence—many lost their clientèle. At the end of three terrible months of unemployment and privation, the 18,000 metallurgic workers won their case, after hunger had taken its toll of victims among their families; some workers committed suicide. The Minister of Labour, pausing for a while in his impertinent mouthings, finally compelled the employers to accept the forty-four-hour week.

Here were three conflicts entailing lamentable consequences, which the Government neither knew how, nor wished to interpret aright. Their system was to oppose any claims by the workers, to which the Minister of the Interior, also working on a system, attributed a revolutionary intent. Such contempt for and hostility to the organized proletariat, especially the proletariat of the cities, was never a feature of the monarchy, still less of the dictatorship of Primo de Rivera.

The Samper Government, which owed its existence to the parliamentary votes of the agrarian oligarchy, was not out to suppress the proletariat only, but the whole work of the Republic, and even things and persons which the monarchy had respected. The Catalan and Basque regions were the next to suffer the assault of the central oligarchy.

The Catalan *Lliga* was heavily defeated in the elections for the Catalan Parliament. The *Esquerra* or Left, the political organization of the *rabassaires* and the small urban *bourgeoisie*, obtained from the regional Chamber the necessary approval for the *Ley de Contratos de cultivo* (Law of Farming Contracts) with which the reader is familiar and which, as he also knows, aroused the protest of the great landowners of the region. The *Lliga*, without sufficient strength in Catalonia to prevent this law from prospering, sought aid from the Madrid Government and Cambó succeeded in getting Samper to lodge an appeal, on the grounds of unconstitutionalism, with the Tribunal of Guarantees which since September 1933 had been dominated by an oligarchic majority. The Tribunal of Guarantees gave its verdict against the Catalan Parliament and the *Esquerra* and for the central Government, the protector of the class interests of the *Lliga*. So the Catalan agrarian law was annulled by law; but the *Generalidad* refused to accept the verdict of the Tribunal of Guarantees. In this case, the Samper Government did not have recourse to violence, since the regional police were under the authority of the *Generalidad*.

While the conflict with the Catalonian middle class was lying dormant, Samper came to blows with the Basques. Incited, no doubt, by the oligarchy, the Minister of Finance, Marraco, resolved to modify the Economic Agreement between the State and the Basque Provinces whereby the Basques and Navarrese collected their taxes and handed over an agreed global sum to the Treasury. For the Basques, the threat was extremely grave, because it touched their pockets. In order to defend the Agreement, the nationalists decided that the municipalities should elect a Commission to replace for the purpose the

497

provincial Committees (*Diputaciones*) of which the Radicals and Monarchists had made themselves master, in a region where neither the Samper Government, nor the Radical-Agrarian coalition, nor the grain and olive oligarchy commanded a visible number of adherents. The step proposed by the Basques was perfectly legal, since the municipalities frequently set up *ad hoc* commissions from among their own numbers, to negotiate with the Government on definite subjects. But, as usual, the Minister of the Interior incontinently qualified the design of the nationalists as a criminal conspiracy and prepared to frustrate it by violence.

The Socialists of the region supported the nationalists and went to the prohibited elections. The police charged the rebels and used their truncheons on councillors, mayors and deputies to the Cortes. There could not have been a situation more insulting to the Republic.

In the meanwhile, those ineffable Ministers, whose idea of government was to suppress every protest with extreme severity, showed the same characteristic lack of moral fibre they had shown in other matters, by concocting their own economic agreement. Once more, it was apparent that the Radicals still clung to the idea that power meant booty. And soon petty larcenies and swindles on a greater scale came to light, which scandalized, though they did not surprise, because they were expected.

The gambling houses, which had been closed by the military dictatorship, began to open their doors in secret, and the Government, far from being deterred by the inevitable public outcry, proceeded to re-authorize gambling *sub rosa*. Attracted perhaps by the private reputation of the political party which was in power, there arrived in Madrid an adventurer of dubious nationality called Strauss, the inventor of a contraption, similar to roulette, called *straperlo*, which afterwards became widely famous. Strauss got in touch with the Radicals, proposed that they should become silent partners in the enterprise, and by way of a trial run, span his wheel in the very buildings of the Ministry of the Interior, while certain Lerrouxist politicians watched for some hours with fascinated curiosity. Play was carried on with this apparatus in the Hotel Formentor de Mallorca, where the foreigner recouped the "expenses" which his contacts with the Ministers had cost him; the Casino de San Sebastián also removed the dust from its card-tables and play would have gone on, had not the Opposition Press made the facts known to the public and the outcry forced Salazar Alonso to order the closing of the establishment.

The oligarchy was not going to break with the Radicals over a question of ethics. The administrative intemperance of Lerroux's followers was tacitly accepted in the pact of the Parliamentary majority with the Government which was kept going by its votes. The oligarchy tolerated the corruption in the Government provided the Radicals carried out the political programme of the Agrarian-Catholics, at least in its initial stages. *Do ut des.*

As might be expected, gloomy forebodings assailed the parties of the régime. However disastrous the Samper Government was, no solution more favourable to the Republic appeared on the political horizon, given the composition of the Cortes. The present was deplored and the future was scanned with deep disquietude. The *C.E.D.A.* had laid its plans to conquer and subdue the Republic. It would support for a certain time a Radical Government, would then divide the power with those false Republicans, and once the combination broke up, would assert its claim, as the most numerous party in the Chamber, to man the Republican ship. The various outrages committed by the Lerroux and Samper Cabinets, which did not even contain *Cedist* Ministers, were obviously but a portent of what Spain could hope for from a coalition Government of Catholics and Lerrouxists, to say nothing of a Ministry in which the *C.E.D.A.* predominated.

From the first moment it was clear to the Socialists that an attempt was being made to corral the proletariat in order to enslave it, a necessary preliminary in the process of abolishing the popular Republic. And with this deep conviction, gravely weighing its responsibilities, the Socialist Party warned the Cortes, with the greatest solemnity and deliberation, that if the paths of right and legality were closed to the proletariat, the Socialist organization would commit itself, before the country, to seek justice by the road of revolution. In this way, the Socialists summoned the Conservative classes to amend their policy which, if they did, would justify *a posteriori* the warning, and, if they did not, would fortify the position of those who placed their last hope in the people's violence.

Unfortunately the oligarchy, far from fearing the insurrection of the oppressed, seemed to desire it. For the oligarchy had hailed with alacrity, at the beginning of 1934, the disappearance of Social-Democratic Austria, annihilated as much by its own revolutionary irresolution as by the bullets of Dollfuss and his Christian Socialists. Nazism had already been ruling for a year in Germany; and Italian Fascism seemed to be firmly in the saddle for decades to come. Nearer home even, in more senses than one, Portugal flaunted its Catholic dictatorship. With its total lack of humanitarian feelings and of the spirit of justice, the Spanish oligarchy was incapable of softening its heart before the pleas of the Opposition. The march of world events, illustrated by the ascending curve of Fascism, would alone have dissuaded it from listening to the people's complaints, if its arrogance had not already precluded it from doing so. Never did an influential social class abuse its power with less circumspection than did the Spanish oligarchy during the year 1934. To contemplate the oligarchy triumphing in all its garrulous nakedness, one would have to go to Parliament to hear what an unexceptional witness had to say: "I was present at the session of the Cortes on Wednesday last. What a spectacle! We saw there a pathetic scene; we saw a man, pierced in his sensibilities as a Socialist, as a Republican and as a Spaniard, by the gravest, most painful, most acute anxieties; we saw him shattered by the inner struggle of conscience; we saw him implore the whole Parliament for a just solution, a way out; we saw him call upon the Government to fulfil its obligations, and before this moving, awful spectacle, do you know what most of them did? They laughed!"[1]

The path of compromise was blocked to the people. And the oligarchy contemplated with inner joy what it should have seen with fear—the desperate attitude of the proletariat. The peasants' strike, which was easily suppressed, seemed to the Government a perfect example of what was going to happen to the working classes in general once the authorities had silenced the clamour of the Socialists, whose conservative spirit now inspired the oligarchy, not with respect, but with jokes in doubtful taste. With a little effort, Spain would be another Austria or another Portugal.

The electoral results had made the oligarchy so overbearingly arrogant that it was quite certain the Republic would be defunct within a matter of months. But if it had been more level-headed and less vengeful, it would have noted that the Republic could not expire without bringing about a national catastrophe of singular magnitude. Azaña had prophesied it when he said "that a monarchy in Spain is physically impossible and that another trial of dictatorship would do no more than precipitate a social cataclysm."[2] The Republic, the Government of the oppressed classes, could not be replaced for a long time in

[1] Azaña, speech in Madrid, Feb. 11th, 1934.
[2] Speech in Madrid, Sept. 14th, 1931.

Spain. Sometimes history takes sides for a cause. And the dilemma which history presented to the wealthy classes in Spain was to accept the Republican reforms or a bloody revolution, another civil war. Less than anyone could the oligarchy fail to recognize in what conditions and by what methods it had risen to power with a parliamentary majority in the November elections. But even admitting that the victory was legitimate, the electoral results did not, in any case, justify the barbarous abuse of power in which the victors were indulging, much less a totalitarian dictatorship.

According to the certificates of election sent to the Congress of Deputies by the provincial Census Committees, the Socialist Party polled 1,627,474 votes. The Catalonian *Esquerra* and the coalition of the parties of the Left polled 850,632 votes. That is to say, the Left, without the Communists, obtained 2,488,104 votes. In sum, the votes of the Left, apart from those of all the other parties, Communists, Independents, Anarchists, etc., amounted to 3,375,432. The *C.E.D.A.* obtained 3,345,504 votes, or 30,000 less than the Left. The Radicals mustered 806,304 votes. But when the Parliament was formed, it could be seen that the Socialists had 61 deputies, while the Lerrouxists had some 100 seats. It was also seen that all the Left parties, with 30,000 votes more than the *C.E.D.A.*, were only entitled to 99 seats, while the Right *bloc* obtained 212.

This analysis is not intended to refute the oligarchic-radical triumph which was assured, for better or for worse, in November; for what interested the Government which ordered the elections and its allies was the number of deputies, not the number of votes. But these figures reveal that the reactionaries did not enjoy sufficient moral support among the nation to change the Republican policy to the point of disinterring, in practice, the old régime.

However, no calculation or reflection was capable of restraining the enthusiasm of the oligarchy for an absolute régime—an enthusiasm which was stimulated, as has been pointed out, by the international situation. But, on the other hand, the international situation showed the Spanish proletariat the dangers of allowing itself to be defeated without a struggle or of offering a flaccid and tardy resistance. And in the face of the formidable menace represented by the *C.E.D.A.*, whose tactics in invading the Republic were infinitely more sinister to democracy than the open and irreconcilable hostility *à outrance* of the Monarchists, the Socialist Party informed the President of the Republic and proclaimed to the nation, as the hour of peril advanced, that the very instant the Catholic-Agrarian Party—that murky equivalent of the Dollfuss and Oliveira Salazar movements—crossed the threshold of the Government, even if they only posted one of their members in the Government of the Republic, in that instant, irrevocably, the Socialist Party would unleash the revolution.

The determination of the *Cedists* to succeed the Radicals in the Government was as resolute and invincible as the will of the Republican proletariat to prevent them was inalienable and decided. All eyes were turned to the Palace. What use of his constitutional faculties would the President of the Republic make? It lay in his hand to open the doors of the Government to the oligarchy or to close them by dissolving a Cortes which frustrated the possibility of a Republican Cabinet being formed. The former course would be the signal for revolution; the dissolution of the Cortes, if it did not avoid civil war, would perhaps postpone it and, in any case, would place the Republic in a better position to defend the régime. Alcalá Zamora, obsessed with the reform of the Constitution, feared less what was to his blindness of soul a hypothetical insurrection of the people than the anathema, or, perhaps, formal excommunication of the Church, which, as a good Catholic, terrified him.

## CHAPTER XVI

## THE OCTOBER INSURRECTION

THE CRISIS WAS foreseen. The Samper Government would present itself in the Cortes on the 1st of October, as stipulated by the Constitution. But Spain had so many ravages to reproach it with, that no one expected its continuation. Either it would be overthrown by the parliamentary majority or the President of the Republic would withdraw his confidence. During all the summer, in the midst of strikes, political crimes and menacing concentrations of Fascist and anti-Fascist crowds, this had been the unanimous conclusion of the political cabal. A speech made by the head of the *C.E.D.A.*, Gil Robles, in which, without irony, he called Samper a "man of little tranquillizing influence at the head of the blue bench", brought down the Government as soon as Parliament resumed its sittings.

In this same speech, Gil Robles announced that his party would not support any Cabinet in which it was not represented.

The President's dilemma was crystal clear: either to authorize a Government based on the parliamentary majority, or to dissolve the Cortes. But Alcalá Zamora clung obstinately to the idea of broadening still more the basis of the régime; he had already closed the constituent Parliament, and with a new dissolution of the Cortes his constitutional faculty in this direction would be exhausted; he would not be able to rid himself of the third Chamber.

The Republicans who made a parade of calling themselves moderates were mysteriously convinced that the President of the Republic would not admit the oligarchy to the Government; the Socialists vacillated in their prognostication. The moderate Republicans supposed that the President would dissolve the Cortes and that it would be they, in a Government of national concentration, who would *make* the elections. Socialist reticence was founded on the state of progressive opinion in the country; they doubted whether Don Niceto would dare to defy it, especially as the Socialists had threatened revolution.

The crisis adjusted itself by the traditional process of those palace consultations where the President listened, or pretended to listen, to both Greeks and Trojans, according to the practice of the Spanish pseudo-constitutional monarchy. With Alcalá Zamora, no Ministerial crisis ever solved itself in less than a week.

All the Republicans—if one rightly exempts the Radicals from this nomenclature—advised the President to form a Government concentrating all the Republican elements except the Socialists, and to dissolve the Cortes. The Socialist Party promised, if the Government were entrusted to them, to form a homogeneous Government, purely Socialist in character, "so as to satisfy the justifiable anxieties of the working class which today is made a mock of". This was a purely theoretical attitude, but one which corresponded to a situation in which the Republicans did not want to be suspected of "Marxism" and the Socialists deplored the timidity of the Republicans.

Naturally there was no party loyal to the essential nature of the Republican régime which did not impress on the President the disastrous consequences which would arise from the admission of the *C.E.D.A.* or Popular Action to the new Government. And there were many outstanding men who reminded Alcalá Zamora of the tense expectancy of the working classes.

In spite of all this, it was known already on October 3rd that the President of the Republic would hand over the power to a Government based on the parliamentary majority in that

503

factious Cortes. On the night of that same day, the order for the quartering of the troops was issued. The streets of Madrid were silent and deserted, except for the tramp of the soldiers bringing their mobilization orders to their officers; over the city lay the brooding calm which, as in nature, presages public disasters. The Socialist Committees were keeping their vigil.

The President's decision was proclaimed after only a few more hours' delay. By the middle of the evening of the 4th, Lerroux was once more Prime Minister, this time with three Ministers from the *C.E.D.A.*

On the following day, a general strike was proclaimed throughout Spain and bloody conflicts broke out in the north. On the 6th, the Government of the *Generalidad* rose and severed relations with the Madrid Government. And every Spanish Republican who was conscious of the issues at stake, saluted with grief, but also with resolute hope, the beginning of a tragedy which dislocated the tortuous designs of Catholic Fascism.

All the reputable Republican Parties condemned the way in which the President had solved the crisis. So did, in substance, the Basque Nationalist Party. These middle-class organizations were not revolutionary, nor did they take up arms like the proletariat, but they divorced themselves on the 5th of October from the corrupt institutions of the régime and, on moral grounds, they represented a cardinal factor in the insurrection.

The passive adhesion of the Republicans to the revolutionary movement took the form of several leaflets which reached the streets at the same time as the first exchange of shots between strikers and troops. The Republican Left (Azaña) declared that "the monstrous deed of handing over the Government of the Republic to its enemies is treason" and stated that they "broke off all relations with the present institutions of the régime and affirmed their decision to adopt all means to defend the Republic". *Unión Republicana* (Martínez Barrio) argued that the entry of the *C.E.D.A.* into the Government obliged it to "sever all collaboration and withdraw all support from the organs of the régime". The *Partido Republicano Conservador* (Miguel Maura, ex-colleague in the Republic of Alcalá Zamora) proclaimed that "hastily and forgetful of all, we are being expelled from our legal position in the Republic" and affirmed "from now on, our essential incompatibility with this sullied Republic, ante-room of a brutal and anti-democratic reaction".

Other small parties of the Left issued similar protests. And the Valencian public must have displayed a certain bewilderment before a paragraph in *El Pueblo*, organ of the Samper Party, which stated that "faced with a period of oppression and shame, no other way remains than the revolutionary volley". Samper himself was Minister of Foreign Affairs in the new Government!

What should perhaps most urgently claim our attention now is the grouping of the social classes in the October conflict. Whenever a decisive political crisis arises in Spain, two national nuclei form themselves spontaneously—the agrarian oligarchy on the one hand and the historic middle class and the proletariat on the other; incontrovertible proof, let us repeat, of the existence of powerful common interests between the Spanish *bourgeoisie* and proletariat, as opposed to the upper classes; and proof also that, if afterwards the progressive nucleus disintegrates, it is due to a lack of clear vision of the national problem among the democratic classes and the want of a man, or men, capable of gathering together and transmuting into action the common sentiment. At bottom, the October revolution is only a reproduction, attuned to other circumstances, of the revolutionary movements of 1917 and 1930. And the survival of the agrarian-aristocratic oligarchy, which neither of those movements succeeded in destroying, however much they weakened or undermined the monarchy, is the *ultima ratio* of the bloody events of 1934.

The rise to power of the agrarian oligarchy provoked anew the *rapprochement* of industrialists, merchants and proletariat in the political arena. Although they were both ardently Catholic, the Castilian-Andalusian agrarian oligarchy and the Basque agrarian and industrial middle class were bound to clash, and, in spite of the fact that the Basque Nationalist Party took care not to appear revolutionary, the aggression against the Economic Agreement, prelude to other aggressions, urged it forward towards the lines of the anti-oligarchic opposition. The same thing happened with the Catalan *Lliga*. The *Lliga* had taken up its stand with the Samper Government long before the heralded revolution was taken seriously. And it was inevitable that this should happen, though the Catalan capitalists accepted the situation with a wry face; for when the *Lliga* was defeated in the elections for the Catalan Parliament and its interests attacked by the *Esquerra*, only from the Samper Government could it hope for a salve to assuage, even slightly, the onslaught of the *Generalidad*. Fleeing from the enemy at his heels, Cambó sought refuge in Samper (that is to say, in Gil Robles) and supported him in Parliament in exchange for concessions like the appeal against the *Ley de Contratos de cultivo*. If the *Lliga* had been in power in Catalonia, it would certainly have been in conflict with the Samper Government, like the Basque nationalists; but as the Samper Government was its only stay and prop, it supported it, though grudgingly, in the Cortes. And when Cambó realized that the October crisis would be solved by the entry into the Government of three Ministers from the *C.E.D.A.*, he declared, alluding to his party's attitude, that as the new Government did, so would they do. That is, the *Lliga* accepted the majority Cabinet of October 4th with the mistrust with which the great industrialists had always viewed the great landowners in power.

When the workers' rebellion had been quelled and the Cortes resumed its tasks on November 5th, the *Lliga* voted its confidence in the Government with obvious displeasure and then only after Lerroux had announced that he would not be surprised if the proletarian rising repeated itself—an absurd suspicion.

Two important lessons can be learnt from the period of history after 1917. The first is that the class struggle in the regions of the industrial *bourgeoisie*, that is, in the Basque Provinces and Catalonia, renders the prosperity of regional autonomies impossible from every point of view and makes of separatism a utopian creed. Because whoever governs in Madrid, the class which has been displaced by the autonomous Government will lean, at the expense of the class which has been brought to the top, upon the centralizing forces of the rest of Spain. And the second lesson is that, in a régime of constitutional liberty, the class struggle between proletariat and *bourgeoisie* frustrates the possibility of establishing a front capable of changing the basic form of oligarchic government in favour of a national democracy, whether agrarian or *bourgeois*, or even a working-class democracy. Hence, it is in the interests of all the progressive classes in Spain to suppress or to mitigate the political differences which divide them, in order to emphasize what distinguishes them in common from the aristocratic-agrarian-financial oligarchy. Naturally, it is absurd to suppose this could be realized at one blow in a system of civil liberty and universal suffrage. But it is not less certain that, if Spaniards could be convinced that the parliamentary path will always lead to civil war in Spain in the present relationship of the classes, the work of the statesman would be greatly lightened.

In 1934 the Liberal Republic had failed in Spain, as it failed in Russia in October 1917. But Spain's political frontiers are very different from the political frontiers of Russia; and as the international situation in 1917 helped Lenin, so the international situation in 1934 helped the Spanish Fascist parties.

But the Spanish revolution of October was, before all, a defensive gesture. However radical the revolutionary propaganda of the working-class parties appeared—a radicalism imposed by the oligarchy which, in resisting every reform, impelled the masses to a desperate extremism—however radical this propaganda may have appeared, none of the proletarian parties had any other thought than to re-establish the popular Republic as it had been conceived, in its social aspect, before the 14th of April, 1931. "*Ils seraient tous morts pour elle; elle leur avait donné l'espérance.*"

The political-social programme of the insurgents, which was not made public until fifteen months after the events of October, gives the measure of the policy the Socialist Party and its associates were pursuing. It consists of ten points, which can be summarized as follows: (1) Nationalization of the land, which was to become State property, except in the regions of the small-holdings where it was to remain in the possession of the actual cultivators; all land rents to be collected by the State, the municipalities or other public communities or corporations authorized by the State; in the regions of the latifundia, collective cultivation to be established; (2) progressive acceleration of hydraulic works and, in consideration of the fact that the supplies voted in the Budget were inadequate, use to be made of the national savings at a moderate rate of interest. "This operation could be carried out through a partnership between the State, the federative entity of the *Cajas de Ahorro* and official banking, mortgaging the lands which were capable of irrigation": (3) higher education to be reserved exclusively for pupils who had reached a satisfactory standard in the elementary and secondary schools; special schools to be created to complete the technical knowledge of the workers and raise their general cultural level: (4) dissolution of all the religious orders and confiscation of their property, plus the expulsion of the Jesuits from the national territory: (5) disbandment of the Army, reduction of its contingents and recruitment of men and officers from among the parties loyal to the Republic; those who had shown whole-hearted adhesion to the régime to be allowed to remain in the Army: (6) dissolution of the Civil Guard and reorganization of the police forces on the same democratic bases as the Army: (7) modification of all the organs of the Public Administration and weeding out of officials hostile to the Republic: (8) the moment not being propitious for carrying out the socialization of the major part of Spanish industry, the programme to be confined to measures for the moral and

507

material betterment of the workers, allowing them to share in the control of those industrial organizations in which they were employed: (9) reform of the taxation system, special emphasis being laid on taxes on unearned income and inheritance: (10) the foregoing programme to be carried out rapidly by decree and endorsed later by legislative organs freely ordained by the people; "and in the belief that this programme would not obtain the assent of the present occupant of the Presidential chair, steps would be taken to relieve him of his office".

As can be seen, if the October revolution had achieved its final objective, the Republic would not have gone much farther than it was intended to go at birth. In fact, only the agrarian oligarchy would have suffered gravely in its interests. And it seems beyond doubt that, on the basis of such a programme, a national movement of democracy versus oligarchy could have been formed, if there had been anyone to initiate it or any understanding of realities among the Republican and working-class parties. The Spanish *bourgeoisie*, including the great industrial capitalists, would have gained rather than lost by the nationalization of the great agrarian properties, the hydraulic works and other economic reforms.

These, then, were the political and social aspirations of the October combatants, or the Workers' Alliance.

In almost the whole of Spain, the distinctive tendencies of the proletarian movement had been united in a revolutionary coalition to resist Fascism. In Asturias, the interpenetration of Socialists, Communists and Anarchist-Trade Unionists was complete. Not so in Catalonia, where, because the *C.N.T.* was more closely controlled by the *F.A.I.*, this popular sector remained on the fringe of the Workers' Alliance.

The revolution spread over the whole of Spain, but with significant lack of uniformity. Except in Barcelona, the Republicans registered a platonic protest in the rest of the country. The peasants did not fight, except in isolated villages of Andalusia, Castile, Navarre and Aragon. The June strike had prostrated the agrarian movement and its effects were felt in October. But the miners of the north—Asturias, Viscaya, León, Santander, Palencia—fought heroically. With few exceptions, military discipline did not crack for a single moment. The proletariat of the great cities did not raise their rebellion much above the level of a general strike. In some towns they did not even stop work; in others, the general strike lasted twenty-four, forty-eight hours. In Madrid the strike lasted nine days and the revolution was not a rising of the masses which imperils the State, but a spasmodic disturbance which harasses the police.

From the 5th to the 13th October inclusive there was a unanimous strike in Madrid. The proletariat gave a marked impression of discipline and resistance. The strike began in the early hours of Friday the 5th. The Government thought that on Saturday the workers would go back to work, driven by the necessity of drawing their week's wages. This did not happen; and then the authorities conceived the hope that the workers would go back to work on Monday. They were soon disabused. On Monday, it was clear from the spirit of the workers that the strike would go on for at least a week. Most of the railwaymen had stopped work, though they were as a rule difficult to draw into a revolutionary strike. On the West and M.Z.A. lines, the workers left their posts in a body and the Government was obliged to mobilize the first and second Railway Reserves. Moreover there occurred in Madrid frequent clashes between strikers and police, bomb explosions, petards, etc.

In the great capitals the people were psychologically prepared for a political, anti-Fascist strike, but not for a fight to overcome the Government. The necessary conditions for social revolution were wanting; and the proletariat lacked arms. But as a political strike, that in Madrid was a splendid sample of civic maturity.

The insurrection in Asturias—comparable with the Paris Commune—can be explained by the revolutionary temper of the miners, who possess one of the oldest and most seasoned Socialist organizations; by the material and strategic possibilities; by the relative weakness of the Government forces, and by the unanimity with which all the workers plunged into the revolution. The Asturian miners have always responded to all insurrections with terrific impetus. In 1917 it was these same Asturian miners who gave the most trouble to the Government troops. In 1934 the revolution in Asturias was a rising of the masses, a social revolution. The miners were joined by the industrial proletariat and by a motley crowd of peasants, whose presence was explained by the fact that the miners raised levies in all the villages of the mining valley where they passed, snatching away useful men. "*Hala! camaradas!*" was their rallying cry. Thus was formed a torrential flood, which swept away the posts of the Civil Guard, set up a new social order, born of the moment and embodying the social ideas predominating in each zone, and passed on to spread towards Oviedo or distribute itself over the mountains. Having overcome the resistance of the Civil Guard and taken their arms, the miners marched in a column on the Asturian capital, into which they penetrated, without military advice worthy of the name, firing off sticks of dynamite which they lighted with their cigars. Five, six or seven thousand warlike men, accustomed to the most arduous labour and the cruellest dangers, fought valiantly in the streets of the city, most of which they occupied during nine terrible days.

To suppress the Asturian insurrection, the Lerroux-Gil Robles Government sent by sea from Spanish Morocco the *Tercio Extranjero*, a shock force which the monarchy had wanted to use in 1930 to quell the Republican movement. The proposal to move these troops, who had been formed to fight the Moors, to the Peninsula, was sharply censured at the time by Alcalá Zamora himself. But where the monarchy did not succeed, the Republic did. And in 1934 the Government did not stop at bringing up a few *banderas* of the *Tercio*; they also sent to Asturias two *tabores* of regulars or Moorish troops. In this way, the Berbers made their appearance in lands that they had never been able to trample underfoot. Mahometans now made war on Spaniards at the command of a Government which was half Catholic, half masonic. But the oligarchy had already given clear proofs that it would stick at nothing if it saw its property menaced; it felt itself so weak, so devoid of moral and material authority to sustain an unjust Government, that already in 1934 it began to have recourse to outside help, to the use of foreign forces—a policy which was to culminate in the civil war, when besides relying on the *Tercio* and the Moors, who were quickly defeated by the Republican militias, it was to open the frontiers of Spain to the regular troops of other nations.

For the Republicans, Catalonia was the last bastion of the Republic. Ruled by a middle-class Government which would not compound with the entry of the *C.E.D.A.* into the Government, Catalonia promised to be, in October 1934, the invincible redoubt of democracy. Like the Basque nationalists, the *Esquerra* had withdrawn from the Cortes and the *Generalidad* had been in a state of rebellion since the verdict on the *Ley de Contratos de cultivo*.

The directors of Catalan Left policy found themselves, on the eve of the event, in the same state of mind as the Socialist and Republican leaders. They prepared to face the delicate circumstances which would be created by the formation of a Ministry with politicians who were not acceptable to the popular Republic. But they could not imagine the thing would really happen. The President of the *Generalidad*, like Azaña, like the

510

moderate Republicans, envisaged the possibility of a Government based on the parliamentary majority with the anxiety caused by things which *may* happen, which may easily happen, but which, owing to the consequences they are bound to entail, usually remain stillborn.

At midday on the 4th, that is, hours before the Ministerial crisis had been solved, the President of the Catalan Government tried to establish communication with the President of the Republic. He did not succeed, but he spoke over the telephone to Sánchez Guerra, Secretary-General of the Presidency of the Republic. Companys asked him to inform His Excellency that the Government of the *Generalidad* would send him a telegram announcing that the admission of the *C.E.D.A.* to the Government would precipitate a catastrophe in Catalonia. At three o'clock in the afternoon, Sánchez Guerra rang up President Companys and told him: "His Excellency begs you not to worry and reiterates his affection towards yourself and his respect for your Government." The fact is that, up to the last moment, Alcalá Zamora was giving the Republicans the impression that no one would be made a Minister unless he had expressly declared himself in favour of Republicanism.

By mid-afternoon of the 4th, the list of the new Cabinet was known in Barcelona. In the Palace of the *Generalidad*, the news came like a thunderbolt. The hour of great decisions had struck; but the men of the *Esquerra* wavered. They feared that the proletariat, the Workers' Alliance and the *F.A.I.* would control the revolution. And while Companys, before rising in rebellion, assured the Catalan people that there, in the Government, stood the defenders of their liberties, Dencás, the Minister of the Interior, summoned the political chiefs and warned them: "Watch the *F.A.I.*" The Catalan middle class was now going through the phase which the Madrid middle class, the Mauras and the Martínez Barrios, had already gone through; fearful that the Republic would escape them through the Left, they did everything in their power to destroy it through the Right.

The night of the 4th passed and the whole of the 5th, without Catalonia coming to a decision. In the rest of Spain, the working classes were carrying on the fight in one way or another. The Republicans had issued their statements of policy. And public opinion was asking: What is the *Generalidad* waiting for? At last, on the 6th, the leaders of the *Esquerra* agreed to rise against the Madrid Government.

The revolutionary movement decreed from Madrid by the workers' centres, except the Anarchists', was, until the night of the 6th, in Barcelona, a general peaceful strike. There it was the Government which had promised to open fire. Consequently, though perhaps with hesitation, President Companys appeared on the balcony of the *Generalidad* in the early hours of the night of the 6th and proclaimed the Catalan State of the Federal Spanish Republic—an absurd, but typical, proceeding.

The phases of the revolution in Catalonia can be summarized as follows: A night of shelling of the buildings of the *Generalidad*. Barricades. Heavy shooting in the streets. The Catalan Councillors resisted the fire of the troops, waiting for the *rabassaires*, the "brothers of the Maresma, of Tarrasa, Hospitalet, Sans", who did not come. At dawn, Companys and his colleagues in the Ministry surrendered to General Batet. Dencás fled.

As in the rest of Spain, except the mining valleys of the north, the masses in Catalonia seemed to be inhibited. Not only did the Anarchists not fight, but on the 8th of October, they asked the military authorities for permission to broadcast an order terminating the general strike. They did much the same thing in other capitals, where they hastened to assure the Governor that they had nothing to do with the revolution. Now, as during Azaña's Government and in December 1933, during the Lerroux Government, the conduct of the Anarchists—except in Asturias —coincided, no doubt fortuitously, with the interests of the aristocracy.

The losses occasioned by the entry of the *C.E.D.A.* into the Government—the cause of the rebellion—were considerable, both in lives and property. The central districts of Oviedo were devastated, the University building with its magnificent library was burnt down, and the cathedral, where the Government troops were posted, suffered some damage.

The number of dead throughout Spain was 1,335 and the wounded 2,951, most of them peasants, that is, insurgents. After October, about 40,000 persons were thrown into prisons and penitentiaries.[1]

But not all the revolutionaries fell fighting; many were murdered by the forces charged with suppressing the conflict, after it had already ceased. For once the rebellion was extinguished, although some combatants still remained dispersed in the Asturian mountains, the repressive measures were ruthless

[1] The data regarding the victims are those published by the Government in Jan. 1935. But some sources give the casualties in Asturias alone as 3,000 dead and 7,000 wounded, figures which, perhaps, correspond more to reality than the official figures. The Government concealed the total losses suffered by the police forces.

and The arbitrary punishment of Asturias by the African troops was carried out with a total disregard for the letter and spirit of the law. And these new horrors, coming on top of the disasters of the struggle, dealt a deathblow to Spanish Fascism in its cradle.

Police repression was characterized by unbounded severity—but it was symptomatic that *political* repression failed. Even though defeated, the people had succeeded in their primary objective. The revolutionary movement of October altered the whole political calendar of the *C.E.D.A.*, dislocating its plans for the pacific conquest of the Government. The repressive measures which the oligarchy was preparing against the time when, advancing from post to post, it would deprive the Socialists of honour, prestige and mass support, were still premature.

For its part, the aristocratic party demanded draconian measures. How this party wished, like Caligula, that the people had only one head! They would have liked the heads of the Socialist leaders, the dissolution of all the non-Fascist parties, the confiscation of the funds of the trade unions, the closing of the Cortes—in short, an implacable dictatorship. Political repression was confined to the suspension of the Socialist Press, a declaration that the Asturian Miners' Trade Union was illegal and the taking over of certain *Casas del Pueblo* to house the Government forces. The workers' organizations, both political and trade-unionist, continued firmly in existence, more firmly than they would have been had the workers accepted without a protest and without sacrifice a Government which was but a prelude to Fascism. From the attack, the Government passed over to the defence, in the face of the universal execration it had aroused for having brought the Moors to Spain and for the excesses committed by the expeditionary forces which invaded Asturias. The oligarchy was not able to instal an even more abominable dictatorship than the one Spanish democracy had endured under the Samper Government.

The *C.E.D.A.* and its offshoots did not expect that the revolution would assume the dimensions it did. They thought that it would not pass beyond the stage of a twenty-four-hour general strike—this was the thesis put forward by *El Debate*—and that once the Socialists had heard the crack of the whip, they could deal with them later with a heavy hand *à la* Dollfuss. This had happened in Vienna, because Social-Democratic Austria had lost a critical year, and when afterwards it plucked up courage to resist, the Catholic party completely controlled the State and had already made its decisive stroke; and while in February

R s

1934 the Socialist militias of the *Schutzbund* were fighting, in Vienna everyone was working—an extraordinary spectacle; not even the working classes were on strike. The danger in Spain was the same—that the proletariat would become demoralized for lack of wise and dynamic leadership, and would become Fascist, or, at least, cease to be Socialist. But October prevented this. The ones who were demoralized were the Fascist parties.

On the other hand, there can be no doubt that, before the October explosion, the Vatican, becoming terrified by the turn of political events, had finally convinced itself of the perils which a totalitarian dictatorship in Spain would bring on the Church, with the various factions fighting each other tooth and nail. Paradoxically enough, the Holy See insisted upon the *C.E.D.A.* acting with greater tact and prudence.[1] Austrian Catholic Fascism had fallen into the crass error of destroying Social-Democracy, the only popular force really opposed to the native Nazis, who, thinking they had as much right as Dollfuss to seize the Government with violence, had tried to do so in July by assassinating the "pocket Chancellor". Rome had reached the point of being persuaded—and the sight of the Spanish cataclysm finally convinced her—that by relying on brute force, the Spanish Catholics were setting a pernicious example which might be imitated by Conservative parties which were not the party of the Church.

After the October insurrection, Gil Robles learnt to moderate his political language. The perplexity and moderation which may be observed now in the speeches of the head of the *C.E.D.A.* are at odds with the arrogance and aggressiveness of his former political declarations. For example, Gil Robles had said in Madrid on October 15th, 1933, a year before the revolution: "We want the whole Government and that is what we are asking for. To realize this ideal, we are not going to be restrained by archaic forms. Democracy is for us not an end in itself, but a means whereby we go forward to conquer the new State. When this moment arrives, Parliament will either submit or we shall sweep it away."[2] Compare this paragraph with the following, of November 20th, 1934: "Confronted with the excesses of political Liberalism, there has little by little arisen in the world

[1] Within the Church itself in Spain, the conduct of the reactionaries was condemned. "For me, the greatest of the present disasters, which today are so overwhelming," said Señor Arboleya, Canon of the Cathedral of Oviedo, "is the inconsistent and unheard-of behaviour of the so-called Right." (In *El Día* of San Sebastian.)

[2] Quoted from *El Debate*.

a doctrinal current, subsequently embodied in political systems, which leads directly to the absorption by the State of all individual activities. The sum and compendium of such a totalitarian doctrine is the celebrated phrase of Mussolini: 'Everything in the State, nothing against the State, nothing outside the State.' Against this political current"—adds Gil Robles—"which is gaining a hold in youth circles, it seems to me necessary to react."[1]

The bloodshed of October which cemented the union of the Spanish working classes, sowed disunity, on the other hand, among the ranks of the conquerors. The Monarchists, in particular, thought there would never again be such a favourable moment for a *coup d'état*. But for the agrarian-Catholics, such aristocratic impatience was the alpha and omega of irresponsibility and demagogy.

With the Republicans out of the fight, national policy was divided, in dramatic monopoly, between three forces in collision —the President of the Republic, the *C.E.D.A.* and *Renovación Española*. The President, seriously perturbed by the catastrophe he had so frivolously precipitated, and morally prostrated, showed nevertheless rare integrity in the face of possible new dangers. The shock of October had forced Don Niceto to awake to realities. A *coup d'état* was to be feared, although the skirmishing in the oligarchic camp diminished, if it did not destroy, the menace. The President of the Republic, in any case, prepared to save what remained of the régime. He placed generals who were in his confidence where they could be useful and personally supervised from his high position the movements of troops. The officers who were hostile to the Republic had not risen this time, and, if they had intended to, their intention was largely frustrated by the resolute action of Alcalá Zamora, who might well have been surprised later by a military *coup* if the popular rising had not occurred in October.

The subsequent political events can be summarized as follows. The President of the Republic refused to sanction or to sign any death warrants, particularly the death sentence passed on the leader of the Asturian miners, Ramón González Peña; and with the struggle which arose on this count between the Right *bloc* and Alcalá Zamora, the discord in the oligarchic camp grew. The Monarchists reproached the *Cedists* for staying in a "soft" Government which did not proceed against the revolutionary chiefs with the inexorability they thought the occasion merited. And Gil Robles, between the plutocratic

[1] Interview in *La Vanguardia* of Barcelona.

Charybdis and the Presidential Scylla, lost for some time his authority over those social classes which saw with malevolent disgust how the opportunity for striking off the most prominent Socialist heads was being lost. The *C.E.D.A.* chief found himself in an impossible situation. Aristocratic extremism threatened to leave him without a party if he temporized with the President of the Republic, but the President of the Republic was holding the sword of Damocles over the head of the Cortes.

, Gil Robles understood, nevertheless, that he had without delay, to offer his defrauded followers authentic proof of his Ministerial power and he made it a point of honour to see that the sentences passed by the military tribunals were carried out. Firmness in this dispute, however, did but show up the impotence of the *C.E.D.A.*, although it enabled it, at least, to save its face before that part of the public which was opposed to clemency. The Government which had provoked the revolution fell, then, on March 29th, 1935. On April 3rd, Lerroux formed a homogeneous Cabinet of Radicals, which did not even get as far as appearing before the Cortes, and at the beginning of May, after a month of arduous negotiation, the *C.E.D.A.* declared itself resolved to re-enter the Government. Gil Robles announced his claim to lead the new Ministry, but the President did not view the project with sympathy. In the end the Catholics agreed to accept five portfolios, two more than in the first majority Cabinet, and Alcalá Zamora had no scruples in augmenting the *C.E.D.A.* contingent since he brought into the Government as Minister of the Interior Portela Valladares, an old and astute politician, very much to the President's taste. Gil Robles took over the War Office himself, appointed General Franco Under-Secretary, and raised the hopes of the enemies of the Republic out of all proportion to the situation. The Catholics did not achieve any more in the War Office than a Señor Hidalgo would have done, if he had been pressed. And the understandable irresolution of Gil Robles or the intemperate haste of his competitors in the oligarchic camp could not but inflame still more every day the intestine strife of the plutocratic parties.

The resurrection of the Republic will be the theme of the next chapter; but it is fitting that this chapter should end on this note—sixteen months later, the popular Republic was to arise, like another phœnix, from the ashes of October.

## CHAPTER XVII

# THE OLIGARCHY IN CONFUSION

THE EXPERIENCE OF other nations and knowledge of the Spanish Conservative classes allow us to infer that, if the Spanish Socialists had remained indifferent to the political changes of October 4th, the working classes and the Republic would not have had to undergo fewer outrages than they did, in fact, suffer. Without the revolution, the Lerroux-Gil Robles Government would have succeeded in muzzling the Left Press, as nearly happened under the preceding Cabinet. And the same thing would have happened in every other direction. Under Samper, the parliamentary majority exercised a dictatorship at the expense of the proletariat and the genuine Republicans; under the Government of October 4th, this dictatorship would have been accentuated, or the entry of the *C.E.D.A.* would have lacked sense. And the inevitable recrudescence of the reactionary policy initiated in November 1933 would have thrown the working class and the Republic, more or less, into the same state of oppression they were in after the revolutionary movement had been stifled. They would have been thrown into the same state of servitude, but without honour and probably without a future.

If the proletariat had not risen, police repression would certainly have been less severe, though it must be remembered that the fact that the Social-Democrats did not defend themselves in Germany and defended themselves but tardily in Austria, did not spare them horrifying experiences at the hands of the police. And the Spanish oligarchy had given conspicuous proofs that, for it, the meekness of its adversary was not an extenuating circumstance in the hour of revenge.

The persecution of the proletariat, both politically and socially, was part of the programme of the new Government. I think I have said enough about the forms which political repression took; here it is necessary to add a few lines about social or economic repression.

In Chapter XV of this Book, I described the vindictive repercussions which the electoral victory of the Right *bloc* in November 1933 had in the countryside. All the work of the Republic on the agrarian side was undone; wages were cut by 50 per cent; in the rural zones—as if the agricultural situation were not already sufficiently complicated—not only frightful poverty, but anarchy, too, stalked the land. One might have said that there remained no precept for the reactionaries to abolish, no law for them to lop off, no vengeance for them to satisfy. But in 1935 the oligarchy went to unimaginable lengths in their oppression of the peasant. The *C.E.D.A.*, already in the Government, resurrected the feudal "lord of the manor", who, besides being invested with monstrous powers over the landless outcast, swindled him in a way that made the agrarian-Catholic Party a worthy rival of the Radicals.

On March 15th, 1935, the Government, for the first time in the history of Spanish agriculture, passed a *Ley de Arrendamientos rústicos* (Law of Rural Leases) which, under colour of regulating this juridical form of property, made the fixing of rents, the right to renew contracts and the faculty to annul them, dependent upon the will of the great landlords. This law did no more than put on paper the state of things which had always existed, before the Republic, in the Spanish countryside without legislation to confirm it. But with the proprietor now spurred on by his own feelings of revenge, and the peasant now lacking the protection even of the Civil Code, economic terrorism reached incredible proportions in the regions of the oligarchy. Notices to quit followed one another at an increasingly alarming rate, and the few long-term leases remaining in Castile, Estremadura and Andalusia were abolished.

Following on this, on August 1st the landed oligarchy published their project of agrarian "reform". The spirit of this law, and even the letter, naturally do not conceal its high degree of consanguinity with the spirit and letter of the *Ley de Arrendamientos rústicos*. It introduced into the rural areas greater confusion and injustices than already obtained there. It is not worth while to describe the oligarchic agrarian "reform", having touched on the *Ley de Arrendamientos* and bearing in mind that it had only an ephemeral existence, since the oligarchy was defeated in the elections of 1936. But we should not pass over certain interesting and significant aspects of this oligarchic "reform"

We have already seen that, under the law of amnesty, the· nobility who had been expropriated without compensation for their share in the events of August 10th, 1932, recovered their lands. But the great landlords wanted to profit to the full from the political change, whilst they put their estates beyond the reach of future Republican interference, and the agrarian "reform" of August 1st, 1935, is permeated by this desire of

518

the corrupt landed nobility. The expropriations without compensation were formally annulled, but the expropriated estates were not handed back to their masters, but were converted into temporary tenancies. The State was to maintain a number of peasants on these estates and pay over the corresponding rent to the owners. From what date? From the date when the oligarchy's agrarian "reform" came into force? No. The collection of rents was to be retrospective, that is, it was to date from the instant when the lands had been confiscated. And the rent was to be calculated, not on the basis of the taxable value of the lands, but according to an expert valuation—the expert valuer in question being in the service of the oligarchy. In this way, two measures of value were introduced; when the State had to levy tax, the estate was worth what the owner said, and when the State had to fix the rent, the estate had another value, no doubt greater, which was settled by the expert. The landed class thus confessed that it had been defrauding the Exchequer for generations and it had no scruples in defrauding it once more.

In addition, the State had paid suitable compensation to the nobility for the improvements effected on the expropriated estates. When the expropriation ceased, the landowners were under an obligation to refund the compensation to the Treasury. No, said the oligarchic agrarian "reform"; the aristocracy would return the compensation at the end of the nine years of occupancy, if the State had not expropriated the lands by then. They would do this, they said, on condition that expropriation did not take place. The point was, that the rapacious ruling classes should run no risk. But the nobility did not mind expropriation, because they were going to receive from the State sums which exceeded the value of their estates and because they were going to receive them in cash, in State Bonds at 4 per cent, with the option of transferring them or mortgaging them immediately. And since there were 383,062 hectares of expropriated lands with an annual rental value of 9,576,550 pesetas (calculating 25 pesetas per hectare), the sale value of these properties, at 4 per cent, would exceed 200 million pesetas, capital—probably inflated by the expert valuation—which the Lerroux-Gil Robles Government were going to hand over, if nothing prevented them, to the great absentee landlords.[1]

Let us leave here the *C.E.D.A.'s* agrarian "reform" to glance at another episode essentially the same, the final touch to the portrait of the oligarchy in our time.

[1] Instituto de Reforma Agraria, ibid., pp. 37 *et seq.*

In the Cabinet of October 4th, the Ministry of Agriculture was taken over by a Catholic, a Professor of the University of Seville and a member of the *C.E.D.A.*, who was soon to achieve national fame through what others remained all their lives a stranger to—namely, common sense. A Spanish Conservative and Catholic with common sense would be bound to achieve rare notoriety. I refer to Señor Jiménez Fernández. This Minister attempted to overcome anarchy in the rural areas, not with the customary violence which added fuel to the flames, but with reforms which aimed at creating smallholdings, at helping the *yunteros* of Estremadura and alleviating the lot of other landless peasants. Needless to say, Jiménez Fernández immediately roused the antagonism of Parliament. The oligarchy thought him a Socialist in disguise, a thousand times worse than the confessed "Marxists", and the epithet of "White Bolshevist" gained rapid currency in a social *milieu* which suffered from terrifying hallucinations and was haunted day and night by Communist monsters and hobgoblins. The laudable intentions of the Minister of Agriculture, who up to that moment had enjoyed a certain authority in the bosom of the *C.E.D.A.*, could not, therefore, make any headway. Like Canalejas, who, when he saw that nothing durable could be done in Spain while the régime of agrarian property remained unchanged, wanted to introduce certain slight reforms, Jiménez Fernández was rejected by his colleagues. All his arguments and exhortations fell on stony ground. It was of no use that he reminded the Catholics of the Church's criterion in social matters or evoked the figure of Leo XIII and his celebrated Encyclical. The oligarchy replied through the mouth of one of the landowning deputies: "If you want to take away our lands with encyclicals in your hand, we shall end by becoming schismatics; the Socialists, at least, are more frank than you in their effort to expropriate us."

When the Government of May was formed, Jiménez Fernández was dropped. The oligarchy, in a fine panic, turned him out as if he was an apostate or a reprobate.

Never was the agrarian-aristocratic-financial oligarchy so powerful economically as in the first thirty years of the present century. Never, also, was it so pusillanimous or so ignorant. Its hysterical timidity, which unmasked an agent of Moscow or a bloodstained Communist in every wretch who begged at its door, converted an imaginary peril into a possible menace.

The philosophic scepticism of Cánovas, who reckoned Spain as irretrievably lost, had its roots largely in an intimate knowledge of the ruling classes whom he thoroughly despised, although his vanity as an intellectual led him to seek or to accept the applause of the *salons*. Intellectually, Cánovas stood head and shoulders above the landed oligarchy; but Silvela, Sagasta, Maura, Canalejas were worthy politicians without pretensions to genius, and, though they had great defects or limitations, they were superior to Cánovas and the oligarchy in civic and humane feelings. But neither Cánovas, nor Silvela, nor Sagasta, nor Canalejas were members of, or presided over the oligarchic parties now. And this in a moment when the disappearance of the Restoration State was forcing the Spanish Conservative classes to improvise new solutions for the national political problem. They might not accept the Republic, might even reject every reform, but confronted with the Republican and democratic State, they had to set up, at least potentially, another State, as Cánovas did when confronted with the first Republic. Nevertheless, the crazy rising of August 1932 revealed already that the oligarchy, under the Republic, was bereft of leaders. The anti-democratic leadership was as insignificant and mean as the classes which followed it, or rather, which urged it on from behind. Neither in numbers nor quality did the *caudillos* of the plutocracy stand comparison with the most eminent politicians of the Restoration régime. In its moment of gravest peril, the oligarchy could count on only two men—Gil Robles and Calvo Sotelo— and so feeble and inane were the men who surrounded them that, by contrast, they could both claim to be a Hercules or a Samson.

José María Gil Robles, son of an illustrious Catholic Professor of Civil Law, ex-pupil of the Salamanca friars, lawyer, Professor of Administrative Law, contributor to *El Debate* and leader of the party of the Church and the great Castilian landowners, was not lacking in qualities indispensable in the political arena. He was a man of action, a skilled organizer, a practised orator and he had character of a sort. Huge interests were entrusted to him, not all of them despicable for an intelligent Spaniard— the interests of the Church, incalculable from both a material and spiritual point of view, as well as the interests of agrarian property. His mission could not have been more delicate, since an hour had struck which was unfavourable to the survival of a great number of privileges and the owner class, whom Silvela, on leaving politics, qualified as ungovernable, continued to justify the epithet. Gil Robles had to govern an oligarchy without peer, besides contending with a fighting democracy. And for such an arduous task, the *C.E.D.A.* chief was not entirely competent. In the Spain of 1933 the Republican reforms, the Constitution and the play of democratic ideas guaranteed that there would be no major conflict, unless the reactionaries willed otherwise. Gil Robles had the merit, perhaps, to persuade his party that it was perfectly possible to achieve the counter-revolution by constitutional roads. The counter-revolution would be, in the end, quite as complete and profound as the most exigent reactionaries could desire. With such assurances, the agrarian-Catholics were appeased. But the Republic, as was natural, placed itself on guard and forbade them access to leadership of the Government. Herein lay the fatal contradiction of Gil Robles' policy. His public, which knew in confidence that the object was to abolish the Republic secretly, followed him; but the Republic was in the secret, too, and would not allow itself to be abolished, though it might have allowed itself to be reformed. The insuperable difficulty of issuing victorious in the teeth of a social class which was obstinately working its own ruin and the ruin of Spain explains, perhaps, the failure of Gil Robles. But by his temperament, his inexperience and his commonplace mentality, Gil Robles was incapable of solving a moral and political conflict of this magnitude without cheating his own class or alarming the enemy. Violent and tempestuous speeches made by the head of the *C.E.D.A.* before the October insurrection bore witness to the fact that either he was not master of his public, a sign of deficient powers of leadership, or that his political career had been too rapid for him to be on guard against the effects of success. With his propagandist ravings, sometimes anti-republican, at other times opportunist, but always vehement, Gil Robles was not the brake the oligarchy needed, but its spur; he was the trumpet sounding the advance, irritating those behind and encouraging the fury of those in front. And though he did not desire civil war, and perhaps feared it, he seemed bent on making it inevitable.

To sum up, it may be said that the agrarian-catholic party lacked the statesman to whom their copious and subtle interests, if not their mentality or want of patriotism, entitled them.

Until the spring of 1934, when Primo de Rivera's ex-Minister of Finance, José Calvo Sotelo, returned to Spain, the aristocratic party virtually remained without a head. Calvo Sotelo, who retired into exile on the fall of the dictatorship, returned under the protection of the amnesty declared by the oligarchic Cortes. Republican tolerance had allowed him, during the four years of his exile, frequent communication with the public which read the monarchist Press in which he published signed articles on economics.

The financial oligarchy, which backed *Renovación Española*, owed an old debt of gratitude to Calvo Sotelo. As I have already stated, under Primo de Rivera's régime he favoured, as never before, the interests of financial capital. That period was a veritable reign of the bankers, who were cajoled not only by all kinds of monopolies, but also when the Minister of Finance had occasion to lend money as a consequence of the gold loan; Calvo Sotelo lent money to the agrarians at 5 per cent, but to the banks at 3 per cent. In this way, he disposed of 584 million pesetas which he had obtained abroad at a higher rate of interest than the Treasury was now exacting, thus obviously favouring private profit at the expense of the public. And the grateful remembrance of the young Finance Minister's past record stamped him as the ideal politician for this branch of Spanish society. His arrival was hailed in the drawing-rooms with fervour and exhilaration. The aristocratic party now had a leader, and an exceptional one, to their way of thinking. On May 18th, 1934, Calvo Sotelo was officially invested with the headship of *Renovación Española*, the ceremony being crowned with a noisy and cordial banquet. The joyous banqueters marched from the festive board to the Cortes, where all, or almost all, held seats, since in the November elections it was rare that a Monarchist candidate, if there was one, was not elected. The *Renovación Española* group entered the Chamber, each wearing a red carnation, and escorting their new chief. The spectacle moved Indalecio Prieto to improvise a timely and biting allusion to the past.[1]

The agrarian-Catholics would never have elected Calvo Sotelo as their leader, first, because neither his birthplace, nor his family connections, nor his vocation enabled him to *sense* agrarian matters as the Castilian oligarchy sensed them; and secondly, because for the landowners, the past, insofar as it depended on Primo de Rivera's ex-Minister of Finance, held

[1] "When I saw Señor Calvo Sotelo enter the Chamber this afternoon with this elegant *cortège* which has been accompanying him since morning, I remembered that this brilliant escort, adorned with carnations, consists of men who have had the Christian humility to forget promptly and totally grave wrongs. For Señor Calvo Sotelo, servant of the dictatorship which rose against the representations of those Monarchist parties which today form his guard of honour—Señor Calvo Sotelo, besides eagerly endorsing those constantly disrespectful phrases with which General Primo de Rivera repeatedly and effectively castigated the Monarchist parties, ended by speaking of them with such deep contempt that he said that the Dictator had no need to unsheathe the sword—it was enough for him to wield the broom to sweep away all the refuse of the parties which served the Monarchist régime—refuse whose flowery representatives have provided him this afternoon with an almost bridal escort."

no great attractions. The oligarchy of the wheat-growing lands had been politically destroyed by the dictatorship, without receiving economic compensation comparable with what the bankers and the aristocrats received. It may be as well to repeat that the dividing line which separates political interests rarely marks with mathematical exactitude, especially in the case of groups which have fundamental values in common, the division of economic interests. But what is necessary to our analysis is the general composition of the political nuclei, and the conflict we are about to witness between the *C.E.D.A.* and *Renovación Española* cannot be satisfactorily explained, in my opinion, by supposed differences as to the form of government. The restoration of the monarchy was far from having been, under the Republic, a dogmatic aspiration of the aristocratic party, still less of the agrarian-Catholic oligarchy. In Spain, the confirmed Monarchists were only a small fraction; the rest, in the oligarchic area, were clerical, civil or military Fascists. And in accepting the mandate of *Renovación Española*, Calvo Sotelo had already shown himself, and his own aides-de-camp had presented him, as in no way bound to the monarchist régime. "Aucune forme spéciale de reconnaissance ne le liait au régime monarchique."[1]

Like the *C.E.D.A.*, *Renovación Española* represented economic interests which were attempting to gain the upper hand over related interests or over the interest of the nation in general; and the restoration of the monarchy was not, for those interests, the cardinal issue of the moment. The chief issue at stake for everybody was to put the Republic *hors de combat* by means of a dictatorship. But in their overweening pride, the party of the *caballeros* forgot that that part of their social power which was not vested in finance, derived from the land; and they despised the agrarians. Moreover, for the Catholics, as such, this question was of the utmost importance; what place was the Church to occupy in the new State? Finally, there was the problem of tactics: by what road were they to travel, and how best could the hazards be avoided, in the process of turning the Spanish people into another Israel in Egypt, hauling the stones in silence for Pharaoh's pyramids.

The October events came like a cold douche to Gil Robles. They made him understand, directly or through the medium of the Vatican, that before attempting to enthrone a totalitarian régime, in the Italian or German manner, a vast work of "education" and proselytizing of the masses had to be undertaken. Of the desire to abolish the political parties, as expressed

[1] J. F. de Lequerica in *Je suis partout*, July 15th, 1938.

by Calvo Sotelo, Gil Robles commented as follows: "Those who want to destroy them and speak of replacing them with advantage should consider first if it is not necessary to strengthen and encourage what, in the realm of social activities, hardly shows signs of true organic life."[1] The head of the *C.E.D.A.* thus proclaimed the *social* weakness of Fascism in Spain, a fact to which his eyes had been opened, no doubt, by the violent opposition of the working classes to the entry of his party to the Government.

For its part, *Renovación Española* did not blench before any difficulty. Its irrational optimism and contempt for public opinion originated in the supposition, nurtured to a certain extent by the weakness of civilian society, that the only force that counted in Spain was the military. The aristocratic party reduced, therefore, the problems of politics and the Government to strangely simple formulas. Of the same order was the adventurous optimism of Calvo Sotelo, in whom Fortune, who had never perhaps denied him a favour, may have implanted the unwavering confidence that the hero is always wont to have in his star.

Calvo Sotelo was born in 1893, in Túy, in the lovely province of Pontevedra. An ambitious and diligent pupil of the monks, he graduated when still very young in Civil and Canonical Law, obtained a University chair, and applied his studious temperament to the Moral and Political Sciences Department of the *Ateneo* of Madrid. His public activities began, within the fold of the Conservative Party, under the aegis of Don Antonio Maura, who took him into his private secretariat. One of the first rank of that brilliant and shrewd company of young men who surrounded the statesman from Majorca, Calvo Sotelo embarked on an unusual political career. In 1919, he took his seat in the Cortes as deputy for a district in his native land. In 1921, we find him Civil Governor of Valencia. Although he owed his rapid advancement, which was only partly due to his own merit, to the *old politicians*, Calvo Sotelo was to applaud, two years later, the military energy with which Primo de Rivera swept away the old parties and their chiefs. His admiration for the Dictator, and the familiarity which he had gained under Don Antonio Maura's wing with the problems of administration, ensured him access to the new régime in which he figured, at the start, as Director-General of Local Administration. And in 1925, when the Government of civilians was constituted, Primo appointed him Minister of Finance. Calvo Sotelo was then in his thirty-second year.

[1] Interview in *La Vanguardia*, ibid.

The dearth of political leaders among the Conservative classes was not palliated, under the second Republic, by the return of the ex-Minister of the dictatorship, but rather became more pronounced. The technical administration of Calvo Sotelo, while he served under Primo de Rivera, was not lacking in acumen, but in general it was, at the most favourable estimate, unfortunate. The idea of his own worth, which perhaps could not be modest in a person with such remarkable antecedents, may possibly explain the excessive confidence with which Calvo Sotelo seized the helm of the Conservative ship in the—to it—tempestuous sea of the Republic. As in the case of Gil Robles, his mission was difficult and the plan which he had matured abroad, without the least hint of having learnt anything, could not have been less adequate to the circumstances or less conducive to tranquillity in Spain. A real Conservative statesman would not have fallen a victim to the illusion, let alone encouraged it among his class, that it was an intelligent and workable policy to set against the democratic Republic in Spain, as the only science of government, the vulgar and problematical solution of a military dictatorship with more or less *corporative* elements.

The moral and civil degradation of the aristocratic nucleus was not even on this occasion, as we have seen, mitigated or disguised by a leading *cadre*, such as the oligarchy possessed under the régime of the Restoration. Their sense of personal dignity and their conception of political efficiency taught the Restoration politicians to fear the disastrous government of soldiers. They installed a system which was perverse, certainly, but a civilian system. And while it had politicians capable of finding a non-military solution to the embittered problem of the class struggle, although in the long run it was no solution, the degenerate oligarchy resigned itself to dispense with the yoke of sword and spur. In every age, it has been an unmistakable symptom of the abjectness of an oligarchy, or a proof of the consciousness of its own ineptitude, that it suffers from an insane desire to be ruled by soldiers; and in fixing all their hopes on the Army, the Spanish Monarchists testified before the country that they were, in the last analysis, a class that was ethically and mentally exhausted, and contemptible in every light, save for their wealth.

The intimate relationship which Carlism established at this period with *Renovación Española* reminds us of the existence of an anti-Liberal force which deserves to be seriously reckoned with. Carlism, during the life of the Republic, was not a party, but a communion, the *Comunión Tradicionalista Española*, a title which expresses its character as a religious movement and which might, very properly, have been given it from the beginning. The Catholicism of the oligarchic parties may appear to us frequently to be more social than religious. In case of a conflict between property and the Christian duties imposed by religion, the oligarchy threatened to become schismatic. Not such was the Catholicism of the Carlists, who were usually small proprietors. The Carlists or traditionalists were not anxious about the social question, which did not exist for them in the archaic and Arcadian economic life of agrarian-pastoral Navarre. The hub of their existence was religion. If Carlism, after the military defeat in the nineteenth century, was disarmed by the policy of compromise, the anti-clerical and laicizing laws of the second Republic breathed new life into it. It reorganized itself under the above-mentioned name of *Comunión Tradicionalista* and allied itself to *Renovación Española*—and not with *Acción Popular*—because the aristocratic party had in common with the traditionalists what *Acción Popular* or the *C.E.D.A.* did not have; the resolution not to come to terms with the Liberal Republic, even in thought, and the principle of monarchy—absolute, dictatorial, defiant. For *Renovación Española*, religion and even monarchy were secondary considerations; at the moment, the vital question was to install a régime which would place their class interests beyond reach of the slightest reform. And the annexation of a movement like the Carlist, the only one with a high, if anachronistic, ideal in the reactionary camp; a political-religious movement impelled by faith, spurred on by fanaticism and burning for a fight, communicated to *Renovación Española* energies and enthusiasms which were absent from that party, while it strengthened the adhesion of the plutocracy to the policy of violent tactics against the Republican régime.

The absolutism of *T.Y.R.E.* (*Tradicionalistas y Renovación Española*, extraordinary amalgam of names difficult to conjugate) had its theoretical organ in the review *Acción Española*, which borrowed its title, and sometimes its ideas, from *Action Française*. These organizations did not constitute a Fascist movement properly so-called; any profoundly anti-Liberal régime could have acted as their mouthpiece in the Government. A new party, still less original, was to undertake to propagate in Spain the demagogic theories and practice of Italian and German Fascism.

José Antonio Primo de Rivera, eldest son of the dead Dictator, more attentive to foreign political trends than to the needs and welfare of Spain, placed himself at the head of a small nationalist group, which, after sorting over innumerable names and rejecting as, perhaps, inadequate or discordant the Spanish name of

*Tercio* and the Roman name of Legion, picked the Macedonian name of *Falange*. The *Falange* was the typical Fascist Party, with its corporativism, its appeal to the rabble, its outstretched arm and its impossible imperialism. It had no scruples in inscribing on its banner the emblems of the Catholic sovereigns nor in borrowing from the Anarchists the colours red and black. And with such attributes and profanations, a turbulent propaganda, and the stimulus of international Fascism, the Falangists promised Spain a régime counselled by resentment and ruled by the worst kind of reactionary—the self-willed, ignorant and cruel *señorito*. A recruiting Centre for young landowners, careerist intellectuals or visionaries and adventurers of the worst type, the *Falange* was one more absolutist party, cold-shouldered by the oligarchy and ignored by the populace. Its most famous figure, and perhaps also the noblest, was the son of the Dictator. The fanatical nationalism of the *Falange* brought a smile to most lips and met with no response from the people, who did not need to know Dr. Johnson's apophthegm to be convinced that here was a case of clear imposture. For the noisy patriotism of the Falangists was no other than that of the oligarchy, and the patriotism of the oligarchy was, as Angel Ganivet said: "that of persons who refused to pay their taxes and then cried, 'To Morocco, infamous *canaille!*'"[1]

The Spanish *Falange* would not have required, or merited, more than four lines from the historian (though it might have occupied more than four pages in the chronicles of political crimes), had it not been a ramification of international Fascism. This party's complete lack of originality gained it the triumph over the other counter-revolutionary groups and, in the end, over the people. The support which was denied it by the Spanish masses was made up for by the adhesion of foreigns arms which, having to choose a party to support or a political instrument to use in order to dominate Spain without a scandal, adopted the hybrid *Falange* as the most genuinely Fascist organization.

However, to return to the period under study, the *Falange*, with its cohort of paid assassins, was from its birth a considerable factor in the programme of agreed violence instigated by the wealthy classes.

Those who expected their salvation from disorder and anarchy —the atmosphere they thought necessary for the military *coup d'état*—adjusted their trouble-making tactics to the political ends they were pursuing. But the agrarian-Catholics, or rather their leading *cadres*, who recognized and proclaimed the absence

[1] *Epistolario*, p. 55.

of conditions for a dictatorship, contributed largely by their economic terrorism and provocative speeches to frustrate the possibilities of living in harmony, without providing a political remedy for the situation which such excesses could not but create. Gil Robles now bitterly condemned the violent tactics of *Renovación Española*, *Tradicionalismo* and the *Falange* which he thought catastrophic.[1] But *Accion Popular* itself did not manage to evolve a just policy; the most it achieved was to accept the Republic in a barely audible voice, as a spectral being, without equalitarian entrails.

If the agrarian-Catholics had confessed themselves loyal supporters of the Republic, their acts would have belied them. The social policy of the *C.E.D.A.* was irreconcilable with any ordered régime. Reactionary dictatorship, though Gil Robles refused to admit it in public, was the natural result of the unbridled anti-reformist fervour of the oligarchy. Given the hypothesis that the party of the Church would have approved the popular régime, how could it have agreed upon such an attitude with the oligarchic dictatorship which lay like a dead weight on the countryside? By drawing back in horror from every gesture towards reform and by annulling the social laws of the Republic in such a way as to weight the scales against democracy, the *C.E.D.A.* showed that it patronized an idea of justice so abominable that it was only compatible with a system of terror. And the contradiction already pointed out, namely, to aspire to govern the Republic after having declared its intention of passing over the popular will, paled before the inconsequence of repudiating the *coup d'état* and of defending a class policy which made the functioning of a moderate régime impossible. There was in all this a profound conflict, a naked struggle, which strangled the policy of the Catholics, condemning it to tragic sterility. Gil Robles gave the fatal impression that he was playing a double game. And if Mirabeau could say of Robespierre: "This man will go far; he believes all he says", it might well be said of Gil Robles that he would achieve nothing; he believed nothing he said.

It should be noted that the most fervent anti-dictatorial manifestations staged by the head of the Catholic party did

[1] On December 22nd, 1934, Gil Robles declared in Madrid: "So long as I have any imfluence over Spaniards of the Right, I will never consent to the adoption of catastrophic tactics. They (*Renovación*) think they can save their ideals by the reaction which would arise after the hecatomb. But it is not easy. After the dictatorship, which I am not out to judge now, came political revolution. A new dictatorship might produce, after a period of calm, social revolution, the Communist Republic."

nothing to dissipate the general suspicion, which was perhaps shared in the end by the President of the Republic, that he proposed to govern, one day or another, in the manner of Dollfuss or Oliveira Salazar. In the meantime, *Acción Popular* came to be like a mammoth vehicle, stuck in the mud up to the axle, and sprawled across the road. Immobile itself, it blocked the way to everyone else. *Renovación Española* followed with nervousness and disgust the manœuvres and counter-manœuvres of Gil Robles' sterile Fabian tactics, execrated his inclination to compromise with the Republic—the spirit of compromise not being really indigenous to the *C.E.D.A.*—and every day discord grew more clamant in the ranks of the two-headed oligarchy.

The oligarchy, obviously, was suffering from undeniable confusion, no doubt as the result of the popular explosion in October, which imposed on the most numerous party of the reaction a wary and cautious policy. But if *Acción Popular* had learnt, as it seems, to moderate its political impatience, it failed to apprehend the social lessons which flowed from the situation in 1935. In their impotence to destroy the proletariat politically, the Conservatives diverted themselves by exasperating them. Each law was a new turn of the screw of economic oppression. And the civil war, which might have been contained or postponed, or perhaps avoided by a few timely reforms and a magnanimous policy, advanced, as a result of this cruel and blind obstinacy, with an inexorable and sinister step; and with the civil war, revolution, in which those who could not bring themselves to yield something were likely to lose everything.

In this impasse, not relieved by even one gleam of light ahead, the Parliament of the oligarchic majority and the Radical-*Cedist* Cabinet held the nation as in a vice. The Budget deficit became again what it was under the monarchy and the dictatorship: 1,028 million pesetas. And the genuine capitalists, the *bourgeoisie*, saw with alarm the collapse of the industrial and commercial economy, a corollary partly of disastrous administration, partly of the general scaling down of wages in the rural areas, and partly of the decline of Spanish credit abroad.

The industrialists and merchants, advised by Cambó, urged the necessity for a change of economic policy, which could not be achieved without the expulsion of the landowners from the Government. The President of the Republic, now seeking a middle class to act as a stabilizing political centre, did not turn a deaf ear to the lamentations and suggestions of the industrial and commercial *bourgeoisie*, nor did he persist in ignoring the ineptitude in government of the agrarian-aristocratic Cortes.

530

The political situation which arose in November 1933 was reaching its climax. And in September Alcalá Zamora handed over the Government to Don Joaquín Chapaprieta, a business man and an ally for the occasion of the deputies of the *Lliga* and of those capitalists who resented the egoism, irresponsibility and ignorance of the landowners.

The Chapaprieta Government had a short life. The Cortes was hostile to him, and this enmity turned to horror when the parliamentary majority heard him declare that he proposed to balance the Budget and for this pecuniary sacrifices must be exacted from all Spaniards, without distinction of class. The oligarchy had few objections to the dismissal of employees and to cuts in the salaries of officials; but when they discovered that death duties were to be increased and a new tax levied on landed property, they preferred to face the chances of another Government crisis.

The oligarchy's decision confirmed once more its obstinate propensity to commit suicide. The Radical Party, mortally wounded by the financial scandals, was morally and politically discredited in Parliament and in the country. The *C.E.D.A.* was not likely to obtain governmental power from the hands of a President who had paid so dearly for having admitted it to the Government. Consequently, with that Cortes, there was no Ministry possible, and even less probability that it would govern with tolerance and decency. And dissolution augured for the Conservatives the almost certain risk of an imminent and terrible electoral defeat.


CHAPTER XVIII

DRIFTING

THE END OF the Chapaprieta Government decided the President of the Republic to sanction the formation of a Cabinet without Ministers from the *C.E.D.A.*, to dissolve the Chamber and to attempt the artificial gestation of a middle-class party which would be the centre of gravity in the future Cortes. The man who was charged with creating such a party, presiding over the new Government and carrying out the elections, was Don Manuel Portela Valladares.

The President of the Republic thought that, by manipulating the electoral machine dexterously from the Ministry of the Interior, in the old way, he might surreptitiously bring to birth, if not the middle-of-the-road movement, oxygen of Parliamentary democracy, at least the organization which would serve its turn in the Cortes. In effect, all the vicissitudes of the régime sprang, in principle, from the lack of a middle class; but Don Niceto erred now in his choice of proceeding—the only one which would occur to a politician of the old régime—to found a Centre Party, as he had erred before by impeding, with the considerable means at his disposal, the rise of a new social class in the countryside or the enjoyment by the peasants of such a standard of living as would dispose them to support the Republic with the enthusiasm of people defending their own property. The President had made the same mistake as almost all the Republicans to the Right of Azaña; they wanted to enjoy liberty and democracy without passing through the troubles of revolution and without destroying the social foundations of absolutism; they trembled before property, feared to alarm the rich, and hastened to rid themselves of the Socialists, ignorant, perhaps, that they were cracking the axle of the Republic, since the Socialists conducted themselves in the Government as if they were the middle class the Republic needed and Spain did not possess. But let us turn to the development of the crisis.

During the course of 1935 the idea had been gaining ground of an imminent change of policy, which now hardened into the dissolution of the Cortes. The torpor of the reactionaries, on the one hand, and the flexibility of the Republicans, on the other, encouraged Alcalá Zamora to smoothe the way to the political rehabilitation of the Republican parties. These parties withdrew their October declarations in which, as will be remembered, they broke with the President of the Republic; they condemned or censured the popular insurrection and made their peace with the political institutions. With this retraction they made possible the free play of the powers of the State, that is, they placed themselves anew in a position to govern during Don Niceto's term of office as President. The Republican recantation was perhaps necessary to redeem the Republic and might be considered prudent tactics if it responded to a high-minded policy and did not imply forgetfulness of what the régime owed to the sacrifice of the proletariat. That the Republic was, miraculously, face to face with its last opportunity must have been evident to everybody. The consternation of the oligarchy when confronted with the dissolution of Parliament foreshadowed the triumph of the Left in the forthcoming elections, fixed for February 1936. The people's optimism proclaimed their confidence in victory.

But beyond the likely, or probable, electoral defeat of the reactionaries the future was shrouded in darkness.

The working classes had radicalized themselves as a consequence of the economic oppression, the political persecution, and the fiasco of Socialist collaboration in the Government. The Socialist masses, and, in particular, the numerous and powerful youth organizations, broke away from their party chiefs, and showed themselves resolved not to accept, inside the party, any leader save one approved by their revolutionary fervour. The Liberal and parliamentary Republic had as yet but few followers, even among the Republicans who followed Azaña. It was recognized and admitted that the régime had sinned in its weakness towards its enemies and it was proposed, when the Republic should recover its strength, to install an exclusive and dynamic system, saying little and doing much. But on the other hand, the bias taken by the class struggle, which grew daily more envenomed, intimidated the Republican leaders, beginning with Azaña.

The convenience of studying in a single chapter the figure of Azaña obliges me to confuse the chronology of events and excuses me here from recording in detail the personal and public tragedy of the Republic's most eminent politician. In 1935 Azaña addressed himself to public opinion with a frequency natural in one who was still, or appeared to be still, the mouthpiece of Spanish democracy. He spoke at public meetings in various capitals, always before immense Republican and working-class crowds. In the spring he spoke at Valencia, in the summer at Bilbao, in the autumn at Madrid. But Azaña was already an exhausted and defeated statesman, with no solution for the great problem which was now confronting him—the same, in substance, as in 1931, but much more pressing. The warm contact with the masses galvanized his energies as an orator, but could not make of the writer a man of action. Azaña's state of mind was that attributed by him in his speech at Valencia to other Republicans: "The fact is that I notice in some Spanish Republicans such a decay of will-power, such a pusillanimity of character that they allow themselves to be taken in by the propaganda of their enemies and, through reading the insolent absurdities which they write against us, are overcome with alarm." There was nobody, nevertheless, more overcome with alarm than Azaña himself, who in this speech proclaimed how much he had changed in how short a time.

The collaboration of Socialists and Republicans in the Government had been a dogma to Azaña; in the first place, because he held it as axiomatic that, free from the responsibilities of government, the proletariat would create enormous difficulties for Republican Cabinets, and also because, according to him, a national policy without the presence of the working class in the Government could never succeed. Azaña always preferred not to govern at all, than to part company with the Socialists, and he fell in 1933 through being consistent in his ideas and sane in his doctrine. But let us listen to him now: "Republican Left affirms that this work, concerted, articulated, and solemnly supported by all, must be carried out from the seat of power, by a Government strictly Republican, purely Republican." Azaña did not now want to alarm the owner classes, nor did he gird himself with energy, as in former days, to resist the assaults of the plutocracy, the criticism of faint-hearted, confused or corrupt Republicans, and the discontent of his friends. The new Republican policy of the Left obviously confirmed the pusillanimity of character and the decay of will-power among the better Republicans. The philosophic middle class showed itself less audacious, or more timid, even than in the first years of the Republic; it was satisfied with less now than then; it was less resolved than ever to take a hand in the reform of the nation. The hostility of the reactionaries, the October disturbances, and the new radicalism of the proletariat had daunted it.

But nothing, unless it be the collapse of his political morale, could justify Azaña in recommending, against his own reason, a Government without Socialists, which, as could be foreseen, would be without authority, without vigour and probably not overburdened with competence. And as the exclusion of the proletariat from the responsibilities of government originated in the Republicans' desire not to provoke the oligarchies, the suspicion that they would derive no benefit from the Government confirmed the Socialist working classes, still profoundly disillusioned, in their intention of demanding for their part, a purely Socialist Ministry. Both attitudes were pernicious, because they implied the widening of the gulf between the proletariat and the middle class; and these social classes needed one another in order to consummate a mutually beneficial anti-oligarchic revolution and also to preserve the Republic.

The new tactics of the Left Republicans did not cause a single Socialist to shed a tear. The Ministerial union of the first two years was held to be well and truly dissolved. The tendency was, through ill-advised *amour propre*, to delimit responsibilities in the next Republican experiment: And the Socialists, divided as to the character the revolution should take—for some, dictatorial and drastic; for others, parliamentary and moderate—showed themselves unanimous, or nearly so, in their refusal to share the burdens and anxieties of government.

The inescapable obligation to set free the 25,000 political prisoners who still lay in prisons and penitentiaries, among them those condemned for their part in the peasants' strike of June 1934, made it absolutely vital for the parties of the Left to exercise intelligence and to come to an agreement before the elections. At the end of the year the Popular Front was born, solidly cemented by the necessity of obtaining, or promulgating, the desired amnesty and repairing the most crying injustices. The alliance was formed by the Republicans of the Left, the followers of Martínez Barrio, the Catalan *Esquerra* and the workers' parties, except the Anarchists and the Anarcho-Syndicalists. The electoral pact presupposed a collaboration far beyond the anticipated triumph in the polling booths and laid down reforms which the Republicans undertook to introduce with the parliamentary support of the proletariat. This part of the programme was regarded as contentious and accepted with scant enthusiasm by both sides. The Socialists proposed the nationalization of the land and the banks, control of industry by the workers and unemployment insurance or a subsidy to relieve the unemployed—in fact, the programme they were putting forward at the time of the October insurrection. Such suggestions, which, set forth or presented in a less doctrinaire manner, were the only ones likely to curb the power of the agrarian-financial oligarchy, did not meet with the approval of the Republicans. In the end, the programme of government of the Popular Front comprised the re-establishment of the rule of the Constitution, the reorganization and independence of the judiciary, the protection of the peasants and small farmers, the settlement of peasant families, the reorganization of industry, the protection of small industries and commerce, a plan of public works, another plan for the construction of dwelling-houses, the placing of the Exchequer and the banks at the service of national reconstruction, equitable distribution of taxation, and lastly, a régime of liberty and democracy. Everything was ambiguous here; each item had the air of a vague evasion. And the fact that, after 130 years of civil war, Spanish democracy had not even been able to agree that, in order to save itself and Spain, it had to do four things—no more than four, of equal importance to each of the victims of the oligarchy—gave rise to reflections of despair. The vital question was the form of government. The first thing necessary in order to make the régime acceptable

535

to all Spaniards, or merely to govern, was a State; but so confused did the democrats appear, on the very verge of their ruin or salvation, that they insisted upon carrying out the national reform under a régime of political liberty, regardless of the fact that civil war was advancing with relentless step. With the agreement to govern on parliamentary lines the Popular Front was condemning the Republic to future impotence and thus introducing the factor of disssolution which was lacking to make the régime, when it was re-established, absolutely ungovernable.

If the elections of November 1933 took place in an atmosphere of civil war, those of February 1936 were civil war itself. The chief political forces of the nation grouped themselves into two irreconcilable *blocs* of equal size. Excited and violent electoral propaganda surpassed in incidents all previous experience of the sort. It was clear that both groups recognized without the shadow of a doubt the decisive character of the fight, with the slight difference that for the Left, always burdened with an extreme conception of legality, the electoral results were going to decide the existence of the Republic, while for the Right, accustomed to understand legality more as the expression of economic and social power than as an immanent juridical concept, and less sure of victory, the February elections would not say the last word in the great historic struggle. This applied, above all, to the aristocratic party and the Carlists, who were entering the fray in company with the *C.E.D.A.* and the Catalan *Lliga*. These forces, if the ballot box failed them, did not feel bound by their own conscience to submit. To democracy's triumph, however well founded in right, they opposed the right of rebellion.

The victory of the Popular Front crowned the desires of the Left parties and exceeded the hopes of the sceptics. The democratic parties gained 266 seats in the new Chamber, the reactionary *bloc* 153, and the Centre, including the Basque nationalists, 54. For the first time, the Communists, who in the Parliaments of the Republic had been represented by a single deputy, acquired a certain importance with fifteen seats. The numerous Radical contingent of the previous Cortes was wiped out, and its eight representatives, faced with the disappearance of their group, modestly incorporated themselves with the twenty-five Centre deputies under Portela Valladares. The strongest nucleus in the Chamber was the *C.E.D.A.* with ninety-six deputies, followed by the Socialists with eighty-seven. And Azaña's Republican Left, which had been extinguished in the November elections, came back with unexpected vigour with eighty-one deputies.

The distribution of the votes made it clear that the phenomenon of 1933 had repeated itself, this time in favour of the Left. The difference in the number of seats in the Cortes corresponding to each *bloc* was, as always, disproportionate to the difference in votes. The Popular Front obtained 4,540,000 and the Right and the Centre 4,300,000.[1] So that without the strength of either of the two great political constellations having perceptibly varied in the country, an oligarchic Parliament, hostile to any transaction with democracy, was succeeded by a popular Chamber with a mandate to carry on the revolution. That is to say, the velleities of the electoral law, which ought not to have obscured the judgment of the oligarchy to the point of compelling it, with a kind of insane fury, to exasperate the common people in 1933, ought not either to have concealed from the Republicans in 1936 the formidable political-social power of the defeated.

The publication of the electoral results announced the end of the Republic's Babylonian captivity. The rejoicings of April 14th, 1931, were repeated—tempered, on the side of the proletariat, by suffering. The Spanish people were awakening from a nightmare, from a frightful dream, in which they had seen themselves condemned, perhaps, to perpetual oppression. It was not surprising, then, that they were impatient to prove that they were awake and ready to enjoy the rights which had been snatched away. Moreover, the policy of the oligarchy had fomented poverty and need. The truth is that the clamour of the streets, the outcry from the prisons and the impotence of the authorities prevented the Portela Ministry from continuing to govern, until they could render an account to the Cortes, as was legally necessary, of their administration. The President of the Republic had hastily to call upon Azaña, who without delay formed a Government, as agreed, which was "purely Republican".

It was clear that, not from the present moment, but ever since national reform through parliamentary methods had failed, the balance of legality had been broken and the constitutional dyke had burst. Once more for the Left, the question was not law or no law, but life or no life. The people had gone to the polling booths, as almost always in Spain, in the most disadvantageous conditions, arising out of their own principles; in voting, nobody doubted that if reaction triumphed, the Republic would disappear and be replaced by a military or Fascist dictatorship, but no one doubted either that the victory of democracy would not entail the disappearance of the oligarchy, a

[1] Final data published in *El Sol* of Madrid, March 3rd, 1936.

conclusion that derived from the Government and the programme of government which the Popular Front was offering the nation. In effect, the new Government was born to rule Spain in strict accordance with the Constitution and Parliament. Its policy had been defined by Azaña—peace and concord. No therapeutic remedy could have been less adequate to that explosive situation. In a régime of liberty, peace was impossible; in any case, *concord* was fatal to democracy. As the oligarchy ought not to have been implacable during the period of its domination, so the Republic could not show signs of weakness in 1936; and as the terroristic policy of the Right was disastrous both for them and for Spain, so would a policy of complacency and compromises be disastrous for the democratic parties and the nation. In the general interest of Spain and the individual interest of each group, it was needful that the Conservative policy should be distinguished by its generosity towards the under-dog and that the Republican policy should be characterized by its severity towards the fortunate, especially on the economic plane. By being loyal to its barbarous principles at the expense, in the long run, of its own interests, the oligarchy had ushered in the civil war; by having, in its turn, honoured its ideals, against the promptings of the instinct of self-preservation, the democratic Republic fanned the flames lit by the absolutists. When the monarchy fell, the only way to save Spain was by a Left dictatorship, or later, when the inevitable and rapid dissolution of parliamentary Government took place, by an enlightened Conservative régime which would accept, and even improve on, the timid Republican reforms. But, as we have seen, the Republicans conducted themselves with the magnanimity and prudence which befitted a Conservative Government, and the Right acted with the severity and destructive energy which should have been the attributes of a Left Government. Each social hemisphere carried out the policy most opposed to its duty and to the tranquillity and prosperity of Spain.

With peace and concord, Azaña recommended calm and moderation. But the people could not wait, however much they wanted to. The amnesty, for example, should have come from the Cortes; but well-meaning officials, either through Republican conviction, or out of panic, were already throwing open the prison doors in some cities. The Constitution was a suit which had been cut too tight for Spanish democracy, which, in two years, had grown out of all recognition! And Azaña could not grow with it. The amnesty, then, had to be proclaimed before the deputies met again.

Crucified on the tables of the constitutional law, the Government of the reconquered Republic had to look on while other saturnalia of liberty took place. The peasants began the agrarian revolution anew on their own account. In Andalusia, Estremadura, and some zones of Castile, lands and estates were confiscated, more out of crying need than a clear revolutionary urge. Clashes multiplied between the people and the Civil Guard in which the *gente de blusa*, the peasants, came off worst, as usual, and the events of Casas Viejas and Castilblanco were repeated on a scale unknown during the first two years.

In the cities, convents and churches burned once more, violent strikes followed one another in swift succession, and shots were exchanged between the political factions, sometimes within the same party or within the body of the working class.

As soon as the Cortes began to function, it paralysed the Government and acted as a sounding-board to civil war by transmitting to the nation its own turbulence, magnified a hundredfold. The deputies hurled insults and abuse at one another—each session was a continuous riot. And as almost all the representatives—true representatives—of the nation went armed, sooner or later there was bound to be a catastrophe. In view of the frequency with which firearms were brandished or hinted at, the disgraceful precaution of searching the legislators for arms on entering the Chamber was adopted. It is superfluous to add that the atmosphere of excitement condemned Parliament to absolute sterility; and yet Parliament was the instrument to which the over-modest reforms and measures of government comprised in the programme of the Popular Front had been entrusted.

The strident disorder which afflicted the nation was, for the most part, the work of the reactionaries, who saw in the public chaos the necessary premise, in the extremity to which they were reduced, for obtaining what had been denied them by the elections—the occasion to establish the dictatorship of the Army. A few days after the victory of the Popular Front, there came into action all those dark and well-known forces which a turbulent and corrupt plutocracy can mobilize in a country which is politically and socially unbalanced. The "clients" of the aristocracy, mingling with the unprincipled rabble and the radicalized proletariat, contributed largely, in every way, to keeping alive agitation and panic in the streets. The Monarchist and Fascist *caballeros* frequently perpetrated crimes and assaults which at times provoked reprisals from the group which had been attacked, the vileness of the struggle being intensified as

539

the ripples of hatred spread in ever-widening circles. Every day, every hour, the confusion and disintegration of the Government grew worse. And even if the Republicans and workers had refused to defend themselves, the disturbing activities of the *agents provocateurs*, the "clients" of the aristocracy, and the elegant followers of the oligarchy who were waging war from *Renovación Española* and the *Falange*, would have been enough to facilitate the no less demoralizing work of the reactionary deputies, who accused the Government of weakness and incompetence.

From the time when the Cortes resumed its sittings, the heads of the oligarchic opposition used periodically to read to the deputies—with the object of having their remarks printed in the newspapers and so coming to the knowledge of the public—circumstantial reports of such incidents, encounters, outbreaks of arson, trangressions, strikes, assaults and crimes as took place throughout the whole country, not forgetting the most remote hamlet. These dangerous tactics of enlarging on the confusion and tumult were crowned by the perverse delight with which the speaker collected and underlined those events which wounded the dignity of the Army and injured the honour of its officers. The function of the legislator was increasingly tarnished by this foul propaganda, while from the same parliamentary benches the oligarchy proclaimed the saving mission of the armed forces, subordinating civilian society to brute force and declaring the Army to be the spinal column of the nation.[1]

As the political affiliation of the promoters of anarchy was never mentioned and the accusations came from the Conservative camp, it appeared that political delinquency was the monopoly of the popular classes. But during the four months which separated the Republican victory from the military rising, as often as the hand that fired the shot or the origin of the calamity could be traced, the evidence was plain that the so-called champions of order were unquestionably guilty. Between the authors of the incidents, and the deputy who exploited them, lay a coincidence which was by no means fortuitous—a suspicion that might be extended to many social conflicts. By means of this double game, only possible in a system of liberty mortal to democracy, the Government was overwhelmed by chaos in the streets and by responsibility in Parliament. And it is sufficient to enumerate the most striking criminal acts to understand the basis and meaning of the alarmist campaign which, in Parliament and Press, was inciting the Army to restore peace.

[1] Tactics of Calvo Sotelo. Speech on June 16th, 1936.

On April 14th bombs exploded under the platform on which the provisional President of the Republic and the entire Government were watching the march past of the military forces. As a result, a lieutenant of the Civil Guard died shortly afterwards, and during the funeral of the victim, at which all the notabilities of the reactionary parties were present, shots were exchanged between the funeral *cortège* and labourers employed on some works near the route of the procession. No other disturbance equalled this in absurd and dramatic incidents, a symptom of the nervous disorder which afflicted the capital of Spain.

On the evening of March 12th, when coming out of his house accompanied by the detective who was acting as his escort, the Socialist professor and Vice-President of the Cortes, Jiménez de Asúa, was the object of a cowardly attempt, from which he escaped unhurt, but the detective with him lost his life.

On another day the hired assassins of the reactionaries placed a powerful bomb in the house of Don Eduardo Ortega y Gasset. The dwelling was destroyed, but as the Republican lawyer and his family were absent at the time, there were no victims.

In Santander the Fascists assassinated the Socialist Malumbres, editor of the weekly *La Región*. Another victim of the White Terror was Don Manuel Andrés Casáus, editor of *La Prensa* of San Sebastián.

A new type of crime, the most repugnant of the series, in my opinion, made its appearance at this time. The White Terror began to choose its victims from a circle which had always commanded respect—the magistracy. On April 13th, Don Manuel Pedregal, a judge who some time before had sentenced a Fascist gunman to thirty years' hard labour, was assassinated.

But as we shall see later, no crime had graver immediate consequences, owing to the special standing of the victims, than the assassination of the Republican officers of the *Cuerpo de Asalto*.

The political classification of the aggressors was apparent in each one of the above-mentioned events. The enemies of the Republic had to suffer nothing comparable in the quality of the victims chosen. No newspaper editor among the Fascists, Monarchists or Catholics suffered the fate of Malumbres or Casáus; no magistrate of the many who judged the workers or the Republicans met with the brutal reprisals which caused the death of Señor Pedregal; no reactionary police or Army officer died through deliberate aggression, a victim of the hatred of the democrats.

For the rest, the profound disturbances which accompanied the triumph of the Popular Front proclaimed that civil war had already broken out and that the Left had not the knowledge, nor the power, to find a way out for themselves or for Spain, from this tremendous impasse. From the beginning of May, the situation steadily deteriorated, owing to the fact that Azaña had exchanged the Premiership for the Presidency of the Republic. On April 7th the deputies had pronounced against the action of the President in dissolving the former Cortes, a political manœuvre which, according to Article 81 of the Constitution, entailed the resignation of Alcalá Zamora. On May 10th Azaña was elected President, through the votes not only of the parties of the Popular Front, but also those of certain components of the anti-Marxist *bloc*, though the *C.E.D.A.* abstained. On May 12th Casares Quiroga formed a Government of Left Republicans and followers of Martínez Barrio. In its hour of greatest crisis, the Republic had its weakest Government.

Moreover, as we have seen, Azaña was not now the man he had been during the first two years. In such a mood, it would have been little use for him to continue in the seat of authority and at the forefront of the fight. But Azaña had something essential to that moment, a virtue or personal endowment which was lacking in all the other politicians in the democratic latitude—authority. Undoubtedly no politician, Republican or Socialist, enjoyed the personal authority which Azaña could exercise over the vast and heterogeneous democratic mass—an authority which transcended party and made itself felt, more tangibly in some zones than others, throughout the length and breadth of Spain. There may have been persons more capable of facing up to circumstances, better endowed with vision and temperament to cope with pandemonium, but these qualities or attributes did not compensate their possessors for the lack of authority from which all the possible leaders suffered, some even in his own party, like Indalecio Prieto, or like the Republicans in their dealings with the working classes. Except Azaña, they were all party men, with a well-defined following behind them, and another, not less well-defined, opposite; mistrustful on occasions, in political matters, of their ally and, as often as not, of their own colleagues.

During the months which preceded the military rising, the only solution, whatever the difficulties, for the Republic, for Spain, for the régime and the nation menaced by collapse, was the total suspension of the Constitution. But only if Azaña had been the incarnation of the new system could such a régime have

542

had any chance of success. Any other Republican would have been unaccepable to proletariat and *bourgeoisie* alike and would have encountered invincible obstacles in imposing obedience, even by force. But Azaña, if he had been cast in a different mould, was in such a singular and such a favourable position to fulfil the task which history had reserved for him, that, representing as he did (or so the Conservatives thought) the last hope of the *bourgeoisie*, he could still count on the affection and confidence of the common people.

It is important to emphasize here that the proletariat was agitating for two or three easily identifiable motives: first, because they were suffering want, then because they wanted to coerce the Republicans in order to force them to proceed with resolution and without weakness in the Government; and finally, because they were enduring constant and criminal provocation from the Fascist aggressors and the landowners. These causes of disorder—the principal ones—would have disappeared once a Government with full powers, led by the person who would have inspired least mistrust in all the social classes, had demonstrated the unshakable intention of preserving formal order without detriment to the progress of the revolution—with the understanding, of course, that order without rapid and obvious reforms would have been as utopian an enterprise as the reforms without order which were the present fare. Needless to say, the difficulty was to take this gigantic step—a step only possible for a great man who, subordinating the personal consequences which such a heroic and perchance unpopular gesture might entail to the more fatal consequences for Spain of allowing civil war to run its course, would sweep away a régime of liberty which was harming everyone and destroying the Republic. Such dubious liberty would willingly have been exchanged by the proletariat for certain radical reforms imposed dynamically and inexorably on the oligarchy. The middle class, and not only the Republican middle class—that is, the neutral classes, would unhesitatingly have exchanged reforms which would have benefited them rather than otherwise, for the sake of personal security and public order, so necessary to commerce and industry. In 1936 no one wanted a Parliament in Spain, and there is no doubt that, by abolishing it, a national aspiration admitted by the majority would have been satisfied. Some— the Fascists, Monarchists and Catholics—were against the Cortes because they were absolutists; others, the Marxists, because of past experience and out of principle; the Anarchists, because they were a-political; many Liberals, because they considered it sterile; others, especially youth, because in latter years they had lost their illusions and had grasped the impossibility of conquering reaction by parleying with it. Going to the root of these attitudes, there can be no doubt that the immense majority of Spaniards agreed upon the necessity of a change. And in 1935, whenever Azaña sought the stimulus of the masses or when he was face to face with his own Republican public, he encountered this feeling. The dictatorship of the proletariat was neither desired nor recommended by the Communists, and in the Socialist Party the desire for it was a sign of desperation or fatalism arising out of the weakness of the Republicans or the fear that other working-class organizations would carry the masses with them; as happened, in spite of all, when Socialist youth went over to Communism.

If we thoroughly analyse the underlying motives of the conflict into which Spain was plunged following the victory of the Popular Front, ignoring what is superficial and demagogic, we cannot fail to be astonished at the extraordinary extent— as always when a people falls into such a state of tumult and convulsion—to which everything depended on the character of one man, on the failure of Azaña. Insofar as they did not depend on his state of mind or character, which was never that of the man of iron, there existed, in my opinion, the perfect conditions for the politician who gathered together in the *Campo de Comillas* half a million Spaniards—an unusual event— to put himself at the head of the nation and to save it, with a hand which, in order not to be heavy, had to be just, from the vortex which was threatening to engulf it. But to the extent that they depended on Azaña himself, the indispensable conditions for this miracle to occur were absolutely lacking.

Azaña, because he felt himself lacking in strength, handed over the wheel, at the steepest point of the incline, to Casares Quiroga, a well-meaning politician, a man of convictions, but not capable of dealing with the situation. Prieto had not succeeded in forming a Government, through the veto of his own party.

As often happens, the shortcomings of the Government and the fear of exceeding their functions, for which they were called to account daily in the Cortes, acted like a brake on their power and led them to make imperfect use of the means at their disposal or to apply them with such caution that, by accident, or through the prevailing confusion, they frequently favoured the cause of their enemies. In the two months that Azaña presided over the Ministry, he adopted certain measures against the conspirator generals, but with such ill luck that he sent General Franco to the Canary Islands where he was nearer his dangerous focus of influence in Morocco, and General Goded to the Balearic Isles where, as in the case of Franco, it was less easy to keep a watch on him and collect complete and authentic information about his intrigues. No less unfortunate for the régime was the removal of General Mola, on February 28th, from the command of the African Army to the military governorship of Navarre, whereby the Republic gave the fanatical *Requetés* the leader they lacked. The Government went ahead like a blind man with his stick, taking such precautions as occurred to them to restrain the enemies of the Republic or possible conspirators. But the purging of the Army, which had received a copious influx of absolutist officers during Gil Robles' term of office, could no longer be carried out save by recourse to collective and drastic expedients. Two-thirds of the generals were resolved or disposed to revolt against the Popular Front Republic, and so little could the Government count on the armed forces that the Inspector-General of the Army, Rodríguez del Barrio, presided over the *junta* of generals which was organizing the revolt.

Until the 17th of April, the Government did not order the dissolution of the Fascist organizations, or, rather, did not decree them illegal, since to dissolve them, in the present eclipse of their authority, was beyond their power.

In the end, Spain entered upon the summer like a rudderless ship embarking upon a stormy sea, buffeted by the waves, and with a crew which was desperate, resigned, or terrified. The horizon of the Republic was already disappearing behind the lowering storm-clouds. Protected by the national confusion, the generals, without serious setbacks, were putting the final touches to their preparations for attack which the common people, with better insight than the Government, were expecting from day to day. Ever since February, the Republic had been living in a constant state of anguish, menaced by the irrevocable peril of a military *coup d'état*, and overwrought nerves had reached the pitch when organized civil war on a grand scale was preferable to the constant bloodletting of partisan clashes and isolated aggressions. If the aristocratic party's ideal was to see Spain rent by civil war rather than pacified under the Republic, there was no doubt that it was finally on the way to complete triumph.

For its part, the revolution—if this word can express that disjointed tumult—continued its career. The proletariat were striding ahead by three distinct routes, and, naturally, without a leader. The revolution was like a serpent; the head advanced, but the motive force came from the tail. And where it was going was difficult to conjecture.

Madrid argued with violence at the feet of a helpless Government. *Agents provocateurs* ranged at will, with a finger in every pie. There was a general strike of waiters, a general strike of liftmen, a general strike of builders. The Anarchists, who had always been in a minority in the capital, now thrived on the confusion and succeeded in imposing their will on the placid proletariat of Madrid. An old tragedy was about to be re-enacted—civil war within the working class. As a result of the builders' strike, which the Anarchists wanted to prolong, workers of the *U.G.T.* and the *C.N.T.* settled their argument with bullets.

The capital of the Republic was suffering, no doubt, the dramatic effects of the desperation of the proletariat, the fruit, in the last analysis, of the soulless policy of the oligarchy. But there were other causes.

During the last ten years, the Telephone Company had attracted to Madrid a multitude of unskilled workers, farm labourers transformed into *peons*, the same human element which formed the leaven of Anarchism in Barcelona. This mass of workers, who were notoriously easy to influence and indoctrinate with violence and utopian theories, united now with the day-labourers in the building industry and brought to Madrid the methods of combat and violent tactics which characterized the industrial centres of Catalonia. For the rest, the disorders of the moment favoured Anarchism, which in a few months took over the moral leadership of the workers' movement in Madrid.

The same confusion which facilitated the conspiracy of the generals assured the impunity of the Fascist terroristic bands which continued to choose their victims at their own discretion. Deputies, magistrates, Republican and Socialist chiefs had their last hour marked in the lists of these ruffians. Until, as I said, they decided to dispatch the officers of the Assault Guard, soldiers notoriously Republican in their sympathies and loyal to the régime, who, because they had suppressed the insurrections of August 10th in Madrid, had earned the hatred of the reactionaries. In May, the Captain of the Assault Guard, Señor Faraudo, succumbed in the streets of Madrid in exceptionally dramatic circumstances, when walking with his wife; the terrorists fired from a car, all the shots lodging in Faraudo's body, which perhaps denotes the professional character of the criminals.

The Republican officers of the Assault Guard, guided by a sense of duty and discipline, controlled their anger and the crime went unpunished.

On July 12th Señor Castillo, a lieutenant in the same corps, was assassinated in similar circumstances, also in the main street and without risk to the assailants. Confronted with this second crime, which promised not to be the last of which this body of officers would be the victims, Castillo's colleagues gave vent to their feelings, their thirst for vengeance over-coming all sentiments of duty and mercy.

Early next morning they commandeered a lorry belonging to the corps, and a group of officers of the Assault Guard, together with an officer of the Civil Guard, drove to Calvo Sotelo's residence. The uniform procured them entry. They went up to the apartment where the leader of *Renovación Española* lived and announced that they had orders to arrest him. Calvo Sotelo suspected a trap and tried to communicate with the heads of the police, but he was frustrated by the officers cutting the telephone wires.

Ignorant of the enormity that was about to be perpetrated against his person, perhaps because it *was* an enormity, or because he was neither a coward nor a weakling, the prisoner descended resolutely with the Republican officers, who were still blinded by the memory of Castillo's corpse. Prisoner and captors got into the lorry, and as soon as they had left the city precincts Calvo Sotelo was killed and his corpse placed in the cemetery *del Este*.

The ultimate barrier of disorder had been passed. Nothing more was required, after this incident, for the Government and the reactionaries to lose, the former, what shreds of authority remained to it, the latter, what judgment they still possessed.

CHAPTER XIX

## THE CONSPIRACY

In view of the bloody convulsions which shook Spain from 1934 on, and, above all, the hostilities which broke out in July 1936, it might perhaps be convenient to glance back at the pacific and hopeful days of April 1931. Thus we shall be able to place the civil war in its right perspective.

There should be no difficulty in recalling that the Republic

547

came into being in answer to the votes of the people, with exceptional simplicity and frankness, without upheavals and without victims, even if we take into account the events of December of the previous year, which left no resentment in any Republican breast and which were unimportant compared with the momentousness of the change. Outside Spain, few could explain the resignation of the Monarchists and fewer still understood, perhaps, the generosity of the Republicans. There was no disturbance or bloodshed, although the people might, with complete impunity, have treated their fallen adversaries with violence. The Royal Family, which was guarded on the last day by the people's militia, left Madrid and crossed half Spain amid the respectful indifference of Spaniards. It was obvious, in every light, that the people wanted to forget the past; they were looking forward with a serene desire for peace and justice and even for harmonious relationships with the classes which had ill-treated them. The dominating desire of the victors, where social welfare was concerned, was to bring Spain into line with the democratic countries. If we bear in mind its miserable standard of living, the proletariat might well have fallen prey to demagogues or to the parties which were the bitterest enemies of the régime of private property. But the Communists were at that time a party without a following, and it would not be untrue to say that they were unpopular. The Anarchist party, though numerous, was far from counting among its numbers the greater or better part of the proletariat, though, in parenthesis, it may be added that the vigour of this weed indicated an extremely rich and fertile soil which might have borne other fruits had those whose duty it was thought fit to cultivate it. Liberal and evolutionary Socialism counted its adherents even in the poorest hamlets, where, if the Spanish people had not been, in general, reasonable and realistic, ignorance and desperation together would have excluded doctrines of compromise and concord. Clearly, the proletariat aspired to better its lot, but the changes it desired were so slight, so moderate and necessary, that, with impolitic confidence, it took them for granted on the fall of the monarchy. During the first years of the Republic, if we discount the complex agitation of the Anarchists, who had never respected a Government of any colour, there was no conflict or turmoil to indicate a love of revolt, impatience to destroy, or itch for vengeance among the people. The needy classes gave ample credit to the new régime and to the possessors of wealth, hoping that everything would come right without violence or catastrophe. Need

548

we recall that the workers in the populous industrial regions, when apprised of the economic crisis, offered to accept less wages in order not to embarrass the Republic?

But there can be no peace in a nation if the Conservative classes, through natural turbulence or extreme egoism, will otherwise. And the Republic had not been in being for a month, before its enemies the *caballeros*, the cause of the disasters of May 11th, joined issue with it. It was, therefore, in spite of the generous and tranquil disposition of the people that, given the political and social elements or factors which characterized the new situation, tragedy was inevitable. However far-reaching the patience of the masses, their need was so great and the anti-reformist obstinacy of those who should have remedied it so persistent, that in a system which smoothed the path of the wealthy and was slow to give satisfaction to the under-dog, as the constitutional and parliamentary Republic was bound to be, it was difficult to avert civil war. If extraordinary social inequality was not enough, in such conditions, to ensure the worst, the existence of a frivolous and irresponsible class—the most powerful in Spain—whose aim was rather to provoke than to avert bloodshed, guaranteed that there would be no repose or harmony in Spain. This will be seen in the history of the conspiracy, whose genesis and development will be the theme of the present chapter. But first, we must recall the objective historical origins of the civil war.

It is necessary to recall that the Spanish Liberal revolution, in all its protracted and tragic progress, always left the landed aristocracy unharmed and, paradoxically, even favoured it. This social class, thanks to its predominating economic power, came to be the literal nucleus of the modern agrarian oligarchy.

Another point should be noted. In spite of the scruples of the grandees, who were wedded to a mediaeval conception of banking, the nobility ended by merging socially with the principal middle-class financiers of the new vintage, in shareholders' meetings and on the Board of the Bank of Spain; and by granting them titles of nobility, procured for them entrance to their drawing-rooms, a privilege which was never extended to merchants and industrialists, classes which were oppressed by the bankers and despised by the aristocrats and landowners. With such interpenetration, the grandees increased their wealth, which was now not only vested in land, and the bankers added lustre to their houses.

The second Republic underestimated the economic power and the trouble-making capacity of the aristocracy and, by abolishing by decree titles of nobility, thought it had done something of note—the same ingenuousness as characterized the Republicans of 1873. The anxieties of the democrats, then as now, centred upon the clerical problem. According to tradition, it was agreed that the Republic's most formidable enemy was the Church. The so-called Monarchists, a reduced minority, without a future, which could only muster in Parliament fifteen or twenty deputies at the most, were hardly taken into consideration by the Republicans. And yet this class proved to be the greatest hindrance to the consolidation of the Republic, besides proclaiming by its mere existence and its economic hegemony the impossibility of founding a democracy without first depriving the *señores* of their immense power.

By way of illustration, let us imagine how stormy would have been the course of democracy in France, or the Liberal and parliamentary system, if the Revolution had left intact the landed power of the 50,000 parasitic and ungovernable nobles who were disorganizing the country in the eighteenth century (Gibbon, Vol. IV, chap. xliv, p. 404). In the same way, let us imagine the convulsions of English democracy, if the middle classes had not reduced the 200 feudal families (ibid., p. 405) which England possessed at a similar epoch to the decorative rôle of a monument to tradition, daily more burdened by taxation. Nowhere has the revolution of the middle classes been more complete or more perfect than in France; nowhere did the aristocracy suffer such social extermination. And to this is due the *fundamental* equilibrium and solidarity of French political institutions. The English *bourgeoisie*, perhaps because it was much wealthier than the old nobility, had no need to condemn the latter to extreme impotence, and although the middle classes share with the aristocracy the moral and political government of the nation, the last word in British politics lies with the capitalists. Compare the position of the nobility, tributary of the *bourgeoisie*, in these two democracies, with the position of the nobility, oppressor of the *bourgeoisie* and the rest of the nation, in Spain.

As has been said, the Spanish aristocracy adopted from the beginning an attitude of turbulent rebellion towards the Republic. Their incredible pride had suffered an affront which was unbearable to the *caballeros*, all the more so as they saw the monarchy fall without lifting a finger to defend it. But the most important thing was that, under the Liberal and equalitarian Republic, their outrageous economic privileges, already inadmissible, were threatened with extinction. Ever since the

Republic came into existence, the policy of this social class was directed towards the organization of civil war. In love of violence, the aristocracy was outdone by the Carlists or Traditionalists, an ultramontane and theocratic movement, which had always been prepared to wage war on the country in the name of religion. Voltaire had a word for such people when he said: "Celui qui fait la guerre à sa patrie au nom de Dieu est capable de tout."

This social class and this Party of superstition became allies in order to destroy the Republic by force of arms, a mad project which was bound to lead, as eventually it did lead, to a gigantic cataclysm. The history of the anti-Republican conspiracy testifies that they were not at all concerned for the consequences which the design to destroy the Republic, in a struggle with the people, might bring on Spain. The insurgents were impelled by a sort of demoniac fury which led them to prefer a Spain in ruins to the consolidation of the Republican régime. With such a preliminary survey of events which are already familiar to us, we can now pass on to unfold the history of the pertinacious conspiracy which, in spite of momentary setbacks and failures, was never successfully thwarted by the Repúblican Governments, and finally exploded, with irreparable effects for Spain, in July 1936. This work would be incomplete if we did not pay sufficient attention to the spring which poisoned the river.

A few days after the proclamation of the Republic, the Marqués de Luca de Tena, owner of *Prensa Española* and paladin of the aristocracy, visited Alfonso XIII in London. Luca de Tena returned to Spain with certain statements by the dethroned monarch, which were published in *ABC*. This first contact with the King in exile and the publicity given to his remarks, stimulated the Monarchists to fight with tardy resolution for the cause and the person whom before, when it would have been timely, they had no will to defend. To begin with, they decided to found a new party, which was soon in full swing. The headquarters of the new political organization, in the calle de Alcalá in Madrid, were inaugurated, with the consent of the Government of the Republic, on May 10th, 1931. The consequences of having permitted this first Monarchist point of assembly were afterwards to be fatal to the Republic. The aristocratic crowd promoted amazing disorder, which overflowed, through speeches, hymns and acclamations, into the streets. Such rash and daring provocation roused passers-by with contrary views; and the sallying forth of the demonstrators gave the signal for the first clashes between Monarchists and

Republicans. Cars were set on fire, and immediately new crowds collected at the place of the incidents: and knowing the political affiliation of the authors of the outrages, the Republican and working-class public decided to attack the Monarchist paper *ABC*. But the newspaper offices were guarded by detachments of the Civil Guard, who at the sight of the menacing attitude of the crowd, fired on it, wounding some and killing others.

The news of the incident spread rapidly in Madrid and swept the provinces like wild-fire. The people who, as happens in such cases, are welded together more closely by outside provocation, reacted on the following day in various regions by attacking their antagonists and setting fire to churches and convents. This was an unhappy day for the Republic, all the more so since the régime had come into being by such civilized methods.

The Government imprisoned the Marqués de Luca de Tena, who remained in custody for three months.

Thanks to the propagandist weapon which the impotence of the constitutional Government placed in the hands of its enemies, and thanks also to the political liberty which the régime guaranteed to its most recalcitrant opponents, the plutocratic classes re-formed their menacing and dangerous ranks. In a couple of weeks, the aristocratic party, which had only succeeded in scraping together a few thousand pesetas for the last electoral campaign under the monarchy, collected a million and a half pesetas.[1] With this sum, not to be despised for a beginning, the Monarchists really began the organization of the civil war. "They agreed to create a research organization to collect and publish texts from great thinkers on the legality of a rising, and with this object *Acción Española* was founded on December 15th, 1931." They also decided to "prepare the atmosphere in the Army, in which certain generals assisted from the first moment". And lastly, they set themselves to "create a party with full legality, at least apparent, which would justify meetings, subscriptions and a network of subsidiaries".[2]

Having adopted these serious resolutions, the conspirators submitted them to the approval of Don Alfonso. The King, a shrewder politician than the authors of the plans, displayed, it seems, a certain anxiety and tried to restrain the impulsive aristocracy by advising them first to find out what line *Acción Popular* would take. But yielding finally to the insistence of his friends, Don Alfonso sanctioned the proposed programme.

[1] Felipe Bertrán Güell, *Preparación y desarrollo del alzamiento nacional*, p. 82. Valladolid, 1939.
[2] Ibid., p. 83.

We are told that he strongly recommended that the new party should only indulge in such political activity as was necessary to justify its existence, that is, that it should limit itself to preparing the insurrection; but this is hardly credible, since it conflicts with Don Alfonso's political sentiments and contradicts his former reservations.

Independently of the preparations in hand to set up a new oligarchic organization, and before the projects and activities just mentioned had been mooted, the aristocracy had established contact with some of the highest-ranking and most restive of the generals. Not much later than June 1st, 1931, that is, after a month and a half of the Republic, the Monarchists were already approaching, with success, Generals Ponte, Cavalcanti and Orgaz, with whom Señores Vegas, Arcentales, Fuentes Pila and the Marqués de Quintanar, among others, opened negotiations. The interviews took place at the residences of Pardo Bazán and Arcentales at Madrid. The result of these preliminary contacts was that the conspirators journeyed to Santander, Seville and Valencia. In Valencia, they got in touch with the Marqués de Villores; others met abroad.[1] Fascist writers, thinking, no doubt, of the responsibility with which such deplorable citizens would be charged before the bar of history and before Spaniards themselves, have adopted the precaution of pointing out that the conspiracy was being formed "to cope with the possibilities of a Communist movement". This pretext is absolutely devoid of any historical truth, as we know, and is a last-minute addition—which eventually came unstuck—to the primitive edifice of the plot.

On September 29th, 1932, there was another meeting in Paris, this time at the residence of the Vizcondesa de Gironde, where almost all the persons already alluded to met, together with the Marqués de las Marismas, Vigón, Calvo Sotelo, Yanguas Messía, Saínz Rodríguez, Barón de Viver, and others. This aristocratic gathering was likewise presided over by Don Alfonso. The leadership of the new party was entrusted to Don Antonio Goicoechea, and it was resolved "to put into practice the plan agreed upon".

For some weeks the subversive labours of the *caballeros* were interrupted, owing to the fact that Goicoechea, while recrossing the frontier on his way home, was arrested, imprisoned in Madrid and later transferred to an Asturian prison. In November, this personage was set free to continue his political activities, seconded by the Conde de Vallellano, the Marqués de las

[1] Bertrán Güell, p. 84.

Marismas, the Marqués de la Eliseda and Señores Fuentes Pila and Yanguas Messía.

In the meantime the military rising of August 1932 had taken place and failed. General Don José Sanjurjo had led the revolt in Seville, but had had to surrender, as stated in another place, for want of sufficient support even among the enemies of the Republic. This rising went beyond the limits of the absurd, and is thus very revealing of the mentality of the protagonists, besides being not wanting in other interesting aspects.

Sanjurjo was a general without great gifts, less imaginative and intelligent than Primo de Rivera, though, like him, an assiduous worshipper at the shrines of Venus and Bacchus. Soldiers of his temperament, courageous in warfare, ambitious for glory, with a purely superficial conception of patriotism, are easily convinced that Providence has reserved for them a mission to save their country, a flight of fancy which the weakness and corruption of civilian society are wont to encourage wherever such circumstances obtain. Behind each *pronunciamiento* there are always certain social forces which are incapable of imposing their will on society by their moral vigour or by their own political means—forces which, when they are, or call themselves, Conservative, are apt to confound their individual interest with the interest of the nation, or their egoism with justice. Soldiers are slow to throw off discipline and break their oaths of obedience and loyalty. But when he is urged by powerful interests, as in the case of Primo de Rivera, Sanjurjo and Franco; daily surrounded by flattery and servile adulation; his vanity, resentment, ambition and pride continually played upon; hearing for weeks and months on end that public order, and even national salvation, depend on his sword, our soldier ends by agreeing to commit a crime, now clothed with heroism and prowess, which at first blush had perhaps terrified him.

Sanjurjo was not of the stuff traitors are made of, and though a person of little intelligence, understood that to rise against the Republic in 1932 was a stupendous blunder. But the perfidy and avarice of certain powerful Andalusians, who saw themselves already expropriated by the Republican agrarian reforms, launched this impulsive soldier on the adventure of August. Sanjurjo was sacrificed to the pride and ignorance of a class which abominated social justice and supposed that all Spaniards shared their disgust and fear. They thought, this class, that it was enough for a soldier of high rank to order the trumpet to be sounded in half a dozen barracks, for the walls of the Republican Jericho to fall down flat. The August conspiracy was formed, if not by the same persons, by the same Conservative forces which put all their trust in violence; in the first place, the absentee aristocracy and other wealthy landlords, with the soldiers who belonged to these social classes or were the object of their flattery.

That Sanjurjo was sure of his failure, seems to be beyond doubt. His office first as Director-General of the Civil Guard, and afterwards as Director-General of the *Carabineros*, had enabled him to travel all over Spain and acquaint himself with the state of public opinion and opinion in the garrisons; the result was to convince him that the projected rising would not be supported by the Army, let alone the people. This impression Sanjurjo conveyed to his followers.[1]

Nevertheless, the small band of conspirators, particularly the young soldiers and the least scrupulous of the grandees, persisted in trying their fortune. Nothing indicates better the social class which supported the rising than the fact that the generals established their headquarters in Madrid in the house of the Marqués de Molins.

The plan consisted of various concerted *coups de main* by which the insurgents were to seize the Ministry of Communications and the War Office.

At the given hour, there advanced on Madrid a detachment of the *Remonta*, quartered in Tetuán de las Victorias, a regiment, like all the cavalry regiments, whose officers belonged for the most part to the aristocracy. Some of the Army chiefs and officers of the Civil Guard who were leading the insurrection went to the Ministry of Communications, others to the War Office. The couple of Civil Guards who were guarding the Ministry of Communications refused to obey a colonel of the same corps who ordered them to follow him. A few minutes later some detachments of Assault Guards arrived to defend this official centre, which was never at any moment in danger of falling into the hands of the rebels, though it was attacked by the forces of Tetuán de las Victorias.

At the War Office, when the rebels—thirteen in number—arrived at the back entrance of the building, they found to their dismay that the guards who had joined the conspiracy had been changed. A few shots were exchanged and some of the attackers fell.

At nightfall on August 10th, Sanjurjo was still in Madrid. He was ordered to go immediately to Seville, where, he was

[1] Bertrán Güell, p. 90.

told, everything had already been settled. The General refused at first, convinced that the whole affair was a leap in the dark.[1] He tried to persuade his friends that the attempt was premature; but they overwhelmed him with entreaties, and Sanjurjo, perhaps afraid his courage might be doubted, set off by aeroplane for the Andalusian capital, with his son Justo and his adjutant, Lt.-Col. Infantes.

In the morning, the leader of the rebellion arrived at Seville and—much to the surprise, no doubt, of Sanjurjo himself—the city surrendered without a blow—so weak is the civic pulse in the important capital of the regions of the latifundia. The people appeared confused or indifferent; the Army, the Civil Guard, the police, being under the authority of the same persons who had commanded them under the monarchy and the military dictatorship, prepared to accommodate themselves to the new situation. Sanjurjo set up his headquarters on the splendid estate of Señor Esquivel, one of the potentates who supported the rising and a typical representative of his social class. From this residence, surrounded by the rebel Civil Guard, the General launched a manifesto stating that the rising was not directed against the Republic, but against the Government.

But on discovering in Seville that in the rest of Spain nothing was happening, or that where incidents had taken place the Government was master of the situation, the Army changed its tone. Colonel Rodríguez Palanca sent a message to the isolated dictator that the garrison could not support him, and Sanjurjo, seeing that all was already lost, decided to make for the Portuguese frontier with General García de la Herrán, his son Justo and his adjutant. A couple of Security Guards arrested the rebels near Huelva.

The people of Seville came out of their stupor then and rioted, setting fire to the *Círculo de Labradores*, the offices of the newspaper *La Unión*, Esquivel's house, Luca de Tena's house, the *Círculo Mercantil*, the *Unión Comercial*, the New Casino, the Church of San Ildefonso, the *ABC* offices and various other buildings—a popular reaction typical of anarchism.

The Government of the Republic fortunately held in its hands the threads of the August intrigue and adopted precautions which proved effective. But the Government could not spare the régime or Spaniards the contretemps of the insurrection. The Constitution converted Ministers into terrified spectators of perils of this kind. The authorities possessed documents proving that General Barrera, a turbulent and impetuous

[1] Bertrán Güell, p. 92.

soldier, was not only one of the conspirators, but the leader of the conspiracy. The Government ordered his arrest . . . but let us listen to Azaña: "General Barrera was arrested, other gentlemen were arrested, some of whom were imprisoned on the evidence of these same documents; but the judge, rightly, on good grounds, found no evidence of guilt in those papers against General Barrera; he had no evidence, no legal grounds, within the strict letter of the law, to commit General Barrera to trial. Yet it was obvious that everything there set forth referred to General Barrera and it was clear to whoever had read those documents; nevertheless, we had no other course open to us but to set General Barrera at liberty."[1]

And so this soldier was able to continue organizing civil war. On August 10th, when the rising in Madrid was quelled, Barrera went to Biarritz in Ansaldo's aeroplane, from whence he made for Seville to join up with Sanjurjo; but when he arrived, the capital had reverted to the Republic.

The courts condemned Sanjurjo to death, but the Government, in order not to make anti-Republican martyrs, suggested to the President that he exercise clemency and commute the extreme penalty to one of perpetual imprisonment. When he was set free by the amnesty proclaimed by the oligarchic Cortes of 1934, the General who led the August rebellion repaired to Estoril in Portugal and began to prepare a new rising. Before the August disturbances, the conduct of Sanjurjo was foolish and disloyal, since he was in the service of a Republican Government in a post of responsibility; afterwards, seeing that he owed his life to the magnanimity of the Republican Ministers, Sanjurjo exhibited a strange sense of honour, all the more curious in a soldier and hardly consonant with his personal dignity.

The August fiasco did not dissuade the organizers of civil war from their criminal intentions. The only thing they learnt then, with perverse understanding, was "that the country was not yet ready for civil war and that the enterprise lacked, moreover, preparation and atmosphere".[2] They had, therefore, to work on the country more conscientiously, in order to prepare it for the fratricidal struggle by creating the right atmosphere.

With this end in view the aristocratic party, as has been stated, gave itself over to the liveliest activity in Spain and abroad during the second half of 1932.

In 1933 *Acción Española* appeared, a review edited by Ramiro de Maeztu, which fulfilled one of the points of the programme

[1] Speech in the Cortes, Nov. 23rd, 1932.
[2] Bertrán Güell, p. 91.

557

mapped out in 1931 by the Monarchists, establishing the foundation of research organizations "which should collect and publish texts from great thinkers on the legality of a rising". "The year 1933 was a year of great political activity as regards the preparation of the *national movement*."[1] In these months, Don Antonio Goicoechea was appointed representative of the conspirators abroad.[2]

Political agitation in the barracks constituted the second point in the Paris programme. One of the generals undertook to deal with this part of the propaganda: "his discreet and painstaking work resulted in the formation of the *Unión Militar Española* in which numerous officers were enrolled under the supreme command of General Sanjurjo."[3]

The third item of the Paris agreements was put into practice on January 12th, 1933, with the foundation of *Renovación Española* under the leadership of Goicoechea. As we have been told, this organization arose "with full legality, at least apparent, in order to justify meetings, subscriptions and a network of subsidiaries".

Among the most active and dangerous members of the *Unión Militar* was Colonel Varela, Commander of the Cadiz garrison during Sanjurjo's rebellion, and a member of the conspiracy, though he did not then take any active part, probably owing to the rapidity with which the movement was quelled in Madrid and Seville. Varela was, nevertheless, one of the soldiers imprisoned by the Government in August 1932. He was kept a prisoner for eight months in Guadalajara. While there, the indomitable Colonel had frequent conversations with the Carlist chiefs, Conde de Rodezno and Fal Conde. These conversations gave birth to the idea of organizing the Traditionalist youth of Navarre in military formations. Once at liberty, Varela departed for that abrupt and fanatical region, went the round of the villages, and drilled hundreds of peasant youths, mostly in barns, in the art of warfare against the Republic.[4] The Colonel, disguised as a priest or a villager, went from village to village through regions profoundly hostile to the new régime, to Liberalism and to civilization. It was of vital importance to the conspirators to turn the *Requetés* into real soldiers to provide a suitable leaven for the regular troops, on whom they could not depend. Just about this time, the Republic raised Varela to the rank of General (having kept him prisoner for eight months as a public danger), or, at any rate, did nothing to

[1]Bertrán Güell, p. 100.    [3]Id., p. 100.
[2]Id., p. 100.    [4]Id., p. 101.

prevent this imprudent promotion. Varela's subversive activities might now give rise to the deepest suspicions, so it was agreed that Lt.-Col. Rada should take over his work with the Carlist masses. "Many *Requetés* went to Italy and Tunisia to drill and receive instruction in throwing hand-grenades. Arms were bought, the contracts being negotiated abroad, especially at Antwerp, by General Ponte."[1]

As will be remembered, in the summer of 1933 the Republic appeared to be firmly established. The Government had quelled both Sanjurjo's rising and the Anarchists' rebellion at the beginning of the year, without much effort. Agrarian reform, though slow and inadequate to the nation's needs, was making headway, enriched by the properties expropriated from the nobles implicated in the August events. Azaña had restored order in the Treasury, within the old framework. The Army, with fewer divisions, was yet more efficient than under the monarchy. The people's standard of living was higher and the social conflicts were on the way to being solved, thanks largely to the presence in the Government of the Socialists. Would the Liberal and parliamentary Republic be, after all, the final régime in Spain?

Before such a sombre outlook for those who had always believed that the new régime would have short shrift, the disquietude and impatience of Monarchists and plutocrats grew. That summer the perfidious and scandalous campaign against the Government on account of the Casas Viejas atrocities was intensified. The corrupt Republicans made common cause with the aristocracy. The Anarchists declared in the columns of *Solidaridad Obrera* that there would be no peace in Spain while the Socialist dictatorship—as they called Azaña's ultra-parliamentary Government—lasted. New elements, interested in making the bloody struggle inevitable, joined the party of the grandees and the generals. In connection with *Acción Española*, the *O.L.S.A.* was born, a company which, "under the pretext of legal research into the Agrarian Law", was but another centre of great landowners and the lawyers of the great landowners, charged with preparing rebellion. The offices of the *O.L.S.A.* were frequently used as the rendezvous of Señores Goicoechea, Sáinz Rodríguez, Sangróniz, Ruiseñada, Arredondo, José Antonio Primo de Rivera and Conde de Rodezno. At other times the conspirators met at the house of Sangróniz in Madrid, where the generals attended—Varela, Mola, Orgaz and the rest.[2]

[1] Bertrán Güell, p. 101.          [2] Id., p. 101.

Finally, to complete the picture, at the vanguard of the forces which were preparing for the civil war came the Fascist *Falange*, which celebrated its first national conference on October 4th, 1934. It was clear that the leading *cadres* of the *Falange* had been recruited essentially from the same social elements as formed the other anti-Liberal parties, namely the youthful landowners of Andalusia and Castile.

The social hurricane of October passed, leaving Oviedo in ruins, the Republic temporarily defeated, and the agrarian-Catholic party confused. The *caballeros* thought the new régime was finished with. The old classes recovered their ascendancy in the State and over the nation. But none of this influenced adversely the organization for civil war, as we shall see later.

In the summer of 1935, General Aranda, Military Governor of Asturias, ordered military manœuvres to take place in the mining *cuenca*. The manœuvres were attended by the Minister of War, Gil Robles; the Inspector-General of the Army of the North, General Goded; the Under-Secretary for War, General Fanjul, and the head of the General Staff, General Franco. All these generals owed their appointments to Gil Robles. The idea underlying the proposal to hold the manœuvres was to prevent the miners from coming to the future defence of the Republic. "These manœuvres"—we are informed—"were one of the foundation stones of the preparations for the *national* rising."[1]

Other military measures were adopted by the conspirators through the Ministry which was ruled by the *C.E.D.A.* To the north of Madrid, in the sierras which separate the two Castiles, fortifications and breastworks were built, for the occupation of troops coming down from the north, should the blow fail in the capital of Spain. During the civil war, these fortifications proved their worth.

The disquieting turn which national policy was taking during the course of 1935—disquieting, that is, for the interests of the reactionaries—gave an added stimulus to the idea of the *coup d'état*. The aristocratic party proposed to prevent at all costs the exit of the *C.E.D.A.* from the Government or of Gil Robles from the War Office. *Renovación Española* and the generals began, therefore, to organize resistance to a change of policy; but the President of the Republic precipitated the dreaded event, and a meeting convened for December on the estate of General Fanjul near Madrid, at which Goded, Franco and

[1] Bertrán Güell, p. 114.

Varela, among others, were to have been present, could not take place. Gil Robles handed over the Ministry of War to his successor without any untoward incidents. The leader of the *C.E.D.A.* certainly did not think seriously at any time of heading an armed insurrection against the Republic. In the instant to which I refer, he explained his docility, it seems, by saying that he had not enjoyed sufficient support to establish himself strongly in the Ministry. But the truth can be inferred from the attitude which the Catholic party always observed under the Republic, even, as will be shown, after the triumph of the Popular Front— an attitude which was opposed to civil war and military dictatorship, although Gil Robles by his violent speeches and tortuous tactics gave to everyone, friend and foe alike, the opposite impression. The organizers of civil war themselves perceived that the Catholic party "lost no opportunity of seeing whether by legal methods bloodshed might be avoided".[1] This was the principal political difference which separated the two heads of the oligarchy at that moment.

At nightfall on February 17th, 1936, when the defeat of the Right *bloc* became known, Calvo Sotelo invited Señor Portela Valladares, who was still Prime Minister, to come to the Palace Hotel, where a long conference was held, at which the leader of *Renovación Española* urged him, with a dramatic appeal to his patriotism, to hand over the reins of power to General Franco. Portela displayed a certain hesitation, either genuine or feigned, but finally refused to lend himself to such an infamous proposal.

Three days later, on February 20th, the generals and civilian heads of the conspiracy met at various places throughout Spain. They sounded the state of mind in the garrisons which, in view of the popular enthusiasm, did not appear much disposed to support the rising. The Government got wind of these intrigues and decided to remove Franco to the Canaries, Goded to the Balearics, and Mola, who was in command of the African Army, to Navarre.

Just before Franco was due to depart to the Canary Islands, there gathered at Madrid, at the house of the Monarchist deputy Señor Delgado, Generals Franco, Mola (on his way north), Villegas and Varela. During these conversations the meeting confirmed the military plans of the insurgents. It was agreed that each general should rise in the region of his command and should declare martial law; afterwards they should establish communications as circumstances permitted. The next day,

[1] Bertrán Güell, p. 116.

some hours before Franco left Madrid—which he was not to see again until three years later, although he swore he would return whenever circumstances required his presence—he met General Varela in Señor Delgado's car "and in the back of the car, both generals perfected the last details of the preparations for the rising".[1]

In the Canaries, far from the watchful eye of the Government, and near the considerable military contingent in Morocco, the generals' conspiracy pursued its course without the obstacles and setbacks it would have encountered in Madrid. Orgaz, Varela, Fanjul, Villegas, Galarza and Rodríguez del Barrio—the last, Inspector-General of the Army, who presided over the league and brought the voice of Sanjurjo into the discussions— saw each other as frequently as they desired. The military *Junta* which was to organize the civil war was forming—Rodríguez Carrasco, Franco, Saliquet, Goded, Fanjul, Ponte, Varela and Orgaz. Of these, Rodríguez Carrasco, Franco and Goded were in command of troops.

During these weeks, the military *Junta* began to send secret instructions to their fellow-plotters throughout Spain, giving them final directions for the rebellion. These documents are of exceptional interest, particularly the first of the series, because it contains the complete organization of the rising and a clear exposition of its character. Fascism or a Fascist régime are not mentioned once, but only military dictatorship—the goal also of the aristocracy. Paragraph 7 of this circular is also worthy of our attention. "Junior officers who take part in the movement shall be recompensed by immediate promotion, or, if they prefer it, a civil appointment with a salary equivalent to that attached to the promotion offered in recompense. Corporals in similar circumstances shall receive a life pension or recompense in cash, or a suitable civil appointment; the rank and file, security of employment at a remunerative wage, in the provinces where they were born."

What was in course of preparation, then, was the classic absolutist *pronunciamiento*, supported by the most powerful part of the agrarian oligarchy, just as occurred in the nineteenth century, the period in which Spain was still living politically— and this last appreciation of events is borne out by the unrealistic politics of the democrats. The Army was preparing to take the lion's share in the conquest of the country and threatening, if it proved the victor, to acquire highly pernicious dimensions and powers.

[1] Bertrán Güell, p. 124.

The document was dated April 1936, and ordained that everything should be ready and under way within a maximum period of twenty days.[1]

For its part, the aristocratic party did not remain idle. Political agitation, street brawls, acts of terrorism, Press campaigns—all the activities of the *caballeros* were directed, as has been said, to preparing the atmosphere for the dictatorship which the generals were maturing. *Renovación Española*, naturally, had large funds at its disposal, partly acquired abroad; and it is typical of the lack of honour and the exorbitant avarice of the Spanish plutocracy that it should solicit or accept, without real need, the financial help of foreign Governments and parties.

It is useful to record here that Don Antonio Goicoechea had been appointed in 1933 as representative abroad of the Monarchist Party. In this capacity, he signed agreements with the Italian Government which were published in official documents during the course of the civil war. The visit to Mussolini was confirmed by Señor Goicoechea on November 22nd, 1937, in a speech at San Sebastian, in which he declared that he and other Monarchists had been to Italy to obtain, not only the help of the Italian Government, but also that of the Fascist Party, should civil war break out in Spain. José Antonio Primo de Rivera was also received by Mussolini on several occasions.

The conspirators also opened similar, but less barefaced, negotiations with Hitler's Government. These negotiations were carried on with greater discretion, through the belief that the introduction of Germany into Spanish politics might awaken misgivings and alarm in London and Paris which would have more serious consequences. Nevertheless, the visit of General Sanjurjo to Berlin in March or April of 1936 leaked out, and the French Ambassador informed his Government of the fact, adding that Sanjurjo had been cordially received in official circles.[2]

In the meantime, the preparations for the insurrection were forging ahead in the Peninsula. It had already been decided that Franco was to go to Africa, where he was to rise with the Army of Morocco. Mola was to rise in Navarre; General González de Lara, at Burgos; Rodríguez Carrasco in Catalonia; Varela and Orgaz in Madrid, the former to seize the War Office, the latter to take the *Capitania General*. In principle, the date of the

[1] Bertrán Güell, p. 124.
[2] Pertinax, in the *Fortnightly Review*, Aug., 1937.

rising was fixed for April 20th, 1936, by agreement between the generals in Madrid, at a meeting in a house in the *Guindalera*. But two days before, General Rodríguez del Barrio sent for General Varela to come to his house and told him that, owing to certain private reasons, the rising would have to be postponed.

The Government, following up the intrigue, though often losing the scent, once more ordered Varela to Cadiz and Orgaz to the Canaries.

In the face of these new difficulties, the plans of the rebel generals underwent some modifications. Mola was appointed head of the rising, in view of the liberty of movement he enjoyed in Carlist Navarre. In Madrid, Varela and Orgaz were replaced by Generals Fanjul and Villegas. At this moment, the conspirators were joined by Generals Cabanellas and Queipo de Llano, Republicans—at least in name.

As we know, the conspirators appreciated the fact that the rising had little chance of success in Madrid. The military plan was adjusted, therefore, to meet this circumstance: troops from Aragon were to be directed on Madrid through Guadalajara; those from Navarre and Logroño, through Somosierra; those from Burgos and Valladolid, through León and Navacerrada; and those from Valencia, through Tarancón.[1]

In June, Pamplona was already the nerve-centre of the rising and General Mola its chief executor. A constant procession came to interview Mola, among them the Traditionalist deputy Señor Oriol; General Queipo de Llano, who breakfasted one day with Mola in an inn near Irurzún; Kindelán, head of the Air Force; Cabanellas, Fanjul, González de Lara, who was still in command of the Burgos division, though the Government was soon to replace him by the loyal Batet.

The Conde de Rodezno visited Mola in the early days of July and the result of these negotiations was that the *Junta Suprema Nacional del Tradicionalismo*, which had its headquarters in San Juan de Luz, placed at Mola's disposal 7,000 men whom the Carlists were already holding "on a war footing, with arms, equipment and in correct military formations".[2]

Meanwhile, there moved from province to province, maintaining relations between the conspirators themselves and between them and their sympathizers abroad, a multitude of soldiers and civilians—Don Juan Antonio Bravo, Captains Sanjurjo, Fernández de Córdoba, Valdesevilla, Ruiseñada, Larduty, Barrera, Lastra, Vicario. Mola was in constant

[1] Bertrán Güell, p. 127.      [2] Id, p. 129.

correspondence with Sanjurjo, with Franco, and with the *Junta* at Madrid which then consisted of Generals Ponte, Saliquet, Fanjul, Villegas and González Carrasco.

The Fleet, as may be supposed, had its due share in the plot and a visit which Admiral Salas paid to the Canary Islands in the *Jaime I*—an event which attracted attention through the long conversations which the Admiral had with Franco— certainly did not pass unobserved by the Government.

"Just at this time, Calvo Sotelo gave many interviews to various civilians and soldiers."[1] He exchanged impressions with General Villegas who was going to direct the rising in Madrid and who, at the last moment, expressed his lack of enthusiasm. In the house of Don Juan Pujol, Calvo Sotelo talked with Gil Robles and in the Ritz Hotel with Ventosa, from the Catalan *Lliga* and an emissary of Cambó. To all these, the leader of *Renovación Española* gave an account of his labours.[2] Nevertheless, Calvo Sotelo spoke after this manner in the Cortes: "When I hear talk in this Chamber of the danger of Monarchist soldiers, I smile a little, because I believe—and you will not deny me a measure of moral authority to formulate this belief— that there does not exist at this moment in the Spanish Army, which respects the Constitution whatever individual political ideas may be, a single soldier disposed to rise in favour of the monarchy and against the Republic. If such a one there was, I say with all frankness that he would be a madman or an imbecile; though I consider that that soldier would also be mad who, in the face of his destiny, would not rise in favour of Spain and against anarchism, if this were to appear."[3] A masterpiece of dissimulation!

It is not a light task to read the mind of Gil Robles on the eve of the military rising. Probably he himself did not know where his interests lay in that instant. Had he wavered in his opposition to the use of force, when he saw the horizon of the Republic closed to his party? A great part of the youth of *Acción Popular* had passed over to the ranks of the *Falange*, in disgust with the vague and indecisive policy of Gil Robles. The last time that the leader of the *C.E.D.A.* openly and resolutely resisted those who were trying to urge him along the path of fratricidal violence was shortly after the victory of the Popular Front, the moment that the generals and the aristocratic party, with singular lack of judgment, thought opportune for a rising.

[1] Bertrán Güell, p. 130.     [3] Speech on June 16th, 1936.
[2] Id., p. 130.

No doubt, the Vatican feared civil war in Spain and was opposed to the Catholic party beginning it.[1]

As regards the *Falange*, when José Antonio Primo de Rivera was imprisoned in Alicante—a circumstance which did not entirely prevent him from taking a hand in the conspiracy—the party was deprived of its most active and authoritative member. The *Falange* was not a danger to the Republic, except as an agent of disorder and turbulence. In Madrid it could only number 2,000 men[2], under the leadership of Fernández Cuesta, whom the Government set at liberty on July 4th, at a moment which certainly could not have been more awkward for the régime. But on the 11th, so inconsequent were the police methods imposed by the Constitution, which its enemies were always able to outflank, that he was back again in prison.

Several times General Mola fixed a date for the outbreak of hostilities, the initiative for which lay with the conspirators in the confusion which tied the Government's hands. Several times the blow had to be postponed. But in the end Mola ordered the chief conspirators to be each at his post, awaiting the agreed signal, on July 15th. The assassination of Calvo Sotelo accentuated the nervous impatience of the rebels, some of whom began operations on their own account; and Mola could no longer delay the outbreak of civil war. All the preparations had been perfected down to the last detail, as is only possible when he who makes them is in possession of the field. The insurrection was to begin in Morocco. Queipo de Llano was to go to Andalusia; Cabanellas was to operate in Saragossa; Saliquet in Valladolid; González Carrasco in Valencia; Goded in Catalonia, having exchanged with the latter; Fanjul in Madrid, through the withdrawal of Villegas; Mola in Navarre and Burgos, and Franco in Africa.

[1] Henry Buckley has given us interesting information about the attitude of Gil Robles during the agitated days of February: "I had rushed to Robles' home on the day following elections to obtain an interview. His secretary showed me into a salon and then went back into an inner room, where he had some visitors whom I could not see and to whom he spoke in quite a loud voice. He said: 'Yes, last night the Monarchists tried to persuade our Chief (he meant Robles) to join in a *coup d'état* to forestall the results of the elections and to prevent the Left from reaching power, as it was clear that they would do, judging even by the early voting returns. Our Chief was furious. He refused point-blank. He told them that they were irresponsible and quite mad to suggest such a thing and that neither he nor his party would consider participation in such a wild adventure.' At this point, the secretary suddenly realized that he had forgotten to close the door and he hurried across the room and slammed it shut" (*Life and Death of the Spanish Republic*, p. 195).

[2] Bertrán Güell, p. 135.

On July 16th Mola informed José Antonio Primo de Rivera that he had fixed the rising for the 18th 19th and 20th.[1] And, in fact, on July 18th, General Franco broadcast to Spaniards from Tetuán, announcing the insurrection. "Spain has saved herself", he declared. "You may be proud to be Spaniards." Tragic words, in truth, which were soon to have a ring of sarcasm.

## CHAPTER XX

## THE CIVIL WAR

DON JUAN: Every idea for which man will die will be a Catholic idea. When the Spaniard learns at last that he is not better than the Saracen, and his prophet no better than Mahomet, he will arise, more Catholic than ever, and die on a barricade across the filthy slum he starves in, for universal liberty and equality.

BERNARD SHAW, *Man and Superman.*

THE REBELS COUNTED on a short war. The confusion and disorder prevailing in the democratic camp, the mutual suspicion between the parties, the hostility between the leaders, the indiscipline of the masses, the weakness of the Government —all led them to believe that the rebellion would not encounter any serious obstacle. The generals had the support of powerful social classes, and on the military plane they would have at their disposal, at a reasonable calculation, two-thirds of the Army officers, the Fleet and the Civil Guard, two Moroccan divisions, the foreign *Tercio* and the fanatical *Requetés*. It is not surprising that in view of the considerable forces they disposed of, the generals and the aristocracy should reckon the Republic already defunct or Spain—in their own words—saved, from the very minute the rising began. In thirty days at the most, they thought, the enemy would be dispatched. Two weeks, perhaps, separated Franco from Madrid. When the Emperor Charles V invaded France, he asked a prisoner how many days' journey Paris was from the frontier. "Twelve, perhaps, but they will be days of fighting", replied the French patriot. The Spanish insurgents were to find the same thing. Their contempt for the people led them to ignore the formidable energy and political maturity of the Spanish proletariat and they did not stop to consider that the discord among the democratic parties might, in no small measure, have sprung from and been nourished by

[1] Bertrán Güell, p. 136.

the lack of a clear common objective. This, the rebellion created. The people rose as one man against the rebels, and the reconciliation of the factions in the street immediately imposed upon the leaders forgetfulness of the past. Not only the immediate past of Spanish democracy, but also the present miseries, inseparable from any war and aggravated by the unavoidable injustices of revolution, were already melting away in the fire of popular heroism.

The lack of weapons of war from which Spain suffered, due to the backwardness of the nation, led naturally to a display of great virtues by the people. Individual man, natural man, still counted in Spain. Six months afterwards, he was to count less, because the war would be waged on modern methods, when, with foreign aid, mechanized warfare superseded the period of street barricades. But in the meantime, the proletariat of Madrid and Barcelona did memorable things and saved the Republic. These signal successes claim our attention here, but first we must glance for a moment at political events of a very different character.

On July 18th, the imminence of the Army rising in Spain was beyond a doubt. It was expected that the Government would authorize the distribution of arms among the parties of the régime. The people waited in the streets, in nervous expectation, their eyes fixed on those places where their own destiny and the fate of the Republic were being decided. The barracks were besieged, rather than watched, by crowds who from a discreet distance followed in suspense the movements and sounds of the troops. The Ministers were continually besieged by the workers' leaders, who urged them to adopt, without loss of time, resolutions of a gravity to match the situation. In this state of tension, alarm and peril, which predisposed the people to desire rather than fear a definite encounter with the enemy, Spaniards heard the announcement, in the early hours of July 19th, of the formation of the Martínez Barrio Government—a Government charged with capitulation. Panic-stricken by the course of events, Azaña and the *moderate* Republicans—the Republicans who handed over the Republic to the reactionaries in 1933—resolved to attempt a reconciliation with the generals in the Peninsula who were on the point of rallying to Franco.

The new Cabinet was seeking an impossible compromise. Neither Azaña nor the *respectable* Republicans had, it seems, realized, or would ever realize, the nature of the men and social classes with whom the Republic had to deal. Above all, they did not grasp the fact that the misfortunes which were over-

568

whelming them at that moment had originated precisely in the pusillanimity of the Republican politicians; and now they proposed to crown the tragedy with another show of civic cowardice, with a lame and bungling policy, as impracticable as it was dishonourable. At bottom, the unfortunate Martínez Barrio solution did not so much derive from a middle-class policy which was fearful of the proletariat, as obey a tradition of moral timidity, which led this kind of Republicanism always to compromise in fundamental things. The most illustrious Republicans certainly had not known how to be on their guard against enemy propaganda, or against the siren songs of class prejudice; nor had they understood that the insurrection which had just broken out had begun to be organized in 1931. In their inmost heart they were convinced that the rebellion had been provoked by Marxism. And perhaps Azaña thought that history had reserved for him the unhappy role of the Spanish Kerensky. All this was stuff and nonsense. There were no Bolshevists in Spain and no Lenin; nor could a Lenin have attempted in Spain what he succeeded in doing in Russia, nor did the Spanish proletariat want anything else but that the Republicans should govern with a firm hand and carry out the revolution to which their political ticket and their speeches committed them.

The absence of firmness, the facile immolation of principles, the flight from national realities—all these faults of the democratic parties had led the Republic to the present abyss, and now they were going to put it out of its misery, with the same fatal sense of duty, by offering the insurgents a share in the Government and Mola the Ministry of War. A spectator might have cause to wonder whether there were not more honour and more loyalty to principles, even if less sense of justice and less patriotism, on the other side. Not without dignity did Mola reply to Martínez Barrio: "If you and I were to seal a bargain, we should both have betrayed our ideals and our men. We should both deserve to be lynched."[1]

Fortunately the Republican working-man understood matters differently. After their past experiences, the people held the profound conviction that in a Spain which burned to regenerate herself, there was no margin for amity with the social classes which had organized the civil war—classes with no notion of the public interest, which preferred the nation to go under rather than lose one jot of their century-old privileges.

The Republic would defend itself, thanks to the popular

[1] Bertrán Güell, p. 76.

integrity; but as a symptom, the Martínez Barrio Government denoted an alarming state of mind in the high places of the régime. Neither the decisive reply of the insurgents to these first tentative approaches—unconditional surrender of the Republic—nor the, in this respect, instructive development of the conflict, could ever persuade certain persons and parties that the Spanish Republic no longer had any option save to resist; that capitulation would not avoid bloodshed, or misery, or grief, but that its consequences might well surpass in gravity the disasters of war; and that, even if this important battle were lost, the salvation of the Republic lay in substituting for a policy of compromise, of not knowing what to do with the régime or its enemies, another policy of clear-cut proposals, knowledge of national problems and incorruptible resolution in execution.

What is certain is that on July 19th a faint-hearted and mistaken attitude to the civil war was already creeping into the most influential circles of the Republic and that this error, if it were favoured by circumstances during the course of the conflict, might prove fatal to Spanish democracy.

The people received the Government of the utopian compromise with such manifestations of disgust and reprobation that the authors of the initiative had to awaken to realities. Don José Giral, a man better endowed for private than for public life, formed another Ministry, with Republican generals in the key Departments. A Republican Government, moderate and all the rest of it, so that neither the rebels nor the chancelleries should take fright! Unfortunately, in the eyes of the rebels and the chancelleries, the inoffensive Señor Giral was as Marxist as Dimitrov. Little or nothing was gained abroad by this farce and much was lost at home in impetus, efficacy and authority.

The formation of the Giral Government coincided exactly with the beginning of the rebellion in the Peninsula. At daybreak in Barcelona the disloyal regiments started to march on a city which seemed to repose in confidence, though it was not asleep.

The moral temper of the populace, whose theme was the spirited and expressive "They shall not pass!" augured the certain failure of the rising in Madrid. The surprise factor had disappeared since the start of the rebellion in Africa. The precautions adopted by the Government in the capital of the Republic were adequate to the danger. Government offices were closely guarded and protected by barricades and sandbags. From the early hours of Sunday, the militia went the rounds of the city in taxis or other vehicles or stationed themselves in front of Government buildings waiting for news and arms, while the danger spots were patrolled by the police. The barracks were closely guarded from outside.

"On Monday", wrote Carlyle of the Paris which was about to storm the Bastille, "the huge city has awoke, not to its week-day industry: to what a different one! The working man has become a fighting man; has one want only: that of arms". July 19th, 1936, was not a Monday, but a Sunday; and for the Spanish people it was not a feast-day that dawned, but a day of very different emotions, and like the people of Paris, they had only one want—arms.

It is not part of my design to write the history of the civil war, if by that is meant a day-to-day narrative of the tremendous events which unfolded in Spain in the thirty-three months during which the Republic put up an organized resistance to the aggression of the rebels and their foreign allies. But I cannot omit from these pages such significant and memorable events as the days of July in Madrid and Barcelona.

Some skirmishing, on the usual lines, between the militia and the Fascists, firing from rooftops and sometimes apparently from churches, announced the outbreak of hostilities in Madrid. The people stormed the political centres of the reactionaries and began once more burning churches and convents. While this was going on, the artillery regiment at Getafe rose and bombarded the neighbouring aerodrome; but after a bloody and stubborn struggle with the loyal Air Force, the Civil Guard and the workers' militias, it had to surrender. The fusion of the Civil Guard and the people in the same cause was a new and significant spectacle, not without its moving side.

The barracks of the Pardo Engineers remained deserted; the officers had led the troops northwards, in search of Mola. Among these soldiers went the youngest son of Largo Caballero.

In the Pacífico, part of the garrison supported Franco and furious fighting took place; but in a few hours the Government forces had suppressed this focus of rebellion. Obviously, the exaltation of the people had a positive effect upon forces like the Civil Guard which would have joined the rebels had they not found themselves surrounded by an atmosphere of enthusiasm and heroism which, like all the passions, are contagious.

The flight of the Pardo regiment was a proof of the sceptical view the rebels took of Madrid. Madrid was the hardest nut the rebels had to crack. It is difficult, if not impossible, to understand why, when the task of conquering the capital of the Republic called for the energies, courage and authority of the best leaders of the plot, the conspirators should have delegated this enterprise first to Villegas, who had sense enough to resign, and then to Fanjul, a general with none of the soldier in his make-up, and so little intelligence, or so timorous or self-effacing, that he did not know how to refuse a commission which everyone else rejected out of hand.

Because of its special characteristics—a vast thick-walled building set on a hill, a few steps from the centre of Madrid—the Montaña barracks, which were in the hands of the insurgents, might have constituted a serious menace to the Republic. Like all the rest, this military centre was closely guarded by the militia. The Government were well aware of the dubious allegiance of the Montaña officers, but, as in the other cases, their policy was to leave the initiative to the enemy and not to go out and meet the danger for fear of making the situation worse.

Consequently, by midday on Sunday, an excited crowd of officers from other regiments, aristocrats and young Fascists, besides some of the commanding officers of the troops garrisoned there, were able to gather in these barracks. From here the principal offensive against the vital organs of the Republican State was to be launched, led by General Fanjul. But the General kept his followers waiting longer than their patience could hold out, long enough to imperil the success of the enterprise, and did not put in an appearance until the early afternoon. Even then, he wasted valuable time in needless speeches and harangues, in declaring martial law, in announcing the establishment of the military dictatorship and in other prolegomena of a political nature. The late afternoon was the moment chosen by the rebels to sally forth into the streets. The barracks were more closely besieged then than at any time before, and the swarms of people in the streets nearby made it a certainty that the rebels would be confronted by an indomitable human mass when they broke out of the fortress.

As the afternoon wore on, the rebels decided not to abandon the barracks, preferring to open hostilities with a burst of rifle and machine-gun fire. This ill-advised aggression was the call to arms which conjured up the resistance of the crowds outside and gave the signal for the beginning of the siege. Firing then became general and both sides prepared to give battle—the one protected by the thick walls of the barracks, the other sheltering in buildings and round corners or taking cover in trees and behind barricades. The Government had at length distributed such light arms as it possessed and the militia was better equipped for fighting; but the number of complete rifles that were service-

572

able was small, since there were, in fact, in the Montaña barracks 50,000 or 60,000 rifle bolts—a circumstance which increased the urgency for the Republicans to extinguish this focus of rebellion.

It was obvious that the insurgents had opted for the defensive. They lacked the resolution to challenge the people in the streets and shut themselves in behind walls, thinking perhaps that other seditious forces would arrive in time to raise the siege. But help did not arrive; and the Assault Guards and the people's militias, swiftly reinforced by new groups of armed workers and by loyal Army officers, would have sufficed to disperse the troops had they attempted to break out. Before this Bastille an infuriated people surged, the desperate mob of every authentic revolution, the under-dogs, equipped with every kind of curious weapon. To complete the comparison with the unforgettable assault on the Parisian fortress, there only lacked, perhaps, the triumphal arrival of the 75-mm. gun, which came on the scene with an enthusiastic escort of young and old, sister procession to the crowds which dragged the cannon of the King of Siam.

The arrival of the artillery reinforced the siege of the insurgents. The street attacked with two 75-mm. and one 155-mm. gun, with machine-guns, rifles and pistols. A powerful loudspeaker on the Government side called on the soldiers to desert. Two armoured cars patrolled the square. The barracks replied with light artillery fire, mortars, machine-guns and rifles. But the situation at Getafe and Cuatro Vientos having returned to normal, the loyal Air Force began to drop leaflets summoning the rebels to surrender and threatening bombardment from the air.

At the end of Sunday, the situation of the besieged was desperate, but they continued to resist. At dawn they rejected an ultimatum, and the Republican airmen bombarded the barracks.

Monday morning was well advanced, when a white flag was seen at one of the windows; the Republicans ceased fire and the militia attempted to approach the fortress. A burst of machine-gun fire brought them up short and there were some casualties. Probably some soldiers had wanted to surrender without the knowledge of their officers. This incident was repeated twice more during the course of the day, exasperating the besiegers, many of whom lacked arms and counted on obtaining them from the rebels.

The Republican officers deplored the spirited rashness of their warlike and indisciplined troops. They ought to let the

573

artillery and the Air Force, they said, force the enemy to surrender. But neither the caution of the professional soldiers nor military science could restrain the impulsive and foolhardy resolution of the people, who, pushing aside their leaders, launched themselves with their precarious armaments on the assault of the barracks. The morale of the rebels was badly shaken. The attacks from the air had unnerved them. The incessant bombardment, the isolation of their position, the demoralization of the troops, showed them already the uselessness of continued resistance.

The militia rushed the barracks. The first rank of attackers fell to the bullets of the enemy—for the masses behind, the danger had already passed.

Few of the besieged escaped with their lives. Some committed suicide, others were killed by the invaders. General Fanjul was rescued with difficulty by the officers of the Assault Guard, who thrust him hurriedly into an armoured car.

Such was the historic assault on the Montaña barracks by the people of Madrid, an exploit which was darkened by tragedy no less horrifying because it was foretold in that sentence which warns us that as we have sown, so shall we reap, as Haman expired on the gallows he had himself erected for Mordecai.

Madrid was awakening slowly from her long and oppressive nightmare. In the capital, the enemy was disorganized and beaten. But for all that, the danger had not passed. Mola was coming down unhindered from the north, over the broad table-land, with 10,000 men, abundant artillery and some aeroplanes. To the cry of "A la Sierra!" the people of Madrid rushed tumultuously to the encounter. In all kinds of vehicles—taxis, lorries, omnibuses, requisitioned private cars—the proletariat, without officers, almost without arms, sped along the roads connecting Madrid with the north. The insurgents had occupied the Alto del León, astride the two Castiles, and had spread out over the breastworks and trenches constructed in the period when Gil Robles was head of the Ministry of War. From these camouflaged positions, they mowed down the crowds which rushed on them blindly, rashly determined to scale the heights. Some militiamen penetrated into enemy territory and continued the advance at the risk of being cut off; others flung themselves on the enemy machine-gun posts; others finally climbed without opposition to places where, thanks to their intrepid enthusiasm, the Republic would soon hold firm bastions. At some points, Mola's forces had to give way, the rebels perceiving at once

574

that they had to deal, so to speak, with the people who discomfited Napoleon.

The Alto del León remained, not without dispute, in the power of the enemy, but the Republican flag waved over the other heights of the Guadarrama. Two columns of militiamen had crossed the Sierra; one with Segovia as its objective, the other making for Avila, which it came within sight of. But it had to turn back for fear of being cut off.

Meanwhile other columns of volunteers, mingling with the Civil Guard and Assault Guards, had broken out of Madrid at various points of the compass. On the road to Saragossa, the militia entered Alcalá de Henares, advanced on Guadalajara, which was holding out bravely against the insurgents under the command of the turbulent General Barrera, who was shot there. Having taken this place, the militia went on to Sigüenza, captured it for the Republic, and continued as far as the border of Aragon.

The people themselves suppressed the Toledo rising, but the rebels, working on a preconceived plan, took refuge with women and children in the impregnable Alcázar, where subsequently scenes took place which might have come straight out of Dante's Inferno.

Madrid, with its broad romantic girdle of mountains, belonged at last to the Republic. The noble people of Madrid and the loyal forces had achieved victory over the insurgents in the most critical days of the régime. And from Barcelona and other provinces came encouraging news. The popular epic of Madrid was not to be an exception.

In the early hours of July 19th, the rebel regiments in Barcelona opened fire on the patrols of the Assault Guards. The troops garrisoned in Pedralbes advanced towards the Plaza de la Universidad and the Plaza de Cataluña, probably with the idea of joining up with the troops from the Atarazanas barracks, which, if they were to go up by the Rambla and establish contact with this column in the heart of the capital, would make the defence overwhelmingly difficult because the Republic had not equivalent means of combat at its disposal there. But the rebel officers of the Atarazanas garrison stood on the defensive, and protected (like the Military Governor's Office and, to a certain extent, the *Capitanía General*, whence Generals Goded and Burriel and Captain López Varela directed the rising) by a machine-gun which the rebels had placed on the Columbus Monument, they expected, no doubt, to hold this important district.

The Civil Guard remained loyal to the Republic, like the Assault Guard. These forces steadfastly beat off the first attacks of the rebels and, supported by the militia, engaged the troops to good effect in the calle de las Cortes and before the University. They could not, however, prevent the Army with its artillery from reaching the Plaza de Cataluña, and occupying the Telephone Exchange, among other buildings of military importance. But by occupying the Plaza de Cataluña and establishing themselves there, the rebels exposed themselves to a siege. The column was fired on from the adjacent streets and the soldiers defended themselves by bombarding the buildings with 75-mm. guns and raking the approaches with machine-gun fire.

Meanwhile, summoned by the sound of battle and the common danger, the proletariat hastened from the Barceloneta and the populous dock areas towards the Plaza de Cataluña. A machine-gun, placed at a street-corner, opened fire on the crowds, but the militiamen in their turn, taking cover behind trees or doors, held up for five precious hours the advance of the army of Pedralbes towards Atarazanas and the *Capitanía General*.

At this point in the conflict, the scene was already dominated by the impetuous people of Barcelona, who, without distinction of age or sex, surged through the streets with a frenzy that was epic in its heroism. Courage is as contagious as fear, that other extreme of mass psychology, and there is no human power which can resist a mob in heroic vein. Once the instinct for self-preservation has given place to enthusiasm, nothing is impossible for the masses. Danger draws crowds like a magnet, sacrifice brings out the best instincts of the human race, and the mob sweeps on with the irresistible grandeur of a natural force. In these conditions, a revolution is like a tempest; everything is swept away before it. Confronted with the frenzied proletariat of Barcelona, the military plans of the rebels were bound to fail; and they did fail. It was impossible to wage war in a great city with an enemy whose ignorance of the rules of warfare led him into incredible and unexpected audacities. Men of the people took with their bare hands machine-gun posts which had seemed impregnable, militarily unassailable. By astonishing methods, the mob seized several guns and were soon bombarding the Telephone Exchange and the *Capitanía General*.

The weakest flank of the rebellion, the lack of popular support, was immediately apparent in Barcelona, as in Madrid. As soon as opportunity occurred, the soldiers passed over to the Republican ranks and fraternized with the militia. The morale of the troops was frankly low.

At midday on Sunday, furious fighting was going on at various points of the capital. But the insurrection had received its death-blow.

On Monday morning, the *Capitanía General* was heavily bombarded and stormed by the militia. Most of the officers in the entourage of the leader of the rising were killed. Goded escaped with his life, for the moment. Conducted to the *Generalidad*, he broadcast an appeal to his friends to surrender, saying that Fate was against them. Goded was a brave man, but an inveterate conspirator.

It only remained to suppress the rebellion in the Atarazanas barracks. The militia decided to storm the place, and mounting two machine-guns on a lorry, they launched an attack on the huge entrance door, in a do-or-die attempt. The insurgents, paralysed, surrendered.

On July 19th the Spanish people saved the Republic, not for the last time. They saved it by sheer heroism and sacrifice, as we have seen. No doubt, the other side also had its heroes and patriots, but they were the tools of an oligarchy which had been demonstrably perverse, and the ideas behind the rebel movement had proved, in the light of reason, to be pernicious. The people were fighting for bread and education, for liberty—even for their enemies!—but, above all, for their life, since the insurgents were trying to exterminate them. The generals and the aristocrats were fighting to perpetuate hunger and ignorance, to subordinate civil society to brute force, to the Army; to ensure licence for the powerful and slavery for the weak. The Republic had never menaced their physical existence as they were menacing that of the people. Fanaticism or blind superstition might inspire some of the rebels with a longing for martyrdom or glory; but history shows, as we have seen, that a degenerate oligarchy may know how to die—a circumstance which does not diminish, but rather augments its potentialities as a source of danger, since it brings to the defence of cruel inequalities, corruption, obscurantism and despotic power, impulses worthy of a nobler cause. In short, abnegation and altruism in a civil war must be appraised in the light of the ideal in whose service they are displayed; and the ideal of the insurgents was fatal to Spain.

Once the military rising in Madrid and Barcelona had been suppressed, the civil war entered upon a new phase in the Republican zone. The revolution which should have occurred in the nineteenth century, or at least in 1931, was on the march. The aristocrats and the generals were responsible for an upheaval which the Republicans had done their best to prevent. The

Ts

rebels had destroyed the remains of the old institutions. They had disbanded the Army. They had broken up the State. They had annihilated the old order. What remained of the pseudo-constitutional monarchy and of the Republic of the lawyers disappeared in a matter of hours in the formless mass of the useless, the utopian and the unreal. The future constitution of the Spanish nation was being *born*, not written in the political arena as in 1931. Society's instinct for self-preservation was seeking an outlet to the new day or the new era. Through the smoke of the temples, and the hail of bullets and the death-rattle of anarchy, painfully, dramatically, another society was coming to birth.

But while the new constitution or the new State was forming in the womb of society, chaos was abroad. Spain—half of Spain, that is—was making her long-deferred French Revolution. The people of Madrid and Barcelona fought like the people of Paris at the close of the eighteenth century. Fundamentally, Spain was living in that epoch. What mattered the distance between one age and another? The social classes which attacked the Republic entertained ideas which philosophers had denounced two centuries ago. And what if this age is the Age of Industry? The Spanish people defended themselves against the rebellion with their bare hands, with pikes and staves, with the tools of their trade or with arms as primitive as those with which the Parisians stormed the Bastille. The theory that in our time a revolution cannot be made with barricades turned out to be inapplicable to the Spain of 1936. The size and intrepidity of the mob kept the arm of the State, the Army, at bay.

All revolutions have much in common, but the Spanish revolution of 1936 was surprising in its curious similarity, both in nature and form, to the French Revolution. The Spanish proletariat bore a marked resemblance to the French proletariat of a century and a half ago. Its mentality was the same; the historical problem it was trying to solve was the same. Foreign intervention in Spain provoked the same rampant nationalism among the people. Madrid and Barcelona and Valencia saw their "infernal columns", and their *Armée révolutionnaire* (expert in unseating the Catholic religion) set out under the command of their Durrutis and Ascasos, counterparts of the Rossignols and Ronsins. (Ronsin admitted candidly that his troops were "the elixir of the Rascality of the earth".) Madrid was to have her November massacres, as Paris had her September massacres, "in other words, the rough justice of the people". And there was to be a "carmagnole complète", especially in Barcelona;

a revolutionary carnival or lupercalia of democracy, such as only occurred during the French Revolution. A Bacchanal of masked men, their faces disguised behind a thirty days' growth of beard; anti-clerical necromancy dancing round the bonfires of missals and soutanes, with real mummies in attendance, and in the belfry a madman furiously sounding the alarm. A Last Judgment, a warning, perhaps, that the Rights of Man are not lightly mocked.

Such were the consequences of the attempt to put an end to disorder by civil war.

In what may be defined as its national phase, the civil war took a bias definitely favourable to the Republic and the revolution. The greater part of the Air Force and most of the Fleet remained in the service of the régime. The legitimate Government held Madrid, Catalonia, all the Levante coast, Murcia, Almería, Jaén, Malaga, part of Estremadura, Ciudad Real, Toledo (with the rebels in the Alcázar), Guadalajara, Cuenca, Bilbao, San Sebastian, Santander, Asturias (except Oviedo). It seemed beyond doubt that the conflict, though widespread and bitter, would end in the defeat of the rebels. Yet, as is well known, the end was very different, a matter that we shall study later on. But first, I think it is of interest to call the reader's attention to a phenomenon which is, to my mind, of enormous significance, although it may only be apparent to those who probe to the very core of the disaster.

This phenomenon was the nation's unequal response to the rising of the oligarchies. In a matter of a few days, Spain split up into rebel territory and loyal territory. Two Spains, each hating the other, were locked in combat. But not the two metaphysical Spains discovered by the Liberals, originating, as they thought, in the Catholic sovereigns or Philip II; not Catholic Spain and Liberal Spain. The two Spains which were tearing each other to pieces were the Spain that was sick, where the structure of property and the character of economic life were concerned, and the Spain that was healthy. The Republic held the two industrial and commercial regions of the north; Asturias and the Basque coast; all the east below Catalonia as far as Almería and Malaga; and Madrid with the part of Castile it dominates. The industrial and commercial regions, the regions of the middle class and modern proletariat, rose then, spontaneously, for the Republic.

On the other side, the insurgents made themselves master with hardly any opposition (which makes the opposition they did encounter all the more honourable and heroic), of the whole of the Spain which was socially sick—of Galicia and Castile with their miserable smallholdings, of Andalusia and Estremadúra with their latifundia. This is, of course, on general lines.

This peculiar division of the country into rebel and loyal, absolutist and Liberal, even were it not so nicely adjusted to social conditions, certainly affords, in my opinion, the most profound historical lesson to be learned from the civil war. It uncovers the root of the national problem of our days and confirms the fact that a Republic or a parliamentary democracy can only flourish where the middle classes predominate, preferably in regions where industry and commerce are fairly well developed. The moral is obvious—just as the *bourgeois*, Liberal or middle-class Republic could not take hold in the regions of the latifundia and minifundia, so absolutism is a plant which does not flourish in Madrid or the Levante or the larger cities of the north, even though these may be Catholic.

That we are confronted with two Spains is evident. Not, however, the Spain of the priests and the free-thinkers, but the Spain whose civic life has been stifled, mediaeval, ecstatic, hating novelty, without commerce with Europe, the Spain of Galicia, Burgos, Salamanca, Pamplona, Seville, Cadiz, etc.; and modern Spain, eager for progress, dynamic, loving novelty, open to the currents of European thought, the Spain of Madrid, Barcelona, Valencia and Bilbao. Half of Spain has progressed; the other half has stagnated; and that is why what might, until the nineteenth century, have been the tragedy of an enlightened minority because the whole nation was equally backward, today expands and resolves itself into a geographical and economic tragedy. The conflict between the two Spains did not really exist until our time. What the Liberals call the two Spains lacked before a geographical expression; in reality, there were not two Spains. On the one hand, there stood the bulk of the nation; on the other, an intellectual élite. Strictly speaking, there were not two nations as such, but an agrarian and superstitious Spain overshadowing a small group of philosophers and humanists without influence over the people or over any social class. The only social class capable of understanding the ideas of the Renaissance, the *bourgeoisie*, did not exist in sixteenth-century Spain, as I have pointed out in the Introduction.

Today, the problem is different. One Spanish hemisphere still lives in the Middle Ages, the other has advanced politically and morally as far as the nineteenth century. Today, Spain really is divided in two. Two systems of land tenure, two economic worlds, two moral and political tendencies which can only blend with difficulty. In contact with the sea, with industry, and with the outside world, the Basque and the Catalan, who until yesterday were Carlist, have embraced religious toleration. Far from the sea, the factories and commerce, the Navarrese and the Castilian continue to abominate liberty and civilization; the Galician, caught in the net of the smallholdings, cannot defend them; and the Andalusian, serf of seigneurial property and humbled by hunger, falls an easy victim to the oligarchy. It is not religion which divides Spain today into, roughly, absolutist and republican, but the conditions of life, every day more divergent, of the two nations, economically speaking. The reaction of each zone to the outbreak of the civil war, the facility with which the Republic lost the west, the north-west and the south, and the rapidity with which the rebels were driven back in the north, the Levante, and in Madrid, emphasize precisely the same incompatibility which led to the explosion of 1936. The effect shows us the cause. And the inference is this: the Republic never existed in the Spain of the latifundia and of the minutely parcelled lands. That Spain not only professed, but was bent on achieving, a régime of absolute monarchy; while the Spain of the great cities, of commerce and industry, held firm to the Republic, which was not only the régime it desired, but also, naturally, the one best suited to its interests.

The situation which arose at the beginning of the civil war and split the nation imperatively into two halves—the agrarian and anti-Liberal, poor in urban centres; and the mercantile, industrial and middle class, represented by the most important cities—is only, in its bare essentials, a more obvious reproduction of the phenomenon which occurred in the elections of April 1931, in consequence of which the Republic was proclaimed. Then, the countryside voted for the continuation of the monarchy; and now it agreed, in the part where it did not rise, in allowing the Republic to perish. The new régime would have had to introduce almost cosmic changes in the regions which were constitutionally sick—formidable transformations in the nation's economy and in the system of agrarian property—if it was to make itself as acceptable and adequate to pastoral and rural Spain as it already was to urban Spain.

# FOREIGN INTERVENTION

IT WILL BE perceived, from the foregoing chapter, that the insurgents were in a desperate situation. They were rising against the State—an always risky enterprise—they had the people against them, and, to complete their discomfiture, the country's important industry, an indispensable factor in war, was located in regions which remained under the legitimate Government. In the first weeks of the civil war, the movement led by General Franco seemed likely, therefore, to end like General Sanjurjo's rising, though the task of suppressing it might be more arduous and lengthy. The confidence or faith of the rebels could only be explained by the negotiations they had concluded with foreign Powers.

The military rising had been mastered; that it finally triumphed was due entirely to the favour, expressed in aid of every shape and form, of the great Fascist and parliamentary Powers.

The aristocratic-military plot against the Spanish Republic had from its inception, as we have seen, international ramifications due, on the Italian and German side, to the determination to weaken France and England economically, politically and militarily. This is the A B C of the whole affair. But in the parliamentary democracies, the sympathy of the extreme Right-wing Conservatives for Fascism was stronger than their sense of nationalism and patriotism. For the decadent *bourgeoisie* of Europe and America, Hitler and Mussolini were heroes, geniuses whom destiny had entrusted with the high and heaven-sent task of saving civilization. In Paris, London and Washington, there was no special alarm over German rearmament or expansion, because it was supposed that these were but preliminaries to a formidable attack on Communist Russia. On this dangerous hypothesis, the great capitalist democracies based their military plans and their diplomacy. (In one aspect, the principal reason for the lightning fall of France in 1940 was that the High Command and the officers of the French Army were not psychologically prepared to fight against Nazi Germany.) The result was that, owing to the indulgence with which international Fascism was treated, every weak nation ran the risk of disappearing.

In this respect, Spain was no exception; but the peculiar

circumstances of the case, the fact that she was the first victim of the military aggression of the Axis in Europe, the stubborn resistance of the Spanish people, Non-Intervention, the duration of the conflict, etc., threw abundant light on both the brutality of Italo-German terrorism and the cynicism of the spectator nations.

As it turned out, the Spanish Republic was not abandoned, outside Spain, by the whole world. The minority in the democratic nations which agitated against the cruel policy of their Governments and the enthusiastic volunteers who hastened to give their lives for the anti-Fascist cause, proclaimed—in strong contrast with the egoistical indifference in which world opinion took refuge—that altruism and the passion for justice were not entirely dead among civilized humanity. These heroes atoned by their sacrifice, even without intending to do so, for the worst actions of their Governments; but at the same time, the very fact that they, and all those who in any way protested against the infamous conduct of which the Spanish people were the victims, were persecuted by their rulers and unapplauded by their fellow-citizens, showed up the deplorable apathy into which the peoples had fallen.

To trace the complete history of foreign intervention in the Spanish civil war would convert this chapter into a voluminous book. To omit the information which makes it clear how the conflict changed from a civil war into the siege of the Republic by the capitalist Powers, would, on the other hand, deprive the story of its most dramatic and important aspect. We will, then, study the question of foreign intervention up to the point at which the data begins to be redundant.

The impression that the military rising was about to take place, or definite information to that effect, led to a great number of aristocrats and members of the oligarchy congregating in the South of France and Portugal during the weeks which preceded this incalculable event. Since 1934, Estoril and Lisbon had been important centres of the conspiracy against the Spanish Republic, and the aeroplane in which Sanjurjo was to have left to lead the rebellion of July 1936 (a step which was frustrated by the mysterious accident which cost this head-strong general his life) started from there.

Gil Robles may, or may not, have been in the plot. When he took leave of Conde de Peña Castillo at the last session of the Permanent Committee of the Cortes, someone remarked that his presence in Madrid was going to be necessary; but the tale runs that the leader of the *C.E.D.A.* replied that he had already done enough when he was Minister of War. At the moment, Gil Robles was living at Biarritz, but when the situation of the insurgents improved, he went with other *émigrés* to Lisbon. Lisbon was already the headquarters of the rebels in foreign territory, and Portugal afforded the curious spectacle of being yet another region of the Peninsula in rebellion against the Spanish Republic. For the rebels, the frontier between the two sister nations had been blotted out; for the Republicans, to cross the border involved as much danger as entering enemy territory.

By the middle of August the fact that the war was drawing closer to Portugal and the presence there of a considerable number of Spanish Monarchists, who were moving about with as much freedom as if they were in rebel Spain, alarmed the nation, and the Lisbon Government, now anxious in good earnest, accentuated its hostility to the neighbouring Republic. Franco's officers penetrated into Portuguese territory at will, bearing arms and flying the proscribed flag; they patrolled the frontier regions looking for fugitive Republicans, and with the sinister help of the Portuguese police, carried them off to Estremadura where they were immediately executed without the formality of a trial. Hundreds of Republicans, among them Madroñero, Mayor of Badajoz, and Nicolás de Pablo, Socialist deputy, were sent back to Spain or handed over to the rebels by the Portuguese authorities.

In Lisbon, a small group of the Spanish aristocratic party, with Gil Robles and individuals who had deserted from the Republican Embassy, had formed a diplomatic and commercial body which was recognized by the Portuguese Government as the legitimate representative of Spain. The Republican Ambassador, Sánchez Albornoz, was virtually a prisoner and subjected to innumerable insults and threats. Communication with Madrid was difficult; he did not know whether the telegrams he sent off were ever transmitted and those addressed to him arrived after incredible delay, mutilated and illegible.

The diplomatic and commercial body created by the insurgents had its headquarters at the Hotel Aviz and among its members the aristocrats (not in perfect harmony with Gil Robles) were prominent, some of whose names will be familiar to the reader who has followed the ramifications of the plot. The Spanish oligarchy was perfectly represented by the Marqueses de Quintanar, Foronda, de la Vega de Anzó, by the Conde de las Torres and the Conde de las Cortes. The Marquesa de Rubio

Argûelles, more active than anybody else, represented, no doubt, those ladies of Spanish society who were wont to declare that a Rolls Royce was not a luxury, but an indispensable necessity.

While part of Estremadura remained under the Republic, Franco in the south and Mola in the north could telephone to one another via Lisbon, a private line having been installed in the Hotel Aviz, connecting Burgos with Seville. The strategic advantage which the Republicans should have enjoyed through the division of rebel territory into two zones, did not exist in practice, since the insurgents passed from one to the other and communicated by telephone through Portugal. But that situation did not last long. Even before the rebellion, Franco's Air Force was using Portuguese ports and aerodromes with absolute freedom. On July 17th, two Spanish Savoia hydroplanes, numbers 23 and 35, on service in Africa, refuelled in the naval port of Bonsuceso, where later, after the outbreak of the civil war, numbers 33 and 34 obtained similar facilities. With the connivance of Portugal, Franco's troops quickly conquered Estremadura. The capture of Badajoz was relatively easy for them, thanks to the German Air Force. The rebel aeroplanes, all German Junkers, which bombarded the capital of this province, had their base two kilometres from the Portuguese village of Caia, where they were refuelled and where they took off to attack.

There is no doubt that the Portuguese dictatorship considered itself, neither more nor less than the Spanish insurgents, at war with the Republic. The Portuguese broadcasting stations were placed at the disposal of the rebels, and one of them, the Union Club, at their entire disposal. The Press, which was controlled by the Government, printed whatever was damaging to the Spanish Republic or was not allowed to print anything that might favour it. There was no form of aid that the Portugal of Oliveira Salazar did not give the rebels, who were even able to raise large loans with the *Banco Nacional de Portugal* and the *Banco de Espíritu Santo*. But no help the rebels received was more fatal to the Spanish Republic than that which concerned armaments. In this connection, Portugal lent Franco aid which was as timely as it was valuable. The first considerable instalment of war material which Franco obtained from Germany was unloaded at Lisbon, as we shall see when we refer to the adventurous voyage of the *Kamerun*. The Barcarena arms factory in Portugal supplied him immediately with machine-guns and hand-grenades and the Bemfica factory undertook to turn over to him its whole production. And with a frequency which had disastrous results on Republican resistance, supplies of petrol —precious and indispensable fuel of which the insurgents were running very short—crossed the frontier at Elvas.

In the last fortnight of August two scandalous events made it perfectly clear that the Portuguese Government considered itself at war with the Spanish Republic. On August 20th the Spanish steamship *Romeu*, proceeding from Teneriffe, entered the port of Lisbon, carrying Falangist troops, the rearguard army, and petrol. The petrol was unloaded and dispatched to Badajoz, after which the *Romeu* weighed anchor for Vigo with the Fascists on board, escorted by the Portuguese destroyer *Lima*.

The other alarming incident was the arrival of the German steamship *Kamerun* with 800 tons of war material for the insurgents at the port of Lisbon. The curious history of this voyage will be told when we deal with German intervention, but here it may be mentioned that on August 25th the *Kamerun* and the Swedish steamship *Wisborg* unloaded at the Santa Polonia quay light tanks, military aircraft parts, aerial bombs and hand-grenades. These ships were unloaded—and guarded at the same time—by Portuguese soldiers of the Corps of Artillery (*The Times*, Aug. 25th).

To continue the history of Portuguese intervention would, as I have said before, make a monotonous and interminable story. The aggressive policy which the Lisbon Government pursued until the total destruction of the Spanish Republic is un-equivocally expressed in these initial incidents.

Portugal made war on the Spanish Republic and declared herself a belligerent against the legally established Government in Spain. The cynicism of the Portuguese delegation in the Non-Intervention Committee must have astonished the most case-hardened diplomats. And British foreign policy at this time was so inept that Portuguese effrontery met with lamentable indulgence in London, partly because the Chamberlain Government was hostile to the Spanish Republic and partly because the prestige of Great Britain abroad had fallen to such a low ebb that England's oldest ally might change its allegiance.

Italian intervention began with significant promptitude. On July 30th, five Italian military aeroplanes appeared over Algerian territory, flying towards Spanish Morocco. Four were Savoia-Marchettis and the other a Savoia. Until July 20th they had formed part of squadrons 55, 57 and 58 of the Italian Air Force. Two of them ran out of fuel and were forced down in the frontier zone. Some of the crew were killed in the crash, some were captured by the French authorities. These aeroplanes had their full military equipment, except bombs, and were well supplied with machine-gun ammunition. They had no identification marks and the national flag had recently been painted over with white.

According to the investigation carried out by the French authorities, the expedition had been prepared in great haste, both by the organizers and the actual crews; and this explains the lack of precautions to hide the true identity of the planes and pilots. The crews were made up of both military and civil pilots. The nationality of the military pilots was clearly shown by special documents found on one of the dead men and by his passport, pilot's licence and military pay-book.

The aeroplanes took off on July 29th from Bologna, whence they flew to the aerodrome of Elmas at Cagliari in Sardinia. At five o'clock in the morning of July 30th, they left Cagliari for Melilla. All the maps found in the machines were of Italian origin and showed the route to Melilla and Ceuta.

The third aeroplane which came to grief disappeared without a trace about forty miles from Oran, on the same day as the other two made their forced landing in French territory. Only two, therefore, of the original five aeroplanes reached their destination.

Hours after the accident, a Spanish aeroplane flew over the Italian machines and dropped a sack containing uniforms of the Spanish Foreign Legion and a message in Italian: "Put on these uniforms and tell the French authorities that you belong to the Legion and your base is at Nador. We will send you two drums of petrol and mechanics, so that you can continue your flight. Don't put your heads in the lion's mouth."

Interrogated by General Denain, the survivors admitted that they were under military orders and that they were handing over the aircraft to the Spanish rebels (*The Times*, July 31st).

On August 1st there were fourteen Italian Savoia-Marchetti aeroplanes at Nador in Spanish Morocco (*The Times*). On the 2nd, twenty-one were counted at the same aerodrome (*The Times*). And on August 24th, three Capronis bombed Irún and the villages along the San Sebastian road, while other machines of the same type attacked the Republican lines near Beobia (*The Times*).

All these incidents had already dissipated, in the first month of the rebellion, any doubts that may have lingered about the Italian Government's policy towards Spain. And with equal

587

swiftness it was apparent that the parliamentary democracies did not consider themselves menaced by such open intervention. In this connection, the sentence imposed in French Morocco on the six captured Italian airmen was highly revealing. They were sentenced to a month's imprisonment, with the promise of being set at liberty before the expiry of the sentence if their conduct was good, and to a fine of 200 francs (*The Times*, Aug. 11th).

Hitler, also, did not hesitate to identify himself immediately with the cause of the Spanish insurgents—a policy which was confirmed by the arrival on August 3rd of the pocket-battleship *Deutschland* at Ceuta, whence the Admiral repaired to Tetuán to have breakfast with General Franco—a sinister portent for the Spanish Republic.

The first material proof which the Madrid Government had of the arrival of German war material for the rebels came a week later with the landing on the Barajas aerodrome at Madrid of a three-engined Junker armed with machine-guns. This machine sheered off so quickly that the Republicans guessed it was a military plane, and it was pursued and dealt with by the loyal Air Force near Azuaga (Badajoz).

In the early days of August the Italian military aircraft in Spanish Morocco were joined by powerful German Junkers. On the 5th, there were already several German three-engined planes at Tetuán (*The Times*). On the 12th, twenty Junkers heavy bombers and five fighter planes were observed in Seville (Dispatch from the correspondent of the *New York Times* at Seville, transmitted from Gibraltar). On the same day, *L'Intransigeant* printed a dispatch from Tetuán describing the preparations for intense activity by the rebel Air Force and the arrival on the previous day of about twenty German military pilots.

Meanwhile, the first ships carrying war material for the Spanish insurgents—the Swedish s.s. *Wisborg* and the German s.s. *Kamerun*—had left German ports.

The *Kamerun* was stopped within the three-mile limit in the Straits of Gibraltar by the cruiser *Libertad* and a submarine, both in the service of the Republic. As a result, the commander of the German naval forces in the Mediterranean intervened, and an uproar ensued which alarmed the Republican Government. The Germans denounced the action of the Republican fleet as a crime against the right of free navigation on the high seas, as piracy, etc., and threatened to take reprisals. On August

20th, the German Official Agency denied in an outraged manner that the *Kamerun* was carrying war material and, appealing to the humanitarian sentiments of the civilized world, affirmed that the object of her voyage was only to take off German refugees in Cadiz. The *Kamerun* remained at liberty and continued her course without having had her cargo examined, although she could not enter her original port of destination owing to the presence of the Republican Fleet. A few days later, as has been related, this ship, whose mission, according to the Germans, could not have been more innocent, unloaded 800 tons of armaments for the Spanish insurgents at Lisbon.

It is superfluous to add that the Republic, having begun the war with superiority in the air, no longer enjoyed this advantage, either in the quality or the quantity of its aircraft. And the highly favourable circumstance that most of the warships continued to serve the Republic was also soon nullified by the action of the German and Italian Fleets which were practically at war with the legitimate Government of Spain. The German and Italian squadrons maintained constant communication with Franco's naval units; lying with their lights ablaze off the coastal towns, they directed the rebel bombers and wirelessed to them important information. The rebels possessed no submarines; yet Government ships were torpedoed by mysterious submarines in the very mouth of the harbours. When the fragments of a torpedo were examined after the attack on the Republican cruiser *Miguel de Cervantes*, it was seen that they belonged to a "White Head" torpedo, No. 533, manufactured in the Italian city of Fiume. This happened in November, when intervention was already well advanced.

These facts are enough to show the danger in which the Spanish Republic stood from the armed hostility of Germany, Italy and Portugal. The scanty and deficient armaments which were all the Republic had at its disposal, the few bombers, the almost non-existent fighter planes, the antiquated artillery, the machine-guns, the rifles, rapidly disappeared or became unserviceable, as was natural when obsolete weapons are used continuously against modern war material. The Madrid Government found it daily more impossible to replace this poor material, while new consignments, each one exceeding the last in quality and quantity, were pouring into the arsenals of the insurgents.

Neutral witnesses recorded the self-sacrifice and enthusiasm of the militiamen and officers of the Republic, while stressing the lack of weapons with which they were contending. There are hardly any—they wrote—who are provided with proper weapons. In many cases the militiamen are defending themselves with shot-guns and some have been armed with museum-pieces which have not been fired for a hundred years (*Manchester Guardian*, Aug. 19th). The advance of the rebel troops—mostly Moors and Legionaries—up the valley of the Tagus was rendered irresistible by the crushing superiority of the rebels in the air (*The Times*, Oct. 19th). Madrid was already in serious jeopardy. Three columns were converging on Navalcarnero to the south-west of the capital. The forces of the Burgos *Junta*—the name of Franco's Government—seemed to have complete mastery of the air. "The Government aeroplanes are conspicuous by their absence in all the sectors I have just visited", said James Abbe, correspondent of the *Morning Post* at Burgos.

The attacks of the rebel army were preceded by heavy aerial bombardment which terrified whole villages and set in motion pitiful columns of refugees, who, with their donkeys, mules, carts and household belongings, filled the roads leading to Madrid. The rebel artillery concentrated its fire on the object of attack and the battle began in earnest when the powerful Capronis, in groups of three or four, appeared with their escorts of Fiats. Then the Government positions were pounded by bombs of all sizes, and the rebel tanks advanced, six at a time, moving rapidly and manoeuvring with ease, but never ceasing their fire over the open lines of the Republican militia. This parade of force would have been enough to reduce the morale of veteran troops if they had not had an equal weight of armour to reply with, and the majority of the militiamen had but poor training in the art of warfare and even poorer weapons (*The Times*, Oct. 23rd).

In vain did the Spanish Republican Government call upon the Governments of Paris, London and Washington, in the name of law and reason, to help them to obtain war material with which to make a stand against the rebellion and foreign aggression. The official world of Europe and America was deaf to the pleadings of the Spanish Republic, whose tribulations it thought were a certain augury of its rapid demise. But if the capitalist democracies, risking their interests as menaced nations in Spain and avowing their contempt for humanitarian and progressive principles, complacently helped in the ruin of the Republic, another Power followed the course of events with just alarm for its interests. The U.S.S.R. could not desire the victory of the insurgents, as the parliamentary democracies appeared to desire it, but if the conflict had remained a purely internal affair, the Moscow Government—though its duty, like all the rest, was to support those who had right on their side—would in all probability have refrained from playing a lone hand. But the intervention of the Fascist States created for the U.S.S.R., both at home and abroad, a delicate and explosive situation. A number of reasons in my opinion, counselled the Russian Government not to shut its eyes to the disquieting events in Spain.

The explosions of feeling which sometimes agitate party politics and incite peoples to action rarely move Governments. to depart from their fixed course. Even when a Government adjusts its policy to the passionate clamour of the street, it keeps. its own interests in view. Soviet Russia had motives for suspend-- ing its passive attitude on the Spanish question as powerful as: they were difficult for the statesmen of Moscow to ignore. If,. as has been foolishly repeated *ad nauseam*, Stalin's policy towards. Spain had consisted in implanting, or helping to implant,. Communism in the Iberian Peninsula, he would have shown for- the first time that he was not the wise politician who had crowned his party and his nation with so many triumphs. The more incapable among the rulers of the parliamentary democracies believed, or stated without believing what they were saying, that Russia proposed to convert Spain into another Soviet Union, because they themselves, in Stalin's position, would not have found any other alternative. The famous Communist plot, organized in Moscow, against which the Spanish generals and aristocrats rose a few hours before it was due to explode, was a fantastic subterfuge, an alarm without serious foundation; although the invention of this bogey gave positive aid to Hitler, Mussolini and Franco in places where any sort of cock-and-bull story about Russia or the Spanish Republic fell on fruitful ground. On the other hand, those who believed in good faith in the existence of a sinister plot against Spain, conceived and organized in Moscow, failed to perceive that, faced with the Hitler menace, it was in the interests of the U.S.S.R. to foster a *rapprochement* with France and England—interests which would not be furthered by Moscow fomenting civil war in Europe or in any isolated country. The Franco-Russian Alliance and the resolutions agreed upon at the VIIth Congress of the Third International showed that Stalin had subordinated the idea of European revolution to the more pressing and vital policy of checking the expansion of Germany. And nothing could have been more foreign to Soviet interests than the hostility which would have been aroused in the capitalist democracies by an attempt to create a new Communist State in Spain.

Since the beginning of 1935, the action of the Communist parties, in tune with Stalin's perspicacity, had been everywhere directed to lulling the *bourgeoisie* to sleep; but the *bourgeoisie* refused to be lulled and remained obstinately wide-awake, because in the period I refer to, it hated anything that was not Fascist. Actually, of all the workers' groups, the Spanish Communist Party sounded the most conservative, or least aggressive, note during the months preceding the insurrection.

On the other hand, those who proclaimed the existence of a Communist plot, like those who were the easy victims of this propaganda, implicitly accused Moscow and the Third International of negligence, which in itself would destroy another of the arguments which were used to terrify devout ladies and owners of property; for it is not clear how the agents of Moscow and the politicians of the Kremlin, who, according to the extreme Right, are so subtle and dangerous, could have organized a conspiracy for the month of July 1936, which would cause civil war to break out and deliver the Government into the hands of the Spanish Communists, and yet forget the absolute necessity for supplying them with arms. War, civil or otherwise, is waged with arms; and those who maintain that Russia provoked the Spanish war, imply that Stalin and the men of the Third International are imbeciles.

The fraudulent story of the Communist plot in Spain—a story about as authentic as the Protocols of the Elders of Zion—has all the characteristics of the mare's-nests invented for political reasons in order to justify the tactics of the opposition. This game is as old as the history of political and religious struggles. It was a fabrication—but one which damaged the Spanish Republic, because vast sectors of world opinion, not all of them capitalist, lent ear to it.

The same crisis—the German menace—which induced Moscow to lend a new orientation to the Third International, impelled Russia not to continue indefinitely with the tragicomedy of Non-Intervention. Nothing caused more anxiety to the rulers of the Kremlin than the diplomatic isolation of their nation. The ancient Russian aspiration to count as a great power in Europe revived under the Soviet régime with a new vigour, due to the peril in which Communist Russia always stood of seeing herself engulfed in a war with the whole capitalist world. The Third International was a political instrument which was effective and necessary to Moscow so long as her diplomatic and military isolation lasted. In case of aggression against the Soviet Union, the Communist parties could do much to weaken anti-Russian action in enemy countries; and as the first task of international Communism lay in avoiding the disappearance of the Socialist system which was already functioning over a sixth part of the globe, the interests of Marxism in general coincided naturally, according to the Communists, with Russian national interests and even with those of Russia as a world Power. It was, therefore, of transcendental importance for the Soviet Union that the Third International should not be discredited so long as the menace of capitalism against the Socialist State lasted.

In 1936 the political, diplomatic and military isolation of Russia was absolute, in spite of the Franco-Russian Pact of Mutual Aid. And the adhesion of Russia to the farce of Non-Intervention—an agreement faithfully observed by her—placed the Third International and the Kremlin in a singularly uncomfortable position. The Soviet Union was under the same obligation as England and France not to flout international law, under which the Spanish Republic was entitled to acquire the means of defence. But the avoidance of this duty raised graver moral issues in Russia than in the other countries, because the Government in Spain was a popular régime which drew most of its energies from the proletariat. If the Soviet Union persisted in observing strictly the dictates of Non-Intervention, the Third International would run the risk of either disappearing altogether, or, in the main, of suffering an essential diminution. The Communist parties had a hard task in justifying the passivity of Russia before the destruction of Spanish democracy.

The Soviet Union could not abandon the Spanish Republic without undermining the foundations of the Third International. It had, therefore, to support the Madrid Government; but this was not, in my view, the sole motive, nor eventually the most important.

Russia, as a probable victim of the military aggression of the Fascist States, understood that the crushing of the Spanish Republic by the insurgents and their foreign allies would mean the victory of Italy, Germany and Japan over the nations which were interested in maintaining the peace. On this point, the coincidence of Russia's interests with those of the democracies was absolute and well-known. Russia feared war; and the *status quo* defended by Soviet pacifism suited the rich and satiated nations. Not only was it important to Russia—as it should have been important to England, France and the United States —that the Spanish Republic should conquer its enemies, thus avoiding the emergence of a Spain allied to Germany; but it

593

was also imperative that Spain, governed by the Left, should be allied to the democratic nations in the inevitable and imminent world conflagration. If the Republic succumbed, there would be one more nation in Europe—and that one splendidly situated —unfriendly to the Soviet Union. This would be a considerable asset to the Fascist international front. The military and economic potential of Italy and Germany would receive notable reinforcements and the isolation of Communist Russia would become again as serious as it was in the most anxious days of Bolshevism.

With the idea always in their mind of breaking the political and diplomatic blockade of their country and warding off isolation, the politicians of the Kremlin no doubt foresaw that, if Russia contributed to the overthrow of Franco and his Fascist protectors merely by fulfilling her obligations under international law, she would be able to count on one really friendly nation in Europe. The diplomatic position of the Soviet Union would take a turn for the better, since the Kremlin would hold in its hand what it had always wanted—an important diplomatic card to play in its relations with France and England, with the aim of creating the conditions for a close tripartite alliance. Threatened by Hitler's Germany and Japanese militarism, Russia, in 1936, felt this necessity more imperiously than ever.

For the reasons already noted, it was not possible for the Moscow Government to continue perpetually subject to a Non-Intervention agreement which apparently was only binding on the democratic States, either because the latter were indifferent to the fate of the Spanish Republic or because they stupidly desired its destruction.

Towards the end of 1936, when German, Italian and Portuguese intervention had already lasted three months, the first Russian aeroplanes and war material appeared in Spain. But the Republic never succeeded in solving the problem of war material and this spelt its doom. Franco had armaments and to spare, but he was always short of men; the Republic, on the other hand, had plenty of soldiers, but no arms. But the rebels could import Italian troops and German technicians without let or hindrance, and the Republican Government encountered insuperable obstacles in obtaining war material. Sometimes the situation improved; the proportion of the Air Forces, which at the beginning was twelve or ten rebel planes to one Republican, was at times two or three to one. But in the air, as in no other element, mere superiority brings decisive advantages; and in the most vital period of the war, as at the battle of Teruel, the rebels had 500 aeroplanes against the Government's 150.

The Soviet Union fulfilled its self-imposed duty; but the duty it had undertaken *vis-à-vis* the Spanish Republic was not the duty which Germany and Italy owed the insurgents. For Hitler and Mussolini, the Spanish war was their war; not so for Stalin. The Russians made an effort which was limited—a limit imposed by distance, transport facilities and the permanent and circumstantial interests of Soviet foreign policy. Russia wanted little from Spain; Germany and Italy had staked everything. Russia was alone; Germany and Italy counted on the complicity of the great capitalist democracies. The Fascist States intervened for reasons of aggressive imperialism; Russia was fulfilling an unavoidable duty, in her own defence.

The difference, both in concept and impulse between Russian help and Italo-German intervention was manifest, although officially the opposite impression was put about in the parliamentary democracies.

CHAPTER XXII

## THE REPUBLIC AT WAR

WAR AND REVOLUTION followed parallel courses in the democratic zone. The problems which beset the Government were those which a civil war of profound social significance always brings on the popular side. Less than any other institutions could property and the economic structure stand aside from the general convulsion. The impulse behind the popular rising to recover the rights of the people was bound to impose great changes in these fields, even if the necessities of war had not required them. But some kind of order was indispensable, if the Republic was to survive and continue the struggle. All this would require time. Some things had to die a natural death; others could only be born after a straightforward period of gestation.

The centre of gravity of the war and of politics was the street. Power was in the hands of the people, the parties, the committees. The revolution, and the war itself, in the territory dominated by the Republicans, followed the process of trial and error. To advance and retreat is the characteristic fluctuation of a society not yet vertebrate, which seeks to find an axis on which to revolve. In the military, as in the economic, order, the revolution attacked and fell back, erred and redeemed its error, and would go on making mistakes and correcting them until the bitter lessons of experience did what even the Government could not do—showed the masses the dangers of indiscipline and the tragic results of ignorance.

The Largo Caballero Ministry which was formed on September 4th, 1936, marked a step forward along this road. The direction of the war and of politics began to pass into the hands of the Government. No one enjoyed more authority then over the proletariat than the old leader of the Socialist trade unions. All the parties of the Republic were represented in this coalition, except the Anarchists. Indalecio Prieto became Minister of Marine and Air, with immediate benefit to order and discipline in these Departments. Don Juan Negrín shouldered the heavy burden of Finance, which, thanks largely to him, was saved from the threatened collapse. Largo Caballero reserved for himself, besides the Premiership, the Ministry of War.

A new and important step was taken on November 3rd with the entry into the Largo Caballero Government of four representatives of the *C.N.T.* If more than once in the past, learned optimists had imputed to Spain the introduction of original elements into the political history of the world, at any rate she now set an incontrovertible precedent in having Anarchist Ministers.

The tyranny of events and changing social conditions were conspiring to transform Anarchism into a constructive and responsible force, in the same way as the revolution, by abolishing luxury and establishing greater social equality, had already taken the beggars off the streets. In that part of Spain which was ruled over by the people, the pathological excrescences of a society which was abnormal in the extreme were being rapidly eliminated.

The people soon felt the liveliest desire for unity and co-ordination. The hour of the saturnalia of liberty was over. What, a short time before, had satisfied, and even flattered, many ears among the populace—the praise of indiscipline, the rejection of law and order—the people now reacted to with weariness and suspicion. On the other hand, the call for concerted action, the demand for a single command, the desire to have an Army and to concentrate every energy on the war, was becoming uppermost in the mind of the workers.

The Largo Caballero Government began the formation of the new Republican Army on the basis of the popular militias. It

596

created the Corps of Political Commissars (*Cuerpo de Comisarios politicos*). For the Republic undoubtedly had to found a political, revolutionary Army, very different from the one which already existed in Franco's Spain. Without discipline, which is simply a corrective against fear, there can be no militia; but discipline under the insurgents was one thing, and discipline under the revolution another. The morale of a regular Army is sustained by fear from above; there can be no Army of this kind, as the old apophthegm runs, if the soldier does not fear his officers more than the enemy. But in a revolutionary Army, this fear produces the opposite effect; it demoralizes; here, severity is not enough; it must be accompanied by political action and intellectual persuasion. History shows this to be the classic method; and so, as I have said in another place, the commissar, the agitator, the political delegate, appear in all revolutionary wars, with both good and bad results, which is why they inevitably conflict with the regular Army officers.

The task of creating the new Republican Army was exceptionally arduous, because it was generally believed that the war would be a short one and each political group wanted to keep its own soldiers and arms in order to assert itself, or not to allow itself to be passed over, when peace returned. The existence of a great number of political groups was to be the most serious obstacle on the home front to a Republican victory.

Largo Caballero became Premier at the most difficult period of the war, just when the old order was crumbling and the new was coming painfully to birth. The former Secretary of the *U.G.T.* began to gather together the dispersed and perplexed forces; he included the Anarchists in the Cabinet, as we have seen; ordered (at the insistence of the Republican Fleet) the withdrawal of the Catalan troops who had landed on the island of Majorca in an adventurous foray; and attempted to create a General Staff. But the military situation deteriorated; the Italians took Malaga without a fight, and the unfortunate and alarming insurrection of May 1937 broke out at Barcelona; events, some of them fatal, which belonged to the period of elimination of the unadaptable and the outworn; others, less disastrous, yet difficult to prevent.

Meanwhile, the dispute between Largo Caballero's Socialist group and the Communist Party, which had perhaps originated in the close philosophic relationship between the two movements, grew more bitter, accentuated as it was by the rivalry between Communists and Socialists of the Left over the leadership of the revolution. This rivalry made Ministerial collaboration between these two Republican groups difficult. No doubt the Communists were unjust to Largo Caballero; while Largo Caballero and his doctrinaire advisers, on guard, even before the war, against the Communists, received the advances of this party with distrust and misgiving. Communist pugnacity inclined Largo Caballero's movement more and more towards a reconciliation with the Anarchists, and the *C.N.T.*, equally menaced by the proselytizing fervour of Communism, far from rejecting political solidarity with this branch of Socialism, went half-way to meet it.

The Communist Party, which had only a few thousand members in 1931, the year of the Republic, had been adding to its numbers in proportion as the proletariat veered towards radicalism as a result of the opposition of the oligarchy to all reform. But the well-established name of the *U.G.T.* and the *C.N.T.*—each in the regions of its traditional predominance—prevented an independent Communist trade union from arising. The Spanish section of the Third International developed, then, with its small *cadres* in the Socialist trade unions, as a minority political force, not entirely free from intellectual middle-class elements. For the rest, internal unanimity, enthusiasm, and a facility for expounding without prolixity constructive formulas of action, made the Communist Party a group which was more important for its methods of combat than for its numbers. Until 1935 this party preached a rigid class policy, which was one of the reasons why it did not advance more rapidly under the Republic.

But if the Spanish Communist Party did not notably increase, the Socialist Party became more radical; Socialist youth, in all its numbers, adopted the Marxism of Lenin and wanted to make of Largo Caballero a revolutionary leader of this stamp. But when Socialist youth perceived that Largo Caballero could not be, nor had ever seriously thought of being, the Spanish Lenin,[1] they changed their mentor and placed their hopes in Stalin. More than 100,000 Socialist youth enrolled *en bloc* in the Communist Party. Hence the old Socialist Party, besides finding itself lamentably divided by personal and tactical questions, lost its youth organizations. Internal dissension deprived it of cohesion; the flight of its youth to Communism robbed it of its dynamism.

That meant that, at the outbreak of the military rising, no party of the Republic was better placed for the struggle than the

[1] Largo Caballero rejected in public the sobriquet of "the Spanish Lenin", accusing his enemies of having invented it.

Communist Party. None was so coherent, so disciplined or so sure of itself. And when the parliamentary democracies—the inspiration of all the other parties of the régime—abandoned the Spanish people, and the U.S.S.R. fulfilled its obligations under international law, the Communist Party inevitably came to the fore in the moral leadership of the régime. The people, contrasting the war material and supplies of all kinds arriving from Russia, with the blockade maintained by France and England,[1] ascribed their salvation to the Soviet State. The Republican middle class, surprised by the moderate tone of Communist propaganda and impressed by the unity and realism which prevailed in this party, flocked in great numbers to join its ranks. Nothing succeeds like success; and the Communists, at home and abroad, were a force to be reckoned with. Army officers and officials who had never turned the pages of a Marxist leaflet, became Communists, some through calculation, others through moral weakness, others inspired by the enthusiasm which animated this organization. And there were moderate politicians who thought it might be a wise policy to encourage the Communists in order to weaken the Socialists.

In May 1937 the Communist Party, in its unmistakable way, submitted to Largo Caballero, and made public, an eight-point programme, to be put into practice immediately by the Government; the aim being to establish better co-operation between the Services and to accelerate the formation of the new Army. The Communists announced that if the provisos were not accepted, they would not support the Government.

Largo Caballero replied with another plan, in which the U.G.T. and the C.N.T. were to have the preponderance over the purely political parties in the Cabinet and a central War Council, presided over by the Prime Minister, was to be set up. Unless this programme was accepted in its entirety, Largo Caballero threatened to resign the Premiership.

The Anarchists embraced the idea with enthusiasm and made it clear that they would not participate in any Government that was not led by Largo Caballero. The Executive of the U.G.T. supported the project. But if the trade unions approved it, no political party considered it appropriate to the occasion.

Popular opinion had changed so much in such a short time, and the Republic stood in such grave peril, that the people did

[1] The British trade unions approved the policy of Non-Intervention at the Plymouth Congress (Sept. 11th, 1936) by 3,029,000 votes to 51,000. The Labour Party also, at its Conference at Edinburgh on Oct. 5th, pronounced in favour of Non-Intervention.

not resent the absence of the Anarchists and Largo Caballero's Socialists from the Government; nor did the men and the organizations who had been excluded—perhaps because they had been excluded through their own choice—lack then the necessary patriotism to leave the government to others.

The new Government was headed by Negrín and besides this innovation contained others, such as a new Ministry of National Defence, under Indalecio Prieto, which was responsible for all the armed forces. Prieto had already organized the Republican Air Force, with marked success.

The Negrín Ministry took office at another critical juncture for the Republic—though, in fact, every moment was critical. The Fascist States were beginning to drop the mask and intervene more openly. The German Fleet bombarded Almería on the last day of May. Bilbao was endangered through lack of aeroplanes and artillery, and fell on June 19th, the whole of the north following it within three months. It was almost unbelievable that England not only permitted the conquest by Germans and Italians of the north of Spain—the region where her interests were most seriously prejudiced—but also tightened the blockade of the Republic by discouraging her merchant ships from entering Spanish waters.

However, apart from these disasters, which only France and England could have prevented, the signs of order and organization increased in democratic Spain and the Republic prepared to survive. From the first moment, the Negrín Government gave an impression of strength. Liberty began to be compatible with authority. Harmful experiments in the revolutionary field were rectified; new war factories were built; arbitrariness in the administration of justice was abolished, and a popular Army, capable of standing up to the disciplined and well-armed forces of General Franco and his Fascist allies, began to take shape.

Here we must glance at the military situation. Madrid had been saved for the second time in November 1936, and saved, at the outset of the new peril, by the same people who had saved her in July. The International Brigade arrived providentially to stiffen the defence; 20,000 rifles sent by Mexico proved invaluable, while the first Russian fighter planes helped to achieve the miracle (for it was nothing else) of preventing the entry of the rebels into the capital of Spain.

The Largo Caballero Government had moved to Valencia on November 7th, leaving the defence of Madrid to General Miaja, who achieved his mission at the head of a *Junta* composed for the most part of young men, some of them almost children. Never did such an arduous and glorious task fall on such young shoulders and never was a trust so nobly and excellently performed.

But the battle of Madrid did not end in November; it was only to end with the war. Impregnable to a frontal attack, the rebels tried to isolate the capital, threatening its communications with the east by a vigorous offensive which led to exceptionally sanguinary fighting on the banks of the Jarama. Here, as before in the suburbs of Madrid, the International Brigade put up a terrific resistance and suffered heavy losses.

In March 1937 the Italian offensive on Guadalajara threatened for a time Madrid's communications with the north-east. However, 30,000 Italians, commanded by General Bergonzoli, suffered a spectacular defeat at Brihuega; and the battle of Brunete in July, one of the most sanguinary and bitter of the whole war, was the first sign that the new Republican Army was already preparing to pass over to the offensive—a fact which received immediate confirmation in the attack on Saragossa by the Army of the east (September), which led to the capture of Belchite and brought the Republicans to within about twenty kilometres of the important Aragonese capital.

The chief cause of anxiety, which was to weigh most heavily on the Republican Ministers right up to the end of the war, was the scarcity of arms—a serious obstacle to the formation of the Army. The Republic suffered virtually a blockade which not only affected war material, but also food and raw materials; in fact, everything that had to be imported. Hence, the greatest privations were endured by the civil population. Where armaments were concerned, the situation, while always remaining acute, varied; some months were not so bad as others. At the moment, the Republic was obtaining what was necessary for survival.

Seeing the complacency with which the Governments in London, Paris and Washington viewed the war of international Fascism against Spanish democracy, Germany, Italy, Portugal and Franco were coming out boldly into the open. In the summer of 1937 the Mediterranean began to be too dangerous for ships bringing Russian supplies to the Republic. Italian submarines were sinking merchantmen right and left. This obliged the Republican Government to seek new routes, or to devise plans to maintain the flow of vital Russian shipments.

The democratic Governments excused their complicity in the Fascist outrage against Spain with the pretext that their intervention would cause Italy and Germany to redouble their efforts and the final result would be another world war. Theoretically this argument could not hold water; and its falseness was soon apparent in practice when the British Fleet decided to put a stop to piracy in the Mediterranean. The Italian submarines disappeared. The fact is that the Fascist Powers were not seeking a world war at that moment; on the contrary, they feared one, as their preparations were not yet complete.

On October 31st, 1937, the Negrín Government left Valencia, where the Government Departments had hardly room to function, for more spacious quarters in Barcelona. Azaña had taken up his residence in Barcelona a few months after the outbreak of the civil war and had been able to observe at his leisure the stupidities of separatism, the weakness of the autonomous Government and the insufficient contribution which this rich and fortunate region was making to the war, and to suffer, as one of the besieged, the turbulent events of May 1937.

In this synoptic account of events, the next place belongs to the operations at Teruel—operations which seemed to change the course of the war and which, with the sinking of the insurgent cruiser *Baleares* by the Republican Fleet, were part and parcel of the days when the hopes of the Republicans stood higher than they had ever been since Non-Intervention began.

The offensive of the People's Army against Teruel began in the early afternoon of December 17th, 1937, in the middle of a frightful hail and snow storm. Since the conflict broke out, the Republican lines had been very close at various points to this desolate capital. With skill and caution the Republican General Staff concentrated near Teruel a large army of between 40,000 and 50,000 men, with all their armament. The task of isolating the city took four hours, the forces under Lister severing the precarious communications which linked Teruel with the world of Franco. Fifteen thousand rebel soldiers and 20,000 civilians were cut off. The troops took refuge in the most solid buildings —the Civil Governor's office, the Bank of Spain, the Seminary and Convent of Santa Clara. Here some 4,000 rebels made ready to resist, while the civil population was removed by bridle-paths.

The weather was vile, but that did not prevent the enemy aeroplanes from putting in an appearance and establishing their usual superiority in the air. Junkers, Capronis and Fiats bombarded and machine-gunned the Republican Army incessantly, while the artillery which the rebels had quickly concentrated kept up a steady fire.

The Republican siege consolidated itself rapidly, sustained by enthusiasm and heroism, in spite of the pitiless weather. On the 28th Franco counter-attacked from the north and the west, with great weight of armour, in the first serious attempt to raise the siege. The Republican troops, all Spaniards, stood firm. On the 31st the enemy launched another still more furious offensive on the Republican lines. That day a terrific hurricane was raging, and to the fury of the elements was added the tireless Italo-German Air Force, always overhead, and the perpetual bombardment of the insurgents. Time and again, the enemy broke on the Republican lines which hardly yielded an inch of ground during the whole of the battle. Outside Teruel, the nearest enemy position was still about four kilometres away.

The Fascists would not renounce their intention of reconquering this mediaeval capital of the Maestrazgo; they could not afford to lose prestige at home and abroad. The rebel troops which were besieged in Teruel surrendered on January 7th, 1938, for lack of food and water. But Franco attacked every day with greater fury, more armour and fresh troops. The Republican command had finally to fling in the International Brigade, but the enemy was splendidly equipped and fought well. The battle lasted for six weeks, until the 22nd of February, when the Republic withdrew from the city.

Teruel was an excessive, though necessary, drain on the Republican troops. The cream of the People's Army was skimmed off, and the best of the Republican equipment was damaged or lost. As a method of depriving the enemy of the initiative—so dangerous when the attack is vastly superior to the defence in weapons—the Teruel offensive no doubt obliged the Fascists to desist from a new operation against Madrid's communications in the Guadalajara sector. From this point of view, the Republican command achieved its objective.

The French frontier was hermetically sealed; nothing entered Catalonia from that direction. And not all the ships bringing armaments arrived. Indalecio Prieto accelerated and multiplied war production, but the problem exceeded the capacities of the Republic.

This was the principal cause of the catastrophe which followed the battle of Teruel on the Pyrenean-Aragonese front.

On March 8th, 1938, the enemy began a general offensive in Aragon—delayed, perhaps, several months by the Republican attack on Teruel—from the Pyrenees as far as the Maestrazgo.

The Republican lines were then within sight of Saragossa, curved round Huesca, almost surrounding it, and passed through the neighbourhood of Jaca. Franco attacked from Huesca towards the north; from Saragossa in the direction of Lérida; from Saragossa with the coast as his objective, through the valley of the Ebro; from Montalbán bearing towards Valencia.

Even though the Republicans knew that the rebels possessed a great weight of armour, such a vast operation surprised them after the disaster the enemy had suffered at Teruel; and the surprise, together with the enormous superiority in armaments, gave the attacking forces an irresistible advantage. The Republic had no aeroplanes, no artillery, no tanks, no shock troops with which to hold back the Fascist Army. Some Republican units went into action, half of them without even rifles, let alone machine-guns or hand-grenades. The Republican front crumbled along its entire immense length.

These days saw one of the greatest feats of the Republican Army—the resistance of the 43rd Division under the command of Colonel Beltrán. Isolated in the foothills of the Pyrenees, this division kept the enemy at bay for several weeks, in an epic struggle. Only when food and ammunition gave out did the 43rd retire into France, in good order, with snow waist-high.

Lérida fell on April 3rd, after holding out for eight or ten days in conditions of tremendous inferiority. The Republican forces possessed, as always, little artillery and the enemy had the mastery of the air. On the same day the Republic lost Gandesa, a position of great strategic value south of the Ebro. The Republican front was disorganized, in utter confusion, the Fascists outflanking numerous Government contingents, with heavy loss to the Republitans.

On April 8th the rebels reached the Noguera-Pallaresa and the Republic lost Tremp and other centres where the electric power stations which fed the industrial regions of Catalonia were situated. This serious setback was counteracted by putting into operation the steam-driven power stations. Actually, Catalonia had been without electricity for days before, when the Fascists occupied Balaguer, to the north of Lérida, a place through which the high tension cables from Tremp, Camarasa and Capdella passed.

General Franco and his German and Italian allies kept up their offensive along the whole line for a month. Partly owing to attrition and partly through the reorganization of the Republican defence which grew daily more effective, the Fascist advance was halted at last, more or less exactly on the borders of Catalonia.

The great natural obstacles, chiefly the rivers—the Noguera-Pallaresa, the Ebro and the Segre—marked, generally speaking, the new division of territory between the belligerents. In the north, the line of fire ran up to the French frontier, to the west of the Seo de Urgel.

But south of the Ebro the offensive which began on March 8th continued unchecked, and the Italians, equipped with aeroplanes, tanks and guns in the usual proportions, were opening a way to the Mediterranean.

Franco left Catalonia alone for the moment while he concentrated on the attack south of the Ebro; and on April 15th, the rebels entered Vinaroz. The Fascist advance continued southwards, along the coast, with Castellón de la Plana and Valencia as its objectives. The territory held by the Republicans was, therefore, divided into two zones.

Meanwhile the civil population in Republican territory was being attacked, against all the rules of warfare, by German and Italian aviators. Since January, air raids on Barcelona and other Catalan cities had been causing innumerable casualties and great damage. Towns like Granollers had suffered more or less the fate of Guernica. The bombardment of open cities, entirely without military significance, is particularly odious when it is carried out without any risk to the attacker; hence, the frankly cowardly nature of the air raids by the Germans and Italians on the cities of Republican Spain.

Barcelona suffered the first serious air raid on January 25th, when some hundreds of people were killed in the centre of the city. On the 30th, another raid by Italian planes based on Majorca caused 350 casualties, eighty of whom were children. But it was in March that the large-scale frequent raids on Barcelona took place which began, at last, to alarm world opinion. These outrages committed by Italian airmen lasted from the night of the 16th, at the rate of a raid every three hours, until the afternoon of the 18th, the number of raids amounting to seventeen and the resulting casualties being very heavy. In one raid alone about 400 persons were killed; and during the two days of aerial bombardment there were 1,300 fatal casualties and more than 2,000 injured.

The excesses of the Fascist Air Forces in Franco's service finally aroused the open disgust of the whole world, though the reaction was not as energetic as the occasion warranted. The Pope protested to the Burgos *Junta* or Government. The Governments of Paris and London agreed to make representations to *both* sides in Spain, with a view to stopping air raids like the ones on Barcelona. Such an admonition to both aggressor and victim—which intentionally ignored the nationality of the airmen and aeroplanes causing the casualties—showed that Franco-British diplomacy could not cease from being perfidious over the Spanish question, even when it came to making a humanitarian gesture.

The succession of events which assailed the Republic in the early months of 1938 were accompanied by political consequences at home and abroad. On April 5th, Negrín, besides his own anxieties as Prime Minister, had to deal with complications in the Ministry of Defence, and came to the conclusion that Prieto's state of mind was not the most appropriate to direct the war. The ensuing Ministerial crisis brought the *C.N.T.* and the *U.G.T.* into the Cabinet, represented respectively by Segundo Blanco and Ramón González Peña.

With the course of the war and the revolution the parties and men of the Republic had suffered, with varied results, a wearing-down process, both political and military. Anarchism was in dissolution; with the disappearance of the social conditions which engendered and nourished it, it was dying a natural death. Neither direct action nor clandestine existence had any longer a *raison d'être*. And no one was surprised when, on July 4th, 1937, the *F.A.I.*, as a body, decided to convert itself into a legal movement. This decision was confirmed on the 11th of July at the regional conference at Valencia. The Anarchist movement became a *political* organization and its members were authorized to accept posts in all public offices.

The avatar of Anarchism was proof of a vital crisis in this important section of the proletariat; and the philosophic and moral crisis of the *C.N.T.* and the *F.A.I.* obviously could not manifest itself without arousing internal divisions in both cognate parties.

The Socialist Party, as we have seen, was seriously weakened by personal animosities and differences of principle. Its three or four leading personalities interpreted the general situation and even day-to-day events in very different, and at times incompatible, lights.

The Republican parties, deprived of Azaña and Martínez Barrio—the former immured in the Presidency; the latter politically immobilized as Speaker of the Cortes—were sunk in torpor, without a leader, and hopelessly bewildered by the dynamism of circumstances. Moreover, numerically they lacked power and, to complete their confusion, they found themselves impeded by conflicts of opinion on the fundamental problems of the revolution and the war.

In the concert—or rather, the confusion—of the parties, the Communists continued to occupy a front rank. Through their unbreakable unity, combative ardour and unanimous resolve never to capitulate (in the other parties there were those who thought a compromise with Franco both desirable and possible), the Communist Party was a war party of much weight in the Republic. The Communists were striving to occupy in the Republic at war, the place that the Socialists had occupied in the Republic of April 14th. The growth and moral leadership of the Communist Party was, nevertheless, imposed by the circumstances (not forgetting circumstances abroad) which have already been emphasized.

At the head of the Government, Negrín not only expressed, through his realism, the popular will, but his most salient characteristics responded to the crying needs of the hour. Negrín was the instrument of powerful circumstances which, as so often happens in history, snatched from the vortex the man who was most fitted to take charge of the situation. In 1937, this man of science became, by force of circumstances, and not by his own wish, the indispensable leader of the war and of the Republic.

Naturally this did not happen—in so far as it depended on Negrín—merely because of his intellectual vigour or his knowledge of national and international problems, still less because of his experience as a politician and a Minister, although his administration in the Ministry of Finance qualified him for more ample scope in governmental affairs. Azaña was also a skilful leader, a well-read, travelled man, with considerable political experience; nevertheless he had gone astray intellectually both before and after the civil war.

It was not enough to be intelligent, cultivated, or a perspicacious politician in order to lead the Republic out of the impasse into which it had fallen. What was needed, primarily, was a man of action; that is to say, the possessor of sufficient moral energy to confront with a clear mind the most formidable responsibilities. Action is the begetter of conflict and conflict involves responsibility, and responsibility cannot be met except by a man of action, who can act in the measure corresponding to the weight of responsibility. Such a man must have greatness of heart, to an exceptional degree. In short, he must be a great man.

These three attributes—intelligence, moral energy and greatness of soul—are endowments which, in effect, are rarely found together; but when they are to be met in any conspicuous measure, in one and the same person, they are the infallible signs of a great man. A great man, according to the classic definition, is one who sees farther and goes deeper into things than the generality of people; who has a standard of ethical values different from that of others; and who has enough energy to impose his vision of reality. And to this minority Negrín undoubtedly belonged.

Negrín was approaching his forty-fifth year when the civil war broke out. Extraordinarily vital, endowed at once with an iron constitution and unusual mental energy, he possessed, in every respect, a kind of excess of vitality which could have launched him with the certainty of success into the absorbing political strife of a nation in mortal peril, like Spain, if he had felt a vocation for political life or had had any ambition to take his place among the immortals. But the former did not appeal to him—the latter aroused his derision. As a citizen, he could not turn his back on the national problems—who could in Spain?—but he had witnessed the tragicomic political scene as an anxious spectator rather than as an actor. In 1928, during the dictatorship of Primo de Rivera, Negrín thought it his duty to join a party and his choice fell on Socialism, with whose postulates and philosophy he had become familiar during his years as a student in Germany. But apart from aspiring, in substance, to the faded laurels of an anonymous and disciplined member of the Socialist Party, Negrín, in becoming part of this organization, was far from desiring to tuck himself away in sectarian pigeon-holes. All he did was to proclaim that the party founded by Pablo Iglesias was, in his opinion, the most solvent party, the party which was called upon to direct the destinies of the nation and the best prepared for this high task. For to Negrín, the party, whatever its label, could not be an end in itself, without running the risk of condemning itself to sterility. Nothing could have been more remote to his anti-demagogic spirit, which had run the whole gamut of life, than to think that the party could sacrifice the nation on the altars of class-interest. That is to say that Negrín, who looked with the eyes of a philosopher on the men of one book, was not a Marxist, nor did he consider himself a link in the chain of one particular social class.

The son of well-to-do parents in the Canary Islands, Negrín was Fortune's favourite from his childhood. He was able to choose a career, to travel, to move about the world at his own caprice. In reality, he was formed intellectually outside Spain,

608

in Germany, during the twelve or fourteen years which are most important to the future of the individual; and there he completed his scientific studies which afterwards earned him a a Chair of Physiology in the University of Madrid.

His residence abroad, his aptitude for languages of which he knew a great many, and his insatiable curiosity, made of Negrín a citizen of the world, an internationalist, without thereby diminishing his sterling patriotism.

In the end, as was natural, Negrín could not stand aside from political activity, any more than could other Spaniards who were eminent in the arts and sciences. In Spain, as in all nations undergoing a mortal crisis, patriotism and aloofness from political strife do not go hand in hand; and in a nation of such striking social inequality any Spaniard less than sixty years of age who is not a revolutionary is an inferior. I have already hinted that Azaña would probably never have broken a lance in the political struggles of his country, had not the national tragedy drawn him away from the literature which was his true and tyrannical vocation. But in Negrín the distaste for the hurly-burly of public life was stronger than in others; partly because he hated publicity (in this respect, he would have liked to possess Gyges' ring and become invisible to the public and to photographers) and partly because he did not consider he had the temperament for politics, which, in view of the crudeness of political life in a primitive nation, was certainly true. Neither was Negrín an orator, as the man of action seldom is. He had none of the demagogue in his composition, as even the most austere politician had; and the desire to proselytize was not included in his make-up; whether he had disciples or not was apparently all one to him. He became a deputy without having made a speech in the accepted meaning of the word, and Prime Minister in a democratic Government (an extraordinary phenomenon in Spain) without having become a well-known figure on public platforms.

Another personal idiosyncrasy divorced Negrín perhaps instinctively from active politics—the desire to defend his personal liberty, the passion for personal freedom of a man used to conduct his life by his own standards, or—to the vulgar observer—by no standards at all. He extracted from life the last ounce of enjoyment, and because of this, those who only knew him superficially might have thought him frivolous. But beneath the mask of frivolity and beneath that other contrasted mask of the hard and reserved man—his second line of defence—

there was a fine, cultivated and serious mind and a sensitive heart.

In his relations with men and parties, Negrín held to a principle peculiar to the superior man: firmness in fundamental things, compromise in unessentials. Such, to my way of thinking, was the man called by circumstances to the outstandingly difficult mission of leading the Republic to victory, in a world which was officially almost entirely hostile to it.

Let us now turn back to the course of events.

The crumbling of the Pyrenean-Aragonese front and the arrival of the insurgents on the Mediterranean confirmed many in the conviction, which some had held since July 17th, 1936, that the Republic had lost the war. For Negrín, the Republic had no option but to resist and, if the worst came to the worst, go down fighting. He argued, therefore, as was his duty to do and, fortunately, also his conviction, that the war could be won.

It cannot be said that there were many Republicans of any class who were in favour of unconditional surrender, though a few would have bought peace at any price. But there were a fair number in influential circles of the régime who thought it worth while to broach the subject of capitulation. This kind of person used to be called "copperheads" during the American Civil War—an allusion to the most poisonous snakes in the United States. To imagine that the Republic could capitulate in any other circumstances than those which would leave it at the mercy of an unscrupulous enemy, crazed by hate and fear, was to ignore supinely the calibre of the Spanish Fascists and, with equal crassness, to fail to recognize the character of the help which Franco was receiving from Italy and Germany. Franco had invariably replied up till then to individual and official soundings on the subject of a compromise peace, with the monotonous and blunt refrain: "Unconditional surrender." Those who thought that the Republic could in any case count on the diplomatic support of the democracies were out of their senses. The ruling classes in England and France desired the victory of Franco—Germans or no Germans, Italians or no Italians—as eagerly as the Governments of Berlin and Rome. The reaction of the French Government to the catastrophe of March and April was to send a cruiser to Catalan waters so that Azaña and the Government could escape. In official circles in London, the splitting of the Spanish Republic into two zones was greeted with satisfaction, since it was supposed that the demise of the Republic could not now be much longer delayed. And this impression was fortified by the words of anguish spoken by individual politicians of the Republic and picked up by the chancelleries; words which were obviously well-intentioned because they sprang from the assumption that the triumph of the rebels was alarming, as it should have alarmed, the Governments of London and Paris; but actually harmful in the extreme, because there was no such alarm in London— quite the contrary—and in Paris, where there was greater anxiety, no Government would lift a finger to help a Republic which was already, according to those who ought to know, on the point of dissolution. The enemies of the Spanish Republic would do nothing to save it, and to go to them with jeremiads was a waste of time; on the other hand, to represent the situation as irreparable to those who might help the Republic with weapons to defend itself with, was to dissuade and discourage them by giving them the impression that anything they did would be too late.

Finally, those Republicans, whatever their political label, who thought a compromise with the rebels was feasible and sought mediators where they thought they could find them, not only shook the Republic's credit abroad (as if it was not already sufficiently shaken), but also spread at home, first among a small group, but afterwards among a great number of Republicans, the tragic mirage that justice could be looked for from the enemy.

In April 1938, the Republic had not lost the war, in spite of the disaster at Vinaroz. The rebel advance towards Castellón was meeting with energetic resistance from the Republicans, and Franco's penetration of 100 kilometres to the south cost him two months of ferocious fighting before he finally took the port. Castellón fell on June 16th and the front was stabilized at about twenty-five kilometres from Sagunto.

During these two months, the French frontier had been open to the passage of war material for the Republic. The Government arsenals received the anxiously awaited reinforcements of light artillery, anti-tank guns, tanks, a few aeroplanes, machine-guns and rifles; arms for the most part acquired in Russia, though some were also bought in the United States and other countries, wherever the Republican Government had been able to obtain them.

In the Levante, the resistance of the Government troops stiffened. Valencia was protected from the north by the Sierra de Espadán and by excellent fortifications constructed by the

Republicans in those winding passes, between Viver and the coast. Persuaded that they could not open a passage through the unassailable fortifications that covered Sagunto, thanks to the tenacious opposition of the anti-Fascist troops, the Italians began a new offensive on July 15th from Teruel, with Valencia as their objective. The rebel forces consisted of the Littorio and "23rd of March" Divisions and the mixed Blue Arrow Division, commanded by Italian officers. The enemy attacked with an enormous weight of artillery (about 600 guns) and about 400 aeroplanes. Franco's forces, with the Italians, numbered about 80,000 men.

The insurgent attack broke with the usual fury. One after another, the first Republican positions were overwhelmed, though the enemy met with heroic resistance at many points, as at Mora de Rubielos. Hundreds of aeroplanes had pulverized the villages on the road from Teruel to Valencia. On the 18th, the Italian columns reached the fortifications which defended Viver. The Republican engineers had constructed very solid strong-points, some of which were capable of withstanding a 1,000-lb. bomb. These fortifications covered all the approaches the rebel troops might use in their advance on Valencia. The Italians, who probably thought Republican resistance had been overcome and saw themselves already in Valencia, threw themselves on the fortified positions. Then began the greatest massacre of the whole war on the field of battle. As the Fascists surged forwards, the Government machine-guns literally mowed them down. According to an English eye-witness, the Nationalists brought up guns and began to shell the defences with an intensity that recalled the World War. It would be difficult to say how many shells a minute fell on the fortifications; and when the guns stopped firing, the bombers appeared, dropped their bombs and returned for more, which they again dropped. It seemed impossible that anyone could still survive in those hills. Yet when the infernal bombardment ceased and the Nationalists tried to advance on the fortifications, the Republican machine-guns again spat fire furiously from among the ruins. Then, more hours of punishment, more bombs. The insurgent bombers could fly as low as they liked, since the Government possessed no anti-aircraft guns in this sector.

On July 25th, the Republicans were still resisting before Viver. In eight days the enemy lost 15,000 to 20,000 men, the greatest massacre, as I have said, of the whole war; losses as great as the combined armies of Wellington and Blücher suffered at Waterloo.

Whatever were the enemy's plans before the insuperable anti-Fascist defence in the Viver sector, a new Republican offensive on the Ebro forced him finally to abandon the conquest of Valencia and suspend offensive operations in Estremadura.

At dawn on July 25th, the first units of the Republican Army crossed the mighty river of Aragon, slightly below its confluence with the Segre. The offensive caught the insurgents unawares. The Republicans penetrated 45 kilometres behind the enemy lines and took a great number of prisoners, mostly Moors and Italians; by the fifth day, they had reconquered an area of 700 square kilometres and widened the bridgehead to an extent of 32 kilometres.

The Government forces performed prodigies in these operations on the Ebro. Within a few days, more than 50,000 men with their equipment, including 300 guns and general supplies, had crossed the river. Incessant enemy air attacks on positions and troops without anti-aircraft defences complicated in no small measure the movements of troops and the work of the engineers. In addition, the rebels opened some of the dikes and the resultant flood carried away some of the improvised bridges, which the Republicans rebuilt with surprising rapidity. But it was obvious that as soon as the battle moved west of the Ebro, the enemy's superiority in armour would destroy the advantages gained by the Republicans by surprise and audacity. In these conditions, the strategically inferior position of the Government Army, practically isolated in what was basically enemy territory and only linked to Republican territory by the railway near Mora de Ebro, was thrown into relief. The Republican Army demonstrated its excellent qualities in an unequal struggle which lasted about four months;[1] on November 15th, its last units crossed to the east bank.

Madrid, Teruel, Sagunto, Viver and the Ebro had proved that the Republic had an Army and that some units of this Army were formidable, taking into account the poverty of their equipment. As in all revolutionary wars, part of the Republican military command devolved upon men of the people, soldiers formed in the struggle, petty Cromwells, until a short while ago absorbed in their obscure professions and, some of them

[1] The correspondent of the Stefani Agency at Saragossa made known on August 8th the support received by the insurgents from Italian airmen in the critical days of the battle of the Ebro. "From July 25th–August 5th, the 'legionary' aeroplanes took part in 1,672 air combats, with a total of 2,817 flying hours. They dropped 462 tons of explosives and fired 5,800 rounds from their machine-guns. The total number of aeroplanes used was 541."

in their Marxist Bible—men who would never have believed it, if they had been told that one day they would command an Army Corps. Among the soldiers of this kind were Juan Modesto, a carpenter, commander of the army which fought on the Ebro; Enrique Lister, a stone-cutter, who achieved particular distinction at Teruel, defended Tortosa and led the 5th Army Corps on the Ebro; Valentín González, *El Campesino*, who, though much inferior to Modesto and Lister, had distinguished himself in Guadalajara and held the enemy in check for a week at Lérida; Cipriano Mera, also a labourer, commander of an Army Corps in the Central zone; Gustavo Durán, a musician, commander of the forces who fought the enemy to a standstill before Sagunto; Tagüeña, a University man, who held the Littorio Division, with its abundant artillery and aeroplanes, at Cherta for two weeks with half a division; and many others, like Medina, *El Campesino's* right-hand man, less known and subordinate to the popular and professional officers.

All these soldiers of the Republic came from the first militias, not from the Academies, and though some of them based their claim to command on the strength of having taken a course of study in the art of warfare, they depended for technical matters on the officers of the old Army. But, in their turn, the professional soldiers were, generally speaking, dependent for leadership on these improvised soldiers. The latter lacked technical knowledge, the former lacked the fire and genius for leadership which revolutionary times demand.

The most eminent of the professionals was Don Vicente Rojo, who was a major at the outset of the war and the most competent and studious of the soldiers who served the Republic in its most critical hour. Rojo had been an instructor in the Infantry Academy of Toledo, and during the civil war he was promoted General and Chief of the General Staff. To sum up, these two types of commander—amateur and professional—were mutually complementary, the one supplying morale and energy, the other, technical knowledge.

The popular Army always suffered, however, like the whole conduct of the war in the democratic camp, from a radical defect. At the beginning, each party founded its militia, and each militia was the fighting arm of a party or trade-union organization. When the militias were converted into the new Army, the existence of the political parties, each firmly planted in its old-time party position, was reflected in the armed forces in a manner which gave rise to disquiet. Although there were no units which were specifically Communist, Socialist, Re-

614

publican, Anarchist, etc., the commanders, both popular and professional, had not lost their clear-cut political bias; most of them were party men, who kept a watchful eye on the political controversies in which the parties in the rearguard were perpetually embroiled. Every officer, every soldier, had in his wallet his certificate of affiliation to a political or trade-union organization. For their part, the party politicians were attentive to, and highly suspicious of, the political bent of the Army.

Imbued with the obsession of not losing the peace, the political parties did their utmost to help the Republic to lose the war. The political sympathies of the Army commanders, especially the men of the people, were so pronounced that, to some extent, no one could triumph or fail without automatically involving his party in victory or in his personal discomfiture. Consequently, no one could be promoted without the displeasure or suspicion of his rivals, who saw in his promotion the political progress and increased influence of his party. The promotion of Lister, a Communist, to the rank of Lt.-Colonel in recognition of his brilliant conduct of the battle of Teruel, was followed a few days later by the promotion to the same rank of Mera, an Anarchist.

All this was absurd, but probably difficult to avoid in a revolutionary war which depended on the moods of political parties, a thing rarely seen in history, at least in the history of successful revolutions.

It is, then, surprising that in such conditions, the Republic should have succeeded in maintaining a disciplined and efficient Army. It speaks very highly of the Spanish people's capacity for constructive effort in the most adverse circumstances, and makes one wonder what Spanish democracy could not do if one day it began to let itself be guided by common sense.

Let us now turn to another subject, equally obstructive to Republican victory. On August 17th, 1938, the Basque and Catalan nationalists had provoked a new Ministerial crisis when Señor Ayguadé, Minister of Labour, and Señor Irujo, Minister without Portfolio, left the Government of the Republic. Their motive for resigning was the promulgation by the Government of three decrees, two connected with finance and the third with the Ministry of Justice. With these measures, the Government of the Republic proposed to withdraw from the jurisdiction of the regional authorities faculties, attributes or organisms in the constitutional competence of the State. The Negrín Ministry was joined by two new Ministers: Don Tomás

615

Bilbao, of *Acción Nacionalista Vasca*, and Moix, of the *Partido Socialista Unificado de Cataluña*.

It was not the first time during the war that the Republican Government had clashed with the autonomous Governments of the Basque country and Catalonia. On the contrary, the conflict over jurisdiction had not ceased for a single moment since the Statutes were promulgated. But the Catalan and Basque nationalists profited by the reigning confusion and the agony of the Republic to repudiate, first in practice, then in both practice and theory, the Statutes of Autonomy.

On July 25th, 1936, a decree was passed by the Catalan *Generalidad* to extend the jurisdiction of the "Rector of the Autonomous University of Catalonia" (until then the Autonomous University of Barcelona) to secondary education, which was in the competence of the central Government. The University passed under the direct jurisdiction of the Council of Cultural Relations (*Consejo de Cultura*) of the *Generalidad* and the representatives of the Republican Government disappeared from the board of the Council.

By another decree the *Generalidad* dissolved the *Juntas de Obras del Puerto* (Harbour Works Committee) of Barcelona and Tarragona, in which the national Government had been represented.

Another similar measure was the decree of August 20th, transferring to the Catalan Department of the Interior all the functions within the national competence of the Republic in Catalonia.

The Official Bulletin of the *Generalidad* was converted into an Official Journal and only the regulations appearing in this publication were to be obeyed and carried out by Catalans.

The *Generalidad* provided an escort for the "President of Catalonia", who changed his title of Honourable for that of Excellency; and on October 15th, the "President of Catalonia" arrogated to himself the right of reprieve, a faculty which was exclusive to the President of the Republic.

Towards the end of August the *Generalidad* presented the central Government with a triply urgent demand for a credit of 50 million pesetas to cover the cost of the war in Aragon and Majorca, another of 30 million francs in Paris in order to acquire raw materials, and an authorization from the *Centro de Contratación de Moneda* to obtain 100 million pesetas in cash. The Government granted all these, subject to certain modifications, on September 8th. On August 22nd, the Republican Minister of Finance requested the *Generalidad* to contribute

373,176,000 pesetas in gold and 1,060,000 pesetas in silver to the national metallic reserve fund. The national Government proposed to concentrate gold and silver in Madrid to prevent secret hoarding and exportation. The *Generalidad* refused. The negotiations between the Government of the Republic and the Catalan Government ended with the deferment of this thorny question until after the war. The same thing occurred over the gold and silver reserves of the Basque Provinces.

The *Generalidad's* reply was not only negative; it foreshadowed the proposal to create an independent financial organization—a tendency subsequently expressed by the appointment of an inspector of the *Generalidad* to each branch of the Bank of Spain in Catalonia. The Catalan separatists were planning the creation of their own system of central banking and note issue. On August 28th, the *Generalidad* founded the Official Discount Bank.

On September 26th, Companys reconstructed the Government of the *Generalidad* and besides confirming Terradellas as Finance Councillor, appointed him First Councillor or Prime Minister of the Autonomous Government. Thus, Companys himself became *de facto* President of the Catalan Republic. The new Government assumed the attributes of sovereign power, including a Ministry of Defence, under Sandino.

On October 21st, the *Generalidad* created a Department of Foreign Trade and all goods for export began to bear the mark "Made in Catalunya". A month later this Department took over all the functions of the Official Chamber of Commerce and Navigation at Barcelona.

On December 11th, the *Generalidad* sanctioned the issue of banknotes, with an initial issue of 20 million pesetas.

On December 27th, the *Generalidad* founded a Secretariat of Foreign Affairs, as an adjunct of the Presidency.

The new independent financial system of Catalonia was expounded by José Terradellas in fifty-eight decrees promulgated by the "President of Catalonia" between the 8th and the 12th of January 1937. By a decree of November 20th, the Finance Councillor of the *Generalidad* assumed full powers to carry out the unification of the Catalan finances. Among other things, the plan provided for the "nationalization" of foreign trade.

"The *Generalidad*", wrote Azaña, "has got away with everything."[1]

No one in the Republic had fought harder or with more success than Azaña to bring Catalan autonomy to fruition.

[1] *La Velada en Benicarló*, p. 107.

Neither his pen nor his voice ever grew weary in proclaiming the good faith of the Catalan nationalists, their moderation—according to Azaña—in viewing the problem of the relations of the autonomous region with the State and their like-mindedness with the non-Catalan supporters of autonomy. "These men", said Azaña of the Catalan autonomists, "represent for us a sense of Republican liberty and a sense of autonomy which coincides exactly with the programmes, ideas and proposals of our Republican Party."[1] The leader of the Republic recognized immediately that "there had arisen in Spain, as a result of the discussion of the Catalan Statute in Parliament, an agitation, a propagandist campaign, a protest, an alarm".[2] Vast sectors of public opinion, in fact,—not all of them reactionary—thought that the Statute marked a great step forward to secession. Even among the middle class, which supported the Republic, particularly among the business world (and not excluding a great number of Catalans themselves), there existed the conviction, as I have said in another chapter, that behind autonomous aspirations lurked a determined separatist design. Azaña took up the challenge of these seemingly passionate voices, stigmatizing their fears as prejudice. "The only way to solve the problem of Catalonia", he asserted, "is to solve it on liberal lines." The Republican middle class and the proletariat agreed with him. For their part, the Catalan nationalists accepted the Statute with words of good faith: "For the first time in history", wrote one of them, "we are on the way to a fitting and just internal political organization. Let us pursue it without hesitation. Our watchword is: complete political and social regeneration, through the sincere fulfilment of the Constitution."

In this atmosphere the Republicans, reassured by the words of Azaña and the Catalan nationalists, thought that the latter would not push autonomy too far or cause serious trouble for the Republic—a régime which, even at the risk of infuriating the oligarchy, alienating the greater part of the Army and exciting the indifference or hostility of many other Spaniards, was adopting a liberal attitude towards their aspirations.

For the man who had fought most fervently for the autonomy of Catalonia, the conduct of the *Generalidad* dispelled his last illusions, if he still had any left. In this spirit, Azaña wrote the most despairing condemnation of his own work. "The Government of Catalonia, through its debility and through the fact that it is pursuing secondary aims under cover of the war, is the most powerful hindrance to our military action. The

[1] Speech in the Cortes, Oct. 22nd, 1931.     [2] Ibid., May 22nd, 1932.

*Generalidad* is in insurrection against the Government. Whilst they say unofficially that purely Catalan questions have taken a back place, that today no one thinks of pushing autonomy to extremes, the *Generalidad* attacks the services and sequesters the functions of the State, moving towards a *de facto* separation. It legislates on what does not fall within its competence, administers what does not belong to it. In many assaults on the State, they shelter behind the *F.A.I.* They take over the Bank of Spain, so that the *F.A.I.* shall not take it over. They take over the Customs, the frontier guards, the direction of the war in Catalonia, etc. Under the miserable pretext of preventing misuse of the trade unions to despoil the State, they complain that the State does not help them and they themselves become prisoners of the trade unions. The Government of Catalonia exists in name only. The trade union representatives in the Government signify little or nothing; their comrades neither obey them nor fulfil the agreements painfully drawn up in council. The decree to collectivize industry was approved, as part of a compromise, in exchange for which the trade unions accepted the decrees of mobilization and militarization. The first was fulfilled, but not the others. When the Government of the *Generalidad* promulgated at one time fifty-eight decrees, each one of which was an infringement of the law, not one of them was observed, because the trade unions did not like them. We have here the double gain that the *Generalidad* interferes in things outside its competence and anarchic disobedience reigns. The repercussions on the war are already apparent. A rich, populous, hard-working country, with great industrial potential, has, as it were, mortgaged its power to make war. While others fight and die, Catalonia indulges in political squabbles. There is practically no front to speak of. It may be wondered why the rebels have not tried to break it; if they had wanted to, they could have been at Lérida by now. In the eighth month of the war, nothing has been done in Catalonia to organize an Army worthy of the name, after objecting to the central Government organizing and commanding one. . . . The newspapers, and even the men of the *Generalidad*, speak daily of the revolution and of winning the war. They talk of Catalonia taking part in the war not as a province, but as a nation. As a neutral nation, some say. They talk of war in Iberia. Iberia? Where is that? An ancient country of the Caucasus. . . . If the war is in Iberia, they can take it calmly. At this rate, if we win, the result will be that the State will owe money to Catalonia. Catalan affairs under the Republic have done more than anything else to arouse the Army's hostility to the régime. During the war the pest of anarchy has come out of Catalonia. Catalonia has been an enormous drain on the strength of the Republic to resist the rebels and to wage war."[1]

These words of Azaña, though denouncing a reality which no one touched so closely as he did, are not, in form at least, free of passion. Companys was not an advocate of separatism, but he was a man of weak will, and in that confusion he allowed himself to be overruled by not too intelligent advisers who, in their self-deception, thought it permissible and practical to take advantage of the situation to exceed the Statute, thus stupidly imperilling the autonomy already achieved and alienating the sympathies of Republicans like Azaña who had done so much to bring it about. On the other hand, the Government of the *Generalidad* found itself, from the moment the war began, outflanked by the proletariat, to whom it owed, in a large measure, its existence; and the workers' parties also wanted to profit by the occasion to carry out their revolution, obliging the *Generalidad* to issue decrees that were contrary to the law.

The Catalan situation lost some of its virulence when the Negrín Government moved to Barcelona. Little by little, the Government of the Republic recovered the attributes and powers that had been trampled under foot. And the decrees on which the representatives of Catalan and Basque nationalism had based their abandonment of the national Government were among the last measures adopted to this end.

As we shall see later, Basque nationalism did not lag behind its Catalan counterpart in justifying the fears of the anti-autonomist Cassandras. "The amateur Basque Government", wrote Azaña, "is meddling in international affairs."[2] In effect, the Basque Government created a Department or Directorate of Foreign Affairs which was entrusted to a member of the Nationalist Party, a person who liked to repeat: "White and Red in Spain, they are the same."[3]

The war in the Basque Provinces ended in June 1937. Nothing had occurred there which was not common to the whole of Republican Spain during the first year of the armed conflict, although the German air terror reached its maximum intensity

[1] *La Velada en Benicarló*, pp. 101 *et seq.*
[2] Ibid., p. 107.
[3] G. L. Steer, *The Tree of Gernika*, p. 132.

with the destruction of Guernica and the maritime blockade caused the civil population sufferings which the rest of anti-Fascist Spain was to endure only later. In sum, heroism, hunger and desperation, tempered at times by faith in the justice of the cause at stake.

The leadership of the war and of politics in this region devolved in actual fact on the most conservative, and at the same time most considerable force, which was Basque nationalism. And the Basque nationalists, with some exceptions, no doubt, lost sight of the fact that besides a war, a national revolution was taking place. The Basque nationalists were offered an excellent opportunity of learning the history of Spain and of understanding other Spaniards—of understanding, on the one hand, Spaniards from Asturias, Santander and Madrid and, on the other, the Spaniards who were attacking from Navarre; in short, of realizing that all were not the same or equal. But the Basque nationalists, with the exception, perhaps, of Aguirre and a small group, understood neither the one nor the other during the war, as they had not understood them, or wanted to understand them, before. It was impossible for the majority to grasp that something more profound and universal was at stake than their Statute. As a Conservative and Catholic party, a party of *order*, most of the nationalists were more anxious about their allies than their enemies, especially if the former were not Basques and the latter were. Obsessed by the desire not to lose their respectability and to maintain their repute as good Catholics, they showed an indulgence towards the Fascists bordering on frivolity. For example, the head of the military censorship was a major attached to the General Staff called Arbex, who exclaimed at a council which had been summoned to decide whether Bilbao could hold out or not: "What is the sense in letting ourselves be killed here?" Naturally, Arbex went over to the enemy a few days later, with all the information in his possession. The head of the Basque General Staff, Colonel Montaud, was also frank: "Our peasantry, if you want to know the truth, is at heart more at one with the other side than with us", he said.[1]

This incredible tolerance of the Basque Government towards suspected or avowed traitors could only lead to a catastrophe. The catastrophe duly occurred. Captain Goicoechea, a Basque and an officer of the old Army, inspector of the ring of fortifications which was supposed to defend Bilbao, one day placed the plans of the fortifications in a brief-case, drove his car to the

[1] Steer, p. 223.

front, and coolly passed over to the enemy. Goicoechea's treachery quickly sealed the fate of Bilbao. Yet the Basque Nationalists did not take his base betrayal seriously. "We knew him well", they said. "He's a pleasant fellow and got on very well with us. He isn't at all a Fascist; he's a Basque at heart. In his case, it wasn't ordinary treason; he was just terrified by the poverty of our resources at the time when he went. He was frequently in the party (Basque nationalist) offices and we could see that he really favoured our cause."[1]

The Basque nationalists thought this was the way a "highly civilized people" should make war. And the thought that they might appear bloodthirsty and brutal if they took the necessary measures against Fascists who had the military plans in their pockets, led them not only to allow these same Fascists to stay at the head of the defence of Bilbao, but even to treat them with respect. Goicoechea was a Basque at heart, and when he went over to the enemy, taking the plans of the fortifications with him, it was not, forsooth, a sign that he sympathized with the Fascists, but simply his love of Bilbao—that love of Bilbao, which, shared by the Basque nationalists, was to produce, weeks later, the catastrophe of Santoña.

With Bilbao in peril, the Basque Government moved to Santander, where they organized the evacuation to France of part of the Basque civil population which had taken refuge there. Aguirre took up residence in a villa at Cabo Mayor.

Between five and six o'clock on the evening of June 19th, 1937, the enemy occupied Bilbao.[2] The Republican Army retreated towards Santander, in good order, with all their equipment. The Basque nationalist units, consisting of about 25,000 men, encamped between Castro-Urdiales on the coast and Valmaseda to the south. In Santander, the Republican forces amounted to another 25,000 men. The equipment of both Armies was, as usual, much inferior in number, and partly also in quality, to what the enemy could bring up. The only novelty in this respect was the addition of nine Russian fighter monoplanes which had been flown direct from Madrid to Santander after the fall of Bilbao. The Government Air Force at the aerodrome of La Albericia at Santander consisted of eighteen Russian fighters, seventeen Gourdous bombers and a collection of obsolete Potezs and Breguets.

On the 14th, the Fascists had begun an offensive against Santander from the south. The forces taking part in this attack

[1] Steer, p. 151.
[2] For the succeeding events, I have followed Steer almost literally.

were mainly Italians, and, with their usual abundance of artillery and aircraft, they soon broke the Republican lines at the Puerto del Escado. On the 18th, Franco's forces were half-way between their point of departure and Santander. (Yet it was almost two months before they entered the capital.)

Some days later the enemy despatched one of his columns towards Asturias with the object of cutting the communications of Santander at Torrelavega. At that moment General Gamir Ulibarri, one of the most competent Republican soldiers, commanding the forces of the Republic in the north, ordered two Basque battalions to cover positions on the Santander line. "For the first time, the Basques refused to fight. They would not kill themselves any more doing *Santander's business*. They had marched far enough from their own country; they would stay where they were, on the borders of Vizcaya."[1]

Later came the order from the Republican General Staff to retreat towards Asturias; but the Basque nationalist army, instead of obeying, began to concentrate on Santoña. The Basque nationalists had another plan. One battalion—the Pandura—occupied Santoña and the other nationalist battalions occupied Laredo and Colindres between them.

The Basque nationalist leaders had decided to conclude a separate peace with the Italians. Juan de Achuriaguera, President of the Executive Committee of the Basque Nationalist Party, had gone to parley with General Mancini, Commander of the Blue Arrow Division.

Aguirre, President of the Autonomous Government, went to France in an aeroplane. Rezola and the rest of the *Departamento de Defensa* arrived at Santoña with the archives. They knew that they would be shortly going to France in English ships, but first they had to be present at the surrender of the Basque Army.

Not without surprise for the most part, those civilians and soldiers who had crowded into Santoña learnt that they could not get to Santander either by sea or land. The Basque nationalist battalions and the Executive Committee had set up a *Junta de Defensa* to carry out the capitulation, had occupied the port, and trained machine-guns on all the roads, holding everybody virtually prisoners.

The conditions of surrender signed by Juan de Achuriaguera and his lieutenant Arteche, with General Mancini were as follows:

[1] Steer, p. 380.

On the part of the Basque troops:

I. To lay down their arms in order and surrender their material to the Italian legionary forces, who should occupy the region of Santoña without resistance.

II. To maintain public order in the zone that they occupied.

III. To assure the life and liberty of the political hostages in the prisons of Laredo and Santoña.

On the part of the Italian forces:

I. To guarantee the lives of all Basque combatants.

II. To guarantee the lives and authorize the departure abroad of all Basque political personalities and functionaries at present in the territory of Santoña and Santander.

III. To consider Basque combatants subject to this capitulation free of all obligation to take part in the civil war.

IV. To assure that the Basque population loyal to the Provisional Government of Euzkadi should not be persecuted.

Certainly no separate peace was ever signed which was more disloyal to an ally—in this case, the non-Basque Republican Army and civil population. The injustice leaps to the eye when we realize that the non-Basque Republicans, deprived of the benefits of the capitulation, were also deprived by the Basque nationalists of the right to escape, by sea or land, to Santander, or· to retreat into Asturias or embark for abroad.

When the negotiations with Mancini began, the Basque nationalists lowered the flag of the Republic and hoisted their own flag in Laredo and Santoña. "For in the interval before surrender, the Basques had declared themselves free of both Spains."[1]

Let us pass over the fact that the Basque nationalists were already annexing territories outside the jurisdiction of the Basque Government, for the striking of the Republican flag at Santoña and the hoisting of their flag signified nothing else.

In the Town Hall of Santoña the political leaders and functionaries of the Nationalist Party were now awaiting the arrival of the ships from France which were to take them out of danger. The Santander campaign lasted until August 26th when the Fascists occupied the capital. On the 24th, Santander had not yet fallen and the Basque nationalists were still waiting in Santoña for the arrival of the Italians. They had had time to walk, not to France, but to the United States.

[1] Steer, p. 386.

On the 25th, the Basque troops began to show signs of discontent. Some said they did not trust the Italians and feared they would be forced to fight for Franco; others came to the Town Hall claiming equal rights of evacuation with their leaders. The more extreme elements took the attitude that if they were not evacuated, no one else should be.

By evening, the port was full of small armed and unarmed trawlers. The most impatient decided to embark. The ships lay in the harbour all night, because the *Junta de Defensa* would not allow them to put to sea. "There was no hurry: the Italians were trusted by the *Junta de Defensa*."

At nightfall the Italians entered Laredo. An Italian lieutenant-colonel preceded the troops in the side-car of a motor-cycle, and as soon as they had occupied Laredo the terms of surrender negotiated with the Basque nationalists were read to the public in the Plaza. The Italian flag was hoisted and, underneath, the document was affixed to a wall.

At dawn on the 26th, the *Junta de Defensa* in Santoña ordered the *bous* and trawlers to draw up to the quay and the people to disembark. The troops were disarmed and ordered to barracks. It was known that the Italians would enter Santoña in the afternoon and regulate the embarkation in accordance with lists which were being drawn up by the Basque leaders in the Town Hall.

In effect, towards five o'clock, the Italians entered Santoña and the *Junta de Defensa* handed over to Colonel Fergosi the administration of the city, a city in which neither the Basque Autonomous Government nor the Basque Nationalist Party had either jurisdiction or subjects. The Basques then handed over their arms, war material and Fascist prisoners. They undertook, further, to maintain public order in that zone, that is, to see that no one moved.

At this moment, two small British ships entered the bay. They had been sent from Bayonne, no doubt by other Basque nationalists, to take off the Basque *responsables*. They were the *Bobie* and the *Seven Seas Spray*. To the captain of the *Bobie*, a Frenchman called Georges Dupuy, we owe a moving and factual account of what happened in Santoña from the time of his arrival to the end of the Basque tragedy. Here it is:

"It was at 4 p.m. on Thursday and we were before Santoña. In our natural uncertainty with regard to the events in that town, we moved somewhat prudently towards the port. At 4.20 a little tug passed the point. A flag flew at its bows, but because of the light we took some time to identify it; at last we were able to assure ourselves that it was the flag of Euzkadi. At that we made rapidly for the harbour and cast anchor.

"The harbour was most animated. A large number of fishing-boats were lying in the anchorage, full of people. The *Gazteiz*, a small armed trawler, and two or three other small vessels were there also, and crowded. On the quay there was a mass of people throwing all their arms in heaps—rifles, revolvers, machine-guns, cartridge belts, everything. Armed men, Basques, guarded the quay and its surroundings. Troops in fair order were coming along the roads which opened on the port, then disarmed and dispersed.

"I went ashore with the captain of *Gazteiz*. In the town great animation, flags, banners, draperies in the colours of Franco, fluttering everywhere. Almost all the women were sporting Fascist ribbons and emblems. On two of the squares Italian soldiers were sitting and singing, their arms piled and unguarded.

"I went to the Town Hall, which was surrounded by a crowd of Basques without arms. Inside, the stairs and corridors were packed with people, and I had great difficulty pushing my way into the room where the leaders were. This room had also been invaded by the crowd, and there were wounded almost everywhere. An open door at the other end showed another room full of wounded.

"I asked for M. Axuriaguera whom I had been recommended to see before anyone else, and learned that he was at Vittoria and was expected back at any moment."

Dupuy, writes Steer, was then fully informed of the conditions of surrender. He asked for instructions about the embarkation of the militia, and was told that they were waiting for news. Though, adds Steer, he advised them to act quickly and send the fishing-boats away that night, nothing was done, and the only orders which he received, and carried out, were to move the archives and the radio equipment aboard *Bobie*.

"On my way back I noted nothing unusual. The streets and the quays were crowded, but order reigned. The Italians did not seem any more aggressive than before, and there was no blue Falangist uniform to be seen. At ten and about midnight, still no news.

"At six next morning, August 27th, I returned to the Town Hall, and found Italians there as well as Basques. The leaders did not seem to have the same control over their men's movements as yesterday. No news of M. Axuriaguera. The Town Hall was surrounded by Italian soldiers.

"At the same time, the Basques began to mass on the quay, in good order, waiting for the embarkation. At nine I received the order to begin to embark all those in possession of a special ticket issued by the leaders, or a passport of the Government of Euzkadi. The officer-observer of the Non-Intervention Committee on *Bobie*, M. Costa e Silva, examined the papers with me and the work went on in a businesslike way on both ships, *Bobie* and *Seven Seas Spray*.

"At ten o'clock an officer in the uniform of the Italian Army, but a Spaniard, and carrying the Falangist badge, came and gave me the order to interrupt the embarkation, and wait for new orders. I asked him who had told him to do so, and he said Colonel Fergosi, commanding Santoña.

"I stopped, and at this moment—about ten-fifteen—sections of Italian soldiers appeared on the quay, closed around the crowd of Basques who were waiting to board us, placed four machine-guns in excellently chosen positions and set a guard on *Bobie's* gangway, composed of a dozen men and a non-commissioned officer. All communication between ship and shore was forbidden.

"Italians piled the material abandoned by the Basques in lorries. I saw quite a column of *gudaris*, disarmed, going along the Laredo road, and also lorries, all of which carried the Italian flag.

"At two that afternoon Silva and I, escorted by four Italian soldiers, visited Colonel Fergosi at the Town Hall. None of the Basque leaders was there now, and it was occupied by Italians entirely.

"Colonel Fergosi told me that he had received formal orders from the Generalissimo—Franco—that no one, Basque or foreign, was to leave Santoña. I drew his attention to the fact that all the Basques on the two ships were now under the protection of the British flag and that if no more Basques could come on board I could nevertheless leave with those there already—and *Seven Seas Spray* too. His answer was definite. 'No one is allowed to leave Santoña, and the *Almirante Cervera*, which is outside, is already so informed.' Silva also insisted, but to no effect. We were separated, and our papers verified. (Their treatment of me having nothing to do with the point at issue, I pass over in silence the petty incident which followed until nine o'clock that night.)

"I returned to the ship at nine. The same Spanish officer ordered all the passengers to leave *Bobie*. All was done in an orderly way and the ship was then searched from top to bottom, by this person and four other Falangist officers. Next, the identity of *Bobie's* crew was verified and their papers examined word by wearisome word by the Falangists, particularly those of the two engineer officers (both Basques) and my own. At last, at midnight, the Falangist officer and his acolytes departed after strictly forbidding all communication with the shore.

"Saturday; and as daylight began to show, I saw the men who had been disembarked that evening walking along the road to Laredo. There were others on lorries which carried the Italian flag, that went away by another road. I do not know where.

"Then other Basques I saw were coming down to the quay to mass there; the Italian guard was commanded by Lt.-Colonel Farina. And there were Colonels Fergosi and Piesch, the latter in charge of concentration camps.

"Two groups formed on the quay; on one side the Basques who had fought in the war and been disarmed, on the other the political leaders. I was allowed to communicate with them, and learned:

( i) That there was no news of M. Axuriaguera, who ought to have left Vittoria the evening before;

(ii) That there was some hope that the negotiations now in progress would end in an order for all to go aboard. I was asked to delay our departure as long as possible for this reason.

"In truth, confidence and hope reigned in Santoña . . . at least among the leaders.

"At the same time, I received the order to disembark the archives and the radio. I resisted as long as I could, but without success in spite of the ardour and ingenuity of my arguments. The disembarkation had to be made and was completed by ten-thirty.

"All this time I was in conversation with Colonels Piesch and Farina. The latter in a frank moment expressed all his bitterness, and said how angered he was to see all that was going on. 'It is disgraceful', says Farina, 'to see that an Italian general cannot keep the promise which he has given (*sic*)' and 'there is no case in all history of such a thing happening'. Colonel Piesch added words of assent.

"Towards eleven, Colonel Farina told *Bobie* to make out to

anchor and await orders, and *Seven Seas Spray* to lay on to the quay and disembark the people aboard.

"Before *Bobie* left the quay, I saw Colonel Fergosi and asked him in the presence of Colonel Farina if the Basques were really prisoners of the Italian Army, and only of the Italian Army. He assured me that such was the case, and that it was not in the intention of General Mancini to deliver the Basques, whoever they were, to the Falangists. I thanked him for this assurance, and expressed a fervent hope that the promise would be kept.

"At the last moment I shook hands with the leaders and asked them if they had any message for the *Presidencia;* unfortunately their optimism was still too strong for them to think of anything to send. They only asked me to stay as long as possible at Santoña, in hope that the conversations would reach a successful conclusion.

"At mid-day we were settled at our anchorage. We could see the Laredo road, and columns of men upon it, every now and again groups of lorries with the Italian flag.

"At 9 p.m. an Italian officer, accompanied by four Falangists themselves officers, came aboard to give us the order to leave. Another search of the ship, and at 10 p.m. she was head on to the open sea. . . . The rest of the night passed without incident except for the appearance on deck of six men who had hidden in the machinery. We were in Bayonne next morning at nine-fifty."

CHAPTER XXIII

# THE REPUBLIC AT WAR
### (*continuation*)

At the end of 1938 the Republic had already exacted from that part of the Spanish people who were not yet under the insurgent yoke such sacrifices that only people well aware of what was at stake in their struggle with the forces of Fascist reaction (both their own and international) could have endured them. On the shoulders of the Spanish people fell all the weight of the conflict between classes and nations which was lying dormant in the world. Many powerful interests clashed on the Spanish battlefields. The Spanish Republicans were paying for everything; they were paying for their resistance to Franco and they were paying for their opposition to the imperialistic expansionism of Germany and Italy.

In general, the mass of the people in Europe and America were incapable of understanding the sufferings of the Spanish people save as a calamity from which they themselves had escaped and from which they proposed to continue escaping, whatever the cost to others.

In that moral unawareness of the West, the Spanish Republicans were the emblem of self-sacrifice. If the Spanish people had not been conscious that they were dying for interests higher than their own freedom, for those "Catholic, universal values" of which Bernard Shaw, in the paragraph with which I have begun one of the preceding chapters, pronounced them to be the champions, they could not have risen to such heights. But this persuasion that their cause was a universal one bred in the Spanish people the energy to persevere in the struggle. And this, and no other, was the secret of the moral grandeur of Madrid.

If the insurgents had not belonged to a social class which was rotten to the core and without honour, they could not have stomached the insult of being forced to remain for two and a half years before the gates of Madrid, impotent before the city walls, especially when they could count on an inexhaustible flow of foreign troops and overwhelmingly superior and up-to-date war material. Never did a proud oligarchy suffer such a great humiliation.

At the end of two and a half years of siege, the heart of Madrid had not changed; it was the same as in July and November of 1936. Bombarded from the air and land, with the front line but a tram fare from the centre of the town, exhausted by hunger and cold and by all the hardships which can make life intolerable and shake the morale of a people, Madrid was the most lively and genuine symbol of those racial virtues which spring perennially in the soul of the Spanish populace.

The scarcity of food, which was common throughout the Republican zone, was extremely serious in the capital of the Republic.

After thirty months of war, with things daily going from bad to worse, the people, in the regions where the Republic still held sway, would not admit defeat. Their bodies might weaken, their spirits never. The Republican soldier was not free from the heartbreaking influence of the privations he was enduring, and not the least of these was the lack of armaments. Nor could the sufferings of his family in the rear fail to leave their mark on him. This soldier might belong to one of the shock detachments of the Republic, or he might find himself in one of the least efficient units; in either case, his heart was with the Republic. Adversity did not succeed in modifying the feelings of the people, who from the first day had proved to the rebels (however much the latter laboured under the delusion that it was not so) that they would never be beloved of the common people. When the 43rd Division retreated over the Pyrenees into France, they were told by the French authorities that they were free either to pass over to the enemy or to continue the fight under the Republican banner. Of 4,000 soldiers, only 168 joined the rebels.

The Spanish people remained faithful to their Republic; and in a satisfied Europe, which placed its precarious peace and its petty diversions above unavoidable universal duties, the prowess of the Spanish Republicans was the hope of the generous and the intelligent. But this same prowess was a continual reproach and an annoying obstacle to the egoists, and a nightmare to the reactionaries. Far from admiring the splendid resistance of the Republicans, the egoists and cynics deplored it. They feared that if the Spanish conflagration were not soon extinguished, it would end by spreading over the whole of Europe and they would be enveloped by the flames. The destruction of the Spanish Republic was an urgent necessity, they thought, in the interests of peace. The ultra-reactionaries went farther. They desired the victory of Fascism in Spain and would have opened the doors of their country to the enemy (as they did in France) if by doing so they could have encompassed the downfall of European liberty.

But let us resume our account of events in Spain.

The campaign on the Ebro had held up the enemy for four months, which was equivalent to a great victory for the Republic; but, as after the struggle for Teruel, Franco was able to dovetail with the Ebro counter-offensive a new offensive as irresistible as that of the opening months of 1938. In contrast, the Republican Government could not replace the losses of equipment suffered in the recent fighting.

In June the French had again closed the frontier to all armaments for the Spanish Republic. The Republican Army salvaged everything that could possibly be salvaged after the bitter fighting on the Ebro; for the retreat to the east bank in November was a brilliant operation carried out with impeccable skill. But both troops and armour were suffering from the effects of the terrific effort expended. At the same time, the blockade which held anti-Fascist Spain a prisoner was at that moment tighter than ever. Once more the situation could not have been more difficult for the Republic. The Government was well aware of the facts, knowing as it did that the rebel forces were concentrating on the Catalan front—a threat which Negrín drew attention to in his words to the Army on December 11th. The battle of Catalonia was due to begin at any moment.

It should have begun on December 15th, but the weather, which was extremely unsettled, obliged the rebel High Command to put off the offensive. On the 23rd, large-scale aerial and artillery bombardments of the Republican lines were the prelude to the great attack. The enemy crossed the Segre south of Lérida with unexpected ease, and this breach endangered Catalonia.

On this sector the Italians, the best armed troops of the Fascist Army, were operating. The Republicans had to evacuate a large section of the river bank to avoid a surprise flank attack, and then the enemy began to outflank one position after another, without encountering any serious resistance. The Republican High Command immediately called up their reserves, throwing in the 5th Army Corps with orders to stem the insurgent advance at all costs.

For nine days the Italians—the spearhead of the attack— broke against the obstinate resistance of the Republicans in the mountains before Castelldans. But a strong enemy column opened up a path towards Borjas Blancas (on the road from Lérida to Tarragona) and on January 4th the Republic lost this important centre of communications.

The Italians could now develop their tactics without serious opposition, though some Republican battalions fought with unparalleled heroism. Nevertheless, the overwhelming and deadly array of armour which the Fascists disposed of on land and in the air had filled the democratic Army with dismay.

The Republican High Command endeavoured to establish a front from Vendrell, on the coast, towards the Tremp sector, but before they could gather sufficient forces to form this front the line was outflanked by the enemy tanks.

On the 15th the Italians entered Tarragona.

In the meanwhile, morale in Barcelona had sunk very low. German and Italian aircraft were bombarding the city, without opposition, as in March of the previous year. Transport was disorganized, the port was put out of action by enemy air raids, and within a few days the problem of feeding the city was hopelessly aggravated. The political bickering, which never ceased, the corrosive action of the separatist minority, personal and party strife, sharpened the public distress. Privations of all kinds, wide-spread suffering, and, above all, the sudden end to the hope of containing the enemy in the mountains, conspired together to announce the end of Republican resistance in Catalonia.

Between January 20th and 22nd, Barcelona suffered fifteen air attacks; between the 24th and 25th, eighteen.

A great part of the civil population of the Catalan capital and of many other places occupied or menaced by the insurgents, were already on the roads, in cars, on foot, hampered by their humble household goods, men, women and children, on the road to France—an exodus as pathetic as any of modern times. By their flight, the Spanish people announced, as clearly as if a plebiscite had been taken, that they preferred expatriation to life under the infamous government of the rebels.

On the 26th, the insurgents occupied Barcelona and the Republican Army retreated towards the frontier in better order than might have been expected (in better order than the French Army observed in their retreat of 1940).

The offensive which culminated in the conquest of Catalonia by the Fascists had been an Italian operation, and as such it will be known to history. In eloquent contrast, all the forces of the Republican Army were Spanish, the Government having disbanded the International Brigades in October.

Italian units constituted the principal and decisive nucleus of the Fascist Army which attacked Catalonia, and the General who distinguished himself in the campaign was also an Italian, Gambara. From the Segre to Gerona—where, in order to deceive the French, the Italians withdrew from the fight—it was the Italian forces which rolled back the Republican Army. The purely Spanish units caused the High Command of the People's Army less anxiety. Their mobility was not so great, no doubt because they did not possess such a great number of automatic rifles and light armoured cars. Entrenched in the mountains of Valls, the Republicans held, and visibly weakened, Franco's Spanish troops who were unable to dislodge them from their positions. Something similar occurred for some time on the Tremp-Balaguer sector. Only weight of numbers and the superior armaments of the Italian troops opened to the Fascists the road to Tarragona which, as we have seen, Mussolini's expeditionary force was the first to enter.

The infantry under Gambara's command numbered 40,000 men; and in addition, he had 15,000 or 20,000 men in the mechanized units or as reserves. These forces were grouped in the Littorio, Ninth of March, Green Arrow, Blue Arrow and Black Arrow divisions; the last three mixed with some Spanish elements, though in a minority. They were mobile units, equipped with enormous quantities of automatic rifles, machine-guns, light artillery and tanks. The light artillery consisted of some 400 Italian guns, and the heavy artillery of about 100 German guns. There were about 200 light Italian tanks and a large number of German *Mercedes*.

To complete the picture of the attacking Army, we must add to the Italian forces the German Condor Legion in the air, several Moorish divisions, a division of *Requetés* and a cohort of Fascist adventurers of various nationalities.

The Republican troops in Catalonia numbered about 120,000 men and they possessed no more than 37,000 rifles. At the beginning of the offensive, the Republican Army deployed from Lérida to the coast only possessed sixty pieces of artillery, and half of these were in poor condition. On the Valls sector there were one or two machine-guns to every battalion and twenty-eight guns to the whole Army Corps. The Republicans were almost entirely without anti-tank guns and heavy artillery; and the Fascists could put between ten and twenty aeroplanes into the air for every Government plane.

In spite of this, more than one French port at that time was overflowing with war material of all kinds belonging to the Spanish Republic, the last consignment of armaments acquired by the Spanish Government from the U.S.S.R.—the last, and the most considerable, since it represented a larger quantity of war material than the Russian Government had hitherto supplied to the Spanish Republic. It included more than 500 aeroplanes and thirty torpedo-boats. If instead of immobilizing it, the French Government had permitted the delivery of such an important consignment of war material in September, before the offensive against Catalonia had begun, the Republican Army would have been better equipped than even before. But all the steps the Republican Government took to gain effective possession of the Russian arms, and other arms acquired in various countries, failed. In the end, the French Government, turning an anxious eye on the Italian advance in Catalonia, paid heed to the anguished entreaties of the representatives of the Spanish Republic, and part of the consignment of war material began to cross the frontier. But the course of events could not now be changed. It was too late—so much so, that some cargoes fell into the hands of the enemy before the Republicans had time to unpack them.

The loss of Catalonia involved the Republican Government in a desperate situation on the frontier. Soon an immense multitude of fugitives, mostly women and children, were crowding together on the French frontier, an exhausted throng, seized with panic which was fomented partly by the German and Italian bombers which machine-gunned and bombed the lines of refugees along the roads from Barcelona, and partly by the fearful prospect of falling into the hands of the Fascists.

The first batch of refugees was relatively well received at the three points of entry; Cerbère, Le Perthus and Bourg Madame. But on the 28th of February, the French closed the frontier and sent back the soldiers to Spanish soil, a decision which even applied to the wounded, unless they were stretcher-cases. This led to heart-rending scenes. In torrential rain, the *Garde mobile* remorselessly escorted to the frontier groups of soldiers who walked with difficulty, some with gangrenous wounds, famished, soaked to the skin.

On the 30th, the number of Spanish refugees who were clamouring to enter France amounted to about 10,000. Thousands of old men, women and children, drenched to the skin in their flight through the mountains on foot, passed the night of the 30th-31st in the open, in icy weather.

Again the French opened the frontier, and on the 31st the number of fugitives in the frontier region was about 35,000. By every road, across the mountains and along the highways, there straggled interminable columns of almost fainting people. On February 2nd, some 45,000 souls were waiting at the frontier, begging to be allowed to enter France. The French reinforced the guard with Senegalese, who forbade the French population to succour the refugees. On the 3rd, the Germans and Italians committed the dastardly action of bombing Figueras from the air when the influx of refugees in the streets was at its highest; the number of victims, both dead and wounded, was about 1,000. On the 5th, the Italians entered Gerona, and 60,000 more refugees fled to Figueras and thence to the frontier.

Except for the units covering the retreat, the Republican Army had fallen back on France at Le Perthus and crossed the frontier in divisions of 5,000 men who, on setting foot on French soil, were marched off by gendarmes, *gardes mobiles* and Senegalese troops to various concentration camps, chiefly that at

Argelès, a sandy expanse surrounded by barbed wire. In these camps, the Republican soldiers were received by more Senegalese with fixed bayonets and *Spahis* with drawn swords. The Spaniards were treated like prisoners of war.

On February 14th, the camp of Saint-Ciprien held about 60,000 refugees, a promiscuous crowd of men, women and children. In the soldiers' camp at Argelès, about 70,000 men were confined.

Under such conditions, human endurance, weakened by two years of privations, succumbed. After long days in the open, without food or medical care, the old, the very young, the sick and the seriously wounded, could not survive the ordeal. In a single night, twelve children died at La Junquera. Others fell on the road, or under a tree, in the arms of their mothers who watched them die, as Hagar in the wilderness sat waiting for the death of her son Ishmael. Ten men died every day in the camp at Argelès.

To the sands of Argelès, Saint-Ciprien and Prat de Mollo came the professor, the soldier, the doctor, the artist, the artisan, the poet, the hero, the flower of the wit and the thought and the liberal youth of Spain. Without drinking-water, without food (it was weeks before the refugees could appease their hunger), on a soil through which the sea water filtered, blinded by the sand of the dunes, the Spanish Republicans peopled those unforgettable shores—some of them, as I have said, for but a short time, since every day Charon ferried a full load across the dark flood. Well might Dante's superscription have been affixed to the barbed wire: "Lasciate ogni speranza, voi ch'entrate."

The Republican Government remained near the Army of Catalonia until the retreat had been completed. When the last units had gone by, the Government removed to Toulouse, whence it proposed to transfer itself to the regions where the Republic still held sway. The President, Don Manuel Azaña, also crossed over into France and found a temporary abode in the Spanish Embassy in Paris.

During those days in the frontier zone, the Spanish Prime Minister and the Ministers who accompanied him had to cope not only with the tremendous problems to which the exodus of the civil population and the retreat of the Army had given rise. The future of the Republic and of Spain was more than ever in jeopardy; and no doubt the tragedy of the general situation struck even deeper into the soul of the Republican leaders than the pitiful events they were witnessing. We have already seen that from the first day of the military rising the Republicans had sought by many ways to make peace with the insurgents. The President of the Republic had sent emissary after emissary to try to reach some understanding with the rebels which might bring the war to an end. There were few of the Republican leaders who did not ceaselessly strive, through private and political channels, with all the weight of their prestige, to mitigate the unyielding and unpatriotic obstinacy of the Spanish Fascists. But at no moment did the sun of hope rise far above this horizon.

Now the Republican Government was again sounding the enemy's generosity with proposals whose modesty was in proportion to the delicacy of the situation in which the Republic stood.

In spite of the unutterable confusion which reigned on the frontier, the Republican Minister for Foreign Affairs had succeeded in maintaining contact with the principal members of the Diplomatic Corps. Now Álvarez del Vayo explained to Mr. Stevenson, the British *chargé d'affaires*, the tragic situation in which thousands of Republicans in the Central-Southern zone, deprived of the means to leave Spain, would find themselves if the defeat in Catalonia were followed sooner or later by a similar catastrophe in the rest of Republican territory. The British diplomat declared his willingness to suggest to the Foreign Office a plan to evacuate the Republicans with the aid of the British and French Fleets, as had been done with the civil population of the Basque Provinces.[1]

As regards the peace proposals, it should be noted that on February 1st, the Cortes, meeting at Figueras, had empowered the Government to negotiate peace, if possible, on the following terms:

(1) Evacuation of foreigners in the service of the rebels.
(2) Freedom for the Spanish people to choose their own political régime without outside interference.
(3) Absence of reprisals.

On this basis, the Government of the Republic, some days later, held conversations with the British *chargé d'affaires* and the French Ambassador, M. Jules Henry.

On February 5th, when the Minister for Foreign Affairs met both diplomats at Le Perthus for an exchange of views, the British representative, acting on instructions from the Foreign Office, asked the Spanish Minister if his Government would

[1] Álvarez del Vayo, *Freedom's Battle*, p. 295. New York, 1940.

consent to British mediation to put an end to the war under conditions acceptable to the Republic.

As a result of these conversations, a meeting took place on the following day, the 6th, at Agullana, where Negrín was residing at the moment, at which the British *chargé d'affaires*, the French Ambassador and the Spanish Prime Minister and Minister for Foreign Affairs were present.

Negrín explained to Mr. Stevenson and M. Henry the meaning and scope of the three conditions laid down at Figueras. He pointed out that the first two conditions could be considered purely theoretical in view of all that had happened since then, and that the third condition relating to reprisals was the only one on which the Republican representatives would insist at all costs. If they were to cease fighting, the Republican Government required guarantees that Republicans would not forfeit their life and liberty for having defended a legitimate régime against a rebellion. If the Republican Government received such guarantees and obtained help in evacuating from Spain those citizens whose life under a rebel régime would be both a material impossibility and a spiritual torture, they would try to find a way of putting an end to hostilities. Otherwise, the Spanish Prime Minister pointed out, if such guarantees were not forthcoming, the struggle would continue to the last man and the last cartridge.

Later Negrín referred to the possibilities of resistance still open to the Republic, mentioning—so far as they could be divulged—the means of combat still existing in the Central-Southern zone, and reaffirming the Government's determination not to lay down their arms until they had received satisfaction on the crucial point of reprisals.[1]

The British *chargé d'affaires* and the French Ambassador understood that the Republicans could not demand less from the rebels, and withdrew after promising that they would bring the Republican Government's point of view to the attention of their respective Governments.

On February 9th, after having been present at Le Perthus when the last of the Republican forces entered France, Negrín and the Ministers with him in the frontier zone left for Toulouse. Here the whole Republican Government met in council at the Spanish Consulate, and after agreeing to remove to Madrid as and when transport was available, the Prime Minister and the Minister for Foreign Affairs set out for Alicante in a French aeroplane of the Toulouse-Casablanca line.

[1] Álvarez del Vayo, p. 297.

Meanwhile, one of the strangest episodes of the whole war had been taking place in the island of Minorca.

Minorca, which had been loyal to the Republican Government since the beginning of the war, still kept her allegiance, firm as a rock, to the Republic. The Republicans had added to the already powerful military defences of the island new fortifications, trenches, shelters, etc., which the whole population had helped to construct. The stoicism with which they endured aerial bombardment and privations of all kinds was a constant proof of the mettle of the 43,000 Spaniards who inhabited Minorca at that time. With such defences and such people, Minorca was impregnable. Her defence against air attack left little to be desired. The Fascist air raids had only claimed twenty-eight victims since 1936, and during the same period the anti-aircraft guns had brought down fifteen Italian planes. Neither the rebel warships nor the Italian and German fleets dared to approach the island. But the Fascists, having subdued Barcelona, decided to add to their recent conquests this Mediterranean fortress.

There is no question but that the commander of the base at Minorca was aware of the loss of Catalonia. Yet the determination of both officers and men to defend the island was as resolute as ever. The Commander-in-Chief was one of the bravest officers of the Republic, Admiral Ubieta, who did not even trouble to reply to an ultimatum sent him by the insurgents in Majorca.

On February 9th, the British cruiser *Devonshire* entered Port Mahón and her captain landed to pay the usual courtesy visit to the Governor of the island. In due course, Admiral Ubieta boarded the *Devonshire* to pay his return visit. At that moment, Italian aircraft based on Majorca bombed Port Mahón with unusual intensity, and disturbances, provoked by the few followers of Franco, broke out in the Minorcan capital.

Once on board the British cruiser, the Republican Admiral was informed that the Conde de San Luis, Fascist Governor of Majorca, was also there; he had come to demand the capitulation of Minorca.

Admiral Ubieta refused to parley with the insurgent chief and prepared to leave in order to return to his post, especially in view of the disturbances at Mahón. The captain of the *Devonshire* pointed out to him the danger he ran in disembarking. The English were opposed to his resuming the command of Minorca; they urged surrender, and Ubieta found himself for all practical purposes a prisoner.

The incident concluded with the capitulation of the Republicans and the *Devonshire* brought off 400 refugees and landed them safely in France.

In the early hours of February 10th, the Prime Minister and the Minister for Foreign Affairs stood once more on Spanish soil. Seldom has a statesman been faced with such dramatic events as confronted Negrín when he reappeared at the head of his Government in the Central zone. (The other Ministers returned to Spain a few days after him.) The dilemma could not have been more tragic. Once Catalonia was lost, only a miracle could save the Republic. On the other hand, the Republic could not surrender unconditionally, which was the only form of surrender the insurgents would accept. That is, the Government *could* do it, if it was an irresponsible and pusillanimous Government capable of taking such a grave course.

In February 1939, with the Republic reduced to this extremity, peace depended entirely on whether Franco would undertake to respect the life and liberty of those Republicans who elected to remain in Spain, and not hinder the flight of those who wanted to leave the country. But no guarantees could be expected from such an enemy; for the rebels were consumed with the desire for revenge, and they would have considered their triumph but a Pyrrhic victory if they had not been able to satiate their thirst for vengeance on millions of Spaniards. The Republic had to deal with a savage deity, a Spanish Moloch or Belial, whose bloodlust would only be appeased by sacrifices of hundreds of thousands of Republicans without regard to age or sex.

Nevertheless, unanimity among the heads of the Republic— unanimity in appreciating that unconditional surrender was out of the question—had been shaken. Azaña, broken-hearted, resigned his office as President of the Republic on February 27th. Martínez Barrio, who, as Speaker of the Cortes, should have succeeded him, was unwilling to return to Spain. Most of the Republican generals advocated putting an end to the war "on any terms". More clear-sighted and more master of himself, Negrín thought that the Republicans should exhaust whatever possibilities of resistance still remained. The Republic had no choice and there was no better alternative to offer the people.

The Government weighed up the means at their disposal for continuing the war and noted that there were still in Republican Spain eight million people spread over a quarter of the national territory, with ten provincial capitals. The Republic's military forces amounted to 800,000 men divided into four Armies:

(1) The Army of the Centre. Four Army Corps to defend the Madrid sector under the command of Col. Segismundo Casado.

(2) The Army of the Levante, under the command of General Menéndez, to defend the provinces of Cuenca and Valencia, and the coast between Nules and Valencia.

(3) The Army of Andalusia, led by Colonel Moriones, to defend a huge expanse of territory from Motril to the district round Cordova.

(4) The Army of Estremadura. Four Army Corps under General Escobar, linked with the Army of the Centre in Estremadura and in the valley of the Tagus.

The Republican Fleet consisted of three cruisers (two 9,000-ton and one 6,000-ton); thirteen destroyers, two gunboats, four submarines, three torpedo boats and auxiliary vessels.

The Republic still held a certain number of important ports— Valencia, Alicante, Sagunto, Gandía, Denia, Torrevieja, Cartagena, Almería.

In the air, the Republic's position was critical, as it had been throughout the war.

As regards war material and munitions, there were still factories in Madrid, Albacete, Ciudad Real, Alicante, Sagunto, turning out munitions and light arms, rifles, machine-guns, mortars and some tanks.

Negrín calculated that, with the means of combat still at the Republic's disposal, resistance could be prolonged for at least six months. In support of his thesis he could argue that though the scarcity of weapons could not be denied, the ratio between the war material in Republican hands and what the rebels possessed was the same as it had been from the beginning; that he was confident he would be able to lay hands on at least part of the armaments belonging to the Republic and at present detained in France; that if there were few aircraft, the Republic had never had enough; that it must not be inferred from what had happened in Catalonia that the same thing would happen in the Central-Southern zone; that if 60,000 men of the Republican Army had been able to contain the enemy for four months in the campaign on the Ebro, it was not too much to hope that the 800,000 men in the Armies of the Central-Southern zone—incomparable human material—would display even greater defensive capacities; that he was not unaware of the truly tragic hunger suffered by the population of Madrid, but it could be alleviated by means which would be immediately adopted; that in the confused and

X s

changing state of Europe, he did not think it extravagant to hope, if they continued to resist for a few more months, that events abroad might modify a state of things so adverse to the Republic; that lastly—and this was the most important—the Republic had no choice but to resist, unless all Republicans were to submit themselves to the pitiless vengeance of the insurgents, and the Government was to assume the incalculable responsibility of handing over a people who had given such proofs of heroism and nobility to the blackest reaction that had ever existed in any country.

With this judgment, these ideas, these proposals, and these hopes of its Prime Minister, the Republican Cabinet began its work of defending the last Republican outposts.

As soon as all or the majority of the Ministers were in Madrid, the Government addressed a proclamation to the people, saying that, so long as there existed no prospect of peace with independence, security and liberty, no other policy was possible save that of defending the regions of Spain which had not yet been invaded. Whether we come safety through this terrible ordeal, said the Government, depends solely on our common resolution and will. Let the spirit which made Madrid immortal in the memorable days of November 1936 be born again; let this spirit spread throughout the whole of loyal Spain, so that, filled with energy, we shall all, without exception, march together, without party rivalries which would be suicidal. Only in this way can the Government accomplish its difficult mission successfully.

But there was no doubt that the policy of resistance, "the only possible policy", ran counter to the will of vast numbers of Republicans. The loss of Catalonia had wrought havoc in the morale of the political and military leaders in the Central-Southern zone; and since Catalonia fell, enemy propaganda had hastened the process of demoralization by insisting that Franco would not take reprisals and would only punish those who had been guilty of crimes and transgressions against the common law. From all quarters there breathed a soft music which was to lull to sleep the people's instinct for self-preservation. The soothing words of the Fascist broadcasters were echoed by those Fascists who had always gone about freely in Madrid under a Republican mask. They were sure that Franco would be generous if the Republicans surrendered, but oh! his fury would know no bounds if the Republic decided to go on resisting. The foreign Press joined in the chorus of those who never doubted for an instant that Franco would treat the Republicans humanely.

*The Times* wrote on February 9th: "Dr. Negrin still has Madrid, the bloodless surrender of which might secure for him mitigation of General Franco's terms. General Franco has not behaved unreasonably in any of the territory he has occupied."

The foreigners living in Madrid—English, French and American—who had nothing to fear from the Fascists; the diplomatic representatives and other agents of the Powers interested in the victory of Fascism or simply in the rapid conclusion of the Spanish war, lost no opportunity of helping to create that feeling of confidence and security which was leading the Republican generals and a large number of political leaders step by step towards the abyss.

Negrín and the Republican Army chiefs had an interminable meeting at Los Llanos (Albacete). The generals expounded their views on the situation at the various fronts and discussed the Republic's military prospects as a whole. General Escobar, Commander of the Army of Estremadura, and Colonel Moriones, Commander of the Andalusian Army, were confident of their ability to resist on their respective sectors. But the other generals did not conceal their pessimism.

Much about the same time, Negrín received the leaders of the Popular Front and discussed the situation with them. He called their attention to the undoubted peril of believing that peace would be possible before Franco and his foreign allies had seen that the Republic had means to resist for longer than was convenient to them, and was prepared to employ those means.

There was one party which did not need the exhortations and advice of the Prime Minister—the Communist Party. Neither the fall of Catalonia nor Fascist propaganda had made the least impression on the Communists. No sooner had that campaign come to an end, than the Communist Army chiefs and political leaders returned from France to the Republican Central zone, determined to fight on as long as was necessary.

The self-seeking policy of the Communist Party, its exaggerated instinct for proselytizing, the absence of scruples with which it often pursued its party ends, marked it out from among all the Republican organizations. And these negative qualities, which were offset, no doubt, by the enthusiasm and resolution with which the Communists were fighting Fascism, nevertheless wounded the liveliest susceptibilities of less combative parties and persons, at whose expense this Marxist movement was growing.

In February 1939 the Communist Party was the only party which continued to urge further resistance. There were men in the other political and trade-union organizations who foresaw

643

the moral and physical disasters in unconditional surrender and rejected this "solution" outright. But those who dared to swim against the pacifist stream were few and far between; so that in this moment of the Republic's peril the Government could not count on any support for their policy save that of isolated individuals of various political affiliations, sections of parties, and the Communist Party *en bloc*. The people had been prepared by recent events and by thirty-two months of privation to believe anything that would satisfy their justifiable desire for peace. The masses, in general, would follow anyone who promised them an immediate peace, guaranteeing them bread and liberty. But only a demagogic and irresponsible Government would have told the people that such a peace was possible.

<br>

CHAPTER XXIV

# THE COLLAPSE

As we know, the Republicans had disdained no means of obtaining peace without reprisals, and now they were formally endeavouring to open negotiations with the rebels through the intermediary of the Powers particularly interested in the rapid end of the war. On February 13th the Republican Ambassador in London, Señor Azcárate, handed the Foreign Office a note expressing the hope that the British Government would approach the insurgents with a view to paving the way for an agreement which would allow of the immediate cessation of hostilities.

Some days afterwards the Republican Minister for Foreign Affairs went to Paris, summoned the Ambassador in London, and with him Dr. Pascua, the Republican representative in the French capital, agreed together that, in the light of the circumstances soon to be created by Azaña's resignation and the imminent recognition of Franco's Government by France and England, it would be useless and even prejudicial to insist upon the evacuation of foreigners and the right of the Spanish people to choose their own Government, as conditions of peace. They decided to concentrate their efforts on the condition relating to reprisals, and endeavour to obtain facilities for those Republicans, both civilians and in the armed forces, who had most to fear if they fell into the hands of the Fascists, to leave Spain.[1]

[1] Álvarez del Vayo, p. 301.

The Ambassador in London was instructed to communicate to the Foreign Office the Republican Government's definitive attitude.

At the same time, Negrín was continuing to study the military situation with the Army chiefs. The Minister of Defence wanted to reorganize the General Staff immediately and create mobile shock units. But the more faint-hearted among the Republican generals privately thought, and sometimes voiced their opinion to all and sundry, that any attempt to improve the fighting dispositions of the Army would be sterile and illusory.

The enemies of resistance, that is, those who wanted to end the war "on any terms", were numerous and influential both in Spain and abroad. Varying sentiments and aspirations moved them to desire the surrender of the Republic. Some, in good faith, hoped for justice from the unjust—an egregious piece of folly: *Justum ab injustis petere insipientia est.* Others were sure of gaining an honourable place in history if they were successful in negotiating peace. Others—the traitors—were flinging themselves at last on their prey, after trying vainly for two and a half years to destroy the unbreakable morale of the people of Madrid. There were also Republicans who, from the first day of the conflict, would have delivered up the Republic if they could, simply because they preferred a Fascist dictatorship to a genuine people's Republic. Finally, there were on the Republican side those base souls who favoured Franco's victory, or would have done nothing to prevent it, for the pleasure of witnessing the downfall of the Republican Government itself which they would have liked to see prostrate and humiliated.

Worthy specimens of human nature in its hour of tribulation and disaster, this melancholy amalgam of soldiers and politicians was already preparing the ruin of the Republic before the Negrín Government had returned to the Central zone.

Don Julian Besteiro was the centre of one of the circles of the conspiracy; the centre of another anti-resistance circle was Colonel Segismundo Casado, commanding the Army of Madrid. Both circles soon came to an agreement.

Besteiro was a politician who was divorced from the realities of the Spanish situation, a Spanish MacDonald, with a utopian policy of compromise utterly unsuited to Spain. He held an indulgent view of Fascism, and wanted to introduce corporative elements into the Republican Constitution, proposing in the Cortes the setting up of a Corporative Chamber. The Russian revolution terrified him and he was one of those who believed that the advance of the Communists in Spanish politics was transforming the Republic into a Soviet.

These mistaken ideas, governed by a character which was extraordinarily complex, dignified but not humble, very sensitive to personal questions, made Besteiro an advocate of capitulation even before the civil war had begun.

In May 1937 Besteiro attended the Coronation of George VI and, as the special emissary of the President of the Republic paid a visit to Mr. Eden with the obvious mission of ascertaining how the Spanish war could be brought to an end. His efforts were no more successful than all the others.

Besteiro's indisputable authority was not intellectual, but moral, and sprang largely from the fact that he had defended the interests of the proletariat and dedicated himself actively to Socialist policy at a time when Socialism hardly attracted the intellectuals and relied only on working-class leaders. During the civil war, Besteiro withdrew into isolation at Madrid, refusing to accept any of the posts offered him by the Government, except the purely nominal one of President of a *Junta* for the reconstruction of the capital; and in this passive attitude, which did not imply indifference, he remained until he judged the situation ripe for the peace he was in favour of, peace on any terms.

From the time that Besteiro joined the Socialist Party, as a convert from Lerrouxism, he was laying up for himself a personal tragedy, engendered more by his character than by his ideas. From the beginning, his position in the Socialist Party was, by his own act, one of isolation. When he might have succeeded Pablo Iglesias in the leadership of the workers' and Socialist movement, he was displaced by the more flexible and more politically-minded Largo Caballero. Besteiro's personal tragedy continued to manifest itself in a persistent tendency to go against the grain of everything that the dynamism of Spanish politics required from a Socialist leader, and culminated in the sentence passed on him by Franco on entering Madrid, though he had not lifted a finger against the insurgents either before or after the war or during the course of hostilities, and had contributed more than anyone to the cessation of resistance.

Whereas among the civilians it was Besteiro who was chiefly responsible for the furtherance of the plot against the Negrín Government, among the demoralized Republican military chiefs Colonel Casado took the lead in persuading political parties and Army commanders that the Negrín Government was the only considerable obstacle in the way of peace. Casado, who had been appointed by Negrín to command the Army of the Centre, was convinced that Franco would never negotiate with the Prime Minister and still more convinced that Franco would make peace with him, Casado, whenever he asked him to. Casado expounded this point of view to General Hidalgo de Cisneros while he was having luncheon with him on March 2nd, 1939, in the Alameda de Osuna, General Miaja's headquarters.

"In the course of conversation, Casado expressed his conviction that Franco was not willing to negotiate with the Negrín Government and that so long as it rested with the latter to enter into peace discussions, nothing could be done. On the other hand, there was no more time to lose. It was essential to arrive at an agreement in two or three days. 'And only we soldiers can do this,' added Casado. He then referred to the interview which he had had in Madrid with British officials. 'I can't go into details, but I give you my word of honour that I can get out of Franco much more than the Negrín Government can.' Later he said: 'I'm quite certain—and I'll pledge you my word of honour on this, too—that it will be possible to make Franco promise that no Germans, Italians or Moors shall enter Madrid, that there shall be no reprisals, that anyone can leave Spain who wants to, and that the military rank of the majority of us soldiers will be recognized.'" Casado thought "that Franco would be forced to maintain a strong army after the war and would therefore need Republican officers to make up for the tremendous losses suffered on the rebel side".[1]

Colonel Casado was firmly persuaded that Franco would make peace with a new Republican Government. "Negrín", he writes, "ended by telling us that he had failed in his efforts for peace and that, therefore, there was nothing to do but resist. It did not occur to him to tell us that, having failed in this intention, he had decided to resign, so that a Government might be formed which could achieve what he was unable to achieve."[2] "Dr. Negrín", he says in another place, "had lost all hope of starting peace negotiations and, instead of making way for a Government which would be in a position to discuss the matter with the enemy, he was determined, or forced, to stick to his cry of resistance at all costs."[3]

What Government would be in a position to discuss peace with the enemy? According to the Colonel, a Government led by

[1] Álvarez del Vayo, pp. 306–7.
[2] Colonel Casado, *The Last Days of Madrid*, p. 119. Peter Davies, 1939.
[3] Ibid., p. 196.

the Army (preferably by himself), or one in which he had part; for he was entirely convinced that he could obtain a peace which would be acceptable to the Republic. Casado did not abandon this idea for a moment. No sooner had Negrín arrived in Madrid than the Colonel, according to his own statement, offered to take part in any peace discussions that were opened.[1] If we are to believe Casado, he told the Prime Minister at another interview on March 1st "that I thought I was fairly respected in the enemy camp, in spite of my well-known Republican and anti-Fascist sympathies, and that I would put myself at his disposal, so that if negotiations were to be opened, he could use my services. The only solution was direct discussion between the two armies"[2]—an opinion which he had already communicated to General Hidalgo de Cisneros, as we have seen.

The new Government recommended by the Colonel would obviously not include the Communists. On February 24th Casado had an interview with two representatives of *Izquierda Republicana* (Left Republican) "and we arranged that they should go to Paris . . . to take a message to Señor Azaña, inviting him to come to Spain, remove his confidence from Negrín's Government, and form another of Republicans and Socialists".[3]

The exclusion of the Communists from a Ministry determined to put an end to the war appeared to these Republicans a *sine qua non*, since they had arrived at the conclusion that the Communist Party was a serious obstacle to peace. They thought that Franco would not negotiate so long as a trace of Communist influence remained in Republican territory, a prejudice which was fostered by Fascist propaganda, according to which the insurgents were fighting solely against Bolshevism. For the Fascists to come to an agreement with the Republicans, thought the moderate Republicans, unequivocal proofs of anti-Communism must be given. Moreover the Communists were fanatics who did not trust Franco's word and were determined to go on fighting. In short, if a *decent and honourable peace* were to be assured, the Communists could not be counted on. The Communist Party must, therefore, be suppressed.

For such a mission, Colonel Casado had the necessary mental preparation, as we shall see from his ideas on national and international politics; and the bitter party strife, in which the Communists thrived lustily with their discipline and tactics, promised ample aid to anyone proposing to enlist the other

[1] Casado, p. 112.    [2] Id., p. 196.    [3] Id., p. 182.

Republican organizations against the Spanish Section of the Third International.

In Colonel Casado's opinion, the Spanish civil war had been engineered on the rebel side by Germany, on the Republican side by Russia.[1] This was also Franco's theory, at least as regards Russia. Germany, writes Casado, wanted to undermine the strategic position of England and France, and Russia wanted "to undermine as much as possible the whole social framework of Europe".[2] The Russians "were simply trying to impose their own political system in Spain".[3] This absurdity, which was the basis of anti-Republican propaganda in the insurgent zone and in Fascist circles abroad, could not deceive anyone outside those circles, unless he were manifestly ignorant of international problems and of the part which the Soviet Union played in them in 1936.

The Colonel goes on to prove that he had completely misread the situation. "I have often thought that the excess of Communist Commands may have influenced France, Great Britain and the United States to abandon us as they did."[4] It may occur to some that if the reason why those Powers abandoned the Spanish Republic was chiefly the Communist Commands, the democracies would not have behaved in exactly the same way towards Abyssinia, Austria and Czechoslovakia, which they abandoned as completely as they abandoned Spain.

No one could have displayed grosser ignorance of the course of world events than Casado when, because he thought he could solve the immense problem which weighed on the Republic, he prepared to overthrow the Government. The Colonel was a consummate schemer, whose ideas on more complex questions were puerile. Thus, he suggested that if the pay of the Republican troops, which according to him, amounted to 600 million pesetas annually, had been reduced by half, the Government could have set aside a minimum of 1,000 million pesetas for propaganda and espionage, "a sum more than sufficient to change the course of the war and even the opinions of the Great Powers, who made such poor use of their Pact of Non-Intervention".[5]

That is to say, the Republican Government could have bought all its enemies in Paris and London with large packets of worthless Spanish notes. Doubtless, by the same curious process, the

---

[1] Casado, p. 43.
[2] Id.
[3] Id., p. 54

[4] Id., p. 87.
[5] Id., p. 98.

Republic could have succeeded, not only perhaps in changing the course of the war, but in turning itself into a Great Power.

Casado's ideas on the subject of Spanish home politics were equally absurd. The reader knows the causes of the conspiracy of August 1932. But, according to the Colonel, these were not the real causes; the real causes were far simpler. "The Left-wing Press never lost an opportunity of criticizing Army officers, without realizing that, by so doing, it provoked them into seeking contact with the forces of capitalism and reaction. In this way, that parody of a military rising was produced in August 1932."[1]

The Colonel announced that he was anti-political—merely "a Spanish soldier anti-political by instinct". Consequently, for him, the last meeting of the Cortes at Figueras had been "one of the many theatrical spectacles of buffoonery and indecency, which politics have presented to us since the world began".[2] And as politics are so despicable, the Army's mission, according to Casado, is "to do the people's will, removing any obstacle which opposes it".[3]

Such was the mental heritage of Colonel Casado. Without knowing it, however summarily, we should not be able to understand fully the tragedy in which he was the chief protagonist. With that intellectual baggage, it is not surprising that the Commander of the Central Army should believe that destiny had entrusted him with the mission of repeating the peace of Vergara and going down to posterity as another Maroto.

In February 1939 the leaders of the Popular Front, with the exception of the Communists, were in a state of tragic perplexity and irresolution, which is understandable if we remember that most of the guiding personalities of the Republican and Socialist movement were not in Madrid, that the political decomposition of the Republic—strangled by party rivalries— was well advanced, and that the situation was desperate in the extreme.

For the most part, the leaders of the Popular Front were opposed to the policy of resistance, but they undoubtedly hesitated before the suggestion of supporting a military rising against the Government, particularly after hearing Negrín. The vacillations of the party leaders (chiefly Socialists and Republicans, for the Anarchists were, as usual, resolved to tempt fortune) exasperated Colonel Casado, who thought they

[1] Casado, p. 49.      [2] Id., p. 152.      [3] Id., p. 192.

650

ought to force Negrín to sue for peace, by radio, apparently, as the Council of Defence subsequently did. The Colonel denounced their "unpardonable weakness, considering the gravity of the situation. This weakness made me think", he says, "that the help which they had on so many occasions offered me, would not be as effective as one could wish".[1]

Casado was growing impatient. The pressure of circumstances had impaired his critical judgment, so that he was sure of the success of his pacifist initiative. The accusation that Casado, in agreement with the enemy, proposed to hand over the Republic to Franco seems to me not sufficiently founded in fact; that that was the intention of some of the gentry who were working along the same lines as he was—people who were conspiring with the Fascists—cannot be doubted; for in the Council of Defence which was subsequently formed, and around this disastrous body, all kinds of persons were to be found. But it is equally certain that Casado's unthinking policy was sure to lead to the Republic being handed over, bound hand and foot, to the enemy—as in fact happened, though this was not perhaps his design.

Casado infected those around or near him with his own desperation and destroyed any lingering remnants of morale in most of the Republican political leaders and military chiefs. He said, for example, that the enemy had concentrated a major part of his reserves in the zone south of Madrid in order to open the decisive battle; that the Fascists could put into the field thirty-two divisions, with abundant automatic arms and great quantities of tanks and artillery; that in this case, if the Republicans waited for the offensive which the enemy had already prepared for the conquest of Madrid, the Republican front would be smashed on the first day of the attack;[2] that if the enemy succeeded in cutting communications with the Levante, as he would try to do, the Republicans would either have to surrender within forty-eight hours or die of hunger; that there was always the possibility that part of the population would perish in the ruins as the result of the terrible air attacks which the enemy would launch to coincide with his powerful artillery bombardment; that the Army lacked weapons; that the food supplies for Madrid which Negrín had promised would not arrive for lack of transport, etc.[3] (A month later, Casado himself offered his services to Franco to help him in solving the problem of feeding Madrid when the Fascist troops entered, using "the supplies which the *Junta* has already acquired abroad

[1] Casado, p. 114.    [2] Ibid., p. 111.    [3] Ibid., p. 109.

and which can be brought to this zone with comparative ease".)[1]

It was obvious that tragic days were in store for the Republican zone. In the impasse in which the Republic found itself, catastrophe was practically inevitable in one way or another. But Casado, who thought that any means were permissible when the prize was peace, unscrupulously exaggerated the weakness of the Republic and the strength of the insurgents.

In the first place, the enemy had not prepared an offensive against Madrid. Moreover, at no moment could Franco have concentrated thirty-two divisions on a single front, still less keep them concentrated on the outskirts of the capital of the Republic at a time when the bulk of the Fascist Army was holding down Catalonia. When, a month later, Madrid capitulated, the insurgents' mobile units were still in that region.

The truth was that the rebels were not proposing to attack at the moment, partly because the best part of their Army was consolidating the conquest of Catalonia (a conquest which was to prove a burden and an anxiety to Franco for some time), and partly because Franco thought that once Catalonia was conquered, Madrid would surrender. Franco had exact information on the success with which his agents in Madrid and abroad were working; he knew that many Republicans were unwittingly acting as if they were his agents and he hoped that they would hand over the Republic to him without the need for further military operations. The Fascists, therefore, were in no hurry to renew the offensive—a policy which would have been imprudent since it might have united the Republicans; on the contrary, they wanted to allow time for the intrigues and feuds which were undermining the democratic parties to bear fruit in their favour.

Apart from the political disintegration of the Republic, the Republic was stronger and Franco weaker than Colonel Casado imagined or said. The fact that the Fascists thought the war had ended with the conquest of Catalonia induced in them a dangerously complacent frame of mind and one that might have obliged them to accept the capitulation of the Republic on the terms put forward by the Republicans, that is, without revenge or reprisals, if there had been a unanimous resolution in the democratic zone to back up the Government. The idea might well have gained ground in the Fascist camp that it was not worth while continuing to sacrifice the Army in several more

[1] Casado, pp. 222–3.

months of fighting, when the price at which Franco might purchase peace was so modest.

The rebels also were suffering from internal strife and general discontent. Political discords and the uneasiness caused by the enormous numbers of foreign troops kept the insurgent zone in a state of lively anxiety. The incurable hostility between Falangists and *Requetés* had recently given rise to violent clashes in the north. The situation was such (though it would not be right to exaggerate it) that Republicans living under Franco kept their faith in a Republican victory even after the Republic had lost the Catalan regions.[1]

Perhaps because he could not conceive of there being anyone who believed in the possibility of solving the tremendous problem confronting the Republic by methods other than the Government's, Negrín does not seem to have entertained the idea of a rebellion against his policy. For what man in his senses would be so bold as to shoulder the responsibilities of usurping the Government, and thereby bring on his head the task of ruling the Republic at that desperate juncture? Nevertheless, the moral collapse of most of the Republican old Army chiefs indicated a latent insubordination.

The Government must have been inclined on the whole to think that only in the Communist leaders could they have entire confidence. The Communist military chiefs who had returned from France had not yet been given new posts; the first to obtain commands were Lt.-Colonels Etelvino Vega and Tagüeña, who took over the military command of Alicante and Murcia respectively.

The intention of the Minister of Defence to create mobile shock units (which would inevitably be placed under the command of Modesto and Lister) to stiffen resistance at the weakest points was taking practical shape; and the news of the Communist appointments, or projected appointments, profoundly disturbed many politicians and soldiers of the other parties; some, because they refused to recognize that the appointment of Communist leaders would help in the prosecution of the war and placed party interests before the interests of the Republic; others, because the creation of mobile units under Communist com-

[1] "One of our greatest surprises was to discover, on establishing contact with the so-called rebel zone, that faith in our victory was infinitely stronger than in our own zone. Most of the population in the zone which was not loyal to the Republic believed unswervingly in our victory and were sure, even after the loss of Catalonia (though in my opinion it was already impossible), that we should win" (Rodriguez Vega, speech at Mexico, March 10th, 1943).

mands signified in no uncertain manner that the Government had decided to resist, that the war would go on, and that the possibilities of striking a successful blow against the Government would vanish in the twinkling of an eye.

Another step which alarmed the conspirators was about to be taken. Negrín announced that he was going to broadcast to the nation, and a few days in advance he communicated the general purport of the speech he was going to make to various politicians and Army chiefs, among them Colonel Casado.

All this precipitated events. Negrín was to have broadcast on March 5th. He was forestalled by Casado; and the nation heard by the same medium a subversive manifesto issued by the *Consejo Nacional de Defensa* (National Council of Defence), an organization which did not so much counsel as "darken counsel", which could not call itself national, since it excluded such an important sector of the Republic as the Communist party, and which did not propose to defend anything, but rather to leave the Republic defenceless.

The manifesto of the rebel *Junta* is a clear example of how easily despair can induce a group of men, until yesterday servants of a noble cause, to lay aside their moral scruples and become the sport of the basest passions. I shall only quote the most important passages in this document.

"Several weeks have passed since the war in Catalonia ended with general desertion. . . . While the people were sacrificing several thousands of their best sons in the bloody arena of battle, the men who had put themselves to the fore in demanding resistance deserted their posts and sought a means of saving their lives even at the cost of their dignity, by the most shameful flight. . . .

"To prevent this, to remove the memory of that shame, to avoid desertion at the gravest moments, the National Council of Defence has been formed. . . . The National Council of Defence which has picked up authority where Dr. Negrín's Government threw it away. . . .

"We affirm our own authority as honest and sincere defenders of the Spanish people, as men who are determined to give their own lives as guarantee, and to make their destiny that of all the rest, so that nobody shall escape the sacred duties which are incumbent upon all alike. . . .

"We have come to show the way which may avoid disaster, and follow that way with all the rest of the Spanish people, whatever the consequences may be. . . .

"We oppose the policy of resistance, to save our cause from ending in mockery or vengeance.

"Either we all are saved, or we all go under, Dr. Negrín has said, and the National Council of Defence has given itself as its first and last, as its only task, the conversion of these words into reality."[1]

After this, Don Julian Besteiro read a speech.

"The truth is, citizens," said Besteiro, "that after the battle of the Ebro, the nationalist armies have occupied the whole of Catalonia, and the Republican Government have been on the move for a long time in French territory.

"The only object of Dr. Negrín's Government, with their concealments of the truth and their captious proposals, is to gain time, time which has been lost so far as the interests of the mass of the citizens, both combatant and non-combatant, are concerned; and this policy of deferment can have no other end than to nourish the morbid belief that the growing complication of international events will let loose a catastrophe of universal proportions in which the working classes of many nations will perish together with our own.

"Republican opinion is already surfeited with this policy of waiting on the final catastrophe, of submission to foreign orders, with complete indifference to the nation's sufferings.

"At this grave hour, I beg you, with all the emphasis at my command, to support, as we are supporting, the legitimate Government of the Republic, which for the moment is none other than the Army."

Last came Colonel Casado, whose words were directed almost exclusively "to the Spaniards on the other side of the trenches", to whom he said that they also were affected by "the phrase with which we have expressed the dilemma confronting us: Either we all are saved, or we all go under".

"Look at the interests of the nation; consider what is best for Spain," he told them. That was the necessary basis for any legitimate aspiration. "We shall not cease fighting till you assure us of the independence of Spain. The Spanish people will not lay down their arms whilst it has no guarantee of peace without reprisals."

The Spanish people had taken up arms in July 1936 in order to put an end to a *pronunciamiento* and finish for ever with the violent usurpation of power by the Army, and here were re-

[1] Casado, pp. 140, 141, 142.

655

spectable Republicans and political parties destroying their own civil Government, proclaiming the Army to be the only legal institution and placing themselves at the orders of a Colonel in just the same way as the parties of reaction had supported Franco.

The Council of Defence was only the grotesque mask of a military dictatorship no different from any other. General Miaja had consented to preside over it, but Casado was the typical military dictator surrounded by a consultative *Junta*.[1]

The Council of Defence hardly encountered any opposition. It was favoured to a marked degree by the passivity of its opponents and by the confusion or the expectation of the mass of the people. Casado, who was not prepared to prosecute the war against Franco, was ready, on the other hand, to war against other Republicans; and as a result, those who would still have liked to fight the Fascists, refused an armed conflict with the new Government. Both attitudes were loyal to the principle which inspired them.

The Council hypnotized the people, or allured them, by the demagogic gesture of promising them an honourable peace, and the faith that this proceeding aroused in the delusive miracle-working capacities of the *Junta*, spurred on the latter to defend their trickery without giving a thought to the means whereby their promise was to be translated into action. The Casadists thought, moreover, that they would be helped in their enterprise by the Powers which wanted nothing better than to liquidate the Spanish war, an illusion which was fostered by the diplomatic representatives and special agents who were carrying on their treacherous work in Madrid.

The expectation with which the Republican working class followed the events of March can be readily explained. The heads of the rebellion were declaring that "they were opposed to the policy of resistance in order to prevent the people's cause from ending in derision or vengeance"; and with these words they were affirming that they had a solution whereby the Republic would not perish without glory or advantage. The people were longing for peace, as was natural, and whoever promised it with certain guarantees, as I said before, would have had them on his side, though the maker of the promise had been Franco himself. But the people did not want to surrender unconditionally, and the policy of the *Junta* was leading to that tragic outcome.

[1] The National Council of Defence consisted of General Miaja, Colonel Casado, Don Julian Besteiro, M. González Marín, M. San Andrés, J. del Río, E. Val, A. Pérez and W. Carrillo.

It is inconceivable that the Commander of the Army of the Centre should not have realized that, by rebelling, he was destroying what chances of resistance still remained to the Republicans and that, therefore, he was leaving the Republic no alternative but unconditional surrender. Casado had said in his broadcast that the Spanish people would not lay down their arms until they had obtained guarantees for a peace without reprisals. This was also the policy of the Negrín Government—only, after the insurrection of the *Junta*, that policy had no chance of being put into practice. The Colonel was saying in effect: If Franco does not concede us the minimum terms we are going to demand, we shall resist; but a few minutes before, in the manifesto and in other speeches, it had been stated that resistance would bring derision and vengeance on the Republic. First the people were being morally discouraged from continuing to defend themselves; then they were being warned to prepare themselves to resist.

In substance, the Council of Defence was announcing to the whole world that the war was ended and the Republic already at the mercy of the enemy. In any case, such was the situation created by the *pronunciamiento* of March 5th.

The first consequences were not slow in making their appearance.

Since the loss of Catalonia, the partisans of surrender "on any terms" had been under the urgent necessity of demonstrating that the Republic could not continue the war. Logically, the weapons still at the Republic's disposal were an obstacle to peace; the greater the demoralization of the people and the fewer the means of resistance available to the régime, the more the cause of peace would gain. This is the explanation of the flight of the Republican Fleet to Africa a few hours after the Council of Defence had been set up.

When the Admiral in command, Don Miguel Buiza, ordered the Fleet to make for Argel, in circumstances which will afterwards be related, it occurred to the captain of the destroyer *Antequera* that instead of deserting, the fleet ought to put itself at the disposal of the Council of Defence; but "the Commander of the destroyer flotilla answered him at seven o'clock that the Admiral's decision was helping the new Government in their mission. . . ."[1]

The desertion of the Fleet was a fatal corollary of the Madrid rebellion. Two days before this event, on March 2nd, Admiral Buiza announced to the commanders of the Republican Fleet

[1] Casado, p. 164.

"that a *coup d'état* against the Government of Dr. Negrín was imminent and that a National Council of Defence would be formed, which would represent the Army and all the political parties and syndicalist organizations."[1] The Fleet was also to mutiny and place itself at the orders of the National Council of Defence.[2]

The Government discovered what was happening at Cartagena, and on the following day, the 3rd, they sent Paulino Gómez, the Minister of the Interior, to warn the naval commanders that the Government were determined to frustrate the conspiracy. On the 4th the Government appointed Lt.-Colonel Francisco Galán to be Commander of the naval base. The appointment of Galán was received with anger and protests, and his presence in Cartagena precipitated the insurrection of Colonel Armentía of the Artillery, of other Army chiefs and officers and of a regiment of marines. The rebels were joined by a crowd of Falangists, who seized the wireless station at the naval base, and the forts and batteries. The co-operation of the enemies of resistance and the *Falange* lent the incidents at Cartagena a suggestion of baseness, from the taint of which the Council was never able to free itself. The revolt of the advocates of capitulation and the Falangists was, however, soon suppressed by forces under the command of a Communist, Rodríguez, who had just returned from France.

The news of the *coup d'état* in Madrid was given to the Admiral commanding the Republican Fleet in a message from the captain of the cruiser *Libertad*. "In the manifesto", the captain of the *Libertad* said, "the people were told the truth about the war and that the Government of Negrin was guilty of treachery to them and had prepared its flight (*sic*)."[3]

During the following hours, the Admiral communicated with the ships' captains and ordered the fleet to sail at dawn for Argel. But when the Republican ships had put to sea, the French authorities signalled to the Admiral that he should take them to Bizerta. For the first time, the battle fleet of the Republic was welcomed in a French port.

Faced with the *coup d'état* staged by the Commander of the Central Army, the Negrín Government prepared to take their stand on the law; but they soon found that their isolation was almost complete. In particular, Fascist propaganda, which coincided with that of the partisans of surrender, had convinced the people that the moment had arrived to make peace, and

[1] Casado, p. 155.        [2] Id., p. 161.        [3] Id., p. 162.

that peace without reprisals was possible, since nothing was farther from Franco's thoughts than to persecute those who had committed no crime.

Again, it was a long time since the people of Madrid had set eyes on the Government, and the absence of higher authority had contributed considerably to the general demoralization. Some of these ill effects began to be remedied with the presence of the Ministers in Madrid; but the Government remained only a short time in the capital. The Prime Minister wanted to find out for himself the position in the provinces and decided to go on a tour of inspection—a decision which greatly facilitated the subversive work of the partisans of surrender in Madrid, not only because it left the field free for their machinations, but also because the uncertainty of the Government's movements weakened their ascendancy over the popular mind.

Negrín proposed to direct the war from the Levante provinces, remembering perhaps the deplorable effect produced by the Government's precipitous flight to Valencia in November 1936 and thinking perhaps that if he remained in Madrid his presence would give Franco's Air Force and artillery additional reason to bombard the city.

Lastly, the presence of Besteiro and General Miaja in the *Junta* led the mass of Republicans to think that they would not be cheated of their hope of obtaining a worthy solution. The Council had a solution (thought the people) that Negrín did not have—an impression constantly fostered by the assurance with which the authors of the *coup d'état* were speaking, as if they already had the guarantees in their pockets, and by the silence of the Government whose declaration had been killed in embryo by the rebel Republicans.

The Government realized their impotence to deal with the rising; they could not establish contact with the loyal Army leaders in the Central zone. Casado had seized control of the communications.

The idea of getting entangled in a Republican civil war was repugnant to every responsible person. Once such a war broke out, everything could be given up for lost. As I said before, the partisans of resistance were psychologically not prepared to fight other Republicans. Acceptable peace conditions could be hoped for from the enemy if the Republic displayed the will to resist. Intestine war among Republicans would destroy, or fatally impair, that weapon. Negrín was ready, therefore, to sacrifice his own position for the sake of bringing all the anti-Fascist elements into harmony. He tried to negotiate with

Casado, offering to hand over the reins of government subject to certain conditions. But the Colonel was adamant.

The Prime Minister sent Casado a message in which he exhausted all the possibilities of reconciliation, suggesting among other things:

"We must all lay our arms on the altar of the sacred interests of Spain; and if we want to come to terms with our enemies, we must first avoid bloodshed between those who have been brothers in arms. The Government, therefore, proposes that the *Junta* in Madrid should appoint one or more persons to settle all differences in a patriotic and friendly manner."

But Casado was so assured of the success of his mission that he behaved in a manner reminiscent of Mola when Martínez Barrio invited him to parley.

When the Government learned that the Council's forces had taken over the command in Alicante and that there was a risk of being made prisoner, they resolved to leave Spain. By absenting himself, Negrín took the best course open to him. The *Junta* was capable of any atrocity, for having come into being in order to placate the enemy and having committed itself irretrievably to pursuing a peace acceptable to Republicans, it might not have hesitated to offer to Franco, if he had demanded it, the head of another John the Baptist.

In the plane that was taking him to France, Negrín may perhaps have consoled himself with the saying: *Nemo propheta acceptus est in partia sua.*

In spite of the fact that the partisans of resistance shrank from civil war in the Republican camp, the conflict flared up, and it was inevitable that it should do so, and Casado knew that he was provoking it. It must be emphasized that the members of the *Junta* were determined to fight the forces and persons who remained loyal to the Government, while the latter were anxious to avoid a collision. The opponents of the Council, therefore, adopted a passive attitude. A great number of Republican soldiers and politicians—among them General Escobar, Colonel Moriones, the Commissar-General Ossorio y Tafall, Rodríguez Vega, Secretary of the *U.G.T.*—declined to have any dealings with the Council. In private, they denounced it in scathing terms; in public, they did not oppose it. For what if the defeat of the *Junta* had led to the formation of another similar body, as lacking in real authority as this one? The situation admitted of no remedy.

But the dispute with the Communists was another thing.

According to Casado, they must be reduced to impotence, if his hands were not to be tied in his dealings with the Fascists. The Colonel had, therefore, taken measures against them "in anticipation of the aggressive attitude which the Communist Party would probably take up, with such of the military forces as might follow it".[1] For "the Communist Party would probably adopt a rebellious attitude".[2] Casado was sure the Communists would rise against the Council, because one of the principal points of the Council's policy was the suppression of Communism, and it was not to be expected that the Communists would resign themselves to disappearing. The Council of Defence "had to suppress the hysterical cries, absurd slogans and intolerable conduct of the Communist Party", declares the Colonel. "From its very first moment in office", he adds, "the Council set out to achieve this, because we were convinced that it was our only way to a decent and honourable peace."[3]

The *Junta* had, then, to try and eliminate Communist influence, not only, as was natural, because the Communists advocated resistance and insisted that the Republicans could not trust Franco's word, but also because, as we have seen, there was a prevalent illusion that, if every trace of Communism were suppressed, the Fascists would view the Republican negotiators as respectable persons with whom it might be possible to come to an agreement.

The defensive character of the Communist reaction against the Council is, therefore, palpable. Casado placed the Communists under the necessity of fighting the *Junta*, and in the course of the conflict the Communist military leaders were obliged, as we shall see, to turn their arms against him.

There were four Army Corps under Casado's authority in the Central zone; the 1st commanded by Colonel Barceló, the 2nd by Lt.-Colonel Bueno, the 3rd by Colonel Ortega—all three Communists. The 4th Army Corps was commanded by Cipriano Mera, an Anarchist, who had been Casado's closest ally in the *coup d'état*.

On the morning of March 5th, the Communist Ascanio, commanding the 8th Division, mobilized his forces against the Council. Bueno being ill, Ascanio took over the command of the 2nd Army Corps before Casado could replace Bueno by Zulueta, an ex-Communist in the service of the *Junta*. Ascanio placed his troops across the roads to Aragon and France, thus preventing the troops under the command of Gutiérrez de Miguel, belonging to the 65th Division, from joining up with the *Junta's*

[1] Casado, p. 131.      [2] Id., p. 184.      [3] Id., p. 198.

troops. Part of these troops, aware of the rôle assigned to them, passed over to Ascanio's Army.

Although the encounter between the Council of Defence and its opponents had begun, the 1st and 3rd Army Corps, commanded by Communists, remained at the front on the fringe of the fratricidal conflict. Only Casado's intention to mobilize them against the forces fighting the *Junta* shook them out of their passivity. When Casado ordered the 200th Brigade to march against the Communists who were fighting in Fuencarral, this unit made ready to move, not to support Casado, but to join Ascanio's troops.

The bias which the military struggle had taken from the outset was unfavourable to the Council. Casado had staked everything on the support of the 4th Army Corps, commanded by Mera, two battalions of which had been sent to Madrid before the *coup d'état*. But a column of this Corps, under Liberino González, proceeding from Guadalajara towards the capital of the Republic, was unable to penetrate beyond Alcalá de Henares, where the population and the troops declared their loyalty to the Negrín Government.

At this moment, the Communists broached the subject of an agreement with Casado and the conflict appeared to be on the way to a solution. Officially, in fact, it was supposed to be ended; but the struggle went on because neither the *Junta* nor the Communists wanted to be the first to fulfil the conditions agreed upon. And as Casado soon saw that the column under Liberino González had finally succeeded in breaking through at Alcalá de Henares—which put the Council in a more favourable position—the possibilities of peace between Republicans not only diminished, but the battle became more bitter and fratricidal.

Next, Casado tried to make use of the 7th Division under another González, a Communist. This division was defending the lines of the Casa de Campo and Rosales and had shown neither hostility nor sympathy to the Council of Defence. But when the Colonel requested González by telephone to send him the artillery and a machine-gun unit, González is said to have replied: "Come and fetch them yourself, traitor." What is certain is that this division refused to obey Casado and the latter ordered the *Junta's* forces in the Puerta del Sol to attack González' headquarters, near the Plaza de España.

What followed was typical: the 7th Division had to meet simultaneously an attack by Casado's troops and the troops of Franco. The latter attacked him along the line of the lake in the Casa de Campo. González defeated the *Junta's* forces, inflicting casualties on them and forcing them to retreat to their point of departure; but in the Casa de Campo he had to give way before the Fascists, who advanced to the very gates of the park.

After having driven back Casado's troops, the 7th Division organized a counter-attack against the Fascists and the next day regained the lost positions, killing 300 of the enemy and taking about ninety prisoners.

In the meantime, Franco's Air Force and artillery were bombarding the sectors held by the Communists who were fighting against the Council of Defence.

In a different order of things, the tragedy of the Fascist zone was now being repeated on Republican territory as a farce. From the outset, the Council of Defence occupied the position in respect to its enemies which Franco occupied in respect to the Republic. The Madrid *Junta* stigmatized the defenders of legality and of the Government as insurgents and rebels, and labelled all those Republicans who were not enthusiastic supporters of Casado's *coup d'état* as Communists.

We can, without any loss to history, pass over the development of the intestine quarrels of the Republic in the streets of Madrid, among an indifferent and tired populace. The Council established its authority after a week of bloodshed; in reality, it owed its triumph to its opponents' lack of enthusiasm for disputing its power on the field of battle. But the defeat of the Communists was accompanied by a savage police persecution in which, as might have been expected, the disguised Fascists who were serving the new organism took part. The Republican gaols filled up with Communists; though many who managed to get away escaped reprisals by taking refuge with the Armies of the South and the Levante where Colonel Casado did not trouble to pursue them.

For their part, the Communists were not guiltless, in the heat of the battle, of detestable excesses which were not justified even by the fanatical conviction that they were fighting against traitors to the people's cause. Among other excesses or outrages may be reckoned the death of the *Junta* Colonels Otero, Fernández Urbano and Pérez Gazzolo. It was never known how these soldiers perished nor who were their executioners. All that is known for certain is that their corpses appeared in El Pardo.

The Council condemned to death two Army chiefs, members of the Communist Party—Lt.-Colonel Eduardo Barceló and

663

Commissar Conesa. Both were shot. In the short and painful history of the *Junta*, there is really no more disgraceful episode than the execution in cold blood of these two Republican soldiers. The reasons Casado gave to justify these death sentences might have issued from one of Franco's tribunals. "There were some Communists who stayed in their positions until the last moment, and among them those most to blame, Lt.-Colonel Barceló and Commissar Conesa."[1] "The Council approved death sentences for Barceló and Conesa, not only as leaders of the rebellion (*sic*), but also because under their authority, or I should say under their command, all sorts of offences had been committed and assassinations done."[2]

Though Casado had promised, during the first peace negotiations with the Communists, that only those who had committed offences against the common law would be punished, the Council's justice was following in the footsteps of Franco's justice. It was the justice of the Fascists, with one important difference, which should be emphasized.

The party factions—which had been used by the reactionaries to destroy the Republic and give it the *coup de grâce*—had culminated in the Republican petty civil war which we have just described; and the *Junta* military chiefs who were assassinated by the Communists fell in the heat of battle when passions were running high. But there were circumstances surrounding the disappearance of Barceló and Conesa which gave this double murder the repugnant character that vengeance always assumes when it is adorned with the trappings of justice. The members of the *Junta* set themselves up as judges in a cause in which they were an interested party, and executed in the name of the law a sentence dictated by party hatred.

Possibly, also, the defeat of the Communists was not enough for the Council, but they must needs offer up victims as a propitiatory sacrifice—hence the execution of Barceló and Conesa.

Not only did the Council display unpardonable Pharisaism in executing the two Communist leaders, but they also plumbed the depths of ignominy in their choice of victims. Barceló was one of the professional soldiers who had best served the Republic during the civil war. Loyal to the popular cause from the first day of Franco's rising, he distributed arms to the people from the Ministry of War and effectively helped in organizing the masses for the struggle. In November 1936 he was seriously wounded in the Pozuelo and Las Rozas engagements. His

[1] Casado, p. 179.      [2] Id., p. 180.

conduct during the whole war was that of a devoted Republican. There was nothing, in conscience, he could be reproached with, and to hold him to blame for excesses committed by fanatical Communists at a time of general anarchy was pure arbitrariness. Barceló's personal moderation was as notorious as his loyalty to the Republic and to his party, which he served quietly and without fuss. Perhaps it was this moderation which led Casado to believe that Barceló was not a Communist at heart.[1]

When the civil war between the Republicans came to an end, the Republic was left as maimed as Patroclus in the Iliad, after Apollo had dealt him the staggering blow which left him unarmed and defenceless. The *coup d'état* of March 5th had cost the lives of 2,000 Republicans; and the victors had suffered as much as the vanquished. Let Casado himself describe the situation: "Unfortunately, our attempts to secure such a peace were opposed by the Communists. Their subversive (*sic*) attitude lasted seven days and its ravages were so great that the National Council of Defence could not take up negotiations, with the ability to quote the power of resistance of the troops and civil population. The struggle between the Communist forces and those of the National Council of Defence caused our effectiveness to be weakened, caused sections of our front to be abandoned and remain for several days at the mercy of the Nationalists, and caused despair among the civil population. . . ."[2] "We were in a most precarious situation as a result of the material and moral ravages which the Communist revolt (*sic*) had produced."[3]

Casado naturally refused to recognize that all these ills flowed from his *coup d'état*, and it is surprising that he should lament them, seeing that on March 5th he did not shrink from the prospect of provoking in the Republican zone precisely that sub-civil war which has been described. Moreover, Casado was to confess later that what occurred was in accordance with his plans (Speech on March 26th).

The formation of the Council of Defence had already had fatal repercussions on the Republic; the Fleet had fled, and demoralization among Republicans had been sharply accentuated; the war was given up for lost. In such conditions, what sort of peace could be hoped for from Franco?

The Council had been occupying itself with the peace negotiations during the struggle with the advocates of resistance and had even arrived at the point of asking by radio for discussions

[1] Casado, p. 187.     [2] Id., p. 198.     [3] Id.

to be opened. In spite of everything, Casado still believed that as soon as he had made contact with the Fascist generals, enemy intransigence would vanish. He thought, as we know, that he was much respected in the Fascist camp and had over-weening confidence in his powers of persuasion. He viewed peace as an affair to be settled by the armies, as between officers and gentlemen.

The *Junta* proposed to treat with the "Nationalists" on the lines that the latter should guarantee the national independence and integrity of Spain, the expatriation of all who wished to leave the country and the absence of all reprisals.[1] The task of parleying with Franco's generals obviously devolved upon Colonel Casado, who was to be accompanied by General Matallana, Commander-in-Chief.

Having settled what peace terms were acceptable to the Republicans and appointed plenipotentiaries, the Council published the document which was to serve as a basis of discussion with the "Nationalists". In the preamble, the Council declared itself to be the living expression of Republican Spain (with evident truth, since, after the defeat of the Communists, the only other expression was a dead or captive one), and apologized to Franco for not having devoted its activities to obtaining peace, owing to the circumstance that "certain Communist elements have carried on an armed rebellion against its authority. . . . Fortunately, the movement has been suppressed and has served to show once more that the Council has the support of all those Spaniards whose sense of honour makes them put their hope of peace before everything".

The *Junta's* conditions of peace followed, namely: (1) Final and categoric declaration of respect for the national sovereignty and integrity; (2) Assurance that all those who had taken part in the war from honourable and sincere motives should be treated, both as regards their persons and their interests, with the greatest respect; (3) Guarantee that there should be no reprisals or other sentences, save those passed by competent tribunals; (4) Respect for the life and liberty of Republican soldiers and Republican political commissars who were not guilty of any criminal offence; (5) Respect for the life, liberty and *career* of professional soldiers not guilty of any crime; (6) Respect for the life, liberty and interests of public officials under the same conditions; (7) Twenty-five days' grace to allow for the expatriation of all persons desiring to leave the country; (8) No Italian or Moorish soldiers to be introduced into the

[1] Casado, p. 199.

Republican zone; (9) This document having been accepted by the Council, it should be presented to the enemy by the Head of the Council and the Commander-in-Chief."[1]

In going to Franco (who had never admitted the possibility of a conditional peace) with the claims set out in this document, the Council showed a complete lack of grasp of the situation. The Negrín Government had been prepared to end hostilities if the enemy guaranteed the absence of reprisals and the safe conduct of Republicans desiring to go abroad. Yet we know that the rebels refused to negotiate even under such favourable conditions. Colonel Casado's *Junta* was more exacting and, over and above the Negrín Government's terms, added the provisos that there should be no Moors or Italians in the Republican zone, that Franco should give a definite and categoric promise to safeguard the national sovereignty and territorial integrity, that he should maintain public functionaries in their office and respect the rank and career of the *professional* soldiers.

As regards the Army of the Republic, the Council traced a dividing line between the professional and non-professional soldiers, including the latter under clause (4) and the former under clause (5). This shows the extent to which the *Junta* was dominated by Colonel Casado and the old Army generals. It was obvious that the professional soldiers who had risen against the Negrín Government were trying to save themselves at all costs; and not only trying to save their lives, but hoping to enter the Fascist Army with the rank they had enjoyed in the Republican Army.

Casado calculated that Franco would need officers and was under the illusion that the Nationalists could not do without the Republican officers of the old Army. And it is highly probable that Franco's agents assured these Republican professional soldiers that their services in ending resistance would be recognized, to the consequent advantage of their career. The Caudillo did, in fact, show himself generous to some of them afterwards.

Negrín had promoted Casado General, and Casado had received the news of his promotion with satisfaction, according to General Hidalgo de Cisneros, in whose presence the Colonel gave orders for the new insignia to be sewn on his uniform.[2] But he changed his mind shortly afterwards, and when he rebelled he did it as a Colonel. He had realized that the rank of General would prejudice him in Franco's eyes; and events justified this fear.

[1] Casado, p. 202.  [2] Álvarez del Vayo, p. 308.

Let us repeat that the nine-point document revealed the Council of Defence as completely divorced from realities. This *Junta*, while militarily much weaker than the Negrín Government, was much more ambitious. Negrín had behind him military forces which, if well led and organized, would have caused Franco serious anxiety; for it can never be sufficiently emphasized that, in spite of his victories, the prolongation of the war was not welcome to him. Colonel Casado's *Junta* had no intention of fighting and had liquidated most of the means of resistance on which it could lay hands. As a result, the Republic was at the mercy of the Fascists, and the Fascists knew it. And whereas before, Franco had spurned the Republicans' request for a conditional peace, he now reacted to the aspirations of the Council of Defence with senseless, but understandable, haughtiness. The Burgos *Junta* declared that "Franco considered all approaches to him for a conditional peace highly insulting, since, as he has repeatedly said, he would only accept absolute and unconditional surrender".

On the morning of March 11th the Council approved the nine-point document and decided to open peace negotiations with the "Nationalist" Government. That is, they had already repeatedly asked for peace over the radio, getting only uncivil replies from the Fascists, and now they were going to see which Fascists in Madrid would be acceptable to Franco as intermediaries.

"This important business", says Casado, "was carried out with the greatest secrecy." A meeting of the Council took place in the morning; in the evening, Franco's representatives in Madrid presented themselves spontaneously to Casado with all the boldness of those who had the whip hand. These representatives were already familiar with the Council's peace conditions as set out in the memorandum.[1] A treacherous member of the Council had betrayed the whole scheme to them.

Franco's principal agent in Madrid was Cendaños, Lt.-Colonel of Artillery and head of one of the military Departments of the Republic! He was accompanied by another individual. Cendaños naturally congratulated Casado on the Council's decision to negotiate peace and declared that he and his companion were entirely at his disposal. Casado was alarmed by his visitors' "impulsive and unexpected" statement. He toyed with the thought of arresting them and passing summary judgment on them for high treason, he says, but eventually decided to accept them as a connecting link in the negotiations with Franco.

[1] Casado, p. 207.

The history of the discussions can be summed up as follows:

Franco's representatives warned Casado that the Council's representatives "would have as their only mission to seek an accord with the Nationalists on the manner of surrendering our zone and the Republican Army, since the Generalissimo would demand its unconditional surrender, and this in a very short space of time".[1]

Casado replied that the Republican Army was prepared to fight to the end, and Franco's agents, no doubt with a smile, handed him a document setting out the terms fixed by the Caudillo.

The Council of Defence studied this document at length. "One could see only too clearly that this document had been drawn up so cleverly that, whilst conceding nothing, it would give a sense of confidence to all those who read it in good faith."[2]

The Head of the *Junta*, who had risen against the Government in the belief that he could obtain better peace terms than Negrín, now perceived—a little late—that it was impossible to come to terms with such an enemy. "The declarations made by the enemy representatives and a study of the concessions offered by the Generalissimo made me doubt whether any negotiations would be possible."[3]

However, Casado kept his impressions to himself. "I did not wish my scepticism to affect the other members of the Council, because we had to avoid depression or excitement, the consequences of which might have been fatal. In spite of my silence, I realized that the other members of the Council supposed, as I did, that General Franco would refuse conversations for peace."[4]

Casado requested Burgos to clarify the meaning of certain proposals, but Franco was not in a hurry to reply. For a week the negotiations hung fire; and the Council, perhaps for the first time, despaired of obtaining the *decent and honourable peace* which had already cost them so dearly in honour and self-respect.

During the interval, the Colonel meditated ordering the retreat of the Central Army on the Tagus and prepared, he says, to organize the evacuation of the civil population of Madrid. But the fear of hastening the process of demoralization decided the Council to postpone all action until the 26th.

The *Junta* did not take any measures because, in fine, it had promised the people a just and decent peace and did not dare

[1] Casado, p. 210.    [2] Id., p. 214.    [3] Id., p. 214.    [4] Id., p. 214.

to confess its failure. The public was told nothing about the state of the negotiations; but the Press (the opposition papers had been suppressed) filled its columns with attacks on Negrín, the Communists, and Russia, while it dinned into its readers' ears the thesis that every Republican who had not committed murder or robbery could look to the future with confidence. The people were being psychologically prepared to greet Franco's troops without alarm.

In his eagerness to placate the wrath of the Burgos Jove, Casado ordered the Fascist prisoners to be set at liberty. The Communists remained in prison.

On the 19th the Colonel was told that Franco's representatives wanted to see him. Cendaño and his companion informed him that the Generalissimo agreed to negotiate, but would not accept him and Matallana as plenipotentiaries on account of their high rank. "In their place, two officers of the Republican Army were to be chosen as representatives, whose only mission would be to settle details of our surrender."[1]

The Council agreed that even if Franco insisted on unconditional surrender, it was not a bad sign that he agreed to negotiate.

Casado chose as the *Junta's* delegates Lt.-Colonel Antonio Garijo and Major Leopoldo Ortega, of the Cavalry, both of the General Staff.

Two days later, the Nationalist agents gave Casado a message from the Generalissimo, saying that the Council's representatives were to go to Burgos on the 23rd by aeroplane, flying by direct route over Somosierra and landing on the Burgos aerodrome between nine and twelve o'clock.

Before Lt.-Colonel Garijo and Major Ortega departed on their mission, Casado informed the British Consul at Madrid of the course of the negotiations, and the latter remarked "that he could not give any official opinion on such an important point, but, privately and in a friendly way, he considered that this was the best and perhaps the only solution. Personally," writes Casado, "I considered that this private opinion of Señor Milanés coincided with that of the British Government."[2]

With a view to sounding the possibilities of evacuating those Republicans most seriously threatened by the vengeance of the Fascists, Besteiro and Casado approached the British and French Consuls. The French Consul promised nothing definite; and Señor Milanés replied that the British Government were quite prepared to help in the humanitarian work of evacuation

[1] Casado, p. 216.    [2] Id., p. 220.

by taking off refugees in the warships stationed off the east coast of Spain, if General Franco agreed. The *Junta* sent the Intendant-General of the Centre, Trifón Gómez, to Paris on a similar mission.

The nations whose agents had led the Council of Defence to believe that they could count on them in an emergency were beginning to lose interest in the Republican tragedy and to leave Besteiro and Casado in the lurch. They did not need them any longer.

The plenipotentiaries of the *Junta* alighted at the aerodrome of Barajas at 10.30 a.m. on March 23rd. With them travelled Franco's agents in Madrid, bearing a message from the "National Council of Defence to the Nationalist Command".

This document, which was signed by Casado alone, expressed the hope of surrendering the Republican zone "in the best possible circumstances, without bloodshed"; the Nationalist Government were asked for facilities for the evacuation of persons desiring to leave Spain, and for an undertaking not to insult Madrid by a march past of foreign troops. It was proposed that the surrender of Republican territory should take place by zones or theatres of operations, so that there might be organization and order, and, finally, the Nationalist Government were promised help with the problem of feeding the Central zone.

The *Junta's* emissaries returned from Burgos at seven o'clock in the evening and recounted their adventures. They had seen some Germans on the Burgos aerodrome, who took several photographs of the Douglas aeroplane in which they had been travelling. They entered a small building set apart for the aviators. They were coldly received by two of Franco's colonels, Gonzalo and Ungría, in the officers' mess on the aerodrome. Garijo and Ortega submitted to their interlocutors the plan drawn up by the Council of Defence, according to which the Republican zone was to be surrendered to Franco within a period of twenty-five days, by theatres of operations—first the Centre, then Estremadura, next Andalusia, and finally the Levante.

Franco rejected surrender by zones and replied with an elaborate and extensive plan of occupation. The Caudillo insisted upon the symbolic surrender of the Republican Air Force before six o'clock on March 25th and the surrender of the other military forces of the Republic on the 27th.

The *Junta's* representatives suggested that a pact should be signed; but the Nationalist representatives made it clear that they would sign no pact, that the concessions would not be amplified and that the Council of Defence would have to keep strictly to the instructions laid down by the Generalissimo.

Casado replied that the attitude of the Nationalists had no precedent in history.

The Council requested Burgos for another interview; and Franco replied on the 25th in the affirmative.

Once more Lt.-Colonel Garijo and Major Ortega appeared at the Burgos aerodrome, to urge the Council's point of view. But again Franco's representatives rejected the *Junta's* desire to hand over the Republic by zones; though they consented to draw up an agreement to be signed by both parties. Lt.-Colonel Garijo was instructed to draft a convention, and while he was occupied in this task, at six o'clock in the evening an emissary from Franco informed him that the negotiations must be broken off, as the *Junta* had not surrendered the Republican Air Force within the stipulated period. With this disconcerting news went an abrupt request for the emissaries of the Council of Defence to leave Burgos immediately.

The Republican officers protested strenuously at being forced to leave at an advanced hour and in bad weather conditions, but they did not succeed in softening their adversaries' hearts. They left Burgos, therefore, feeling greatly humiliated.

At 7.30 in the evening, the disappointed plenipotentiaries arrived at Madrid, and the Council, having heard their story, resolved to surrender the Republican Air Force on the following day, the 26th. They informed Burgos by telegram; but Franco replied with another, inviting the Council to instruct the front-line Republican troops to raise the white flag and start surrendering.

The Burgos ultimatum was followed by three attacks by the Fascist forces, one at Pozoblanco towards Almadén, one from Toledo to Mora, and the other towards the hills of Ocaña. Only on these sectors were Franco's troops fighting the Republican Army, and even these offensives were carried out "with very small forces", according to Casado himself. "In the armies of the Levante and Andalusia", adds the Colonel, "our forces remained in their positions without being attacked by the enemy. It is certain that the latter advanced on Almadén and Mora de Toledo, not with the idea of isolating the Estremadura Army, but simply with the object of making our forces retreat, so that they could occupy the zone quickly without fighting."[1]

[1] Casado, p. 252.

At that moment, as after the fall of Catalonia, Franco's chief anxiety was to avoid new battles. The dictator feared that the Republican forces, disobeying the Council of Defence, would offer resistance; and the benevolence with which the Fascists received Republican soldiers who surrendered (in contrast with the cruelty with which they were afterwards treated) was due to "the fear that acts of violence on their part would provoke a reaction among the Republican forces".

Franco had good grounds for fearing opposition, since Casado's *Junta* was already no more than a tragicomic figurehead. It could not hand over the Air Force, in spite of having agreed to do so, because many of the pilots had fled to Orán with their planes. And when the people knew that they were required to surrender unconditionally, they naturally felt lost and despairing. As I have repeatedly said, the people longed for peace, but no one envisaged the surrender to the enemy of eight million inhabitants, ten provinces and an unconquered Army of 800,000 men without any counterbalancing concession or guarantee.

The public alarm and discontent forced the Council to appeal to Republicans by radio. During the night of the 26th, various members of the Council and leaders pledged to Casado's policy came in turn to the microphone. José del Río, Secretary of the Council, said among other things: "The National Council of Defence has been astonished by what has happened and cannot understand the intentions of the Nationalist Government, to whom it offered everything necessary for the surrender of the Republican zone in the best conditions possible."[1]

Colonel Casado must have amazed his hearers with this revelation: "I can assure you that in the whole of the loyal zone nothing has happened contrary to the plans conceived by us in taking over the constitutional power of Republican Spain on the 5th of March."[2]

But the most striking speech was delivered by González Marín, an Anarchist, and the Councillor for Finance and Economy in the *Junta*: "To achieve a total reorganization of this country and *dedicate the energies of the people to war*, we had no remedy but to remove the Negrín Government, acting above considerations of a constitutional and juridical kind."[3]

On the evening of March 27th, the Republican soldiers began to desert from the front lines. The Commander of the Central Army appealed to Casado for instructions, and the Colonel ordered him not to oppose the desertions.

At seven o'clock on the morning of the 28th, the same officer

[1] Casado, p. 239.     [2] Id., p. 245.     [3] Id., p. 243.

received orders to get into contact with the Nationalists to arrange for the formal surrender; and as soon as he appeared before Franco's generals in the *Hospital Clínico*, Casado considered his mission in Madrid was ended and prepared to leave for Valencia "to liquidate the other armies in the same way".[1]

The Colonel went in his official car to the aerodrome where a plane was waiting to take him to the capital of the Levante. From the aeroplane he could see "strings of lorries and groups of soldiers going home, realizing, perhaps, the uselessness of their magnificent sacrifice".[2]

The Colonel found the Valencia garrison in a state of alarm. He ordered the troops to parade and told them "that according to Franco's promises, those who had not committed crimes of bloodshed would go free".[3]

In Valencia itself, Casado declared "before members of the International Delegation and a dozen persons: 'General Franco has promised me that he will not oppose the evacuation. He has signed no document because that would be a humiliation which one cannot ask from a victor. But you can trust his word. All the promises he has made to me have been kept.'"[4]

On the beginning of the 29th, practically all the Republican armies had been disbanded, and at eleven o'clock Casado gave orders for the surrender, though he realized that such an act had no meaning.

The *Junta* had advised Republicans that all those who wanted to flee the country should congregate in Alicante,[5] and about 10,000 persons who desired, with understandable anxiety, to leave Spain, soon gathered in the port.

The members of the Council of Defence who had joined Casado in Valencia—except Besteiro and one other who elected to remain in Madrid—decided unanimously to go to the port of Gandía, whence they left for England with a hundred other Spaniards in the British warship *Galatea*.

At Alicante there were no ships to evacuate the vast throng of fugitives (among whom were two to three thousand women and children) and they were immediately surrounded by General Gambara's Italian troops. Many gave way to despair and there were forty to fifty suicides within the space of a few hours.

Most of the men were moved from Alicante to the concentration camp at Albatera, where soon 17,000 or 18,000 Repub-

[1] Casado, p. 251.
[2] Id., p. 254.
[3] Id., p. 255.
[4] Id., p. 296.
[5] Id., p. 256.

licans were crowded into a space intended for 800 persons. For several months they lived exposed to the elements, practically without food, often without water. Twice or three times a week, the prisoners heard bursts of rifle fire when Republicans who had attempted to escape, or been unjustly accused of having tried to do so, were shot.

"It was then that a reaction set in, which enabled us to see why we had been fighting and why it would have been better to continue to resist."[1]

## CHAPTER XXV

## THE FALANGIST STATE

AFTER A LAPSE of several months, the Republicans were leaving the concentration camp at Albatera, to be charged and brought to trial. "The entry into Madrid", relates Rodriguez Vega, "gave us an idea of what was to be the panorama of terror, grief and tragedy which we would have to witness or endure for the space of some years; the maltreatment of one's comrades, the routine bludgeoning of old men and women, without respect to age or sex; refined tortures which, during the time I was in that *Comisaria* in the calle de Almagro, led to three suicides."[2]

"On the plea of rebellion, hundreds of thousands of Spaniards are being condemned to death, hundreds of thousands are being condemned to thirty years' imprisonment, and hundreds of thousands more are being condemned to twenty, to twelve, or to six years' imprisonment."[3]

According to Mr. Phillips, towards the end of 1939, 100,000 Republicans had already been executed by Franco in what was at the beginning of that year Republican territory. Franco's tribunals were passing death sentences at the rate of a thousand

[1] Rodriguez Vega, speech at Mexico, March 10th, 1943. Rodriguez Vega, Secretary of the Socialist General Workers' Union, was taken to Madrid and condemned to death by Franco's tribunals, but owing to an error, he escaped with his life, recovered his liberty and was able to leave Spain.

[2] Rodriguez Vega, id.

[3] A. V. Phillips, author of the pamphlet *Spain under Franco* (London, 1940), from which I have taken these data, lived in Madrid from 1927 to 1939. He was correspondent at various times to Reuter, the Exchange Telegraph Company, and the *News Chronicle*. During the civil war he broadcast in English for the Republicans. In August 1939, he was arrested by Franco's police and thrown into the Polier prison, where he remained for more than four months without being charged or brought to trial.

a month. And Rodríguez Vega points out that in December 1939 there existed in the Ministry of War more than 69,000 dossiers relating to persons who had been condemned to death. As regards the loss of personal liberty, the Secretary of the *U.G.T.* calculates that, from the capitulation of Madrid to the b'eginning of 1942, more than two million persons had passed through the prisons and concentration camps. Mr. Phillips gives the figure of 100,000 persons detained in the prisons of Madrid during the period of his incarceration in the Polier prison, and considers that at least a million Spaniards had been deprived of their liberty at that moment. "It may easily be much higher than the million mark. Franco himself seems to be alarmed and referred to the problem in his New Year's speech. Indeed, he placed the question in the foreground of his message and says that it affects 'a large portion' of the population of Spain. How large a portion it is difficult to ascertain, but personally I should say that in one way or another quite half the population is affected. I should say that in Madrid there are 100,000 in prison, that is to say, one-tenth of the population. If the same is the case all over Spain, we should arrive at the two-million figure. Many women", continues Mr. Phillips, "have to take food to their husbands in one jail and to a brother or sister in another. The strain of visiting one and the other, the worry of getting food for them, utterly upsets their nerves, so that in some ways they are far worse off than those in jail. I have heard some say that they would prefer to be inside. This great human tragedy extends from one end of Spain to the other. A tragedy of immense human suffering."

As regards the food situation, it is interesting to recall that in 1938 and 1939, towards the end of the war, the amount of food received by each person in Republican Spain, during the period of the greatest scarcity, was 150 grammes of bread daily and 100 grammes of other foodstuffs. Under Franco, as late as 1942, Rodríguez Vega tells us that "the official ration was 100 or 200 grammes of food a week. In many Spanish towns there was no bread for weeks at a time. Broadly speaking, it may be stated that the weekly ration was hardly enough for one day. The situation as regards official supplies", he adds, "was worse than the worst situation that any Spanish city could have had to endure at any period of the civil war".

The Spanish people's justifiable and deeply-felt longing for peace was iniquitously drowned in fresh blood by the vengeful ferocity of the conquerors. The innumerable arrests and executions which followed Franco's victory decimated the productive population again, causing irreparable ruin. Industry, the mines, agriculture, suffered from lack of man-power. The triumphant reactionaries were like the Louisianian savages who, when they wanted to pluck the fruit, cut down the whole tree (Montesquieu, I, V, chap. xiii).

The flower of Spanish intellect perished or went into exile, and the intellectual and moral level of the nation which Franco had subdued soon sank to the obscure depths where it had lain in the days of Ferdinand VII. All of a sudden, in the intellectual, moral and political order, Spain appeared with the repulsive mask of 115 or 120 years ago. The *Falange* was but the resurrection of the royalist volunteers of 1823. The clergy, as uncultured and as base as they had been a century ago, fell upon the stricken conscience of the conquered with a kind of violence more odious than physical repression.

The most grinding poverty and the most exorbitant luxury, existing side by side in startling contrast, were proof that the oligarchy was once more ruling the nation. The landed and financial nobility saluted the New Era of absolutism with provocative impatience and the newspaper columns were once more filled with frivolous society items and titled names. The aristocracy recovered their outrageous economic power and used it, with characteristic insensitiveness, to parade their wealth. A good example of this was the reception given by the Duke of Alba on April 27th, 1943, at his palace in Seville, to celebrate the coming of age of his daughter Doña María del Rosario Cayetana. "Some 2,000 people filled the drawing-rooms and the beautiful gardens," wrote a journalist. The reception did not begin until midnight and went on till the early hours of the morning. Grandees of Spain, the lesser nobility, diplomats, powerful landowners, bullfighters, and breeders of bulls for the ring were regaled by the Duke with a splendid banquet and a brilliant ball. In the traditional Seville Fair, General Franco presented the young Duchess with a gold cup won in the Women's Competition.

"In the ancient palace of Las Duenas", wrote another society journalist, "there was an atmosphere of grandiose splendour." It was, in fact, the greatest social event Spain had witnessed for many years. According to the *Daily Mail*, the reception cost the Duke of Alba £10,000 or about half a million pesetas.

In that same city of Seville, some 40,000 Republicans had been executed by the Fascists during the civil war and the majority of the population were starving. Seville—at all times

677

the seat of millionaires and beggars, and in 1943 the emblem of the national grief and misery—was still shaken by the terror of the executions and prostrated by the hunger of the people. Only an oligarchy devoid of all virtue, without conscience or patriotism, could have put the finishing touch to the civil war by displays like the one I have described. Nowhere, not even, perhaps, in Czarist Russia before the Bolshevist Revolution, could one find an aristocracy capable of showing such indifference to the nation's suffering.

The dream of those who had acclaimed the Army's rebellion as the herald of order soon vanished into thin air. As always when the Army seized the Government, Spain was in a state of anarchy.

The *Falange* completed the disorganization of the country's economic life with its arbitrary *corporative* system and aggravated the moral and financial instability caused by the civil war by the systematic and perverse corruption which it introduced into every branch of the public administration.

The infamous nature of the new régime was shown in the State Budget. The Falangist Party was awarded an annual grant of 160 million pesetas. The Army took the lion's share, or 21·4 per cent of the public funds; next came the Ministry of the Interior, responsible for all the police forces, with 10·8 per cent. The other Ministerial Departments found themselves relegated to the background or ignored. It might have been thought that a nation devastated by war would have been in urgent need of reconstruction, but this was not the view of the new rulers of Spain. The estimates for Public Works, therefore, amounted to only 11·4 per cent of the Civil Estimates. Only 4 per cent was allotted to Education; and Agriculture, although Spain was an agricultural country, had to be content with a mere 9 per cent (Budget 1944–45).

As on previous occasions, the oligarchs found a useful ally in the Army, the hub of the new dictatorship. They had recovered their fortune and lands with the triumph of the counter-revolution; for though the *Falange* appeared before the public with a plan of agrarian reform the counter-revolution in the country-side was characterized by cruelty which was unprecedented even in Spain. In favouring the proprietors at the expense of tenants and landless labourers, the new Government's agrarian decrees exceeded anything the imagination could devise. Rents were raised everywhere, with retroactive effect in what had been Republican territory during the war; that is, the tenant had to pay the landlord the arrears of rent which had accumulated during the war, and not at the old pre-war rate, but the new and much higher rate.

These decrees were so iniquitous that before they were passed they gave rise to acrimonious disputes among the Fascists in the Cabinet, and the Government was occupied for several weeks in discussing and approving them.

The officially controlled price of wheat rose from about 50 pesetas in 1939 to more than 80 in 1941, with a consequent rise in the price of bread, the people's staple food.

As might have been expected of a régime whose principal objective was the merciless exploitation of the people, the cost of living rose sharply without an equivalent rise in wages.

The oligarchy, therefore, maintained and improved its economic position, as it had always done whenever the Army installed a dictatorship; but it was the soldiers and the *Falange* who enjoyed the political power. Once more in the history of Spain, we find the oligarchs excluded from political power by the Army. They had appealed to the Army to save them, and the Army had duly done so—with the decisive help of foreign troops—but the result was, as always, not altogether advantageous to the oligarchy.

As in the nineteenth century, when the Republican and proletarian menace disappeared, the propertied classes began again to hanker after a régime other than the military—a more stable régime, controlled by themselves, which would avert once and for all the danger of another rebellion—in short, the monarchy.

In June 1937 Gil Robles broke with the insurgents and declared himself in favour of the restoration of the monarchy. There is no doubt that the wheat-farming oligarchs of Castile supported the man who had been their leader under the Republic in his aspiration to change the régime of the Army and the *Falange* into a régime which would have restored to them their political power. Gil Robles, whose conflict with the aristocratic section of the oligarchy, or rather with the great landowners of the south, had arisen under the Republic through his refusal to support a monarchist restoration, now became the champion of this policy.

We have already seen that *Renovación Española*—the aristocratic nucleus of the landed oligarchy—embarked upon civil war with the sole object of saving its lands. So long as its property was threatened, *Renovación Española* considered the return of the King a subsidiary matter, as we learnt from Señor Lequerica, whose remarks are quoted elsewhere. But when the social danger was past, the aristocracy resumed with ever increasing intensity its demand for the restoration of the monarchy. Politically speaking, the aristocratic oligarchy had been thrust into the background of the Falangist State. Don Antonio Goicoechea had been adequately rewarded for his conspiratorial activities by being promoted to the Governorship of the Bank of Spain. That was all. On personal grounds, another source of grievance between the new régime and the aristocratic party was the incident which obliged the Marqués de Luca de Tena, owner of *ABC*, to leave Spain.

To sum up, we find the Spanish oligarchy endeavouring, as in the nineteenth century, to confine the Army to barracks and to found a permanent civil State in which its interests would prevail and prosper under the protection of the law. The oligarchy considered that the Army had accomplished its mission by destroying the people's Republic and demanded that it should leave the Government, give up politics, and make way for an oligarchic régime founded not on force, but on law. It was the same need as led Cánovas del Castillo to found the institutions of the Restoration.

Nevertheless, the national and international situation was now very different from what it was in 1874. In 1874 there were hardly any Republicans in Spain; in 1940 those Spaniards who still placed any faith in the monarchical form of government were in a minority. Not even the oligarchy was unanimous in its desire for the restoration of the monarchy. For General Franco and the Falange to make way for a new king was, in the last instance, as dangerous as to accept the return of the Republicans to power. For if the monarchy was to have any permanency, it could only return to Spain as a régime hostile to Fascism. Anything that implied continuity between Franco's system and the restored monarchy was bound to add to the latter's unpopularity. It was incumbent, therefore, on the Pretender Don Juan—the younger son of Alfonso XIII—to establish beyond a doubt that his monarchy was anti-Fascist. And in those circumstances Franco could not lend himself to the change. On the other hand, the Monarchists were convinced in their heart of hearts that the monarchy could hardly survive without leaning on a military dictatorship. This was the solution which Gil Robles recommended. But a monarchy based on dictatorship of this kind would endure only as long as the military dictatorship lasted—which is precisely what happened to the monarchy of Alfonso XIII. In his negotiations with

Franco, Don Juan requested the *Caudillo* to hand over the power to a *Junta* of generals who had taken no part in the reprisals against the Republicans. This *Junta* was to maintain order for two or three months and organize a national plebiscite to determine the question of Monarchy or Republic. Faced with the impossibility of reaching an agreement with the usurpers of power, Don Juan launched the manifesto of March 22nd, 1945 from Lausanne. After vehemently attacking the régime, he ordered Monarchists to break with Franco. But the manifesto did not produce the desired effect. Only a few of Don Juan's supporters left the service of the Falangist State. The oligarchy, as usual, did not keep faith, nor did it seriously believe in anything. Just as in 1931 it played the coward and deserted Alfonso XIII, so in 1945 it was not going to risk anything for its king. Moreover, not a few Monarchists rejected the manifesto and continued to serve Franco, openly saying that the manifesto went too far and questioning its discretion and opportuneness. On the other hand Don Juan had forgotten that the Falange reckoned him among its adherents, that he himself had applauded Franco and that his followers had been the real instigators of the civil war.

So much for the Monarchists, the opposition of the oligarchy to the Falangist system.

The Republican opposition inside Spain was obviously in a state of complete impotence. For Franco established, as we know, a police State the like of which, for sheer ferocity and relative size, never existed in Italy or Germany. The numerous armed forces of the State, the serried ranks of the secret police, the Falange—every one of whose members was a police agent—had come to represent in Spain an incredible percentage of the total inhabitants of the country. Such an imposing apparatus of terror, clamped down on a people who had been deprived of political guidance by the emigration of innumerable anti-Fascist leaders and the execution of almost all those who had been unable to flee, was in itself an assurance of the impossibility of overthrowing the Falangist régime from inside Spain. Those political and trades union leaders who remained alive in Spain—even those of secondary importance—could be counted on the fingers of the hand.

The radical extermination of the opposition, the immense coercive machine of the Government, the domination of the country by a party sustained by State funds, excluded the possibility of Franco being overthrown by an internal revolt. Besides the nation was worn out by civil war and disorder. Even to-day, six years after the end of the Spanish war, a large body of opinion which loathes Franco and the Falange accepts them resignedly for fear that a change of régime would bring in its train new intestine struggles, reprisals and chaos. The memory of the horrors of civil war—palpable and evident horrors, suffered by all Spaniards—exercises a much more powerful influence on the majority of the population than the tragedy of frightful poverty and tyranny—less visible and less apparent, and only suffered by the proletarian classes—which the Fascist régime has created in Spain. Finally, the economic and financial privileges extended by this régime to the agrarian oligarchy and capitalists of all kinds entail the appearance of new and very powerful interests which, if the march of events had been less unfavourable to Fascism, would have helped decisively, taken in conjunction with the terroristic methods of the State and the desire for peace among the majority of Spaniards, to keep Franco in power for decades. Nevertheless, underground resistance existed from the first moment of Franco coming into power. When the civil war ended, the worker's parties began to print clandestine leaflets and newspapers, an activity for which the inexorable penalty was death. Hardly had Franco installed himself in Madrid in April 1939 than the Communists resumed the secret publication of *Mundo Obrero*. The Socialists also immediately began to print anti-Fascist propaganda leaflets. Later the Republican middle class launched forth on the dangerous adventure. In time, all parties were taking a hand in the game. The underground political movement, growing daily ever bolder, was already in 1944 a matter of serious concern to the Falange. In the long run, the inexorable Falangist terror had fundamentally failed.

Such was the state of affairs in the cities. In the mountains, resistance had not ceased either since the civil war ended. Thousands of men took refuge or defended themselves in the principal mountain ranges of the country. Franco used the Moors and the *Tercio Extranjero* against them without succeeding in subduing them. The authorities frequently called upon them in siren tones to surrender, with marked lack of success.

·  ·  ·  ·  ·

Franco's attitude to the war between the Axis and the democracies was consistent with the fact that the new Spanish régime owed everything to Hitler and Mussolini. When Italy entered the war in June 1940 in order to attack France, Franco declared himself a non-belligerent. If at that moment Britain had shown any weakness, Fascist Spain would probably have joined in the hostilities in order to share the booty. She did not do so, no doubt because Hitler preferred a non-belligerent Spain. Franco did for his allies all he possibly could do in his curious state of non-belligerence. He had signed the Anti-Comintern Pact and had united himself to the Axis from a military point of view. He placed at Germany's disposal maritime and air bases, which played an important part in the Battle of the Atlantic. He declared to the world at large that the Allies had lost the war.[1] He promised Hitler to send a hundred thousand workers to Germany. And the Spanish Fascist State openly took part in the war against the Allied Nations by sending the Blue Division to the Russian front. Franco even went so far as to announce that "if the road to Berlin were opened, then not merely would one division of Spaniards participate in the struggle, but one million Spaniards would be offered to help."[2]

.    .    .    .    .

Republican opposition to Franco outside Spain showed itself chiefly in the enlistment of great numbers of Republicans in the Allied armies. Thousands of Spanish Republicans gave their lives for the cause of democracy at Narvik and Bir-el-Acheim, in Syria, Tunis, Italy, Normandy, Paris; enlisting in the guerrillas of the French *Maquis*, in the Navy and the merchant service, in the Army and the Air Force, in the ranks of the parachutists and special services of the United Nations.

When France fell, Negrín went to London "because he wanted to symbolize by his presence there his adhesion to the cause of which Great Britain was then the only champion".

The immense majority of the Spanish exiles remained in France; others stayed in North Africa and a considerable number went to Mexico and other Central and South American Republics.

Party struggles—inflamed in exile by the frustration and bitterness which always accompany defeat—seriously weakened the Negrín Government, the legitimate Government of Spain according to the Constitution. Nevertheless, this Government had received the mandate of the last Cortes to meet on Spanish soil to continue its mission even if it had to leave Spain, and moreover, since the office of Head of the State was vacant, Negrín could not hand in his resignation to the only authority

[1] Speech to the National Council of the Falange, July 17th, 1941.
[2] Speech to the Officers of the Alcázar in Seville, February 15th, 1942.

which was constitutionally entitled to accept it. But when the defeat of the Axis was certain, the Republicans felt the urgency of restoring the Republican institutions abroad, and as soon as it was practicable the exiled deputies met in Mexico on August 22nd 1945 and elected as provisional President of the Republic Don Diego Martínez Barrio.[1] Negrín handed in his Government's resignation to the new President and Don José Giral[2] formed a new Cabinet which was immediately recognized by Mexico.

In 1946 Franco's régime finds itself attacked by the same malady which destroyed the Spanish Republic—it is suspended in a void, surrounded by the hostility of the nations. As we have seen, the diplomatic isolation of the Republic in 1939 was almost complete. The Allied victory brought about a diametrically opposed state of affairs. At the Crimea Conference, held at the beginning of 1945, the Allied Powers sealed the fate of Franco's régime. In the Declaration which was published on February 13th, it is stated:

"By this declaration we reaffirm our faith in the principles of the Atlantic Charter, our pledge in the declaration by the United Nations, and our determination to build in co-operation with other peace-loving nations a world order under law, dedicated to peace, security, freedom, and the general well-being of all mankind."

The ostracizing of Franco's régime, that is to say, of Spain as governed by Franco, was carried a step further at the San Francisco Conference where it was unanimously decided on June 20th, on the initiative of the Mexican delegation, that the future international organization should not include those States "whose régimes have been established with the help of military forces belonging to countries which have waged war against the United Nations—as long as those régimes are in power."

The resolution passed at the San Francisco Conference made a tremendous impression in official circles in Madrid. Franco's Minister for Foreign Affairs felt obliged to reply with a note of protest and Franco himself devoted the major part of the speech which he made at the inauguration of a new radio service to South America to complaining of the diplomatic severity with which the United Nations were beginning to treat his régime.

[1] See p. 484.　　　　[2] See p. 570.

For the first time, Spaniards—oppressors and oppressed alike—perceived that the reigning dictatorship which was so impossible to dislodge at home, was being seriously menaced from abroad.

At this juncture, the Declaration of Potsdam appeared on August 3rd, in the following terms:

> "The three Governments feel bound to make it clear that they for their part would not favour any application for membership put forward by the present Spanish Government which, having been founded with the support of the Axis Powers, does not, in view of its origin, its nature, its record, and its close association with the aggressor States, possess the qualifications necessary to justify such membership."

The decisive character of these words finally destroyed any hope that Spanish Fascism might still have entertained of saving itself from the general shipwreck of Fascism.

Labour's victory at the polls in Great Britain on July 5th, which preceded the Declaration of Potsdam, was naturally a new and formidable *contretemps* for the Spanish Fascists.

The growing general sentiment against Franco's régime was later emphasized—among other hostile measures taken by France, Great Britain, and the United States—in the resolution adopted almost unanimously by the Assembly of the United Nations in its London meeting of the 9th February 1946. In this the Members of the new world organisation agreed to act towards Fascist Spain in accordance with the letter and spirit of the Crimean, San Francisco and Potsdam Declarations.

The truth is that the destiny of Franco's régime was inseparably bound up with the fate of Fascist Italy and Nazi Germany. When the Allies overthrew the Nazi State, they dealt a mortal blow to the Falangist State. But there is no doubt—and the democratic forces in Spain should see in this a grave warning not to forget the teachings of history—there is no doubt, I repeat, that if the three great victorious Powers had not planned to make the life of Fascist Spain impossible abroad, Franco would have maintained his dictatorship for a long time yet. Though the Axis was defeated, the Spanish people ran the risk of enduring the Falangist system for, perhaps, the twenty or thirty years that Mussolini lasted in Italy—a catastrophe which would certainly have brought about the moral annihilation of Spain, the total paralysis of her vital forces.

# INDEX

## A

Abadal, Raimundo de, 170, 179–80
Abbé, James, on Republican lack of aeroplanes, 590
*ABC*, Monarchist paper, 285–6, 289, 551, 552, 556
Abd el-Krim, routed, 201
Absolutism: *versus* Liberalism, 26–9; of Ferdinand VII, 31–2
*Acció Catalana*, founded 1922, 396
*Acción Española*: Newspaper of *T.Y.R.E.*, 527; founded 1931, 552; in 1933, 557–8
*Acción Nacionalista Vasca*, 616
*Acción Popular*, 552; and *Renovación Española*, 527; youth goes over to *Falange*, 565
*Acción Popular Agraria*, Agrarian Popular Action Party, in November elections, 1933, 487 *et seq.*
*Acción Republicana*, 207
Achuriaguera, Juan de, surrender of Basques to Italians, 623–4, 627, 628
*Action Française*, 527
*Administración Local*, Maura's law, 141
Agrarian-aristocrats, and October insurrection, 1934, 505 *et seq.*
Agrarian laws, under 2nd Republic, 336–52
Agrarian party, 131–5; and Joaquín Costa, 160; and Primo de Rivera, 193
Agrarian problem, importance of, 265–6
Agrarian reform: Absent under 2nd Republic, 283 *et seq.*; and Azaña, 314–16; programme of landed oligarchy, 1935, 518–19
Agrarian repression after October insurrection, 1934, 517–18
Agrarian resources, 212–15
Agrarian revolution in Catalonia, 350–2
Ágreda, Sor Maria de, 34
Agriculture, 21–2; and Cortes of Cádiz, 47–8; development of, 100–1; importance of, in national economy, 127–9; policy of Primo

de Rivera, 194 *et seq.*; profits from, 233; credit and banking, 252
Agronomy, 215–18
Aguilera, Alberto: And general elections, 119; survey of textile industry, 244
Aguilera, General, 205
Aguirre, José Antonio, 623; on Basque Carlism, 408; on Basque nationalism 416; President of Basque Autonomous Government, 424, 623
*Afrancesados* (Francophiles), 24–5
Africa: Spain in, 87–8; garrisons in, 97; Army reform in, 326
Air Force: 1931, 325; loyalty of, 571, 573
Alameda, Father Cirilo de la, and the Freemasons, 44
Alava, under Castile, 411 *n*
Alba y Bonifaz, Santiago, 177
Alba, Duke of: And agrarian reform, 343; Liberalism of, 451; reception in Seville, 677–8
Alba, Santiago: Minister of Education, 179; reforms, 180; fall of National Government, 180–2; in the Governments of 1918–23, 184; and Primo de Rivera, 188; quarrel with Cambó, 395; Finance Minister, 396
Albigenses, 14
Albornoz, Sánchez, Republican Ambassador in Portugal, 584
Alcalá de los Gazules, rising of Quiroga, 1820, 44
Alcalá Zamora, Niceto, 140, 208–10, 342; founder of Republican Liberal Right and first President of 2nd Republic, 267, 268; Catalan separatism, 278; importance of his policy, 284–5; aims of, 300; disagreement with Parliament, 301; displaced by Azaña, 301; Catalan autonomy, 399, 400; President of the Republic, enemy of the Constitution, 445, 481; exit from Republican Government, 445; sincerity of his Catholicism, 450; *Ley de Congregaciones*, 1933, 454; exit from Cabinet, 1931, 478; his

gramme, Oct. 1934, 507; Azaña's efforts to purge, 545; Monarchists' organization for civil war, 552; military manœuvres, 1935, 560; military dictatorship the aim of the 1936 conspiracy, 562; new Republican Army, 1936, 596 et seq.; soldiers of the Republic, 614–15

Arrazola, absolutism of, 413
Arredondo, an organizer of the Civil War, 559
Arteche, Basque nationalist, 623
Asamblea Nacional, 193
Ascanio, Communist soldier, 661
Ascasos, 578
Asensio, Calvo, 91
Asensi, Botella, resignation of, 490
Asociación Republicana Militar of Ruiz Zorrilla, 126
Assault Guard, loyal to Republic, 576
Asturias, 97; in October insurrection, 1934, 508, 509
Augereau, Pierre-François-Charles, Duc de Castiglione, 79
Austerlitz, Battle of (1805), 24
Austria: Surrender at Austerlitz, 24; the Hapsburgs, 358–9; disappearance of Social-Democratic régime, 1934, 499–500
Autonomy: Regional, 53, 54; Galician, 279; nature of in Soviet system, 401–2; municipal, of Basque cities, 411 n; Statutes of Autonomy repudiated by Basques and Catalans, 616
Avance, confiscations and fines, 492
Ayguadé, Minister of Labour, leaves Government, Aug. 1938, 615
Azaña, Manuel, 171 n, 207, 300–24, 491; Minister of War, 1931, 268 n, 269; on Socialists in Casas Viejas, 293–4; Prime Minister, 301; influence on 2nd Republic, 301; early life, 302–4; and Juan Valera, 304–8; study of military questions, 308–9; politics and literature, 310–11; on general elections, 312–13; emphasis on moral problems, 313–14; agrarian questions, 314–16; counter-revolution, 316–17; his failure, 317 et seq.; his Liberalism and democracy, 319–20; his fear

of action, 320–4; President of the Republic, 323–4; political testament, 323; the lost chance, 324; reform of the Army, 325–36; neglect of agrarian problem, 337; and Catalan autonomy, 1932, 399, 404; on Basque Carlism, 408; and Protestant Church, 429, 429 n; "Spain has ceased to be Catholic!", 437; error on Church-Republic relationship, 441–2, 455–6; and religious Orders, 446; and teaching by clergy, 451; and secularization of education, 453–5, 484; on public health, 458; Minister of War, 465; and tax on unearned income, 467; and gold reserves, 467; and Bank of Spain, 469; and Republican Budgets, 471; efforts to avoid social revolution, 472–3, and the Socialists, 473–4, 476; the only possible Prime Minister, 1933, 481; on conduct of proletariat, 482 n; Ley de Congregaciones, 484; fall of his Government, 484; opposition of Barrio, 486; on the Samper Ministry, 1933–4, 492; on the Government and the Cortes, 934, 500; on impossibility of a monarchy, 500; and October insurrection, 1934, 504 et seq.; his followers in 1935–6, 532–3; his 1935 campaign, 533 et seq.; his theory of coalition, 533–4; his party after the February elections, 1936, 536; formation of Republican Government, Feb. 1936, 537; policy, 538; President, May 1936, 542; the lost opportunity, 1936, 544; on Barrera's conspiracy, 557; conciliation with the Generals, July 1936, 568–9; in Barcelona, 602; immobilized as President, 606; compared with Negrín, 607; French scheme for his escape, 610; and Catalan autonomy, 617–20; on Basque autonomy, 620; in Paris, 636; resignation from Presidency, 640, 644; invited to return to replace Negrín, 648

Azcárate, Ambassador in London, efforts for peace through British Foreign Office, 644
Azcárate, Gumersindo de, 125, 171 n

Zs

# B

Babeuf, François-Noel, French Communist, 274
Badajoz: Military rising, 126; strike of *braceros*, 292; captured by Franco, 585
Bakunin, Mikhail (1814–76), 102, 147–8
Balance of power, and independence of Portugal, 354 n
*Baleares*, insurgent cruiser, sunk, 602
Balearic Islands, 97, 356
Balkans, ascendancy of the Army, 334 n
Balmes, 34
*Banco de Bilbao*, 254
*Banco de Espiritu Santo*, loans to rebels, 585
*Banco Exterior de España*, 343
*Banco Herrero*, 254
*Banco Hipotecario* (Mortgage Bank), 342
*Banco Nacional de Portugal*, loans to rebels, 585
*Banco Urquijo*, 254–5
*Banco de Vizcaya*, 254
Bank of England, 469
Bank, National Agrarian, 342
Bank rate, 254–5
Bank of Spain, 254, 286, 342; political power of, 444–5; struggle against the Republic, 468–70
Bankers: Widespread directorships of, 254; growth in power of, 549
Banking, 315; policy of Primo de Rivera, 193; in Asturias and Bilbao, 237; private, 239–40; credit system, 252–5; and agrarian reform, 342–3; in Catalonia, 1936, 616–17
Barceló, Colonel Eduardo, Communist officer, 661; shot, 663–5
Barcelona: Commercial classes in, 19 n; and the Spanish revolution, 26–9; Liberalism in, 27; burning of convents, 36; Carlism, 68; in O'Donnell's rising, 1856, 82; journals attacked by Army, 1906, 142–3; First Socialist Congress, 1870, 148; *Semana trágica* (tragic week), 1909, 143; terrorism, 153; establishment of Infantry *Junta de Defensa*, 1917, 169; Catalan capitalist Cabinet proposed 176–7; terrorism of Martínez Anido, 1918, 23, 182, 199; telephone strike and general rising, 1931, 297–8; and political unity of Spain, 358; cotton looms of, 376; the first bomb, 1892, 390; at outbreak of Civil War, 571, 575 *et seq.*; insurrection of May 1937, 597; capital of Negrín Government, 602; Italian air attacks, 605, 632–3; occupied by insurgents, 633

Barcia, Roque, leader of Cartagena Federalists, 104, 393
Barley, rise in cultivation of, 128
Barnés, Domingo, and *Ley de Congregaciones*, 455 n
Barnés, Francisco, and *Ley de Congregaciones*, 455 n
*Barranco del Lobo*, disaster of, 1909, 143
Barrera, Captain, 564
Barrera, General, leader of conspiracy: Arrest and trial of, Aug. 1932, 556–7; shot, 575
Barrio, Diego Martínez, 511, 659; Minister of Communications, 1931, 268 n; head of Radical Government, Nov. 1933, 484 *et seq.*; compared with Lerroux, 485; the November elections, 1933, 486 *et seq.*; "mud, blood, and tears", 486; leaves the Radical Party, 491; the October insurrection, 1934, 504 *et seq.*; and the Popular Front, 535; and Government of Casares Quiroga, 1936, 542; Government of, July 19, 1936, 568; policy of capitulation, 569; speaker of the Cortes, 606; refusal to return to Spain, 640; provisional President, 1945, 684
Barriobero, 205
*Bases de Manresa*, 390
Basque Cultural Congress, 1918, 421
Basque nationalism, 392, 393, 403, 405–24
Basque Nationalist Party (*Partido Nacionalista de Euzkadi*), 278–9, 416; in elections, Feb. 1936, 536; and Civil War, 615
Basque Provinces, 22, 97; autonomy granted, 53; Carlist war in, 72; separatism, 154; land tenure, 219–20; differentiations, 415–16; Church in, 433; Civil War in, 620–9

Basques: Resistance to Spanish unity, 366; regionalism of, 382–3; geographical distribution of, 405; part played in Spanish history, 405–6; language and traditions, 406, 420; Carlism of, 407–8; the Inquisition, 407; insurrection against Espartero, 1841, 412; counter-reformation, 418–19; town *versus* country and nationalism, 420; plebiscite and autonomy, 1933, 422–3; Samper Government and, 497–8; October insurrection, 1934, 505 *et seq.*

Batet, General, 512; loyal to the Government, replaces González de Lara, 564

Beaucaire Fair, 20

Belgium: Capital in Spain, 257; Church in, 432–3

Belchite, captured by Republic, 601

Belloc, Hilaire, 41

Belluga, Cardinal, 35

Beltrán, Colonel, leader of 43rd Division, 604

Beni-bu-Ifrur, iron mines, 143

Benlliure y Tuero, 205

Berbers, 9

Bergonzoli, General, defeated at Brihuega, 601

Bermudo III of León, 354 *n*

Bertran de Lis, 26, 62

Bertrán y Musitu, 184

Besteiro, Julián, 173, 659, 670; Deputy President, 270 *n*; conspiracy for peace, 645–6; speech on need for peace, March 1939, 655

*Bienes concejiles* (common lands), under Liberal policy, 57–8

*Bienes comunales* (common lands), 21–2

*Bienes de propios* (lands rented to peasants), 22, 47, 48, 49, 56, 101, 345

Bilbao: Carlist insurrection, 68; siege of, 72; proclamation of *padres de provincia* and Civil War, 1833, 407; fall of, 600, 622

Bilbao, Tomás, joins Negrín Government, 615–16

"Black Hand" (*La Mano Negra*), 121

Blanco, Segundo, in Negrín Government, 606

Blockade, 601

*Bobie*, British ship, 625, 627–9

Bofarull, Antonio, Catalan anthologist, 377

Bolsheviks, 275

Bolshevism: International instructions of, rejected by Spanish Socialists, 197–8; reasons for separatism of, 394

Bonald, Leopoldina, 146

Bonaparte, Joseph: In Spain, 24–5; and Spanish Freemasonry, 42

Bonaparte, Napoleon, dictatorship of, 317–18

Books, 20, 247–8

Borbolla, Rodríguez de la, 140

Borbón, General, 176, 177

Borjas Blancas, loss of, 632

Boscán, 357 *n*

*Bourgeoisie. See* Middle class

*Braceros* (landless labourers), 60, 225, 226; and Catalan freedom, 277; strike at Badajoz, 292

Braga, Archbishop of, 369

Brañas, 393

Bravo, González: Civil Guard founded, 51; absolutist dictator, 53, 89, 413

Bravo, Juan Antonio, 564

Brihuega, Battle of, 601

Broca, on French and Spanish Basques, 405

Brunete, Battle of, 601

Bryan, Jennings, and Republican monetary policy, 467

Buckley, Henry: *Life and Death of the Spanish Republic*, 296 *n*; on Gil Robles during Feb. 1936, 566 *n*

Budget for Public Worship and the Clergy, 53, 54, 114, 435, 444, 494

Budget, Republican, 470–2

Bueno, Lt.-Col., 661

Buiza, Admiral Miguel, and desertion of the fleet, 657–8

Burgos, headquarters of Franco's "Government", 590

Burriel, General, director of rising at *Capitanía General*, 575

## C

*Caballeros*, and the 2nd Republic, 288–9

Cabanellas, General, 329; Republican, joins the conspirators, 564; to rise in Saragossa, 566

Cabezas de San Juan, the first *pronunciamiento*, 1820, 39–40, 44

Cabinet of monks, 81, 82

in power by peaceful methods, 1843–68, 413; *fueros* as a *casus belli*, 414; crisis in Basque Provinces, 415; and *Renovación Española*, 526–7; elections, Feb. 1936, 536; readiness for Civil War, 551

Carlyle, Thomas, 571

Carlos María (son of Don Juan and g.s. of Don Carlos), Pretender, proclaimed King by Carlists, 1868, 75–6, 105

Carlos Maria Isidro de Borbón (Don Carlos, s. of Charles IV, b. of Ferdinand VII, g. uncle of Q. Isabel II, Pretender), rise and history of the Carlists, 66–78, 407–8

Carner, Jaime, Finance Minister, 471, 479

Carrel, Armand, on toleration under Cromwell in England, 319–20, 320 *n*

Carrillo, W., and Council of Defence, 656 *n*

Cartagena: Falangist rebellion, 104; desertion of the fleet, 658

Cartagena, Marqués de, bequests for education, 231

Cartels, 239, 246–8

Casado, Col. Segismundo, conspiracy for peace, 641, 645, 646–74

Casas Viejas, rising of the peasants, 1933, 292, 298, 299, 481, 486, 539, 559

Casaú, Manuel Andrés, victim of the Terror, 1936, 541

Cascajares, Cardinal, encouragement for Costa, 161

Cassola, Manuel, Minister of War in Sagasta's Government, 116–17

Castañera, Conde de, 369

Castel-Rodrigo, Marqués de, 367

Castelar y Ripoll, Emilio, 98–9; leader of Republican group, 125–6; and Costa, 159

Castellón, loss of, 611

Castilblanco, strike of the peasants, 1932, 292, 539

Castile, 22, 97; toleration for Jews, 14; cloth factories, 23; beginnings of rural revolt, 60; and Carlism, 70–1; favourable to Socialism, 148–53; wheat-growing oligarchy under 2nd Republic, 285–6; Counts of, 353; kingdom estab-

lished, 354, 355; legal unification of, 355; importance of, 356; effects of union with Aragón, 365; and the wars of religion, 365–6; and the War of the Spanish Succession, 371 *et seq.*; Catalonia inimical to, 378–9; Liberalism in, 381; and Government of Vizcaya, 411 *n*; and the counter-reformation, 419

Castillo, Lieutenant of Assault Guard, assassinated, 547

Casualties, October insurrection, 1934, 512

Catalonia, 22, 97; cotton mills of, 23, 375–6; autonomy granted, 53; clergy in rural crusade against Monarchy, 67; and Carlism, 68; Carlist rising, 1847, 72; landing of pretender Montemolín, 1860, 74; support for protectionism, 132; Nationalist movement, 145; favourable to Anarchism, 148–53; the "Catalan question", 153–5; and the Army rebellion, 1917, 170 *et seq.*; separatism abandoned, 1918, 179–80; new demand for autonomy, 181–2; chaos, 1918–23, 183–4; and military dictatorship, 185–7; electrification of, 215; land tenure, 220–2; Canadian capital invested in, 258; separatism, 266, 277–8; Monarchists, 266; insurrection of *F.A.I.*, 1932, 298; decree relating to leases, 1931, 340; agrarian revolution, 350–2; modification of Constitution under Ferdinand the Catholic, 355; "Castilianizing" of, 357 *et seq.*; feudalism of, 358; resistance to Spanish unity, 366; rebellion of 1640 and civil war, 368 *et seq.*; anti-French tradition, 370; Philip IV and, 370 *et seq.*; War of Spanish Succession, 371 *et seq.*; enfeoffed to France, 1640, 372; independence after 1716, 373; nationalism, 374–405; commerce and industry in 18th century, 375; exclusiveness of Nationalist movement, 377; disappearance of autonomy, 1822–45, 379; error of "oppressed minority", 380; first newspaper, 381; two social movements of political Catalanism, 381–2; Peasant movement, 382–3; "regionalism", 388; economics of

Fonseca, Archbishop of Toledo, 12
Ford, Richard: On failure of Espartero, 66 n; on Basque *fueros*, 409–10
Foreign exchange and Spanish currency, under Republic, 466–7
Foreign intervention, 582–95
Foreigners, in industry and commerce, 22–3
Forestry, and National Plan of Hydraulic Works, 462
Foronda, Marqués de, in Lisbon, 584
*Foro* (payment in kind), 223
*Foros* (Galician leases), in agrarian problem, 339, 344, 345
Fouché, Joseph, Duke of Otranto (1763–1820), 25
Fourier, François-Marie-Charles, 127
Franche Comté, 356
Francisco de Asis (King-Consort of Isabel II), instrument of the Carlists, 73, 413
France: Wars with Spain, 7–8, 364–5; army of occupation in Spain, 1823, 8; the Albigenses, 14; "French ideas", 19; contrasted with Spain, 19; vigour of the middle class, 20; revolution, 24; attacked by English in Holland, 24; number of clergy, 32; expulsion of the French, 1813, 25; revolution and the landowners, 59; commercial treaty denounced, 1890, 133; and the Moroccan War, 201; French capital in Spain, 255–6, 258; revolution compared with Spain, 1931, 273–4; and Catalonia, 370; Church in, 432–3; loan to Spain, 1931, 465–6; Republic contrasted with Spanish Republic, 475; eradication of nobility, 550; and the Fascist Powers, 582; protest against air attacks on civilians, 605–6; cruiser sent to Catalonia, April 1938, 610–11; the Spanish refugee 43rd Division, 631; refugees, 1938–9, 635–6; recognition of Franco's Government, 644; welcome to Republican fleet, March 1939, 658
France, Anatole, 468
Franco, General Francisco, 318, 329, 554; corrupt regime of, 251; and nationalization of railways, 251; and foreign capital, 257; agreement with I.T.T.C., 260–1; and

the Church, 456; Under-Secretary of War, April 1935, 516; sent to Canary Islands, 545, 561; head of General Staff, at military manœuvres, 1935, 560; perfecting of insurrection, 562; to rise with Army of Morocco, 563, 566; in touch with Mola, 565, 585; rising in Tetuán and broadcast to Spaniards, July 1936, 567; early threats to his success, 582; military situation, 1937, 600; counterattack at Teruel, 602, 603; advance to Catalonia, 604–5; advance on Santander, 623; the campaign after the Ebro, 631 *et seq.*; peace terms, Feb. 1939, 640 *et seq.*; and Fascist Republicans, 1939, 642–3; reported unwilling to negotiate with Negrín, 647; and Communist opposition to Council of Defence, 663; negotiations with Casado, 666 *et seq.*; Spain under his rule, 675 *et seq.*; and Don Juan, the Pretender, 680; and Axis Powers, 682 *et seq.*; the internal and external Republican opposition, 683 *et seq.*
Franco-Russian Alliance, 591
Franco-Russian Pact of Mutual Aid, 593
Franklin, Benjamin (1706–90), 103
Freemasonry: And Liberalism, 27, 42–6; November elections, 1933, 489–90; in Lerroux–Gil Robles Government, 510
Free-trade *v.* Protection, 129–35
Friars: Murdered, 1834, 36; expelled and houses confiscated, 1836, 50; and Carlist insurrection, 68
Fuel-oil, 214
Fuentes, Pila, an organizer of the Civil War, 553, 554
*Fueros*, Basque: And Liberalism, 409; after first Carlist War, 1839, 410; and Civil War of 1833, 407; and Cortes of 1839, 410–11; abolished by decree of Espartero, 1841, 412; survival of, 412 *et seq.*; abolished by Alfonso XII, 1876, 414
*Fueros*, Catalan: Attempt to suppress, 368–70; and Philip IV, 370–1; abolition decreed by Philip V, 372
Fulgencio, Father, 73, 413

# G

Gálán, Lt.-Col. Francisco, 658
Galarza, on eve of Civil War, 562
Galiano, Alcalá, 27; Freemasons' envoy to the absolutists, 44; abandons reforms, 61; interview with Fray Cirilo, 73
Galicia, 97; land tenure, 222–3; autonomists of, 279; separatism, 392–3; regionalists under the Republic, 403–4
*Galleguismo* (Galician nationalism), 393
Gamazo, leader of agrarian Liberals, 131, 133, 161
Gambara, General, Italian offensive in Catalonia, 634, 674
Gambling houses reopened, 1934, 498
Gandesa, loss of, 604
Ganivet, Angel: On national character and tradition, 424–6; on oligarchy, 528
García de la Herrán, General, 556
García el Mayor, 411 *n*
Garijo, Lt.-Col. Antonio, 670, 671 *et seq.*
*Gazteiz*, armed trawler, 626
Gazzalo, Pérez, murder of, 663
General Union of Workers=*Unión General de Trabajadores*, q.v.
*Generalidad* (Government of Catalonia), 399; and Madrid, 497, 504; and *C.E.D.A.*, 511; and October insurrection, 1934, 512 *et seq.*; and Negrín Government, 616 *et seq.*
Geography and political parties, 148
George VI, Coronation of, 646
Germany: The Reformation, 12–13; capital in Spain, 257; Church in, 432–3; triumph of Nazis, 499; support for Spanish Monarchists, 563; determination to weaken France and England, 582; intervention in Spain, 588–90; Third International, 592; bombardment of Almería, 600; air raids on Spanish civilians, 605; forces in Catalonia, 1938, 634
Gerona: Siege of, 79; taken by Italians, 635
Gibbon, Edward, 211, 269 *n*, 332, 432
Gibraltar, Strait of, and Moroccan War, 201
Gijón, Socialist Congress, 1902, 156
Gil Robles, José María, 574; leader of Castilian oligarchy, 285; head of *C.E.D.A.* and October insurrection, 1934, 502–16; on Samper, 502; after insurrection, 514–15; loss of authority, 515–16; Minister of War, 1935, 516; career of, 521–2; effect of October insurrection, 1934, 524; on abolition of parties, 525; on danger of violence, 529 *n*; and the Army, 545; military manœuvres, 1935, 560; replaced at Ministry of War, 561; conversation with Calvo Sotelo, 565; eve of rising, 565–6; and the conspiracy, 583–4; and the Monarchy, 679 *et seq.*
Giner de los Ríos, Francisco (Don Hermenegildo), 171; founder of *Institución Libre de Enseñanza*, 126; and Cánovas decree against universities, 114; a founder of the new Spain, 158, 160
Giral, José, Government of, 570, 684
Gironde, Vizcondesa de, an organizer of Civil War, 553
Goded, General: Chief of Central General Staff, 329, 330; sent to Balearic Islands, 545, 561; military manœuvres, 1935, 560; eve of Civil War, 562; to rise in Catalonia, 566; director of rising at *Capitanía General*, 575; escape of, 577
Goicoechea, Antonio, 559; on Committee of Monarchists, 266; leader of the Civil War Party, 553; arrest and imprisonment, 553; representative of conspirators abroad, 558; agreements with Italian Government, 563; Governor of Bank of Spain, 680
Goicoechea, Captain, treachery of, 621–2
Gold, and Republican monetary policy, 467–8
Gómez, Carlist General, 71
Gómez, Paulino, and desertion of the fleet, 658
Gómez, Trifón, 671
González Carrasco: Gen. of Madrid *Junta*, 565; to rise in Valencia, 566
Gonzalo, Colonel, 671
Gonzalez, Communist, 662–3
González, Count Fernán, 353
González de Lara, General: To rise at Burgos, 563; ·replaced by Batet, 564

701

the fall of the Monarchy, 210; and local unemployment, 340

Murcia, 97; burning of convents, 36

Muret, Battle of, 14

Murguía, 393

Murillo, Bravo: Reform of Charter of 1845, 51; and the Carlists, 73; constitutional reforms of, 73; absolutist reaction of, 413

Mussolini, 195, 515, 563, 682

## N

Naples, 356, 365

Napoleon Bonaparte, war in Spain, 8, 23–5

Narváez, Ramón Maria, Duke of Valencia, 26, 38, 40, 60, 80–2, 318; on the Army, 37; dictator, 1856, 52; and Mendizábal, 61; Battle for Madrid, 63; and Espartero, 64; and the Carlists, 73; and Isabel II, 74; Charter of, 83; opposition to, 84; opposition of Prim, 90; absolutist reaction, 413; anti-clericalism of, 451

National Debt, 47, 48–9, 57, 87

National Government, Maura's, 1918, 178–9; fall of, 179–82

National Militia, 48, 82

National Plan of Hydraulic Works, 462

Nationalist Party, Basque, 278–9

Navarre, 97; Carlist war in, 72; kingdom established, 354; incorporated in Castile, 356; resistance to Spanish unity, 366; and Government of Vizcaya, 411 n

Navy, Spanish: Destroyed by American Navy, 111; and conspirators, 1936, 565

Necker, Jacques (1732–1804), Administration des Finances, 20

Negrín, Juan: Finance Minister, Sept. 1936, 596; Government of, 600 et seq.; in Barcelona, 602; change of some Ministers, 1938, 606; leadership of, 607–10; belief that war could be won, 610; on the Catalan front, 632; on peace offer, Feb. 1939, 638; return to Spain, Feb. 1939, 640; the final stand, 642 et seq.; efforts to create shock-units, 645, 653; resistance

at all costs, 647 et seq.; contemplated broadcast, March 1939, 654; isolation of, March 1939, 658 et seq.; escape to France, 660; terms of peace, 668; in London, 683; resignation, 684

Nelson, Lord, Battle of Trafalgar, 406

"Neutral" classes, 159, 207; and military dictatorship, 203; and the 2nd Republic, 264–5

Neutrality, in First World War, 134

New Granada, 356

Newspapers, 247–8; first Catalan, 1860, 377. And see Press.

Nicolau d'Olwer, Luis, Minister of Trade, 1931, 268 n

Nieremberg, Father, on Church and people, 431

"Night of St. John" Conspiracy, 204–6

Nobility. See Hidalgos

Nocedal, Cándido: Carlist Minister of the Interior, 1856, 52, 73, 74; and Carlos María, 76; absolutism of, 413

Nocedal, Ramón, break with the Carlists, 1888, 112

Non-Intervention Committee, London, 586

North African plazas, 356

North American Telephone Company, 258

Novaliches, Manuel Pavia, Marquis of, 90

Nueva Federación Madrilena, founded 1872, 148

Nueva Planta decree of Philip V, to modify Catalan institutions, 373

Nuns, statistics, 32, 49

Nuts, tariffs on, 1926, 194–5

## O

O'Donnell, Enrique, 79–80

O'Donnell, José Enrique, Conde de La Bisbal, 38; summary of activities, 1856–68, 52–3; disloyalty of, 64–5; and Carlists, 73; and Isabel II, 74

O'Donnell, Leopoldo, 114, 119, 318; and the new oligarchy, 78–88; intrigue, 80–1; revolt at Vicálcaro, 82; Minister of War, 82;

713

on loyalty of Army to Republic, 555; arrested, 556; amnesty, 1934, 557; head of *Unión Militar Española*, 558; consultations for Civil War, 562; visit to Berlin, 1936, 563; in touch with Mola, 565
Sanmarti, Teresa, 146
Santander, Bishop of, 31
Santo Domingo, war against Haiti, 88
Santo Domingo de la Calzada, military rising, 126
Santoña, catastrophe of, 622 *et seq.*
Saracen invasion, 711 A.D., 8–9
Saragossa: Chair of Economics founded, 20–1; burning of convents, 36; Chambers of Commerce, 1898, 134; Congress, 1872, rupture between Anarchists and Socialists, 147; general strike, 1933–4, 495–6
Sardinia, 356, 365
Sartorius, Luis José, Count of San Luis, 73
Savigny, Friedrich Karl von, 280
Savings and bank deposits, 472
Savoy, captured by France, 24
Schoolmen, 10
Schools: *Grupos escolares*, 457; building under the Republic, 457
Scotland, in United Kingdom, 380
Secret societies, 41 *et seq.*
Security Guards, 196
Sédan, Battle of, 99
Seguí, Salvador, 199
Segura, Pedro, Cardinal-Archbishop of Toledo: Pastoral letter on the Republic, 437–8; expelled from Spain, 438; and the Vatican, 438–9
Seigniories, jurisdictional: The law of Aug. 1911, 47; repealed, 48
Semprún, Civil Governor of Toledo, 438
Senate, conditions of membership, 1876, 58
Senén, Valentín Ruiz, business manager of the Jesuits, directorships held in 1934, 436 *n*
*Señoríos*, abolition of, 59
*Señoritismo*, 233–4
Separatism: And terrorism in Barcelona, 154; under the 2nd Republic, 266–7; in Catalonia, 1906, 391. *And see* Catalonia, Basques
Serrano Dominguez, Francisco, Duke de la Torre, 64, 80, 137; and

Francisco de Asís, 73; O'Donnell's rising, 1856, 82; Prime Minister, 92; regency of, 90; defeated at elections, 94; Government of, 107; leader of Liberals in Senate, 131
*"Serviles"* (lackeys): Absolutists, 79; enemies of the Constitution, 381
Sesame-seed, tariffs on, 1926, 194–5
*Seven Seas Spray*, British ship, 625, 627–9
Sevillano, Liberal banker, 99, 236
Seville, 40; people's rebellion, 104; Sanjurjo's rebellion, 290; Holy Week celebrations forbidden, 450
Seville Waterworks Co., Ltd., 258
Share-croppers, Catalan, 350
Shaw, Bernard, 630
Shipping, at Cádiz and Barcelona, 26
Sicily, 356, 365
Sieyès, Comte Emmanuel-Joseph, 282
*Siglo de Oro*, 15
Silió, on committee of monarchical party, 266
Silk, 23, 244–5
Silvela, Francisco, leader of Conservatives, 134, 279, 521
Silver, 213
Silvestre, Fernández, Moroccan campaign, 1921, 183
*Sindicato Unico*, 199
*Sindicatos Libres*, 199
Sismondi, on prosperity of States, 387
Slate, bituminous, 214
Smallholders of Galicia, 222–3
Small holdings, in agrarian problem, 339, 344
*Soberano Capítulo*, 42
Social legislation, 153
Socialists (Socialism): Riff War, 1909, 145; Spanish Socialism, 146 *et seq.*; First Congress at Barcelona, 1870, 148; geographical distribution, 148–53; elections of 1901 and 1905, 156; Parliamentary Assembly, 171–2; Moroccan catastrophe, 1922, 185; military dictatorship, 1923, 185, 197–200; membership, 1923, 198; "collaboration" with dictatorship, 199–200; "Night of St. John" conspiracy, 205; bodyguard for deposed royal house, 1931, 262; and 2nd Republic,

716

Rivera, 194–5; on land, 223; agricultural, 227–8; compared with other countries, 240; on unearned income, 240, 467; Catalan land taxes, 351; lower, of 18th century, 375; Basque, 419; insurgents' programme, 1934, 508

Tedeschini, Monsignor, Papal Legate at Madrid, 439

Telephone, automatic, political consequences of its installation, 256, 260–1

Templars, 14

Tercio Extranjero, used for suppression of Asturian insurrection, Oct. 1934, 510

Teresa, Santa (1515–82), 35

Terradellas, José, Prime Minister of Catalan Autonomous Government, 617

Territories, 97

Terror: After 1823, 31–2; in Barcelona, 153; from 1918 to 1923, 182; the White Terror, 1936, 541

Teruel, siege of, 602–3

Textiles, 23, 243–6, 258, 375; Catalan, 215, 238

Tharsis Sulphur Copper Mines Ltd., 259

Thiers, 475

Third International, 591–5

Tierra y Libertad, 148

Timber industry, 257

Times: On Portuguese help to rebels, 586; on Italian intervention, 587–8; on rebel air superiority, 590; on poverty of Republican arms, 590; on Franco and Republican surrender, 643

Tithes: Abolished, 1837, 50; restored, 1845, 50

Toca, Sánchez, and Catalan autonomy, 400

Toledo: Centre of learning, 13; and Carlism, 70

Toledo, Councils of, 29

Toledo, Cardinal-Archbishop of, and the Carlists, 89, 209

Torpedo attacks on Republican ships, 589

Topete, Admiral: Juan Bautista, Pronunciamiento at Cádiz, Sept. 1868, 27, 90, 91, 92; defeated at elections, 94

Torcuato Luca de Tena, Marqués de Luca de Tena, founder of ABC, 286–7

Toreno, José Maria Queipo de Llano, Conde de, 25, 27, 61, 62; expulsion of Jesuits, 50

Torquemada, 363

Torras y Bages, Bishop of Vich, leader of Catalan peasant movement, 382

Torrero, Muñoz, 27

Torres, Conde de las, in Lisbon, 584

Toulon, Napoleon the hero of, 24

Toulouse, Count of, 14

Toulouse, Spanish Government at, 636

Towns, and Carlism, 68–9

Trade, 23; and Republican monetary policy, 469–70

Trade unions, 148, 599 n

Traditionalist Youth of Navarre, 558

Trafalgar, Battle of, 406

Tramways, 257

Transport, 23

Treasury, the 1931 situation, 465–6

Tree of Guernica, 406–7

Tremp, loss of, 604

Trent, Council of (1545–63), 35

Tribunal of Constitutional Guarantees, 53

Tribunal de Defensores de la Fe, 28

Tribunal Supremo de Justicia, for trial of military offences, 326

Turks, in Asia Minor, and Catalonia, 357

Turreau de Linières, Baron, 70

T.Y.R.E. (Tradicionalistas y Renovación Española), 527

## U

Ubieta, Admiral, Commander-in-Chief of Minorca, 639

Ukraine, in Poland, 380

Ulibarri, General Gamir, 623

Un troç de paper, first Catalan newspaper, 377

Unamuno, Basque philosopher, 35, 139, 406

Unemployment: In agriculture, 226, 339–40; under Republic, 471–2

Ungría, Colonel, 671

Unión Comercial, Seville, 556

Unión General de Trabajadores (U.G.T.) (General Union of Workers):

# WORLD AFFAIRS: National and International Viewpoints
## An Arno Press Collection

Angell, Norman. **The Great Illusion, 1933.** 1933.

Benes, Eduard. **Memoirs:** From Munich to New War and New Victory. 1954.

[Carrington, Charles Edmund] (Edmonds, Charles, pseud.) **A Subaltern's War.** 1930. New preface by Charles Edmund Carrington.

Cassel, Gustav. **Money and Foreign Exchange After 1914.** 1922.

Chambers, Frank P. **The War Behind the War, 1914-1918.** 1939.

Dedijer, Vladimir. **Tito.** 1953.

Dickinson, Edwin DeWitt. **The Equality of States in International Law.** 1920.

Douhet, Giulio. **The Command of the Air.** 1942.

Edib, Halidé. **Memoirs.** 1926.

Ferrero, Guglielmo. **The Principles of Power.** 1942.

Grew, Joseph C. **Ten Years in Japan.** 1944.

Hayden, Joseph Ralston. **The Philippines.** 1942.

Hudson, Manley O. **The Permanent Court of International Justice, 1920-1942.** 1943.

Huntington, Ellsworth. **Mainsprings of Civilization.** 1945.

Jacks, G. V. and R. O. Whyte. **Vanishing Lands:** A World Survey of Soil Erosion. 1939.

Mason, Edward S. **Controlling World Trade.** 1946.

Menon, V. P. **The Story of the Integration of the Indian States.** 1956.

Moore, Wilbert E. **Economic Demography of Eastern and Southern Europe.** 1945.

[Ohlin, Bertil]. **The Course and Phases of the World Economic Depression.** 1931.

Oliveira, A. Ramos. **Politics, Economics and Men of Modern Spain, 1808-1946.** 1946.

O'Sullivan, Donal. **The Irish Free State and Its Senate.** 1940.

Peffer, Nathaniel. **The White Man's Dilemma.** 1927.

Philby, H. St. John. **Sa'udi Arabia.** 1955.

Rappard, William E. **International Relations as Viewed From Geneva.** 1925.

Rauschning, Hermann. **The Revolution of Nihilism.** 1939.

Reshetar, John S., Jr. **The Ukrainian Revolution, 1917-1920.** 1952.

Richmond, Admiral Sir Herbert. **Sea Power in the Modern World.** 1934.

Robbins, Lionel. **Economic Planning and International Order.** 1937. New preface by Lionel Robbins.

Russell, Bertrand. **Bolshevism:** Practice and Theory. 1920.

Russell, Frank M. **Theories of International Relations.** 1936.

Schwarz, Solomon M. **The Jews in the Soviet Union.** 1951.

Siegfried, André. **Canada:** An International Power. [1947].

Souvarine, Boris. **Stalin.** 1939.

Spaulding, Oliver Lyman, Jr., Hoffman Nickerson, and John Womack Wright. **Warfare.** 1925.

Storrs, Sir Ronald. **Memoirs.** 1937.

Strausz-Hupé, Robert. **Geopolitics:** The Struggle for Space and Power. 1942.

Swinton, Sir Ernest D. **Eyewitness.** 1933.

Timasheff, Nicholas S. **The Great Retreat.** 1946.

Welles, Sumner. **Naboth's Vineyard:** The Dominican Republic, 1844-1924. 1928. Two volumes in one.

Whittlesey, Derwent. **The Earth and the State.** 1939.

Wilcox, Clair. **A Charter for World Trade.** 1949.